The Treasury of Precious Instructions: Essential Teachings of the Eight Practice Lineages of Tibet

Volume 2: Nyingma
Part 2

The Tsadra Foundation Series

published by Snow Lion, an imprint of Shambhala Publications

Tsadra Foundation is a US-based nonprofit organization that contributes to the ongoing development of wisdom and compassion in Western minds by advancing the combined study and practice of Tibetan Buddhism.

Taking its inspiration from the nineteenth-century nonsectarian Tibetan Buddhist scholar and meditation master Jamgön Kongtrul Lodrö Taye, Tsadra Foundation is named after his hermitage in eastern Tibet, Tsadra Rinchen Drak. The Foundation's various program areas reflect his values of excellence in both scholarship and contemplative practice, and the recognition of their mutual complementarity.

Tsadra Foundation envisions a flourishing community of Western contemplatives and scholar-practitioners who are fully trained in the traditions of Tibetan Buddhism. It is our conviction that, grounded in wisdom and compassion, these individuals will actively enrich the world through their openness and excellence.

This publication is a part of Tsadra Foundation's Translation Program, which aims to make authentic and authoritative texts from the Tibetan traditions available in English. The Foundation is honored to present the work of its fellows and grantees, individuals of confirmed contemplative and intellectual integrity; however, their views do not necessarily reflect those of the Foundation.

Tsadra Foundation is delighted to collaborate with Shambhala Publications in making these important texts available in the English language.

Nyingma

Mahāyoga, Anuyoga, and Atiyoga
Part 2

THE TREASURY OF PRECIOUS INSTRUCTIONS:
ESSENTIAL TEACHINGS OF THE EIGHT PRACTICE
LINEAGES OF TIBET
VOLUME 2

Compiled by Jamgön Kongtrul Lodrö Taye

TRANSLATED BY THE
Padmakara Translation Group

SNOW LION

Snow Lion
An imprint of Shambhala Publications, Inc.
2129 13th Street
Boulder, Colorado 80302
www.shambhala.com

Cover art: Thangka "Longchenpa." Collection Eric Colombel.
Photo: Rafael Ortet, 2018. © Eric Colombel, New York.

9 8 7 6 5 4 3 2 1

First Edition
Printed in the United States of America

Shambhala Publications makes every effort to print on acid-free, recycled paper.
Snow Lion is distributed worldwide by Penguin Random House, Inc., and its subsidiaries.

LIBRARY OF CONGRESS CATALOGING-IN-PUBLICATION DATA
Names: Kong-sprul Blo-gros-mtha'-yas, 1813–1899, compiler. | Comité de traduction Padmakara, translator.
Title: Nyingma: Mahāyoga, Anuyoga, and Atiyoga, part two
Other titles: Gdams ngag mdzod. English
Description: Boulder: Snow Lion, 2024. | Series: The treasury of precious instructions: Essential teachings of the eight practice lineages of Tibet; volume 2 |
Includes bibliographical references and index.
Identifiers: LCCN 2023037343 | ISBN 9781645472926 (hardcover)
Subjects: LCSH: Rnying-ma-pa (Sect)—Doctrines. | Rdzogs-chen. | Tantric Buddhism.
Classification: LCC BQ7662.4 .K669513 2024 | DDC 294.3/420425—dc23/eng/20231026
LC record available at https://lccn.loc.gov/2023037343

Contents

Foreword

In his vast work *The Treasury of Precious Instructions* (*gDams ngag rin po che'i mdzod*), Jamgön Kongtrul Lodrö Taye, that most eminent of Tibetan Buddhist masters, collected all the empowerments, instructions, and practices of the eight great chariots of the practice lineages. Not only that, but he himself received the complete transmissions for all the practices, accomplished them including the retreats, and preserved them in his own mindstream. He then passed on the transmissions to his own students and all who requested them.

The Treasury of Precious Instructions exemplifies how Jamgön Kongtrul Lodrö Taye's whole life was dedicated to teaching and spreading the dharma, whether it be sutra or mantra, *kama* or *terma*, old or new translation school, free of sectarian bias. Without his supreme efforts, many traditions of Tibetan Buddhism would have been lost.

The teachings of the Buddha have now spread throughout the Western world, and there is a growing need for major texts to be translated into English so that Western dharma students and scholars have access to these essential teachings. I was, therefore, delighted to hear that having successfully published a translation in ten volumes of Jamgön Kongtrul Lodrö Taye's *The Treasury of Knowledge* (*Shes bya kun khyab mdzod*), the Tsadra Foundation has embarked on a second major project, the translation of *The Treasury of Precious Instructions*, and I would like to express my gratitude to them.

May their work be of benefit to countless sentient beings.

His Holiness the Seventeenth Karmapa, Ogyen Trinley Dorje
Bodhgaya
February 21, 2016

Series Introduction

The *Treasury of Precious Instructions* (*gDams ngag rin po che'i mdzod*) is the fourth of the five great treasuries compiled or composed by Jamgön Kongtrul Lodrö Taye (1813–1900), also known as Karma Ngawang Yönten Gyatso, among many other names. Kongtrul was one of the greatest Buddhist masters of Tibet. His accomplishments were so vast and varied that it is impossible to do them justice here. The reader is referred to an excellent short biography in the introduction to the first translated volume of another of his great works, *The Treasury of Knowledge*, or the lengthy *Autobiography of Jamgön Kongtrul*. Even if his achievements had consisted solely of his literary output represented in these five treasuries, it would be difficult to comprehend his level of scholarship.

Unlike *The Treasury of Knowledge*, which is Kongtrul's own composition, his other four treasuries may be considered anthologies. Kongtrul's stated mission was to collect and preserve without bias the teachings and practices of all the lineages of Tibetan Buddhism, particularly those that were in danger of disappearing. The English publication of *The Treasury of Knowledge* in ten volumes and the forthcoming translations of this *Treasury of Precious Instructions* in some eighteen volumes can attest to the success of his endeavor, perhaps even beyond what he had imagined.

The Treasury of Precious Instructions is, in some ways, the epitome of Kongtrul's intention. He first conceived of the project around 1870, as always in close consultation with his spiritual friend and mentor Jamyang Khyentse Wangpo (1820–1892). The two of them, along with other great masters, such as Chokgyur Dechen Lingpa, Mipham Gyatso, and Ponlop Loter Wangpo, were active in an eclectic trend in which the preservation of the texts of Tibetan Buddhism was paramount.[1] It was with Khyentse's encouragement and collaboration that Kongtrul had created *The Treasury of Knowledge*—his incredible summation of all that was to be known—and compiled the anthologies of *The Treasury of Kagyu Mantra* and *The Treasury of Precious Hidden Teachings*. This next treasury expanded the scope by aiming to collect in one place the most important instructions of *all* the main practice lineages.

Kongtrul employed a scheme for organizing the vast array of teachings that flourished, or floundered, in Tibet during his time into the eight great chariots of the practice lineages (*sgrub brgyud shing rta chen po brgyad*), or eight lineages that are vehicles of attainment. He based this on a much earlier text by Sherab Özer (Prajñārasmi, 1518–1584).[2] The structure and contents of that early text indicate that the seeds of the so-called nonsectarian movement (*ris med*) of the nineteenth century in eastern Tibet had already been planted and just needed cultivation. The organizing principle of the scheme was to trace the lineages of the instructions for religious practice that had come into Tibet from India. This boiled down to eight "charioteers"—individuals who could be identified as the conduits between India and Tibet and who were therefore the sources of the practice lineages, all equally valid in terms of origin and comparable in terms of practice. This scheme of eight practice lineages became a kind of paradigm for the nonsectarian approach championed by Kongtrul and his colleagues.[3]

The Treasury of Precious Instructions implements this scheme in a tangible way by collecting the crucial texts and organizing them around those eight lineages. These may be summarized as follows:

1. The Nyingma tradition derives from the transmissions of Padmasambhava and Vimalamitra during the eighth century, along with the former's illustrious twenty-five disciples (*rje 'bangs nyer lnga*) headed by the sovereign Trisong Detsen.
2. The Kadam tradition derives from Atiśa (982–1054) and his Tibetan disciples headed by Dromtön Gyalwai Jungne (1004–1063).
3. The Sakya tradition, emphasizing the system known as the "Path with Its Result," derives from Virūpa, Ḍombi Heruka, and other mahāsiddhas, and passes through Gayadhara and his Tibetan disciple Drokmi Lotsāwa Śākya Yeshe (992–1072).
4. The Marpa Kagyu tradition derives from the Indian masters Saraha, Tilopa, Naropa, and Maitripa, as well as the Tibetan Marpa Chökyi Lodrö (1000?–1081?).
5. The Shangpa Kagyu tradition derives from the ḍākinī Niguma

and her Tibetan disciple Khyungpo Naljor Tsultrim Gönpo of Shang.
6. Pacification and Severance derive from Pa Dampa Sangye (d. 1117) and his Tibetan successor, Machik Labkyi Drönma (ca. 1055–1143).
7. The Six-Branch Yoga of the *Kālacakra Tantra* derives from Somanātha and his Tibetan disciple Gyijo Lotsāwa Dawai Özer during the eleventh century and was maintained preeminently through the lineages associated with Zhalu and Jonang.
8. The Approach and Attainment of the Three Vajras derives from the revelations of the deity Vajrayoginī, compiled by the Tibetan master Orgyenpa Rinchen Pal (1230–1309) during his travels in Oḍḍiyāna.

The very structure of *The Treasury* thus stands as a statement of the nonsectarian approach. With all these teachings gathered together and set side by side—and each one authenticated by its identification with a direct lineage traced back to the source of Buddhism (India)—maintaining a sectarian attitude would be next to impossible. Or at least that must have been Kongtrul's hope. In explaining his purpose for the collection, he states:

> Generally speaking, in each of the eight great mainstream lineages of accomplishment there exists such a profound and vast range of authentic sources from the sutra and tantra traditions, and such limitless cycles of scriptures and pith instructions, that no one could compile everything.[4]

Nevertheless, he made a good start in *The Treasury of Precious Instructions*, which he kept expanding over the years until at least 1887. The woodblocks for the original printing—carved at Palpung Monastery, where Kongtrul resided in his nearby retreat center—took up ten volumes. An edition of this is currently available in twelve volumes as the Kundeling printing, published in 1971–1972.[5] With the addition of several missing texts, an expanded and altered version was published in eighteen volumes in 1979–1981 by Dilgo Khyentse Rinpoche. Finally, in 1999 the most complete version became available in the edition published by Shechen Monastery, which is the basis for the current translations.[6] The structure of this enhanced edition, of course, still centers on the eight lineages, as follows:

1. Nyingma (Ancient Tradition), volumes 1 and 2;
2. Kadam (Transmitted Precepts and Instructions Lineage), volumes 3 and 4;
3. Sakya, or Lamdre (Path with Its Result), volumes 5 and 6;
4. Marpa Kagyu (Precept Lineage of Marpa), volumes 7 through 10;
5. Shangpa Kagyu (Precept Lineage of Shang), volumes 11 and 12;
6. Zhije (Pacification), volume 13, and Chöd ("Severance"), volume 14;
7. Jordruk (Six Yogas [of Kālacakra]), volume 15; and
8. Dorje Sumgyi Nyendrub (Approach and Attainment of the Three Vajras, also called after its founder Orgyenpa), volume 15.

Volumes 16 and 17 are devoted to various other cycles of instruction. Volume 18 mainly consists of the *One Hundred and Eight Teaching Manuals of Jonang*, a prototype and inspiration for Kongtrul's eclectic anthology, and also includes his catalog to the whole *Treasury*.

Translators' Introduction

In all the annals of Tibetan Buddhism, Jamgön Kongtrul Lodrö Taye must appear as in many ways incomparable. His five great treasuries together with his own compositions fill a library of over one hundred volumes. As a founding member of the *rime*, or nonsectarian movement, he demonstrated a prodigious erudition and assiduity, collecting together the texts and lineage transmissions of the whole of the Tibetan tradition, thereby preserving many that were threatened with extinction. Tireless in promoting and preserving these same lineages, he spent many years in solitary retreat, meditating on them in his hermitage of Tsadra Rinchen Drak. To be sure, when one considers all the details of his life, one is bound to conclude that Jamgön Kongtrul was not only one of the greatest masters ever to have appeared in the history of Tibetan Buddhism but also one of the greatest scholars and religious leaders of all time.

He worked constantly in close consultation with his friend and mentor, Jamyang Khyentse Wangpo, whom, though seven years his junior, he did not hesitate to regard as his "lord guru." It was to him that in 1862 he offered his first massive work, the ten-volume Buddhist encyclopedia known as *The Treasury of Knowledge*. Jamyang Khyentse Wangpo responded with the prophecy that it was only the first of five great treasuries that Kongtrul would eventually produce. Of these, and from the point of view of the Tibetan tradition as a whole, *The Treasury of Precious Instructions* must rank as one of the most important, for it brings together in a single place important texts of all Tibetan schools envisaged as eight chariots of transmission. Its aim was to establish in the face of threat, and to protect from the danger of decay, the full range of the eight great practice lineages of Tibet. "To preserve these," Ringu Tulku observed in his preface to the translated catalog, "is to preserve Vajrayāna Buddhism."[1]

It was not a moment too soon. Until the nonsectarian movement breathed new life into them, many of the Tibetan traditions of learning and practice were, after centuries of proscription and neglect, already in a lamentable state of decline. And yet more terrible dangers threatened. From the completion of *The Treasury of Precious Instructions* and its first transmission to a small group of disciples in 1882, less that seventy years would pass before Tibet was itself assaulted and overrun by the Chinese communist forces. And in the cultural and religious wreckage that followed, Kongtrul's great treasuries would be among the most important sources from which Tibetan masters could reassemble their teaching traditions in exile and rebuild anew the tattered remnant of their immense heritage, eventually transmitting it to the West.

The Treasury of Precious Instructions has grown with time. The original ten volumes first printed at the monastery of Palpung in Kham were again printed in the twelve volumes of the Kundeling edition in the early 1970s. Many more texts were subsequently added until a new edition in eighteen volumes was assembled and published under the auspices of Dilgo Khyentse Rinpoche at Shechen Monastery in 1999. It is this Shechen edition that has been followed for the translation into English.

The first of the eight lineages, preserved in the first and second volumes of *The Treasury*, is the one that historically appeared first: the Nyingma, or Old Translation, school. In his autobiography, Kongtrul records that from what he regarded as the most important and representative elements of the Nyingma school, he selected texts related to what he called the "three yogas"—by which he meant the teachings and practices of the three inner tantras according to the nine-vehicle structure used in the Nyingma tradition. The texts selected as representative of the first two yogas, the generation-stage practices of mahāyoga and the perfection-stage practices of anuyoga, together with those belonging to the outer "mind class," and the inner "space class" of atiyoga, *mahāsandhi*, or the Great Perfection, are assembled in the first Nyingma volume. Subsequently, the texts belonging to the "pith-instruction class," specifically those related to the unsurpassed secret section—the Heart Essence, or Nyingtik—form, for the most part, the contents of the second Nyingma volume, which is translated here.[2]

It is easy to see why Kongtrul followed this scheme. Although, rarely, lineage holders of the Great Perfection can be found in other Tibetan schools, it is true nevertheless that its teachings constitute the most treasured and distinctive feature of the Nyingma tradition. In order to introduce and contextualize the Heart Essence teachings, we will endeavor to provide a theoretical explanation of its doctrine followed by a brief history of its origins and transmission to Tibet in a manner coordinated with the contents of the present volume.

The Great Perfection and the Heart Essence

The most profound and essential tenet of the buddhadharma, at least in the understanding of the Nyingma school, is that within the mind of every being, as its bedrock, fundamental stratum, or element, lies the buddha nature. Though utterly hidden by layers of obscuration accumulated from beginningless time, this nature is perfect. It is not an existent thing in the ordinary sense of that expression since it lies beyond even the distinction between existence and nonexistence. And yet it is blissful and replete with all the qualities of enlightenment. Concealed and unrecognized, its presence is nevertheless felt, dimly and confusedly, even in the most elementary organisms of sentient life in the ignorant clinging to self-identity and the ever-present thirst for satisfaction and happiness.

Expressed in more sapiential terms, the buddha nature is equated with the mind's true nature, primordial wisdom, the limpid, clear state of awareness (*rig pa*) that precedes and remains unmodified, though obscured, by discursive, dualistic cognition. It is like the surface of a vast, immaculate mirror in which the whole range of phenomenal existence appears reflected. In usual circumstances, the surface of this mirror is undetectable, invisible, and yet it is the one factor that makes the vision of those reflections possible. Transcendent in the sense of forever remaining pure and unspoiled by any adventitious circumstance, awareness is nevertheless immanent in every experience. All that appears, whether good or bad, is the display of awareness—awareness, the nature of the mind, the ground of both samsara and nirvana.

The direct introduction to the nature of awareness and the sustained experience of it leading to manifest enlightenment constitute the essential method of the Great Perfection teachings, the purpose of which is to break through the all-enveloping shell of the thoughts and emotions of the ordinary mind, like clearing away the clouds in order to reveal the ever-present, yet hitherto obscured, sun.

In order to define and situate the teachings of the Great Perfection within the doctrinal scheme of Mahāyāna Buddhism, it is helpful to refer to the doctrine of the three kāyas: the dharmakāya, the body of ultimate reality, followed by the rūpakāya, or body of form, which in turn comprises the sambhogakāya, the body of enjoyment, and the nirmāṇakāya, the body of manifestation, whereby the path to enlightenment is revealed to beings.

Tracing the activities of the three kāyas in reverse order, we may say that for the sake of beings in samsara, who are strongly caught up in the desire to achieve happiness and escape suffering, and who are therefore in need of instruction in ethical discipline, meditative concentration, and wisdom, the teachings, mainly in the form of sutras, are set forth in the causal vehicle of characteristics by the supreme nirmāṇakāya, the Buddha Śākyamuni, appearing in the form of a renunciant.

For beings of higher capacity, who are able to penetrate more deeply into the nature of things and who are able to transform defilements into their corresponding wisdoms, the teaching of the tantras, the resultant vehicle of skillful methods, is set forth by the sambhogakāya, the buddha Vajradhara, arrayed in the silks and ornaments that symbolize the qualities of enlightenment.

Finally, for fortunate disciples of the highest capacity, the teachings of the Great Perfection, which introduce the nature of the mind, are directly set forth, not by the rūpakāya, but by the dharmakāya, the primordial buddha Samantabhadra, who, as the expression of the mind's most fundamental ground, is naked and has the deep-blue color of unfathomable space.

This presentation of the Mahāyāna teachings in terms of the three kāyas raises a number of important points. First, just as the three kāyas are facets of the same awareness, the nature of the mind, so too the different vehicles are all expressions of the same dharma. However different they may be in teaching and methods, they are essentially one and without contradiction, suited to the different capacities and aspirations of beings.

The second important point is that, whereas the sutra and tantra teachings are set forth by the rūpakāya in its varying forms, the teachings of the Great Perfection belong, as we have said, to the level of the dharmakāya. This means that, although the Great Perfection, or atiyoga, is generally classified as the highest of the inner tantras, it nevertheless stands apart from them and in fact transcends them. The Great Perfection speaks of the primordial ground, which is prior to the division between samsara and nirvana and is the ultimate expanse of self-arisen awareness. Those who are able to follow this path do not purify or remove mind-obscuring defilements through the use of antidotes as in the lower vehicles. Instead they recognize directly the present, intrinsic, primordially immaculate "great perfection" of the mind itself, which is pure from the beginning and has never been stained.

The eight lower vehicles, from the Sūtrayāna to the anuyoga instructions of the inner tantras, are designed to cater to the needs of practitioners of lesser capacity, and their teachings are set forth and implemented on the level of the ordinary discursive mind. By contrast, the Great Perfection takes as the path not the ordinary mind but the nature of the mind, the primordial wisdom of awareness. And it is with the introduction and recognition of that nature that the path of the Great Perfection begins. The difference between these two approaches is stated clearly by Khangsar Khenpo Tenpa'i Wangchuk in his commentary to Longchen Rabjam's *Treasury of the Dharmadhātu*:

> There are two kinds of dharma. One appears in the eight successive vehicles (up to and including anuyoga) where the ordinary mind is taken as the path and the result is accomplished through the concerted effort of adopting and rejecting. Contrasted with this is the teaching of the Great Perfection, in which primordial wisdom, unstained by the ordinary mind, is taken as the path. . . . Now the ordinary mind is a consciousness that apprehends the objects of the senses; it is a consciousness that accumulates various propensities . . . and all of the lower vehicles, which take the ordinary mind as the path, are therefore based on methods that are by nature manifestations of the *display* of awareness's creative power [not awareness itself]. They were set forth as a means to relinquish or clear away the mental factors and manifold habitual propensities of the ordinary mind. For according to the eight gradual vehicles, pure primordial wisdom is actualized when the mind and mental factors are relinquished. By contrast, the tradition of atiyoga states that, without relying on an object or subject of purification, the mind and mental factors are already—in their very nature and in this very instant—the indwelling primordial wisdom.[3]

It is for this reason that although the teachings of the Great Perfection are set forth in a vast collection of scriptures, which are of necessity couched in human language, it is important to realize that they are constantly straining to express meanings and experiences that lie beyond the reach of ordinary thought and word. This is why the Great Perfection is not a tenet system in the commonly accepted sense: a body of theoretical propositions culminating in an intellectual position, or view, *about* the nature of the mind and phenomena. The "view" of the Great Perfection *is* the actual vision or experience of this nature. It is revealed as the nature of the mind itself and must be pointed out, directly introduced, to a qualified disciple by an accomplished master and holder of the lineage. It is only when this introduction takes place, and the disciple sees the nature of the mind, that the path and practice of the Great Perfection begins.

The Transmission of the Great Perfection Teachings

In recent years, the Great Perfection has stimulated a good deal of interest in the Western Buddhist academy. The research is ongoing, but already much scholarly work has been done in the attempt to clarify questions about the origins, dating, and transmission of texts, the manuscript lineages and the complex relations between them, and possible links between the Great Perfection teachings of the Nyingma Buddhist school and those of the indigenous Tibetan tradition of Yungdrung Bön, and so on. These questions are of abiding interest, but in the present context—namely, the Nyingma section of *The Treasury of Precious Instructions*—it seems more appropriate to sketch out the story of the arrival of the Great Perfection in Tibet according to the traditional account with which Jamgön Kongtrul was familiar and which is taken for granted by Tibetan masters, scholars, and practitioners down to the present day. Beginning in a mythical past and gradually coalescing into recorded history, it is a rich and fascinating tale, filled with superhuman figures and miraculous events, and a line of masters that comes down in unbroken sequence to the flesh and blood, if highly extraordinary, figures of our own time.[4]

Originating from an utterly transcendent source—namely, the dharmakāya—and appearing gradually in the human world through the activity of the rūpakāya, the teachings of the Great Perfection are said to pass through three kinds of transmission: the mind-to-mind transmission of the victorious ones, the transmission through symbols of the vidyādharas, and the oral transmission of spiritual masters.

In the mind-to-mind transmission of the victorious ones, the teachings are said to arise from the primordial buddha Samantabhadra himself. In the eternal present of the "fourth time," they pass directly to his retinue, the sambhogakāya buddhas of the five families, who, as his outward reflection, are of the same nature as himself. This first transmission, from the dharmakāya to the sambhogakāya, beyond time and place, thought and word, occurs entirely within the realm of natural and effortless luminosity.[5] Subsequently, the sambhogakāya buddhas Vajrasattva and Vajrapāṇi transmitted the teachings—in a form accessible to beings—to Adhicitta in the Heaven of the Thirty-Three Gods and to the nirmāṇakāya Garab Dorje in the human world.

Garab Dorje

There are several stories of the appearance in this world of Garab Dorje. Miraculously born of a virgin, and a being of preternatural beauty and spiritual and intellectual gifts, he received directly from Vajrasattva, appearing to him in a vision, the six million four hundred thousand verses of the Great Perfection tantras, all of which were delivered according to the mind-to-mind transmission of the victorious ones.

Withdrawing to the Śītavana charnel ground, Garab Dorje is said to have instructed the ḍākinīs and other disciples who gathered round him. As the first human teacher of the Great Perfection, at once a figure of legend and of history, Garab Dorje acts as the bridge between the transcendent realm of the buddhas and the human world. It is with him that the transmission through symbols of the vidyādharas is said to have begun.

Mañjuśrīmitra

The next master in the lineage of the Great Perfection is Mañjuśrīmitra. He became the principal human heir of Garab Dorje and received from him the full transmission of the six million four hundred thousand verses of the Great Perfection. When the time came for Garab Dorje to depart from this world, dissolving into a mass of light, he miraculously bestowed upon his disciple as his parting testament, *The Three Statements That Strike upon the Vital Points*, written on a parchment in ink of lapis lazuli and enclosed in a tiny casket the size of a fingernail. This teaching is the first of *The Parting Testaments of the Four Vidyādharas* translated in the present volume.

Having received the transmission of the full range of the Great Perfection teachings, Mañjuśrīmitra arranged them into the important threefold classification of mind class, space class, and pith-instruction class.[6] In his commentary to Longchen Rabjam's *Treasury of the Dharmadhātu*, Khangsar Khenpo Tenpa'i Wangchuk defines the three classes as follows:

> Practitioners of the mind class of the Great Perfection consider that phenomena are the mere display of the creative power of awareness, the enlightened mind. They therefore assert that phenomena are the outward arising of awareness. Practitioners of the space class say that since within the expanse of awareness, phenomena are the self-experience of that same awareness, they are its ornaments in beautiful array. In other words, they say that phenomena are simply the self-experience of awareness; they do not speak of them as being its outward arising. Finally, for practitioners of the pith-instruction class, the whole of phenomenal existence manifests within the state of awareness. Phenomena are nonexistent and appear in the manner of a magical illusion. And since phenomena are posited as being empty forms, which merely appear, they are neither the mind nor different from the mind.[7]

Within this threefold classification, the pith-instruction class is the most important and the one most practiced nowadays. Mañjuśrīmitra is said to have remained in the charnel ground of Sosaling absorbed in meditation for a period of over a hundred years. Here it was that Śrīsiṃha, the next great holder of the Great Perfection teachings, encountered him.

Śrīsiṃha

Śrīsiṃha was born in China. In early adulthood, he ordained as a monk and spent ten years at Wutai Shan, the Five-Peaked Mountain sacred to Mañjuśrī, where he studied and practiced the outer and inner tantras. At length, Avalokiteśvara appeared to him and told him to go to India and seek out his master in Sosaling. Following these instructions, Śrīsiṃha remained with Mañjuśrīmitra for twenty-five years, in the course of which he received the entire range of teachings and pith instructions of the Great Perfection.

When the time came for Mañjuśrīmitra to leave this world, there occurred a scene similar to the one that had attended the departure of Garab Dorje. As the master disappeared into a mass of light, he bequeathed his parting testament to his lamenting disciple. This teaching, *The Six Meditative Experiences*, is the second of *The Parting Testaments of the Four Vidyādharas* translated here. Śrīsiṃha went on to make a second important innovation, dividing the teachings of the pith-instruction class into four sections: outer, inner, secret, and unsurpassed secret, the last of which is generally referred to as the Heart Essence, or Nyingtik. From the point of view of the Tibetan tradition, Śrīsiṃha was a lineage holder of particular importance since all the great masters who brought the Great Perfection teachings to Tibet were his disciples: Vimalamitra, Guru Padmasambhava, and Vairotsana.

Jñānasūtra and Vimalamitra

Next in the lineage of holders of the Great Perfection teachings are Jñānasūtra and Vimalamitra. They were contemporaries, friends, and both became scholars of great eminence. Vajrasattva appeared to them in a vision and told them that if they wished to attain full enlightenment in their present lives, they should seek out Śrīsiṃha and request his guidance. For reasons unknown, Jñānasūtra was detained in India, and so Vimalamitra set out alone, traveled to China, and met Śrīsiṃha at his residence in the legendary Bodhi Tree Temple. From him Vimalamitra received the oral transmission of the first three sections (outer, inner, and secret) of the teachings of the pith-instruction class. He then returned to India, met again with Jñānasūtra, and transmitted to him all that he had learned. Thereupon, the two friends set out together for China with the intention of requesting further instruction. They stayed with Śrīsiṃha in the charnel ground of Sosodvīpa and after twelve years of study and practice under his direction, Vimalamitra, content with what he had received, returned to India. Jñānasūtra however stayed on and at length received the full transmission of the pith-instruction class, which included the unsurpassed Secret Heart Essence.

The time eventually arrived for master and disciple to separate. Some days after Śrīsiṃha had departed on a journey, Jñānasūtra beheld him in a glorious vision shining with light and realized that he had passed into nirvana. In great lamentation, he fell to the ground weeping, whereupon he received the last testament of his master, once again written in precious ink and enclosed within a tiny casket. This was the teaching called *The Seven Nails*, the third of the four parting testaments.

Returning to India, Jñānasūtra was reunited with Vimalamitra in the charnel ground of Bhaseng. He transmitted to him all the additional teachings that he had received from Śrīsiṃha, in particular the Heart Essence section of the teachings of the pith-instruction class, which Vimalamitra had not yet received. Finally, the moment arrived for Jñānasūtra himself to pass away. Appearing in a mass of light before his desolate friend and disciple, he bestowed on him *The Four Methods of Leaving Things as They Are*, the last of *The Parting Testaments of the Four Vidyādharas*. Jñānasūtra's final gift to Vimalamitra brought to a conclusion the symbolic transmission of the vidyādharas, which had begun with the transmission of Garab Dorje to Mañjuśrīmitra. Henceforth, it is with the teaching of Vimalamitra to his Tibetan disciples that the oral transmission of spiritual masters begins.

Transmission to Tibet

The transmission of the Great Perfection teachings in Tibet passes through three important masters, all of whom were, as we have said, disciples of Śrīsiṃha: Vimalamitra himself, but also Guru Padmasambhava and the great translator Pagor Vairotsana. The contributions of the latter two masters will be discussed presently, but for the moment, the traditional account continues with Vimalamitra.

Tradition has it that within thirty years of receiving the final transmission from Jñānasūtra, Vimalamitra attained the rainbow body of great transference. This is the supreme accomplishment, rarely achieved, of the teachings of the Great Perfection, in which the attainment of buddhahood is accompanied by the dissolution of the gross elements of the physical body, which are transformed into light. No longer subject to ordinary death, the yogi is able to remain indefinitely in this world, visible to other beings according to need. Vimalamitra gradually made his way to Oḍḍiyāna, and it was there, toward the end of the eighth century, that he received and accepted the invitation of King Trisong Detsen to go to Tibet. He remained there for about thirteen years, during which time he transmitted the full range of the Great Perfection teachings. He eventually withdrew, reputedly at the age of over two hundred years, to Wutai Shan in China, where he is said still to reside.

With the assistance of Yudra Nyingpo, Kawa Paltsek, and others, Vimalamitra presided over the translation of many scriptures of the Great Perfection. Most importantly, he conferred the teachings of the Heart Essence in conditions of the strictest secrecy to a small group of disciples consisting of King Trisong Detsen, Prince Mune Tsenpo, Nyangben Tingdzin Zangpo, Kawa Paltsek, and Chokro Lui Gyaltsen.

The scriptures of the Heart Essence, thus transmitted by Vimalamitra, fall into two groups: the oral pith instructions and the seventeen tantras translated from Sanskrit. Tibetan tradition tells us that, for the sake of future generations, Vimalamitra himself committed the pith instructions to writing in four volumes in inks of different colors: gold, copper, turquoise, agate, conch, and turquoise. And since the time had not arrived for these teachings to be disseminated beyond the select group just mentioned, Vimalamitra hid them, together with the translated tantras, in the cliff of Gegung at Chimpu near Samye.

As a means of preserving the teachings of the Heart Essence till times more propitious for their propagation, Tingdzin Zangpo, one of the small group who had received them, constructed the temple of Zhai Lhakhang in Uru, and concealed there the seventeen tantras of the Heart Essence and other scriptures. Before attaining the rainbow body, he ensured the continuation of their oral transmission by giving it to his close disciple Be Lodrö Wangchuk. Keeping these teachings secret throughout his life, this master also attained the rainbow body but not before passing the transmission to Drom Rinchen Bar, who again attained the rainbow body after giving the transmission to Neten Dangma Lhungyal. When the time arrived for the written teachings to reappear, Dangma Lhungyal, already in possession of the oral transmission, recovered the texts that had been hidden by Tingdzin Zangpo over a hundred years before in Zhai Lhakhang. At length, he transmitted these texts to the celebrated yogi Chetsun Senge Wangchuk and instructed him to make copies of them. Chetsun did so and then reconcealed the originals though not, it seems, in their original hiding place.

At some later point, Vimalamitra appeared in a dream to Chetsun and told him to find the texts of the pith instructions that he himself had hidden in Gegung at Chimpu. Chetsun successfully recovered the treasure texts and, following Vimalamitra's instructions, took them to Oyuk Chigong in Tsang, where he practiced them in secret for seven years. During that time it is said that Vimalamitra came to him in person from his mystic abode in Wutai Shan and stayed with him for two weeks, teaching him and bestowing on him directly the full oral transmission. So it was that Chetsun Senge Wangchuk brought together the pith instructions, the written scriptures, and oral transmission of what would eventually be known as *The Heart Essence of Vimalamitra* (*Vima Nyingtik*).

Chetsun eventually gave the transmission of these teachings to Gyalwa Zhangtön Tashi Dorje and shortly afterward disappeared in a mass of rainbow light in his meditation cave at Chigong at the age, so it is said, of one hundred and twenty-five years. It was from this point onward that the transmission passed, in a clear historical succession of lineage holders, from Gyalwa Zhangtön (1097–1167) down to Rikdzin Kumaradza (1266–1343) and from him to Longchen Rabjam (1308–1363). *The Heart Essence of Vimalamitra* represents the unbroken oral lineage, or *kama*, of the Heart Essence teachings as distinct from the teachings of *The Heart Essence of the Ḍākinīs* preserved as spiritual treasures, or *terma*.

Guru Rinpoche and The Heart Essence of the Ḍākinīs

In addition to the Great Perfection teaching coming down from Vimalamitra, we should also consider the lineage that passes through Guru Padmasambhava. Like Vimalamitra himself, Padmasambhava was a disciple of Śrīsiṃha. In addition, he received in direct transmission from Vajradhara the so-called Chitti and Yangti yogas which are similar to the Heart Essence but are found only in certain revealed treasures. The body of the Great Perfection teachings, the seventeen tantras and pith instructions of the Heart Essence, were transmitted by Padmasambhava to his consort Yeshe Tsogyal and to a great multitude of ḍākinīs. For this reason, this tradition is known as *The Heart Essence of the Ḍākinīs.* Concealed as a spiritual treasure, it was eventually revealed in the thirteenth century by Pema Ledreltsal, and from him it passed through the intermediary of Gyalse Lekpa Gyaltsen to Longchen Rabjam.

Vairotsana

For the sake of completeness we should briefly mention the part played by Vairotsana in the transmission of the Great Perfection teachings to Tibet. A disciple of both Vimalamitra and Guru Padmasambhava, Vairotsana also encountered—admittedly under extraordinary circumstances—Śrīsiṃha, himself, the master of his masters. From him he received directly the teachings of the mind class and space class and became the holder of a lineage that came down eventually to Longchen Rabjam. He also received the Heart Essence teachings directly from Garab Dorje in a pure vision. These teachings, henceforth known as *The Heart Essence of Vairotsana* (*Vairo Nyingtik*) were concealed as treasure.

Longchen Rabjam thus inherited the two great streams of the Great Perfection tradition: the oral transmission of *The Heart Essence of Vima-*

lamitra, which he received from his master Kumaradza, and *The Heart Essence of the Ḍākinīs*, which had been preserved as treasure. For *The Heart Essence of Vimalamitra*, he composed a collection of thirty-five commentarial instructions known as *The Innermost Essence of the Master*, and for *The Heart Essence of the Ḍākinīs*, he composed the fifty-five instructions of *The Innermost Essence of the Ḍākinīs*. All together, these collections are referred to as *The Four Parts of the Heart Essence*,[8] which, despite its name, contains a fifth, concluding commentary called *The Profound Innermost Essence*,[9] which summarizes the contents of both commentarial collections.

Within the terma tradition as a whole, *The Heart Essence of the Ḍākinīs* occupies a position of particular importance, for according to the mysterious working of terma revelation, it is regarded as the "mother" of all subsequent Heart Essence teachings that appeared as treasures in the ensuing centuries.

The Second Nyingma Volume of *The Treasury of Precious Instructions*

As Kongtrul himself states in *The Catalog of "The Treasury of Precious Instructions,"* the main component of the second Nyingma volume consists of texts belonging to *The Heart Essence of Vimalamitra* and *The Innermost Essence of the Master*. Nevertheless, *The Heart Essence of the Ḍākinīs* was not entirely forgotten. Originally, and again according to the catalog, a text of pith instructions titled *The Precious Golden Garland according to the Tradition of Padma*, which belongs to *The Innermost Essence of the Ḍākinīs*, was also selected for inclusion.[10] However, for reasons unknown, both the Kundeling and the Shechen editions of *The Treasury* omit this text and replace it with a collection of instructions by Guru Padmasambhava, which are found in both the scriptural and terma collections of the Nyingma school.

Following the Heart Essence scriptures and the empowerments written by Longchenpa, Kongtrul included his own composition on the practice of the Heart Essence, the celebrated *Mother and Child* commentary. The volume continues with a series of other auxiliary texts belonging to the Great Perfection generally: the essential instructions of Guru Padmasambhava and the *Guide for Meditation* written by Longchenpa for his *Finding Rest in the Nature of the Mind*. This is followed by elements taken from The Trilogy of Natural Openness and Freedom, again by Longchenpa. The volume concludes with several ritual texts composed by Kongtrul himself.

Acknowledgments

It was an honor to be invited to participate in the mighty work of translating Jamgön Kongtrul's *Treasury of Precious Instructions*. Therefore, first of all we would like to express our admiration and gratitude to Eric Colombel and the Tsadra Foundation for their extraordinary and generous commitment to the completion of this great project.

Many of the texts contained in this volume were difficult to understand and translate, but we have been very fortunate in the assistance that we have received from Tibetan masters, both tulkus and khenpos. Of these we wish first to express our gratitude to our personal teachers Taklung Tsetrul Pema Wangyal Rinpoche and Jigme Khyentse Rinpoche. We must then give thanks to Khenchen Pema Sherab, to whom we owe an unrepayable debt of gratitude, and to his faithful assistant, Khenpo Sonam Tsewang, both of Namdröling Monastery, Mysore, India. In addition we would like to express our special thanks to Shechen Khenpo Gyurme Dorje and to Dagpo Tulku Rinpoche of Mindröling. Finally, our thanks are also due to Nikko Odiseos and to our patient and long-suffering editor Anna Wolcott Johnson of Shambhala Publications. This volume was translated by Helena Blankleder and Wulstan Fletcher of the Padmakara Translation Group.

Technical Note

This translation was made primarily from the second volume of the Shechen edition of *The Treasury of Precious Instructions*. We did not refer to the Kundeling printing of the Palpung woodblocks, which contains the same texts in the same order, because both editions contained the same misspellings, had the same omissions, and so on. In the quest for accuracy, we have relied instead, wherever possible, on other sources. These include the most recent Shechen edition of *The Four Parts of the Heart Essence* by Longchenpa, several texts by the same author published by Dodrubchen Rinpoche in the 1960s, and a Chinese edition of *The Expanded Collection of the Nyingma Kama*.

It was not practical to cite every error or textual variant, and therefore only the most significant are mentioned in the notes. Throughout the volume, numbers in curly brackets embedded in the translations indicate the Arabic page numbers of the Shechen edition.

The use of square brackets to indicate words that were added by the translators has been kept to a minimum. Textual annotations inserted by the author and also rubrical instructions in the sādhanas and empowerment rituals are set in small type.

Standard diacritics have been retained for Sanskrit terms. Tibetan and Sanskrit terms that now appear in *Merriam-Webster's Collegiate Dictionary* have been treated as English words and spelled phonetically (e.g., lama, sutra, chakra, mandala). Nevertheless, standard diacritics have been retained for mantras. Seed syllables (*oṃ, āḥ, hūṃ, hrīḥ*, etc.) are all indicated in lowercase with the exception of the basic vowel *A* (ཨ), which has been capitalized in order to avoid any possible confusion with the Tibetan *a chung* (འ) or with the English indefinite article.

In the bibliography and notes, various references from classical Indian works in the Kangyur and Tengyur are identified whenever possible according to the numbers in the Tohoku catalog of Kangyur and Tengyur texts

(Toh.), Peking Tengyur (P.T.), and Nyingma Gyubum (*NG*) as cataloged in the Tibetan and Himalayan Library (THL) Master Edition of the Collected Tantras of the Ancients. Whenever possible, citations and references found in the various texts have been identified and located manually and with reference to the Buddhist Digital Research Center (BDRC) library and the THL digital library.

The texts in this volume are replete with the specific doctrines and recondite terminology belonging to the tradition of the Great Perfection. On numerous occasions, definition and explanation are both called for—not only in relation to the teachings themselves but also to the way in which the terms themselves are translated. Since it was not feasible to provide extensive notes, we have indicated places to which the interested reader may refer, notably in the second volume of *The Treasury of Precious Qualities* (hereafter *TPQ, Book 2*) by Jigme Lingpa and Kangyur Rinpoche.

PART ONE

Primary Texts for the Heart Essence Teachings

The texts in this section fall into two groups: *The Three Testaments of the Buddha* and *The Parting Testaments of the Four Vidyādharas*. *The Three Testaments of the Buddha* are taken from *The Gold-Lettered Instructions* preserved in *The Heart Essence of Vimalamitra*. This group of texts in fact contains two sets of three testaments. Coming from a transmundane source, they are all referred to as tantras, they were all delivered under similar circumstances, and, in their varying ways, they all cover the same subject matter—the Great Perfection practice of tögal. The first set of testaments, translated here, is also contained in *The Heart Essence of the Ḍākinīs*. In his general colophon to these testaments, Kongtrul refers to them as the essence of the seventeen tantras of the Heart Essence, the unsurpassed secret section of the pith-instruction class of the Great Perfection.

The Parting Testaments of the Four Vidyādharas are likewise taken from *The Gold-Lettered Instructions*. In the version preserved in *The Heart Essence of Vimalamitra*, the testaments contain textual annotations probably added by Vimalamitra himself. They have not been translated here since, for reasons unknown, Kongtrul did not include them in the version contained in *The Treasury of Precious Instructions*. Naturally, these annotations were of help for the translation and were of course taken into account, although it must be said that on occasion their pertinence to the texts themselves was not always evident.

For both of these collections of source texts, no commentaries are to be found, with the exception of the testament of Garab Dorje to Mañjuśrīmitra. Although this testament as a whole is here referred to as *The Three Statements That Strike upon the Vital Points*, the celebrated pith instruction of that name consists only of three sentences within that testament: "Recognize your own nature. Come to a decisive certainty about one thing. Be confident in the subsiding [of thoughts]."

In the period between Garab Dorje and Longchenpa, no commentaries seem to have been made on this teaching—indeed, it is only in the form recorded in the present testament that it was preserved at all. Subsequently, a short commentary was composed on it by Longchenpa and forms part of one of the pith instructions of *The Innermost Essence of the Master.*[1] Only in the nineteenth century was an extensive commentary composed on it by the celebrated Nyingma master Patrul Rinpoche with the title *The Special Teaching of the Learned Śrī Gyalpo*. Since then, and in that form, it has been widely used as a pointing-out instruction in the Nyingma school. Inasmuch as this teaching is available in modern publications, it is usually in the form of transcriptions of oral teachings given by various masters. However, a written commentary on it has been published by the twentieth-century Tibetan scholar Khangsar Khenpo Tenpa'i Wangchuk.

The absence of commentaries always presents difficulties for translators. For the rendering of these parting testaments, we have had recourse to whatever authorities we have been able to consult. The reader should be aware, however, that in several places the translation, though as accurate as we could manage, is conjectural. And in the spirit of the tradition, we implore the indulgence of Ekajaṭī and the other protectors.

1. The Three Testaments of the Buddha

The Quintessence of the Key Points of the Pith-Instruction Class of the Luminous Great Perfection[1]

The First Testament of the Buddha

In Sanskrit: *Buddhadhekarayedhunāma* {2}
In Tibetan: *Sangs rgyas kyi zhal 'chems dang po zhes bya ba*

Homage to Vajradhara, the sixth completely perfect buddha.

Kyema, kyema!
Children of my lineage, bring all the key points of the Secret Mantra into one and put it into practice.

Here are the preliminaries
Concerning body, speech, and mind.
Meditate upon impermanence, compassion, and bodhicitta.
Because this body is engendered, caused by ignorance,
The six migrations lie indeed in their seed syllables.
Because awareness is indeed the triple kāya,
The triple kāya also manifests in its three syllables.
In these syllables, train yourself,
And apply the separating *rushen* practice.

Then settle in the natural state
And afterward refresh yourself:

Adopt the gazes of the śrāvakas,
The bodhisattvas, and the wrathful deities.

Then when you have gained confidence
In stillness, firmness, letting go,
Outwardly and inwardly relinquish all activities.

Assume the postures of the elephant, the lion, and the rishi.
In speech, cut through the stream of words,
And for the mind, from in between your eyebrows,
Concentrate on space.
And in accordance with the crucial points
Of sense door, field, and breath,
Primordial wisdom manifests within the visual field.
Perception of this is a key point—do not separate from it.

With the basis laid through the three kinds of motionlessness, {3}
Achieve the warmth of the four visions.
Make assessment with three kinds of settling,
And drive in the rivet of the three attainments.

It is my pledge that you will not return to the three worlds.
There is no doubt that you will pass beyond all sorrow.

In the southern region of the Heaven of the Thirty-Three, in the garden of Jīvaka, the physician, when the great Vajradhara displayed his passing into parinirvāṇa, Garab Dorje fell to the ground and lamented sorrowfully:

> *Kyema, kyihu!* Sorrow and sadness!
> If now the radiance of the lamp, our teacher, sets,
> Who will drive away the darkness of the world?

When he revived from his faint, he saw before him in a mass of light the right hand and arm [of the Buddha] as far as the elbow, from which there dropped into the palm of his own right hand a casket of precious crystal no larger than a fingernail. He opened it and there discovered this instruction written in letters of melted lapis lazuli upon a precious blue surface. And Garab Dorje gained the confidence of realization.

Samaya.

The Second Testament of the Buddha

In Sanskrit: *Buddhadhekaramadunāma*
In Tibetan: *Sangs rgyas kyi 'das rjes gnyis pa*

Homage to the completely perfect Buddha, the heroic mighty subjugator. {4}

If you truly wish to gain enlightenment,
You must train yourself in this preliminary.
If you do not properly perform the separating rushen practice
With regard to body, speech, and mind,
You will not free yourself from the three worlds.
Therefore train in this preliminary.
If you gain dexterity in its key points,
You will be skilled in common and supreme accomplishments.

For the preliminary practice linked with body,
Stay alone in solitude.
Engage in all the various behaviors of the six migrations,
And also the behavior of the Triple Gem.
Sit upright with the soles of your feet joined
And with your palms together at your crown.
The body of the one who sits in such a posture
Will not fall back [into samsara]—
Obstacles will be dispelled,
Strong clinging to it will be overcome,
Obscuring veils will dissipate.
The body will subside in the nirmāṇakāya;
It will not be different from the body of a buddha.
Nothing will be left behind.

For the preliminary practice linked with speech,
Imitate the different cries and tongues of the six realms.
And likewise imitate the various sounds
Belonging to the peaceful and the wrathful deities
And all the elements.
For three days, implement instructions
For the placing of the seal, developing of skill,
Search for mental pliancy, and journeying on the road.
For those who practice in this way regarding speech,
Strong clinging to it will be overcome.
Their obscuring veils will dissipate.
Their speech will not fall back [into samsara]
But [from buddha speech] will not be different.
It will subside in the sambhogakāya.

For the preliminary practice linked with mind,
Bring to mind the six realms and their sorrows,
Then search from where this mind arises.
You will not find it but will meet the dharmakāya.
Search for where it dwells.
Not finding it, you will encounter the sambhogakāya.
Search for where it goes.
Not finding it, you'll meet with the nirmāṇakāya.
For those who practice in this way regarding mind,
Strong clinging to it will be overcome.
Obstacles will dissipate, and obscurations will be purified.
And they will not fall back into the triple world.
Their minds, subsiding in the dharmakāya,
Will pass beyond, not different [from the buddha mind].

Then gain skill in bringing to their natural state
Your body, speech, and mind. {5}
And afterward, refresh them.
Make effort in this practice.
Once you have completed these preliminaries,
Put them from your mind.
Come now to the key point of the seeing [of awareness]
Through relinquishing all acts of body, speech, and mind.

In the eastern quarter of the great Blazing Mountain charnel ground, a trysting place for ḍākinīs of various clans, when the completely perfect Buddha displayed his passing into parinirvāṇa, Garab Dorje fell to the ground and in sorrow lamented:

> *Kyema, kyihu!* Sorrow and sadness!
> If now the radiance of the lamp, our Teacher, sets,
> Who will drive away the darkness of the world?

When he revived from his faint, he saw before him in a mass of light, the right hand and arm [of the Buddha] as far as the elbow, from which there dropped, enclosed within a casket of precious crystal, the above instruction. It was written in self-arisen letters inscribed with the inks of five different gemstones upon a parchment the color of melted lapis lazuli. This sublime instruction, laden with blessing, is the second testament of the Buddha. It appeared thus so that the nirmāṇakāya Garab Dorje might remember it. It is in the manner of an instruction bestowed by all the enlightened ones, who have passed beyond sorrow. It is the condensed essence of all their teachings, bestowed upon their only heir.

Samaya.

The Third Testament of the Buddha

In Sanskrit: *Buddhadhekarayatrināma*
In Tibetan: *Sangs rgyas kyi 'das rjes gsum pa*

Homage to Vajradhara, the natural state of openness and freedom.

Kyema, kyema!
Listen to me, children of my lineage.
If bodily you wish to pass beyond all sorrow,
Train in these postures of the triple kāya.
Those who do so pass beyond all sorrow
In the dimension of the enlightened body
Of the buddhas of the past, the present, and of time to come.

Concerning speech, observe the stages of the training
Till you gain stability and firm conviction.
Those who do not disregard this training
Will pass beyond all sorrow
In the dimension of the enlightened speech
Of the buddhas of the past, the present, and of time to come.

The crucial point concerning mind
Is mastery of the three ways of gazing. {6}
Watch a sky devoid of the three defects—
This is the key point of the visual field.
Gaze upward, downward, to the side—
This is the key point of the sense door.
Train yourself in breathing very slowly—
This is the key point of the breath.
Through taking pains in these three crucial points,

Empty awareness, the three kāyas, will arise.
Imprison the awareness-chains,
For thus—and this is a key point—
You will undoubtedly perceive it.

Through the vision that perceives the dharmatā directly,
All conceptual, fixating views subside.
Through the vision of the enhanced experience of awareness,
Primordial wisdom in the bardo is made manifest.
Through the vision of the climax of awareness,
You recognize the sambhogakāya.
Through the vision of the exhaustion of phenomena in dharmatā,
The state of great perfection, the result beyond all action, is achieved.

If, therefore, you accomplish the four visions,
You have no need to seek nirvana in some other place.
Lay the ground with the three kinds of motionlessness.
Make assessment with three kinds of settling,
And in your body, speech, and mind, the signs will manifest.
Fix it with the rivet of the three attainments.
Beyond this there is nothing left to teach. *Samaya.*

Keep close this teaching that has been bequeathed to you,
Perfectly inscribed in precious inks.
Those who honor it will surely gain their freedom.
At times of rainbow lights, of thunder, earthquakes,
Frost, or hail, of famine or eclipse,
To read this text aloud in the appropriate direction
Is more meaningful than offerings made to all the buddhas
Who have manifested in a billion universes.

When our teacher displayed his passing into parinirvāṇa, this instruction, imbued with the blessing of uncontrived and self-arisen teaching, and written in self-arisen letters with inks of five gemstones, fell into the palm of Garab Dorje's right hand in response to his lamentation, upon the Vulture Peak to the south of Rājagṛha. This final testament of the Buddha was uttered for the sake of Garab Dorje, the only heir of all his teachings.

Samaya.
Sealed. Sealed. Sealed.

The culmination of all true paths is the Luminous Great Perfection, within which there are three classes of teaching. The highest of these is the class of pith instructions comprising limitless cycles of outer, inner, secret, and most secret teachings. {7} Furthermore, the essential core of the renowned six million four hundred thousand ślokas of the tantras of the most secret pith instructions, or Heart Essence, is explained in terms of seventeen kinds of utterly refined light. These are said to be the seventeen tantras, of which *The Word-Transcending Tantra* is regarded as the root, or foundation, the precious seed of their origin. Now the essence of the key points of all these tantras is further expressed in the unequaled tantras known as *The Three Testaments of the Buddha*. They, together with the following *Parting Testaments of the Four Vidyādharas*, are set down in the form of vajra verses.

The actual meaning of *The Three Testaments* may be summarized as follows. *The First Testament* briefly sets forth the entire corpus of the pith instructions (primarily on tögal) related to the sphere of luminosity belonging to the uncommon secret pith-instruction class of the Great Perfection. *The Second Testament* sets forth the preliminary for the tögal practice, while *The Third Testament* gives detailed instruction on the main practice, distinguishing the four visions. A detailed understanding of the meaning of all of them may be gained by consulting manuals of instruction such as the treatise titled *The Precious Treasury of the Supreme Vehicle* and the text of pith instructions known as *The Innermost Essence of the Master: The Wish-Fulfilling Gem*, composed by the omniscient master Longchenpa.[2]

2. The Parting Testaments of the Four Vidyādharas[1]

The Parting Words of Garab Dorje to Mañjuśrīmitra

The Three Statements That Strike upon the Vital Points[2]

Garab Dorje

namo śrī guruye

I bow down to the confidence of realization of self-cognizing awareness.

This awareness, which is not established as existent,
Arises unimpeded in its various self-display.
All phenomenal existence therefore manifests
As the field of dharmakāya.
This arising naturally subsides,
And in this point the wisdom of all sugatas resides.
The threefold pith instruction, given to revive you from your faint,
Will cut the ties that bind you to samsara and nirvana.
Hide these, my parting words, deep in your heart.

ati
Here is the pith instruction that reveals awareness directly.

Recognize your own nature.
Come to a decisive certainty about one thing.
Be confident in the subsiding [of thoughts].

There is your own nature, and there is your perception of other things. {8}
The two united, this is recognition.

ithi

Whatever appears is yourself,
And your strength is the greatest.
You recognize yourself.

The mother is recognized in the mother.
The child is recognized in the child.
And in one, the one is recognized.

You are linked to awareness alone.
You are linked to yourself alone.
You are linked to openness and freedom alone.

Outer appearances are resolved in yourself.
Your self-experience is resolved in one thing only.
Doubts are resolved in openness in freedom.

ithi

To have power over yourself is like having the self-assurance of a rich and wealthy person.
To have power over others is like having the self-assurance of a cakravartin king.
To have the power of the place of freedom is like having the self-assurance of space dissolving into space.

ithi

In yourself, you are open and free.
The one is free in one.
The two, the mother and her child, are joined together.

ithi

When you recognize your own nature, you recognize the ground. Thus it is like a mother meeting with her child. It is the recognition that there is but one sole place of freedom. Knowing that through yourself you are open and free, you gain a clear certainty in primordial awareness. You thus acquire a clear conviction that through stain, the stain is cleansed—that for thoughts there is no other antidote to rely upon than thoughts themselves. Since you are free within the very ground, you gain trust in it. Therefore, just as a knot tied on a snake unties itself, the cognition that depends on something else is worn away, and you settle in the very ground.

ithi

When Garab Dorje displayed his passing beyond sorrow, Mañjuśrīmitra fell fainting to the ground, lamenting greatly. From within a mass of light there appeared the right hand of the Blissful Resurrected One,[3] and in order to bring him to his senses, there fell into the palm of Mañjuśrīmitra's right hand these parting words in the form of three statements, spontaneously penned in deep-blue ink of molten lapis lazuli. To contain them, there fell also a precious crystal casket the size of a fingernail. Mañjuśrīmitra, reviving from his swoon, gained the confidence of realization.

Conceal these words, therefore, in the mandala of your heart. This instruction on the three statements, this final testament given at the moment of its author's passing—the distilled essence of the tantras and a golden teaching on the view—came down in the great charnel ground of Śītavana. This supreme instruction, appearing at the source of the river Danatika, is the path that brings release to every being. It is a pith instruction that brings instant freedom in a buddha field. It is now complete.

The Parting Words of Mañjuśrīmitra to Śrīsiṃha

The Six Meditation Experiences[4]

Mañjuśrīmitra

namo śrī guruye {9}

I bow down to the confidence of realization of self-cognizing awareness.

This awareness, which is not established as existent,
Arises unimpeded in its various self-display.
All phenomenal existence therefore manifests
As the field of dharmakāya.
This arising naturally subsides,
And in this point the wisdom of all sugatas resides.
The sixfold pith instruction, given to revive you from your faint,
Will cut the ties that bind you to samsara and nirvana.
Hide these, my parting words, deep in your heart.
Samayam atikramatha.

I bow down to confidence in the indwelling nature!
This is my ultimate instruction, a teaching on the great primordial wisdom.
This great primordial wisdom appearing in its own domain[5]
Is to be watched in the sky devoid of all activity
Like fencing in a deer.
According to the realization that arose within my mind,
In order to revive you from your faint,

My parting words I will declare
And now reveal six pith instructions
Concurring with the key points of the body
And the target of awareness.

Kyema, kyema, my great noble son!
If you wish to look directly at awareness in its nakedness,
Search for its domain and
Focus on the key points of the body.
Stop the path of movement in and out.
Home in upon the target that you focus on. {10}
Lay the ground with motionlessness, and
Hold the vast expanse within your grip.

Its natural domain is the original primordial purity.
Its domain of spontaneous presence is hallucinatory appearance.
Its bodily domain is its supporting place.[6]
Its domain of the unclouded sky is the object of the practice.
Its domain of colored light is the visions of luminosity.
Its domain of self-experience in the bardo is its final destination.

With the lion's posture is awareness mastered.
With the posture of the elephant is awareness watched.
With a vulture's flight, you soar in the vast spaces of the view.
With a vixen's crafty step, you travel through the grounds.
With the stretching manner of man, the mind is fixed upon the sky.
And in the way a knot is tied, the chains are held in place.[7]

The breath is drawn in for a while through nose and mouth,
And thus the karmic wind of ignorance is stopped.
The mind is focused on the sky,
And thus the movement of your thoughts is stopped.
Awareness is directed to the eyes,
And thus there's no delusion with regard to ultimate nature.
The outer and the inner spaces blend,
And thus awareness does not move.
This is itself not different from the ultimate expanse,
And thus discursive mind is halted.

Awareness merges with the ultimate expanse,
And thus delusion dissipates within the ground.

The sky devoid of clouds,
The pure and ultimate expanse devoid of stains,
Perceptions free of all obscuring veils,
The disks of light that neither radiate nor reabsorb,
Luminous appearances that do not intensify or dim,
The chains that neither come nor go—
Regarding all of these, you focus on awareness as it is.

Unmoving is your body; thus you rest in the four visions.
Unmoving is your gaze, and thus you halt the movement of the chains.
Unmoving is awareness, thus phenomenal existence sinks into the
 dharmakāya.
Suchness is unmoving, thus all false appearances are halted.
Dharmakāya is unmoving, thus primordial wisdom is recognized.
From emptiness there is no moving, thus all thoughts are naturally
 purified. {11}

Phenomenal existence arises as awareness, luminous and empty,
Thus from mindless matter you are free.
The sky's expanse is filled with chains of light,
And therefore you are free in dharmatā, the mother.
All that is perceived is simply luminous appearance,
And therefore you are freed from the five demons of the elements.
The nature of samsara and nirvana is recognized,
And therefore you do not depend on anything.
In awareness emptiness and luminosity are blended,
And therefore you are free from words of tantra teachings.
Enhanced is the vastness of the ultimate expanse,
And therefore you are said to grasp awareness in your hand.

ithi

When Mañjuśrīmitra ascended into the sky enveloped in a mass of rays of light and passed utterly beyond all sorrow, Śrīsiṃha fell fainting to the ground and cried out in all the ten directions. A great sound came from the sky and brought him to his senses. As he gazed into the sky, there appeared in a blaze of light the right hand of Mañjuśrīmitra. And as if to wake him from his swoon, there fell into the palm of his hand a precious casket containing this instruction written of its own accord in dark-blue ink of melted lapis lazuli. This event occurred in the great charnel ground of Sosaling, and through the simple falling of the casket into his hand, Śrīsiṃha gained the confidence of realization. These parting words of Mañjuśrīmitra, known as *The Six Meditation Experiences*, are a pith instruction that causes one to pass beyond sorrow in the expanse of unborn emptiness. More secret than all secret instructions, it is taught in order that it may be practiced. It is now complete.

The Parting Words of Śrīsiṃha to Jñānasūtra

The Seven Nails[8]

Śrīsiṃha

sarva santika

Homage to Perfect Wisdom, empty and luminous.

Self-cognizing primal wisdom,
All-pervading, variously appearing,
Unconfined, beyond extremes—
That I might fix it motionless to the unchanging ground,[9]
I joined with seven nails the perilous paths:
Samsara and nirvana.
Thus I felt within my mind a great unchanging bliss. {12}

Like a sunbeam is the pith instruction thereupon.
To rouse you from your faint,
The door of wisdom's treasury I open wide
And speak with clarity this secret teaching.
Grasp its meaning, which is like a wish-fulfilling gem!

At the border of samsara and nirvana,
Drive in the nail of primal wisdom, open, unimpeded.
Between the objects of the senses and the mind,
Drive in the nail of the lamp's self-experience.
Between the mind and matter,
Drive in the nail of ultimate, pure nature.

Between discontinuity and permanence,
Drive in the nail of the vast, free, and open view.
Between phenomena and their nature,
Drive in the nail of dharmatā,[10] awareness.
Between the states of dullness and wild movement,
Drive in the nail of the five open, unrestricted sense doors.
Between appearance and emptiness,
Drive in the nail of the primordial and perfect dharmakāya.

ithi

Luminosity, by its nature unobscured, is wisdom, which is naturally open and free. Applying it to what is seen as something other is like a fire that touches grass.

Appearances are a state of naked openness and freedom. To know this is to gain control of memories and thoughts. It is like light that touches a dark house.

To recognize awareness, the pure, primordial state that is the ground, is like the loving touch of man and woman.

Since primordial wisdom, free by nature of extremes, arises as its own condition, it is beyond the estimate of both being and nonbeing. It is as when a face meets with a mirror.

When there is freedom from both view and meditation, all manifold cognitions occur as a display. It is as when the frost meets with the sun.

Since the primordial seal of the uncontrived state is placed upon phenomenal existence, the knowing subject is recognized as the state of evenness. It is as when you meet your only child.

Because primordially and without effort, the dharmakāya is never parted from them, the world and beings are both free and open in themselves. It is like the meeting of a pauper with a treasure trove.

ithi

When Śrīsiṃha passed utterly beyond all sorrow, dissolving into the sky in a mass of rays of light, Jñānasūtra with great lamentation fell fainting to the ground. A great sound came from the sky and brought him to his senses. As he gazed into the sky, {13} there appeared in a blaze of light the right hand of Śrīsiṃha. And as if to wake him from his swoon, there fell into the palm of his hand a precious casket no bigger than a fingernail. Through the simple falling of the casket into his hand, Jñānasūtra gained the confidence of realization. This happened in Tashi Trigo. *The Seven Nails*, the parting words of Śrīsiṃha, are now complete. There are like a guide for the blind.

The Parting Words of Jñānasūtra to Vimalamitra

The Four Methods of Leaving Things as They Are[11]

Jñānasūtra

sarva ekara

I bow down to the state of emptiness primordially pure.

Herein is contained
The secret fundamental meaning of the Secret Mantra.
The wisdom mind of all the buddhas of the three times
Manifests as a great lamp of light
That drives away the darkness of the mind.

O you, a yogi who renounces all,
In order to dispel the false perceptions of the world,
Catch with the net of changeless skillful means
Primordial wisdom, self-cognizing, hard to realize.
Place it in the vast and ultimate expanse extremely deep,
And rest in the one sole sphere, beyond all ontological extremes.

This instruction, which revives you from your swoon,
Is known to be the equal of the buddhas.
Fortunate indeed you are
Who in the broadness of your mind
Desire to gaze upon awareness
Not to be attained through grasping.
Meditate at all times on this teaching.

Emaho! If you always meditate on this instruction,
Bliss will naturally arise.
Kyema! If you wish to gain the state of great equality,
At all times meditate on this instruction.

If you wish all your activity to be refined,
Leaving all appearances just as they are,
Let them settle in their naked state.
If you wish for strength in all your meditations,
With a state that's like an ocean where all is left just as it is,
Blend mind and matter into one.
If you wish for freedom from all views,
With a view that's like a mountain where all is left just as it is,
Bring all things to their exhaustion.
If you wish to dwell within the very state of all results,
Through the pith instruction of the view, awareness left just as it is,
Leave all delusions to subside just where they are. {14}

When appearances are left alone,
They are from the outset joined with emptiness.
When the mind is left alone,
It is from the outset joined with matter.
When phenomena are left alone,
They are from the outset joined with ultimate expanse-awareness.
When delusions, too, are left alone,
They are from the outset joined with natural openness and freedom.

Place upon appearance one that's evanescent, that leaves no trace—like drawing on the water.
Place on thought one that's traceless like a bird's flight in the sky.
Place on emptiness one that, like a bird's flight from a trap, is delusion's own intrinsic purity.
Find freedom in awareness with one that is unalterably pure, like someone cured from smallpox.

ithi

When you are able to experience and transform appearances—
A power that's like intoxicating wine—
The five elements are settled in the natural state.
When the mind has been completely stilled—
Like a deer caught in a hunter's snare—
It is settled in the natural state.
When the mind does not dwell on phenomena
But sees awareness like a face appearing in a mirror,
All phenomena are settled in the natural state.
When delusion sinks into the mother—
Like a knot tied on a snake—
The nonexistence of delusion and its contrary is settled in the natural state.

The state of natural openness and freedom of appearances
Is like a person in a temple who does not discriminate.
When thoughts dissolve into the ground,
It's like a sea untroubled by the wind.
When you meet awareness and the ultimate expanse,
It's like arriving at the summit of Mount Meru.
When you reach the level of the irreversible three kāyas,
It's like the *se* tree's fruit.

This [instruction] is the life tree of view, meditation, action.
It breaks the neck of those who are inflexible
And tracks down all that has been lost.
It is a board for stretching what is bent.

It is a pith instruction whereby the vast is grasped in hand.
It is a pith instruction that keeps in check what is untamed.
It is a pith instruction whereby intelligence is honed.
It is a pith instruction that settles all deeds in their natural state.

ithi

It is the foot that carries different things upon the path,
The hand that cuts the string of thought, {15}

The eye that sees awareness face-to-face,
The laundering whereby delusion is all rinsed into the ground.

It is the path on which appearances are encountered.
It is the ground on which awareness is encountered.
It is the sphere where vision is encountered.
It is the fruit where freedom is encountered.

When Jñānasūtra passed utterly beyond all sorrow, Vimalamitra with great lamentation fell fainting to the ground. A great sound came from a mass of light appearing in the sky and brought him to his senses. As he gazed into the sky, there appeared the right arm, from hand to elbow, of Jñānasūtra, which dropped into the palm of Vimalamitra's right hand a precious casket no bigger than a fingernail. He opened it and looked within, and there he saw a sheet of paper of five jewels on which was this instruction written of its own accord in deep-blue ink of lapis lazuli. Simply by seeing it, Vimalamitra gained the confidence of realization. This happened in the mighty charnel ground of Bhaseng.

The Four Methods of Leaving Things as They Are, the parting words of Jñānasūtra, are now complete. They make possible the attainment of buddhahood on a single seat and are like a lamp that shines in the darkness. They are the pith instructions on leaving action in its natural state, on leaving meditation in its natural state, on leaving the view in its natural state, and on leaving the result in its natural state.

Samaya ithi.

The first of *The Parting Testaments of the Four Vidyādharas* teaches the primary introduction to the practices of trekchö and tögal. The second speaks mainly of tögal meditation. The third explains how to enhance these meditations and dispel obstacles. The fourth discourses principally on the methods of trekchö. But all four topics are touched upon in each of the four. And so it is that all aspects of the path to enlightenment for a single person are completely revealed.

Mangalaṃ bhavatu.

PART TWO

Ritual Texts Taken from *The Innermost Essence of the Master*

These texts are principally the rituals for the four special empowerments of the Great Perfection: elaborate, unelaborate, extremely unelaborate, and supremely unelaborate. Composed by Longchen Rabjam, they are taken from *The Innermost Essence of the Master* of *The Four Parts of the Heart Essence* but are very similar to the corresponding empowerments contained in *The Heart Essence of Vimalamitra*. They contain a great deal of explanatory material in the form of rubrics for the rituals and prescribed discourses to be given by the vajra master. Therefore, although as empowerment rituals they are probably of limited use to Western readers, they nevertheless remain extremely interesting on the doctrinal level.

The first, third, and fourth empowerments are each followed by rituals of mandala offering designed to enable students to accumulate the merit necessary for the reception of empowerment. The second empowerment on the other hand is followed by two supplementary texts: a ritual for the "descent of primordial wisdom" and an explanation of the symbolism of the ritual vases used in the empowerment mandala. The entire section concludes with an elaborate gaṇacakra feast offering ritual.

3. The Net of Purity

A Ritual for the Elaborate Empowerment[1]

Longchen Rabjam

Within the space of dharmakāya {18}
Unfolds the mandala of the sambhogakāya.
The rays of light of the nirmāṇakāya
Scatter the darkness in the minds of beings.
The primordial lord, together with the lineages of the five families,
Is a wish-fulfilling treasure,
Naturally present in the temple of my mind.

From the vast and secret Nyingtik teachings,
Which directly show the vajra of the minds of all the buddhas,
I shall elucidate the stages of the detailed ritual
Of the first of the four ripening empowerments.

This exposition discusses three topics: (1) the necessary qualifications of those taking part in this ritual; (2) the correct preparation for the ritual; and (3) the main section—namely, the granting of the empowerment itself.

The Necessary Qualifications of Those Taking Part in This Ritual

First, the masters who grant the empowerment must have three qualities. They must be learned in the teachings of the sutras and tantras. Crucially, they must have direct experience of awareness. Finally, having brought their own minds to maturity, they should be able to bring to maturity the minds of others.

Second, the disciples on whom the empowerment is bestowed must themselves have four characteristics. They must give rise to the attitude of considering as a buddha the master who directly reveals to them the ultimate quintessence. Grounded in the good soil of faith, they must reject the poisonous serpent of nonvirtue. Conscious of their deluded condition, they must be very generous in the offering of worldly wealth when requesting true and authentic instruction. {19} Sparing neither their bodies nor their lives, they must be prepared to give everything to their master, whom they must serve with intense devotion and respect.

The Preparation

For the mandala, take a square surface, smooth like a mirror and an arm-span in breadth. Sprinkle it with saffron and the five substances deriving from a cow. With five-colored powders that have been empowered as the five primordial wisdoms, trace lines on it beginning with a central perpendicular line and progressing to the other lines as far as the apertures of the doors. In the center of a circle of blue light, draw an eight-petaled lotus in beautiful colors—white in the east, yellow in the south, red in the west, and green in the north. Then draw the square platforms for the deities, the doors, verandas, and door buttresses, together with the buddha field. Finally draw the seat in the form of a solar disk and a vajra fence surrounded by a ring of five-colored lights. In the center and in the four directions of the mandala, place precious vases colored according to the five enlightened families, each one marked with its respective indicator (that is, *oṃ āḥ hūṃ svā hā*) and equipped with ornamental stoppers and ribbons. They should contain the five kinds of gem, five kinds of grain, five kinds of medicinal substances, five kinds of incense, pure water, and milk. These ingredients should be sprinkled with the three white and three sweet foodstuffs. Each of the five ornamental stoppers of the vases should be decorated with an arrow, a mirror, {20} a crystal, a silk ribbon, a peacock feather, and an image of the appropriate buddha family. A kapāla filled with amṛta should be placed in the mandala. This will be the substance for the secret empowerment. A phurba should be placed at each of the four doors, and a sword in each of the intermediate directions. Then all around the mandala arrange the outer and inner offerings, together with tormas and a vast feast offering. Positioned in the mandala, the perfect support for the third empowerment should itself be adorned with a canopy, a painted image, and so on.

The Granting of the Empowerment

This is the main section and comprises three stages: (1) the self-blessing and the blessing of the mandala, (2) the entry of the disciples into the mandala, and (3) the empowerment itself.

The Self-Blessing and the Blessing of the Mandala

Here, there is no elaborate practice of the generation and perfection stages as one finds in the lower tantras of the Secret Mantra. In a single instant, the master brings to mind that he or she is the buddha in the primordial mandala—blue Samantabhadra (ground awareness) in union with his consort. His two hands are in the mudra of meditation, and he is seated in vajra posture. Measureless rays of light radiate from him. The master recites the syllable *A* one hundred and eight times. In an instant, he visualizes the mandala in front as the mandala of the five enlightened families and seals it with the syllables *oṃ āḥ hūṃ svā hā*. He then pronounces the syllables *oṃ āḥ hūṃ*. In so doing, he blesses the whole of phenomenal existence, the universe and beings, transforming it into a pure field with palaces of the five primordial wisdoms filled with male and female deities and blessing the samaya substances as ornaments delightful to the senses. All this is clearly described in *The Tantra of Self-Arisen Perfection.*

The Entry of the Disciples into the Mandala

The entry of the disciples into the mandala unfolds in eleven stages.

First, the Supplication

The disciples offer a mandala and with joined hands make the following supplication three times.

> *Emaho!*
> Great lord and master, protector of all wandering beings!
> I am a fortunate child of wisdom.
> I belong to this tradition of the ultimate great secret.
> Accept me therefore as your disciple.

Second, the Master Consents

Ema!
Fortunate children of wisdom,
If you commit yourself to this profoundly secret vehicle,
The teachings of myself, the holder of the vajra, {21}
It is certain that you will achieve its fruit.
Banishing your every doubt,
As though you saw me as a perfect jewel,
Do you willingly regard me as your master?

The disciples reply, "Yes, we do so willingly."

Third, the Disciples Take Refuge

They recite three times after the master,

The five winds purified are the essential body.
The five defilements purified are the five primordial wisdoms.
Seeing that the Three Jewels
Are the perfect action of the triple kāya, I bow down.

The master then gives the following explanation:

> Fortune disciples! The radial channels of the four chakras of your bodies are the sangha. The essence drops are the dharma. The five quintessential winds are the buddha—that is, the five primordial wisdoms, the five defilements in their primal purity. With the intention of meditating on these Three Jewels as the triple kāya, take ultimate refuge.

Fourth, the Generation of the Two Bodhicittas

For bodhicitta in intention, the disciples repeat three times after the master,

Emaho!
Ignorance is this world's dark abyss.

With the lamp of skillful means and wisdom
And owing to the kindness of my master,
I will realize the primordial wisdom dwelling in myself.

The master then says,

> Cultivate a mental attitude never before experienced, the intention to implement the four visions, the manifest appearance of the path of your awareness, which is primordial wisdom.

For bodhicitta in action, the disciples recite three times,

Emaho!
Final buddhahood is [the union] of awareness and the
ultimate expanse—
The three kāyas, freedom from the four extremes,
Primordial wisdom beyond the reach of words.
All this I shall accomplish in this very moment.

The master then declares,

> Give rise to ultimate bodhicitta, intending to recognize the primordially pure expanse, the space-like, unborn dharmakāya, together with primordial wisdom, spontaneously present awareness, which is endowed with the nature of the three kāyas, transcends the four conceptual extremes, and is beyond the reach of words and syllables—a sublime state, ineffable, inconceivable, and inexpressible.

Fifth, the Tying of the Protection String {22}

In order to protect the disciples from the mental states of samsara by means of the five primordial wisdoms, the master should make mantra knots on braids made of five-colored strings while saying *oṃ āḥ hūṃ svāhā oṃ svabhāva śuddhāḥ sarva dharmāḥ svabhāvaḥ śuddho 'haṃ*. The braids should be tied on the right arms of the men and on the left arms of the women.

Sixth, the Proclaiming of the Samaya

Pouring water from the activity vase, the master says,

> *hūṃ*
> Here is the water of your vajra pledge.
> If you spoil this, you will burn in fires of hell unbearable.
> For countless kalpas your pains will be past numbering.
> If you keep your samaya pledge,
> You will naturally attain all wonderful accomplishments—
> All without exception.
> Therefore, keep samaya, the water of life.
> Observe it; keep it in your heart.
> *oṃ sarva pañca amṛta samaya hūṃ hrīḥ tha*

The master then goes on to say,

> *Kye!*
> Fortunate disciples! If you let your samaya pledge decline, you will never be free from vajra hell and you will have to endure unbearable pain for many kalpas. But if you keep samaya and do not break it, you will accomplish every excellence in this and future lives, and you will quickly gain enlightenment. Therefore, keep your samaya well!

Seventh, the Descent of Wisdom

Incense and the "great fat" are now burned. The disciples, seated in vajra posture, are instructed to meditate on Samantabhadra in union with his consort. Holding the vase breath, they should gradually visualize the channels, the four chakras with their root syllables, and the luminous essence drops. Then, with this clear visualization, they should meditate without distraction on the words of the master. Playing the ḍamaru from time to time, the master should chant the following verses slowly, carefully, and with a pleasant melody.

> *Ema!*
> Children of the lineage, blessed with fortune!

The chakras of formation in your navel centers
Are the dwelling place of the nirmāṇakāya.
The five winds are beyond intentioned movement.
The shining essence drops are aswirl and swaying.

Ema! {23}
Children of the lineage, blessed with fortune!
The chakras of the dharmatā within your hearts
Are the dharmakāya's dwelling place.
Here reside five buddha families.
The shining essence drops are aswirl and swaying.

Ema!
Children of the lineage, blessed with fortune!
The chakras of enjoyment in your throats
Are the dwelling place of the sambhogakāya.
The major and the minor marks of buddhahood are present of themselves.
The radiating essence drops are bright and sparkling.

Ema!
Children of the lineage, blessed with fortune!
The chakras of great bliss in the crowns of your heads
Are the dwelling place of the union of the three kāyas.
In the tip, within the place of the result,
Amazing is the peal of laughter of the wrathful king.

The disciples should clearly concentrate on these words.

Eighth, the Casting of the Flower

In order to symbolize that their eyes of wisdom have been blinded by ignorance from beginningless time, the disciples cover their eyes with a band of black silk. Holding a silk tassel of five colors in their joined hands, they say,

Emaho!
Starting from the primal essence of luminosity,
Until this moment of encountering this supreme vehicle,

> Thanks to training in the fundamental ground,
> May this tassel fall upon my supreme family.

With these words, the disciples throw their tassels into the middle of the palace.

Ninth, the Granting of the Name

For the male disciples, if the flower tassel falls into the middle of the palace, the name will be Natsok Rangdröl. If it falls in the east, the name will be Dorje Nyingpo. If it falls in the south, the name will be Döyön Rangshar. If it falls in the west, the name will be Dechen Gyalpo. If it falls in the north, the name will be Gonga Chadral. For the female disciples, if the flower tassel falls in the middle, the secret name will be Khalong Yangma. If it falls in the east, the name will be Ngadrang Ösal. If it falls in the south, the name will be Gangshar Chönyi. If it falls in the west, the name will be Pemai Longchen. If it falls in the north, the name will be Khyabdal Chikchö.

Tenth, the Removal of the Eye Covering

The disciples ask the master,

> *Kyema!*
> O Lord and holder of the vajra!
> In the three realms of samsara, I am blind.
> With your compassionate wisdom,
> Dispel my ignorance, I pray.

The master then says, {24}

> My children, fortunate and noble!
> You were once blinded by delusive dualistic clinging.
> You left the wish-fulfilling jewel within yourselves and looked for it elsewhere.
> This scalpel is the tool that will fulfill your wish.

As the master removes the eye covering with the golden scalpel, the disciples consider that their ignorance has been dissipated. The master then explains,

All this symbolizes that although you all have within you a wish-fulfilling jewel—the quintessential, fivefold, self-cognizing, primal wisdom—you fail to see it. The eyes of your minds are blinded by the ignorance of subject-object dualistic clinging. Looking for that jewel elsewhere, you have wandered in samsara. Now through the compassion of me, your master, this golden scalpel (the instructions on primordial wisdom) removes the cataracts of ignorance and reveals, directly for your eyes to see, the light of your awareness residing in your hearts.

Eleventh, the Way in Which Four Things Should Be Seen

The Way of Seeing the Master

The master asks,

> Look, my noble children, look!
> Undistracted, look within your minds.
> Of the several ways of seeing me,
> How, my children, do you see me? Speak!

And the disciples answer,

> I see my master as a buddha.

Disciples of pure karma may well see their master in the form of a deity, or as a mass of light, and so on. They may well see him as a buddha through the power of their devotion.

The Way of Seeing the Mandala

> Look, my children, gifted with both sight and fortune.
> Look upon this perfect mandala.
> The time has come to cultivate great trust.
> How now do you see this mandala?

The disciples then answer according to how they actually see the mandala, whether as predominantly white, yellow, red, green, or blue. In this way, the family of primordial wisdom to which they belong is determined. The master then explains the meaning of the different elements of the mandala, pointing them out one by one with his golden scalpel. {25}

> The round blue center of the mandala indicates the fact that within the ground, the dharmatā, there are no antidotes to be applied [for there is nothing to eliminate]. The beautifully colored eight-petaled lotus indicates that the ground is endowed with the quintessence of the five winds. The four square platforms symbolize the lights of the four elements. The four courtyards together with the four doors indicate that the four activities are complete within you. The five walls of ruby and so on symbolize the radiance of the five primordial wisdoms. The four buttresses indicate that the four boundless attitudes are present of themselves within the ground. The eight gazelles are the symbols of the purity within the ground of the eight consciousnesses. The four wheels symbolize the primordial turning of the wheels of outer, inner, secret, and unsurpassed teachings. The four parasols mean that you dwell primordially within the expanse of the ground, which is everlasting, stable, unchanging, and spontaneously present of itself. The crossed vajras indicate that all phenomena partake of primordial enlightenment and abide within the state of great perfection. The projecting platform of the palace, where the offering goddesses stand, indicates that all the delights of the senses arise as ornaments and that there is no need to relinquish them. The cornices symbolize the fact that all that is desired arises by itself, while the lattices are symbols of the perfection of the qualities of the ground. The balconies indicate the impartiality of compassion, while the balustrades symbolize the essence of luminosity. The buddha field symbolizes the spontaneous self-experience of awareness. The solar seat indicates the wisdom that dwells in the ultimate expanse. The fence of vajras means that the ultimate expanse is without movement or change. The ring of light rays that surrounds [this fence] symbolizes the spontaneous display of the kāyas and the five primordial wisdoms in the ultimate expanse.

The Way in Which the Articles [in the Mandala] Are to Be Considered

The master asks, {26}

> *Ema!*
> Children of good fortune, understand these signs—
> These symbols all arrayed, the substance of samaya.
> Look at all these things that indicate the fundamental nature,
> And tell me what you see.

Each of the disciples answers,

> I see that all are the display of dharmatā.

The master then explains how the articles are to be considered, indicating them with his scalpel.

> *Kye!*
> Fortunate children of the noble lineage. The five vases indicate that the five enlightened families dwell within you. The five ribbons fastened to their necks are meant to show that the five female and male buddhas are inseparable. The ornamental stoppers show that the [enlightened] body, speech, mind, qualities, and activities are primordially complete within you. The five crystals indicate the ultimate nature, primordial purity, the ground of dharmakāya. The five iridescent peacock feathers mean that the luminous character [of awareness], the radiance of the five lamps manifesting within you, is spontaneous presence, [awareness,] the ground of the sambhogakāya. The five mirrors indicate that the cognizant potency, the five primordial wisdoms, the essence of awareness, are the ground for the unfolding of the nirmāṇakāya. The five arrows and the five-colored ribbons respectively symbolize the five wisdoms and the five winds within the ground. The four phurbas show that there is no movement or change in the ground. The four swords indicate that the doors of the four ways of taking birth are closed. The tormas and the offerings, which adorn the mandala, show that the pleasures of the senses appear as the self-experience of awareness.

How the Vajra Kindred Are to Be Regarded

Ema!
Wondrous children of the lineage!
Your sublime friends, kindred in the mandala—
Tell me how you see them.
The time for pure perception has arrived.

In reply, each of the disciples says,

> I see my friends, yogis and yoginīs, companions in the quest for liberation, as male and female deities.

The Granting of the Empowerment

There are four empowerments.

The Vase Empowerment {27}

The disciples sit in vajra posture. The master takes the vase from the center of the mandala and, placing it on the head of each disciple, says,

hūṃ
This vase of the expanse of dharmatā
Is filled with the self-arisen water of empty luminosity.
I grant you empowerment, my fortunate son [or daughter].
Realize now the fundamental nature of the ultimate expanse.

The master then recites the consonants of the Sanskrit alphabet,

ka kha ga gha nga
ca cha ja jha ña
ṭa ṭha ḍa ḍha ṇa
ta tha da dha na
pa pha ba bha ma
ya ra la va
śa ṣa sa ha kṣa

pha phā phi phī ma mā mi mī
ba bā bi bī nya nyā nyi nyī
ka kha ga gha nga
ca cā cha chā ṭa ṭā ṭha ṭhā pa pā na

Having thus granted empowerment with the consonants together with the root syllables of the chakra at the crown of the head, the master pours a drop of water on to the head of each disciple, after which the ablution should be made.

The master goes on to explain,

> Within the empty expanse of the dharmatā, primordial wisdom subsists as phenomenal appearance. This is symbolized by this vase and the water it contains. Be certain that the primordial wisdom of the dharmadhātu dwells within you.

The master then takes the vase from the eastern quarter of the mandala and, placing it at the heart of each disciple, says,

hūṃ
This unborn quintessential vase
Is filled with ceaseless, self-arisen substances.
I grant you empowerment, my fortunate son [or daughter].
Realize now the meaning of the four fearlessnesses.

a ā i ī u ū ṛ ṝ ḷ ḹ e ai o au aṃ aḥ
ka ca ḍa ta pa ya svāhā ka gha bha jha

After pronouncing the vowels together with the root syllables of the thought-gathering chakra, the master anoints the heart of each disciple with a drop of water and performs the ablution with the remaining water. The master then explains,

> Within the unborn, space-like nature of the mind, there dwells unceasing, self-arisen awareness, the primordially pure nature of the ground. This is symbolized by this vase and the water it contains. Recognize it as mirrorlike primordial wisdom.

The master then takes the vase from the southern quarter of the mandala and, placing it at the throat of each disciple, says, {28}

> *svāḥ*
> This vase of self-arisen primordial wisdom
> Is filled with self-arisen substances that delight the senses.
> I grant you empowerment, my fortunate son [or daughter].
> May you have the power to achieve spontaneously your every wish.

After reciting the consonants together with the root syllables of the taste-gathering chakra (*ra rā ḷ ḹ aṃ e a ā*), the master pours a drop of water on the throat of each disciple, performs the ablution and then explains,

> Whatever perfect quality may be wished for is possessed spontaneously from the very beginning by awareness, self-arisen primordial wisdom. This is indicated by this vase and the water it contains. By the recognition of it, all wishes are accomplished. Be certain that it is the primordial wisdom of equality.

The master then takes the vase from the western quarter of the mandala and, placing it at each disciple's navel, says,

> *āḥ*
> Unborn and free of all attachment,
> This vase is filled with the joyful substance of continuous great bliss.
> I grant you empowerment, my fortunate son [or daughter].
> Receive the power of passion free of clinging.

The master then pronounces the vowels followed by the root syllables of the chakra of formation: *a ta li ha udha raṃ yaṃ ṇaṃ najaṭi sakha raṃ yaṃ.*

The master pours a drop of water at each disciple's navel and with the remainder performs the ablution. He then explains,

> The unborn nature of the mind, primordially free from attachment, is great bliss manifesting from the stream of quintessential amṛta that fills the chakras of your body. This is symbolized by the

> vase and the water it contains. Recognize the descent, reversal, and holding of the quintessential element of great bliss, free from dualistic apprehension, as all-perceiving primordial wisdom.

The master than takes the vase from the northern quarter of the mandala and, placing it at all four places of each disciple, says,

> *hāḥ*
> The vase of open, unimpeded primal wisdom
> Is filled with the substance of the five unceasing winds.
> I grant you this empowerment, my fortunate son [or daughter].
> Attain the power of complete and perfect strength.

Pronouncing the consonants, vowels, and root syllables of the four chakras, the master says *ha he ho* and pours a drop of water on each of the four centers of the disciples, after which the ablution is performed. The master then explains,

> In self-cognizing primordial wisdom, the state of primordial unimpeded openness and freedom, {29} the five quintessential winds are present as primordial wisdoms. This is indicated by the vase and the water it contains. The great strength of self-cognizing awareness, self-arisen primordial wisdom, in which everything "self-arises" and "self-subsides," is perfect and complete from the very beginning. Recognize it as all-accomplishing primordial wisdom.

All these empowerments constitute the empowerment of the vajra master and reveal the nature of the five kāyas and five primordial wisdoms.

The Secret Empowerment

The master takes the kapāla filled with amṛta and places it at the four places of the disciples' bodies. Invoked through the symbolic union of Samantabhadra and his consort in the center of the four chakras, the bodhicitta flows and fills the chakras, the channels, and the whole of the disciples' bodies. The disciples rest for a while in the state of great bliss. The master then says,

hūṃ
The self-arisen kapāla of infinite great bliss
Is filled with the essence drops of Samantabhadra free from desire.
I grant you this empowerment, fortunate son [or daughter] of the great lineage.
Gain power over your channels, winds, and the supreme bodhicitta.

The master then recites the consonants, vowels, and all the syllables of the four chakras. The disciples then take a sip from the kapāla and consider that their bliss is thereby increased. The master then explains,

> In the state of self-arisen primordial wisdom, which is blissful from the very beginning, the flow of the quintessence of Samantabhadra father-mother appears in you as bliss. Recognize that this is the dharmakāya, the nondual state of complete openness and freedom.

The Wisdom Empowerment

According to their ability, the disciples should then embrace either an actual mudra or a mentally visualized one. The master then says,

Phenomenal existence is a buddha field filled with great bliss—
A great bliss that is the display of primordial wisdom.
Freedom is the intercourse of skillful means and wisdom.
It is great bliss. Enjoy it without ceasing.

As the master utters these words, the disciples should consider that they are Samantabhadra father-mother in union. The essence drops stirring in the crowns of their heads introduce them to the primordial wisdom of joy. As they reach their throats, {30} the primordial wisdom of supreme joy is introduced. Descending then to their hearts, the primordial wisdom that is beyond joy is introduced. Then, as they flow from the navel to the secret center, the wisdom of coemergent joy is introduced. The master then explains the meaning of the empowerment:

> Fortunate disciples! The universe and the beings it contains, the whole of phenomenal existence, are deities by nature from the very beginning. Beings who appear in the form of men and women are linked from the first as skillful means and wisdom. The bliss of their mutual enjoyment is the primordial wisdom of the victorious ones, which dwells [within them] as the four primordial wisdoms. Do not renounce it, therefore, but enjoy it together. It is primordial wisdom itself. Certain it is that freedom will quickly come to you.

The Fourth Empowerment

This is an introduction, by means of words, to the nature of the mind. The master gives the following symbolic indication:

> *Kye!*
> Listen, O fortunate children of my lineage!
> In the vast abyss of space, the sun and moon rise and remain upon the wish-fulfilling jewel. Do you see it?
> The rainbow in the intervening air is caught by the lasso of the wind-breath. Do you see it?
> The ocean jewel astride the supreme horse of crystal soars above the sun and moon. Do you see it?
> The soldiers of the six kinds stationed in the city of five elements, human beings who went upon Mount Meru, and the man of crystal imprisoned in the dangerous paths of the three worlds—they turned in an instant round the three worlds, and they fell asleep in their own home. Do you see?

The master then reveals the meaning of these four symbolic indications:

> The first symbolic indication means that when the jewel of the chains of awareness arises in the vast expanse of space, the sun and moon, namely, your two eyes, see them. It is in the center of the mass of light at your heart (the lamp of the inner pure expanse) that awareness dwells. The luminous channel of the jewellike chains of awareness branches into two extremities (located in

your eyes). From these there issues a radiance that appears as the lamp of the empty disks of light, which is like the sun and moon.

In the cloudless sky of the outer expanse, the radiance of the chains of awareness appears like jewels, and these can be watched by the eyes. {31}

The second symbolic indication means that when the five lights, the radiance of inner space, manifest in the sky, and when awareness fixes on them without distraction, the halting of your in-breath and out-breath prevents the disks of light from moving.

The third symbolic indication means that the radiance of awareness residing in the heart enters the channel that is like a crystal tube and arises unobstructed through your two eyes. These elements are respectively referred to as the jewel, the horse, and the sun and moon.

The fourth symbolic indication shows that when awareness stirs from the expanse of the ground, and when there is the failure to recognize its nature, beings wander in samsara. Their minds—namely, the soldiers of the six kinds—are stationed in their individual bodies, the cities of the five elements, and seem to be born and to die. The deluded minds in their bodies turn around Mount Meru and are subject to joy and sorrow. The basis for the manifestation of their deluded minds is the stainless, self-cognizing, primordial wisdom that is their minds' nature. This is the man of crystal. Both the ordinary man and the crystal man are imprisoned in impure body, speech, and mind upon the treacherous path of the three worlds of samsara. Similarly, there is, on the one hand, the [ordinary] mind and that which appears to it. On the other hand, there is primordial wisdom. When this wisdom is held, imprisoned by the [ordinary] mind, beings wander in samsara. But if the nature of the mind is recognized, the three realms will in an instant appear as the state of total openness and freedom. Dissolving in primordial wisdom, which is its home, the mind then "falls asleep" in the state of dharmakāya, which rests in the expanse of primordial wisdom.

In brief, the mind unfolds from primordial wisdom. When primordial wisdom is imprisoned in the mind, one wanders in the three worlds of samsara. But when the nature of primordial

> wisdom, the utterly pure expanse of the mind, is recognized, ignorance dissipates, and the citadel of the primordial state is captured.

Having thus explained in detail the meaning of the symbolic indications, the master exhorts the disciples with this inspiring song:

> *Emaho!*
> Noble children, listen undistractedly!
> Samsara and nirvana are not present in the ground.
> How wonderful, therefore, is their arising!
> Realization of the ultimate is not within the reach of words.
> How wonderful, therefore, is faith derived from seeing it directly! {32}
> Awareness is free indeed from birth and diminution.
> How wonderful, therefore, its visions that occur while on the path!
> Primordial purity is not something to be freed.
> How wonderful, therefore, the means whereby the wind-mind may be cleansed!
> Numberless are the approaches of the vehicles of teaching.
> How wonderful, therefore, is instantaneous attainment!
> The ways in which experiences arise are vast.
> How wonderful, therefore, to be convinced of their true nature!
> Manifold indeed are the descriptions made with words.
> How wonderful, therefore, to see the meaning of the symbols!

The master then proceeds to explain the meaning of the song:

> The ground—that is, the fundamental nature—does not exist either as samsara or nirvana, and yet when the display of awareness occurs, the recognition of it brings forth nirvana. The failure to recognize it leads to the manifestation of samsara. The ultimate nature cannot be known by means of verbal descriptions, but it is seen directly by means of awareness. The primordial expanse of ultimate reality, the naturally present potential, or buddha essence, knows neither increase nor diminution, and yet thanks to the practice, the four visions gradually manifest. The

> fundamental nature is primordially pure and is not something that is to be freed. Nevertheless, thanks to profound instructions, the wind-mind can be purified into the ultimate expanse. According to the many expositions of the [different] vehicles, buddhahood is gained in the course of time. And yet through the instantaneous recognition of one's nature, freedom is achieved [at once]. Although there are limitless aspects of meditative experience, one should be determined never to depart from the ultimate nature. Even though there is no end to verbal descriptions, the understanding of a single symbol brings realization of everything. Each of these points is truly wonderful.

Concluding Celebration

The master then says,

> Now that you have received this empowerment, you are authorized to engage in the practice of the generation and perfection stages as well as in the practice on the fundamental nature. You are permitted to meditate on the channels and winds and also the bliss of primordial wisdom. Even if you do not make much effort in the practice, you will nevertheless gain freedom within three lifetimes.

The disciples should then offer a mandala and outer and inner offerings and enjoy a gaṇacakra feast. It is said that only two to seven people of the best karmic fortune are allowed to take this empowerment at one time. If the empowerment is given to more than that, the ḍākinīs will inflict punishment, and so the number should not be exceeded. One should moreover examine the people concerned to see whether or not they are proper recipients. {33}

The purpose of this empowerment is to bring its recipients to a state of spiritual maturity so that they will be in a position to liberate others. If the empowerment is given by an impure vajra master to impure disciples, it is said that this will cause them both to be reborn in the lower realms. It is therefore important that both the giver and the receivers be pure. If, however, it is certain that the candidates for the empowerment are of good karmic fortune, then even if there are many of them, there is no conflict, for this is not incompatible with the stipulation that no more than seven people should be accepted. How is this? Because those concerned are people who will purify the spheres of the seven consciousnesses. This is taught in *The Manual of the Crucial Instructions concerning Empowerments.*[2] Indeed, if they are not proper recipients, even one is too much. Bereft of proper fortune, such a person will distort the secret words of the dharma.

Regarding the time of the empowerment, it is said in *The Subtle Explanation of Empowerments*,

> The elaborate empowerment ritual should be performed especially in the mouse, dragon, horse, and pig years. Of the four seasons of the year, the first four months are propitious. The empowerment should be given then, for it is at that time that it will yield results. Regarding the days [of the month], [the empowerment may be given] from the first day of the waxing moon until the moon's disappearance [at the new moon]. As for the hour, the empowerment should be given at noon or midnight. In accordance with their physical disposition, the yogis should receive the empowerment in the years of their specific elements. It is thus that the empowerment ritual will be realized. At such times, for disciples who keep samaya and whose bodies accord with the element [of the year of empowerment], there is no numerical limit. If the recipients are in harmony with the elements, there is no conflict even if there are fifty or a hundred.[3]

Therefore, when the outer elements [of the yogis' birth years and the year of the empowerment] are compatible and in accord, and when the inner karmic fortune is in harmony, there may be any number of recipients of the empowerment.

By the merit of explaining as they have been taught
These stages of elaborate empowerment,
May every being gain the majesty of supreme power,
Spontaneously achieving, as they wish, the twofold goal.

Although the sublime masters of past ages
Perfectly set forth this ritual, {34}

It had become unclear and muddled, uncertain in its meaning.
Therefore, I have clearly set it forth, in proper order and without mistake.

In this practice I had trained in earlier times,
So in this life it was accomplished naturally, directly.
Therefore, without adulteration of the sublime lineage,
I, Longchen Rabjam Zangpo, have composed it properly.

May this deep supreme instruction,
Which through its crucial points brings freedom,
Rejoice the hearts of all the fortunate!

This completes the elucidation of the elaborate vase empowerment, *The Net of Purity*, one of the various empowerments of the Secret Heart Essence. It was written by Longchen Rabjam, a yogi of the supreme vehicle.

4. A Clear Exposition of the Names for the Elaborate Mandala[1]

Longchen Rabjam

With reverence to my teachers {36}
I shall now set forth
The list of names for those who enter
The elaborate mandala.

In the beginning, in order to determine which of the five primordial wisdoms of the vajra essence of luminosity is the principal wisdom and mandala to which disciples belong, they each throw a flower into the mandala.

When the flower is thrown and falls in the center of the mandala, the name is derived from Vairocana of the tathāgata family of the wisdom of the dharmadhātu. The names given indicate the fundamental nature:

Natsok Rangdröl,
Chöying Drime,
Lhundrub Gyalpo,
Gyurme Yeshe,
Khalong Yangpa,
Mimik Chönyi,
Yedröl Nyukma,
Lhunyam Chadral,
Kunche Gyalpo,
Longchen Rabjam,
Khanyam Chöku,
Zhidral Chönyi,
Samdzok Gyalpo,

Jöme Tsönde,
Changchub Nyingpo,
Nyukma Chamdal,
Yetong Tsadral,
Kundröl Yeshe,
Malu Chönyi,
Rolang Yeshe,
Gangshar Rangdröl,
Yedröl Dzinme,
Matsal Rangdzok,
Charme Rangjung,
Sangye Rangche,
Mingyur Lhundrub,
Khyabdal Chenpo,
Nangsi Chöku,
Tsalchen Dzokpa, and so on.

These names derive from the name of the ultimate expanse beyond movement and change and should be given, as appropriate, to both the men and the women.

When the flower falls in the eastern quarter, the names derive from Akṣobhya of the vajra family of mirrorlike wisdom. The names given indicate luminosity:

Dorje Nyingpo,
Dorje Sempa,
Dorje Lekpa,
Önga Lhundrub,
Yeshe Drime,
Ngangdang Ösal,
Lhunyam Miyo,
Chamchik Changchub,
Saltong Dzinme,
Rangsal Chöku,
Malu Lhundrub,
Döne Changchub,
Miksam Trödral, {37}

Gakme Rangsal,
Rangjung Yeshe,
Ösal Nyingpo,
Nyime Yeshe,
Chokme Rangyen,
Mikme Kundröl,
Yangpa Chenpo,
Drowa Chönyi,
Samdzok Döma,
Charme Namkha,
Makye Chönyi,
Mine Rangjung,
Melong Yeshe,
Rölpa Gakme,
Gyayen Rangdröl,
Tadral Uma,
Dzokpa Rangjung,
Rikpa Drime,
Rangshar Gakme,
Tadröl Longchen, and so on.

Deriving from clear and limpid luminosity, all such names should be given, as appropriate.

If the flower falls on the southern quarter, the names are derived from Ratnasambhava of the jewel family of the wisdom of equality. The names indicate nonduality:

Döyön Rangshar,
Gyachen Paljor,
Yönten Rangjung,
Samdzok Gyalpo,
Tsokchen Lhundzok,
Dögu Rangshar,
Yizhin Nyingpo,
Peme Rangdröl,
Döndrub Nyingpo,
Zhingkham Namdak,

Lhundrub Yeshe,
Mache Rangdzok,
Zhide Chönyi,
Yeshe Gyepa,
Chönyi Ngawang,
Longdzok Gyalpo,
Rangjung Longye,
Rölpa Rangshar,
Gangshar Chönyi,
Chirnang Nyamdröl,
Langdor Nyime,
Teme Yongdröl,
Kusum Rangdzok,
Yeshe Ngaden,
Zungtrin Nyingpo,
Yeshe Nyima,
Lhundrub Zakar, and so on.

Beginning with the names that reflect nonduality, these are the names to be given.

If the flower falls on the western quarter, the names derived from Amitābha of the lotus family of all-discerning wisdom are as follows:

Dechen Gyalpo,
Khamsum Yongdröl,
Masam Chönyi,
Chirnang Yeshe,
Lhunyam Dechen,
Pema Longchen,
Longsal Drime,
Dechen Rangjung,
Tamche Babde,
Zhime Rangsal,
Drowa Changchub,
Tamche Chönyi, {38}
Khorde Yedröl,

Mapang Yongdzok,
Rangsal Dechen,
Ösal Longye,
Changchub Rangjung,
Khanyam Dechen,
Zitsa Changchub,
Rangjung Chönyi,
Yöme Tadral,
Yangdok Nyime,
Chöku Rangluk,
Mimik Chamdal, and so on.

These and other names are given to reflect the luminosity of primordial wisdom.

If the flower falls on the northern quarter, the names for Amoghasiddhi of the karma family of all-accomplishing wisdom are as follows:

Gonga Chadral,
Lhundzok Chöku,
Rangshar Rime,
Dzinme Gyalpo,
Malu Yongdröl,
Kunyam Yangpa,
Lhunyam Yongdröl,
Chamchik Sangye,
Yene Charme,
Chatsal Kundröl,
Khyabdal Chönyi,
Trinle Lhundrub,
Yongdzok Changchub,
Rangzhen Döndrub,
Mapang Yongdzok,
Tsöldrub Charme,
Chöku Rangdzok,
Lhundrub Dzinme,
Yongdröl Chenpo, and so on

These names should be given to reflect a vastness free of hope and fear.

If the flower falls on the cusp between two quarters, the names are taken from one [or other] of the quarters or else from both.

This instruction on the list of the secret names was composed in the place of the Self-Arisen Lotus by the yogi Natsok Rangdröl, also known as Longchen Rabjam.

Virtue!

5. The Net of Precious Gems

A Ritual for the Unelaborate Empowerment[1]

Longchen Rabjam

O wishing-gem, fulfilling every hope, {40}
Sublime teacher, ocean of good qualities,
May the feet of your compassion rest firmly on my head,
Upon the lotus of my faith a hundredfold.

Of the four empowerments of the Secret Heart Essence,
The supreme vehicle of the vajra essence of luminosity,
Here I shall explain the ritual of the unelaborate empowerment
As set forth in *The Pure Gem of Subtle Explanation.*[2]

In a pleasant, solitary place, set up a mandala two cubits in size. In its center, trace with colored powders two vases drawn in crisscross fashion. They are red in color with ornamental stoppers and ribbons round their necks. Around them, draw five concentric circles of five lights. Within the surrounding fence of the five lights, draw rays of light in blue color adorned with spheres of light. In the four directions of a centrally placed precious vase filled with incense, blessed medicine, and milk, trace four *A*-syllables, white in color. To the ornamental stopper [of the vase] attach three mirrors, three peacock feathers, and three crystals. Tie a red ribbon around its neck. Arrange the required substances all around—namely, the outer, inner, and secret offerings; the offerings for the gaṇacakra feast; the tormas; the liquid for ablution consisting of milk mixed with saffron; gugul incense; and so on.

The master then visualizes himself as Samantabhadra in union with his consort. He is blue in color and is seated in vajra posture. He recites the three syllables, the vowels and consonants, as much as possible. Considering that the vase filled with incense, blessed medicine, and milk is replete with the wisdom amṛta and is filled with white *A*-syllables, he recites the syllable *A* one hundred times, sealing it with the view of the unborn nature. {41}

It has been said that the master should have previously recited seven thousand syllables of the body, one hundred thousand syllables of speech, ten thousand syllables of the mind, and seven hundred thousand of the unborn, self-arisen vowels and consonants. For if the speech of the master is not pure, it will be impossible for the disciples to receive the empowerment.

Outside [the place where the empowerment is to be given], the disciples perform an ablution before being permitted to enter. Obstacle-creating spirits are driven away by the smoke of the gugul, the sound of cymbals, and the visualization of the Great Wrathful One accompanied by the recitation of his wrathful mantra. The boundary is set up by visualizing the circle of protection, the blazing mountains, and the masses of fire. The disciples sit in rows, a mandala is offered, and the master gives them a teaching explaining how they should transform their mental attitude. He says,

> You have gained a precious human life endowed with eight freedoms and ten advantages—all so hard to find. You have been born in this world of Jambudvīpa, the best of cosmic continents, and you have met a holy teacher and the teachings of the Great Vehicle. Having entered the path to liberation, you must embrace the holy dharma. You must now achieve your liberation from the unbearable suffering of wandering endlessly in samsara. You are like merchants whose boat is adrift on the sea. You are like birds caught in a net, like people lost in a terrifying place, or surrounded by those who seek to kill them. Now you must free yourselves from all of this. Liberation is a state of freshness, peace, fearlessness, and supreme happiness.

The master then goes on to bestow the actual empowerment. This has three parts: (1) entry into the mandala, (2) the empowerment itself, and (3) the concluding celebration.

Entry into the Mandala

Some authorities say that the entry of the disciples into the mandala {42} should begin with the uncommon mandala entry (that is, specific to this empowerment). For if it is combined with the manner of entry of the elaborate empowerment, the [unelaborate] empowerment will not be received. This appears to be slightly incorrect. For as it is said in *The Subtle Explanation of Unelaborate Empowerment*, "Preliminary prayer is necessary because one needs to receive blessings."[3] In addition, it is said, "The samaya of the inseparable body, speech, and mind is bestowed. To violate it will bind you; to keep it will certainly bring supreme benefit." This indicates that it is the common entry that is being taught.

At this point and in accordance with the traditional practice of the masters, a short restoration prayer is recited in order to repair all the degenerations and breaches of samaya. For if the mindstreams of the disciples are not pure, no empowerment will be received. In the presence of the master and the visualized mandala of peaceful and wrathful deities, the disciples imaginatively emanate countless bodies and prostrate and confess as much as possible. It is then that they are allowed to enter the mandala. The entry is twofold: (1) the common entry and (2) the uncommon entry.

The Common Entry

This is performed in five stages. First, the disciples pray to their master, reciting three times the following words:

> Teacher, holder of the vajra,
> Sole friend in the three worlds of samsara,
> Refuge of those who wander unprotected,
> Great stair that leads to liberation,
> Lost in darkness, I now come to you for refuge,
> Ignorance-dispelling light!
> Protect me, who, protectorless,
> Am sinking in the murky ocean of samsara.
> Cool me with the draft of your compassion,
> Tormented as I am by fires of my defilements.

The disciples then repeat the following three times:

Great teacher, holder of the vajra, turn your mind to me!
Buddhas and bodhisattvas, who reside in all the ten directions,
Who belong to the enlightened families
Of vajra, jewel, lotus, karma, and tathāgata,
Turn your minds to me!
From this day forward till the time {43}
When I, (*the disciples say their names*), attain the essence of enlightenment,
Great teacher, holder of the vajra,
I pray you, bless my body.
I pray you, bless my speech.
I pray you, bless my mind.
I pray you, bless all my perceptions.
I pray you, bring me to maturity.
I pray you, cause me to be free.
I pray you, cause me to be filled with perfect qualities.
I pray you, help me to develop.
I pray you, help me to grow great.

Second, the disciples take the vows. The disciples recite the following declaration three times.

Great vajra-holding teacher, turn your mind to me!
Buddhas and bodhisattvas residing in the ten directions,
Who belong to the enlightened families
Of vajra, jewel, lotus, karma, and tathāgata,
Turn your minds to me!
From this time forward till the time
When I, (*the disciples say their names*), attain the essence of enlightenment,
I bow before the Buddha, dharma, sangha—
The Three Jewels unsurpassed together with my teacher.
In my vajra-holding teacher and the Three Jewels I take refuge.
I confess my sinful actions, each and every one,
And cultivate the unsurpassed and sacred
Attitude of bodhicitta.
Guarding the samayas of the five enlightened families,

I will keep a vajra and a bell
And all the other articles of the samaya pledge.
I will never leave the unsurpassed Three Jewels.
I will not forsake the vajra master.
I will never disrespect the vajra kindred.
I will do no injury to sentient beings.
I will not impugn the noble ones
Or scorn the śrāvakas and pratyekabuddhas in the slightest way.
I will not forsake the mantrikas
But will practice stages of approach, accomplishment, and activation. {44}
From this very moment, all these things I will uphold.
The samayas and the vows I will observe,
Never to transgress samayas of my body, speech, and mind.
I will kill no living beings.
I will not forsake the sacred dharma.
I will not turn away from what my master does.
I will not perform mistaken acts.
I will bring beings to maturity.
I will carry over those who have not fully crossed.
I will set free all beings who are not yet freed.
I will bring relief to those not yet relieved.
I will place all beings in the state beyond all sorrow.
I will not despise the teachings.
I will make good offerings to my teacher.
I will cast samsara far away and will adopt nirvana.
I will not offend the bhikṣus.
I will not disturb their meditation.
I will not impugn the dharma or the people.
Most especially, I will meditate upon the mandala
And always practice the perfection stage.
All that the teacher may enjoin
I will not transgress.

Third, the water of samaya is distributed. Pouring a drop of milk mixed with blessed medicine and incense into the palms of the disciples, the master says to each of the disciples,

This is the samaya water of hell.
If you break your pledges,
You will burn for countless eons in the fires of hell.
Great suffering will be yours to bear.
Therefore this living water of samaya
Keep within your hearts, observing it.
If samaya is not broken, it becomes
The samaya water of accomplishment.
Enjoying the supreme and ordinary accomplishments,
You will gain the fruit of perfect buddhahood.
Therefore, keep your pledge.

Fourth, the samaya pledge is taken. The disciples repeat the following three times:

From this moment onward,
Till enlightenment is gained,
I vow to keep myself from all mistaken acts.
I vow that I will never disregard my teacher's words.
I vow that I will keep from harming beings. {45}
I vow that I will never leave the path of perfect bliss.
I vow not to pursue the cravings of the world.
I vow that I will never, even though it cost my life,
Forsake the view, meditation, and action.
I vow that, from this moment onward,
I will never cease to stay
In charnel grounds and so forth, haunts of solitude.
In brief, I promise to relinquish worldly deeds.
I vow that I will not forsake the deeds related to nirvana.

Fifth, the samayas are proclaimed and the vows are granted.

Kye!
Listen, fortunate, dear children of my heart!
Pledge yourselves to implement the sacred dharma
Of the outer, inner, secret vehicles.
From this moment onward, never turn away
From loving-kindness for all sentient beings.

Do not turn away from meditation on the mandala.
Never turn away and leave your teacher.
Have no hatred for the vajra kindred.
Venerate the Triple Gem.
Keep the samayas of the Mantrayāna
And all the vows just as they have been taught.
Do no harm to any of the teachings,
Pursue the path to liberation.

Kye!
Fortunate children endowed with perfect qualities,
Do not discuss with others
This ritual of empowerment.
Never talk about samaya or the words of mantra
To those who did not take empowerment.
Cast samsara far away.
Never turn away from the accomplishment
That causes one to be a vajra holder.

The Uncommon Entry into the Mandala

This is performed in three stages. First, a prayer is addressed to the master. The disciples offer a mandala and recite the following three times:

We fortunate children of the guru's heart
Will confidently heed our teacher, holder of the vajra.
As we receive empowerment
Of the Natural Great Perfection,
We pray that our intrepid vajra master
Show to us the mandala of Ati,
The fundamental nature of the mind. {46}
Perfectly we enter, never to regress.

Second, the master gives consent. The master says once,

My children, great is your good fortune!
Fortunate great bodhisattvas,
Till now you have not entered the empowerment

Of the Natural Great Perfection.
Tonight, I will reveal to you,
My children blessed with fortune,
The mandala of the Great Perfection.
Clear away your thoughts,
Release all worldly ties.
This mandala is free from all conventions
Of acceptance and rejection.
Your mind and lineage are pure,
Your body and your speech are the supports for bliss.
From now on you must not regress!

Third, the flower of awareness is thrown. This is the entry into the mandala of the mind, devoid of the four doors (the four conceptual extremes). The disciples remove their upper garments, and joining their hands at their hearts, they fix their gaze on the master's heart, imagining that the garlands of vowels and consonants are turning there. They relax in a state of undistracted calm, free of clinging. This is what is called the uncommon mingling [of teacher's and disciples' minds].

The Empowerment Itself

This consists of two parts: (1) the empowerment of the wheel of syllables and (2) the ultimate empowerment of the dharmatā.

The Empowerment of the Wheel of Syllables

This is performed in three stages. First is the empowerment of the syllable of the dharmadhātu. The master says,

> Pronounce melodiously a long syllable *Ā*, imagining that your heart is completely filled with white *A*-syllables. Rays of light of five colors radiate upward from them into the sky and strike the point of union of Samantabhadra father-mother. A rain of five-colored amṛta flows down and enters through the crowns of your heads, filling and covering your body inside and out. Concentrate your mind on this. When a drop of saffron milk is placed on the crown of your head, at your throats, and at your hearts, visualize

> these drops as the union of the sun and moon. Consider that on them, the body, speech, and mind of the buddhas {47} become spheres of five lights and that, as they descend into your hearts and melt into light, your own body, speech, and mind become respectively blissful, clear, and free of thought.

During that time, the syllable *A* should be recited gently and slowly, and the master should give a secret name to each of the disciples and say, "I ask you to conceal this name in the unborn state [of emptiness]."

At the conclusion of the recitation, the *A*-syllables gather into the center of the four chakras and the disciples meditate for a moment in the state of emptiness.

Second is the empowerment of the source syllables. This is performed in two stages. First, the vowel empowerment is given. For the vowels, the visualization is the same as for the other empowerments, the only difference being that one should imagine that within the channels there are red vowels that shimmer with a radiant light that pervades the whole of space—as does the resonance of their sound. The vowels should be recited evenly, not too quick and not too slow:

> *a ā i ī u ū ṛ ṝ ḷ ḹ e ai o au aṃ aḥ*

When this is done, the master presses the channel inside the cavity of the disciples' eyes and applies a drop of saffron milk. The syllables are concealed in the four chakras of the disciples who then rest in the unborn state.

Second, the consonant empowerment is given. The consonants should be visualized as white in color and should be recited as previously, the difference being that one should imagine them as entirely filling the interior of the body:

> *ka kha ga gha nga*
> *ca cha ja jha nya*
> *ṭa ṭha ḍa ḍha ṇa*
> *ta tha da dha na*
> *pa pha ba bha ma*
> *ya ra la va*
> *śa ṣa sa ha kṣa*

At the end of this recitation, the master presses the channel behind the ears of the disciples and anoints the place with a drop of saffron milk. All the syllables are concealed within the four chakras of the disciples, who then meditate on emptiness.

Third is the empowerment of the self-arisen syllables. This is performed in three stages. First is the empowerment of the syllables of the enlightened body. A drop of saffron milk is placed on the crowns of the heads of the disciples, who imagine that it is the white letter *oṃ* from which rays of light emerge and pervade the whole of space. The disciples imagine that in the midst of these lights there are many shimmering *oṃ* syllables, whose sound fills the entire world. Sharply uttering the syllable *oṃ*, the teacher presses the channel in the disciples' throats, and all is sealed with emptiness.

Second is the empowerment of the syllable of enlightened speech. {48} A drop of saffron milk is smeared on the disciples' throats. The disciples imagine that it is a red syllable *āḥ*, which they recite, considering that its sound and the light that it radiates fill the whole of space. The channel in their armpits, or the nectar-controlling channel, is pressed, and all is sealed with emptiness.

Third is the empowerment of the syllable of the enlightened mind. A drop of saffron milk is smeared on the disciples' chests at the level of their hearts. The disciples imagine that it is a blue syllable *hūṃ*, which they recite. The master pronounces it and presses the throbbing channel beneath the left breast of the disciples, and all is sealed with emptiness.

The Ultimate Empowerment of Dharmatā

This is performed in four stages. First is the empowerment of great bliss in its immediacy. The master smears two drops of saffron milk, one on top of the other, on the same spot of the disciples' foreheads. These drops become the sun and moon conjoined. The disciples are then instructed to meditate on the nature of the mind free of the movement of thoughts, whereupon the vase is placed on the crowns of their heads. The disciples imagine that inside the vase, words resound clearly and spontaneously, introducing the dharmatā. The master sharpens his awareness, within the state of dharmatā, and melodiously sings the following words:

> Ineffable are all phenomena—inconceivable, beyond all indication, beyond all watching, definition and all expectation. They

> are beyond the elaboration of the mind, free of all conceptual extremes.

The master then says,

> The mind of the present moment is pure intrinsically. Its great, primordial openness and freedom is beyond the reach of ordinary speech, beyond the mind's conceiving. No example can express it. The eyes cannot behold it; it cannot be identified as "this." It is beyond the elaboration of false thoughts. It is beyond all expectation as something to be gained. It is free of the ontological extremes of existence and nonexistence. Recognize it thus.

At that moment, the master pours water from the vase into the cupped hands of each of the disciples one after the other and, uttering the syllables *a āḥ*, plays the cymbals.

Second is the sealing empowerment of purity. The master says, {49}

> *Emaho!*
> Dharmatā, great bliss, beyond the mind's construction,
> Cannot be watched. It is beyond all thought—how wonderful
> that is!
> Primal wisdom, naturally manifest, nondual, all-pervading,
> Awareness self-cognizing, is actually perceived—how wonderful
> that is!
> The fundamental nature of the natural great perfection free of
> action
> Is self-arisen and beyond all effort—how wonderful that is!
> The ultimate, beyond conceptual elaboration, completely pure in
> nature,
> Transcends the two extremes of virtue and of sin—how wonderful
> that is!
> Awareness self-cognizing, free of mental movement,
> self-experiencing,
> Appears as view, as meditation, and as action—how wonderful
> that is!
> The lamp of self-arisen light

> Becomes an object of direct perception—how wonderful that is!
> The all-pervading nature, character, cognizant power
> Primordially arise as the triple kāya—how wonderful that is!
> Primordial wisdom, pure and inexpressible,
> Appears in the pure bodies—how wonderful that is!
> The empty disk of light that drives away the dark of ignorance
> Appearing as an object of the senses—how wonderful that is!

The master then explains the meaning of his words.

> Awareness in its present immediacy, which is empty, luminous, and free of mental elaboration—which cannot be watched and is beyond conception—is not opposed to that which appears as its experiential field. And this is a marvelous thing. Nondual, self-cognizing awareness and your own state of awareness—these two are not in opposition. How marvelous that is! And marvelous too is the fact that the natural great perfection, primordially free of action and effort, and that which occurs to you through skillful means are not in opposition either. Awareness is beyond both good and bad. Awareness appears as the view, meditation, and action. The radiance of dharmatā is directly perceived. The manifestation of empty luminosity is the arising of the three kāyas. Primordial wisdom, inexpressible as it is, is perceived as awareness. And the lamp of the empty disks of light appears before your very eyes. How marvelous are all these things!

Third is the empowerment of the power of awareness. {50} The master then says,

> Things have no intrinsic being. As such, you cannot watch them. They are lifeless and without essential core; they are hollow. They are beyond the reach of words and syllables and language. They are beyond designation; they are beyond expression.

The master then explains further,

> Since the mind has no existence in itself, it lacks intrinsic being. Since it cannot be identified, it cannot be watched. Since it is

> neither existent nor nonexistent, it has no life. Since it is not both or neither, it has no essential core. Appearing while being nonexistent, and empty of itself, it is hollow. It does not exist as a thing, and thus no words describe it. Being beyond conception and thought, it cannot be expressed by syllables. Beyond speech, it is beyond language. Beyond word and thought, it is beyond the conventional. It is beyond description and thus is inexpressible.

Fourth is the empowerment of Samantabhadra, spontaneously present dharmatā. The master says,

> All phenomena are empty and devoid of self.
> The mind that wants and clings to them is utterly deluded.
> The dharmadhātu is indeed beyond conceptual construction.
> To trace its attributes with words is utterly deluded.
> Self-arisen is the essence, ultimate primordial wisdom.
> To strive for it as something that arises from elsewhere is utterly deluded.
> The nature of the mind transcends both birth and death.
> To hold that it arises and then ceases is complete delusion.
> The fruit, complete within yourselves, transcends all expectation.
> To think that it depends upon intelligence is utterly deluded.
> All happiness and sorrow are awareness's display.
> To think of them in terms of taking and rejecting is complete delusion.
> Samantabhadra rests within yourselves.
> To seek elsewhere a yidam deity is utterly deluded.
> You are, yourselves, primordially enlightened.
> To hold that there are lower destinies is utterly deluded.
> The deployment of samsara and the lower realms primordially arises.
> The wish for perfect buddhahood is utterly deluded.
> Do not reject five poisons—they are great self-arisen wisdom.
> To think defilement is a thing you should reject is utterly deluded. {51}
> Hallucinatory appearances are naturally manifest as dharmakāya.
> To think of things as self-possessing is utterly deluded.
> All nine vehicles arise in you.
> To cling to their respective texts is utterly deluded.

The master then gives an explanation of what he has just said:

> *Kye!* Fortunate beings! Everything in phenomenal existence, in both samsara and nirvana, is primordially empty and devoid of self. All things, therefore, are beyond affirmation and negation, acceptance and rejection. Recognize that this is so! If you fail to understand, fixating upon and clinging to the self of persons and phenomena, in terms of independently existent subjects and objects of apprehension, samsara will continue. This is the very essence of delusion.
>
> The dimension, or source, of all externally appearing things—the elements of earth, wind, fire, and water, and the inner aggregates, constituents, sense fields, and so on—is the space-like state devoid of all conceptual construction. Recognize this as the nature of your minds—open, unimpeded, and self-arisen primordial wisdom, devoid of substantial being. If you fail to understand, you will cling strongly to appearing things and to the mind itself. And entranced by the many propositions and statements imputed by the intellect that assumes the reality of things, you will be deluded.
>
> Recognize the essence, the ultimate primordial wisdom that is your birthright. Present of itself, it dwells within you at this very moment. If you fail to understand it in this way, you may believe that, by causes and conditions, you may contrive it and at some later time attain to pure primordial wisdom. But you will be deluded, for it is not thus that it is recognized.
>
> The nature of the mind is devoid of substantial being. It is ungraspable. Recognize that it is free of birth and death. If you fail to understand this and fix upon the notions of birth and death, you may conclude that is arises and ceases. But in this you will be deluded.
>
> Since the three kāyas inseparably united is your natural birthright, you should understand that empty awareness is the dharmakāya. If you fail to do so and think that buddhahood is something to be attained only after many kalpas of exertion, you will be deluded.
>
> {52} Happiness, suffering, and neutral feelings are equal in that they all arise within the mind and are without intrinsic

being. Recognize them, therefore, as the manifestation of awareness, free and open from the very beginning. If you do not understand this and cling to happiness and sorrow as though they were different—striving for what you like and rejecting what you do not like—you will apprehend as different that which is not different. And this is the very nature of delusion.

Know that your awareness is Samantabhadra, self-arisen buddha. If you fail to understand this and, through a dualistic conceptual meditation, you look elsewhere for a yidam deity, all you will find will be mental fabrication and nothing else, and you will be deluded.

Within awareness, the purification of karma and defilements and the development of the wisdom of omniscience are present from the very first. If you fail to understand this and feel fear and dread that you might go to hell, your mind is deluded.

The way that self-cognizing awareness appears is, on a lower level, samsara, the field of the six migrations. On an upper level, it is nirvana, the display of the trikāya. Both these manifestations occur primordially and subsist within the dimension of spontaneous presence. Recognize that this is so. If you fail; if you think that samsara and nirvana are different and wish to dispel delusion and accomplish the true state beyond delusion, your mind is mistaken and deluded.

Understand that what appears as the five poisons is the radiance of primordial wisdom, aware yet empty. If you fail to understand this and fixate on their appearance aspect with the attitude of adoption or rejection—even if you wish to eliminate the five poisons, you are deluded.

All the many outer and inner hallucinatory appearances of the universe and beings—not one of them has ever existed! Recognize them as empty forms, the self-experience of the dharmakāya. If you do not see this and assume that self and other, and all that you engage in or reject, are real, you will experience nothing but a deluded clinging to self; and you will be in error.

Finally, all nine vehicles and all the various tenet systems are simply conceptual imputations. Within the fundamental condition of the nature of the mind, there is no such thing as a hierarchy of vehicles and tenets. {53} Appearances and imputations

> are but configurations traced by your own minds. And yet in truth, they transcend all the elaborations of thought and word. Recognize that this is so. If you fail to do so, you will end up thinking that the various theories of ground, path, and result, as expounded by the different schools, from the Śrāvakayāna to the Vajrayāna, are all truly real. And you will be deluded.

Explaining clearly in this way, the master will bring the disciples to a state of confident certainty.

In addition, there now follows an introduction to the purity aspect [of the different elements of the mandala]. Attaching the eye of a peacock feather to a golden scalpel or long stick, the master indicates as follows the elements of the mandala one by one.

The round shape of the mandala serves as a symbol of the dharmadhātu, which is utterly pure in nature. The fact that it measures two cubits represents the inseparability of skillful means and wisdom or appearance and emptiness. Its flat and even surface indicates the absence of extreme positions. The flowers and gaṇacakra offerings, placed outside the mandala, represent the spontaneous perfection of the two accumulations. The mandala's surrounding fence, composed of five lights, symbolizes the inseparability of the kāyas and wisdoms—that is, the radiance of primordial wisdom. The blue coloring of the interior and its ornamental rays and disks of light indicate that the radiance of the ultimate expanse—that is, great primordial purity (namely, primordial wisdom)—is also adorned with lights and disks of light. The two red vases, drawn in crisscross fashion with colored powders and surrounded by concentric areas of the five lights, indicate the radiance of the five wisdoms. The red color symbolizes the activity of magnetizing and represents great compassion. The crossed configuration of the vases indicates the indivisibility of the ultimate expanse and primordial wisdom. The ornamental stoppers of the vases and the ribbons attached to their necks indicate the spontaneity of the enlightened qualities and activities. The three vases—that is, the actual vase and the two vases drawn in crisscross fashion on which it stands—which appear separately but occupy the same space, indicate that the three kāyas are one in the ultimate expanse, the primordial inseparability of the spontaneous presence of primordial wisdom within the state of primordial purity. The [actual] vase, made of precious materials, and the substances contained within it indicate that awareness is the spontaneous source of the fulfillment of every wish. {54} The hollow cavity of the vase reveals that emptiness is identical with the ultimate expanse. The milk symbolizes quintessential primordial wisdom. The five gems represent the five enlightened bodies. The five kinds of incense indicate five kinds of enlightened speech. The five medicinal substances indicate the five enlightened minds. The five kinds of grain represent the five enlightened qualities. The five kinds of fragrance indicate the five enlightened activities. The four *A*-letters around the outside of the vase symbolize the four activities as being one in the ultimate expanse. The vase's ornamental stopper symbolizes the inconceivable qualities of the ten strengths, four fearlessnesses, eighteen distinctive qualities, and so on. The ribbon on the vase's neck symbolizes the boundless ornaments and arrays of the buddha fields. The crystal, peacock feather, and mirror indicate the ultimate nature, character, and cognizant potency. In addition, the mirror symbolizes the wisdom that knows the nature of phenomena and the wisdom that knows all phenomena in their multiplicity. The placing of a drop of saffron water on it indicates that the nature of primordial wisdom is stainless and pure. The eye of the peacock feather symbolizes the fact that the five primordial wisdoms and their radiance all arise as light and disks of light. The crystal indicates the inconceivable and inexpressible primordial wisdom of the empty but luminous dharmakāya. The three vases coinciding in a single place inside the outer rim indicate that within the inseparability of the ultimate expanse and primordial wisdom, all the qualities of buddhahood are from the very beginning spontaneously and naturally complete within awareness. In the ultimate sense, the appearance of the vase here means that within the field of the ever-youthful vase body, the primordial teacher Samantabhadra himself displays for his retinue (the inconceivably infinite assemblies of primordial wisdom) the dharma of the Great Perfection—while never stirring from the dharmatā and in the time that is beyond the mind's conceiving.

In brief, all these features may be summarized in the inseparability of awareness and the ultimate expanse. And it is revealed when the disciples are asked to focus on the mirror of Vajrasattva, which the master presents to them as follows.

> Look upon this stainless crystal. The five lights naturally present within its empty expanse indicate the spontaneous presence of

> primordial wisdom. {55} They indicate how the nirmāṇakāya of luminous character, the nirmāṇakāya guide of beings, and the diversified nirmāṇakāya[4] work for the welfare of beings by means of the two kinds of wisdom. The crystal also indicates that the five lights within the ultimate expanse are the five families of enlightened body, speech, mind, qualities, and activities—the spontaneous self-experience of awareness within the buddha field of Dense Array. Moreover, the crystal shows that the five lights within the primordially pure ultimate expanse are the naturally and spontaneously abiding primordial wisdom—in other words, the dharmakāya of inner luminosity, the field of the ever-youthful vase body.[5]

It is thus that the master performs the introduction.

Furthermore, the classification of the nature, character, and cognizant potency of the ground (and similarly for the path and result) are introduced by using the vases drawn with colored powder and the crystal. The indivisibility within the primordial expanse of the three kāyas is indicated by the three vases in the blue expanse within the outer surrounding area of the five lights.

At the time of the path, within the primordial purity that is the ground, the radiance of the unmoving empty nature in the heart arises outwardly as three things: the visions of tögal, the wind with which it is blended, and trekchö. These three items are introduced by means of the three vases in the expanse of blue light.

At the time of the result, within the primordial expanse, the three kāyas of awareness assume their natural condition. Again, this is introduced by means of the three vases in the center of the expanse of blue light.

The immaculate crystal symbolizes the emptiness aspect of primordial purity of the ground, path, and result. Its five inner lights indicate and introduce the appearance aspect of spontaneous presence—the radiance of the kāyas and wisdoms.

These key points are extremely important; it is vital to introduce them with the greatest care.

Concluding Celebration

There are three aspects to this. First, the master says,

> It is predicted that through the reception of the unelaborate empowerment, your obscurations of speech will be purified and, in the future, you will be reborn in a sambhogakāya buddha field. You have permission to recite the mantra {56} and meditate upon the channels, winds, and essence drops, as well as on the direct perception of the lamp of the empty disks of light. If, after you have received this empowerment, you observe your samaya perfectly, you will not turn endlessly in samsara, the door to rebirth in the lower realms will be closed. Even if you do not persevere in the practice, you will find freedom in your next life without delay. If, on the other hand, you make an effort, you will achieve buddhahood in this very life.

The gaṇacakra feast offering, together with the tormas, should be blessed, offered, and enjoyed. The master and those who are powerful yogis should then intone the vajra songs. Then the rest of the gaṇacakra ritual should be performed right through to the dedication of merit and the prayers of good fortune.

The conclusion then follows. Everything is dissolved and disappears. Verses of auspiciousness should then be recited, the house where the empowerment has taken place should be decorated with flowers and a celebratory feast should be held on the following day. This will ensure the achievement, in this and future lives, of the four activities, the two accomplishments, and the perfection of the two aims.

This ritual was composed in a former time, but it had become somewhat fragmented and unclear, with the result that the manner in which it should be performed as it had been taught was no longer understood. Therefore, by combining the teachings of such texts as *The Subtle Explanation of Empowerments*,[6] *The Innermost Essence*,[7] and *The Manual of the Crucial Instructions [concerning Empowerments]*.[8] I have set it forth in proper order.

May every being, leaving none aside,
Achieve, by virtue of this merit,

Qualities of realization and elimination.[9]
Never to be parted from the primordial Lord,
May they themselves become the lords of dharma,
Accomplishing quite naturally the twofold goal.

In the middle of the ocean of the teaching of the tantras,
The wish-fulfilling nāga king spreads out his blazing hood—
The elucidating pith instructions—
Ornamented with his blessings' roaring cry.
I have explained them on the slopes of Kangri Tökar. {57}

All the fortunate of future times who wish for freedom
Should constantly exert themselves in this instruction.
And thus replete with all the wealth and riches of the holy lords,
They will bring joy to beings, raising high the banner of their victory.

With the lotus of my faith a hundredfold,
I bow before the feet of my teacher,
The glorious, unequaled Lord of Dharma,
And offer now a garland of the dazzling flowers
Of his words and meaning
Within the sight of beings who are fortunate.

The Net of Precious Gems, belonging to the category of empowerments of the Secret Heart Essence of the Great Perfection, is now complete, elucidating the ritual of the unelaborate secret empowerment. It was composed by Longchen Rabjam, a yogi of the supreme vehicle.

Virtue!

The Descent of Primordial Wisdom Called Massing Clouds of Blessing Power[10]

To my teacher rich with blessing power in massing clouds,
I bow with body, speech, and mind.
The descent of wisdom in the entry to the unelaborate empowerment
I shall now explain.

When the common entry into the mandala is completed, one should, at the beginning of the uncommon entry, perform the ritual by means of which one receives the blessing of the teacher, the yidam deity, and the ḍākinī.

Confidently arising in the form of a wrathful deity, the master banishes all obstructive forces. To the sound of cymbals, the place is fumigated with the smoke from burning gugul incense, "great fat," a fragment of a loin cloth, grains of black sesame, sulfur, and the frog of a horse's hoof. The master then instructs the disciples to meditate on a ḍākinī of the lotus family, red in color, holding a curved blade and a kapāla and having a turning swastika of five colors in her heart. The disciples stand with their ankles close together, the palms of their hands pressed together above their heads, and their eyes closed. The master then speaks to them as follows,

> *Ema!*
> My children, listen undistractedly with devotion and one-pointed faith. Visualize in the middle of the sky, within a blazing mass of light, the dharmakāya Samantabhadra. He is blue in color and is in union with his consort. He is surrounded {58} by a dense cloud of teachers of the lineage, who come down upon the crowns of your heads.

Then, beginning with the words *oṃ guru kuntuzangpo ja jaḥ*, the master recites the names of all the lineage masters down to his root master. Then, to the sound of cymbals, he says *jaḥ hūṃ baṃ hoḥ āveśaya āveśaya a āḥ*. He then continues:

> Most especially, imagine that the guru Vimalamitra arrives flying through the sky from the Five-Peaked Mountain in China. Surrounded by a throng of paṇḍitas and ḍākinīs, he is yellow-green in color, attired as a paṇḍita, and holding a book. He dissolves into the crowns of your heads.
> *oṃ guru vimalamitra samaya ja jaḥ āveśaya āveśaya a āḥ*
>
> Imagine that from Oḍḍiyāna in the western direction, the great Master Padmasambhava arrives. White-yellow in color, holding

> a vajra and bell, and surrounded by the five classes of ḍākinīs, he dissolves into the crowns of your heads.
> *oṃ guru padma siddhi āḥ hūṃ samaya ja jaḥ āveśaya āveśaya a āḥ*

All this is proclaimed to the sound of cymbals. Then comes the descent of the blessing power of the five classes of the yidam deities. The master says,

> Imagine that Vairocana arrives from Akaniṣṭha. He is white and holds a wheel. From Manifest Joy, the buddha field in the east, Akṣobhya arrives. He is blue and holds a vajra. From Glorious, the buddha field in the south, Ratnasambhava arrives. He is yellow and holds a jewel. From Mound of Lotuses, the buddha field in the west, comes Amitābha. He is red and holds a lotus. From Perfect Activity, the buddha field in the north, Amoghasiddhi arrives. He is green and holds a crossed vajra. All these buddhas are surrounded by countless myriads of bodhisattvas. They all dissolve into the crowns of your heads.
> *oṃ āḥ hūṃ svāhā samaya ja jaḥ āveśaya āveśaya a āḥ*

There now follows the descent of the blessing power of the ḍākinīs. The master says,

> Imagine that there arrives, through the expanses of the sky, blue Vajravārāhī together with a white ḍākinī of the vajra class, a yellow ḍākinī of the jewel class, a red ḍākinī of the lotus class, and a green ḍākinī of the karma class. They are all holding a curved blade and a kapāla, with a khaṭvāṅga in the crooks of their arms. They are in dancing posture; they sing, dance, and play the cymbals. They arrive in great multitudes—and fill the whole of space and dissolve into the crowns of your heads.
> *oṃ vajra vārāhī harinisa āveśaya āveśaya hriṃ hriṃ phem phem mi mi yaṃ yaṃ jaḥ jaḥ* {59}
>
> Now imagine that the five classes of ḍākas arrive in great multitudes and dissolve into you.
> *oṃ vajra kiṃkara rāja hriya āveśaya āveśaya samaya jaḥ jaḥ ha ha he he hi hi hūṃ hūṃ phaṭ*

In this way, the blessings descend. As a result, the nature of the mind will be recognized, and the two accomplishments will be quickly achieved.

This completes *The Descent of Blessing Power*, set forth in accordance with the practice of the holy masters by Longchen Rabjam, the yogi Natsok Rangdröl, in the place of the Self-Arisen Lotus.

Virtue! *Mangalaṃ.*

An Essential Instruction on the Meaning of the Vases[11]

This is an essential instruction on the symbolism of the unelaborated empowerment.

Within the pure primordial space,
Awareness self-cognizing,
The changeless king, the nature of the mind,
Is present of itself.
And there the palace of five families
Of luminosity is likewise self-arisen.
To the cognizant power that spreads in all the ten directions,
I bow down.

Beings have within their hearts
A mass of brilliant light.
It rests there by its nature,
A state primordial and free of obscuration.
That it might shine within their minds,
I shall now explain, of all the four empowerments,
The one that is without elaboration.

As a means to show through symbols
That within the purity of mind
There dwell the luminous vase body
And the three aspects of the ground, the path, and the result,
Clearly trace the lines for the two crossed vases.[12]

Divide the quadrangle into four parts.
The two inner parts are the bellies of the vases.
In the east and south are the vases' feet.
In the west and north are their mouths.
In the eastern and southern directions, draw the bases of the vases.
Draw their ornamental stoppers toward the west and the north.
Turning sideways from the eastern quarter to the south, {60}
There are the vases' bases.
From the western and the northern quarters,
And as far as the surrounding rims, draw the wish-fulfilling trees
With green leaves and red stems
And yellow fruits.
The red vases are surrounded by five lights.
Their bases are multicolored lotuses.
The space around them is the color of the empty clear sky.
And all is surrounded by a fence of five-colored lights,
Which, counted from within, respectively,
Are white, then red, blue, yellow, green to symbolize
The body, speech, mind, qualities, and action.
As a reminder of their purity—
Since the mandala is free of limits and extremes—
For one brief moment it seems round,
But then, upon examination, it is not.
Luminosity subsists as the five kinds of radiance.
Therefore, the surrounding fence is of five colors.

As symbols of emptiness and appearance—
Dharmakāya, rūpakāya—
There are two vases corresponding to two ways of seeing.
Since everything that can be wished for
Comes from them spontaneously,
Their ornamental stoppers are wish-fulfilling trees.
Since emptiness and luminosity
Are displayed in various ways,
The base on which the vases have been drawn
Has the outline of a multicolored lotus.
They are surrounded by five lights,

Which symbolize the five primordial families
Present naturally of themselves.
Vases that have such a character
Abide primordially in every being,
Whose minds are boundless light.
The nature of their minds
Is dharmakāya, pure from the beginning,
And luminosity arising as the rūpakāya—
Namely, the five buddhas and the five primordial wisdoms,
Whose radiance appears in form of the five lights.
Therefore, since the dharmakāya and the rūpakāya
Are perfectly included in the ground,
And represent emptiness and appearance,
These vases symbolize the ground itself.

The path dwells also in primordial purity
And in spontaneous presence.
Through their creative power,
The moving mind occurs
Together with a body made of the four elements
And all material objects.
To cleanse the two kinds of creative power,
There are the practices of trekchö and tögal. {61}
By "cutting through," which leaves thoughts as they are,
Allowing them to subside naturally,
The moving mind, called forth through the creative power
Of emptiness, is brought to its exhaustion.
By "leap over" the light arising in the ultimate expanse
Is fixed with the nail of immutable equality.
The body of flesh together with material objects
Thus are made to disappear,
Subsiding in the five lights of primordial luminosity,
Brought to openness and freedom
In the state of their exhaustion.
Trekchö and tögal work respectively
With emptiness and appearance,

With the dharmakāya and the rūpakāya.
The two vases, therefore, are the symbols of this path.

The fruit is thus primordial purity and spontaneous presence.
Indeed, it is the state of freedom
On the level of phenomenal exhaustion—
That is, awareness, the primordial ground
Endowed with radiance of five lights,
Spontaneously present as the five enlightened families.
Their mere appearance dwells
In great and inexpressible primordial purity.

Awareness self-cognizing is the place of Akaniṣṭha,
Which does not dwell in any of the ten directions
And is devoid of center and periphery.
Within the pure field of awareness—
The universe a billionfold—
The mind appears as light, as domes of light,
As deities amid their perfect retinues.
This pure land of the buddhas,
The heart of the spontaneous expanse,
Is the field of Dense Array, completely pure.
Within that field, the multitude of the victorious ones
Is beyond activity: they neither stir nor teach.
It is through their blessing power that
Secret teachings as well as deeds appear all by themselves
In all the ten directions.
Thus, through the very nature, perfect and spontaneous,
Of their great body, speech, and mind,
Wherever there are worlds of beings to be trained,
It's there that emanations will arise to guide them.
Thus, the benefit of beings is wrought all by itself
In accordance with their needs.
Beyond the reach of words,
Their nature is the dharmakāya,
Their character is the sambhogakāya,
Their cognizant power unfolds as the nirmāṇakāya.

Likewise the result—
The dharmakāya and the rūpakāya both—
Is represented through the symbol of these vases.

These words set down by Charme Longyang—
The Vast Expanse Devoid of Action—
Were completed on the slopes of glorious Samye Chimpu.

Virtue! Virtue! Virtue!

6. The Net of Lotuses

A Ritual for the Extremely Unelaborate Empowerment[1]

Longchen Rabjam

To my teacher who embodies all the buddhas, {64}
For the sake of gaining siddhi, I bow down.
I will clearly set forth here the ritual of empowerment
Of the extremely unelaborate mandala.

The ritual has two sections: (1) the preliminary practice and (2) the granting of the empowerment itself.

The Preliminaries

The master and disciples must go to a remote valley or some other solitary place, where, in preparation, they should perform a gaṇacakra feast and offer tormas and a mandala of gold.

Having thus performed pleasing service to their teacher and the ḍākinīs, the disciples should demonstrate the fact that their awareness is not covered by obscuring veils by stripping naked or at least removing their upper garments. Then, in order to purify the eight consciousnesses and clear away all obstacles, the disciples should "don the armor." That is, they should visualize their teacher in terrifying form, dark-blue in color, with his hair streaming upward. He bears his fangs, and his tongue is curled back. On the crown of his head is the syllable *laṃ*, yellow in color. In his forehead is a blue syllable *e*. On his chin is a yellow syllable *su*. In his throat is a smoke-colored syllable *khaṃ*. His two nipples are marked with the syllable *ha*, white in color. {65} In his navel is the syllable *raṃ*, red in color. Finally, the sole of each foot is marked with the syllable *yaṃ*, green in color.

The disciples should consider that a blue syllable *hūṃ* emanates from the heart of their teacher and enters their hearts, which then assume the form of the syllable *hūṃ*. The teacher cries *ha ha* sharply three times, and the disciples, with clear visualization, carry away the tormas and offer them to the owners of the ground and to the ḍākinīs, proclaiming the following injunction: "We will be practicing in this place for three days. Do not create obstacles!"

The disciples then begin with the physical activities. Naked, they each play the ḍamaru and brandish a trident. With hair bristling and unkempt, they run upright and walk bent. They jump, fight, shake themselves, stand on their heads, walk backward, lie down, and recline. They dance and make all sorts of gestures. They shake their limbs and wag their heads. Snarling, they bite down on their lower lips. {66} They swagger from side to side. They slither along the ground like worms, jump like tigresses, and so on, performing all kinds of physical movements and expressions. Finally, they make prostrations and circumambulations. They adopt the posture and appearance of deities and make the mudras. Concluding their practice in the evening, they should lie motionless on a comfortable bed and take their rest. By practicing in this way, they experience the signs of rushen practice, the separating of samsara from nirvana, on the physical level. Developing a sense of freedom from the attachment and fixation to the body, they will begin to feel that they no longer have a body. They will cease to feel heat and cold. They will have neither hunger nor thirst and will lose all sense of tiredness and fatigue. They will feel as though they are walking on air, and a blissful sense of warmth will be ignited. All such signs will occur. Indeed, the rushen practice that separates samsara from nirvana on the physical level should be performed until the signs do occur. The purpose of this practice is to dissipate all bodily obstacles, to purify negative actions and obscurations, to bring about the state of freedom on the level of the nirmāṇakāya, and to join the practitioners inseparably with the unchanging vajra body of all the buddhas.

The practice connected with the speech faculty now follows. Considering that their voices are inseparable from their teacher's voice, the practitioners should make all kinds of utterances. Imitating the voices of the gods, they should sing sweet songs, intoning the vowels and consonants with pleasant and resounding melodies. In imitation of the nāgas, they should make sounds like a lute or else yell loudly. They should imitate the speech of the yakṣas with cries that sound like collapsing cliffs; the speech of the kiṃnaras with sounds like a sitar or thunder; and the speech of the rākṣasas with the sounds of thunderous hail, *rala rala, rili rili*. They should imitate the soft thunder of the voices of the asuras, the lamentations of the suffering from heat and cold of the hell realms, the groans and sighs of the pretas, the hissing and grunting cries of animals in pain. They should make the sounds associated with the birth, sickness, old age, and death of the human state. They should {67} imitate all the cries that they know—of animals like horses, cows, goats and sheep, donkeys, jackals, tigers and leopards, vultures, owls, crows, magpies, dogs, and foxes. And, interspersed among these different sounds, they should shout *phaṭ* repeatedly. They should also utter the dharma sounds *ha*, *hūṃ*, and *oṃ*. And in conclusion, they should recite the teachings of the dharma. At night, they should sleep quietly. This is how they practice the separation of samsara from nirvana on the level of speech.

It is by this means that the Sanskrit language naturally unfolds from within, and likewise many teachings that were previously unknown. Sweet music is heard and so forth. Along with a disinclination to speak, many blissful and inexpressible states of mind will occur. The exercise described should be practiced until all such signs manifest. Its purpose is to dissipate obstacles to the speech faculty, to purify all negativities and obscurations associated with speech, to bring about the state of freedom on the level of the sambhogakāya, and to join the practitioner inseparably with vajra speech.

The practice connected with the mind is as follows. Considering that the whole gamut of their thoughts and memories are at one with the mind of their teacher, the disciples should experience all the states of happiness and grief of every kind of being in the six realms, the states of samsara and nirvana, and the whole variety of thoughts belonging to both spiritual and worldly conditions. They should project their minds into the heart of the sky, into the depths of the ocean, and into the middle of rocky mountains without impediment. They should be joyful or displeased, happy or sad. They should experience birth and death, hunger and thirst, and so on. In their imaginations, they should revisit places where they had been in the past and explore places where they have not yet been—imagining that they are in the different dwelling places of the beings of the six realms. They should imagine that the earth and sky are filled with hell beings, pretas, animals, humans, asuras, and gods—and also buddhas, bodhisattvas, {68} śrāvakas, pratyekabuddhas, stupas, temples, gardens, and the pure fields of the buddhas. Imagining also that earth and sky are filled with beings—friends, enemies, and those about whom they have no particular feelings—they should allow themselves to feel attachment and aversion and train themselves in causing all such feelings to subside. Finally, they should focus on the dharma in word and meaning, keeping in mind the view, meditation, action, and result. They should practice like this until the following signs appear. Their minds become light and clear, all deluded thoughts cease, and a state of joy arises. The concentrations of bliss, luminosity, and no-thought appear, and the space-like realization of primordial openness and freedom manifests from within. The purpose of this practice is to cause mental obstacles to subside, to purify negativities, and to gain freedom in the dharmakāya, thus achieving the vajra mind—that is, buddhahood.

While the disciples enact these three preliminary practices, the master should remain in meditation, in the direct vision of the dharmatā. Afterward, the disciples should go to an easily accessible place in the mountains, and the teacher should question each of them whether they have experienced any signs of success in the rushen practice. If the signs have not occurred, the master should instruct the disciples to repeat the practices. By day they endeavor in the practices related to body, speech, and mind all together, and at night they rest in a state of calm and ease. If, thanks to such practice, the signs occur within three days, the disciples in question are of the highest capacity. the signs appear within five days for those of medium capacity and within seven days or more for disciples of least capacity.

If at that time the sky becomes clear and is suffused with rainbow light, this is a sign that the disciples have mastered the practice and their negativities and obscurations have been exhausted. On the other hand, if the disciples experience many negativities and obscurations, they should continue to endeavor in the practice. The goal of the practice of separating samsara and nirvana is to prevent any regress from taking place. This completes the description of the disciples' preparatory practice.

The Granting of the Empowerment Itself

The actual empowerment unfolds in three stages: First there is (1) a preliminary preparation. This is followed by (2) the empowerment itself, which is brought to conclusion with (3) a celebration. {69}

The Preparation

In the place just mentioned, the master prepares a round mandala [anointed with] saffron. It has a center, surrounding rim, and courtyard. It is decorated with four round lights. Thereupon he arranges five heaps, each composed of five flowers, and all around he places outer, inner, and secret offerings. If he is able to procure the necessary ingredients, he also makes five more mandalas composed of five heaps of five kinds of fragrant substances, five kinds of incense, five kinds of jewels, five kinds of medicines, and five kinds of grains.

The Empowerment

When the sun rises over the crest of the mountain, the disciples approach, each holding a flower. They are purified with saffron water. They remove their upper garments and with hands joined at the level of their hearts, they sit in front of their teacher, who asks each of them three times, "My child, who are you?" To this the disciples answer three times, "I am the dear and fortunate child of your mind." To which the teacher replies, "Enter, therefore, into this excellent and delightful mandala of the Natural Great Perfection. And why? Because samsara has no essence and therefore has no permanence; and it is fraught with sorrow. The supreme method of escaping it and of attaining buddhahood in a single life is the Natural Great Perfection and nothing else. Have great confidence, therefore, and for the sake of every being, repeat this litany addressed to me, your teacher.

> Great teacher, holder of the vajra, turn your mind to me!
> Buddhas and bodhisattvas, who reside in all the ten
> directions,
> Who belong to the enlightened families
> Of vajra, jewel, lotus, karma, and tathāgata,
> Turn your minds to me!
> From now until I, (*name*),
> Attain the essence of enlightenment,
> Great teacher, holder of the vajra,
> I pray you, bless my body. {70}
> I pray you, bless my speech.
> I pray you, bless my mind.

I pray you, bless all my perceptions.
I pray you, bring me to maturity.
I pray you, cause me to be free.
I pray you, cause me to be filled with perfect qualities.
I pray you, help me to develop.
I pray you, help me to grow great.

After reciting this general litany three times, the disciples should then specifically invoke the teachers of the lineage:

Kye!
O you who have the body, speech, and mind of all the buddhas
And who appear in bodies emanated from the ultimate expanse
Where all stains are exhausted,
Look upon us from that same expanse where all impurity is cleansed,
And in your great compassion bring about the benefit of beings.
With all the knowledge of the world possessed by all the blissful buddhas,
You are never parted from their one sole wisdom, whence you do not stir.
In times now past, when you were dwelling in the charnel grounds, you held all beings in your minds.
And though you do not act in ordinary ways,
I pray you, come in aid of my devoted mind.

Emaho!
First in line of all the teachers, root of blessing power,
Passed down to us from one to one,
Great master Garab Dorje, Blissful Resurrected One;[2]
Mañjuśrīmitra, wisdom's emanation,
Supremely trained with mastery of knowledge;
Śrīsiṃha, venerable, supremely loving,
Who with compassion took away all beings' pain;
Jñānasūtra, who dispelled the darkness of this world,

Learned one who utterly removed mistakes regarding all the
vehicles;
Vimalamitra, greatly learned master who,
With power over life, were free of birth and death;
Tingdzin Zangpo, who gained power over mind,
For whom meditation and post-meditation were not different;
Dangma Lhungyal, who revealed the essence of amṛta,
Whose mind was free of ordinary delusion; {71}
Senge Wangchuk, mighty siddha,
Predicted by the ḍākinīs and taken in their care;
Master Jetsun Tulku Zhangtön,
Emanated bodhisattva, guide of beings;
Learned Nyibum, dispeller of the gloom of ignorance,
Who guided beings with the light of knowledge;
Great knowledge-holding Guru Jober,
Who spread the essence of the Great Perfection unsurpassed;
Senge Gyapa, great destroyer of delusion,
Who mastered bodhicitta and became the glory of all
beings;
Munsel Dawa, hidden yogi, who realized great bliss,
The inseparable union of luminosity and emptiness;
Kumaradza, great vidyādhara,
Who had unmoving realization of the luminous dharmatā;
Longchen Rabjam, all-knowing and compassionate,
Who, when delusion utterly collapsed, beheld the meaning
of the Heart Essence—
All you learned beings endowed with an unchanging
realization,
Who came and passed away and dwell within the stainless
ultimate expanse,
May you manifest the deep compassion in which you trained
of old
And turn your minds to me with blessing.
oṃ āḥ hūṃ guru sarva siddhi hūṃ

oṃ āḥ hūṃ
The holy one endowed with essential amṛta, who looked
upon the face of all the buddhas,

Blissful Resurrected One, supreme of the supreme,
Emanation of the buddhas, who removes the torment of all
beings—
To him, amṛta blissful and sublime, I bow in praise.

And to his disciple, emanation of Mañjuśrī,
Free from all defilement, endowed with wisdom mind,
Who with the light of speech removes the suffering of beings—
To Yizhin Nyugu, Sublime Wish-Fulfilling Scion, I bow
down in praise.

To his descendant, learned in the scriptures,
Great compassion's emanation, adornment of the world, {72}
The resting place of beings, endowed with stainless speech—
To Sherab Nyugu, Wisdom's Scion, I bow down in praise.

To his erudite disciple, lord of the three worlds,
Vajrasattva's emanation, who cuts through the fetters of my
mind
And who, endowed with Brahmā's eloquence, enthralls the
minds of beings—
To the Sublime and Blissful Scion, Dewai Nyugu, I bow
down in praise.

To his descendant, whose learning came from many lives of
study,
Who possesses supreme wisdom, knowing all the sections of
the scriptures,
Who, fearless of birth and death, helps beings through his
emanations—
To sublime Desel Nyugu, Scion of Limpid Bliss, I bow in praise.

To his disciple, who possesses the pure eye of flesh,[3]
Who with perfect thought-free concentration found the
vital point of mind
And knew the minds of beings in this world without exception—
To sublime Tokme Nyugu, Scion Freed of the Conceptual
Mind, I bow in praise.

To his fortunate disciple, who held the treasury of dharma,
Who discovered precious treasures and drove away the dark of beings' ignorance,
Upholder of the teachings of the sugata and the instructions of his teacher—
To sublime Pema Nyugu, Scion of the Lotus, I bow down in praise.

To his disciple, master of the treasury of Secret Mantra,
Who having gained supreme accomplishment, the body of radiant light,
Compassionately leads us to the primal ground of phenomenal exhaustion—
To sublime Yeshe Nyugu, Scion of Primordial Wisdom, I bow down in praise.

To his venerable disciple, the lord protector of all beings,
Who mastered all the Secret Mantra teachings and was led by prophecy
And who accomplished supreme luminosity, which scatters ignorance—
To sublime Rinchen Nyugu, Precious Scion, I bow down in praise.

To his valiant disciple, refuge from samsara, {73}
Protector of all beings, lord of stainless glory,
Who, graced with supreme excellence, traversed the sea of wisdom—
To sublime Losal Nyugu, Scion of Clear Intelligence, I bow in praise.

To his disciple, who caused the spread of the essential doctrine,
Who attained the supreme level and mastered all the meanings of the tantras,
And who with the single eye of wisdom had the vision of all things—
To sublime Lotso Nyugu, Scion of the Ocean of the Mind, I bow in praise.

To his disciple, who subdued the forces of the dark of ignorance
And who with endless myriads of wisdom's rays of light
Dried up the sea of beings' pain—
To sublime Nangche Nyugu, Scion of Shining Light, I bow
in praise.

To his disciple, who with understanding of the supreme
vehicle
Cut through the webs of bondage, fulfilling every
expectation,
Who journeyed to attainment's lofty ground whereby all
wishes are fulfilled—
To sublime Chönyi Nyugu, Scion of the Dharmatā, I bow in
praise.

To his disciple, who attained the essence of the sun of
luminosity,
Who utterly destroyed the dense black darkness hard to cross,
Who with compassion's myriad rays illuminates the world—
To sublime Rikdzin Nyugu, Scion of Vidyādharas, I bow
down in praise.

To his disciple, who passed over to the far shore of the
teachings,
Who mastered all the meanings of the tantras and was
learned in the teachings of the vajra essence,
Who with unmoving concentration is absorbed within the
peaceful dharmadhātu—
To sublime Chöchok Nyugu, Scion of the Supreme Dharma,
I bow down in praise.

And you my teacher, source of all accomplishment and ocean
of good qualities,
I pray to you devotedly—in your compassion, bless me.

oṃ āḥ hūṃ guru namo mahāsiddhi samaya
dharmakāya samantabhadra
vajravāgiśu namo yaya siṃ mahāsiddhi samaya

sambhogakāya {74} *vajradhara namo samārthāya siṃ mahāsiddhi samaya*
nirmāṇakāya vajrasattva namo samārthāya siṃ mahāsiddhi samaya
vajrapāṇi nama samārthāya siṃ mahāsiddhi samaya
prajñābhava guru namo samārthāya siṃ mahāsiddhi samaya
mañjuśrīmitra guru namo samārthāya siṃ mahāsiddhi samaya
śrīsiṃha guru namo samārthāya siṃ mahāsiddhi samaya
jñānasūtra guru namo samārthāya siṃ mahāsiddhi samaya
vimalamitra guru namo samārthāya siṃ mahāsiddhi samaya
samādhibhadra guru namo samārthāya siṃ mahāsiddhi samaya
bhahirahe guru namo samārthāya siṃ mahāsiddhi samaya
siṃhaśvara guru namo samārthāya siṃ mahāsiddhi samaya
svastiśrī guru namo samārthāya siṃ mahāsiddhi samaya
suryalakti guru namo samārthāya siṃ mahāsiddhi samaya
jober guru namo samārthāya siṃ mahāsiddhi samaya
yogijñāna guru namo samārthāya siṃ mahāsiddhi samaya
dhekivajra guru namo samārthāya siṃ mahāsiddhi samaya
kumarāja guru namo samārthāya siṃ mahāsiddhi samaya
śīlamati guru namo samārthāya siṃ mahāsiddhi samaya

oṃ āḥ hūṃ

Ema!
Sublime Lord and sire of all enlightened ones,
Teacher, you who rule the mandalas of a thousand buddhas,
Vajrabhava, Garab Dorje, valiant lord of devas,
That I might overcome the dark of my mind's ignorance,
I pray you, show your face to me.

Unstained by the impurities and defects of this world and free of faults,
Supremely pure of mind, endowed with wisdom of three thousand buddhas—{75}
Mañjuśrīmitra, that I might destroy all hatred in my mind,
I pray you, show your face to me.

Radiant with light and tuneful with the melody of Brahmā,
Who with compassionate speech draw beings from the mire,
Śrīsiṃha, that my mental arrogance be purged,
I pray you, show to me your changeless vajra face.

You who teach all vehicles as they appear within your mind,
Who with unchanging wisdom strive to benefit all beings—
Jñānasūtra, free of worldly ignorance, I pray to you,
That I might free my mind of all impure attachment, show
  your face to me.

You whose many writings are replete with marvelous
  knowledge,
Protector of all beings, the sunlight of whose wisdom fills the
  world—
Vimalamitra, that I might halt all impure envy in my mind,
I pray to you, who are beyond both birth and death, show
  your vajra face to me.

You who, with your constant wisdom, stopped the ebb and
  flow of breath,
For whom all things arise as friends in nondual utter
  purity—
Tingdzin Zangpo, that I might end the anger in my mind,
I pray to you, who are beyond duality—show your face to me.

You who have attained primordial equality, the single taste
  of all phenomena,
Where you and others are inseparable within the pure
  condition of enlightenment—
Lhungyi Gyaltsen, that I might cleanse the five defiling
  poisons from my mind,
I pray to you, who shine with merit, show your face to me.

You for whom attachment to your body, speech, and mind
  has ended,
For whom, as fruit of mastery, phenomena have reached
  exhaustion, delusions purified—

Senge Wangchuk, that I might bring my false perceptions to exhaustion,
I pray you, show your face to me.

The final teaching, essence of the Vajrayāna, celebrated as the stem of Secret Mantra,
You have realized and possess a space-like mind beyond duality—
Tashi Mingyur, that I might still the movements and the habits of my mind, {76}
I pray you, wish-fulfilling vajra holder, show your face to me.

Boundless is your wisdom and your knowledge of the essence of the supreme vehicle.
With precious rays of light, you clarify the teachings handed down to us.
Dönyö Dorje, that I might end the defects of samsara in my mind,
I pray you, great and venerable nirmāṇakāya, show your face to me.

Realizing that the limitless expanse of samsara
And the pure space of the dharmatā are one,
Great and perfect lord, that I might still the good thoughts in my mind,
I pray to you, spontaneous, primordial equality, show your face to me.

Manifest form of luminosity, free of all deliberate activity, all duality,
You are the luminous character of spontaneous presence—
Samantabhadra, that I might exhaust the grasping thoughts within my mind,
I pray you, ever motionless, to show your face to me.

You who have attained the Great Perfection, vast as space,
Revealing all as one in natural equality,

King of the two accumulations, that I might drive away the ignorance within my mind—
I pray to you, immaculate and self-cognizing, show your face to me.

In the ultimate expanse of the primordial nature,
Freedom from elaboration dwells without contrivance,
Luminosity devoid of change or movement,
Great vidyādhara, that I might end my mind's adopting and rejecting,
I pray you, you who free the three worlds, show your face to me.

Endless are your qualities ablaze with primal wisdom's glory,
All clinging to reality has naturally collapsed and clinging to a self is utterly transcended,
Drime Pema, Spotless Lotus, that I might bring my mind's deluded thoughts to their exhaustion,
I pray you, sovereign of spontaneous openness and freedom, show your face to me.

oṃ āḥ hūṃ svāhā

The disciples should repeat this prayer three times.

The disciples should then prepare material mandalas of precious things, such as gold, grains, fragrant substances, medicines, flowers, and so on. {77} When they offer them one after the other, they should imagine that they fill the whole of the three thousandfold universe. This offering has two purposes, sublime and ordinary. The sublime purpose of offering precious substances is to experience the five primordial wisdoms. The common purpose is simply [to create the cause for] perfect and abundant possessions in this present life. Likewise, through the offering of grains, on the one hand, one [creates the cause for gaining] the five kāyas, and on the other, one will escape the harm of famine. By offering fragrances, one will attain the ultimate expanse of primordial purity and possess clearly functioning sense organs. By offering medicines, one will be free of the suffering of samsara and be untouched by disease. By offering flowers, all that one perceives will become a buddha field of the five lights, and one will have perfect wisdom and freedom.

The disciples then stand, and removing their upper garment, they join their hands at the level of their hearts. Standing with their ankles close together, they fix their gaze with undistracted minds on the teacher's heart. The teacher then exclaims, loudly and in a brief staccato manner, the syllable *A* six times. The bodies of the disciples will tremble, they will speak [Sanskrit] clearly, and their minds will be free of thought. Primordial wisdom will come down on them.

The disciples then enter the mandala of the enlightened mind. Standing in the way just described, they face the eastern sky while, with a gentle voice, the teacher says three times: "*Ema!* Fortunate disciples, go forth into the heart of the eastern sky." He continues, "When you go there, do you reach a place or destination? And is there someone who goes?" The same procedure is repeated for the southern, western, and northern directions. The disciples leave their minds in the state of emptiness free of thought. The teacher then raises his index finger and, making a circle three times in the air, says (on each occasion), "Watch the expanse of space!" It is thus that he reveals the mandala of the dharmakāya, which is pure like space. {78}

The teacher then gives the introduction to primordial wisdom. He instructs the disciples to put on their upper garments and to sit in the vajra posture. He then speaks as follows: "Imagine the sun aloft in the sky surrounded in the four directions by four other suns. Think that these five suns then rise higher and higher in the sky until they disappear." The teacher then explains the meaning of this by saying three times,

> *Ema!* Fortunate disciples, focus your minds in the sky above on the mandala of five suns radiant with light. Watch as it ascends higher and higher.
>
> Do not regress! Do not regress! Do not regress!
>
> The five suns symbolize the light of the five primordial wisdoms. The fact that they ascend higher and higher until they disappear indicates that they dissolve into the ultimate expanse. The words "Do not regress" uttered three times indicate that you, my disciples, should not regress from the state of the three kāyas.

The teacher then stands up. With his right leg stretched and his left leg bent, he points his index fingers at his eyes and pronounces the syllable *A* repeatedly. He does this in the four directions—four times all together.

The teacher then explains that stretching his right leg symbolizes the fact that the proliferations of samsara are severed. The bending of his left leg indicates the perceptions of nirvana. By pointing his fingers at his eyes, he indicates that primordial wisdom arises from the eyes. The repetition of the syllable *A* indicates that freedom in the unborn nature will be gained in this very life.

The teacher then raises his forefinger skyward, and staring fixedly at the sky, he says three times, "Space is vast."

He then goes on to explain that his raised finger indicates the [vajra] chains that appear in the sky. The fixed stare of his eyes refers to the methods of gazing. Finally, his statement indicates that when hallucinatory appearances cease, the appearances of wisdom arise and dissolve into the ultimate expanse.

The teacher takes this opportunity to explain the pure elements of the mandala. {79}

> *Kye!* Fortunate disciples! The heaps of flowers placed upon the mandala of saffron symbolize the inseparability of the support and the supported. Primordial wisdom spontaneously dwells within the primal purity of the primordial expanse. The support at the time of the path is the precious *citta*, or heart. In its center, there dwells that which is supported: awareness that has the character of luminosity. At the time of the result, when the four visions are perfected, the support is the ultimate expanse of dharmatā. And this is where that which is supported—namely, the radiance of the five primordial wisdoms—dwells. This is the meaning [of these heaps of flowers]. You should understand too that the five offering mandalas of five substances represent the skillful means of enjoying the twenty-five primordial wisdoms.

Concluding Celebration

The teacher now declares,

> Now that you have received the extremely unelaborate empowerment, you will enjoy the buddha field of the dharmakāya. Your

mental obscurations will be purified, and you will reign in the immeasurable palace of blazing skulls within the wrathful buddha field. Even if you make no effort, you will gain freedom in the bardo of your next life. If you do make effort, you will gain freedom in this very life. You are now empowered to meditate on emptiness, the dharmatā.

This extremely unelaborate empowerment is thus set forth
According to *The Subtle Commentary: Bedecked with Precious Ornaments*.[4]
Through the merit of composing it for those who in the future have good fortune,
May every being attain enlightenment, Samantabhadra.

This concludes an elucidation of the extremely unelaborate ritual of the wisdom empowerment *The Net of Lotuses*, which figures among the various categories of the empowerments of the Secret Heart Essence. It was composed at Kangri Tökar by Longchen Rabjam, a yogi of the supreme vehicle.

Virtue! Virtue! Virtue!

7. The Adornment of the Four Continents

An Offering Ritual of the Five Mandalas[1]

Longchen Rabjam

{82} When the extremely unelaborate empowerment is bestowed, five mandalas of five substances should be successively offered. They should be visualized as filling the whole of space and expressed clearly in majestic style as follows:

> *oṃ āḥ hūṃ*
> I visualize a buddha field adorned with wishing gems. Its ground is made of various jewels and covered with golden sand. There are mountains, trees, parks, vast palaces filled with light—all contrived of seven jeweled substances. The ground is a beauteous array of a powerful, vast, and varied richness of precious gems—tönka, great tönka, golden beryl, ruby, emerald, musaragarbha, and wishing-cloud. Its unbounded sky is completely filled with nets of wish-fulfilling jewels. All this I offer in a wheel of everlasting continuity to my teachers, to the multitude of deities of the yidam mandalas, and the ocean-like infinity of the hosts of guardians, until the very emptying of samsara. {83}

An array complete with canopies adorned
With traceries of wish-fulfilling clouds
And glorious rains of all that might be wished,
Which fill the whole expanse of the unbounded sky—
This inconceivable display of concentration,
Like Samantabhadra's offering clouds,

I offer with an attitude of perfect virtue
To you who are the glory of samsara and nirvana.

By virtue of these offering clouds adorning the four continents,
And through this whole array of wish-fulfilling gems,
May every being here and now attain what he or she may wish,
And ultimately come to have experience of the five primordial
wisdoms.

oṃ āḥ hūṃ
I visualize a buddha field, a vast expanse adorned with precious qualities. Its ground is made of every kind of jewel and has a rich array of many trees, medicinal plants, flowers, grains of health-giving crops and fruits. All this I offer to my teachers, to the multitudes of deities of the yidam mandalas, and to the ocean-like infinity of the hosts of guardians, until samsara utterly subsides.

A wealth untold of grains, the sustenance of concentration, {84}
And health-bestowing plants and trees, well ripened crops,
And marvelous cultivated fruits—
All these wish-fulfilling clouds of things,
Which fill the whole expanse of the unbounded sky,
I offer to my teachers, to the hosts of deities
Residing in the yidam mandalas,
And to the ocean-like infinity of guardians.

Through this mandala contrived of a sublime variety of grains,
Utterly replete with every precious quality,
May every being here and now possess an endless wealth
And ultimately have enjoyment of the fields of the five kāyas.

oṃ āḥ hūṃ
I visualize a buddha field adorned with precious primordial wisdom, fragrant with essential perfumes, imbued with various scents of sandal, pervaded by the sweet smell of medicinal plants and flowers, lovely with the ornaments of incense-scented trees and nets of jewels, watered by a myriad gently flowing streams of ravishing fragrance. This powerful domain, this boundless array

of perfect qualities of a buddha field, I offer to my teachers, to the multitude of deities of the yidam mandalas, and to the ocean-like infinity of the hosts of guardians, until all beings rest within the state where all the four extremes have utterly subsided.

An array of health-bestowing trees, sweet-scented flowers,
Fragrant incense, nectar filled with healing substances
Suffusing all the air with fine, sublime aromas free of all impurity,
Lovely with the fragrance of unnumbered buddhas,
Powerful and free of all encroaching dust—
Utterly replete with a wealth of different qualities,
All this I offer with great joy.

Through the perfect offering of these nectar clouds
Of medicine and sublime incense,
Which fill the vast unbounded reaches of the sky, {85}
May every being now have clear unhindered faculties
And ultimately come to the enjoyment of the primal ground.

oṃ āḥ hūṃ
I visualize a buddha field formed of wish-fulfilling clouds, a ground contrived of various jewels, adorned with health-bestowing trees of paradise. Here all forms, sounds, tastes, smells, tactile sensations, and the objects of the mental sense are themselves a source of limitless healing properties that have the power to dissipate the diseases of defilement. The vast expanses of the sky are filled with masses of clouds, self-arisen and in an endless, brilliant, ravishing display. This is a buddha field completely filled with various medicinal roots, trees, and fruits, together with the nectar-essence of the elements: earth, water, fire, wind, and space. I offer it to my teachers, to the multitude of deities of the yidam mandalas, and to the ocean-like infinity of the hosts of guardians until all beings attain the city of great liberation.

This buddha field, completely filled with various medicines,
endowed with an auspicious splendor,
Pervades the whole expanse of earth and sky—above, upon, and
underneath it is the ground of bliss.

It causes all defilement, all the ailments of the elements, to subside
And is endowed with the essential nectar of our freedom.
This array of everything without exception I now offer to the teacher of all beings and to his bodhisattva children.

Through the offering of this nectar mandala,
Which is the supreme sacred cure that dissipates all sickness,
May every being now enjoy long life untouched by any ill,
And ultimately may they come to the enjoyment of the field of great felicity.

oṃ āḥ hūṃ
I visualize a buddha field that is an array of precious luminosity, the ground of which is a ravishing display of parks and flower gardens perfectly adorned with lotuses, {86} great lotuses, lilies of the night, utpalas, and udumbara flowers. It is perfectly adorned with great rivers and vast plains and gardens. I offer this to my teacher, to the multitude of deities of the yidam mandala, and to the ocean-like infinity of the hosts of guardians. It fills the whole of space and all the dharmadhātu. I offer it for as long as they remain.

Imagining that all the reaches of the sky are filled
With lotuses in full and pistil-brilliant bloom—
Whole gardens of them blossoming with light,
Adorned with many-splendored flowers of different colors—
With deep respect I offer them.

Through the offering of this mandala
Of space-pervading clouds of flowers,
Adorned with traceries of countless gems,
May every being now have perfect wisdom,
And ultimately, may they come to the enjoyment of the field of the five lights.

Recite these mandala offerings three times with tuneful melody.

This ritual should only be performed before a great empowerment or teaching. It is not to be done in ordinary situations. It is said that merely to offer it once will perfect the two accumulations and will bring about the experience of the twenty-five kinds of primordial wisdom.

This concludes the mandala offering titled *The Adornment of the Four Continents* composed by Longchen Rabjam, a yogi of the Great Vehicle.

Virtue!

8. The Net of Light

A Ritual for the Supremely Unelaborate Empowerment[1]

Longchen Rabjam

To the three transmission lineages—
By mind-to-mind, by symbols, and by mouth-to-ear— {88}
I reverently bow and here explain the ritual
For the supremely unelaborate empowerment.

In a completely solitary place, set out a row of five mandalas each consisting of five heaps of different substances: a mandala of five heaps of precious stones, a mandala of five heaps of grains, and then medicines, fragrant substances, and incense. Decorate them all around with the outer and inner offerings and the gaṇacakra feast offering.

If this empowerment is given at the same time as the extremely unelaborate empowerment, then, apart from a single offering mandala, there is no need to prepare other mandalas. Otherwise, it is necessary. On a clean white cloth spread out five pieces of silk of different colors. On each of them, trace a circle either with a thread or by drawing it. Each of these circles contain five further circles. In the traditional way, place some precious stones on the blue silk in the center, some flowers on the white silk to the right, some grains on the yellow silk below it, some medicinal substances on the red silk to the left, and some perfume and incense on the green silk below it.

The disciples are purified with saffron, blessed medicine, and incense. They then make prostrations to the master who is facing the east. {89} The disciples, facing the west and imagining that the entire universe is filled with precious stones and the other substances, offer the five mandalas one after the other. The master then explains the benefit of doing so in the following words.

> It is thus that you will enjoy the common and supreme accomplishments. In particular, through the offering of precious stones, you will enjoy the inexhaustible dharma. Through the offering of different fragrances, you will enjoy the melodious teaching of the pure dharmatā. Through the offering of medicinal substances, you will enjoy the happiness of freedom from all suffering. Through the offering of incense, you will enjoy the taste of concentration and enlightenment. And through the offering of grains, you will enjoy endless wealth.

The actual empowerment unfolds in four stages: the entry of the disciples into the mandala, the empowerment itself, the introduction received in the course of the empowerment, and finally, the feast of celebration.

The Entry of the Disciples into the Mandala

This has three stages. First, the disciples answer the master's questions and receive his consent.

The master asks three times, "Who are you?" and on each occasion, the disciples answer, "I am the fortunate dear child of your mind." The master then says, "So it is. {90} Enter, therefore, this mandala of the primordially unborn nature of the mind."

Second, the disciples join their hands and recite the following prayer three times.

> *Kye! Kye!*
> Teacher, holder of the vajra, think of me!
> Long have I lingered—far more than I remember—in the
> three worlds of samsara.
> That I might leave samsara, I appeal to you, my teacher.
> For many a hundred kalpas I have turned and turned within samsara.
> When I asked and searched for Vajrasattva, primal wisdom
> self-arisen,
> I found that buddhahood arises in the mind.
> Show me now, I pray, my mind's sublime condition.

Third, the nature of the mind is then revealed. As the disciples gaze fixedly and without distraction at their master's heart, the latter suddenly exclaims three times, "What is the mind?" And in that very instant there arises [in the disciples] a natural state of mind that is empty, clear, and free of thoughts of subject and object—the dharmakāya. The descent of primordial wisdom has occurred.

The Empowerment Itself

This is threefold. There are three empowerments through which three mandalas are entered.

First, the Empowerment through Which the Nirmāṇakāya Mandala Is Entered

The disciples should adopt the lion posture, and staring straight ahead with the elephant's gaze, they should project their awareness in the form of a ball of light in the eastern direction, like a shooting star. They should leap like a lion and then rest in the state of the unborn dharmatā. The disciples should be instructed to concentrate on the following gradual description, which the master should give in a clear and pleasant voice. The master says,

> *Ema!* Listen, fortunate children of my mind. In the eastern direction, in the buddha field of Manifest Joy, {91} which is so pleasant and ravishing in its beauty, there resides the truly perfect buddha, the bhagavan Vajra Akṣobhya. Blue in color, he is arrayed with precious ornaments and is in inseparable union with his consort. On each and every atom, many buddhas form his retinue, as numerous as there are atoms to be found. They listen to the teachings of their teacher and in turn explain it to their own close retinues. They reveal the sublime state of the mind, luminosity, the suchness of the Secret Mantra. My children, watch this with the elephant's gaze and leap there with the lion's leap.
>
> *a a āḥ*

Pronouncing these syllables, the master places on the disciples the seal of nonregression from the triple kāya.

Then the disciples should turn their gaze to the south. Adopting the elephant posture and staring straight ahead, they should, as previously, project their awareness into the buddha field called Glorious and leap there with the waist-stretching movement. Relaxing in the unborn nature, they should attend to the following words of their master:

> *Ema!* Listen, fortunate children of my mind. In the southern direction, in the buddha field called Glorious, which is so pleasant and ravishing in its beauty, there resides the truly perfect buddha Ratnasambhava. Yellow in color, he is arrayed with precious ornaments and is in inseparable union with his consort. On each and every atom, many buddhas form his retinue as numerous as there are atoms to be found. They listen to the teachings of their teacher and in turn explain it to their own close retinues. They reveal the sublime state of the mind, luminosity, the suchness of the Secret Mantra. My children, watch this with the lion's gaze and leap there with the tigress's leap.
>
> *a a āḥ*

Pronouncing these syllables, the master places on the disciples the seal of nonregression from the triple kāya. {92}

The disciples should now gaze in the western direction. Adopting the rishi posture and slowly shifting their gaze from the left until they are looking straight ahead, they should project their awareness and leap into the western buddha field with the flight of the garuḍa. These stages should be visualized in step with the master's words:

> *Ema!* Listen, fortunate children of my mind. In the western direction, in the buddha field Mound of Lotuses, which is so pleasant and ravishing in its beauty, there resides the truly perfect buddha, the bhagavan Amitābha. Red in color, he is arrayed with precious ornaments and is in inseparable union with his consort. On each and every atom, many buddhas form his retinue as numerous as there are atoms to be found. They listen to the teachings of their teacher and in turn explain it to their own close retinues. They reveal the sublime state of the mind, luminosity, the suchness of the Secret Mantra. My children, watch this with the gaze of the ferocious Great Glorious One and leap there with the flight of the garuḍa.
>
> *a a āḥ*

Pronouncing these syllables, the master places on the disciples the seal of nonregression from the triple kāya.

The disciples should now gaze in the northern direction. Adopting the vulture shoulder posture, turning their eyes upward and visualizing the northern buddha field, they should thrust their fists outward from their hearts and simultaneously leap. They concentrate their minds on the visualization as follows in accordance with their master's words:

> *Ema!* Listen, fortunate children of my mind. In the northern direction, in the buddha field of Perfect Action, which is so pleasant and ravishing in its beauty, there resides the truly perfect buddha, the bhagavan Niśitatejorāja.[2] Green in color, he is arrayed with precious ornaments and is in inseparable union with his consort. On each and every atom many buddhas form his retinue as numerous as there are atoms to be found. {93} They listen to the teachings of their teacher and in turn explain it to their own close retinues. They reveal the sublime state of the mind, luminosity, the suchness of the Secret Mantra. My children, watch this with the gaze of Vajradhara and go there like a flash of red lightning.
>
> *a a āḥ*

Pronouncing these syllables, the master places on the disciples the seal of nonregression from the triple kāya.

In this way, the disciples enter, through the four doors, the mandala of the self-experience of awareness. If they do not have time to practice in this life, they will be born in a nirmāṇakāya buddha field of luminous character. And this is the purpose of this empowerment.

Second, the Empowerment through Which the Sambhogakāya Mandala Is Entered

The disciples should adopt the vajra posture and a staring gaze. They should focus their minds on the buddha field of Densely Adorned Array. They should project their awareness, leap there in an instant like a lion, and rest in the state of the unborn nature. These stages should be visualized one after the other according to the master's words:

> *Ema!* Listen, fortunate children of my mind. Far beyond the buddha fields just mentioned is the buddha field of Densely Adorned Array, pervaded and illumined by the five primordial wisdoms, utterly even and unmoving. There the sugata resides, the knower of the world, the guide of beings, the teacher of gods and humankind, the arhat free of all impurity, endowed with wisdom and the feet of wisdom, the truly perfect buddha Amitābha. He is surrounded by a countless retinue of hundreds of billions of buddhas—the display of the unconditioned nature of his mind. My children, watch all this with the elephant's gaze and go there with the lion's leap.
>
> *a a āḥ*

Pronouncing these syllables, the master places on the disciples the seal of nonregression from the triple kāya. {94}

Third, the Empowerment through Which the Dharmakāya Mandala Is Entered

The disciples should adopt the lion posture and gaze upward, downward, to the right, to the left, and straight ahead. They should watch their awareness empty and naked, primordial wisdom, the great, luminous, empty state devoid of all clinging. As a reminder of this, the master says,

> *Ema!* Listen, fortunate children of my mind. Far beyond the buddha field of Densely Adorned Array, there is the nature of your mind, which is free of any kind of thought. It has no limit and is beyond all measure. It cannot be observed; it is emptiness. It is called the utterly undifferentiated dharmatā. My children, keep your awareness high like a garuḍa hovering in the air. Sit there in the manner of a rishi. Rest there evenly in the manner of a sleeping elephant. Lie like an iron tree trunk, facedown with your limbs drawn in.[3] Stretch out like a man, lying on his back. Draw backward in the slinking manner of a vixen. Stoop with shoulders hunched up like a vulture. Striding like a giant, traverse the grounds while remaining in a state of rest. Like a sucking leech, adhere to the union of awareness and the

ultimate expanse. Like a leaping tigress, become proficient in the experience of awareness. Like a sheep, shake off at once all tendency to dualistic perception. And with the lofty demeanor of the lion, lay hold of the union of awareness and the ultimate expanse.

Ema! Listen, fortunate children of my mind. The mind itself rests in emptiness. Seize this as your basis. The mind itself is stable, ever empty but aware. Hold it firmly. The mind itself is ceaselessly in movement. Master its creative power. The mind itself manifests as primordial wisdom, so train in it as your path. The mind itself {95} is all-pervading, so look for signs. The mind itself is swift in its immediacy, so have confidence. The mind itself does not amalgamate with various phenomena, so keep it separate from them. The variety of things is the unfolding of the mind itself, so do not cling to them as real. Do not regress from this primordial wisdom! Do not regress from the essential sphere [of the dharmakāya]! Do not regress from the enlightened body.

The master then gives a brief explanation of the meaning of his words:

Since the dharmakāya is the ground from which the sambhogakāya and nirmāṇakāya arise, it is said that it transcends them both. Now the buddha field is the primordially empty nature of the mind. Therefore, self-cognizing primordial wisdom is the teacher. As you implement the practice, mastering the postures and ways of gazing, you will recognize this wisdom quite spontaneously, and freedom will be gained within the ground.

According to the level of your own experience, recognize the aware and empty nature of your minds, and firmly take your stand on it. Train in the skill of self-arising and self-subsiding. Rest effortlessly in the inborn clarity, which is luminous and empty. Experience the fact that all arisings disappear without trace. Have certainty in the primordial state of natural openness and freedom. Do not be distracted, but recognize whatever arises. Do not cling to the experience of bliss, luminosity, and no-thought. If you practice in this way, the result, the triple kāya, will arise naturally. Do not regress!

The Introduction to the Nature of the Mind Gained through This Empowerment

The master should tell the disciples to adopt, one after another and according to his words, the postures and gazes of the three kāyas. Then he should say clearly three times,

> *Ema!* Fortunate children of my mind! Listen to the truth of deep insight. The empty nature of the mind is endowed with the character of primordial wisdom. Master the nature of your minds—the union of bliss and emptiness, the ground of Mahāmudrā, the five primordial wisdoms. Dispel your ignorance with the open and unhindered primal wisdom of the empty nature of your minds. Cause the different vehicles, through which one engages in the nature of the mind according to one's capacity, to disappear in the one sole sphere. {96} Orient your dharma practice to the empty nature of the mind—the totally perfect sphere free of all conceptual extremes. Understand the vital point of the spontaneous self-experience of awareness, the indivisible, united state of the nature of the mind. Firmly settle your wind-mind in the mind's pure nature, the union of awareness and the ultimate expanse—that is, the luminosity issuing from between your eyebrows. Now, how should this be done?
>
> Bend your neck slightly, rolling your eyes upward. Breathe normally and press you right hand down over your right eye. Then, with your left eye, look at the sky. This will increase the visions of primordial wisdom. You should understand that in the nature of the mind—the dharmakāya, the uncontrived, self-arisen state—the outer and inner worlds are one and the same. Do not regress from [this experience of] the nature of the mind, unadulterated [by thought]—the completely perfect one sole sphere, free of all extremes. Proceed to the nirmāṇakāya. Proceed to the sambhogakāya. Proceed to the dharmakāya. Do not grasp at the dharmakāya, and yet do not fall back from it. Do not grasp at the sambhogakāya, and yet do not fall back from it. Do not grasp at the nirmāṇakāya, and yet do not fall back from it.

At first, the posture and gaze [for the nirmāṇakāya] should be demonstrated. For the other kāyas, the other instructions are the same except that for the second, the sambhogakāya, the neck should be straightened with the gaze turned slightly downward. In the third case, the dharmakāya, the neck should be stretched upward slightly with the gaze directed straight ahead. The master then proceeds to give a brief explanation.

> Within the seed of samsara—that is, the discursive mind—there dwells primordially the nature of the mind as undeluded, ultimate, primordial wisdom. The nature of the mind is empty. Its character is luminous. The radiance of its cognizant power is unceasing. This is the one sole great fundamental nature. Recognize it. On previous occasions, in the context of all the vehicles up to and including the anuyoga, the nature of the mind, the union of awareness and emptiness, is recognized as the Great Seal, or Mahāmudrā. Here, however, in the context of the vajra essence of ati, it should be recognized as awareness endowed with fivefold luminosity. Brush aside the ignorance of deluded dualistic perception by means of the empty and luminous nature of the mind, the primordially pure, self-cognizing, primordial wisdom. {97} All the different levels of mental capacity according to which one adheres to one or another of the nine graded vehicles are primordially open and free in a state in which there is no such thing as tenet systems. Recognize that all that arises as the dharma never stirs from the great sphere beyond all conceptual extremes. Understand that the two stages do not exist as such. They are the great primordial wisdom of union [of appearance and emptiness], the self-experience of awareness. Strive gradually in the luminosity of the union of awareness and the ultimate expanse, which appears between your eyebrows and is seen thanks to the crucial points of the instructions. In other words, practice in accordance with the crucial points of the postures, gazes, breath, and awareness. The nature of the mind, the self-arisen dharmakāya (the pristine state of primordial purity in which phenomena are exhausted) and the self-experience or display of spontaneous presence (completely perfect and distinct) should be respectively experienced by means of the practices of

> trekchö and tögal. Place yourself in a state in which the spontaneous appearances of the three kāyas gradually manifest. Whatever visions or experiences of awareness arise, do not grasp at them, and in that ground, where they are all exhausted, attain the ultimate primordial expanse within this very lifetime.

This is how the master should introduce the nature of the mind, explaining it calmly and slowly. These words are indeed the introduction that leads to the direct seeing of awareness itself. In the root text, as well as in *The Subtle Explanation*,[4] the only rubric given is "Then give the introduction." The way in which this should be done is not mentioned. But here, this matter is set forth following the presentation in *The Manual of the Crucial Instructions [concerning Empowerments]*. On the other hand, there is no conflict if the introduction is not made here, since it is also presented in the guiding instructions. However, if the guiding instructions are not applied, the introduction should be given.

The Concluding Celebration and the Enjoyment of the Feast

First comes the celebration. The master says,

> Now that you have received the empowerment, your ignorance will be completely cleared away and your minds will blossom into primordial wisdom. You are empowered to meditate on the direct vision of the self-experience of awareness. Even if you do not have the leisure to practice, {98} you will be reborn in a nirmāṇakāya buddha field of luminous character. Those of you whose meditation is of medium strength will gain freedom in the bardo, while those of superior capacity will find freedom in this very life, mastering the vajra-like primordial wisdom of all the buddhas.

Then follows the enjoyment of the feast. When the empowerment is completed, the master and the vajra kindred who surround him must offer a sacred gaṇacakra feast, during which the disciples make offerings to their teacher. If these offerings are not made, accomplishment will not occur. As it is said in *The Classification of Empowerments*,

> If, when empowerment is bestowed,
> No feasts are celebrated, no accomplishment will come.
> The accomplishments will all be spoiled.
> Perform, therefore, the gaṇacakra feast.[5]

If the feast is celebrated, all excellence will be gained in this and future lives. All defects will be banished, and all that one wishes will be accomplished. *The Classification of Empowerments* says,

> Those who offer a great feast
> To the teacher and his retinue and spouse
> Will acquire great excellence,
> Dispelling every defect.

There is, moreover, a considerable difference between the merits deriving from the offerings made at the moment of empowerment and offerings made at other times. *The Classification of Empowerments* says,

> Offerings in their hundred billions
> Presented to the teacher at times other than empowerments
> Do not compare with the limitless, unnumbered merits gained
> From offerings made at even one empowerment.

The reason for this is that the time of an empowerment is an extraordinary moment. For then all the gurus of the ten directions, as well as all the deities of the yidam mandalas, are indivisibly gathered in the person of the master and share his nature.

Accordingly, a gift made to a single woman at the time of an empowerment has the same merit as nine hundred feast offerings made at other times to hundreds of wisdom mamos or to Vajravārāhī herself. As it is said in *The Subtle Explanation*, {99}

> The merit of a little gift of food and drink
> To one yoginī at the time of an empowerment
> Is equal to the merit coming from nine hundred gaṇacakras
> Offered to a hundred mamos or Vajravārāhī.
> In this world one will gain

One's every wish, and in the future
One will have experience of the space of wisdom.
One will, with all one's retinue,
Accomplish the pure celestial realms.[6]

Here, most clearly, I have shown
The meaning of the ritual
Of empowerment, supremely unelaborate.

Like night-flowering lilies
In the white light of this merit,
May every wandering being attain enlightenment.

This supreme and essential explanation,
White like the moonlight on the mountains clad with snow,
Was set forth for the sake of generations yet to come
By Longchen Rabjam on the slope of Kangri Tökar.

This completes the elucidation of the supremely unelaborate word empowerment, one of the various empowerments of the Secret Heart Essence, composed by the yogi Longchen Rabjam.

Virtue! Virtue! Virtue!

9. The Wish-Fulfilling Net

An Offering Ritual of the Five Mandalas of the Five Offering Substances[1]

Longchen Rabjam

{101} When the supremely unelaborate empowerment is given, the disciples should offer, one after the other, the five mandalas of the five substances, reciting the following text three times in unison:

> *oṃ āḥ hūṃ*
> The buddha fields of the ten directions, vast as the unbounded sky; with grounds contrived of various precious stones and strewn with boundless perfumes, medicines, incense, grains, and flowers; densely filled with mountains made of various jewels, trees and gardens, measureless palaces, parasols, and countless arrays of victory banners, ensigns, canopies, and music; together with the unnumbered regions of the universe; all with an excellent abundance of great and boundless riches of both gods and humankind—all this I offer for the sake of every being in a wheel of everlasting continuity to my teachers, to the hosts of deities of the yidam mandalas, and to the ocean-like infinity of the hosts of guardians until the very emptying of samsara.
>
> The ground of gems with scents and flowers strewn,
> With groves of healing plants, with incense and abundant grains,
> And heaps of jewels that fill the vast expanse of space,
> Great clouds of endless offerings, display of my imagination—
> All this I offer with a virtuous mind to liberate all beings in the times to come.

Through the offering of these five mandalas
Contrived of the five substances,
These clouds of different brilliant gems and all the rest,
May beings gain at once a high rebirth
Endowed with all the wealth of gods and humankind
And ultimately have enjoyment of Samantabhadra's buddha field.

From the clouds of sublime offerings
Presented by a pure and virtuous mind,
May gifts pour down in rains on boundless realms.
May the two accumulations both of wisdom and of merit
Be complete, and may the wishes of all beings be fulfilled.
May all these realms be filled with all the riches of the buddhas
and their heirs. {102}
May every being practice virtuous dharma constantly.
May all progress together to the place of freedom,
Spontaneously accomplishing the kāyas and the wisdoms.

This concludes *The Wish-Fulfilling Net*, a ritual of mandala offering composed by Longchen Rabjam, a yogi of the supreme vehicle.

Virtue! Virtue! Virtue!

10. The Wish-Fulfilling Sea

A Ritual for the Offering of Gaṇacakra[1]

Longchen Rabjam

The glorious, brilliant wish-fulfilling jewel of the three kāyas {104}
Perfectly arises from the sea isles of the two accumulations.
The four activities are naturally and spontaneously accomplished.
I bow in homage to the sugatas of the five families.

Here in brief I shall explain
The stages of the ritual of the practice
Of the unsurpassed and joyful gaṇacakra
As the tantra *Essence of the Sun* has taught.

Whenever empowerments are granted, and when teachings are given, a gaṇacakra feast is offered. This may be described under three headings: (1) the preliminary for the gaṇacakra feast offering, (2) the stages of the ritual, and (3) the benefits that accrue from it.

The Preliminary for the Gaṇacakra Feast Offering

Given that you are visualizing yourself as a deity, it matters little whether or not you have a support for your concentration in the form of a painting or a statue. If, however, you have one, you should prepare the offerings in front of it. Then you should perform the self-visualization (*samayasattva*), invoke the wisdom deity (*jñānasattva*), make offerings, and so forth. If you have no support, arrange either in front or to the right of yourself the five outer offerings and the inner offerings of amṛta, rakta, and a kapāla filled with nectar, together with offerings of food and drink—specifically meat, alcohol, and so on. Begin by cleansing the offerings by reciting the *sumbhani* mantra and purify them with the *svabhāva* mantra. Then, as you pronounce the syllables *oṃ āḥ hūṃ*, they are, from within the sphere of emptiness, instantly empowered as amṛta.

The Stages of the Ritual

The ritual comprises three sections: (1) the preparation, (2) the main practice, and (3) the conclusion.

The Preparation

All the participants gather together and sit in rows. The master of ceremonies makes prostrations and says,

> *hoḥ!*
> Master, great vajra holder, lord of yogis, and you, heroes and yoginīs assembled here, pay heed to me. For the sake of all beings, beginning with our patrons, in your great concentration consider all phenomena as a mandala spontaneously present, which has the nature of enlightenment from time without beginning. I request you to remain within this inconceivable state.

So saying, the master of ceremonies scatters flowers all around and then proceeds to give a torma to the obstacle-creating spirits. Then, in an instant, all the participants visualize themselves as Vajrasattva and recite the mantra of one hundred syllables.

The Main Practice

This unfolds in five stages: {105} (1) the self-visualization, (2) the presentation of offerings, (3) the praises, (4) the restoration of spoiled or broken samaya, and (5) the enjoyment of the feast.

Self-Visualization

Take refuge in the teacher and the Three Jewels, and then recite the following:

> I and sentient beings without end
> Are buddhas from the very first.
> And yet, because of thoughts, we wander in samsara.
> I therefore generate the wish to gain supreme enlightenment.

Cultivate the mind of enlightenment by thinking as follows:

Even though beings are primordially enlightened, they are nevertheless deluded through their thoughts. Therefore, I will establish them all in the state of buddhahood.

Then recite the following:

The great space of the nature of the mind is inconceivable.
The expanse of the mind's nature is devoid of thought.
And just as space is unobservable, so too this inconceivable expanse,
The nature of the mind, cannot be seen.
oṃ dharmadhātu jñāna prajñā vajra svabhāva ātmako 'ham

As you recite these words, think as follows:

All phenomena become the natural state of great perfection—the state of emptiness beyond all conceptual extremes.

Then, reciting *hūṃ* ten times, think as follows:

From within the state of emptiness, there manifests an enclosure of burning mountains and wisdom fire in all the cardinal and intermediate directions, zenith, and nadir. Within this space—above, below, and on every side—are fences, nets, tents, canopies of vajras, and a sphere of weapons. And in the midst of this, I suddenly arise as the Great Glorious One.

Visualizing yourself in this form, command the obstacle-creating spirits as follows:

Ema!
I am the self-arisen king of wrathful ones,
The great and glorious.
All you who hinder my accomplishment
Do not remain but go elsewhere.
If you refuse, I shall smash your heads into a hundred shards
And your bodies in a thousand pieces.
oṃ rulu rulu hūṃ bhyo hūṃ

So saying, drive the obstacle makers far away. Then recite the following:

The obstacle-creating spirits are my thoughts.
From my own mind do all such spirits come—
There are no obstacles elsewhere.
The nature of the mind is pure from the beginning.
vajra ātmako 'ham

As you say this, all the obstacle-creating forces dissolve into emptiness: {106}

hūṃ
In the main and intermediate directions, in the zenith and
the nadir,
The massive fires of wisdom blaze.
Vajra fences, nets, canopies and tents, and a sphere of
weapons fill the whole of space.
Assemblies of wrathful gods and goddesses of the Great
Glorious One
Gather in dense clouds, all a-murmur with the sound of *hūṃ*.
hūṃ hūṃ hūṃ

If you prefer a more elaborate ritual, you should perform the three concentrations and meditate on the different elements of the peaceful or wrathful mandala. If you are inclined to a simple practice, simply meditate on the lord of the mandala.

Within the sphere of emptiness, in the center of a lotus and on a sun and moon, I appear as Samantabhadra father-mother, the basis of the mandala. He is blue with one face and two arms. He sits with his legs crossed in the vajra posture, and his hands are in the mudra of meditation. From his body pour forth rays of five-colored light that fill the sky. The whole of space is filled with teachers and the host of the deities of the yidam mandalas.

(Imagine as many as you can.)

hūṃ
From the mandala of the primordial essence of enlightenment,
And from the enlightened mind that is devoid of reference,

I invoke all mandalas.
They steadily remain inseparable from myself.
jaḥ hūṃ baṃ hoḥ vajra samayas tvām

As you say these words, think as follows:

The hosts of teachers, the deities of the yidam mandalas at once come from the expanse of space and steadily remain in me.
oṃ āḥ hūṃ svāhā (Repeat the mantra as much as you can.)

The above should be visualized even if you have a support for the practice.

The Presentation of Offerings

This has five sections.

First, the Outer Offerings

oṃ
I emanate vast clouds of offerings:
Precious blossoms, incense, lamps and perfume,
Offerings of food, and tuneful melody, which fill the sky.
All these I offer to my teacher
And to the host of deities of the yidam mandala.
oṃ vajra puṣpe āloke gandhe naividye śabda āḥ hūṃ

With the appropriate mudras, make offerings to both deities—namely, to yourself visualized as the deity and to the deity represented by an image. {107}

Second, the Inner Offerings

With your thumb and ring finger scatter drops of amṛta and rakta from the kapālas.

To the enlightened body, speech, and mind, I make
respectful offerings
Of the substances whereby the five wisdoms and five families
are attained.

Grant, I pray, supreme and ordinary accomplishment.
sarva pañca amṛta hūṃ hrīḥ tha

Third, the Secret Offering

Pressing your palms evenly together, make a circular gesture and focus on the bliss of union with the consort.

āḥ
By offering joyfully and evenly the indivisibility of means and wisdom,
The vast space of the mother's womb, primordial wisdom of great bliss,
May this essence of enlightenment
Delight the host of the victorious ones.
anurāga pañca hrīḥ ṭha

Fourth, the Unsurpassed Offering

Recalling the nature of the mind, recite as follows:

hūṃ
All phenomena are pure and one within the nature of the mind.
The nature of the mind is great perfection from the first.
In the expanse of dharmakāya free of any reference,
Unborn, beyond expression, the vast abyss of space—*alala!*

Fifth, the Offering of Torma

With *raṃ yaṃ khaṃ*, all impurities, all dirt and stains of the torma, are burned up, washed away, and scattered.
With *oṃ āḥ hūṃ*, the torma's color, taste, and potency are rendered perfect and equal to the vastness of the sky.

Offer the torma to the protectors, both worldly and beyond the world, using their respective mantras, or recite the following:

oṃ āḥ hūṃ
Root and lineage teachers, glorious and sublime, residing in the ten directions and four times, hosts of deities of the yidam mandalas, five classes of ḍākinīs and the endless multitude of guardian spirits, worldly and beyond the world—I offer you this torma, *balinda kha kha khāhi khāhi.*

I pray you, grant that all diseases, evil forces, and obstacles subside. Grant accomplishments, supreme and ordinary.

The Praises

Recite the following verses and other praises: {108}

You who in illusory form have arisen from the dharmadhātu,
Teachers and compassionate lords of beings, past, present,
and to come,
Endless throngs of deities, peaceful and ferocious, and
wisdom ḍākinīs,
Multitudes of guardians, helpers who behave according to
my word,
I bow down to you in praise.

Confession and Restoration

With feelings of regret and sorrow, recall your spoiled and broken samayas and recite the following with joined hands:

Overwhelmed by ignorance and delusion,
I have transgressed and broken
The root and branch samayas of your body, speech, and
mind.
With great remorse and sorrow, I openly confess.

Overwhelmed by beginningless deluded habits,
I have intentionally and unintentionally spoiled and broken
my samaya.

In your presence, great compassionate ones, I confess
And pray you, grant accomplishment of ultimate purity.

Failure to complete the recitations of approach and of accomplishment,
Defilement of the first part of the offerings, ritual uncleanliness,
Failure to make offerings at the proper times, laziness and avarice,
Failure in the view and unclear meditation, careless conduct—
All these things I openly confess.

Disrespect toward my teacher and the vajra kindred,
Careless negativity, defilement,
All short-lived and lasting obscurations,
I openly confess with deep regret and sorrow.
I pray you, grant that I attain the ultimate purity.

hoḥ
Within the nature of the mind, there is no defect, no impurity:
No one who confesses, nothing to confess.
I confess them merely in the way of relative illusion.
May all be cleansed within the nondual mind.

The nature of the mind is spoiled by the perception of duality.
But in the space of nonduality, all is from the first spontaneously present.
Therefore, all is great perfection, similar to space—
It is the unborn dharmatā, ultimate reality, completely pure.

When you have purified your spoiled and broken samaya, take the vows that restore them. With your hands joined, recite the following three times:

Teacher, holder of the vajra,
Buddhas gone in bliss of five enlightened families—
Turn your minds to me, I pray. {109}

From now until the gaining of the essence of enlightenment,
I take refuge in my teacher and the Three Jewels, unsurpassed
Buddha, dharma, and sangha.
All my evil actions I confess.
I rejoice in all good deeds
And generate the enlightened mind.
Properly observing the samayas of the five enlightened families,
I will perfectly possess the vajra, bell,
And all samaya substances.
I will not forsake the unsurpassed Three Jewels.
I will never leave my vajra master.
I will never scorn the vajra kindred.
I will do no harm to sentient beings.
I will never criticize the noble ones.
I will not despise the lower vehicles.
I will never turn away from those who practice tantra.
I will bring to their conclusion
The stages of approach, accomplishment, and activation,
And at all times, I will meditate upon the mandala.
Observing all the vows and the samayas,
I will not perpetrate deluded action.
I will utterly subdue my mind,
Accomplishing the welfare, unsurpassed,
Of those who dwell in all the ten directions.
I will carry over those who have not crossed.
I will set free all who are not free.
I will bring relief to those not yet relieved.
I will place all beings in the state beyond all sorrow.

The Enjoyment of the Feast Offering

If you have not already laid out the offering substances for the feast, do so now. The master of ceremonies then makes prostrations and addresses the vajra master, saying,

hoḥ
I pray you to attend to me.
That we may now enjoy these ornaments—
All that is delightful to the senses—

In the greatly blissful mandala of phenomenal existence,
I ask you now to bless the ingredients of the feast.

Taking amṛta from the small kapāla, the master sprinkles the offerings using his thumb and ring finger.

With *raṃ yaṃ khaṃ*, all impurities are burned up, washed away, and scattered. From the syllable *A* there appears a skull cup free of suture lines. Outside it is white; inside it is red. All the offerings placed in it are blessed with *oṃ āḥ hūṃ* and are transformed into amṛta. In the middle of the skull cup's lid, upon the disks of sun and moon, {110} there is a blue, five-pronged vajra. In its center are the three syllables radiating beams of light. A stream of blessings of the body, speech, and mind of all the buddhas in the ten directions falls and fills the kapāla, whose contents are inconceivably multiplied and fill the entire sky.

Put the first portion of the offering into a vessel, and offer it in front of the mandala. Then offer a portion to the torma, saying,

I offer this to the sacred root and lineage masters in the four times and the ten directions, to the victorious ones of the mind-to-mind transmission, the vidyādharas of the transmission through symbols, and to the yogis of the hearing transmission, to the hosts of the deities of the yidam mandala, to the five classes of ḍākinīs, together with the endless host of guardians of the doctrine, and to all the guests of both samsara and nirvana.

gaṇacakra khāhi

If the offering is made in an elaborate manner, present the offerings to the recipients one by one, beginning with the root teacher and mentioning all their names together with their mantras. The master of ceremonies makes prostration and, making the mudras of the five sense pleasures, addresses the vajra master directly.

Pay heed to me, great hero!
Consider all these offerings as perfect,

And cast away all doubt and hesitation.
Enjoy them in the knowledge
That brahmins, dogs, untouchables
Are in their nature all the same!

In reply, the master makes the mudra of acceptance and takes the pledge:

The blissful buddha is the dharmakāya—
The cleansing of all stains, all clinging, and the rest.
To suchness free of all duality,
I pay homage. *alala hoḥ*

Considering that the five fingers of your right hand are the five ḍākas, and the fingers of your left hand are the five ḍākinīs, joyfully partake of the feast, offering the first part to your teacher and yidam deity. Then consider that the interior of your body is an elaborate mandala of peaceful or wrathful deities, or again that your head is the teacher, your throat is the yidam, and your heart is the ḍākinī—and enjoy the feast as a means of offering it to them. During that time, {111} make sure to abstain from all activities incompatible with the dharma—such as criticism, ribaldry, gossip, and quarreling. Enjoy the pleasing substances in the knowledge that the outer environment is a pure field, that the beings within it are wisdom deities, and that your body is a mandala.

The Conclusion

When the vajra master has explained the history [of the sādhana], the master of ceremonies prostrates to him and says,

hoḥ
Please pay heed to me!
Now that we have performed the feast offering, ocean-vast, in the manner of Samantabhadra, in the mandala of perfect mastery, I pray you to allow the singing of the vajra song of realization and action, the dedication of the torma of the remainder, and the singing of the verses of aspiration and good wishes.

Cymbals are played and the torma of the remainder is offered.

I offer this torma of the remainder to the twenty-eight powerful mothers and to the host of Rāvaṇa, the rākṣasa of Laṅka. Ensure that the four enlightened activities of the yogis—ourselves and our attendants—be accomplished easily without impediment.

All mistakes and insufficiencies,
And everything I could not do,
Whatever faults occurring or that have occurred—
I pray you, Lord, to pardon them.

Make amends by reciting thus the hundred-syllable mantra:

oṃ vajrasattva samayam anupālaya vajrasattva tenopatiṣṭha dṛdho me bhava sutoṣyo me bhava supoṣyo me bhava anurakto me bhava sarvasiddhiṃ me prayaccha sarvakarmasu ca me cittam śreyam kuru hūṃ ha ha ha ha hoḥ bhagavan sarvatathāgata hṛdaya vajra mā me muñca vajrī bhava mahāsamayasattva āḥ

Then dedicate the merit by joining your hands and praying as follows:

Teacher, deities within the yidam mandala, pay heed to me.
Through making gaṇacakra offerings within the city of the
glorious heruka,
May I and every being, leaving none aside, {112}
Achieve accomplishment in this same mandala.
Through the four unimpeded enlightened deeds,
May we all achieve spontaneously our own and others' benefit,
Attaining the supreme and ordinary accomplishments.

Then recite the following:

oṃ
You who bring about the benefit of beings,
Grant us the accomplishment that we might do likewise.
Depart now for the enlightened realm,
Only to return again, we pray.
vajra muḥ

As these words are said, the wisdom deities and all the guests of the torma offering depart. If you have visualized the deities within the configuration of a mandala, dissolve them into yourself. If, on the other hand, you have performed this practice using the support of a tangka painting, and so on, do not ask the deities to depart and do not dissolve them. For it is said that this practice is the supreme consecration.

Then as a means to enhancing your view, meditation, action, and result, intone the vajra song and scatter flowers.

> The massing clouds of teachers, deities of the yidam mandalas, and infinite guardians fill the earth and sky. Sending down a rain of flowers, they now recite the following auspicious prayers.

Then with one voice sing together with them:

Good fortune is spontaneous, not stirring from the ultimate expanse.
The perfect Buddha is the nondual indivisibility of the kāyas and the wisdoms,
The primordial lord, the glory of samsara and nirvana,
Samantabhadra, with unnumbered buddhas of the five enlightened families.
With the good fortune of them all without exception, may all things be auspicious.

The essence of luminosity, the supreme path where all contrivance has been stilled,
Free from all impurity, endowed with virtuous qualities, all of them distinct,
Is the vast domain of primal self-cognizing wisdom.
With the fortune of the sun of sacred dharma, may all things be auspicious.

Ruler of the wish-fulfilling treasury of freedom, field of merit for all beings,
The noble sangha with unnumbered vidyādharas and guardians of the doctrine,
And worldly ḍākinīs in brilliant clouds—
Grant good fortune of supreme accomplishment! May all things be auspicious.

When this has been recited, play the cymbals and scatter a rain of flowers. {113} Then bless yourself with the protective syllables *oṃ āḥ hūṃ*, and complete the sādhana—bearing in mind that phenomena never stir from the state of one taste, the taste of the great perfection.

The Benefits of the Practice

By this means, the accumulations of merit and wisdom will be completed, and all spoiled and broken samayas will be restored. The ḍākas and ḍākinīs will gather. Your teacher and the deities of the mandala will be pleased, and you will receive the protection of a multitude of guardians of the teachings. Your present life will be long and free of ailment. You will have great renown and your wealth and social standing will increase. All that you wish will be accomplished and in your next life you will attain unsurpassed enlightenment. You will achieve the supreme and ordinary siddhis.

By whatever merit I have gained through this brief exposition
Of the practice of the gaṇacakra offering,
May all complete the two accumulations.
May they swiftly reach the state of buddhahood.

People, these days, wish for teachings that are short and few in words.
May this terse concise instruction,
Set forth upon the slopes of Kangri Tökar,
Be a source of pleasure for the fortunate.

This concludes the gaṇacakra ritual called *The Wish-Fulfilling Sea.* It was composed by Longchen Rabjam, a yogi of the supreme vehicle.

Virtue!

PART THREE

Commentarial Material on *The Heart Essence of Vimalamitra* and *The Innermost Essence of the Master*

The Heart Essence Mother and Child is a composition of Jamgön Kongtrul himself. It sets out the path of practice related to *The Heart Essence of Vimalamitra* in conjunction with Longchenpa's *Innermost Essence of the Master*, which are respectively the mother and child texts. It explains how this path was practiced in the tradition of Minling Terdak Lingpa and is based on the commentary *The Excellent Path of Great Bliss* composed by Terdak Lingpa's daughter, the celebrated Mingyur Paldrön. The text also contains short explanations of how this path was practiced in the traditions of the third Karmapa Rangjung Dorje and Rikdzin Tsewang Norbu of Katok. A contemporary of Longchenpa, Rangjung Dorje received the transmission of the Heart Essence directly from Kumaradza himself.

The main part of *The Heart Essence Mother and Child* covers the whole range of preliminary practices: the usual preliminaries for tantric practice and the special preliminaries for the Great Perfection, briefly expounded in *The Heart Essence of Vimalamitra* itself and expanded by Kongtrul's explanations. It should be noted that, in this context, even tantric practice is regarded as a preliminary to the Heart Essence. The text continues with detailed instructions on trekchö and tögal. After an explanation of the bardo and the yogas related to it, the text concludes with an exposition of the resultant state of buddhahood.

In brief, this extraordinary work constitutes a comprehensive guide for the practice of the Great Perfection. The translation was greatly facilitated by notes taken from oral explanations given by Dilgo Khyentse Rinpoche in France in the early 1980s.

11. The Heart Essence Mother and Child

The Stainless Words, a Guide That Brings Together the Two Traditions, Mother and Child, of the Secret Heart Essence of the Great Perfection[1]

Jamgön Kongtrul Lodrö Taye

Textual Outline

Preamble

I. The introduction
- A. The qualifications of the teacher
- B. The qualifications of the disciples
- C. The manner in which a teacher is to be followed
- D. How to lay the foundations of the practice with propitious circumstances of place and time, necessary equipment, and good assistants
  1. Place
  2. Time
  3. Equipment necessary for the practice
  4. Assistants in the practice

II. The guiding instructions: A detailed explanation
- A. The historical background
  1. The mind-to-mind transmission of the victorious ones
  2. The symbolic transmission of the vidyādharas
  3. The aural transmission of the yogis
- B. The empowerment that brings [practitioners] to spiritual maturity
  1. The foundation: The granting of empowerment
  2. The samaya pledges
- C. The liberating instructions
  1. The liberating instructions for those of greatest diligence
     - a. The preliminary instructions

i. The preliminaries to the practice sessions
ii. Laying the foundations with seven mental trainings specific to the Secret Heart Essence
  A) Training the mind by reflecting on impermanence
  B) Training the mind by reflecting on temporary and lasting happiness
  C) Training the mind by reflecting on a variety of circumstances
  D) Training the mind by reflecting on the futility of action
  E) Training the mind by reflecting on the qualities of enlightenment
  F) Training the mind by reflecting on the pith instructions of the teacher
  G) Training the mind on the basis of the absence of discursive thought
iii. The purification of the mind through the practice of the four common preliminaries
  A) Instructions on relative and ultimate refuge
    1) Relative refuge
    2) Ultimate refuge
  B) Instructions on relative and ultimate bodhicitta
    1) Relative bodhicitta
    2) Ultimate bodhicitta
  C) The meditation and recitation practice of Vajrasattva
    1) General instructions
    2) Specific instructions
  D) Instructions for the mandala offering whereby the two accumulations are brought to completion
    1) The offering of the nirmāṇakāya mandala
    2) The offering of the sambhogakāya mandala
    3) The offering of the dharmakāya mandala
  E) Guru Yoga
    1) General instructions
    2) Specific instructions
iv. The training of the body and mind in accordance with the general path of the Secret Mantra
  A) Training in the winds for those who are free of desire

1) Training connected with the color of the wind
2) Training connected with the "shape" of the wind
3) Training connected with the number of respirations
4) Training in the exhalation and inhalation [of the wind vajra]
5) Training in the vase breath

B) Training in the yoga of the essence drops for those who have desire

v. The natural dissolution of the five [inner] elements

A) The practice related to the unborn nature of the five *A*-syllables

B) The dissipation of the hindrances of drowsiness and agitation occurring through the disturbance of the elements

b. The main practice

i. Essential instructions on trekchö, the ground, through which certainty is reached concerning the ordinary mind

A) Essential instructions for an action or conduct that is free of clinging

1) Directions for beginners in the practice
2) Directions for those who apply themselves to the essential teachings
3) Directions for practitioners of the path of yogic discipline

B) Essential instructions for a meditation that is free of conceptual fixation

1) Guiding instructions in relation to the ordinary mind

a) The preliminary training of the body

b) The preliminary training of speech

i) Placing the seal

(I) Placing the seal on outer appearances

(II) Placing the seal on your own body

ii) Developing skill

(I) Developing skill with regard to outer appearances

(II) Developing skill with regard to your own body

i) Searching for mental pliancy

ii) Journeying on the road

a) The preliminary training of the mind
i) An examination of the place from where the mind arises and of the arising mind itself
ii) An examination of where the mind dwells
iii) An examination of where the mind goes
2) Guiding instructions for bringing the mind to its natural state
C) Essential instructions for the view that is free of dualistic fixation
1) The implementation of the view
a) The theoretical understanding of the view
b) The actual implementation of the view
2) A direct and naked introduction to the nature of the mind
a) An introduction through the transmission of blessing power
b) An introduction based on meditative experience
i) An introduction based on the mind's stillness
ii) An introduction based on the mind's movement
iii) An introduction based on the indivisibility of stillness and movement
D) Essential instructions for a result that is beyond both elimination and attainment
ii. Essential instructions for the path of tögal
A) The preliminary practice
1) Separating samsara from nirvana
2) Relinquishing the nine activities of body, speech, and mind
B) Seeing awareness directly
1) Taking support of immaculate primordial wisdom
a) The key point for the body
b) The key point for speech
c) The key point for the mind
d) The key point for the sense door
e) The key point for the visual field or object
2) Introduction to the direct vision of awareness
C) The manner in which the four visions arise

            1) The direct vision of the dharmatā
            2) The vision of the enhanced experiences of awareness
            3) The vision of the climax of awareness
            4) The vision of the exhaustion of phenomena in the dharmatā
          D) Supporting instructions
            1) The three kinds of motionlessness
            2) The three kinds of settling
            3) The three kinds of attainment
            4) The four kinds of confident certainty
      c. Conclusion: The way of constant practice
        i. The sealing of appearances during the day
        ii. Striking on the key point of primordial wisdom during the night
          A) The evening practice of gathering the faculties within
          B) The midnight practice of causing one's consciousness to enter the vase
          C) The dawn practice for making awareness lucid and clear
      d. Additional instructions
    2. Instructions for practitioners of moderate diligence
      a. The nature of the bardo
      b. The classifications of the bardo
      c. The practices connected with the different bardos
    3. Instructions for those of least diligence
      a. Training during the natural bardo of this life
      b. The transference of consciousness while in the bardo
        i. The teaching of this text
        ii. The sudden transference of consciousness into a buddha field
      c. Gaining freedom in the nirmāṇakāya buddha fields
  D. The results of the practice
    1. Different ways of achieving buddhahood
    2. The compassionate activities of buddhahood
    3. The moment when the result is gained
  E. Additional teachings
    1. A general outline of the instructions
      a. Teachings given as guiding instructions
      b. Teachings given as an introduction to the nature of the mind

c. Teachings given as essentialized but complete instructions for departing travelers

2. A classification of the practice

Preamble

namo guru samantabhadraya {116}

Primordial Lord, wisdom self-arisen, all-pervading;
Sambhogakāya, light of the ultimate expanse endowed with seven features;
Nirmāṇakāya, luminous in character, guide of beings, in various forms appearing—
To you my sovereign lord and teacher, I pay homage.

And to the teachings of the Vajra Peak of Luminosity, I bow.
These instructions, space-like, deep and difficult to realize,
Are free from the extremes of things to be abandoned and their remedies.
For those who meet with them, they transfigure the four elements into light.

Garab and the other vidyādharas of both India and Tibet,
Especially Vimalamitra, lord of learned ones,
Longchen Rabjam, magical display of primal wisdom,
And Dorje Ziji—all these I venerate until I gain enlightenment.

Lady of the Single Tress, protectress of the tantras, seventeen in number,
Queen of mantra, mistress of the vast expanse of both samsara and nirvana,
Permit the writing of this text so that no hindrance may impede
Its setting forth and practice. Cause it to be perfectly accomplished. {117}

The Heart Essence of Vimalamitra,
Teachings that transform samsara into the primordial expanse,
Brilliant in their blessing power, undimmed by scholarship,
Distilled into their essence by the omniscient Lord of Dharma,

And extracted from a perfect vessel,
Words of the great tertön and his daughter,[2]
These same instructions that I well received
Through kindness of my sovereign lord and teacher,

Unspoiled by anything that I myself invented—
I will now set forth with clear concision
In the form of gradual instructions,
Intending thus to be of benefit to others.

The summit of the teachings of the victorious buddhas of the three times and the ten directions, the quintessence of all the turnings of the dharma wheel, the swiftest of the swift paths of the Vajrayāna, the very essence of the six million four hundred thousand tantras and the most secret section of the pith-instruction class of the Luminous Great Perfection—all this is embodied in the two traditions, mother and child, of the Heart Essence of the great master Vimalamitra (*Vima Nyingtik*). It is my purpose in the present work to explain the profound instructions that combine these two traditions into a single stream.

By way of introduction, I shall show how, through the bringing together of favorable circumstances, one may gain access to the body of spiritual instructions. This will be followed by an explanation of the instructions themselves in the form of a practical guide. {118}

I. The Introduction

This consists of four topics: (1) the qualifications of a teacher able to set forth the guiding instructions, (2) the qualifications of the disciple who is to receive the instructions, (3) the manner in which a teacher is to be followed, and (4) a description of how the foundation of the practice is laid through favorable circumstances.

A. The Qualifications of the Teacher

It is said in *The Great Array of Ati Tantra*,

> Learned, free of worldly tasks,
> With perfect realization of the dharmatā,

Well versed in all instructions that disciples may require—
This defines a teacher of the Mantrayāna.[3]

In general, teachers in this tradition must be adept in all the doctrines of the various classes of tantra of the Secret Mantrayāna and must be able to distinguish their different views. More specifically, in the case of the path of the Heart Essence, they must have the warmth of experience and must be skilled in explaining its essential instructions. They must be free of attachment, aversion, and so on, and must not be distracted by the busy preoccupations of this life. Having already accomplished the practice of the twin stages of generation and perfection, which strike upon the key points of the aggregate of the vajra body, they must have perfectly accomplished the mandala of primordial wisdom—that is, the direct perception of the dharmatā. Thanks to such a realization, their own minds are free, and through their compassion they are able to bring to spiritual maturity the minds of others. Profound knowledge frees them from all misconceptions concerning the fundamental nature, and their wisdom equips them to answer with dexterity the questions of their disciples. Teachers who possess all these qualities are known as vajra holders.

One should not rely on an unqualified teacher, one whose character is the opposite of what has just been described. As we read in the tantra titled *Awareness Self-Arisen*,

Ignorant and arrogant,
He has no realization of the Secret Mantra
And foolishly keeps only to the words.
He is offensive and speaks boastfully.
He has embarked upon a false path
And has not beheld the mandala of the empowerment.
His samaya pledges are corrupted.
Small in learning, great in self-promotion,
He cannot answer people's questions.
An unexamined teacher
Is a demon for disciples.[4]

Any teacher who displays such a character should be avoided from the very beginning. {119}

B. The Qualifications of the Disciples

As it is said in *The Tantra of Awareness Self-Arisen*,

> Strong in faith and great in diligence,
> Wise and free of clinging and desire,
> Respectful, apt for practice of the Secret Mantra,
> Of undistracted mind, defilement free,
> Observant of samaya and persevering in the practice,
> Obedient to their master's words.

True disciples have vivid faith—they are enthusiastic with regard to the teacher and his instructions, and they do their best in them. They have yearning faith; they long for the results of the practice. They have confident faith, being free of doubts. Finally, they have consummate faith thanks to which they are not swept away by trivial circumstances. They therefore possess all the ways by which the power of blessings may enter them. Without procrastination and without excessive tightness or looseness, they are steadfast in their courageous commitment to the practice whereby unsurpassable enlightenment is attained. They examine the profound, fundamental nature with an extremely clear discernment with the result that meditative experience and realization come easily to them. Worldly comforts, in the way of food and clothing, have little attraction for them. Finally, they have the greatest respect for their teacher and for their supreme yidam deity. Thus equipped, authentic disciples possess all the avenues whereby the power of blessings may penetrate their being.

Eliminating all their doubts and misconceptions concerning the path of the Secret Mantrayāna, they are able to implement its profound practices. Their minds are uncluttered by ordinary thoughts prompted by desire, aversion, confusion, and so on, and they are without distraction. Their resolve never to transgress but to keep all the root and branch samayas is constant. They meditate tirelessly on the profound path, and they fulfill the instructions of their teachers. Disciples of this caliber must be accepted as recipients of the teachings.

Those who are unsuitable to receive the teachings are the reverse of what has just been described. *Awareness Self-Arisen* describes them thus:

Without respect or reverence for their teachers,
They practice in distorted ways the Secret Mantra, {120}
With which they have no links of lineage or of character.
They have little knowledge, and they disregard
The kindness of their teachers,
Twisting senselessly their teachings.
Unexamined students may become the teachers' enemies.

If teachers grant the profound instructions to those who are not worthy to receive them, they will be punished by the ḍākinīs and protectors. Such teachers will be barred from accomplishment and will become an object of reproach and slander. They should therefore reject the kind of disciples just described.

C. The Manner in Which a Teacher Is to Be Followed

In order to be cured from the sickness of samsara, disciples endowed with the necessary qualities should, like sick people entrusting themselves to a physician, serve and honor their teachers with respectful body, speech, and mind, free from any pretense or deceit. Like people wanting to cross a river, who must rely on the directions of a ferryman, disciples should, in fear of samsara, always obey their teachers' instructions. Yearning for liberation, they should serve and respect their teachers in the same way that merchants must rely on their guide and escort. Specifically, disciples must please their teachers with appropriate service. And the best of all ways to serve a teacher is through the practice whereby the teachings of the practice lineage are upheld. The second kind of service is offered through physical or verbal action whereby the obscurations of the three doors are removed. The last and least kind of service consists in making material offerings whereby the two accumulations are perfected. As it is said in *Awareness Self-Arisen*,

Thus one should rely upon the teacher of the pith instructions
To whom one offers one's own body
And all that one possesses that is rare and of great value.

As for the benefits of making such offerings, it is said the tantra *The Source of Amṛta*,

Though you may offer worlds a millionfold—
Worlds adorned with every gem—
To all enlightened ones who fill the whole of space,
The merit will not match a hundredth part
Of that deriving from anointing
With a single drop of oil a single pore
Of your own teacher's body.[5]

Moreover, it is through serving and pleasing their teacher that disciples purify the obscurations of their body, speech, and mind. They become delightful in the sight of everyone, {121} their merit and wealth increase, and they are befriended by the ḍākinīs and achieve without difficulty the supreme and ordinary accomplishments. *The Supreme Samaya Tantra* says,

For devoted students who desire to gain it,
Accomplishment derives from pleasing service
Offered to their teacher.[6]

D. How to Lay the Foundations of the Practice with Propitious Circumstances of Place and Time, Necessary Equipment, and Good Assistants

1. Place

The Luminous Expanse Tantra says,

Empty valleys, snowfields, mountain tops and charnel grounds,
Extremely lonely places, clear and high and fresh,
Are places where the fortunate may practice.
There stability is swiftly gained and concentration grows.[7]

Generally speaking, the place where one practices should be congenial and safe from the predations of enemies, thieves, and the like. It should be undisturbed by the noise and passage of travelers. It should be an auspicious region, where the spirits of the place are well disposed to the dharma—a place blessed by the masters, ḍākinīs, and siddhas of the past. Snow mountains, forest glades, rocky prominences, and so on cause one's awareness to become clear. It is said too that high places "catch the radiance of the rising sun and gather in its westering rays." This means that in places where the sun rises early and sets late, the days are long. One should practice in places that are pleasant, where there is a supply of good water and where all favorable conditions are easily found.

2. Time

With regard to the time of one's practice, one should begin at the right time and on an auspicious day, marked by the right constellation of stars and planets. In particular, for the practice of tögal, it is said,

> Late winter, spring, and summer's end
> Are praised as the best times for the two rays.[8]

In these seasons of the year, the weather is fairly warm, {122} and conditions that might induce drowsiness and mental lethargy are few. Specifically, since the rays of the rising and setting sun are the conditions favorable to the arising of primordial wisdom, it is said that these are the best moments of the day for the introduction to the nature of the mind. Therefore, one should take care to practice accordingly.

3. Equipment Necessary for the Practice

The equipment necessary for the practice includes, first of all, the supplies that are essential for life—namely, food, drink, clothes, and a cushion. Then one needs the supports for the practice, such as the articles of samaya; indispensable equipment such as a vajra and bell; beneficial materials such as medicines and substances auspicious for the practice; and finally, items that are specifically required, such as offerings for empowerments and the ingredients for making tormas and the celebration of gaṇacakra. In short, one should assemble beforehand all that one might require so that one will not need to rush around frantically in search of them should they prove necessary. As it is said,

> Gifts in homage, flowers, offerings for empowerment,
> Materials for tormas and the gaṇacakra feasts,

> Protections for your health in times of practice—
> All these necessary things you should possess.[9]

4. Assistants in the Practice

When speaking of assistants in the practice, *The Luminous Expanse Tantra* says that one should rely on someone who has experience of the profound path or, failing that, on a person whose mind is properly trained and peaceful, whose samaya is pure, and who is well trained in the practice of pure perception. Such a person should have few defilements, should be of a warm-hearted disposition and untiring in providing all favorable conditions.

II. The Guiding Instructions: A Detailed Explanation

This section is divided into five subsections: (1) The first is a description of the historical background and is intended to inspire confidence in the teachings. (2) The second is a discussion of the empowerment, which brings practitioners to spiritual maturity. (3) The third is an exposition of the liberating instructions. (4) The fourth describes the results of the meditation, and (5) the fifth supplies additional teachings that set forth the distinctive features of the practice itself.

A. The Historical Background

It is said in *The Luminous Expanse Tantra*,

> To bring conviction to the fortunate disciples,
> Explain the history of the transmission.

The historical background is considered under three headings: (1) the mind-to-mind transmission of victorious ones, (2) the symbolic transmission of vidyādharas, and (3) the aural transmission of yogis.

1. The Mind-to-Mind Transmission of the Victorious Ones

In the primordial expanse, the expanse of the ultimate nature of phenomena, the primordial purity that is beyond all conceptual extremes, {123} the glorious buddhas, Samantabhadra father and mother arise as the embodiment of primordial wisdom spontaneously present. And to the assembly of their retinue, which is their own self-experience—namely, the five families of the regent buddhas, their bodhisattva offspring, and so on, who themselves are not different from the Samantabhadra father-mother—they teach without teaching, in the equality of the three times, the Great Perfection beyond word and expression.

2. The Symbolic Transmission of the Vidyādharas

The symbolic transmission of the vidyādharas occurred in the following way. In the Blazing Mountain charnel ground, speaking in words of perfect eloquence, Vajrapāṇi, Lord of Secrets, expounded the ultimate reality, the ultimate fundamental nature that transcends relative phenomena and is beyond all striving, to the great nirmāṇakāya Garab Dorje. In the charnel ground, the Cool Grove of Śītavana, Garab Dorje taught this ultimate reality, beyond all action and effort, to the master Mañjuśrīmitra. In the charnel ground of Sosaling, Mañjuśrīmitra expounded the ultimate reality directly and exactly as it is to the vidyādhara Śrīsiṃha. In the charnel ground of Cooling Moon, Śrīsiṃha transmitted it to Jñānasūtra directly and in a manner beyond discursive thought. In the great charnel ground of Bhaseng, Jñānasūtra revealed the fundamental nature, which lies beyond the reach of intellectual understanding, to the great paṇḍita Vimalamitra, transferring his primordial wisdom to him by means of symbols. The symbolic transmission of the vidyādharas persisted as far as Vimalamitra.

3. The Aural Transmission of the Yogis

The aural transmission of the yogis thus begins with Vimalamitra, the great paṇḍita who gave these sublime and perfect teachings, the instructions of the secret unsurpassed, to the lord King Trisong Detsen, Nyangben Tingdzin Zangpo, and others. Nyangben then gave the teachings of the aural lineage to Drom Rinchen Bar and Be Lodrö Wangchuk, thus ensuring that this tradition of transmission was not lost. Moreover, mindful of the beings of future generations who might be guided, {124} he concealed the volumes of the tantras in the temple of Zhai Lhakhang in Uru. These were discovered in the course of time by Neten Dangma Lhungyal, who took them from the place of their concealment. Now Neten Dangma Lhungyal had sought and received the aural transmission of these instructions, and so it was that through him the long oral (*kama*) transmission and the treasure (*terma*) transmission were blended into a single stream. Neten Dangma Lhungyal bestowed these teachings on Chetsun Senge Wangchuk, who in turn revealed the treasure of the four profound volumes.[10] Moreover, at Chargyi Pudra, a rock shaped like a white staircase, he received during a period of seven months the entire set of instructions directly from Vimalamitra himself. Finally, at Dzayi Rawa in Oyuk Chigong, he dissolved into a body of light.

Chetsun transmitted all these teachings to Zhangtön Tashi Dorje, who in turn gave them to Chetsun's son, the learned Nyima Bum,[11] who passed them on to the Lord of Dharma Guru Jober. The latter gave them to Trulzhik Senge Gyapa, who transmitted them to the siddha Dawa Munsel,[12] who transmitted them in turn to the great vidyādhara Kumaradza. And it was Kumaradza who bestowed them on the crown ornament of all learned and accomplished masters, the peerless, omniscient king of dharma, Longchenpa.

This sublime master was prophesied in *The Word-Transcending Tantra*. It is said by some authorities that the line "Then the supreme Lodrö will uphold it" refers to Longchenpa, not only in terms of his names, one of which was Tsultrim Lodrö, but also in terms of its meaning. For the power of Longchenpa's discernment was fully developed regarding objects of knowledge, free of attachment and impediment.[13] Other authorities identify references to Longchenpa in another verse of this tantra, which reads, "Later it will be upheld by one known as the glory of those learned in the [Sanskrit] language." Generally speaking, the life and liberation of Longchenpa was beyond imagining. In particular, he turned the wheel of the teachings of the Luminous Great Perfection without depending on others. He was therefore Samantabhadra himself appearing in the form of a spiritual master.

In *The Word-Transcending Tantra*, we also find the text,

> A bodhisattva dwelling on the ground of realization {125}
> Will propagate the teachings as far as to the ocean shore.[14]

This was a prediction referring to the third Gyalwang Karmapa [Rangjung Dorje], who first received the complete instructions of the Secret Heart Essence from the vidyādhara Kumaradza and later was directly guided by Vimalamitra himself.

As the Karmapa said in his own vajra words,

Vimalamitra has bestowed on me his blessing.
Once when I was staying in the solitude of Karme Yangön,
In the final moments of the rising dawn,
He came, appearing from the east,
So beauteous in the light.
My gaze could not be satisfied.
Into the center of my brow he melted.
Thus all the teachings now I effortlessly grasp.[15]

As the Karmapa said, it was thanks to Vimalamitra's blessing that he easily understood the view of the six million four hundred thousand tantras of the Great Perfection. And thus he was able to compose *The Heart Essence of Karmapa*,[16] which had burst forth from within the expanse of his realization. Karmapa commanded his four learned and accomplished disciples to propagate the teachings of *The Heart Essence of Vimalamitra*[17] and *The Heart Essence of Padma*[18] throughout the central provinces of Ü and Tsang, in Kham, and also in China and elsewhere. And thus the words of the prophecy were fulfilled.

These two great beings, Longchenpa and Karmapa Rangjung Dorje, are thus in all respects incomparable masters of the teachings of the Great Perfection. Their common teacher was the vidyādhara Kumaradza, and indeed, but for a few minor differences in expression, *The Heart Essence of Karmapa* is in word and meaning the same as *The Heart Essence of Vimala*. Furthermore, for all the teachers of the past, the tradition of *The Heart Essence of Vimala Mother and Child*[19] and the tradition of *The Heart Essence of Karmapa* mingled into a single stream so that, as the omniscient Tenpai Nyinche[20] and others have repeatedly said, whichever of these two systems is practiced, taught, and propagated, the understanding of the one is certainly the same as the understanding of the other.

It is our intention in the present text to explain the transmission lineage of *The Heart Essence of Vimala Mother and Child*. {126} The omniscient Longchenpa had many disciples—great beings who accomplished the two goals. The principal lineage of transmission begins with the learned and accomplished master Khyabdal Lhundrub and passes through Jamyang Drakpa Özer, Trulzhik Sangye Önpo, the omniscient Dawa Drakpa, the great siddha Kunzang Dorje, the peerless Gyaltsen Palzang, Tulku Natsok Rangdröl, the greatly accomplished Tendzin Drakpa, the learned and accomplished

Dongak Tendzin, the vidyādhara Trinle Lhundrub, and finally to Orgyen Terdak Lingpa,[21] king of dharma.

In Terdak Lingpa's tradition, the instructions known as *The Great Heart Essence*—that is, the pith instructions of *The Heart Essence of Vimala*—are taught separately and independently from *The Innermost Essence of the Master* composed by the king of dharma, the great and omniscient Longchenpa, Drime Özer, as an elucidation of their profound key points. However, Terdak Lingpa chiefly brought together topics figuring in both texts (henceforth called the mother and child) that are the same in meaning and are similarly enumerated (as in the seven mind trainings described below), combining them with the particular pith instructions that belong specifically to both texts. He thereby established a system that is easy to implement, a system in which the profound key points of an unmistaken practice are presented in a complete and mutually supportive manner. Therefore, to receive the present teaching is to receive all the instructions [mother and child] at a single stroke. And this is why Terdak Lingpa's system of practice is adopted here.

This great master and treasure revealer bequeathed his teachings to his son, Gyurme Rinchen Namgyal, who was himself an emanation of Vimalamitra, and to his daughter, the Venerable Lady Mingyur Paldrön[22] and others. {127} In *The Word-Transcending Tantra*, there is the following prophecy:

> Then Paldzinma, the ḍākinī,
> Will keep this doctrine, spreading it
> Till human life span is reduced to just ten years.
> The teaching then will fade away.[23]

In knowledge and realization, Mingyur Paldrön was unequaled, and her kindness in maintaining and preserving the doctrine was immense. She composed many textbooks that were to be like the eyes of the teaching tradition of the Heart Essence—in particular, *The Excellent Path of Great Bliss*,[24] a guide to the mother and child texts of *The Heart Essence of Vimalamitra*.

From the two sublime children of Terdak Lingpa, brother and sister, the teaching was transmitted to the great scholar Khenchen Orgyen Tendzin Dorje (a tulku of Yudra Nyingpo) and thence to Trichen Trinle Namgyal (a tulku of the great Nubchen). He transmitted it to Trichen Pema Wangyal (a tulku of the great tertön himself, Terdak Lingpa), who transmitted it to Palden Pawo Tsuklak Chögyal, who bestowed the entire collection of empowerments and reading transmissions on the holy being Göntrul Karma Shenpen Taye. It was from him that I myself first received it.

There is also another lineage passing from Trichen Trinle Namgyal to Jetsun Rinpoche Gyurme Trinle Chödrön. She passed to Dorje Zijitsal (Jamyang Khyentse Wangpo), who was himself an emanation of the great paṇḍita Vimalamitra and was like a second Longchenpa. And in an act of supreme kindness, Jamyang Khyentse Wangpo gave these essential teachings, this ocean of maturing empowerments and liberating instructions, to me. This unbroken lineage of empowerments, reading transmissions, and instructions—and also the uninterrupted lineage of meditative experience and realization—are of the greatest eminence.

Generally speaking, the renowned *Four Parts of the Heart Essence* comprises the two parts of *The Heart Essence of Vimalamitra* and the two parts of *The Heart Essence of Padma*. Most Nyingmapas identify the two parts of *The Heart Essence of Vimalamitra* as *The Great Heart Essence of Vimalamitra* and its quintessential commentary, *The Innermost Essence of the Master*. They identify the two parts of *The Heart Essence of Padma* as *The Heart Essence of the Ḍākinīs*[25] (the treasure text revealed by Pema Ledreltsal) together with a text of profound key points—namely, *The Innermost Essence of the Ḍākinīs.*[26] {128} The two *Innermost Essence* texts are mind treasures of the omniscient Longchen Rabjam.

On the other hand, Kongpo Dzokchenpa and Rikdzin Tsewang Norbu[27] present *The Four Parts of the Heart Essence* differently. They count *The Heart Essence of Vimalamitra, Mother and Child* separately but *The Heart Essence of the Ḍākinīs, Mother and Child* as a single entity. To these three sections they then add *The Heart Essence of Vajrasattva.*[28] This is a token representation of *The Heart Essence of Vairotsana*[29] and possesses a threefold lineage of transmission.

Other authorities do not include *The Heart Essence of Vajrasattva* and complete *The Four Parts of the Heart Essence* by adding *The Heart Essence of Karmapa.* Finally, there is also an uninterrupted terma lineage still in existence coming from the lord Rangjung Dorje, who received *The Heart Essence of the Ḍākinīs* directly from [Pema] Ledrel[tsal].

I am most fortunate to have received all these transmissions which, coming through all these different avenues, are now blended into a single stream. Moreover, regarding the individual and separate lineage of *The Heart*

Essence of Karmapa, all the instructions, garnered from personal meditative experience, were gradually and uninterruptedly handed down from Karmapa Rangjung Dorje through Palden Pawo Tsuklak Gawa, the omniscient Chökyi Jungne, the thirteenth lord Karmapa Dudul Dorje, Pawo Tsuklak Chögyal, to the omniscient [fourteenth] Gyalwang Karmapa Tekchok Dorje, who himself kindly granted it to me through reading transmission and explanation.

This is only a brief digest of the historical background. It could however be explained in greater detail following *The Way of Transmission of the Secret Heart Essence*, otherwise known as *The Garland of Gems: The History of the Secret Heart Essence*,[30] which is to be found in *The Innermost Essence of the Master*. One should also consult *The Supplement to the Lineage of the Heart Essence Mother and Child*, also known as *The Hook That Induces Certainty*,[31] composed by the precious tertön Terdak Lingpa.

B. The Empowerment That Brings [Practitioners] to Spiritual Maturity {129}

This has two sections: (1) a discussion of the foundation provided by the granting of empowerment followed by (2) an explanation of samaya, which is the very life of the empowerment itself.

1. The Foundation: The Granting of Empowerment

It is said in *The Word-Transcending Tantra*,

> The fortunate are ripened
> By four kinds of empowerment:
> Elaborate, and unelaborate,
> Extremely, and supremely unelaborate.
> These, distinguished fourfold,
> Bring the mindstreams of the fortunate
> To the state of spiritual maturity.

Generally speaking, those who are engaged in the three yogas [mahā, anu, and ati] do not have recourse to difficult practices as is the case in the lower vehicles. Thanks to their extraordinary methods, the instructions on how to take the five poisons as the path purify the ripened propensity to discursiveness and directly reveal primordial wisdom. The Sanskrit word *abhiṣiñca* means to scatter or to pour. Empowerments in fact scatter or clear away all samsaric tendencies that one may have with regard to phenomena, which, though they appear, have no existence. They "scatter" them and clearly reveal the nature of the ground—in other words, the three kāyas, which are naturally and primordially present. This, moreover, is described as a "pouring out" [of good fortune]. In the particular context of the Heart Essence, when one receives an empowerment of the Natural Great Perfection beyond all mental elaboration in the mandala of ultimate bodhicitta, the dharmatā—namely, the mandala of primordially pure phenomenal existence—one is introduced to the vision of it in its naked state. In the case of persons of the highest capacity, freedom is gained then and there at the time of the empowerment. In the case of those of medium capacity, the meaning of the symbols is understood, and primordial wisdom is experienced. In the case of those of basic capacity, the seed of liberation is planted in the mindstream. As it is said, "It is through empowerment that the shoot of liberation manifestly grows. The capacity for the ineluctable arising of liberation will ripen."

In the present context, although the pith instructions are given in a manner that combines the two *Heart Essences*, mother and child, the empowerments are bestowed exclusively according to *The Innermost Essence of the Master*. Traditionally, the elaborate empowerment is given before the instructions. {130} Before the teachings on trekchö, the unelaborate empowerment is given. Before the teachings on tögal, the extremely unelaborate and supremely unelaborate empowerments are granted together.

2. The Samaya Pledges

It is said in *The Word-Transcending Tantra*,

> The samayas that are grounded in empowerment
> Are countless in variety. In brief, however, they consist in guarding
> The enlightened body, speech, and mind.

Samaya is said to consist in the intention not to transgress the precepts that are to be observed—together with the seed of that intention. As it is said in *The Subtle and Extensive Samayas*,

Not to transgress the pledges no matter what occurs,
And even in one's dreams, is said to be samaya.
To promise this is said to be the vow.[32]

The samayas may be classified as follows. If each of the samayas related with [the teacher's] body, speech, and mind is divided into outer, inner, and secret sections, each of which is again further divided into outer, inner, and secret sections, we come to a total of twenty-seven samaya pledges.[33] In addition, there are samayas regarding things that are to be kept secret, such as the five meats and the five nectars (belonging to the samaya substances of the Secret Mantra). Then there are the samayas concerning secrets entrusted by one's teacher and the vajra kindred concerning what one should do or should not do. In short, without ever losing one's carefulness, mindfulness, and vigilant introspection, one must observe all the root and branch samayas to which one has pledged oneself. It is said in *The Stainless King of Confession Tantra*,

In such a ground provided by samaya,
A harvest of all fruits will ripen.[34]

And *The Supreme Samaya Tantra* also says,

If samaya is not contradicted,
Attainment of the state of Vajradhara, perfect buddha,
Is sure within a single life.[35]

It is indeed said that the development or otherwise of the fruits of the main practice within one's mind depends entirely on samaya.

C. The Liberating Instructions {131}

This section has three parts: (1) the liberating instructions for those of greatest diligence, who achieve liberation in this very life; (2) the instructions for those of moderate diligence, who achieve liberation in the bardo; and (3) the instructions for those of least diligence, who gain freedom in the buddha fields of luminous character.[36]

1. The Liberating Instructions for Those of Greatest Diligence

In *The Great Order of Meditation: The Lamp That Elucidates the Focal Points of Practice*, we find the following text:

> If at the beginning you do not have a confident trust in the naked vision of awareness, you are likely to regress into a false tenet system. For this reason, you should begin with the pith instructions on how to train in bodhicitta, the mind of enlightenment. When you have definite signs of warmth, indicating that bodhicitta has been mastered, you should be guided on the path with the help of the pith instructions of the Secret Mantra. When you have determined whether you are a person with or without desire, you should train accordingly in the channels, winds, and essence drops. Then, when definite signs of warmth appear in relation to the channels and winds, you should draw your awareness away from the elements by means of the pith instructions that sever the flow of thought. When awareness is turned away from the five elements, you should observe the nature of conduct, meditation, view, and result by means of the pith instructions that open one's eyes to what is hidden.[37]

The detailed guiding instructions for conduct, meditation, view, and result, coupled with the textual outline from *The Wish-Fulfilling Gem: The Innermost Essence of the Master* are implemented in three stages. The first consists of the preliminary instructions through which one becomes a proper vessel, able to meditate on the path. The second is the main practice, which, in accordance with the meditation instructions of *The Essence of Luminosity*,[38] establishes what is mind and what is awareness. The third is the conclusion, which, in accordance with *The Three Key Points of the Wheel of Dharmatā*,[39] sets forth a way of practice that is constant like a flowing river.

a. The Preliminary Instructions

The preliminary instructions cover five topics: (1) the preliminaries to the practice sessions, which act as an indispensable link with the meditation on the profound path; {132} (2) the laying of the foundation of the path through the seven mental trainings specific to *The Secret Heart Essence [of*

Vimalamitra]; (3) the purification of the mind through the four common preliminaries; (4) the training of body and mind through the practice related to the winds and essence drops, the common path of skillful means belonging to the Secret Mantra; and (5) the dissolution of the five [inner] elements simply and naturally by means of the pith instructions that sever the stream of thought.

i. The Preliminaries to the Practice Sessions

On a comfortable seat in a solitary place, sit straight in the seven-point posture of Vairocana. Then, according to the gradual stages of the meditation laid down in the instructions, adopt the general and specific key points of physical posture according to the practice you are doing. You should never remain in an ordinary posture, such as lying down or leaning against something. The reason for this is that the body is like a kind of city. Its channels are like streets, the winds are like horses, and the consciousnesses are like crippled riders mounted on the horses. Consequently, if the city of the body is locked down, the entrances to the city's streets will be closed, and the mounted riders will be trapped in the streets that they have entered and will be unable to get out. It is said that a snake has four legs but they are invisible unless the snake is squeezed. In the same way, unless the body is mastered, the mind will not be still. But because of the way that they are connected, if the body is properly positioned, states of realization will manifest within the mind. This is why the masters of the past considered physical posture to be the first of the profound instructions.

Then expel your stale breath nine times in the first session and three times in those that follow. To begin with, expel your breath three times from the left nostril, first gently, then a little more energetically, and then powerfully. Do the same from your right nostril. Finally, expel the stale breath from both nostrils at the same time, gently, more energetically, and then powerfully. In the following sessions, expel the stale breath once from the left nostril, once from the right nostril, and once from both nostrils together. And as you do so, consider that all the negativities and obscurations accumulated from time without beginning in the lives of every being, yourself and others—together with all obstacles, hindrances, and adversities—are brought together {133} and, with the breath in your nostrils, completely driven out of your body so that its interior is cleaned out and becomes pure. This is just like washing a vessel before pouring a precious elixir into it.

When you have done this, generate a powerful sense of bodhicitta and an attitude of thinking, "I am now going to implement the pith instructions of the Great Perfection for the sake of all beings as infinite in number as the whole of space." Then recite the following prayer:

> Glorious root teacher, precious master,
> Remain upon the lotus seat above my head.
> In your supreme kindness guide me.
> Bestow, I pray, accomplishment of your body, speech, and mind.

Visualize above the crown of your head your kind root teacher in the form of Vajrasattva seated on a lotus and disks of sun and moon. His body, complete in its major and minor marks, is adorned with silk garments and precious ornaments. He holds in his two hands a vajra and a bell and he is seated in the posture of a bodhisattva [with his right leg slightly extended]. Then recite the following:

> Precious teacher, embodiment of all the buddhas of the triple time, I place my trust in you.
> I pray you, bless me so that my mind be brought to maturity and freedom.

This is the only thing to be recited although you might also add the following:

> I pray you, bless me so that in my mind
> Be born extraordinary realization of the profound path.
> I pray you, bless me so that in this life
> I swiftly gain supreme accomplishment of Mahāmudrā.

As you make this fervent prayer from the depths of your heart, there flows from the toe of the teacher's right foot a stream of white nectar, which enters through the Brahmā aperture on the crown of your head. {134} It completely fills your body and engenders the primordial wisdom of great bliss. Finally, the teacher melts into light and dissolves into you. Considering that your mindstream is now blessed, remain in a state of awareness free of concepts and clinging.

In the oral tradition of Rikdzin Tsewang Norbu, it is said that one should pray to one's teacher in the form of Samantabhadra—that is, the ground [awareness]—visualizing him in front of oneself in the center of a sphere of blue light. The teacher then takes the form of a dark-blue syllable *hūṃ* and, as will be explained in due course, enters into the center of the vajra [namely, oneself visualized in vajra form].[40] Although this is not actually explained in the texts of the instructions of the omniscient Longchenpa, nevertheless, since it sets forth the "path of the vajra" and since Tsewang Norbu has said that one should meditate on it in the post-meditation periods, this is the practice of that tradition. Rangjung Dorje, for his part, explains the practice in the same way but specifies that one may meditate on one's teacher either in the teacher's natural form or in the form of Vajrasattva. As previously, one finishes by meditating on oneself in the form of a three-pronged vajra, adopting the vajra posture. This constitutes the auspicious environment for the banishing of all obstacles and is the supreme, ultimate sphere of protection.

ii. Laying the Foundations with Seven Mental Trainings Specific to the Secret Heart Essence

In *The Copper-Lettered Instructions*, we find the following text:

> *Kyema! Kyema!* Listen, children of the lineage! There are those who may not be drawn to the direct experience of awareness, for their mental scope is meager, their karmic fortune is weak, and they have no confidence in these teachings. For them to have an experience of awareness, they must train as follows. In a place that is free of unpropitious circumstances, they should give up all outer and inner activity. Abandoning everything that weakens meditative absorption, they should first train their minds.[41]

The text then proceeds to give a detailed explanation. In all, there are seven trainings of the mind: (1) reflection on impermanence, (2) reflection on temporary and lasting happiness, (3) reflection on a variety of circumstances, {135} (4) reflection on the futility of all one's activities, (5) reflection on the qualities of enlightenment, (6) reflection on the pith instructions of one's teacher, and (7) the training of the mind based on the absence of discursive thought.

A) Training the Mind by Reflecting on Impermanence

In the outer world, observe the passage of the seasons. Day and night, there is not even an instant of permanent duration. Inwardly, the body, composed of the four elements, changes. It is impermanent. Like foam, it is without solidity and is quickly destroyed. Secretly, all your relations are impermanent: your parents, relatives, and friends all pass away. And you should remind yourself that you too are in the same predicament—that at any time, the same can happen to you. There is no certainty that death will not come for you today or tomorrow. Bearing this in mind—that you could die this evening or tomorrow—reflect sincerely on all this without a moment of distraction. And when you see others, remember that they too must die, the only uncertain thing being the moment when. All conditioned things are impermanent. Seeing this impermanence, be free of excessive worry for the future. To have such an attitude is a sign that you have gained proficiency in this kind of training—the purpose of which is to turn the mind away from samsara. And as a way of jogging your memory, recite the following:

> Outwardly, come night, come day, the seasons pass.
> Inwardly our bodies change,
> And secretly our friends and loved ones also.
> All conditioned things are passing, soon to end.
> Nothing in them is there that persists;
> They are but bubbles on the water.

B) Training the Mind by Reflecting on Temporary and Lasting Happiness

Negative actions are the source of the lower realms and of every kind of suffering. Virtuous actions are the source of higher destinies and every kind of happiness. But the higher and lower states of samsara are like buckets on a waterwheel. {136} They are fluctuating and impermanent—that is their great drawback. Liberation, enlightenment, is the only way to escape this situation. Nothing else can be relied upon, and no other solution is worthy of your trust; the situation is truly dire. If, on the other hand, you set out on the path to liberation, you will in truth attain the temporary happiness of the higher destinies. Like the bodhisattvas, the offspring of the buddhas, you will enjoy the presence of excellent qualities within your mindstream.

And, like the buddhas, you will achieve a happiness that lasts, the unsurpassed condition of enlightenment. Therefore, form the intention in your mind "I will accomplish the perfection of happiness, both temporary and everlasting."

If, on the other hand, you do not engage in the path of liberation, you will, through negative action, be reborn in the lower realms, or through virtuous action, you will be reborn in the higher destinies only to return to the lower realms eventually. If deeply from the bottom of your heart you think that all action is the source of suffering, you have gained proficiency in this training, the whole purpose of which is to feel revulsion for the sufferings of samsara and to acquire a powerful sense of weariness in its regard. As a way of reminding yourself, recite the following verse:

> Virtue and nonvirtue both will lead
> To wandering in the six migrations.
> Wealth and happiness enjoyed now in this life
> Are nothing more than poisoned food.
> They only look like happiness
> And are the causes of your future pain.
> Thus the path to freedom
> Is the only way to lasting joy.

C) Training the Mind by Reflecting on a Variety of Circumstances

Nothing is reliable or trustworthy for those born in samsara. You may do good to people, but they harm you in response. The food and drink that you consume are causes of disease and death. You accumulate wealth but only for the benefit of enemies and thieves. Hoping for kindness, you look to your friends only to find that they have turned against you. You don't put a foot wrong, but all you get for it is slander and criticism. {137} No matter what you do, people are not pleased. There is no end to this kind of thing, and it is a great source of trouble.

When you reflect honestly about the attitude and behavior of beings, you will see that whatever you may do to help them, there will always be some who are satisfied and some who are not. But however you may look at it, no [real] benefit is ever accomplished. All actions have the nature of suffering. They are themselves the manifold causes of disease and death, and nothing really helpful is achieved. Indeed, there are no infallibly trustworthy objects other than the teacher and the Three Jewels. And if you venerate them with devotion, this itself is a cause of happiness in this and future lives.

Therefore, with the thought that you must turn your mind exclusively to virtue, and reflecting on all the circumstances good and bad of the past, present, and future, you should grow sick and tired of them and make plans for only the short term. To think how truly wonderful it would be to have compassion for all the beings in the six realms, and to honor and venerate your teacher and the Three Jewels, is to gain proficiency in the present training. The aim here is to prepare for the practice by cultivating an attitude of faith and confidence. As a reminder, recite the following verse:

> Endless are life's circumstances and experiences—
> Never-ending are deluded deeds.
> No matter what I do, there is no satisfaction.
> I'm like a deer attracted to the water of a mirage.
> Let me therefore turn my mind to virtue.

D) Training the Mind by Reflecting on the Futility of Action

All the actions of this present life done to protect family and friends or to get the better of one's enemies; all farming, all interest in commerce with its desire for profit, wealth and reputation; all animosity, all attachment, all aggression or affectionate advice for others, desire for approval and pleasant words, spending time with family and friends, accumulating wealth and connections, building houses {138} and mansions—all such activities are useless. None of them will go with you when you die. All that has been done till yesterday is but an object of memory; it will never come back. It is like yesterday's dream. Today's experiences are like the dream that you will have tonight. All that will be done tomorrow will be like tomorrow night's dream. To spend your time in different pursuits related with your loves and hates, your conflicts and quarrels, your praise and blame, happiness and suffering, and the accumulation of property—all this conceals the same fatal flaw. You should remember that worldly concerns are seductive and deceptive illusions, and, but for what you have to do this very day, you should give them all up and instead bring into your experience the instructions of your holy teacher. If the idea strongly arises in your mind that since there is nothing on which you can rely, you should pay heed to the instructions of your teacher, this is a sign that you are proficient in this training, the purpose of which is to engender a desire for the teacher's instructions. As a means to remember this, recite the following poem:

> Worldly works are useless,
> Ground and base of hatred and attachment—
> Nothing but the dreams, both good and bad,
> That fill the one same sleep.
> To be seduced by such illusions is a fatal flaw.
> Away with them! I will now practice
> The profound instructions!

E) Training the Mind by Reflecting on the Qualities of Enlightenment

Buddhas transcend all the defects of samsara. Their bodies are ablaze with the major and minor marks, their speech is the turning of the wheel of dharma, and their minds never stir from the state of primordial wisdom. They are the holy guides of the entire world and all the gods besides. They are the main, indeed the only, refuge and source of kindness for all. It is important that you decide that it is precisely this state of buddhahood that you must gain. If you are not enlightened, you are of no real benefit to anyone. And if you do not train on the path, you will never reach enlightenment. {139} By all means, therefore, meditate and walk in the footsteps of the great and extraordinary siddhas of the past, practicing one-pointedly. They indeed went through many trials and attained freedom by meditating alone in solitude. You should therefore think that you too should abandon the activities of this life and practice alone in solitude. The appearance in your mind of the resolve to meditate—for without this, enlightenment will not be gained—is the sign that you have become proficient in this training, the purpose of which is to induce an enduring perseverance in meditation. As a reminder, recite the following verse:

> The unbounded qualities of buddhahood,
> The triple kāya—these I too possess.
> Through meditation, I will make them manifest.
> The pox, when cured, cannot return.
> So too, through hardships now endured,
> I strive to gain the state of everlasting bliss.

F) Training the Mind by Reflecting on the Pith Instructions of the Teacher

Your teacher is the guide who can save you from the measureless abyss of samsara. The way of liberation, his teaching, is a lifeboat. You must practice it just as he teaches it. If you fail to do so, the disease of suffering will remain an endless torment. Great is the kindness of your teacher, the king of physicians! Therefore, night and day, persevere in the practice of his instructions, which are a nectar-like medicine. Meditate, reflecting on the many reasons why you should do so. To think that you should do nothing but practice your teacher's instructions, in the knowledge that all worldly activities are pointless, is a sign that you have become proficient in this training, the purpose of which is to encourage you to do nothing but implement your master's teaching. As a reminder, recite the following verse: {140}

> My teacher is my healer—
> His teaching is the draft of immortality.
> It is the ship that frees me from the ocean of samsara,
> The mighty stair that leads me to the perfect house of freedom.
> I will practice it persistently both night and day.

G) Training the Mind on the Basis of the Absence of Discursive Thought

> Great ignorance—that is, discursive thought—
> Causes you to fall into the ocean of samsara.

As these words declare, until the present time, ignorance and discursive thought have caused you to wander in suffering, turning again and again in the three realms of samsara. But now you should train yourself with the thought that you must achieve unsurpassable enlightenment. There are three trainings: in empty bliss, in empty luminosity, and in the ultimate reality that is devoid of discursiveness.

First, the training in empty bliss is as follows. Assume the seven-point posture. In the center of your body, which you imagine to be empty and transparent, visualize the central channel, the *avadhūtī*, the width of a medium-sized bamboo arrow. On the outside it is white; on the inside it is red. It is brilliant, radiant, hollow, and empty. Its upper extremity is in the Brahmā aperture, and its lower end extends to four fingers below the navel.

It is very straight. At the upper end of the central channel thus imagined, visualize an inverted syllable *haṃ*. This represents skillful means. It has the nature of bliss and is on the point of dripping. At the lower end of the central channel, visualize an upright, red syllable *A*. This represents wisdom and is about to blaze up. When the visualization is clear, expel your stale breath three times. Then, as you take a deep upper breath, and as you pull up the lower breath, the tummo fire endowed with four features[42] blazes upward from the letter *A*, and the interior of the central channel quickly turns red with the heat of the flames. When the fire touches the syllable *haṃ* in the crown of your head, a whitish stream of blissful bodhicitta immediately flows down from it, and like ghee moistening the wick of a butter lamp, it causes the fire from the syllable *A* at the navel to blaze up even more intensely. {141} Then imagine that the quintessence of the melted lunar amṛta fills the central channel, the four chakras, and the interior of your whole body and engenders the primordial wisdom of blissful warmth. Then without focusing on the *haṃ* and *A*-syllables, concentrate on a brilliantly white and radiant syllable *A* in your heart and hold the vase breath. When you cannot hold it any longer, take in a little more breath and swirl the air around your abdomen. Then expel your breath at first gently but with increasing force. Endeavor in this way until you are able to hold either the great, medium, or small vase breath. When you are not in training, do not hold the breath too forcefully but gently and moderately. As you meditate in this way, the resulting bliss will act as a skillful means giving rise to wisdom, the primordial wisdom of emptiness.

The second training is in empty luminosity. Breathe out completely, gently and with increasing force through both nostrils and consider that all the objects of the six consciousnesses melt away and become a blue space. Focus on this, and hold your breath outside. Then take in a deep breath and imagine that this blue space [into which all phenomena have melted] enters through both your nostrils and remains, still blue, in your navel. Then hold the vase breath, uniting the upper and the lower winds. If you are predominantly of a hot constitution, meditate on the breath as being cool. If your constitution is predominantly cool, meditate on the breath as being hot. As you strenuously practice the four stages of the vase breath [inhaling, filling, turning, and exhaling], if you find that you are not tired, even if you stop breathing for a long time, this is said to be a sign that you have mastered this practice. As you meditate in this way, the skillful means of luminosity will bring forth in the mind a state of emptiness devoid of discursive thought.

The third training has to do with dharmatā, the state of ultimate reality devoid of discursive thought. The key points of bodily position should be adopted as previously described. The key point of speech is to breathe naturally. The key point of the mind {142} is to refrain from mental movement—do not think, do not imagine anything connected with the past, present, or future. Without correcting or modifying anything, just leave your mind in its natural flow, relaxed and at ease in a simple, uncontrived state, wide awake and undistracted. When you leave your mind like this, it will focus and rest wherever it is directed. And if you can remain in this space-like state, luminous and free of thought, you have completely mastered the training, the purpose of which is to intensify [the ultimate] enlightened mind. To remind yourself of this, recite the following verse and meditate on its meaning:

> The mind is tamed through sublime blissful concentration
> On bliss, on luminosity,
> And on the spacious state of no-thought.
> Just as in a fertile soil good harvests grow,
> I practice thus the basis of all concentration.

In the tradition of the great Rikdzin Tsewang Norbu, after training in impermanence, [the first of the seven preliminary practices,] one engages in the practices related to refuge. After the second training, [the reflection on temporary and lasting happiness,] one cultivates bodhicitta. Following the third and fourth trainings, [reflection on different circumstances and the futility of all activities,] one practices the mandala offering. After the fifth training, [reflection on the qualities of enlightenment,] one practices the meditation and recitation of Vajrasattva. After the sixth training, [reflection on the pith instructions of the teacher,] one practices the guru yoga. Finally, after the seventh training, one begins the training on the winds and essence drops.

iii. The Purification of the Mind through the Practice of the Four Common Preliminaries

Although it is not explicitly stated either in *The Copper-Lettered Instructions* or in the instructions of the great omniscient master, it is said nevertheless in the supportive teachings to *The Red Instructions*[43] that one should begin by accumulating merit in solitude. It is thus that the fourfold common preliminary practice is alluded to only indirectly. It is, however, the unbroken practice of all the teachers in the lineage of the great tertön Terdak Lingpa, his offspring, and others.

The present section comprises five topics: (1) teachings on a refuge that is superior to that of the lower paths; (2) teachings on bodhicitta for those of lowest and highest capacity; (3) teachings for the meditation and recitation practice of Vajrasattva, the essential purification of negativities and obscurations; {143} (4) teachings on the mandala offering, which brings to completion the two accumulations; and (5) teachings on the guru yoga through which blessings are swiftly received.

A) Instructions on Relative and Ultimate Refuge

1) Relative Refuge

It is thanks to positive action such as ethical discipline, whereby the ten unvirtuous actions are abandoned, that beings are born in the happy destinies. If, however, they fail to achieve unsurpassable enlightenment, which is liberation from suffering, they will—when the propelling karma of past action is consumed—fall once again into the lower destinies. And for a long time they will have to experience many severe and unbearable pains. Only the precious Three Jewels, and nothing else, can protect beings from such a predicament.

Your own sublime teacher is the buddha actually appearing to you, for he is inseparable from the body, speech, and mind of all the buddhas of the three times. With the attitude of thinking "I implore the protection and help of the Three Jewels, object of refuge," leave your body and mind in their natural state. Then imagine that the ordinary place and environment [where you happen to be] is a beautiful, delightful buddha field made of precious substances. In its center is a wish-fulfilling tree in full flower, spreading out and filling the whole of the sky. In the middle of the central trunk, there is a precious lion throne. There, on a high broad seat made of a multicolored lotus and disks of sun and moon, your kind root teacher is sitting in the form of Samantabhadra arrayed in the vestments of the sambhogakāya. He is dark-blue in color and yet brilliant and shining, radiant with light. He is beautifully arrayed with perfect, silken garments and jeweled ornaments. His two hands are in the mudra of meditation, while his legs are in the vajra posture. He is completely beautiful and adorned with all the major and minor marks of buddhahood. He is surrounded by all the teachers of the lineage.

On the principal branches that extend in the four directions, there are high and ample seats. On the front branch, there is the buddha Vajrasattva, glorious and eminent, {144} surrounded by the yidam deities of the six classes of tantra. On the seat on the right branch is the Powerful Sage (Śākyamuni), the buddha commonly revered in all vehicles. He is surrounded by the buddhas, the supreme nirmāṇakāyas, appearing in the ten directions and throughout the three times. On the seat on the branch at the back of the tree is the jewel of the holy dharma of transmission and realization in the form of a multitude of books. On the seat of the left branch is the jewel of the sangha represented by the bodhisattvas such as Avalokiteśvara, Mañjuśrī, and Vajrapāṇi, together with the sangha of the śrāvakas, such as Śāriputra and Maudgalyāyana. And between the branches are dense clouds of the special sangha—the ḍākinīs, dharmapālas, and guardians who have the eyes of wisdom.

Imagine that you are standing in the front of this tree of refuge in the company of all living beings as numerous as the grains of dust that fill the earth. With great respect in body, speech, and mind, all are yearning to take refuge. Then formulate the following prayer: "I beg your protection. In this very moment, I pray that you will lead me and all beings, as infinite as space, out of samsara, this great ocean of suffering." Then recite the following prayer without distraction as many times as you can—a hundred times, a thousand times, and so on,

> In the teachers, yidams, and ḍākinīs, who fill the whole of space,
> In the buddha, dharma, and the noble sangha,
> I and every being in the six realms of samsara
> Respectfully take refuge.

At the end of the meditation session, imagine that from the objects of refuge there radiate rays of light that, touching you and all beings, cleanse away all negativities and obscurations. Imagine that, like birds escaping from a cage, you all depart for the pure realms. All around, the teachers of the lineage, the Three Jewels, and so on all dissolve into your root teacher. {145} Then your root teacher melts into light, and you imagine that, entering through the crown of your head, this light quickly dissolves into your heart. Then you remain for as long as you can in a state of meditative evenness, in which there is neither an object nor a taker of refuge. When you lie down at night, you should not dissolve the field of merit but, imagining it in front of your pillow, fall asleep in a state of longing, devotion, and respect. Also in the periods between the sessions of meditation, it is important to visualize the field of merit and to persevere in maintaining an attitude of reverence and homage.

In the tradition of the great Rikdzin Tsewang Norbu, it is taught that one should visualize the root teacher in the center of the space in front of oneself. The teacher is in his actual form, and all around him, in the cardinal and intermediate directions, all objects of refuge are present like dense gatherings of clouds. Alternatively, one may consider that the objects of refuge are spread out like masses of flowers or like stars in the sky, without any space between them. And other than being positioned above or below, higher or lower, some in the middle, some all around, one should not consider the objects of refuge as qualitatively different in any way.[44] Finally, according to this tradition, one should settle in a state devoid of all points of reference, a state free from the concepts of the objects of refuge either dissolving or departing. If more details are desired regarding the meaning, classification, and benefits of refuge, these should be explained in the usual way.

2) Ultimate Refuge

The channels and the radial channels of the four chakras of the body correspond to the sangha. The essence drops correspond to the dharma, while the five quintessential winds correspond to the five primordial wisdoms. Recognizing that they (the channels, winds, and essence drops) have the nature of the three kāyas of the state of buddhahood—the primordial absence of defilement—recite the following verse as many times as possible with the conscious intention of training in them.

> The five winds in their perfect purity
> Are the essence of the body.
> Defilements in their perfect purity
> Are the five primordial wisdoms.
> By realizing that the Three Jewels
> Are the perfect action of the triple kāya, I pay homage.

Finally, you should rest in meditative evenness in the luminous nature of your mind.

B) Instructions on Relative and Ultimate Bodhicitta

1) Relative Bodhicitta

{146} With regard to relative bodhicitta, you should begin with the following reflection: "Although on the ultimate level, everything is primordially pure, nevertheless, our mother sentient beings, deluded on the relative level, constantly experience the inconceivable causes and effects of suffering. I will engage in the practice related to the four visions on the path of manifest primordial wisdom, awareness itself, and place them in the state of the primordial lord [Samantabhadra]." With this intention, cultivate an unprecedented attitude of bodhicitta and recite as much as you can the following formula, which is related to aspirational bodhicitta.

> *Emaho!*
> The darkness of this world is ignorance,
> And means and wisdom are my lamp.
> I shall realize through my teacher's kindness
> The wisdom that resides within myself.

Think then as follows: "The ultimate expanse of primordial purity, unborn space-like dharmakāya and spontaneously present primordial wisdom, self-cognizing awareness (endowed as it is with the nature of the three kāyas), lie beyond the four conceptual extremes. No word or letter can express them. I will recognize this state that is beyond both thought and word and cannot be explained." Thinking thus, recite the following aspiration as much as you can.

> *Emaho!*
> The final state of buddhahood,
> The union of awareness and the ultimate expanse,
> The nature of the triple kāya, the ground beyond extremes,
> Is ineffable, primordial wisdom, self-arisen.
> In this very instant, I will realize it.

This is how to cultivate bodhicitta in action.

2) Ultimate Bodhicitta

With regard to ultimate bodhicitta, you should reflect as follows. All phenomena, from the very beginning and on the level of their ultimate nature, are beyond acceptance and rejection, beyond bondage and freedom. Equal and perfect, they are the enlightened state. Samsara and nirvana, buddhas and beings, self and other, and good and bad are not separate and distinct. Knowing that this is so, think, "I am utterly convinced of the state of primordial openness and freedom that transcends the karmic law and all effortful striving. I have complete confidence in the immense vastness of the dharmakāya, my natural birthright." In such a state of mind, recite the following verse:

> I and every living being
> Are enlightened from the very first. {147}
> In knowing this is so,
> I cultivate the supreme bodhicitta.

For a more elaborate bodhicitta practice, you should, for relative bodhicitta, mainly concentrate on *tonglen*, the exchange of happiness for suffering in conjunction with the expiration and inhalation of the breath. In the case of ultimate bodhicitta, you should stay in meditative evenness in the very nature of bodhicitta—that is, the unreality of the three spheres [of subject, object, and action itself].

An explanation of the essential meaning of bodhicitta, its characteristics, the way to develop it, its precepts, and so on, may be done in the usual way.

C) The Meditation and Recitation Practice of Vajrasattva

For the meditation and recitation of Vajrasattva, which purifies negativities and obscurations, the instructions are both general and particular.

1) General Instructions

Above the crown of your head and on a lotus and moon disk, visualize a white syllable *A*. This radiates and reabsorbs rays of light and transforms into Vajrasattva, whom you consider to be inseparable from your teacher. He is white in color. In his right hand he holds a golden five-pronged vajra at the level of his heart. In his left hand he holds a silver bell against his hip. Embracing his consort, he is seated with his legs in the bodhisattva posture. His consort, white Vajratopa, is in union with him, and holds a curved knife and skull cup. Both are clad in silken robes and jeweled ornaments. In Vajrasattva's heart on a moon disk, there is a white syllable *hūṃ* encircled by the hundred-syllable mantra, which turns clockwise and emits glittering rays of light.

Devotion toward your teacher Vajrasattva above the crown of your head as the embodiment of all refuges constitutes the power of the support. With a strong sense of regret and sadness for all the negative actions you have committed in the past, you should think, "O glorious teacher Vajrasattva, I place my trust in you. I and every other being openly confess all past evil actions until this present moment. {148} I pray you, cleanse and purify them." This constitutes the power of regret. You should then decide, "From now on, even at the cost of my life, I shall never again commit such evil actions even in my dreams, let alone my waking life." This is the power of resolution. Finally, to practice the meditation-recitation of Vajrasattva as a remedy to actions previously performed constitutes the power of the practice as an antidote.

As you recite the mantra prayerfully as much as you can (one hundred thousand times)—with these four powers constantly in mind—visualize a stream of white nectar that flows down powerfully from the mantra garland and, issuing from the point of union of Vajrasattva and Vajratopa, enters your body through the Brahmā aperture. You should consider that all diseases, negative forces, sins, and obscurations—in the form of black ooze, pus, blood, grime, small insects, and so on—are expelled from the body through the pores, anus, and urinary tract, as if they were being flushed out by a powerful current coming down from above. As a memory aide, you should recite the following

> Above my head (myself in ordinary form),
> Upon a lotus and moon disk,
> The letter *A* transforms into white Vajrasattva.
> Holding vajra and bell, he wraps his consort in his arms.
> Arrayed in jeweled ornaments, he sits in bodhisattva posture.
> In his heart upon a moon disk, there is a letter *hūṃ*
> Encircled by the mantra of one hundred syllables.

> From his body and the mantra, a stream of white amṛta flows,
> And through the opening upon my head,
> It enters me and fills my body.
> All sins and obscurations thus are cleansed away.
> My body is now stainless like a crystal sphere.

Focusing one-pointedly upon this visualization, recite the hundred-syllable mantra. When you finish, think that your body has become a sphere of stainless crystal completely filled and brimming over with the flow of amṛta. You should then consider that you have attained the accomplishments of enlightened body, speech, and mind, qualities, and action. In conclusion, pray the following with a sense of fervent devotion:

> Lord, in my ignorance and in confusion {149}
> I have transgressed and broken my samaya.
> Protect me now, my lord and teacher!
> Supreme holder of the vajra,
> Embodiment of great compassion,
> Lord of beings, I come to you for refuge!
> I acknowledge and confess
> All breaches and deteriorations
> Of samaya, root and branch,
> Of body, speech, and mind.
> I pray you, cleanse and purify
> The stains of all my negativities,
> My obscurations, faults, and downfalls.

When you have finished, imagine that Vajrasattva accedes to your request and says,

> My child, you are most fortunate! All your evil deeds and obscurations are in this instant cleansed away.

Vajrasattva then melts into light and, dissolving into you, becomes inseparable from your own mind in a state in which neither object nor subject of confession can be found. Remain then in this state for as long as it lasts. Persevere in this practice until you discern signs that your negative deeds and obscurations have been purified. For a detailed account of the faults, downfalls, and antidotes, as well as all the benefits of the meditation and recitation of Vajrasattva, consult the general explanations.

2) Specific Instructions

In an instant, in the center of a lotus upon a lunar disk, you become white Vajrasattva with one face and two arms. In your right hand, you are holding a vajra at the level of your heart. In your left hand, you are holding a bell at the level of your hip. Your legs are in the vajra posture, and you are arrayed in silken robes and jeweled ornaments. In your heart, in the center of a lunar disk, there is a white vajra, the size of your thumb. It is marked at its center with the syllable *hūṃ* surrounded by the hundred-syllable mantra. These syllables shed a pale-yellow light like that of a butter lamp, which purifies the obscurations of yourself and every other being. Considering that all appearances become Vajrasattva and that all sounds become the resonance of the hundred-syllable mantra, recite the following:

> *oṃ vajrasattva samayam anupālaya vajrasattva tenopatiṣṭha dṛdho me bhava sutoṣyo me bhava supoṣyo me bhava anurakto me bhava sarvasiddhiṃ me prayaccha* {150} *sarvakarmasu ca me cittam śreyam kuru hūṃ ha ha ha ha hoḥ bhagavan sarvatathāgata hṛdaya vajra mā me muñca vajrī bhava mahāsamayasattva āḥ*

Recite this mantra as much as you are able. Finally, all appearances dissolve into the syllable *hūṃ* in your heart. This itself then disappears, and you rest in a state beyond reference. When you finish, dedicate the merit. The purpose of this practice is to purify all the negative actions and obscurations accumulated in many hundreds of thousands of kalpas and to restore the spoiled and broken samayas so as to be able to realize the very nature of your mind.

This then is the actual description of the uncommon teaching on the training of the mind by means of the Vajrasattva practice, which clears away all obscurations. It is taken from the short teaching passed down from mouth-to-ear titled *The Self-Experience of Primordial Wisdom*,[45] a root teaching of *The Innermost Essence of the Master: The Wish-Fulfilling Gem*.[46]

In the tradition of the great Rikdzin Tsewang Norbu, the practice is as follows. On the outer level, in accordance with the kriyā tantra, you meditate on Vajrasattva above the crown of your head. On the inner level, in accordance with the caryā tantra, you meditate on him in your heart. On the secret level, in accordance with the yoga tantra, you meditate on the three beings, or sattvas, each enclosed within the other. On the most secret level, and in accordance with the unsurpassed tantra, you meditate on the threefold practice of Vajrasattva. Finally, at the level of suchness, you settle with decisive confidence in the dharmadhātu.

With regard to the outer practice, you should visualize a white lotus flower above your head. It has eight petals, and from each of them other petals branch out until the whole of space is filled with them. Beneath each of these petals, imagine that there is a sentient being, and on each petal above their heads, there sits a Vajrasattva. All the Vajrasattvas are in their usual form, without consort, and seated in the posture of a bodhisattva. In their hearts the seed syllable [*hūṃ*] is surrounded by the garland of mantra. Rays of light radiate from them and make offerings to the buddhas and bodhisattvas and gather back their blessings. With the recitation of the mantra, a stream of amṛta flows down and cleanses away all obscurations. In conclusion, recite the customary formula beginning "O Lord, through my ignorance and my confusion, my samaya pledges were transgressed and weakened." This is then followed by the praises beginning "O great being Vajrasattva . . . ." {151}

The outer practice and the inner practice are combined in the following way. From the deity visualized above your head, the blessings of Vajrasattva's body flow down in the form of the nectar of bodhicitta and fill your body up to the level of your throat. Consider that the obscurations and negative actions you have committed physically are purified and that you receive the blessings of Vajrasattva's body. Vajrasattva then descends into your throat. The blessings of his speech in the form of a flow of nectar again fills your body as far as the level of your heart, purifying the obscurations of your speech. Then Vajrasattva descends into your heart, and a flow of nectar that is the blessing of his mind fills your body to the level of your navel. Persist [in this stage of the practice] for a long time, after which you should consider that you have gained the blessing of Vajrasattva's mind. Throughout each of these stages, recite the hundred-syllable mantra.

The preceding practice is then combined with that of the secret level. The stream of amṛta fills the whole of your body, and all obscurations are purified. Your own body, which is the ripened effect of past actions, is transformed, and you become Vajrasattva himself. In your heart there is the wisdom being (*jñānasattva*) in the same form, and in the heart of the wisdom being there is the samādhi being (*samādhisattva*) in the form of a white five-pronged vajra, in the center of which there is the syllable *hūṃ*. Focusing on this visualization, recite the hundred-syllable mantra.

In conclusion, and at the most secret level, consider that all appearances, sounds, and thoughts are respectively the body, speech, and mind of Vajrasattva, and continue with the recitation of the hundred syllables. On the level of suchness, it is taught that you should remain in meditative evenness in the state of primordial purity beyond all reference.

D) Instructions for the Mandala Offering Whereby the Two Accumulations Are Brought to Completion

When the field of merit is set forth as the object of refuge, many details of the visualization may not be mastered. When on the other hand it is reduced to the central figure, the practice becomes more manageable. This is perfectly permissible. In the present context, the mandala practice will be gradually explained according to this uncommon tradition, beginning with the outer aspect.

Gold and silver are the best materials for the mandala plate. In the middle range, copper and so on may be used. Last of all, {152} if a humble material like stone and wood is used, the mandala plate should not be less than one cubit in size. As for the substances to be offered in heaps, the best are precious gems and so on. Conch and cowrie shells are materials of medium quality, while offering substances of least quality would be saffron colored grains mixed with medicinal plants, roots, and so on—whatever you can gather. The mixture should be sprinkled with saffron water that contains the five ingredients deriving from a cow.[47] Then, imagining yourself in the company of all beings, perform the threefold activity of physically arranging the offering, verbally reciting the offering prayer in a clear and audible voice, and mentally concentrating on its meaning without being distracted by anything else. The actual practice of the mandala offering has three sections: (1) the nirmāṇakāya mandala, (2) the sambhogakāya mandala, and (3) the dharmakāya mandala offering.

1) The Offering of the Nirmāṇakāya Mandala

In front of the field of merit, visualize a vast, pure, vajra buddha field made of precious substances, complete with Mount Meru and the four continents. On the summit of Mount Meru, on a seat of a lotus and moon disk, visualize your root teacher in nirmāṇakāya form. He is surrounded by the teachers of the three transmission lineages: mind-to-mind, by means of symbols, and from mouth-to-ear. In each of the four continents and subcontinents, the Three Jewels are present in the form visualized during the practice of refuge.

First, to symbolize the perfectly pure nature of the mind, wipe the mandala base three times, and so that the moisture of bodhicitta does not evaporate from it, sprinkle the base with saffron water mixed with the five ingredients deriving from a cow. Then it is said that for the best kind offering, you should arrange on the base forty-one heaps of offerings. For an offering of moderate size, make twenty-three heaps, and for a condensed offering, make nine heaps. In the case of a moderate offering, thirteen heaps are positioned to represent Mount Meru, the four continents, and the eight subcontinents. Then in the interstices, eight heaps are placed to represent offerings such as the eight auspicious substances. Finally, two heaps are placed, one in front and one behind, to represent the sun and the moon. Consider that from these heaps of offerings are emanated the infinite glory and wealth of the worlds and inhabitants of boundless universal systems—the array of the buddha fields of five enlightened families of Mahāsāgara.[48] On this array, which pervades the whole of space, is based the field of Mahābrahmā's Eon.[49] {153} As you make the offering, one after the other, combine the recitation of the offering formula with the appropriate visualization.

> *oṃ āḥ hūṃ*
> The golden base is of vast strength.
> Here is Sumeru, the king of mountains.
> To the east is Purvavideha,
> And in the south is Jambudvīpa.
> Aparagodānīya is in the west,
> And to the north is Uttarakuru.
> Then come Deha and Videha, Cāmara and Aparacāmara,
> Satha, Uttaramantrina, Kurava and Kaurava,
> The seven golden ranges and the seven pleasant seas,

The seven precious attributes of kingly rule,
The eight auspicious substances,
The vase of treasure and the wishing-tree,
The harvest grown without the tiller's care,
And everything delightful to the senses.
Here are lovely goddesses, the sun and moon—
On all sides everything delightful
To both gods and humankind.

This array of the infinite reaches of the universe, adorned with boundless buddha fields belonging to the field of Mahābrahmā's Eon, is based on the wheels of inexhaustible ornaments of the body, speech, and mind of Mahāsāgara in the aspects of the five enlightened families—Vairocana and so on—together with the tathāgatas of the ten directions. Offer this vast array—visualized as the inconceivable masses of the clouds of Samantabhadra's offering—to the teachers, the deities of the yidam mandalas, and the ocean-like infinity of the hosts of guardians.

All the universes—each endowed
With Meru and four continents—
As many as the grains of dust
In buddha fields innumerable,
Great heaps of substances
That please the senses of both gods and humankind,
Clouds of offerings to the blissful buddhas,
Adorned by Mahābrahmā's Eon,
A field of merit of unending joy and wealth— {154}
All this I offer to my teachers,
To the deities of the yidam mandalas,
And to the ocean-like infinity of the hosts of guardians.

This precious mandala—these clouds of pleasing offerings,
Together with the boundless riches of the conquerors—
These adornments of unbounded space, I offer to them all.
Thus may I enjoy nirmāṇakāya buddha fields all luminous in
character.

Make the mandala offering as much as you can, accumulating the recitations of this last stanza, adding on each occasion something extra to the heaps of offerings on the mandala plate.

2) The Offering of the Sambhogakāya Mandala

Imagine that the field of merit is the Akaniṣṭha buddha field of Dense Array, inconceivable in its foundations, dimensions, and adornments. Here reside the teachers, the five families of the sambhogakāya in company with their countless retinues. For the best offering, arrange twenty-five heaps of offering substances, thirteen heaps for an offering of moderate dimensions, and seven heaps for a simple offering. This inconceivable configuration of the buddha field of Dense Array, with its immeasurable palace of great liberation, is filled with ravishing goddesses all holding marvelous offerings and is adorned with traceries of precious clouds of the primordial wisdom of the great buddha field known as Drumbeat of Brahmā.[50] Consider that you are offering it all, in a wheel of permanent continuity, until the whole of samsara is emptied.

> *oṃ āḥ hūṃ*
> The Dense Array of Akaniṣṭha, blissful field,
> Appears but lacks intrinsic being.
> In this buddha field there is a palace,
> Beauteous, immeasurable.
> Four doors it has, four corners, and four steps,
> A precious parasol, a dharma wheel with beautiful gazelles,
> And banners of victory devised of precious silk
> Prevailing over every evil force.
> The palace is adorned with decorative tassels,
> Moon disks moving in the wind,
> Jewel-handled tail fans, golden bells, and tinkling garlands.
> It is surmounted with a vajra and a jewel. {155}
> The five concentric walls have ledges made of gems,
> Lattices of different jewels,
> Balustrades with precious stones, and traceries between,
> And banisters and railings—
> A very lofty structure and surrounding plinth

Where stand the offering goddesses
Of charm, of garlands, song, and dance,
Of flowers, incense, lamps, and perfume,
Food, and melody.
All around, both outside and within,
The palace is adorned with heaps and clouds
Of offerings inconceivable.
This wondrous buddha field, Drumbeat of Brahmā,
Adorned with nets of precious clouds of primal wisdom—
All this I offer to my teachers,
To the deities of the yidam mandalas,
And to the ocean-like infinity of the hosts of guardians
In a turning wheel of constant continuity
Until the emptying of samsara.

This place of bliss amid the vast savannas
Of the clouds shot through with light,
Ornamented with four doors, four corners,
Four steps, and walls of the five wisdoms,
With goddesses of charm, of garlands,
Precious song, and dance,
All radiating clouds of offerings—
All this I offer to my teachers,
To the deities of the yidam mandalas,
And to the ocean-like infinity of the hosts of guardians.

I visualize a palace, precious, measureless,
Within the Akaniṣṭha field of utter bliss,
With canopies of clouds
Of various offerings that fill the sky.
Offering it thus, may I indeed enjoy
Sambhogakāya buddha fields,
Spontaneously present.

This is how you should offer the mandala, accumulating the recitation of the final stanza.

3) The Offering of the Dharmakāya Mandala

For the field of merit, call to mind the one sole sphere of the dharmakāya, the buddha field of the Vajra Essence of Luminosity, in which, in a nondual and spontaneous manner, the dharmakāya teacher, the primordial lord, resides accompanied by a retinue of infinite assemblies—the self-experience of primordial wisdom. {156} For the most detailed offering, arrange twenty-five heaps of offering substances. In the case of an offering of moderate size, arrange five heaps, and for a brief, condensed offering, make three heaps. The dharmadhātu, the buddha field of the Luminous Vajra Essence, is unfathomable. It is an infinitude of space, wherein the radiance of awareness, shimmering and dazzling, courses in the form of large and small disks of five-colored lights, of rainbow lights, and beams of light and which is adorned with limitless displays of the kāyas and wisdoms. Consider that the dharmakāya mandala is offered though there is neither an object nor a subject of offering and in a manner that is utterly self-arising, self-manifesting, and self-subsiding.

> *oṃ āḥ hūṃ*
> The field of the luminosity of dharmatā
> Is primordially, intrinsically pure.
> Space-like, it is empty, free of center and periphery.
> Like sun and moon, it shines, spontaneously present.
> Within it there's no way to separate samsara and nirvana—
> They cannot be distinguished.
> It is the great unfathomable source
> Of buddha fields and of the six migrations.
> It is the sphere of precious and spontaneous presence,
> A space that from the triple kāya is inseparable,
> The primordial wisdom of the fourth time of equality.
> The field of the ever-youthful body closed within a vase
> Has neither out nor in.
> It is the innermost essence of all things.
> Radiating lights—yellow, blue, red, white, and green—
> In all the ten directions, it governs a dominion
> Of limitless arrays adorned with vast displays
> Of kāyas and of wisdoms
> Throughout the vast infinity of space.

The field of Vajra Essence of Luminosity
Is completely pure and present of itself.
This is what I offer, within a perfectly immaculate
Expanse of realization, as the perfect gift of primal wisdom—
To my teachers, to the deities of the yidam mandalas,
And to the ocean-like infinity of the hosts of guardians. {157}

This field of luminosity, primordially pure,
Is unoriginate, present of itself, and unconditioned.
In its boundless palace of the five primordial wisdoms,
No diversity is found for all conceptuality subsides.
Spontaneously present, this field,
Wherein the light of the activities
Of the three kāyas radiates—
All this I offer to my teachers,
To the deities of the yidam mandalas,
And to the ocean-like infinity of the hosts of guardians.

The field of the five kinds of primal wisdom,
Luminosity, spontaneously present,
Primordially adorned with kāyas and with drops of light,
Is the pure self-experience of awareness.
Through making such an offering, may I too enjoy
Samantabhadra's dharmakāya buddha field.

Accumulating the recitation of the final stanza, offer the mandala as many times as you can. In conclusion, imagine that the object of the mandala offering, together with all the substances of oblation all dissolve into the blue syllable *hūṃ*, which in turn dissolves into yourself. By this means, you will quite naturally gather a vast accumulation [of merit and wisdom]. Then remain in meditative evenness in the state of luminosity. Additional presentations, general and particular, of the mandala offering—together with explanations of its purpose, benefits, and so on—must be looked for in other texts.

E) Guru Yoga

For the practice of guru yoga, whereby blessings are swiftly received, there are (1) general and (2) specific instructions.

1) General Instructions

The support for the invocation should be visualized as follows. The universe and the beings that it contains constitute an infinite, pure buddha field. There, in the space above the crown of your head, in the midst of a shining tent of five-colored rainbow lights, which are themselves the radiance of the five primordial wisdoms, there is a throne supported by lions. Upon it, on a seat composed of a lotus and disks of sun and moon sits your root teacher inseparable from [and in the form of] Samantabhadra. He is dark-blue and dazzling in his splendor, like a mountain of pure sapphire in the light of the rising sun. His two hands are in the mudra of meditative evenness. He is seated with his legs in the vajra posture, and he is beautifully adorned with the five silken garments and eight jeweled ornaments. {158} His body displays the thirty-two major and eighty minor marks of buddhahood. From his resplendent body radiate immaculate beams of six-colored light, each beam radiating millions of other beams. Within this dazzling expanse, he is vividly and clearly present.

He expounds the dharma with the sixty branches of melodious speech, and his mind dwells in the state of meditative evenness in hundreds of different concentrations. He is the manifest embodiment of wisdom, love, and power. [In the space] above his head are the teachers of the lineage, and all around are the yidam deities, buddhas, the volumes of the holy dharma, and the sangha of the greater and lesser vehicles, together with the hosts of ḍākinīs and faithful protectors. Imagine that they are present in dense and massing clouds. And as a means of remembering all this, recite the following:

> In the center of a vast pure buddha field,
> The world and all who dwell within it,
> In the sky before myself, within a mass of five-colored light,
> Upon a throne upheld by lions
> And a seat of lotus, sun, and moon—

There it is that my root teacher sits,
Embodiment of every refuge,
Inseparable from and in the form
Of Samantabhadra, the primordial lord.
He is dark-blue, radiant, with one face,
And with his two hands in the meditation mudra.
Arrayed in silk robes and jeweled ornaments, he sits,
His legs in vajra posture.
The teachers of the lineage are above his head,
And all around the Three Jewels and the hosts
Of ḍākinīs and guardians of the dharma.
His wisdom body is illusory,
The union of appearance and emptiness.
With clouds of limitless adornments
Of the three secrets—body, speech, and mind—
He manifests in any form required to benefit
All beings according to their needs and aspirations.

Imagine that you are accompanied by all beings, as many as the particles of dust that cover the surface of the earth. Your hands joined in reverence, pray devotedly with a voice neither too loud nor too soft, like the humming of bees. Filled with reverence, turn your mind completely to your teacher, thinking, "In happiness and sorrow, whatever good or ill may come, I place my trust in you." {159}

The body of the teacher is the sangha, his speech is the holy dharma, and his mind is the Buddha. And whereas you did not have the good fortune to meet the buddhas of the past and to hear their teachings, it is now in the present time that your own holy teacher performs their activity. He is your unsurpassable guide, able to point directly to the buddha present within your mind. You should therefore consider him to be even greater than all the buddhas and even more kind. With a focused and ardent devotion, recite the lineage prayer titled *The Mass of Wish-Fulfilling Clouds* or the shorter prayer composed by Minling Terchen, together with the supplement composed by our own lord and teacher [Jamyang Khyentse Wangpo]. Mindful of all the qualities of your root and lineage teachers, address your prayers to them.

Then pray to your root teacher with great fervor,

> *Kye!*
> Teacher, holder of the vajra,
> Sole friend in the three worlds of samsara,
> Refuge of those who wander unprotected,
> Great stair to liberation—
> Lost in darkness, I now come to you for refuge,
> Ignorance-dispelling light!
> Protect me, who, protectorless,
> Am sinking in the murky ocean of samsara.
> With the rain of your compassion, cool me,
> Who am burning in the fire of my defilements.
> Apart from you, my teacher, precious Buddha,
> I have no other hope.
> From now until enlightenment is gained,
> In joy and sorrow, you are my reliance, my recourse.
> In compassion, look at me, who am protectorless.
> Drive away disease and evil forces,
> All hindering influences, and obstacles.
> Grant accomplishments, supreme and ordinary. {160}

Pray like this until a feeling of genuine reverence and devotion arises. Then for the reception of the four empowerments, recite the following text:

> The deities all around dissolve into you, my teacher, and you become yet more magnificent. Your three places are marked with the syllables *oṃ*, *āḥ*, and *hūṃ*, white, red, and blue, which blaze with light. They are the three vajras of all the tathāgatas. I pray you, through the transmission of the four empowerments, grant your blessings, that I and all beings as infinite as space be brought to maturity and freedom.

As you pray in this way, rays of white light radiate from the syllable *oṃ* at the crown of the guru's head. They dissolve into the crown of your own head, and you receive the vase empowerment. All the defilements of your body are cleansed away, you are empowered to meditate on the path of the generation-stage practice, and you acquire the fortune of being able to accomplish the nirmāṇakāya.

From the syllable *āḥ* in the guru's throat, rays of red light radiate and dissolve into your own throat. You receive the secret empowerment. All the defilements of your speech are cleansed, you are empowered to meditate on the path of the channels and winds, and you acquire the fortune of being able to accomplish the sambhogakāya.

From the syllable *hūṃ* in the guru's heart, rays of blue light radiate and dissolve into your own heart. You receive the wisdom empowerment. All the defilements of your mind are cleansed away, you are empowered to meditate on the path of the essence drops, and you acquire the fortune of being able to accomplish the dharmakāya.

From the guru's three places, rays of white, red, and blue light radiate and dissolve into the crown of your head, your throat, and heart. You receive the fourth empowerment. All the defilements related to primordial wisdom are cleansed away, you are empowered to meditate on the path of the Great Perfection, and you acquire the fortune of being able to accomplish the svabhāvikakāya.

> I pray to you, O glorious and holy teacher, {161}
> Essence of all buddhas past, present, and to come,
> Embodiment of the four kāyas.
> I pray you, bless me through the granting of empowerment.
> I pray you, bless me that there may arise in me
> A special realization of the path profound.
> I pray you, bless me with the realization of the view
> Of primal purity, the fundamental nature.
> I pray you, bless me to perfect the primal wisdom
> Of the fourfold vision of spontaneous presence.

With these words of fervent and devoted prayer, consider that the teacher transforms into a sphere of light, which quickly enters and vanishes into the Brahmā aperture in the crown of your head. Consider then that your three doors of body, speech, and mind become inseparably one with the three vajras of the teacher, and then remain in a state of meditative evenness in your own true nature beyond the ordinary mind.

2) Specific Instructions

The following are the specific instructions for the guru yoga practice according to *The Ocean of Accomplishments*:[51]

> *oṃ āḥ hūṃ*
> I take refuge in the Three Jewels,
> Who protect me from the fear of lower realms.
> I cultivate the ultimate enlightened mind,
> And for the sake of beings, I will meditate upon my teacher.

Understanding that all phenomena are unborn by their very nature, imagine that above your head there is a white lotus on which there is a casket made of the disks of sun and moon. Within this casket is a white syllable *A* that radiates light and invites the presence of your root teacher. Imagine him sitting in the half-vajra posture. All the teachers of the lineage and all the teachers with whom you are connected through the reception of teachings dissolve into him. All around in infinite numbers are deities of the yidam mandalas, ḍākinīs, and dharma protectors. They are like dense and massing clouds.

It is taught that one should make mental offerings and praises. Simply to imagine them is sufficient. Nowadays, however, most people are unable to visualize such things without the recitation of an appropriate formula. Therefore, recite the following text taken from *The Great Dharma Prayer Book*:

> *oṃ āḥ hūṃ* {162}
> From the dharmadhātu palace,
> O teacher, unborn nature, come, I pray.
> From the sambhogakāya palace,
> O teacher, spotless luminosity, come, I pray.
> From the nirmāṇakāya palace,
> Come, Compassionate One, I pray.
> Come in rainbow lights a-swirling,
> With deities and disks of light pulsating.
> Sit steadily above my head upon a seat
> Of sun and moon, and never leave.
> Devotedly with body, speech, and mind,
> I reverence you and lay before you

Outer, inner, secret offerings.
I confess the breaches and degeneration
Of my samaya with your body, speech, and mind.
I request you for empowerment that brings maturity
And for instructions that set free.

oṃ
Radiant and clear, your body is unborn.
I pray you, by your vajra body
May my body now be blessed with bliss.

āḥ
Your speech is the unceasing word of dharma.
I pray you, by the vowels and consonants
May my speech be blessed with power.

hūṃ
Your mind is great primordial purity, the expanse of
Samantabhadra.
I pray you, with the state beyond the intellect
Bless me to attain the level of phenomenal exhaustion.[52]

Then fervently recite the following:

Kye!
Teacher, holder of the vajra,
Sole friend in the three worlds of samsara,
Refuge of those who wander unprotected,
Great stair that leads to liberation—
Lost in darkness, I now come to you for refuge,
Ignorance-dispelling light!
Protect me who, protectorless,
Am sinking in the murky ocean of samsara.
Cool me with the draft of self-arisen wisdom
For I am tortured in the fires of the three poisons.
My body of flesh, my speech, and mind,
Entrapped in ignorant delusion—

Cause them to dissolve in light
That I attain remainderless nirvana.
O my teacher, precious Buddha, {163}
I have no other hope but you.
I pray you, look upon me with compassionate eyes,
And free me from the ocean of samsara.
Grant that I achieve within this very life all excellence,
And free me from all obstacles and hindrances.
Grant that at the moment of my death,
I recognize deep luminosity
And be delivered from the bardo's dangerous paths.

I pray that all my deeds of body, speech, and mind
Be always for the benefit of others
And that from this day forward,
Every circumstance be changed into the supreme path
That leads me to enlightenment.

However much I labor, freedom is so hard to gain.
Lord, in the boat of your compassion,
Bring me and all who are protectorless
To the land of liberation.

May all those who have faith in me
And also those who scorn and criticize
Be free of evil actions and defilements.
May they be delivered from the river of existence.

And when at last my simple name
Will bring to beings all that they desire,
May clouds pour down a rain of offerings
In all the buddha fields that fill the ten directions.

By this virtue, may all beings
Be liberated from samsara.
May they gain the two supreme primordial wisdoms,
Spontaneously accomplishing the twofold aim.

At the conclusion of this fervent prayer, a stream of amṛta flows from the teacher's toe and enters the crown of your head and the heads of every being, so that your bodies are filled with it inside and out. The obscurations of your body are cleansed, and you accomplish the enlightened body. Then the amṛta flows into your throat. All obscurations of speech are purified, and you accomplish the enlightened speech. The amṛta then flows into your heart. The obscurations of your mind are purified, and you accomplish the enlightened mind. Flowing then to your navel, it cleanses away all impurity, and {164} you accomplish all enlightened qualities. As it descends into your secret center, you accomplish the enlightened activities in the inseparability of bliss and emptiness. Finally, through the strength of your devotion, the teacher melts into light and dissolves into you so that you can consider that you and he are inseparable. Remain as long as possible in the state of self-cognizing awareness, free from all contrivance and distortion. Conclude the session with the prayer of dedication, thereby establishing a link with your conduct in the post-meditation period.

> Through this spotless virtue
> May the abysses of samsara's lower destinies be churned.
> May beings dwell no longer in samsara
> But swiftly come to buddhahood.

Between the sessions, bring all appearances, sounds, and thoughts onto the path by regarding them as the primordial wisdom of the teachers' three secrets. Strive in this way in the practice that unites the two accumulations.

This exposition could be elaborated further, in which case, the theoretical basis, the benefits and so forth of the guru yoga, should be explained according to the general procedure.

Striving in these stages [of the preliminary practices], whereby the accumulations [of wisdom and merit] are gathered, you should practice them in formal sessions, accumulating one hundred thousand recitations for each. And you should seal your practice with prayers of dedication. Between the sessions, you should implement the key points of conduct associated with each of the practices, according to the general procedure.

These general explanations of the preliminary practices are treated at length in Minling Terchen's instructions. The meditation and recitation of the preliminaries according to the usual guiding instructions are simple and easy and should be adopted as your main activity.

By contrast, the specific teachings are the uncommon instructions elucidated in *The Innermost Essence of the Master: The Wish-Fulfilling Gem.* My lord teacher [Jamyang Khyentse Wangpo] has said that it is very good to continue practicing them. And since they appear also in the teaching of the great Rikdzin Tsewang Norbu, I think that it is important to perform the meditation and recitation of these preliminaries. Consequently, I have not hesitated to set them forth regardless of their length. {165}

iv. The Training of the Body and Mind in accordance with the General Path of the Secret Mantra

This has two parts: (1) training in the winds for those who are free of desire and (2) training in the essence drops for those who have desire.

A) Training in the Winds for Those Who Are Free of Desire

This section has five topics: (1) training connected with the color of the wind, (2) training connected with the shape of the wind, (3) training connected with the number of respirations, (4) training in the exhalation and inhalation [of the wind vajra], and (5) training in the vase breath.

1) Training Connected with the Color of the Wind

The key point of bodily posture is to sit up straight in the seven-point posture. Your eyes should look either up into the sky or down, depending respectively on whether your mind is dull or agitated. The key point for speech is to expel the stale air from both nostrils three times with slow and gentle breaths. The key point for the mind is to visualize in between your eyebrows the essence of all the wind in the form of a white sphere, bright and sparkling, the size of a mustard seed.

Leave aside all discursive thoughts related to past, present, and future—all expectations or fears, all judgments, and all acceptance and rejection—and simply focus one-pointedly on the white sphere. Whatever gross or subtle thoughts arise, leave them to themselves, without following them and letting them continue. Just be completely focused on the sphere between your eyebrows. If your mind is distracted and becomes agitated, just relax, keeping watch, as if from afar, on the bright imagined object (the white sphere) with a mindfulness that is not too tense. Do not regard the sphere and your self-cognizing awareness as two different things. Remain instead in a state in which they are inseparable (a state in which the sphere is simply present), but do not fixate on it excessively. As you bring the form of the sphere into focus, your visualization will become steady. The brilliant light of the sphere will fill your head, then your whole body, then the space around you, and then the whole world. In conclusion, just be aware of the fact that everything that appears is pervaded by the shining white light, which itself has the nature of wind.

While mainly focusing on the sphere between your eyebrows, allow the visualization to fade away gradually. {166} As you train in the alternate process of expanding and dissolving the visualization, your body will start to feel light, your speech will become clear, and your mind will be still. As with all the other trainings, practice this meditation until these signs appear.

2) Training Connected with the "Shape" of the Wind

Visualize at the tip of your nose [the wind in the form of] a bluish white sphere the size of a Tibetan pea. When the visualization is clear, breathe gently through your nose, and consider that when you exhale, the sphere of the wind goes with the out-breath and everything becomes whitish. When you breathe in, the sphere returns and remains cool and fresh on the tip of your nose. If your bodily constitution is predominantly cold, meditate on the wind in the form of a red sphere that is hot to the touch. It is also said that this practice can be done visualizing the sphere in between your eyebrows.

3) Training Connected with the Number of Respirations

In this practice, mind and breath are brought together. Concentrate one-pointedly on counting the three phases of respiration: out-breath, in-breath, and the resting of the breath inside the body. Breathe naturally and count the three phases as a single cycle. Count these cycles without distraction. Train yourself until the movement of the breath gradually becomes slower and longer and until the breath remains stationary inside your body for a long time.

4) Training in the Exhalation and Inhalation [of the Wind Vajra]

Visualize your body as empty and transparent. In your navel imagine that there is a skull cup, white on the outside and red on the inside, with its forehead turned to the front. Focus on a blue vajra of the wind standing vertically inside the skull cup. It is the size of a barley grain. Meditate on this as much as you can. When your visualization is clear and stable, breathe through your nose, considering that as the breath is expelled, the vajra shoots out through your right nostril in a flash of blue light. When you inhale, the vajra enters through your left nostril and comes to rest in the skull cup. As you imagine this, in a state of physical and mental ease, keep your mind vibrant and clear. As you get used to this practice, your mind will become increasingly stable and still. {167} The distance at which the vajra is exhaled grows gradually shorter until, in the cycle of exhaling and inhaling, you consider that it reaches a distance of sixteen fingers from the tip of your nose.

5) Training in the Vase Breath

When you have performed the previous respiratory exercise several times as the basis of meditation and concentration, you should exhale your breath gently and slowly, imagining that the vajra goes far away from your right nostril. Hold your breath outside. Then as you breathe in, think that the vajra enters your body through your left nostril and quickly dissolves into the skull cup at your navel. Then hold the vase breath, uniting the upper and lower winds. The skull cup dissolves and becomes a red syllable *ha*. Concentrate on this. Think that the breath and your body become insubstantial like mist melting away. Then hold strongly the vase breath, which is characterized by four features.[53] When you breathe out, the wind-mind mixes with space and you rest in a state free of thought. If you are already proficient in holding the vase breath, it is enough just to meditate on this. If not, you should train until you are proficient in the best, moderate, or basic vase breath. If in the beginning you hold the vase breath moderately and not too strongly, you will avoid many obstacles. The key points of the body and of the expulsion of stale breath are generally applicable and should be added to all the trainings as they have just been described.

B) Training in the Yoga of the Essence Drops for Those Who Have Desire

Since training in physical bliss with the assistance of an actual consort is not implemented at this point, it is not discussed in the tradition of general instructions. It is however set forth in texts such as Longchenpa's *Ambrosial Clouds of Bliss and Emptiness*.[54] In the present context, the training in bliss, while being in harmony with the text just mentioned, is related to the winds and essence drops.

The key points related to the body are as follows. First, sit with your legs crossed. Make fists with your hands turned up, placing them at the top of the thighs, with your arms stretched rigid. Your eyes should look straight ahead with unmoving gaze. Do not raise your eyebrows.

The key point of the mind is to consider your body to be empty yet luminously appearing, transparent like an inflated membrane. In its center, visualize the avadhūtī, the central channel, as thick as a bamboo arrow of moderate length. {168} It is light red in color or else white on the outside and red on the inside—whichever you find easier. Its upper extremity is in the Brahmā aperture, and its lower end extends to four fingers below the navel. It is straight like a reed and as bright as the flame of a lamp of sesame oil. It is radiant with light. It is extremely delicate like the petal of a lotus flower. To the right of the central channel is the rasanā, the red channel.[55] To the left of the central channel is the lalanā, the white channel.[56] The diameter of these two lateral channels is half that of the central channel. Their upper extremities bend at the level of the forehead and, curving down between the eyes, enter the two nostrils. The lower extremities of these channels curve up into the lower end of the central channel. The three channels are close to each other so that at the level of the four chakras, the lateral channels merge with the central channel and their inner spaces coincide. The four chakras should be visualized as spreading out at these four locations. At the crown of the head, at a distance of two fingerbreadths above the upper end of the central channel, is the peak-arrayed chakra. At the throat, at the level of the shoulders, is the taste-gathering chakra. At the level of the heart and chest is the thought-gathering chakra. And at the level of the navel is the chakra of formation. Visualize all these chakras as being light red in color, brightly luminous and hollow.

In the center of the peak-arrayed chakra at the crown of your head, visualize a luminous essence drop, gleaming white and empty, the size of a pea.

Concentrate on it one-pointedly. While focusing on it, expel the stale breath three times and inhale deeply. Then press down the upper wind, keeping it at the level of the navel and pull up strongly the lower wind by contracting the lower parts of your body. The luminous essence drop will, as a result, begin to pulsate, and a blissful stream of bodhicitta, in drops the size of small peas, will begin to drip down one after the other with a pleasant dripping sound. Alternatively, the bodhicitta flows down from it in a continuous stream like the thread of spider silk. You can visualize whichever you find easier. {169} And as the four chakras at the crown of the head, throat, heart, and navel fill up one after the other, you should imagine that the primordial wisdom of the four joys comes to birth in you. When the essence drops are firmly present in the secret center, consider that you are experiencing the ultimate, coemergent primordial wisdom [of empty bliss]. In order to preserve the glow of each of the four joys, hold the vase breath as much as you can, thus increasing the sensation of bliss.

Your body and mind are now suffused with bliss. Then, as the essence drops are gradually drawn upward, you experience the four joys one by one in reverse order, borne up from below. Gradually they dissolve into the luminous essence drop in the crown of your head and become stable, and you consider that you are experiencing the natural coemergent wisdom. Try to maintain the glow of it as long as you can. In conclusion, this luminous essence drop grows smaller and smaller until it disappears. Then rest as long as you can in a state devoid of thought, free of all mental elaboration. Even during the post-meditation period, maintain as much as you can the union of bliss and emptiness—self-cognizing, self-illuminating awareness.

The fact that you do not meditate on the *A*-stroke[57] in the navel center is a particular feature of this essential instruction. By contrast, when training the body according to the instructions in the text *Ambrosial Clouds of Bliss and Emptiness*, it is said that one should meditate on the *A*-stroke in the navel center. For this is clearly beneficial for those who find it difficult to generate the warmth of bliss.

As you strive in this way, you will experience your body and mind in a state of blissful emptiness. The winds and essence drops will become wholesome and well-tuned, and you will not be hindered by any of the five elements. You will be free of any craving for food and drink. You will gain control over your mind and acquire the innumerable qualities of the limitless meditative stages of the Natural Great Perfection.

If the yoga of the winds for those who are free of desire and the yoga of the essence drops for those who have desire are not explained to people who are already proficient in the practice of the winds based on other paths, there will be no fault of omission. Moreover, since the great omniscient Longchenpa himself did not explain them in the *Meditation Guide for "Finding Rest in the Nature of the Mind,"*[58] {170} it is clearly permissible for these yogas to be withheld from those who have no mastery of their channels and winds.

v. The Natural Dissolution of the Five [Inner] Elements

The essential instructions that sever the continuum of thoughts cause the elements to subside naturally. The key points fall into two sections: (1) the practice related to the unborn nature of the five *A*-syllables and (2) the dissipation of the hindrances of mental drowsiness or agitation occurring through a disturbance of the elements.

A) The Practice Related to the Unborn Nature of the Five *A*-Syllables

The Exhaustion of the Four Elements Tantra says,

> Within the space of the great mindstream
> Where the four elements reach their exhaustion,
> Awareness, wild and free, is found,
> Wherein the basis of delusion is itself exhausted.
> In the palace of appearance, various and all-pervading,
> Within the heart of luminosity, wherein there is no up or down—
> There, without distraction, you should grasp
> Awareness through exhaustion of all thought
> With the hook of the exhaustion of a tense, fixated, mindfulness.[59]

With the conscious intention of performing the practice related to the unborn nature of the five *A*-syllables, adopt the seven-point posture of Vairocana. Breathe in and out gently through your mouth for a short time and in a relaxed manner. In your heart, visualize a blue syllable *A*, the size of the width of your finger. It has the nature of the pure [element of] space. As you concentrate on it, all the movements and elaborations of the wind-mind dissolve [into the *A*]. And as you rest in a state free of all cognitive activity and movement of thought, your space element is purified.

Similarly, either in the chakra at the crown of your head or in the space just in front of the tip of your nose, concentrate on the nature of the pure [element of] wind in the form of two green *A*-syllables, stacked vertically one above the other. All movement of the winds and mental activity dissolve into these syllables, and as you meditate in the way just described, your wind element is purified.

Then, either in your heart or again at the tip of your nose, concentrate on the nature of the pure [element of] water in the form of three white *A*-syllables stacked vertically. Let go of all your thoughts, all ideas and movements of the wind,[60] and holding your breath outside, rest for a little while without breathing. This will purify your water element. {171}

Then, in your throat or in the space in front of you, concentrate on the pure [element of] fire in the form of four red *A*-syllables stacked vertically. By this means, the visual consciousness, essential to the process of perception of objects of apprehension, is naturally purified.[61] As you concentrate on it, your fire element is purified.

Then at the navel or in the space in front, concentrate on the pure [element] of earth in the form of five yellow *A*-syllables stacked vertically. All apprehended objects, as they unfold, dissolve into them. And as you leave the sense doors free of clinging and fixation, your earth element is purified.

Karmapa Rangjung Dorje says in his essential instructions that once the stale breath is expelled, one should hold the vase breath, visualizing the three channels and the four chakras. In the middle of each chakra, one should meditate on a stack of five *A*-syllables in the colors associated with the elements as previously described. The wind-mind dissolves into each stack of letters, and one holds the vase breath as long as one can. Finally, all the *A*-syllables dissolve, and one rests in a state that is free of thought.

B) The Dissipation of the Hindrances of Drowsiness and Agitation Occurring through the Disturbance of the Elements

If, as you meditate in this way, a disturbance arises in the elements and you are overtaken by drowsiness or agitation of mind, here is an essential instruction on how to dissipate such states. It is taken from *The Great Heart Essence [of Vimalamitra]*.

When, owing to a disturbance in the earth element, your body seems heavy and your mind sinks into a dull drowsiness, meditate on a dark-green syllable *yaṃ* in the chakra at the crown of your head, and mingling it with the wind-mind, hold the vase breath. As you release the vase breath, think that physical heaviness and mental drowsiness are driven out into space in the form of blue-colored smoke. This is the way to dispel this disturbance.

When, because of a disturbance in the water element, you feel cold and are shivering, meditate on a blazing, red syllable *raṃ* in your throat chakra. Strongly pressing down the breath, think that there is a red syllable *ha* located below your navel at the point where the three channels join. From this a fire blazes out and fills your whole body. This will rid you of the problem.

Again, when, through a disturbance of the fire element, you have a fever, your body is aching, and so on, meditate on an ice-cool, white syllable *khaṃ*, either in your heart or in your stomach. {172} As you exhale between your teeth with a whistling sound, the problem will be solved.

Finally, when the wind element is disturbed and your mind becomes unstable, and you have pain in the upper part of your body and so on, imagine a heavy, yellow letter *laṃ* in your navel center. Focus the wind-mind into it. This will remove the problem. During all these meditations, you should hold the vase breath, uniting the upper and lower winds.

According to *The Innermost Essence of the Master: The Wish-Fulfilling Gem*, you should meditate on the cool, white, essence drops flowing down from the syllable *haṃ* in the chakra of great bliss [in the crown of your head]. All diseases are healed thereby. You should exhale your breath completely and hold it outside. In the case of cold diseases, visualize the syllable *raṃ* in the chakra of manifestation at your navel. Imagine that fire blazes from it and burns away the disease. Hold the vase breath, uniting the upper and lower winds [in the navel center].

For disorders of the phlegm, you should meditate in the same way but with the following difference. Consider that the nectar flows from the syllable *traṃ* in the chakra of enjoyment and purges all disease. Exhale three times, and between each exhalation take and hold your breath inside. If your mind is agitated and you have many thoughts, concentrate on the blissful warmth blazing from the syllable *haṃ* located in the bliss-preserving chakra, and hold your breath. When you meditate, if no matter what you do, concentration [on the various syllables] does not come, you should visualize the syllable *hūṃ* in the chakra of ultimate reality. This will stimulate the nectar flow from the *haṃ* in the crown of your head. Again hold your breath inside. This is a remedy for all maladies. Concentration will arise quite naturally. These are all sublime instructions. It is said that when you practice, you should pronounce all these letters. The method is to recite the syllables *ha*, *hūṃ*, and *A* many times.

b. The Main Practice

Guiding instructions related to the essence of luminosity are now given that establish what is mind and what is awareness. The explanation is divided into two sections: (1) The first comprises the essential instructions concerning trekchö, the ground, through which certainty is reached concerning the ordinary mind. This is followed by (2) the essential instructions for the path—namely, tögal—whereby certainty is reached regarding awareness.

i. Essential Instructions on Trekchö, the Ground, through Which Certainty Is Reached concerning the Ordinary Mind

The Key to the View, Meditation, and Action, Which Opens the Eyes to What Is Hidden contains the following passage: {173}

> Through the essential instructions for the kind of action that is free from clinging and attachment, appearances are overcome. Through the essential instructions for a meditation that is free from conceptual fixation, the discursive mind is overcome. Through the essential instructions for a view that is free of dualistic clinging, the defilement that underpins all clinging is overcome. And through the essential instructions for a result that is beyond both elimination and attainment, awareness is definitively revealed.[62]

Each of these essential instructions comprises two aspects: an overall aspect related to the teachings of the Great Perfection generally and a specific aspect related to the essential instructions of the tradition of the most secret Heart Essence.[63] Each of these instructions is discussed under four headings, which deal with the agent, object, manner [of the practice], and result obtained.[64] An understanding of the instructions should be gradually acquired by studying such texts as *The Fourfold Cycle of the Lamps:*[65] *The Lamp That Gathers All Action*[66] and so on. These instructions—which refer to action, meditation, view, and result—are explained here only in very general terms.

A) Essential Instructions for an Action or Conduct That Is Free of Clinging

These instructions are three in number.

1) Directions for Beginners in the Practice

Thanks to their understanding of what is to be avoided and what is to be adopted, practitioners refrain from even the slightest negative action and take care to practice even the slightest virtuous deed. They go into the presence of their holy teachers, listen to their teachings, and understand what is right and what is wrong according to the dharma. They receive the complete range of profound instructions and clear away any possible misunderstanding regarding the words in which they are expressed. They reflect on them, correctly assimilate the key points of their unmistaken meaning, and train in methods that turn their minds away from samsara.

2) Directions for Those Who Apply Themselves to the Essential Teachings

This done, they go to some remote place and all alone like a beggar or wild animal, they apply themselves to the practice of their teacher's instructions. Satisfied with only the bare necessities in food and clothing, and without allowing themselves to be distracted by other teachings, {174} they place their trust solely in the instructions that they have received. Leaving aside all thoughts and deeds pertaining to this life, and whatever ties they may have, they persevere with great endurance.

Through the preliminary rushen practice of separating samsara from nirvana,[67] they turn away from the clinging and attachment they have to their body, speech, and mind. Then, all alone without friends or acquaintances, they behave as though they were mute and keep completely silent, abstaining even from making signs. With their six consciousnesses completely relaxed, like a tiny child, they meditate on the dharmatā, the ultimate nature of phenomena.

3) Directions for Practitioners of the Path of Yogic Discipline

Then, without restraint, doing whatever they would normally never dare to do, they forcefully cut through all inhibitions. Like dogs or pigs, they abandon any distinction between what is clean and what is dirty, and they let go of any fixed notions of what is to be adopted and rejected. As they behave spontaneously and without restraint, as though they were insane, they fully experience open and unimpeded awareness, and all appearances become their friends. It is thus that, later on, they are able to transform the attitude of people who have no faith or confidence in the dharma. They have the power to revive those who have been killed and to gain mastery over the four elements and the wind-mind. All their latent attachments are severed. They can practice the yogic discipline of awareness even in markets [and large gatherings] and thus can uproot defilements at the same time as gaining control over outer appearances. This is consequently referred to as "action whereby mastery over phenomena is gained." In brief, one should train in the way that corresponds to the stage in the practice that one has reached.

B) Essential Instructions for a Meditation That Is Free of Conceptual Fixation

The pith instructions for meditation that is free of conceptual fixation are twofold: (1) the guiding instructions in relation to the ordinary mind (the preliminary practice for body, speech, and mind) and (2) instructions for bringing the mind to its natural state.

1) Guiding Instructions in Relation to the Ordinary Mind

These instructions are threefold according to body, speech, and mind. {175}

a) The Preliminary Training of the Body

The training of the body consists in adopting the vajra position. When you implement this practice, you should completely give up all mundane activities and remain alone in a solitary place. In the sky before you, visualize your incomparably kind teacher in a sphere of blue light. He is in his usual form. He is naked but for an *angrak*, a pair of short yogic britches, and is standing in the vajra position. Pray to him with great fervor. Prepare the ground properly, spreading out a large soft mat or cushion so that you do not hurt yourself when you collapse on to it. Then, naked, clad only in an angrak, adopt the vajra position. Standing upright, join the soles of your feet, push out your knees, stretch out your elbows and touch the palms of your hands together above, but not touching, your head. Then with your eyes staring straight ahead into space, visualize your body as a blue vajra blazing with fire. Your teacher, visualized in front, transforms into a dark-blue syllable *hūṃ* and takes up his position in the round hub of the vajra (your body thus visualized). Concentrate on this for a short while. Then consider that the *hūṃ* disappears and becomes inseparable from the quintessential and indestructible sphere in your heart. Then recite the six syllables of the Great Perfection: *'a A śa sa ma ha*. Then halting all thoughts related to past, present, and future, remain there in a perfectly thought-free state, untouched by even the slightest mental movement. Continue this meditation until your body is exhausted and you fall to the ground. When you collapse, leave your body as it is, without moving or altering its position however that might be. For a short while, leave your mind also in a state devoid of thought. Repeat this exercise as many times as you can in the session, beginning with the visualization of your teacher and practicing as before. Persevere in this practice for the space of three days.

{176} To begin with, your body will ache and tremble, and like an old house collapsing to the ground, you will be unable to stand firm. But if you persevere in this practice, you will finally experience a great sense of physical well-being and a sensation of blissful warmth. Indeed, if this happens, it is a sign that your practice has gone to its vital point. The general purpose of this practice is to avert all clinging to the body, to make obstacles subside, and to purify all negativities. Its end purpose is to prevent entry into the city of a physical womb, to discover the freedom of the level of the nirmāṇakāya, and finally to become inseparable from the vajra body of buddhahood.

b) The Preliminary Training of Speech

The preliminary training of speech has four stages: (1) placing the seal, (2) developing skill, (3) searching for mental pliancy, and (4) journeying on the road.

i) Placing the Seal

This has two aspects: (1) placing the seal on outer appearances and (2) placing the seal on your own body.

(I) Placing the Seal on Outer Appearances

Pray with fervent devotion to your teacher visualized in his usual form and seated in vajra posture in the center of a sphere of blue light in the sky before you. Adopt the seven-point posture of Vairocana, and focusing your gaze on the tip of your nose, imagine a blue syllable *hūṃ* (the ground awareness) in your heart. Then imagine that your teacher visualized in front of you transforms into a *hūṃ* and dissolves into the syllable in your heart. Relax for a moment, and then recite the syllable *hūṃ* not too loud and not too soft, with neither lips nor teeth touching. As you do so, many *hūṃ* syllables emerge from the *hūṃ* in your heart, leaving your body through the right nostril. They gradually fill up your entire dwelling place, and finally all outer appearances are completely filled with them. Vibrating and quivering, everything now resounds with the murmuring sound of *hūṃ*. Concentrate on this, and then relax for a brief moment.

(II) Placing the Seal on Your Own Body

Continue the meditation by considering that the *hūṃ* syllables enter you left nostril {177} and completely fill your body from the crown of your head to the nails on your toes.

In the tradition of the great Rikdzin Tsewang Norbu, these two meditations are practiced separately and in the case of the second meditation, you imagine that many *hūṃ* syllables suddenly appear in the outer world and then enter through your nostrils. He stated moreover that it is unnecessary to imagine that all the *hūṃ* syllables that fill the outer world gather inside oneself.

ii) Developing Skill

This also has two aspects: (1) developing skill with regard to outer appearances and (2) developing skill with regard to your own body.

(I) Developing Skill with Regard to Outer Appearances

Pray to your teacher in front of you using the same visualization as before except that, this time, the ground awareness, the blazing *hūṃ* in your heart, is blue black in color. Your teacher transforms into a syllable *hūṃ* and dissolves into the syllable in your own heart. Recite *hūṃ* in a fierce staccato fashion, imagining that from the syllable in your heart *hūṃ* syllables erupt, hot like fire, swift as lightning, razor-sharp, and as powerful as thunder. To begin with, like sparks of fire striking a piece of paper, they pierce and pass back and forth through whatever is in front of yourself, rendering it insubstantial. Gradually, they pierce and purify all things, causing them to disintegrate, so that in the end, nothing real and solid is left even down to the size of a sesame seed. Imagine that everything is totally filled with myriads of *hūṃ* syllables moving and jostling around. Remain for a short moment in meditative evenness.

(II) Developing Skill with Regard to Your Own Body

Practice the guru yoga as described previously. Then imagine that from the syllable *hūṃ* in your heart, many *hūṃ* syllables endowed with the four qualities just mentioned are projected out and pierce through your body from the crown of your head till the soles of your feet, passing back and forth, up and down, and not leaving anything untouched, even down to an area as wide as a split horsehair. Moreover, *hūṃ* syllables endowed with the same four features, abruptly and spontaneously appear and enter your body from outside, piercing and penetrating it without difficulty {178} and rendering it completely empty. As you visualize the *hūṃ* syllables and recite them forcefully in a sharp staccato manner, this will bring on a throbbing sensation in your flesh and you will have the feeling that your whole body has become insubstantial. If you are being attacked by negative forces and so on, this practice will overcome them, and as a sign that these forces are being exorcised, you will tremble and shake. If you continue to train like this, taking occasional rests, you will be freed from negative forces. At the end of the session remain in a space-like state beyond all reference.

i) Searching for Mental Pliancy

Place a stick, three feet in length, in front of you. Concentrate on your teacher, and imagine that he dissolves [into the *hūṃ* in your heart] as previously described. Then from that same syllable *hūṃ* in your heart there emerges a second identical syllable. It passes easily from your heart and positions itself—clear, firm, and blazing—on top of the stick. Focus on this. It then dissolves back into the ground awareness, the *hūṃ* in your heart, only to emerge once again. Repeat this process several times thus creating a basis for your concentration. Now place in front of you a stick, one arm-span in height, and imagine that many *hūṃ* syllables emerge from the *hūṃ* in your heart continuously one after the other, like a string of beads. Beginning from the bottom of the stick, which is in front of you, the string of *hūṃ*s curls round the stick in a clockwise movement, gradually climbing up it. When the first *hūṃ* reaches the top of the stick, which it does quite quickly, place your mind on it for a short while. Then imagine that, starting with the last *hūṃ*, all the syllables come swirling back, moving counterclockwise and dissolve into the *hūṃ* in your heart. Then relax your concentration on the syllables. Then, once again, the string of *hūṃ* syllables begins to emanate and so on as before. Throughout this exercise, recite the syllable *hūṃ*, chanting it slowly and softly. When you have grown used to this practice, you can use a stake two arm-spans in length and, in your visualization, transform it into a wish-fulfilling tree, the top of which reaches to the very Peak of Existence. {179} Once again, you should chant *hūṃ*, repeating the process of emanation and reabsorption of the syllables as just described. Subsequently, train in this way in regard to all things [not just the stick]. If you feel that wherever you focus your mind, it will stay there, and if you gain a vivid clarity regarding all the previous concentrations, this means that you have acquired proficiency in this practice.

ii) Journeying on the Road

As before, meditate on your teacher and on his dissolution into the *hūṃ* in your heart. And as it is commonly visualized, imagine that in your heart there is a white syllable *hūṃ* radiant with five-colored light. Then as you recite *hūṃ* slowly and gently, the syllable shoots out to a great distance from your heart and begins to journey on the road, winding its way like a worm. Imagine that it moves out of your dwelling place and that, little by little, it traverses all the areas that you can see—mountains, cliffs, ravines, and so on—traveling to the unimaginable limits of the universe. Imagine that in some places it lingers a little and its vivid presence is reinforced. Think from time to time that as you slowly recite *hūṃ*, the syllable moves slowly. At other times, imagine that when your recitation is quick and staccato, it shoots like an arrow. Finally, imagine that gradually it returns and rests either just in front of you or in your heart.

When you recite the *hūṃ*, it is important to blend your awareness with your breath, focusing one-pointedly on the movement back and forth of the syllable both outside and inside your dwelling place. It is said that you can pause for rest at the bends in the *hūṃs*' serpentine path, and at that moment you should exclaim *hūṃ* in a short and forceful way.

In particular, according to the oral explanation of the teacher's uncommon essential instructions, {180} concentrate on the primordial, ultimate nature of the body, speech, and mind in the form of a white syllable *hūṃ*, shining with five-colored lights. Imagine that the syllable departs on its meandering course but does not leave behind the body and the syllable from which it had emanated. The *hūṃ* travels to the buddha fields and so on. It is said that this visualization is much more profound than the previous one. Then imagine that after visiting many buddha fields, the *hūṃ* syllable travels to Abhirati, the eastern buddha field of Perfect Joy, where it mingles inseparably with the great bliss of the vast expanse of the mind of the lord and teacher Akṣobhya. And without gathering back the *hūṃ* into yourself, rest in meditative evenness free of thought. Adapt this same procedure [when visiting] the buddha fields [of the rest of the buddhas of the five families].

The *hūṃ* syllable also travels to the hells and the other impure realms. And all the places that it visits are vividly transformed into pure lands with pure inhabitants—deities and immeasurable palaces. In conclusion, imagine that they all disappear along with the *hūṃ*, and then rest in meditative evenness in emptiness, the state free of all thought and mental elaboration. In all these different scenarios, train yourself to imagine that the *hūṃ* travels slowly, as if at a walking pace. It must not move quickly. And wherever the *hūṃ* syllable goes, it is as if you are there in reality. Meditating in this way, you will come to the point where these places are experienced so vividly that it is exactly as if you were actually there. You will have no difficulty in recognizing your dreams as dreams, in multiplying your dream visions, in transforming them, and so forth. It is also said that, through this practice, you will actually be able to go to the buddha fields and the other realms.

As you make effort in this preliminary practice related with speech, the result will be, in the immediate term, that all your clinging to speech as being really existent will be averted and all obstacles will be eliminated. All your obscurations connected with speech will be cleansed away. As for its higher purpose, your speech will not be involved in the things of samsara but will subside into the sambhogakāya, and you will acquire the vajra speech of all the buddhas. {181}

a) The Preliminary Training of the Mind

This preliminary practice is threefold. First one examines where the mind arises, then where it dwells, and, finally, where it goes. *The Word-Transcending Tantra* says,

> First, where the mind originates,
> Then where it dwells, then where it goes—
> Examine these three aspects.
> With this training on the mind, one sees its fundamental nature.

i) An Examination of the Place from Where the Mind Arises and of the Arising Mind Itself

As with all the practices, sit in the seven-point posture of Vairocana, and, as before, meditate on and pray to your teacher visualized in front of you. Your teacher then dissolves into you, blending inseparably with your own mind. For as long as you can, rest in meditative evenness in the natural state that is free of thoughts. Then look within yourself and ask yourself what—among your body, speech, and mind—is the main factor. What is it that throws you into samsara, and what is it that obtains nirvana? Is it your body, your speech, or your mind? When you come to the conclusion that it is principally your mind, proceed to examine it. Where has your mind come from, unfolding in all its multitude of thoughts? Has it come from the outer, extramental, elements? Has it come from your body, which is itself like an illusion? Has it come from empty phenomenal appearances, from your father or your mother? And so on. Has your mind arisen from your mind? Where has it come from? Look for it—here and there, up and down. As you investigate in this way, you will find that the mind has no place of origin and indeed that there is no mind that actually originates. And although thoughts occur to you just as before, [you will see that] in the very moment of their arising, they have no existence. This lack of existence constitutes their "absence of origin," their primordial fundamental nature; it is the way of being of the dharmakāya. This search for the origin of your mind is meant to help you recognize its nature.

ii) An Examination of Where the Mind Dwells

Now whether you think of the mind as something arising from the kinds of entities just described or as something that simply manifests when thoughts suddenly occur, the question you should ask yourself is: Does this mind dwell in outer phenomena or is it inside your body?

{182} Examine whether the mind that dwells [in the present moment] is a truly existent thing or not. What is its shape? What is its color? And so on. Examine how it is. And when the understanding arises that it does not exist as a thing—that it is empty and yet luminous, like the sky—this is the recognition that the mind has no dwelling place. The final purpose of this examination is the accomplishment of the sambhogakāya.

iii) An Examination of Where the Mind Goes

Now regarding the thoughts that seem to appear suddenly and then vanish, ask yourself: Where do they go? What is their destination? And indeed, what are the thoughts like that go there? You may think that they completely vanish, but if you search for where they vanish, you find that they only seem to depart, whereas in fact they go nowhere. They only seem to cease, but in fact they do not do so. To understand this is to recognize the nature of the mind as empty awareness, where there is no trace of anything. The final purpose of this examination is the attainment of the nirmāṇakāya.

Furthermore, is this mind a truly existent thing or not? If it is, by what shape, color, size, function, or nature is it characterized? Look over here at the mind that is examining; and look over there at the mind that is being watched. Are these two minds the same or different? Tracing these thoughts back to awareness, which is their source, watch your mind without being distracted even for an instant. After examining and searching up and down for your mind, relax and rest like an old person sitting in the sun or like a workman who has completed his task.

Again, when thoughts burst forth strongly, one after the other, do not let them go unnoticed but take hold of them firmly and mindfully and look from where they arise. If you think that they have emerged from your mind, ask yourself from where the mind itself has come. Could it have arisen from something that exists? If so, where has that thing itself come from? Could it have arisen from something that does not exist? If so, can you find a point of reference for it? {183} Search without a moment's distraction, and when you fail to find it, rest relaxed in the state of not seeing anything. Again, when thoughts suddenly appear, watch them as before until you reach a decisive certainty about your mind.

An examination of this kind, in which you find nothing at all, should be done repeatedly until you come to the conclusion that there is nothing to identify, no circumscribed thing to examine as being "your mind." As you strive in this way, the immediate goal is to avert any kind of clinging to the mind as something truly existent. It is to cause obstacles to subside and to purify negativities. The ultimate purpose of such an examination is to prevent the mind from engaging in samsara and to cause it to subside into the dharmakāya, the one and only sphere. Your mind will become indivisible from the vajra-like indestructible mind of all the buddhas. As it is said in one of the tantras, "When the mind is driven to its extremity, thinking is brought to exhaustion." And this is the purpose of this investigation.

At this point, if you wish to perform this practice in a more elaborate way, follow the instructions given for the preliminary practice known as "destroying the house of the mind," according to the instructions for the trekchö meditation titled *Natural Rest in the Primordial Flow*.[68] By examining the three aspects of arising, dwelling, and subsiding, you will come to see the ineffable nature of the mind. And through investigating whether these aspects are the same or different, you will come to a realization of the mind's fundamental nature. By discerning this naked experience of the nature of the mind, you will recognize the primordial wisdom that transcends the ordinary intellect. It would be truly excellent if you were able to practice all these instructions in detail.

2) Guiding Instructions for Bringing the Mind to Its Natural State

Visualize in the sky in front of you, in the middle of an empty sphere of blue light, your benevolent root teacher. His body is immovable, his eyes half-closed, his speech inexpressible, and his mind free of all mental contrivance. Concentrate on a white syllable *A* in his heart. As you pray to your teacher, he dissolves into you. Then leave your body completely relaxed and comfortable, just like a bale of straw when its binding string has been cut. {184} As for your speech, leave it completely inactive, like a lute with broken strings. And leave your mind in its natural state with nothing to think about or examine, like a mill wheel once the millrace has been closed. If your body, speech, and mind are left in this way, virtue and nonvirtue, adoption and rejection, and so on—all mental elaborations—will subside like salt dissolving into water. Just rest free of all contrivance in this primordial state of empty, luminous, coemergent wisdom.

Whatever objects appear in the mind or whatever mental states you experience with regard to those objects, do not block what appears in the outer world, and do not get engrossed in what you perceive within. Rest in a state of awareness, vividly awake and nakedly fresh, in which object and subject cannot be identified. For appearances and the mind are indivisible.

The previous, strenuous, and tensely focused exercise of searching the mind is undoubtedly tiring. But now, by relaxing in the natural state, you should feel rested, and there should arise a state of deep concentration—which is of course the purpose of this training. While you are in this state, if you feel the urge to move your body, and if there is the movement of thoughts in your mind, you should nakedly watch their nature and relax at ease. If you feel the urge to speak, just utter the syllables *A A A* without focusing on anything. Moreover, if at this time, an obstacle in the form of a state of wild agitation occurs, you should think of your body-mind as though it were a square block of diamond and remain in meditative evenness. If, on the other hand, you are "spaced out" in a state of dullness, think of your body-mind as a white syllable *A* and focus your attention on it. Finally, if you are overcome with a sense of lethargy, think of your whole body as being a brilliant blazing flame or concentrate on a flame in your heart center. These three lesser concentrations—the block of diamond, the letter *A*, and the bright flame—will dispel these obstacles and bring progress on the path.

In the post-meditation period, you should attend to whatever happens to you, neither accepting nor rejecting it, without any expectation or fear. It is in such a way that all appearances become friends and helpers for your practice. {185} If you forcibly suppress your thoughts, you will never gain stability of mind and you will experience only hindrances. It is important not to cling to the objects of the sixth, or mental, consciousness, and not to manipulate them with antidotes.

When you settle in the state of primordial purity, thoughts arise just as they did before, but now you understand that they do not in fact arise. Recognizing open, unimpeded awareness nakedly, you will come to a clear certainty regarding primordial purity—empty awareness beyond all mental elaboration.

C) Essential Instructions for the View That Is Free of Dualistic Fixation

These instructions are in two stages: (1) the implementation of the view and (2) the direct, naked introduction to the nature of the mind.

1) The Implementation of the View

Here an explanation is given, (1) first, of the theoretical understanding of the view and then (2) of its actual implementation.

a) The Theoretical Understanding of the View

This should be studied in the supporting texts for the trekchö practice, such as *Stainless Space* and *Clouds in the Thought-Free Sky*.[69]

b) The Actual Implementation of the View

Begin with the practice of guru yoga. Then, on the basis of *The Three Statements That Strike upon the Vital Points*,[70] the parting testament of the nirmāṇakāya [Garab Dorje], come to the realization that your own awareness is the stainless dharmakāya.

THE FIRST STATEMENT:
Recognize your own nature.

Your present mind, your mind in this very moment—free of all contrivance, all distortion, all antidotes, and whose nature exceeds all possible definition—is awareness. Awareness is not an entity endowed with attributes. It is primordial wisdom, empty but luminous. It is that great, lucid, vivid, and all-pervading state that is beyond the ordinary mind with its memories and thoughts. It is this awareness that is to be recognized as primordial wisdom, the dharmakāya, primordial purity.

THE SECOND STATEMENT:
Come to a decisive certainty about one thing.

This means that you should rest without moving in the dharmakāya beyond the mind—a fourth state that is free of the other three [namely, thoughts related to past, present, and future].[71] Past thoughts and memories are gone, the future ones have not yet arrived, and in the state of the present mind, completely free of contrivance and alteration, the clarity of awareness is unobstructed. It is as when muddy water is left to stand undisturbed. It becomes naturally limpid and clear. {186} It is only in this state, a state that is not produced by deliberate effort, that that you should settle—the uncontrived, "plain and ordinary" mind[72] that is aware, vivid, lucid, and clear—without slipping into distraction or mental dullness.

THE THIRD STATEMENT:
Be confident in the subsiding [of thought].

When you settle in a state of limpidity free of all mental contrivance—like a clear and pellucid lake—although the plain and ordinary mind unfolds toward objects, these spontaneous arisings steadily and continuously subside, just like the ocean's waves, which naturally sink back into the water. When thoughts arise, if you relax in a state that is free of distraction, if you do not contrive or try to alter anything, these memories and thoughts just vanish, leaving no trace. You become confident that all perceptions dissolve into the ground in a process called "spontaneous subsiding" and that the way these thoughts spontaneously arise is beyond any preference and clinging that you may have—that it is beyond all effort, all adoption and rejection, and beyond all antidotes.

2) A Direct and Naked Introduction to the Nature of the Mind

There are two kinds of introduction to the nature of the mind. There is (1) the introduction through the transmission of blessing power and (2) the introduction made on the basis of meditative experience.

a) An Introduction through the Transmission of Blessing Power

In a solitary place, the disciples should prepare a vast gaṇacakra offering complete with tormas. Make a mandala offering, and, sitting straight, take as the primary object of concentration the master who is introducing you to the nature of the mind. Visualize the guru as has been explained in the guru yoga practice. Then cultivate an extraordinary sense of conviction that the guru is free from all faults and is endowed with every perfect quality—that the guru is the one who satisfies all needs and wishes and is the embodiment of all objects of refuge. You should rely on your guru completely as a person whose every action is perfect. Pray to all the holy root and lineage masters to look upon you with unbounded compassion and to bestow on you their blessings. And with a fervent yearning devotion that brings tears to your eyes, pray to your guru to bless you so that in this very moment you might experience the birth of an extraordinary realization of the profound path. {187} Burn incense and *gugul*, and while your teacher plays the ḍamaru and bell, recite the lineage prayer that mentions all the teachers by name and begins with these words:

> To the dharmakāya Samantabhadra I pray.
> Grant your blessings that experience and realization
> Of the profound path take birth within my mind.

It is thus that the blessing power will come down upon you. In conclusion, the teacher, with immeasurable compassion, melts into light and enters through the crown of your head. Your body, speech, and mind fuse inseparably with the three vajras of your teacher, and you settle in a state of complete relaxation free of all mental contrivance.

This stimulates the blessing power of the teacher. All the experiences of your body, speech, and mind blend with those of your teacher, and all your thoughts are vividly infused with devotion and respect. Free of fixation and clinging, the fundamental condition of the mind is a state of wide-open openness and freedom. And to rest at ease in this state, completely relaxed and without any contrivance, is called "finding openness and freedom in self-cognizing awareness, the expanse of the primordially pure dharmakāya."

The present section is not part of the root teachings [of *The Heart Essence of Vimalamitra* and *The Innermost Essence of the Master*]. However, since it brings an enhancement to one's experience, and since it belongs to the tradition of the great tertön Terdak Lingpa, it is said to be a source of very great blessing power.

b) An Introduction Based on Meditative Experience

The introduction based on meditative experience is threefold: (1) an introduction based on the mind's stillness, (2) an introduction based on the mind's movement, and (3) an introduction based on the indivisibility of stillness and movement.

i) An Introduction Based on the Mind's Stillness

Once it has been thoroughly established that [the mind] is by nature unborn, it is on the basis of the mind's stillness aspect that the fundamental nature of the ground is introduced. This fundamental nature is beyond both freedom and bondage. It is the state of primordial purity in which all phenomena come to exhaustion. The introduction happens in the following way. The teacher addresses the disciples saying:

> As on previous occasions, the key point of the body is to assume the seven-point posture of Vairocana. The key point of speech is to breathe naturally and comfortably. The key point of the mind is that when the past thought has ceased and before the next thought arises, awareness appears in its present immediacy. This is the fourth state, the state that is free from the other three [namely, thoughts related to the three times].
>
> Although it does not exist as anything at all, the radiance of awareness is an unceasing state of great bliss, and its creative power manifests in all kinds of ways. However, the nature of awareness is ineffable, beyond word, thought, and expression. Going beyond the sphere of the ordinary mind, awareness is lucid, open, and awake. {188} It is vivid, nakedly fresh, and pure. It is self-arisen primordial wisdom, the dharmakāya, the great state beyond the mind. You must recognize this directly, face-to-face, and then rest for a moment in meditative evenness in a space-like state that is free of all ontological extremes.

When you rest in this way, mental contrivance subsides. All deeds and doers of deeds, and all thoughts manifest as the display of primordial wisdom, blissful, luminous, and free of ordinary cognition. There is then no difference between sessions of meditation and post-meditation periods, no difference between day and night. The pitfalls of permanent existence and annihilation are no more, and there is no longer anything to accept or reject. You have a decisive certainty regarding the fundamental nature beyond both meditator and object of meditation, the state of primordial purity where all phenomena come to exhaustion. As it is said in *The Most Secret Words Tantra*,

> Free of all past memories and future thoughts
> Is mind in its immediate nowness—
> Vivid, clear, and utterly alert.
> Recognize it as the dharmakāya, the fourth state.[73]

At that moment, the mind devoid of mental contrivance is the dharmakāya. Its blissful luminosity, free of fixation, is the sambhogakāya. In being the ground for the ceaseless manifestation of all appearances, it is the nirmāṇakāya. And the inseparability of these three kāyas is the inseparability of ultimate nature (*ngo bo*), the luminous character (*rang bzhin*), and cognizant potency (*thugs rje*). *The Array of Studded Jewels Tantra* says,

> Your awareness is the perfect Buddha.
> Its nature in the three times is unchanging.
> Constantly unceasing is its character.
> Its cognizant potency appears in all.[74]

Now with regard to this point, there exists a traditional method that is uncommon and unique. When you try to focus suddenly on three objects all at once (a pillar, a table, and a book) or the three times (past, present, and future), trying to concentrate not just on their general aspect but on their subtle particularities, you will undergo a certain experience. And on the basis of this, your teacher will introduce you to the "fourth state free of the other three." As it is said, "The 'fourth' denotes the absence of a real foundation." {189}

ii) An Introduction Based on the Mind's Movement

When you understand that the display of the creative power [of awareness] is unceasing, it is on the basis of this aspect of the mind's movement that the spontaneous subsiding of this movement is introduced. There is no longer any need to reject it or to apply antidotes to it. Within the nature of the mind, blissful, luminous, and free of ordinary cognition, there appears an unceasing variegated display: all the thoughts and memories that arise and dissolve. Even though external appearances do not cease, nevertheless you are not hampered inwardly by having to apply antidotes to clinging and fixation. This state is free of contrivance and alteration, such as seeing off the past and welcoming the future, accepting and rejecting, and affirming and negating. It is awareness, bare, vivid, naked, clear, and awake. Stay quite naturally within its radiance, letting it take its course. Whatever waves arise in the ocean, they are nothing but the water of that same ocean. And so whatever thoughts arise, there is no need for you to push them away or to change them, for they are the display of the dharmatā and nothing else. Although your awareness is displayed externally, appearing in all sorts of ways, these same appearances do not stir from the mind itself, which, like a skilled magician, remains unconcerned by them and does not cling to them. And although awareness manifests internally in all kinds of ways, the mind itself does not cling to or become fixated on these manifestations—like a baby that does not cling to or get involved with what it sees. It is thus that all thoughts naturally vanish and melt away, like salt dissolving into water. This is the "natural subsiding of all appearances." For as it is said in *The Word-Transcending Tantra*,

> No matter the arisings of awareness,
> They subside all by themselves like knots tied on a snake.
> There is no need for antidotes—all effort falls apart.
> They are by nature free and open from the outset.

iii) An Introduction Based on the Indivisibility of Stillness and Movement

When you have a clear conviction that you cannot separate stillness from movement, it is then that on the basis of this inseparability, all that arises is introduced as naked awareness. Leave your three doors relaxed and in their natural state. Even though the display of the creative power of awareness is unceasing and all kinds of thoughts arise, nevertheless if you leave these thoughts in their natural course, without rejecting or encouraging them, without repressing or indulging in them, {190} you will remain unmoving in the state of dharmatā. Since the display of the mind's stillness aspect subsides without impediment, the stillness and the movement aspects are not two separate things. They are inseparable. And because the stillness and movement are [consequently] not posited in relation to each other, if you simply rest in naked awareness without clinging to any of the perceptions of the six consciousnesses, all thoughts, gross and subtle, simply arise and then disappear, like a block of ice that melts into water, or mist evaporating into the sky. You will see that they are just the display of the dharmatā—they do not stir from the dharmatā. As it is said in *The Tantra of Marvels*,

> Just like the waves arising on the sea,
> The moving waves of mind
> Dissolve into the ocean of the primal ground.[75]

So it is that when the mind is still, it is in its primordial state; when it moves, it is the play of primordial wisdom. When stillness and movement are seen to be the same and equal, [one understands that] they are indivisible from each other. No matter what arises, it does not fall outside the radiance of dharmatā. So do not try to *accomplish* the equality of stillness and movement. Do not block movement; do not look for stillness. Everything that manifests is just the play of awareness. It is as the teachings say:

> Buddhahood, immaculate and free from stain,
> Is your own awareness, the unchanging dharmakāya,
> Limpid, crystal clear, and vivid,
> Like the cloudless autumn sky.
> Stay like a mountain: firm, unchanging.
> Stay like the ocean: unmoving in its clarity.
> Stay like the sky: limitless, unbounded.
> However you may stay, it is awareness—rest in it.
> In movement or in stillness,
> Rest within awareness, clear and wakeful.
> Birds fly in the sky; they cannot fly beyond it.
> Likewise, things appear within and do not go beyond
> Awareness. It is there that you should rest.[76] {191}

When you relax in the mind's natural flow devoid of fabrication and alteration, you discover a state of peace and comfort in which there is nothing to do and nothing to avoid, nothing to adopt and nothing to reject—a state in which there is nothing that you still hope for and nothing that you are afraid of. Understand that this is the state of awareness, the indwelling samādhi of awareness.

Here is how to recognize it. At all times, whether the mind is still or moving, whether it is adopting or rejecting something, whether you have good thoughts or bad thoughts, you should simply watch, nakedly and directly, the state of awareness, which is self-cognizing, spontaneous, and naturally luminous. The samādhi that dwells within you and is devoid of clinging[77] will arise, nakedly fresh and clear. Keep within this state through simple mindfulness—effortlessly, without striving to do so—like a steady flow of a river.

All that has been said so far is but an introduction to the view that all phenomena that appear and are experienced are actually beyond the realm of conceptual fixation—adoption and rejection, repression and indulgence, hope and fear.

It is also beneficial if, instead of the foregoing pointing-out instructions, teachers give introductions "to the awareness that dwells within" and "to the memories and thoughts that are beyond arising and subsiding" according to the instructions for the trekchö meditation titled *Natural Rest in the Primordial Flow.*[78]

When fortunate disciples, who have practiced the view in meditation, are introduced by their teachers to the nature of their minds, they remove any misconceptions they may have regarding the profound fundamental nature. And by powerfully and constantly preserving this view, they will rapidly achieve stability in it. By contrast, if you have no meditative experience of the view and have only a theoretical understanding of it, then even if you are given an introduction to the nature of the mind, it will have no effect. On the other hand, if you work hard at the meditation until you gain experience in the different stages of the practice, and if the introduction is given according to that same level of experience and understanding, you will come gradually to the experience of the nature of the mind.

D) Essential Instructions for a Result That Is beyond Both Elimination and Attainment

The result itself is empty awareness, and this is the dharmakāya. You will be completely convinced that since awareness is open and free from the very beginning, there is no need to make it so again. {192} Thoughts are naturally open and free, and therefore you will be quite sure that their subsiding does not depend on antidotes. And since they are utterly open and free by themselves, you will become confident that there is nothing that you need to add or rid yourself of, for thoughts subside all on their own. You will be certain that in the uncontrived state of empty awareness, where thoughts leave no trace, everything is totally perfect and complete, and has been so from the very beginning. And so you will quite simply remain without fabricating anything, without hope or fear.

It is thus that your mind will be at ease and will find freedom in the dharmatā, the fundamental nature of the primordial ground. Recognizing that awareness, in all its present immediacy, dwells within you constantly, you will be able to relax without effort, contrivance, or alteration, quite naturally and in an ordinary way. To experience a complete confidence that the dharmakāya dwells within you—this is the uncontrived, spontaneously present result.

In brief, being now certain that the nature of your own mind is buddha, you will remain without any expectation or doubt, without contriving or altering anything, in that very state of your awareness. As all the notions of action, agent, effort, and striving fall apart, your mind will be deeply relaxed in the state of leaving everything as it is—the great and primordial openness and freedom. This is the fundamental nature of the Great Perfection. It is thus that you should train in the yoga free of all deliberate action, which is like the natural flow of a river.

In the earlier teaching tradition,[79] action and result were explained in only general terms. But because the key points of the view and meditation were explained in that tradition in the uncommon way [of Nyingtik], the action and result are set forth also in the present text in conjunction with the most secret key points found in the supporting trekchö texts *Stainless Space* and *Clouds in the Thought-Free Sky*.[80]

The foregoing teachings have thus set forth the essential instructions whereby one is able to reach a clear-cut certainty with regard to the mind. They explain the principal stages of the trekchö instructions through which all mental contrivance dissipates.

ii. Essential Instructions for the Path of Tögal

The essential instructions through which one reaches decisive certainty with regard to awareness are four in number: (1) the preliminary practice—namely, the training in the key points pertaining to body, speech, and mind; (2) the actual seeing of awareness by taking the support of five key points; (3) a description of the way the four visions arise on the basis of the practice; and (4) the supporting instructions. {193}

A) The Preliminary Practice

The preliminary practice has two stages: (1) rushen, separating samsara from nirvana, and (2) relinquishing the nine activities of body, speech, and mind.

1) Rushen, Separating Samsara from Nirvana

To protect the practice from obstacles, first prepare, if you are able, a feast offering complete with the requisite tormas, and offer it according to *The Wish-Fulfilling Sea: A Ritual for the Offering of Gaṇacakra.*[81] Offer a mandala of gold to the teacher. Then as a symbol of awareness that is free of all veils and obscurations, the disciples should strip naked or, if they are not comfortable doing so, they should at least take off their shirts.

With your palms joined at the level of your heart, stand with your ankles touching, facing your teacher who is also standing and turned to the east. Fix your gaze on your teacher's heart. In order to protect the practice from hindrances and to prevent the eight consciousnesses from being drawn away to sense objects, visualize your teacher as dark-blue and in terrifying form, with hair standing up, fangs bared, and rolled back tongue. His left hand is at his left hip, and, with his arm outstretched, his right hand is in the mudra of threatening. Starting from the east, he glares in all directions, thus repelling all negative forces.

Then from your teacher's heart, there issues a chain of *hūṃ* syllables, one after the other, which enter your body through the crown of your head. Imagine then that your body becomes a dark-blue *hūṃ* syllable. Throughout that time, you and your teacher both recite *hūṃ* with a humming sound. You should then visualize different syllables in the various places of your teacher's body. Imagine that they radiate outward and dissolve into the corresponding places of your own body. Visualize a green syllable *yaṃ* in your teacher's left foot, a red-green syllable *raṃ* in his navel, a smoky gray *khaṃ* in his throat, a blue *e* in his forehead, a yellow *suṃ* in his chin, a white *ha* in his right knee, and a blue-black *phaṭ* in his right foot. {194} As each of these eight syllables radiates outward [and dissolves into your body], you should, in one breath, recite the syllable in question twenty-one times. In this way, you will be protected.

In the tradition of *The Heart Essence of Karmapa*, the protection is created by both the teacher and disciple reciting twenty-one times the syllable *phaṭ*. In the tradition of the great Rikdzin Tsewang Norbu, on the other hand, once the preceding visualization has been done, *hūṃ* syllables stream from the *hūṃ* in the teacher's heart and enter the heart center of the disciple. Imagining that the body of the disciple is filled with *hūṃ* syllables, both teacher and disciple utter sharply three times the syllable *ha*. It is permissible to perform this practice simply—without making the feast offering at the beginning. It is thus that with the eight-syllable practice, one is protected from hindrances.

The rushen practice, the separation of samsara from nirvana, is then performed in the following manner. It is said in *The Word-Transcending Tantra*,

> If you do not separate samsara from nirvana,
> You will never break the bonds that bind
> The three worlds to your body, speech, and mind.
> Samsara and nirvana, therefore, are to be distinguished.

The body, speech, and mind of all beings are by their nature utterly pure from the very beginning. They are, however, temporarily veiled by deluded perception. This is why, from beginningless time, we circle without interruption in the worlds of the six classes of beings, experiencing their different, countless physical appearances, vocal expressions, ideas and thoughts, and suffering and pain—all of which are utterly bereft of meaning. What is the point of continuing to cling to this endless activity? The moment has come to separate the samsaric actions of body, speech, and mind from those of nirvana, thereby severing the root of samsaric birth. But how is this separation to be made? It is by taking as the path the various actions typical of the different karmic experiences of samsara that we will understand the defect of all the futile activities in which we have immersed ourselves. In so doing, {195} we will rid ourselves of our deeply ingrained clinging to such actions. It is said even in the common [teachings] of the Secret Mantra,

> Thought is purified by thought,
> Samsara by samsara.
> Just as water clears away
> The water trapped inside one's ears,
> Likewise, thoughts that cling to things
> Are purified by other thoughts![82]

Go therefore to a solitary place, a charnel ground, or an empty valley, and offer a torma to the ḍākinīs and the local spirits, commanding them not to interfere with your rushen practice of separating samsara from nirvana. Then give rise to the bodhicitta attitude, specifying that, for the sake of all beings, you will distinguish samsara from nirvana so that you will never be born in samsara again. Then imagine that you are experiencing the heat and cold of the hell realms, the hunger and thirst of the pretas, the slavery and exploitation of the animals. Then imagine the experience of birth, sickness, old age, and death of the human condition, the strife of the asuras, and finally the transmigration and fall of the gods and so on. Feel physically, express vocally, and experience mentally all the activities, sufferings, and joys of the six classes of beings. Make great effort in this until physically you are completely exhausted, you have no voice left, and the movements of your mind just stop—like the snapping of a weaver's thread.

It is also said that while you are doing this practice, you should imagine that your teacher in wrathful form performs all the same actions of the three doors as yourself. Later, when you are exhausted, on the physical level, sit upright; on the level of your speech, breathe naturally; and on the level of the mind, look directly at the one who is the subject of all these experiences. Settle yourself naturally and rest.

Then adopt all the physical demeanors of the sugatas and the peaceful and wrathful deities—uttering their mantras and speech, focusing mentally on their vivid and radiant forms. {196} Every so often, recite *A A* and preserve the nature of the ensuing mental state. When you manage to cut through the chain of thoughts, sit in the posture of the buddhas, recite the syllable *A*, and rest in a state of meditative evenness, leaving your mind in a thought-free state.

It is said that it is very important to perform this practice again and again until, on the physical level, you reach the point where you are free of all likes and dislikes and beyond refusal and acceptance in relation to heat, cold, hunger and thirst; until, on the level of speech, you have complete confidence in your teacher's instructions and your understanding naturally unfolds; and until your mind, luminous and empty, manifests unceasingly and without effort as self-arisen primordial wisdom.

The general purpose of this practice is to purify all negative actions of your body, speech, and mind and to remove hindrances. Your attachments and cravings will disappear. The final purpose of this practice is the attainment of manifest enlightenment, the vajra body, speech, and mind.

Once you have completed this practice, you should receive the extremely unelaborate and the supremely unelaborate empowerments and do as *The Testament* declares:

> Then acquire skill in bringing
> Your body, speech, and mind to their natural state.[83]

The practice mentioned earlier of separating samsara from nirvana will provoke disturbances in the elements of your body and you will feel exhausted. In order to rest, you should implement the practice of "bringing to the natural state" as described in the trekchö section. The extraordinary signs that may occur in this practice are explained in *The Great Heart Essence* and [Longchenpa's] *Precious Treasury of the Supreme Vehicle.*

2) Relinquishing the Nine Activities of Body, Speech, and Mind

It is said in *The Luminous Expanse Tantra,*

> That you may strike the crucial point of the direct perception [of awareness],
> Release your grip on actions, outer, inner, secret:
> The nine activities of body, speech, and mind.[84]

For the three activities of body, you should stay alone, outwardly relinquishing all deluded worldly deeds and distractions; inwardly leaving aside all lesser virtuous activities, such as prostrations, circumambulations, and so on; and secretly {197} refraining from all distracting physical movements.

For the three activities of speech, you should outwardly abandon all kinds of deluded, mundane talk; inwardly stop reciting prayers, mantras, and so on; and secretly refrain from any kind of utterance and vocal sound.

For the three activities of mind, you should remain in a state devoid of any support, outwardly relinquishing all conventional and deluded states of mind, inwardly leaving aside all the concentrations required for the generation- and perfection-stage practices, and secretly abandoning the appearing and subsiding of all thought processes.

This is how your three doors should be. And as you acquire stability in this, let go of even this state of being free from any action.

Throughout this period, you should practice as much as you can the extraordinary outer, inner, secret, and most secret guru practice according to *The Magical Ambrosia-Granting Tree: The Crucial Instructions on Luminosity.*[85]

B) Seeing Awareness Directly

For the direct vision of awareness[86] by relying on the five key points, (1) one takes support of immaculate primordial wisdom, after which (2) one is introduced to the direct vision.

1) Taking Support of Immaculate Primordial Wisdom

The teachings on tögal have seven special features on account of which they are superior to the teachings of trekchö. These seven features are as follows:

1. Phenomena are perceived as being made of light.
2. The implementation [of tögal] is related to [or depends on] practical guidance or demonstration.[87]
3. The self-experience of awareness is directly perceived.
4. The channels are controlled through the key points of bodily posture.
5. Awareness is seen through the [refined] organ of sight.
6. Objects are experienced by self-cognizing awareness.
7. Meditative experiences are greatly enhanced.

Endowed with these seven extraordinary features, the tögal teachings are implemented on the basis of five key points, which concern (1) body, (2) speech, (3) mind, (4) the sense door [of the eyes], and (5) the visual field or object.

a) The Key Point for the Body

This refers to three physical postures. The first is the dharmakāya posture of the lion. {198} Place the soles of your feet together pushing your knees apart. Make vajra fists, pressing the base of your ring fingers with your thumbs, and place the base of your wrists on the ground. Your arms should be held straight with your torso upright, your shoulders pressed back, and your neck bent slightly upward. Keep your eyes steady, not moving and without blinking. Your gaze should be relaxed, and you should look into the space in front at the level of your forehead. Your tongue should be slightly rolled upward.

The second posture is the elephant posture. Crouch down in a kneeling posture with your chest on your knees. Place your elbows on the ground with the palms of your hands supporting your chin and your fingers touching your cheeks. Keep your spine straight with your head turned slightly upward. Turn your eyes to the right and left gazing narrowly into space.[88]

The third posture is the nirmāṇakāya posture of a rishi. With your ankle bones close together, sit on the ground, your legs bent with your hands covering your knees. Keep your spine straight, and with half-closed eyes look into the sky.[89]

The first posture (the dharmakāya posture) purifies the elements. The second posture (of the elephant) settles the moving winds. The third posture (of the rishi) generates heat and balances the elements of the body. Ultimately one will find freedom in the three kāyas and pass beyond suffering. Self-cognizing primordial wisdom does indeed dwell within the body, but if the body is not skillfully pressed at its vital points, there is no possibility of seeing this wisdom in reality. It is like a snake, which does indeed have limbs though these are not visible unless the snake is squeezed.

b) The Key Point for Speech

Without uttering the slightest sound, breathe slowly and gently through your mouth with your lips and teeth apart, not touching. Train in holding your breath for a short time outside. {199}

c) The Key Point for the Mind

The view of trekchö is the basis for tögal. Considering that your eyes, the sky, and your awareness are not separate entities but are indivisible, watch a clear and empty sky, free from clouds and mist.

d) The Key Point for the Sense Door

The key point for the sense door [the eyes], is threefold. First, the dharmakāya gaze (looking at the sky with eyes turned upward as though looking at one's uṣṇīṣa) will produce a great increase in the [experience of the] ultimate expanse-awareness. Second, with the sambhogakāya gaze (looking narrowly like an arrow maker checking to see that his arrow is straight), the display of primordial wisdom will be seen. Finally, by means of the nirmāṇakāya gaze (looking slightly downward like a meditating rishi), the lamp of the disks of light will become visible.

In general, when you meditate, looking straight forward into the outer sky—as if you were throwing a spear into space—you will see the "outer expanse." By looking to the right or left or with half-closed eyes, you will behold the "inner expanse," awareness. As you focus your eyes [with these different ways of looking] and gaze into the sky, hallucinatory appearances will manifest as a buddha field. Whichever of the three gazes you train in, you should maintain it comfortably as you focus on the visual field concerned. If you persist too strongly in any of the gazes, the wind will be forced,[90] and this will result in obstacles. It is important to train yourself gently.

e) The Key Point for the Visual Field or Object

In the morning, look westward into a clear sky, free of clouds—or eastward if you perform the practice in the afternoon or evening. Moreover, for luminosity to arise easily, you should, in the morning, watch the sun's rays in the east (or in the west in the evening)—at the distance of a cubit, so to speak, beneath the sun itself. {200}

The key point here is that as you train, you should start by watching the light rays far from yourself [that is, closer to the sun] and then gradually draw them closer and closer to yourself [until they are right in front of you].

It is said that, at first, you create the foundation for the practice by adopting the sambhogakāya posture. Then, as you focus on the light rays, you bring your body under control by adopting the nirmāṇakāya posture. Finally, as you adopt the dharmakāya posture, you focus strongly on awareness and train in it.

On the other hand, it is also said that you should practice gazing in the dharmakāya posture mainly in the morning, in the sambhogakāya posture at noon, and in the nirmāṇakāya posture in the afternoon or evening. It is also said that once you have become proficient in the three main postures, you should continue the training by adopting the seven complementary postures. As it is said,

> There are seven postures for the body's seven vital points:
> Of tiger, of garuḍa, and of man,
> Of fox, of vulture, and of wrestler,
> And, added to these six, the posture of the crocodile.[91]

It is said in *The Extremely Profound Wheel of Dharmatā*,[92] that other postures and gazes, principal and complementary, are needed. When the appropriate moment comes, you should learn them from this text.

Furthermore, it is good at the beginning to combine the postures and gazes of the three kāyas. It is also said that it is good for beginners to practice mainly in the lion posture. On the other hand, *The Lamp for the Key Points of the Practice* in *The Innermost Essence of the Master* states, "Of the three, the sitting posture of the rishi is the one that should be practiced most. And of the three gazes, one should mainly look slightly downward. The other postures and gazes should be used only in a complementary fashion."[93] Given that the rishi posture is easy, it is the one most practiced nowadays.

As you use these key points [the postures and gazes] to train in the direct vision of primordial wisdom, you will gain, among other things, an unprecedented stability in awareness. The six crucial points of this training should be understood according to *The Three Key Points of the Wheel of Dharmatā*.[94] {201} Nevertheless, the present explanation, though brief, is a complete exposition of their meaning.

Everything that is to be understood in the present context is explained in *The Lamp for the Key Points of the Practice* as follows:

> If while practicing you do not see the disks of light but only some vague white glow, look straight ahead with both your eyes evenly focused. If you do not see a [five-colored] expanse, look toward the sun and then gradually to the side. If the disks of light are predominantly white, look rather at their right side. If they are predominantly yellow, look at their top part. If they are predominantly green, look at their left side. If they are predominantly red, look downward at their lower part. If they are predominantly blue, concentrate more on their center. Finally, if the five colors are evenly balanced, it is important to maintain the adopted gaze unchanging.
>
> In the daytime, train yourself using the sun as the support for the dharmakāya posture and gaze. Look at a point one cubit

below or to the left of the actual sun in the sky. It is thus that within an expanse of five colors, you will see vajra chains and disks of light. Then, adopting the sambhogakāya gaze, draw the rays of light further and further away from the sun, whether up or down, or laterally to the right or left, and settle your gaze directly on them. Alternatively, having adopted the nirmāṇakāya gaze and with your mind undistracted, look downward with your eyes unmoving, without speaking, and maintaining a motionless posture. It is thus that the visions of the five-colored expanse and of the vajra chains of awareness and the disks of light will intensify.

During the night, train in the way just described but this time with the moon as the support for the sambhogakāya posture and gaze. The particular feature in this case is that through staring undistractedly at the center of the moon, your perceptions of luminosity will develop. Moreover, if as a result of the daytime practice with the sun, there is an increase of heat in your eyes so that the clarity of the visions has been impaired, this will be counterbalanced by the coolness of the moon, and the visions will become very clear. This is a very important point. {202}

The training with lamps and so forth, as the support of the nirmāṇakāya, is similar though with the particular feature that in the course of your meditation you draw the light rays away from the center of the flame.

The purpose of these practices is as follows. Thanks to the daytime training with the fire crystal of the sun, luminous appearances will increase. Deluded daytime perceptions will come to an end and you will pass beyond suffering. By training during the night using the water crystal of the moon or other sources of light, five-colored lights will appear and the delusions of the night, together with all the different aspects of samsara, will be purified into the two form bodies. And freedom in the primordial state will be achieved.

In the early morning, you should focus mainly on the eastern direction until a white light appears. You should then draw the light to the south and rest there for a short while. Then drawing the light yet further, you should focus on the five-colored lights that fill the western direction. In the afternoon and early evening,

> train again, drawing toward the north the multicolored lights that appear in the west like an unfurled roll of brocade. If you are unable to lead the rays and they disappear, you should train yourself for a long time, focusing on the rays themselves without looking at their source and drawing them gradually further and further away. The most important thing is to watch the vajra chains that can be seen among the luminous appearances.[95]

For the practice of drawing the light from the east to the south and so on, you should stay in a "tögal house."[96]

2) Introduction to the Direct Vision of Awareness

For the introduction to the direct perception of awareness,[97] the visual field is the empty sky free of all adverse conditions [clouds and so on]. The sense organ is the unimpaired far-catching water lasso. The place required is a solitary and quiet location at a high altitude and free of all adverse conditions. In such a place, with your mind focused on the visual field, you will be naturally relaxed and without expectations and apprehensions, fabrication and alteration. In such conditions, the teacher should present the introduction to the visions as follows:

> In the sky in front of you, visualize five disks of light of five colors each one rimmed with rainbows. In the central disk, visualize me, your teacher, in the form of Samantabhadra in union with his consort and having the nature of Vairocana. {203} In the four disks in the four directions, visualize the buddhas of the four families in union with their consorts, and pray fervently to them.

Now recite sincerely and ardently whatever prayers are appropriate:

> When you have finished, all the buddhas dissolve into your heart. Mingle yourself with the indestructible quintessence—the state of ultimate nature, luminous character, and cognizant potency—in other words, self-cognizing luminous awareness. Remain in a state of meditative evenness and recite the six-syllable mantra of the Great Perfection [*'a A śa sa ma ha*] as much as you can.

After indicating all the visions that it is possible to perceive, depending on whatever postures and gazes one adopts, the teacher goes on to say:

> Now, according to the teachings of the sutras and the tantras, the sugatagarbha and the cause tantra[98] are explained and meditated upon on the level of the ordinary mind. Here, however, by means of profound essential instructions, it is awareness itself that is introduced directly, awareness that dwells as the ground and is endowed with the three primordially pure wisdoms—namely, its three aspects of ultimate nature, [luminous] character, and cognizant potency. In other words, unceasing, empty, and luminous awareness beyond all ontological extremes—beyond words and the ordinary mind—is here introduced directly. And the manner in which this is done is according to the three following instructions, which are intended for fortunate disciples of the highest capacity:
>
> Go to a solitary place and implement the key point for the body as I have explained. The visual field is the clear and cloudless sky. Watch therein awareness as I have said.
>
> The meaning of this is as follows. When you practice in this way, the outer expanse, the empty sky, is like a mirror. It supplies the space for the appearance of the visions of luminosity. The inner expanse, referred to as the "lamp of the utterly pure expanse," is like your own face. It is, in the beginning, an all-pervading deep-blue light, within which different colors—like rainbows or the iridescent eye on a peacock's feather—will gradually unfold. It is said in *The Blazing Lamp*,
>
> > Radiant lights of fivefold hue—
> > These become extremely bright.[99] {204}
>
> In the midst of these, there appears the "lamp of the empty disks of light." These disks are like the round ripples appearing on the surface of a lake when you throw a stone into it or like round shields. At first, the disks of light are vague, but gradually they will become increasingly radiant, red, and round. Inside will appear the vajra chains of awareness—your own mind, as it were. The vajra chains are very fine like strings of knots tied on

a horsehair. You will also see golden strings and strings of pearls, crisscross configurations, clusters of flowers, and nets of flowers. At first these will be unclear, vague, and trembling. Now leading them with your gaze, bring them into the fence or boundary of the expanse. Fix on them unwaveringly in a manner unspoiled by any kind of hope or fear, and meditate in such a way that you are conscious of them without stirring from the state of awareness.[100] In this way, they will become ever more firm and stable.

As it is said in *The Word-Transcending Tantra*,

> The chains of one's awareness
> Neither come nor go; they are simply in the sky.

As you watch the very face of the ultimate expanse-awareness in a manner free from all mental fabrication or alteration, these outer appearances will be unobstructed and unspoiled by inner clinging. As you remain steadily in this ineffable state, free of all mental elaboration, [knowing] subject and [known] object blend together inseparably and the appearances of luminosity emerge from the point between your eyebrows, neither too bright nor too dim. If this luminous display is not clear, if it is vague and fluctuates to the right or left, up or down, do not immediately follow it with your gaze or your attention. Instead draw it with your gaze into the place where it had previously arisen, and focus your mind on it—though not too tightly.

By training in this way, you will experience awareness. You will see directly awareness itself—the very face of the vajra chains. {205} And it is said that at that moment, you will be equal in fortune to Samantabhadra. It is as we find in *The Testament*:

> Whoever sees the key point that is the perception of
> awareness
> Will not return to the three worlds.[101]

And it is said in *The Tantra of Secret Action*,

> For the way of gazing at the ultimate expanse-awareness,
> Look into the stainless sky.

Rest in evenness upon the [vajra] chains
Within the ultimate expanse, and do not stir from them.
Those who see them so are, in their karmic fortune,
Equal to primordial Samantabhadra.[102]

Therefore, if you gain certainty in this and if you practice with diligence, you will progress in the experience of the four visions.

This completes the introduction [to the direct vision of awareness]. It is also specified in *The Great Order of Meditation: [The Lamp That Elucidates the Focal Points of Practice]*[103] that once it has been shown how the practice is to be implemented, it is important to understand it in light of the supporting essential instructions and thus gain confidence.

The supporting instructions for awareness contained in *The Copper-Lettered Instructions*, *The Conch-Lettered Instructions*,[104] and elsewhere explain the causes and conditions for the arising of the ultimate expanse-awareness. They clarify what is meant here by delusion and the absence of delusion. They demonstrate the authenticity of this practice and present the result in terms of the three kāyas. The causes and significance of the visions of the ultimate expanse-awareness are thus well explained, and this gives rise to a sure conviction.

If you wish and are able, work through the eight stages of the introduction according to *The Lamp That Illuminates the Metaphors and Meanings*.[105]

C) The Manner in Which the Four Visions Arise

1) The Direct Vision of the Dharmatā[106]

When, having relinquished all activity, you practice one-pointedly, gazing steadily at the vajra chains, you will first see, within the rainbow lights of the lamp of the utterly pure expanse, {206} the lamp of the empty disks of light—that is, as many as two linked orange disks of light the size of your thumb and encircled by two rims. Sometimes these will appear, sometimes not. The vajra chains will tremble and move around. Stop them from doing so by staring at them intently. In order to do this, the pith instructions say that you should focus your awareness without distraction on the lamp of the utterly pure expanse, which has emerged from between your eyebrows, and watch it. This is similar in shape to the Tibetan vowel sign *naro* and is in rainbow colors. This is said to be an extremely profound instruction called the "hook of stable holding."

2) The Vision of the Enhanced Experiences of Awareness[107]

At this stage, the five lights and the disks of light are constantly perceived. The luminous visions of five colors are like a tent of brocade. These, together with straight bands of light, both vertical and horizontal, also emerge from between your eyebrows at a distance of four fingers and then extend as far as you can see in the sky in front of you. Within the round disks of light, which are the display of the ultimate expanse, there appear fourfold clusters of what look like lotus petals. Thus far, this level of vision is referred to as the enhanced experiences of awareness.

3) The Vision of the Climax of Awareness[108]

The sky is filled with the luminous display of five-colored light, in the midst of which, within disks of light bounded by five rims, there appear, first, the uṣṇīṣa of a deity, and then gradually as much as half of the deity's body, then its entire body, and finally groups of five deities and so on until there are countless deities filling all the buddha fields.

4) The Vision of the Exhaustion of Phenomena in the Dharmatā[109]

Outwardly all appearances, inwardly your own illusory body, and secretly the wind-mind—together with all the enhanced experiences of awareness—come to exhaustion. Your body subsides into a body of light; your speech becomes the indestructible spontaneous sound of the dharmatā; and your mind with its duality of apprehender and apprehended, merges with the dharmakāya.

The details of these visions should be studied in the writings of the great omniscient Longchenpa, Lord of Dharma.

D) Supporting Instructions

The supporting instructions comprise a sequence of four stages. First the foundation [for the perfect stability of the ultimate expanse-awareness] is laid by the three kinds of motionlessness. Second, this [stability] is measured according to the three kinds of settling. {207} Third, it is riveted by three attainments. Fourth, freedom is measured through the four kinds of confident certainty.

1) The Three Kinds of Motionlessness

When practicing, you should stay physically motionless in one of the three postures. This will ensure that the channels and winds are naturally settled and thoughts will cease. Keep your eyes motionless, maintaining one of the three ways of gazing. It is thus that you will clearly see the dharmatā and will be freed from all misconceptions in its regard. The winds and awareness must also be motionless, free, and relaxed. It is thus that you will be in the state of the dharmatā and the mother and child luminosities will blend indivisibly. These three kinds of motionlessness are necessary if you are to remain in the primordial expanse.

It is at that time that the meaning of the four lamps may be discerned. In the channel of light[110] in the center of the heart,[111] the great primordial wisdom resides. Its empty nature inseparable from cognizant potency (that is, awareness), constitutes the "lamp of self-arisen wisdom."[112] The luminous character [of this great primordial wisdom], the palace of rainbow light, is the "lamp of the utterly pure expanse."[113] In its midst are clusters of disks of five-colored lights in which the buddhas of the five families are seen. This is the "lamp of the empty disks of light,"[114] which resembles the eye in a peacock's feather. When the inner radiance shines out through the pupils of the eyes, a reddish light appears, which is called the lamp of the empty disks of light. In fact, however, it is the radiance of this same lamp. Furthermore, the display of light that appears in the sky is called the lamp of the utterly pure expanse, but it is in fact no more than the radiance of this same lamp. Likewise, when one speaks of the vajra chains of awareness, these are simply the radiance of these vajra chains. As you meditate undistractedly, focusing outwardly on the vajra chains appearing within the expanse of light, primordial wisdom will arise inwardly, empty but luminous and free from all mental contrivance. This is "the lamp of self-arisen wisdom." {208} It is designated thus when this primordially present wisdom is reached through the implementation of the practice. This does not mean, however, that the lamp of self-arisen wisdom was somehow absent in the past and is now newly arisen.

2) The Three Kinds of Settling

As a consequence of this training, outer appearances will settle and adverse conditions will become auxiliaries to your practice. Inwardly, the illusory body will settle, and you will no longer engage in deluded action. Secretly, the wind-mind will settle, and it will be impossible for thoughts to arise.

It is at this time that you can take the measure [of your stability in the ultimate expanse-awareness]. This is done in relation to your dreams and by means of other signs manifesting on the level of body and speech. Regarding dreams, in the case of practitioners of the greatest diligence, dreams will come completely to a halt. Those of moderate diligence will experience lucid dreams, recognizing their dreams as such. As for practitioners of the least diligence, they will experience only good dreams, never bad ones.

There are four kinds of signs that appear in relation to body and speech. At the time of the direct vision of the dharmatā, your body will be powerless to move from the adopted posture, like a tortoise placed in a metal bowl. In the case of speech, you will be as if dumb; you will have literally nothing to say. And like a bird caught in a trap, your mind will not move from the ground nature, even though thoughts seem to arise.

At the time of the enhanced experiences of awareness, you will be like someone suffering from a serious illness; you will neither wash nor take care of your appearance. Your speech will be like that of a madman, completely incoherent and uninhibited. Your mind will be like that of someone who has been violently poisoned, the coming and going of thoughts will stop.

At the time of the climax of awareness, you will be able to pass unhindered through rocks and mountains like an elephant pushing its way unobstructed through the mud into which it has fallen. Your speech will be pleasant and beautiful like the voice of the young of the *kumbhanda* spirits.[115] Your mind will be like the mind of one who has been shot through the heart with an arrow—all movement and dissolution of thoughts and memories will cease. At the time of the exhaustion of phenomena in the dharmatā, physically you will not be caught up in any deluded acceptance or rejection—like a corpse in a charnel ground. As for your speech, you will merely repeat what others say to you, like an echo. Your mind will be like the mind of someone who has been cured of the plague—all {209} your thoughts and memories will subside into the ultimate expanse, and your awareness will be luminous and clear.

3) The Three Kinds of Attainment

Now that you have mastery over outer appearances, the phenomenal world will be as open and free as a buddha field. Inwardly, because you have mastery over the five aggregates, the illusory body will subside into the state of luminosity. Secretly, through your mastery over the ultimate expanse-awareness, deluded thoughts will cease.

4) The Four Kinds of Confident Certainty

[At this stage,] there is no hope of gaining buddhahood and no fear of not gaining it. There is no hope of escaping birth in samsara and no fear of being born there. One reaches decisive certainty with regard to awareness. All that has been said delineates the practice of tögal, which takes as the path the direct vision of this ultimate quintessence.

c. Conclusion: The Way of Constant Practice

The way of practicing this yoga constantly like a flowing river, as described in *The Three Key Points of the Wheel of Dharmatā*,[116] has two stages: (1) the practice itself followed by (2) additional explanations. The practice itself has in turn two instructions: (1) how to seal appearances during the day and (2) how to strike on the key point of primordial wisdom during the night.

i. How to Seal Appearances during the Day

According to *The Wheel of Most Profound Wisdom*,[117] the ground, path, and result must be protected with thirteen great samayas. Briefly, this means that you should not stain outer appearances and inner awareness (everything within phenomenal existence, samsara and nirvana) by conceptualizing and clinging or by becoming entangled in obsessive concerns about meditative experiences. Instead, train yourself in the attitude of thinking that whatever appears is like a dream or magical display. The mind too is empty and appears like a dream or magical illusion. It is a space-like state beyond all contrivance. It transcends the extremes of existence, nonexistence, both, and neither. It is beyond all partial attitudes, good and bad, and acceptance and rejection. Settle, therefore, in this state without removing or adding anything.

In the post-meditation periods, also, {210} do not lose yourself in distraction. Be mindful and tell yourself firmly that it is certain that all appearing phenomena are like magical illusions and tricks of sight. They are no more than the reflections of the moon in water, emanated apparitions, or castles in the clouds. Not even for an instant is there an atom of real existence in them. This is how you should train yourself. In the same way, you should practice bringing all dualistic perceptions—such as desire and aversion, acceptance and rejection, and hope and fear—into the nondual, primordially free state of awareness, which is open and unimpeded, preserving this state nakedly and free of thoughts.

ii. How to Strike on the Key Point of Primordial Wisdom during the Night

This is practiced in three stages: (1) in the evening, the faculties are gathered within; (2) at midnight, consciousness is made to "enter the vase;" and (3) at dawn, awareness is rendered lucid and clear.

A) The Evening Practice of Gathering the Faculties Within

Half of human life is spent in sleep. To make your sleep profitable, you should do the following. First, sit in the rishi posture of the nirmāṇakāya and visualize in the middle of your body the avadhūtī, or central channel—either white on the outside and red on the inside or else just pale-red and radiant. It is hollow like a bamboo shaft and is straight from the crown of your head to your secret center. In the navel center, there is a red lotus flower of four petals, in the middle of which there is a red *A*-stroke. It is as hot as when one blows on a charcoal brazier. In the upper extremity of the central channel, visualize a white letter *haṃ*. It is upside down. It has the nature of bliss and is glossy, as if drops of oil are about to drip from it. Concentrate on this for a short moment, laying the foundation for the experience of blissful warmth. Then expel the stale breath three times. Slowly inhale the upper breath while pulling up the lower wind from below. As you do this, red fire begins to burn vigorously from the *A*-stroke. As it reaches the letter *haṃ* in the crown of your head, a continuous stream of blissful bodhicitta flows down from it and feeds the fire, which blazes up more and more, burning away all the results of your karma together with your habitual tendencies. The nectar, the melted lunar essence, fills the central channel and all the other channels in your body. {211} An extraordinary experience of the blissful warmth of primordial wisdom will then arise. Focus on this, holding the vase breath as much as you can. When you get tired, start again, training yourself in the visualization just described as much as you are able, breathing normally.

B) The Midnight Practice of Causing One's Consciousness to Enter the Vase

Although it is taught that you should assume the sambhogakāya posture or lie on your right side, it is said here that for the actual sleeping practice, you should sit in the rishi posture. As before, visualize the central channel in the middle of your body, but this time, concentrate for a moment on a white syllable *A* blazing with light in the center of a slightly opened, red, four-petaled lotus in your heart. Now visualize another white syllable *A* in the crown of your head. Between these two syllables visualize a series of twenty-one *A*-syllables. They are very fine and as if threaded on a string. If you are proficient in the wind yoga, hold the vase breath, thereby joining together the upper and lower winds. Otherwise, hold the gentle vase breath and meditate as much as you can on the vivid state of primordial wisdom, empty yet luminous. When you are on the point of falling asleep, the *A*-syllables gradually dissolve, one into the other, down to the syllable in your heart, after which the *A*-syllable in your head also quickly dissolves into the syllable in your heart. The lotus in your heart then closes and you imagine that the *A*-syllable is like a flame enclosed within a vase.

It is thus that—neither too tight nor too lose—you should go to sleep, with the conscious desire to recognize your dreams as dreams. If sleep does not come, repeat again and again the foregoing visualization. Until you sleep and begin to dream, it is important to train without being interrupted by other thoughts. If thoughts arise, however, neither suppress them nor get involved with them, neither encourage nor stop them. Do not block or follow them. Instead, bring your mind back, and place it on the *A*-syllable. Before falling into a light sleep when dreams occur, you will have vague thoughts—images of people, buildings, and so on. {212} Since these are the causes of your dreams, you should, without opening your eyes, think strongly that these thoughts *are* dreams, focusing and settling your mind on the *A*-syllable. By doing this you will be able to recognize your dreams as dreams. It is like when you are trying to thread a needle. It is easier to do it if you twist the end of the thread. After you have trained like this for some time, you will find that even when you are in a heavy and dreamless sleep, you will have a vivid experience of primordial wisdom that is like an empty, luminous sky. And if this experience is maintained, you will arise in a body similar to the illusory body of a yidam deity and you will rest in a state devoid of clinging and mental contrivance. If you do dream, you should dissolve all your dreams and thoughts into the *A*-syllable in your heart and meditate as before. It is thus that the state of luminosity, self-arisen primordial wisdom, will arise.

Even during the day, train yourself by strongly reflecting that everything is just a dream. Transform appearances into peaceful and wrathful deities, and multiply their number. From time to time, change and multiply all the different karmic perceptions of samsara. Travel to pure and impure fields and examine their way of being. Moreover, when you actually come across terrifying sights and situations—such as fires, floods, precipices, and wild and ferocious animals—train yourself to overcome your fears keenly and with great energy, telling yourself that they are just dreams. The result will be that, at night, just as you have trained yourself during the day, you will be able to transform and multiply according to your wish the things encountered in your dreams. It is said that, at first, such visions will be vague but that in time they will become clearer and more stable. When you fall asleep, moreover, you will see what is happening around you, you will hear sounds, perceive odors, tastes, and tactile sensations, and hear conversations, but no thoughts will arise. And at such a time, it is not that you are not asleep, for it is a state from which you can be roused.

If you fail to recognize your dreams as such, then even though you are trying with great endeavor to do so, this is due to some sort of deviation, of which there are four kinds.[118] The methods with which to eliminate them, {213} the key points for the moment when dreams are recognized, and the classification into subtle luminosity and the luminosity of deep sleep and so on are as described in the texts of general instructions.

C) The Dawn Practice for Making Awareness Lucid and Clear

During the dawn session, assume the lion posture and again visualize a shining syllable *A* in your heart. Stare into the sky and breathe out three times [through your mouth] with the sound *ha*. The lotus in your heart (which was closed when you went to sleep) now opens and the syllable *A* shoots up straight through the Brahmā aperture and remains above your head at a distance of a bow-length, about four cubits. Concentrate on the syllable, and train a little in holding your breath outside. This will bring about an excellent state of concentration free of any thoughts. If your mind becomes wild with distraction, bring the syllable lower and lower and when it is again in your heart, focus on it. Meditate with half-opened eyes and with your gaze lowered. If your mind sinks into dullness, meditate as before [on the *A*-syllable in the space above your head]. Freed in this way from agitation or dullness, primordial wisdom devoid of all ordinary cognition will manifest like a flowing river.

As you practice in this way in the three successive sessions of the night, the excellent concentration of bliss [in the evening], luminosity [at midnight], and no-thought [at dawn] will occur, and you will certainly acquire all kinds of preternatural knowledge, swiftly gaining freedom in the expanse of Samantabhadra, beyond all effort and striving. The great omniscient Longchenpa has said,

> In all your meditation sessions, day and night, see to it that your eight freedoms do not go to waste, for all such freedoms, as well as the ten advantages, are difficult to find. Knowing that life is impermanent, do not postpone your practice. Knowing that samsara is suffering, feel great weariness with the world. Knowing that phenomena are without intrinsic being, do not cling to them as truly existent things. Knowing that nirvana, the state beyond suffering, is supremely blissful, practice with the aim of acquiring the peace of enlightenment. And since the Secret Mantrayāna is accomplished with skillful means, train yourself in various paths. {214} The Mahāyāna depends upon compassion, so cultivate bodhicitta for the sake of others. Blessings depend upon devotion to one's teacher, so train yourself to see your teacher as fully enlightened. Everything comes down to your own mind; so train yourself in impartiality and pure perception. Samsara appears because of deluded thought; so cut the root of dualistic clinging to apprehender and apprehended. Happiness and suffering derive from past action; so practice virtue and abandon evil. And since samsara and nirvana both arise from awareness, recognize that their crucial point is awareness itself. To tame

your mind by means of these twelve points is a most important instruction. Reflect on them sincerely.[119]

d. Additional Instructions

The visualizations described above—their meaning and purpose, the signs of their success in terms of physical and mental experiences, the elimination of obstacles and the enhancement of the practice, together with the ways to introduce students to the nature of the mind according to their meditative experience should be grasped in light of scriptures such as the root text of *The Copper-Lettered Instructions*[120] and *The Innermost Essence of the Master: The Wish-Fulfilling Gem*, which is a commentary on its meaning. You should keep these two texts close to you without ever parting from them. In particular, your own body is the basis of the practice. If, therefore, it is hindered by illness or negative forces, you should rely on the text titled *The Wish-Fulfilling Tree of Nectar for the Removal of Hindrances.*[121] And since the key point of the direct seeing of the dharmatā has to do with the eyes, if any harm comes to them, you should rely on *The Illuminating Lamp for the Removal of Hindrances.*[122] Finally, since awareness is the root of the mind practice, if the mind itself falls prey to obstacles, you should rely on *The Stainless Wisdom for the Removal of Hindrances.*[123] Do not leave the words of these instructions unimplemented on the page.

The crucial method for the enhancement of both trekchö and tögal practice is found in the instruction on the three skies. The outer sky, clear blue and cloudless, is uncompounded space unstained by dust. The inner sky is the secret avadhūtī, the secret central channel. This is the *kati*, the crystal channel that rises from the oceanic golden sun and is connected with the water lamp of the far-catching lasso. These two {215} are pervaded by the secret sky, the indestructible sphere in the heart. This threefold sky is not a composite, consisting of three impure expanses. It is by nature the pure, indestructible luminosity, which is altogether characterized by the three aspects of ultimate nature, [luminous] character, and cognizant potency. The example given for the first sky is that of a mirror free of dust. The example for the second sky is the eye of an archer.[124] The example for the third sky is the *ketaka* jewel.

Generally speaking, the so-called central channel is visible to the eye consciousness. This channel is present now in the body and is located just behind the backbone. It is also called the life channel, and it is this that generates the dualistic perceptions of samsara. By contrast, the secret avadhūtī, or central channel, which is posited as the inner sky, is not within the domain of the visual consciousness. It is a channel endowed with the five essences and dwells within the heart of embodied beings. Two channels branch out from this central channel and enter the eyes. The channel located in the heart is referred to as the oceanic golden sun, and the two channels that branch out from it are called the water lamp of the far-catching lasso. These three channels constitute the "support-sky," the sky pervaded [by the secret sky]. They form the central channel, the nature of which is utterly pure. This is the great and quintessential avadhūtī. It is the very nature of the two [branch] channels. It is subsumed within them, with the result that these two branch channels are called by the same name. They are both the inner sky.

Now the secret sky is the sphere endowed with the five quintessences. It is intrinsically luminous. It is marked by the three aspects of ultimate nature, [luminous] character, and cognizant potency. It is moreover the "supported," that by which [the inner sky] is pervaded.

According to this understanding, when you look at the limpid outer sky, adopting any of the physical postures just described, it is through focusing on the inner sky that you focus on the secret sky. It is thus that primordial wisdom, which is beyond all ordinary cognition, will manifest unobstructed within your mental continuum. {216} For the practices and so on of the dark retreat, you should consult *The Wheel of the Primordial Wisdom of Luminosity*.[125]

Instructions for the dissipation of obstacles, the enhancement of the practice, and the conduct to be adopted in the post-meditation periods have been set forth concisely by the omniscient Lord of Dharma as follows:

> Understanding that all appearances are unreal in the manner of the eight examples of illusion, free yourself from the defilements of attachment, aversion, and so on. In the clear conviction that all that arises as the display of the affirming and negating mind is groundless and rootless, do not cling to anything; do not adopt or reject anything. Until your ego-clinging vanishes into the ultimate expanse, meditate on the profound instructions and be attentive to the law of karma. Practice pure perception, cultivate devotion, and render your mind free of faults. Keep your vows

> and samaya pledges, and remain alone in solitude. Rid yourself of distraction and busy activities, and keep to the attitude of thinking that you have no need of anything. Be without attachment and craving, and take freedom from clinging as your path. At all times be mindful of death, and your diligence will blaze like a fire. Practicing virtue day and night, leave aside this life's activities. Rely at all times on your teacher and pray devotedly to him. Take as your path the absence of any target, and rest in the state that is free of action. Let go of the dualistic thought of self and other, and thereby free yourself of fear and expectation. Bringing all adversity onto the path, consider as your teacher every situation that arises. Knowing that everything is the self-experience of awareness, throw away your ego-clinging and desires. Since all things are without any core, keep to the view that they are devoid of true existence. Because you know that all things are naturally—primordially—empty, everything will arise quite naturally as the self-experience of awareness. Spend your days and nights in all such skillful ways.
>
> As long as your mind is influenced by circumstances, train yourself skillfully in awareness and devote yourself to practice in solitude. As long as you have clinging—as long as you affirm and negate—you should engage in positive action, avoid all evil doing, and train yourself in nonduality. For as long as every circumstance does not yet manifest as a friend, school your mind by implementing the instructions and watch the state of awareness. {217} As long as you fear death and rebirth, train yourself in [the understanding of] unborn reality. But when all phenomena, outer and inner, arise as the dharmatā, rest in the riverlike stream of the yoga of nonmeditation.[126]

Hold these counsels dear as a nectar for your mind. In addition, the essential teachings on how to distinguish awareness from the ordinary mind—which are very important in the present context of guiding instructions—should be understood according to texts like *Stainless Space: A Supporting Instruction for Trekchö*.[127]

2. Instructions for Practitioners of Moderate Diligence

For practitioners of moderate diligence or medium capacity, who find freedom while in the bardo, the instructions fall into three sections: (1) the nature of the bardo is defined, (2) the classifications of the bardo state are explained, and (3) the practices connected with the various bardo states are described.

a. The Nature of the Bardo

Whatever is perceived as separate from the primordially pure ground is a bardo state. The appearances of the ground—namely, the appearances that arise as primordial wisdom—are the bardo of pure dharmatā. By contrast, hallucinatory appearances, the phenomena of the six realms of beings, are the bardo of impure delusion. This is the bardo of the ordinary mind together with its seed. It begins from the point when it arises from the primordially pure expanse and lasts until it ends in the ultimate expanse, the ground from which it has arisen.

b. The Classifications of the Bardo

The bardo may be classified into four states. There is the bardo of this life, between birth and death, which is sometimes called the natural bardo. Then there is the bardo of the moment of death, which is followed by the bardo of ultimate reality, followed by the bardo of becoming. The bardo of this life corresponds to the period beginning with the moment of conception in the mother's womb and ending with death due to some physical deficiency. The bardo of the moment of death is the period between the beginning of the death process and the stopping of the inner breath. The bardo of ultimate reality begins with the cessation of the inner breath and the arising of the display of luminosity and lasts until the appearances of spontaneous presence cease. The bardo of becoming is the period between the dissolution of the appearances of spontaneous presence and the creation of the next life.

c. The Practices Connected with the Different Bardos

The practices connected with the four bardos are indicated through examples and the meanings that these examples convey. The practice for the bardo of this life has to do with the elimination of all kinds of misunderstanding. It is illustrated by the way the swallow enters its nest, [directly and without hesitation]. The meaning indicated here {218} is that when you follow a teacher and when you listen to the teachings and reflect on them, you eliminate misunderstanding. Then you unerringly experience the fundamental nature in meditation. And as all misconceptions about awareness are eliminated, the four paths of learning and the qualities of the ten grounds are perfected, and the resultant path of no more learning is actualized.

[The practice for] the bardo of the moment of death concerns the way you remind yourself [of the teachings]. This is illustrated by the image of a beautiful lady gazing at herself in a looking glass. At the moment of death, you should recall all the instructions on which you have previously meditated. How is this done? Keeping clearly in mind the crucial points set forth in the instructions regarding the luminosity at the time of death and the various associated stages of dissolution, you should watch the luminosity and settle your awareness in a state of clarity and emptiness. It is thus that the luminosity of the present moment, which acts like an escort, and the luminosity of the bardo, which comes forth to welcome you arise simultaneously—just as on the fifteenth day of the lunar month, the sun sets at the same moment that the moon rises. And at that moment, you will find freedom.

It is said in *The Union of the Sun and Moon Tantra,*

> When earth dissolves into the earth,
> The body is weighed down, takes no more food.
> It has no further strength to rise and walk.
> When water into water melts,
> Moisture drips from nose and mouth.
> So too when fire melts into fire,
> The mouth and nose completely dry,
> From limbs the body's warmth escapes.
> And when the wind dissolves into the wind,
> The breath comes wheezing, and the limbs will tremble,
> While eyes turn up with backward gaze.
> Those in whom these signs appear
> Are certain now to pass from life.
> Let them then recall and concentrate
> Upon the teachings of their master.[128]

If at this moment you can recall lucidly and without a moment's distraction the instructions that you have received, then when the wind dissolves into consciousness, the mother and child luminosities—the one already present beforehand and the other arising later—will meet, and you will gain freedom in the primordial expanse.

{219} While in the bardo of ultimate reality, you should have trust in the self-experience of awareness. This confidence must be like that of a child climbing into its mother lap. Once you have experience of the truth of the instructions, then no matter how the appearances of ultimate reality arise, you will be without fear and you will recognize them—throughout the five stages of dissolution—as but the self-experience of awareness, the display of primordial wisdom. First, when consciousness dissolves into space, awareness enters into the channel of light and rests in the eyes. In that first instant, there will arise the vision of primordial purity, a luminosity without center and periphery, like the cloudless sky of autumn. Second, when space dissolves into luminosity, this vision instantaneously changes,[129] and there arise the perceptions of the five lights and the three factors (sounds, lights, and luminous rays), which fill the whole of space. Third, when luminosity dissolves into the state of union, there gradually arise—in the course of five days of samādhi[130]—the gatherings of the five buddha families. Fourth, this state of union dissolves into primordial wisdom and the bands of colored lights of the four wisdoms and disks of light occur. Fifth, when primordial wisdom dissolves into spontaneous presence, the buddha field of the primordial purity of the dharmakāya appears in the upper area, the fields of the five families of the sambhogakāya appear in front, and the buddha field of the nirmāṇakāya, guide of beings, appears in the lower area. But no matter what vision of ultimate reality arises at that time, you will be without fear. And just as if you were meeting an old friend, you will have a clear certainty that all is but the self-experience of awareness, the display of primordial wisdom. Whether or not these dissolutions appear successively and in order is not certain, for this reflects the varying capacities of beings. According to *The Union of the Sun and Moon*, practitioners of the highest capacity will gain freedom just at the moment when the body is discarded and luminosity arises. Those of medium capacity will gain freedom in any of the visions of the state of union or visions of primordial wisdom. Practitioners of least capacity will gain freedom in the visions of spontaneous presence.

These visions will moreover continue to occur until the vision dawns in which you find freedom. After that, they simply dissolve into the ultimate expanse and arise no more. {220} When the vision in which you are to find freedom arises, in the first instant, you recognize it as the self-experience of awareness. In the second instant, you rest in this recognition. In the third instant, resting thus, you are liberated. In the fourth instant, being liberated, you emanate different forms in the fields of beings, and in the fifth instant, you dwell in the vase body of inner luminosity. For the most part, these instants are "instants of the completion of an action," and their duration is altogether uncertain. A "meditation day" refers to a period of meditation in one's preceding existence in which one remained in a state of perfect concentration until an ensuing thought occurred. This is only a summary description of these instants. On the basis of *The Lamp of the Crucial Points of Practice*,[131] you should grasp the crucial point of understanding that you are experiencing the visions of the bardo of ultimate reality,[132] the crucial point of gaining stability in the state of openness and freedom,[133] the crucial point of perfect recognition,[134] and so on.

In the bardo of becoming, residual karma continues to manifest as though through an extension inserted into the end of a broken water pipe. Terrible and fearful hallucinatory appearances will arise, but thanks to your previous training in the teachings, you will be able to set out on the path to a pure rebirth.

The following events may occur depending on the varying capacities of different practitioners. Even if you have recognized awareness directly [when it was introduced], if you have not meditated on it sufficiently, you will gain freedom only after several lifetimes. And even if you have meditated but are weak in concentration, it may happen that when the appearances of spontaneous presence manifest and, respectively, the earlier and later luminosities simultaneously subside and arise, you will fail to recognize these spontaneously present appearances as the self-experience of awareness. The appearances will vanish and because your consciousness is now free of its bodily shell, the karmic winds of the subtle four elements will now arise in reverse order, and your mental bardo body will be formed. Your perceptions will be hazy, evanescent, and fitful. All sorts of things will manifest, like feathers blown along by the wind. In your mental body you will be able to pass unhindered through objects composed of the four elements, and you will have all kinds of preternatural karmic abilities. You will have a subtle clairvoyance, sharpened sense faculties, and a clarity of mind not possessed before; and with the pure divine eye you will be able to perceive other beings in the same predicament as yourself [that is, in the bardo]. {221} Thanks to the habitual tendencies that you have acquired, you will be able to visit the places where your relatives live and speak to them. They will not answer, of course, for they will neither see nor hear you. It is then that you will realize that you have died, and remembering the instructions that you have received, you will recognize the nature of all the terrors and hallucinatory appearances of the entire bardo.

Depending on the varying mental capacities of practitioners, the following will occur. Practitioners of superior capacity will take devotion to their teacher as their path. And understanding that all phenomenal appearances included within the two categories of objects of apprehension and the apprehending mind are devoid of real existence and are like magical illusions, they will gain freedom.

Practitioners of medium capacity will gain freedom by relying on the practice of the union of the stages of generation and perfection related to their yidam deity. Practitioners of least capacity, keeping in mind a pure field, should visualize in the space in front of them two red interpenetrating trihedrons [three-dimensional three-sided pyramids] with bases uppermost and points downward. They should then imagine that in the center of their flat base is their own minds in the form of a white syllable *A*. With strong prayer, they should imagine that this double trihedron is projected like a shooting star into the pure field, where the practitioners in question, resting in a state free of all mental elaboration, gain freedom. And even if they fail to achieve liberation, they will escape a bad rebirth in their subsequent existence, selecting a good one in the following way. They should meditate on their future parents in the place of their next life in the form of father-mother yidam deities and should visualize the womb of their future mother as a lotus surmounted by a sun and moon disk on which there is a white syllable *hūṃ*. They should then pray one-pointedly that when their consciousness enters the womb [thus visualized], they will be able to work greatly for the doctrine and beings in the bodily support that they will receive. Visualizing themselves in the form of Vajrasattva, they should imagine that they dissolve into the *hūṃ* in the womb of their mother. Resting in the state of emptiness devoid of all mental elaboration, they will be born as children of parents devoted to the dharma and will encounter the teachings already in their childhood. They will be intelligent and diligent, and when the residual karma of their previous training awakens, they will meet the essential doctrine and continue on the path that remains to them. {222} They will surely attain enlightenment in that very life or in the bardo state.

3. Instructions for Those of Least Diligence

The instructions for practitioners of least diligence or capacity, who achieve enlightenment in the nirmāṇakāya buddha fields of luminous character, cover three topics: (1) training during the natural bardo of this life, (2) the transference of consciousness while in the bardo, and (3) gaining of freedom in a nirmāṇakāya buddha field.

a. Training during the Natural Bardo of This Life

For practitioners who train themselves night and day in the direct vision of the dharmatā, bad dreams cease and only good dreams occur. Such practitioners remain moreover for a long time in the concentrations of bliss, luminosity, and no-thought. At that stage, they should, during the day, visualize the nirmāṇakāya buddha field and project their awareness—in the form of a ball of light—from their eyes into the heart of the main deity of the buddha field in question. At night, as they lie down, they should visualize their surroundings as a nirmāṇakāya buddha field of luminous character, their own body as an immeasurable palace, their heart as a lotus with sun and moon, in the center of which are the buddhas of the five families. And they should fall asleep concentrating on them without distraction. If they manage to do this, it is certain that they will visit that same buddha field in their dreams. This extremely profound instruction is taken from the commentary to *The Union of the Sun and Moon Tantra*.

b. The Transference of Consciousness while in the Bardo

This instruction covers two topics: (1) the teaching contained in this text and (2) a description of the way in which lazy practitioners are reborn in a buddha field on the basis of a pith instruction for the sudden transference of consciousness.

i. The Teaching of This Text

When the self-experience of awareness, the luminosity of the bardo, dissipates, there comes the realization that one is in the bardo. At that moment, and thanks to the previous visualization of a buddha field, it will be possible to go and be born there. This happens through the blessing of the truth of the dharmatā and thanks to the compassion of the vidyādhara teachers. It is also possible because beings in the bardo possess supernatural powers and are able to go wherever they wish. It is said that some people are reborn in the buddha fields as soon as their body and mind separate, whereas others do so at the point when the state of luminosity dissipates. Some remain in the bardo of becoming as though in a dream state for a period of seven days and more, {223} after which, as though awaking from a dream, they are miraculously born in the eastern buddha field of Abhirati and so on. These three ways of birth in a buddha field correspond to the strength of one's practice—superior, medium, or lesser.

ii. The Sudden Transference of Consciousness into a Buddha Field

This describes how lazy practitioners are reborn in a buddha field on the basis of an essential instruction for the sudden transference of their consciousness. Such practitioners should implement the instruction known as *The Essence of Luminosity*,[135] which is found in *The Golden Garland.* If [the transference] is performed according to this method, the directions given in the present text are unnecessary. Otherwise, one should proceed as follows.

First take refuge, generate the attitude of bodhicitta, and practice the guru yoga. Then, sitting on a comfortable seat in the seven-point posture, implement the following six steps: concentration on the "fence of emptiness," visualization of the [central] channel, gathering the wind-mind [into the heart], training in "departure and reception," dispelling obstacles, and finally the actual transference.

First train yourself by considering that within the boundary of your body's skin, there is an empty space free of any obstruction. Second, meditate on the central channel in the middle of your body. It is radiantly clear and as straight as a bamboo arrow, running from the crown of your head to your secret center. Third, in a sphere of five-colored light visualized within your heart, concentrate on the unchanging quintessence of the wind-mind in the form of a white syllable *A*. It is bright and sparkling and the size of a small pea. When ordinary thoughts cease and you are one-pointedly concentrated on the *A*-syllable, this is a sign that the meditation has succeeded. This is what is meant by the state of Samantabhadra in union with his consort, the ground for the arising of the sambhogakāya.

Fourth, visualize within the space at the crown of your head the buddha field of Akaniṣṭha, the field of precious spontaneous presence. In the center of a sphere of five-colored, swirling light, visualize Vairocana in union with his consort. He is inseparable from your own root teacher. He is in the attire of the sambhogakāya and is surrounded by Akṣobhya and the rest of the buddhas of the five families, together with ḍākas and ḍākinīs. {224} Arouse within yourself a powerful feeling of devotion toward them all. Melodiously chanting the syllables *A āḥ* one hundred and eight times, imagine that the syllable *A* in your heart rises higher and higher, quickly dissolving into the heart of Vairocana. Rest in meditative evenness and then imagine that with a feeling of vibrant bliss, the *A* descends from the heart of Vairocana and returns to your own heart.

In order to reduce obstacles to a minimum, visualize within your Brahmā aperture a white syllable *haṃ* from which a stream of nectar flows and dissolves into the luminous sphere of your consciousness [the syllable *A* in your heart]. Finally, this sphere blends into a single taste with the syllable *haṃ* and dissolves into the heart of Vairocana. Then imagine that the buddhas of the five families ascend higher and higher, becoming smaller and smaller, until they vanish like a rainbow melting into the sky. You should then recite the syllable *A* as many times as is appropriate and rest in a state of luminosity and emptiness devoid of all mental contrivance.

If in the past you have trained successfully in the transference of consciousness, it is enough to perform it only when the need arises. On the other hand, if you have not so trained, you should perform this meditation for up to seven days until you receive a sign of success.

In order to dispel obstacles, the fifth step is to practice the vajra recitation as much as you can—that is, the recitation combined with the inhalation, retention, and exhalation of the breath. You should then dedicate the merit.

The sixth step is to perform the actual transference of consciousness when the signs appear indicating that the death process has irreversibly set in and cannot be avoided. Thinking that the Brahmā aperture at the crown of your head is wide open, imagine, as before, that the sphere of light (your consciousness) dissolves into the heart of Vairocana. This time, however, it does not fall back. Visualize this once, twice, or three times as appropriate. In conclusion, and as before, the group of the buddhas of the five families ascends higher and higher. Finally, within the state in which there is nothing to be transferred and no one who performs the transference, release your mind into a state of blissful purity. It is thus that you will recognize the luminosity of the bardo state but will not go on to perceive the abyss of the bardo of becoming. You will thus attain enlightenment in the buddha field of the ever-youthful vase body, the state of Samantabhadra, and will gain mastery of the enlightened activities that spontaneously accomplish the twofold goal. {225}

c. Gaining Freedom in the Nirmāṇakāya Buddha Fields

Practitioners who have directly beheld the dharmatā but have not yet gained stability in it, must continue to meditate. There are others who have meditated but whose concentration is weak and who are thus unable to gain freedom in the bardo. Consequently, when the bardo of ultimate reality arises, they fail to recognize it, with the result that the bardo of becoming unfolds for them like the deluded visions of a dream. When this occurs, it is through the blessing power that results from having seen and understood the teachings of the Great Perfection that they are reborn in a pure buddha field, such as Abhirati—as if they were waking from a dream. They see the tathāgatas, hear their teachings, and receive empowerments and transmissions. They are encouraged, receive predictions, and are uplifted in praise. And they are released from the fetters of their defilements and in an instant come to freedom in the primordial buddha field.

D. The Results of the Practice

Here three topics are discussed: (1) the various ways of achieving buddhahood, (2) the compassionate activities of the buddhas, and (3) the moment when the result is gained.

1. Different Ways of Achieving Buddhahood

Three ways of gaining freedom have been explained in this text [according to the three capacities of disciples]. In addition, one speaks of two ways of gaining buddhahood: buddhahood without remainder and buddhahood with remainder.

Nirvana without remainder occurs when all gross and subtle defilements and the physical body itself (composed as it is of the elements) are purified and are no more. Since the ultimate nature of the mind awakens into the kāyas, the three kāyas are inseparable. Since the luminous character blossoms into the primordial wisdom of omniscience, this wisdom is inseparable from the five lights. And since cognizant potency blossoms into the activities of enlightenment, compassion is uninterrupted. This constitutes "perfect genuine buddhahood." It is, moreover, considered to be a buddhahood occurring in the course of the present life or in the nirmāṇakāya buddha fields of luminous character.

Nirvana with remainder refers to the manner in which the result—namely, the qualities of the path—is achieved on the basis of the practice related to primordial purity and spontaneous presence. {226} It is thus that by progressing gradually through the qualities of the grounds and paths, and after leaving behind the physical body as a kind of residue, one achieves buddhahood in the bardo. This event is attended by all the outer and inner signs: lights, sounds, earthquakes, images of deities in the bones, large round indestructible relics, and so on. This is also described as "perfect and manifest buddhahood."

2. The Compassionate Activities of Buddhahood

However one may achieve buddhahood through the three ways of gaining freedom, compassionate enlightened activities always follow. According to the limitless aspirations of beings, and through the two form bodies present within one's continuum, one will display the "sambhogakāya that appears to others"[136] for the bodhisattvas residing on the grounds, and the "nirmāṇakāya that guides according to need" for ordinary beings who are to be trained.

While never stirring from the inner luminosity in which the kāyas and wisdoms are inseparably merged—the expanse that is motionless and unchanging throughout the passage of time—the sambhogakāya and the nirmāṇakāya strive for the sake of others in the buddha fields of the ten directions in just the same way that the moon aloft in the sky is reflected in many vessels filled with pure water. They work for beings as long as samsara lasts, effortlessly, spontaneously, and uninterruptedly, like the wish-fulfilling jewel and the tree of miracles.

3. The Moment when the Result Is Gained

It is said in *The Instructions on the Testaments*, "Whoever makes direct connection with the pith instructions of the utterly secret Heart Essence will be linked directly to the state beyond all sorrow."[137] So it is that if the instructions of the unsurpassed secret are one-pointedly practiced, those of highest capacity will gain freedom in one life and one body. Those of high capacity will come to freedom in the space of three lives, those of medium capacity in five lives, and those of least capacity in seven lives. This is proclaimed unanimously by the tantras and the assemblies of accomplished vidyādharas. {227}

E. Additional Teachings

The key points of the practice are now laid out as an appendix. There are two parts to this: (1) a general outline of the instructions and (2) a classification of the practice.

1. A General Outline of the Instructions

It is said that there are three ways in which the teachings of the Great Perfection are given: (1) by way of guiding instructions, (2) as an introduction to the nature of the mind, and (3) as essentialized but complete instructions given to departing travelers.

a. Teachings Given as Guiding Instructions

When disciples have completed any of the three preliminary practices, they are introduced to the main practice and receive supporting teachings that are designed to bring them to a state of conviction. Those who have many thoughts and who like to see signs of success or warmth in the practice should first train in the instructions associated with the three kāyas—that is, in the nature and sound of the four elements. They are then introduced to the main practice. Diligent disciples who are drawn to yogic discipline first train in the instructions related to awareness—namely, the rushen practice through which samsara is separated from nirvana. They are then introduced to the main practice. Lazy disciples, who prefer analysis, first train in the guiding instructions in terms of the ordinary mind—that is, the preliminary practices of body, speech, and mind. They are then introduced to the main practice.

b. Teachings Given as an Introduction to the Nature of the Mind

Certain practitioners, thanks to the awakening of their residual karma, are introduced to the nature of the mind at the conclusion of an empowerment. They are able to implement the practice as if they were taking hold of an ear of wheat by the stalk. This refers to the introductions that set forth the trekchö and tögal teachings. Connected with them are twenty-one introductions, such as the introduction in which a mirror is used to exemplify the ultimate expanse, the introduction using the eye of a peacock feather to symbolize primordial wisdom, the introduction by means of a crystal to symbolize the state of union, and the introduction to the nature of the mind by means of the "fivefold sections of five."

c. Teachings Given as Essentialized but Complete Instructions for Departing Travelers

At the end of their lives, dying practitioners are like travelers setting out on a journey, and the pain of death is like a high pass that lies before them on their way. If they fail to recognize all the various appearances that they are about to perceive, these same appearances will become their enemies, whereas if they succeed in recognizing them, they will act as friends. {228} It is therefore said that at the time of death, the introduction to the nature of the mind should be done in the most essentialized but complete way possible. The second and third of these three ways of teaching the Great Perfection are in fact included in the first way of guiding instructions.

2. A Classification of the Practice

If one wishes to give instructions on the perfection stage in a truly perfect manner and in accordance with the maturity of the disciple, it is important to begin with the preliminary practices for the session itself, followed by the seven preliminary mind trainings. The disciples should then continue with general and particular accumulations of merit and wisdom and should then be instructed in the yoga of the winds for those who are without desire and the yoga related to the essence drops for those who have desire. This is followed by the uncommon preliminary practices; the various instructions for primordial purity—namely, trekchö; and then, beginning with the rushen practice for separating samsara and nirvana, the pith instructions for tögal practice. The latter includes the training in the postures of the three kāyas and the pith instructions that strike upon the key point of primordial wisdom for the three nighttime sessions. Then the disciples should strive in all the stages of the training in the recognition of their dreams and in the methods for increasing and transforming them. They should train and meditate on each of these until an authentic experience is gained. The disciples should act and conduct themselves in harmony with any given situation so that, without any doubt, they will attain the primordial place of freedom.

If practitioners who have trained in other perfection-stage practices wish now to engage in the main practice of the present path, they should begin with the practice of the seven mind trainings as appropriate. After completing the uncommon preliminary practice of the yoga of the five elements that cuts through the stream of thoughts—as well as the preliminaries related to body, speech, and mind—they will be able to engage in the actual practice of trekchö and tögal. This is entirely permissible.

Those who are old and those who are unable to master the yogas of the channels and winds, and who are thus unable to achieve the fruit of such practices, may omit the yogas related to the winds and essence drops. There is no fault in this. Moreover, those whose eyes are not clear and who are thus unable to practice tögal should only receive the teachings on trekchö. On the other hand, those who have not already practiced trekchö in the proper way should on no account be given the teachings on tögal alone.

Generally speaking, trekchö is a path through which one can gain freedom without effort. {229} One implements the practice of naked awareness without depending on the visions of luminosity. It is a teaching for those of sharp faculties—lazy people who achieve buddhahood without meditation. Tögal on the other hand is a path through which freedom is gained with effort. By depending on the visions of luminosity, diligent practitioners are able to purify their physical forms into bodies of light and gain enlightenment in this very life.

Whether the way in which the instructions are given is detailed or brief, it is essential that the empowerments of this tradition be granted beforehand. Moreover, whether or not one is able to gather other accumulations of merit or undertake other means of purification, the practice of the guru yoga called *The Ocean of Accomplishments* is indeed extremely important. The meditation and recitation of the three cycles of *The Wish-Fulfilling Gem*[138]—the sādhanas of the guru, deva, and ḍākinī—are also of crucial importance for practitioners. One should furthermore rely on the text of key instructions,

The King of Amṛta,[139] and other texts related to the enhancement of one's practice.

In brief, thanks to this profound teaching, it is impossible for practitioners of superior capacity not to gain freedom in this very lifetime, impossible for practitioners of medium capacity not to gain freedom in the bardo, and impossible for practitioners of least capacity not to gain freedom in the nirmāṇakāya buddha fields of luminous character. Those who encounter these profound teachings, the heart essence of the primordial lord, who practice them diligently, one-pointedly, and as much as they can, without neglecting them will without doubt spontaneously accomplish the twofold goal.

The Vajra Heart of Luminosity,
The path that cannot be surpassed,
The last of the nine vehicles,
Which is endowed with fourfold liberation,
Together with its Inmost Essence,
In all the vast expanse of buddha fields—
Even just their names, Heart Essence
And *The Wish-Fulfilling Gem,*
Are rare indeed.
Supreme among the four traditions
Are the mother and child instructions
Of *The Heart Essence of Vimalamitra.*
The three streams of its teaching gathered into one
Is the sublime possession
Of all learned and accomplished beings;
Its instructions are the quintessential distillation
Of all teachings.
Hard it is to understand
These deep, these perfect vajra teachings,
Ceaselessly watched over by protective guardians.

Free of self-promoting action, {230}
And commanded by my sovereign lord and teacher,
I have set these teachings down in writing.
Though I am supported
By the perfect teachings of my forebears,

My mind is weak, and meager is my strength of meditation.
Of whatever errors have occurred herein,
May the Three Roots and the dharma guardians
Purify me that these faults may do no harm
And cause no hindrance now or in the future.

The supreme diadem of wise Vimalamitra
Is Dorje Ziji, Longchenpa come again.
The nectar of his teaching is unstained
By spoiled samaya.
Let all who have good fortune
Take it as their healing remedy.
In the stainless perfect purity
Within the light of luminosity,
May all delusion now be swept away.
May beings, with whom the whole of space is filled,
Gain manifest enlightenment
Within the primal place of freedom.
May this teaching, like the sun and moon,
Be present everywhere.
Like a wish-fulfilling jewel,
May it now grant the wishes of all beings.
Like an ever-flowing stream, may it not cease
But bring about the deeds of the primordial lord.

When with great kindness the omniscient and primordial lord Dorje Ziji, Jamyang Khyentse Wangpo, bestowed on me the ripening empowerments and liberating instructions [of the Secret Heart Essence], he entrusted to me the task of composing the present text, which gathers into a single stream the systems of instruction belonging to *The Heart Essence, Mother and Child.* He told me to explain it in the way that he had done. Later, when this teaching was required for the practitioners of Kunzang Dechen Ösal Ling, the retreat center of Palpung Monastery, I again requested my lord and teacher, and again he gave me explicit permission to compose this text. Therefore, I, Pema Garwang Trinle Drodultsal, the very least of the disciples of the kind lord Jamgön Tai Situ, took as my basis the manual of instructions composed by Mingyur Paldrön, the Venerable Lady of Mindröling, and enriched it with the addition of appropriate vajra words taken from *The Heart Essence of Vimala* and *The Innermost Essence of the Master*, adorning them with some crucial points taken from the teachings of Dorje Tsewang Norbu and from *The Heart Essence of Karmapa*. I composed this book in Kunzang Dechen Ösal Ling itself, on the day commemorating the Buddha's first turning of the wheel of dharma. May it be of great benefit to the doctrine and beings.

Let virtue increase!

PART FOUR

TEXTS TAKEN FROM *THE PROFOUND INNERMOST ESSENCE*

The Profound Innermost Essence is the concluding supplement to *The Four Parts of the Heart Essence* and is a commentarial summary of both *The Innermost Essence of the Master* and *The Innermost Essence of the Ḍākinīs*. The present section comprises a long empowerment ritual followed by two texts of guiding instructions. The first of these, *A Great Guide for the Supreme Secret Path*, contains several extremely concise (and therefore not easy to understand and translate) descriptions of methods for introducing the nature of the mind. The second text, *The Heart of Practical Instructions*, is related to the practice of tögal.

12. The Luminous Lamp

An Empowerment Ritual for the Secret Cycle of the Great Perfection[1]

Longchen Rabjam

oṃ āḥ hūṃ {234}
I pay homage to the primordial lord endowed with every excellence,
Samantabhadra, beyond all change, spontaneously present,
And to the assembly of my teachers, lords of glory.
The empowerment ritual of the hearing transmission lineage of the
secret cycle I will here set forth.

In a solitary place, on a mandala base rinsed with saffron, draw the central perpendicular and diagonal lines, and within the innermost of three concentric circles, draw an eight-petaled lotus. In the surrounding space of the intermediate circle, draw a sixteen-petaled lotus, and in the surrounding space of the outer circle, draw a twenty-four-petaled lotus. Color the center of the mandala blue, the eastern quarter white, the southern quarter yellow, the western quarter red, and the northern quarter green. The intermediate and surrounding spaces should be in beautiful colors. Upon a tripod placed in the center of the mandala, set a glorious torma containing spices and alcohol and, surrounding it, the five tormas for the general dharma protectors; Ekajaṭī, protectress of mantra; Rāhula; Damchen Dorje Lekpa; and the ground-owning spirits. In addition, lay out the outer and inner offerings and the substances for the gaṇacakra feast offering.

The master then takes refuge, generates the attitude of bodhicitta, {235} purifies all phenomena into emptiness with *ō yogaśuddhāḥ sarvadharmāḥ svabhāva ātmako 'haṃ*. Then, from within the state of emptiness, he visualizes a sphere of protection that covers every direction including zenith and nadir. In the center in the midst of a blazing mass of wisdom fire, the syllable *bhrūṃ* transforms into an immeasurable palace composed of rainbow light. Within this palace, upon a precious lion throne, on disks of sun and moon, the master visualizes Samantabhadra seated in vajra posture in union with Samantabhadrī. The master recites *oṃ āḥ hūṃ* one hundred and eight times, and in an instant he perceives the entire mandala together with the tormas as a palace made of the five lights, generated from the syllable *bhrūṃ*. In its center, he visualizes Vajrasattva surrounded by the rest of the buddhas of the five families and, all around them, the teachers of the vidyādhara transmission through symbols, together with the teachers of the hearing transmission. On every side, the master imagines dense clouds of ḍākinīs of the four families and the infinite assemblies of the dharma protectors. Then, accompanied by drum and cymbals, he chants as follows: {236}

hūṃ
Although not stirring from the peaceful state of dharmatā,
O deities, display of primal wisdom, skilled in methods of
compassion,
Together with the buddhas of the three times and the vidyādhara
teachers,
Arise in illusory bodies from the dharmadhātu!

hūṃ
Do not delay, do not delay, O host of knowledge holders.
Do not delay, do not delay, O host of yidam deities.
Do not delay, do not delay, O multitude of dharma guardians.
Wherever is the palace of the king,
There the people of the kingdom gather.
Wherever is the essence of the teachings,
Ocean-like assemblies of the guardians gather.
Where the sun's essential orb appears,
There the red beams gather and shine forth.
So too when the vast expanse of bodhicitta manifests,
The peaceful and the wrathful deities assemble in vast multitudes.
Like southern clouds appearing in the empty sky,
Assemblies of vidyādharas and guardians gather.
Like streams and rivers flowing to the sea,
There gather vast assemblies of sister ḍākinīs.

Do not delay, vidyādharas of spontaneous accomplishment.
Vidyādharas of Mahāmudrā, you with power over life,
And you of karmic body, come, do not delay!

hūṃ
From your palace that is like the sun itself,
Samantabhadra dharmakāya, together with your consort,
Surrounded by an ocean of primordial wisdom,
Come and bless me in this very place.

From the mandala of refulgent rainbows,
Sambhogakāya father-mother buddhas of five families,
Surrounded by a retinue of bodhisattvas,
Come and bless me in this very place.

From Akaniṣṭha, palace of the dharmadhātu,
Nirmāṇakāya Vajrasattva,
Surrounded by the Buddha's eight close sons,
Come and bless me in this very place. {237}

From the summit of Mount Meru,
Teacher Garab Dorje,
Surrounded by a throng of ḍākinīs,
Come and bless me in this very place.

From the charnel ground of Śītavana,
Guru Mañjuśrīmitra,
Surrounded by a throng of ḍākinīs,
Come and bless me in this very place.

From beneath the bodhi tree,
Guru Śrīsiṃha,
Surrounded by a throng of ḍākinīs,
Come and bless me in this very place.

From the charnel ground of the great Bhaseng,
Guru Vimalamitra,

Surrounded by a throng of ḍākinīs,
Come and bless me in this very place.

From Gekong near to Samye Chimpu,
Nyangben Tingdzin Zangpo,
Surrounded by a throng of ḍākinīs,
Come and bless me in this very place.

From the palace of Yoru Zangpuk,
Venerable Lodrö Wangchuk,
Surrounded by a throng of ḍākinīs,
Come and bless me in this very place.

From the palace of Drakar Taso
Guru Rinchen Barwa,
Surrounded by a throng of ḍākinīs,
Come and bless me in this very place.

From Lungshö Zhai Lhakhang,
Neten Dangma Lhungyal,
Surrounded by a throng of ḍākinīs,
Come and bless me in this very place.

From the Dole Zamkha palace,
Chetsun Senge Wangchuk,
Surrounded by a throng of ḍākinīs,
Come and bless me in this very place.

From the Yoru Drakmar palace,
Guru Shangwa Repa,
Surrounded by a throng of ḍākinīs,
Come and bless me in this very place.

From the Yupuk Selwa palace,
Lama Zabtön Chöbar,
Surrounded by a throng of ḍākinīs,
Come and bless me in this very place.

From the Nyangme Chugö Monastery,
Sublime Gyertön Zhikpo,
Surrounded by a throng of ḍākinīs,
Come and bless me in this very place.

From Nyangme Chugö Mengang,
Nyentön Sherab Tsemo,
Surrounded by a throng of ḍākinīs,
Come and bless me in this very place. {238}

From the sublime place of Yönten Gang,
You, the most kind Choktrul,
Surrounded by a throng of ḍākinīs,
Come and bless me in this very place.

From the stainless palace of luminosity,
Lama Namkha Dorje,
Surrounded by a throng of ḍākinīs,
Come and bless me in this very place.

From the palace of primordial wisdom, self-arisen,
Vidyādhara Kumaradza,
Surrounded by a throng of ḍākinīs,
Come and bless me in this very place.

From the palace of awareness, present of itself,
All-knowing Natsok Rangdröl,
Surrounded by a throng of ḍākinīs,
Come and bless me in this very place.

Following this invitation, the vajra master visualizes the masters of the lineage appearing in the sky above him like massing clouds. They bless and empower him, the torma generated as the deity, and the entire place as being inseparable from themselves. Everything—the earth, the sky, and the intermediate air—is now considered to be the pure field of the masters.

[Next is] the raining down of blessing upon the master and the mandala:

From the different solitudes of the vidyādharas,
Teachers, holders of the vajra, who have gone in bliss,
Surrounded by the masters of the lineage,
Send down blessings on this supreme place,
With dense arrays of parasols and victory banners,
Chiming, tinkling bells and precious ornaments,
All to the sound of melodies and clashing cymbals.
Bestow empowerment upon myself, a supreme siddha.

hūṃ
From Akaniṣṭha, palace of the dharmadhātu,
Victorious yidam deities of the five families,
Surrounded by the sixteen bodhisattvas,
Send down blessings on this supreme place,
With dense arrays of parasols and victory banners,
Chiming, tinkling bells and precious ornaments,
All to the sound of melodies and clashing cymbals.
Bestow empowerment upon myself, a supreme siddha.

hūṃ
From every natural charnel ground,
Enlightened mothers accompanied by wisdom ḍākinīs,
Surrounded by a multitude of male and female warriors,
Send down blessings on this supreme place,
With dense arrays of parasols and victory banners,
Chiming, tinkling bells and precious ornaments,
All to the sound of melodies and clashing cymbals.
Bestow empowerment upon myself, a supreme siddha. {239}

hūṃ
From the retinue of the essential doctrine,
Mantra masters of great strength,
Surrounded by an oceanic multitude of guardians,
Send down blessings on this supreme place,
With dense arrays of parasols and victory banners,
Chiming, tinkling bells and precious ornaments,
All to the sound of melodies and clashing cymbals.
Bestow empowerment upon myself, a supreme siddha.

As these words are spoken, the lineage masters and deities fill the entire space where the empowerment is to be given and become inseparably one with the master and the tormas. Then an offering is made.

hūṃ
Phenomenal existence, utterly immaculate—
The precious outer offering—I present it as a gift.
Please enjoy it, free of all arising and cessation.

Five things pleasing to the senses—
The precious inner offerings—I present them as a gift.
Please enjoy them without ceasing.

Anger, the five poisons—
The precious secret offerings—I present them as a gift.
Please enjoy them without coming, without going.

Wisdom and absorption—
The precious and most secret offering—I present them as a gift.
Please enjoy them without increase or decrease.

This is followed by words of praise.

hūṃ
Samantabhadra, Vajrasattva, buddhas of five families, and
  vidyādhara masters—
Self-arisen primal wisdom, lords and deities of compassion—
All within primordial dharmadhātu,
To you I bow in praise.

Ocean-like assemblies of protectors,
Great is your miraculous power, vast as the extent of space.
With boundless strength, you guard the buddhadharma,
Protecting all who practice it as though they were your children.
To you I bow in praise.

This completes the preparation for the empowerment. {240}

The empowerment is bestowed in two stages. As a preliminary, the extensive or condensed prayer of *Confession and Restoration That Churn the Depths of Hell* is recited together with prayers of fervent devotion. Then the disciples make a mandala offering and remain with hands joined as the master introduces them to the sacred teaching.

> I pay homage to glorious Vajrasattva. Generally speaking, the perfect Buddha, with skill in means and great compassion, expounded an inconceivable array of vehicles and approaches to the dharma for the sake of beings. These are, in brief, condensed into the Hīnayāna and Mahāyāna, of which the Mahāyāna will be set forth here. The Mahāyāna is in turn divided into the vehicle of Secret Mantra and the [sutra] vehicle of the pāramitās. Of these, I will now expound the resultant vehicle of the Secret Mantra—namely, the Vajrayāna. The Secret Mantra is also twofold, outer and inner, and of these I will now expound the inner mantra, the tantras of skillful means. The inner mantra is again divided into three: the generation stage of the mahāyoga, the perfection stage of anuyoga, and the pith instructions of atiyoga. I shall now speak of atiyoga. Ati comprises three cycles: outer, inner, and secret, the third of which I shall now teach to you. The secret cycle has a textual lineage and a hearing lineage of transmission. Here I will speak about the hearing lineage, which has two aspects, written and unwritten. And now I will set forth the instructions called *The Mirror of the Secret Key Points*,[2] which are of the unwritten hearing lineage. Herein there are two parts: (1) an empowerment, which brings maturity to those who lack it, and (2) the instructions, which grant freedom to those who are thus matured. Now I shall bestow the empowerment on you. This has two parts: {241} (1) a presentation of the history of the transmission lineage, and (2) the empowerment that derives from this lineage.

At this point, the master gives an account of the history of the transmission lineage, concise or extensive, as befits the occasion.

The empowerment itself has two parts: (1) the entry of the disciples into the mandala and (2) the actual granting of the empowerment. The entry of the disciples into the mandala is in five stages.

First is refuge and bodhicitta. For the common taking of refuge and the generation of the bodhicitta attitude, the disciples recite three times:

> I take refuge in the teacher, holder of the vajra,
> And the Three Jewels.
> I cultivate the supreme attitude of bodhicitta
> For the benefit of every sentient being.

For the special refuge, the disciples recite the following three times:

> I and sentient beings without end
> Are buddhas from the very first.
> As one who understands that this is so,
> I generate the supreme attitude of bodhicitta.

Second, in order to take the vows, the disciples recite the following three times:

> My teacher, holder of the vajra,
> And all ḍākas and yoginīs, turn your minds to me, I pray.
> From now until enlightenment is gained
> And for the benefit of every being,
> I will cultivate the bodhicitta attitude
> And maintain the vows.
> Preserving the samayas of the five enlightened families,
> I will keep a vajra and a bell,
> And all samaya substances.
> I will not forsake the vajra master.
> I will not abandon the Three Jewels.
> I will not scorn the vajra kin.
> I will not despise the lower vehicles.
> I will do no injury to sentient beings.
> I will not disparage persons or their doctrine.
> I will not engage in actions of delusion.
> I will not despise the buddhadharma.
> I will not trouble those in meditative concentration. {242}
> I will not transgress supreme samayas
> Of body, speech, and mind, belonging to the Secret Mantra.

I will constantly engage in practice of the generation and
perfection stages.
I will do whatever is commanded by my teacher.
To the mighty citadel of liberation
I will carry over those who have not fully crossed.
I will liberate all those who are not free.
I will bring relief to those not yet relieved.
I will place all beings in the state beyond all sorrow.

Third, the disciples are established in samaya in two stages. For the proclamation of samaya, the master pours the water of pledge from the skull cup into the disciple's hands and says,

hūṃ
Here is the water of the vajra samaya.
If you break your pledge, you will be burned in fires of hell.
If you keep it, you will gain the unsurpassed accomplishment.
Therefore, this is the supreme vajra samaya.
Take it to your heart. Observe it.
oṃ samaya pañca amṛta hrīḥ ṭha

For the granting of samaya, the master says,

Kye!
Children of my heart, endowed with fortune, listen!
You have entered now this perfect mandala
Of the Natural Great Perfection.
Pledge yourself to practice holy dharma
Of the outer, inner, and secret vehicles.
Keep the samaya pledge of mantra
And likewise all the vows as they have been explained.
Do not speak of secret matters—
Samaya substances and mantra teachings—
To those who have not been empowered.
Abandon harmful acts toward the teachings.
Thus you will reach supreme attainment
As a vajra holder.

Fourth, the master accepts the disciples. First, the disciples recite the following prayer three times:

> Teacher, holder of the vajra,
> Sole friend in the three worlds of samsara, {243}
> Refuge of those who wander unprotected,
> Great stair that leads to liberation,
> Lost in darkness, I now come to you for refuge,
> Ignorance-dispelling light!
> Protect me, who, protectorless,
> Am sinking in the murky ocean of samsara.
> Cool me with your waters of compassion,
> Tormented as I am by fires of my defilements.
> Give me leave, I pray, to enter now
> The perfect mandala of the enlightened mind.

The disciples then should recite three times,

> To you my teacher, holder of the vajra,
> Devotedly I pray.
> As you now admit me to the granting of empowerment
> Of the Natural Great Perfection,
> Reveal to me the Ati mandala
> Of the fundamental nature of my mind.

The master then gives his consent with the following words:

> *Ema!*
> Great is your good fortune, dearest child!
> Now I shall reveal to you the Great Perfection mandala.
> Clear away all concepts from your mind.
> Let go of everything that binds you to this world.
> This mandala is free of all conventions of acceptance and
>   rejection.
> Your lineage and mind have now been purified,
> And so your body and your speech are the supports for bliss.
> From this day forward, then, do not fall back.

Fifth, the raining down of blessing power. The disciples now stand. They join their hands at their hearts, and with their eyes closed, they generate a sense of faith and devotion. They imagine that their root and lineage teachers, together with the five families of yidam deities and dense clouds of ḍākinīs also of the five families come gradually to the crown of the master's head and merge inseparably with him. The names of each of them resound, the cymbals clash, incense and "great grease" are burned, and primordial wisdom descends. {244}

The actual empowerment is now conferred. The disciples sit in vajra posture and are instructed to meditate on themselves in the form of Vajrasattva. When the torma is placed upon their heads, from the crown protuberances of the teachers, yidam deities, and ḍākinīs just visualized—as well as from the crown protuberance of the master himself, visualized in the form of Samantabhadra in union with his consort—there radiate countless rays of white light. These touch the bodies of the disciples and cleanse away their physical obscurations. The blessings of the enlightened body fill the bodies of the disciples in the form of nectar. The vase empowerment is thus received, and as a sign of this, the disciples consider that their heads are adorned with the presence of Vairocana, who is the size of a thumb. The master then goes on to say,

> *hūṃ*
> The empowerment of the enlightened body
> Is bestowed upon your body.
> The obscurations of your body are thus purified,
> And you attain the accomplishment of the enlightened body.
> Let this complete the precious vase empowerment.
> *oṃ kāya kalaśa abhiṣiñca oṃ*

When the torma touches the disciples' throats, rays of red light issue from the throats of the yidam deities and the teachers. As they touch the disciples' faculty of speech, they purify the obscurations thereof, and the nectar of the empowering blessings of enlightened speech fills their bodies. At that point, they should consider that they have received the empowerment of enlightened speech. The master then says,

> *hūṃ*
> The empowerment of enlightened speech

Is now bestowed upon your speech.
The obscurations of your speech are purified.
You thus attain accomplishment of enlightened speech.
Let this complete the precious secret empowerment.
āḥ vāka guhya abhiṣiñca āḥ

When the torma touches the disciples' hearts, rays of blue light issue from the hearts of the yidam deities and the teachers. As they touch the disciples' hearts, they purify the obscurations of their minds, and the nectar of the empowering blessings of the enlightened mind flows down and fills their bodies, giving them the single taste of great bliss.

The master says,

hūṃ
The empowerment of the enlightened mind
Is now bestowed upon your mind. {245}
The obscurations of your mind are purified;
Thus you attain this same enlightened mind.
Let the empowerment of primordial wisdom now be gained.
hūṃ citta prajnā jñāna abhiṣiñca hūṃ

The fourth or precious word empowerment is the Great Perfection empowerment of the power of awareness. As they relax in the uncontrived nature of the mind, the disciples are introduced to the spontaneous manifestation of their awareness as the dharmakāya, open and unimpeded—the one sole perfect sphere. As it is said in *The Wheel of Precious Empowerments*,

Once upon a time, in the Indian city of Kapilavastu, the son of a king set out on an adventure. He wandered far, was lost, and eventually became a beggar. At length, however, he was recognized by a minister of the land. He was taken home and crowned, and he brought beneath his power all his many subjects.

In just the same way, sentient beings[3]
All possess the nature of primordial buddha.
This they do not recognize
And therefore languish in delusion.
The nature of their minds

Is now revealed to them.
Because with primal, self-cognizing wisdom
They are now empowered,
All the signs of the samsaric state
Subside quite naturally.[4]

In this tale, the prince is the symbol of self-knowing awareness, which is the point to which the story refers. Moreover, the evidence for this awareness is the natural and spontaneous radiance of the mind of the present moment, which is introduced and recognized with certainty as the state of buddhahood.

The gaṇacakra is now enjoyed, together with the torma—it being understood that the torma represents accomplishment. Then all the various stages—dedication of merit, prayers of aspiration, vajra songs, the giving of the torma of the remainder, and prayers of good wishes—should all be performed without error.

Everything that is slightly incomplete or slightly concealed in the previous instructions should be set forth without omission according to the traditional practice of the teachers.

By this virtuous deed may I and every being
Set out upon the path of Natural Great Perfection.
Without striving, without effort, may we all spontaneously achieve {246}
The two objectives. May we thus be kings of dharma.

This ritual of precious empowerment titled *The Luminous Lamp*, which opens the door to the lineage of the unwritten mouth-to-ear transmission, was composed by Natsok Rangdröl (Longchenpa), a yogi of the Natural Great Perfection.

Virtue! Virtue! Virtue!

13. Guiding Instructions

A Great Guide for the Supreme Secret Path[1]

Longchen Rabjam

oṃ āḥ hūṃ {248}
To my sublime and venerable teacher, I bow down.

For the sake of future generations, I shall here condense
Profound and crucial points of gradual instruction
For the introduction to the nature of the mind,
Taken from the unwritten, secret sphere.

This text has three parts: (1) the preliminaries, (2) main part, and (3) conclusion. First of all, there are seven preliminaries to be implemented.

The Preliminaries

First, Guru Yoga

Considering the whole of phenomenal existence as the buddha field of Samantabhadra, the disciples should visualize above their heads, the root teacher and the teachers of the lineage, and address their prayers to them.

Second, the Mandala Offering

Heaps [of grains and so on], arranged on a mandala plate to symbolize Mount Meru and the four cosmic continents, should now be offered. They should be visualized as buddha fields replete with all that is pleasing to the gods and humankind.

Third, Vajrasattva Practice

The disciples should then visualize Vajrasattva, white in color, holding vajra and bell, and with the hundred-syllable mantra in his heart. The disciples recite the mantra.

Fourth, Understanding Life's Impermanence

Outwardly, the disciples should meditate on the passage of the four seasons. Inwardly, they should meditate on the changes occurring in the physical and mental aggregates. Secretly, they should meditate on the bardo state as though they are passing through it.

Fifth, Cultivating a Sense of Weariness with Samsara

The disciples should reflect on the sufferings of each of the six classes of beings. {249}

Sixth, Meditation on Bodhicitta

The disciples should train in the alternating practice of giving their happiness to beings as infinite as space is vast and of taking their sufferings on themselves. They should meditate on great compassion.

Seventh, a Threefold Investigation of the Status of Appearing Objects and the Apprehending Mind

First the disciples should train themselves in the understanding that the five outer objects of apprehension are devoid of intrinsic being. They should meditate on the fact that all things perceived as the objects of the five senses appear but have no existence. They are like magical illusions, like the things experienced in dreams. In the very moment that they are perceived, they are without support or location; they have the nature of space.

Examining the inner apprehending mind, the disciples should search for where the mind arises, appearing as it does in the form of thoughts of rejecting and accepting. And they should ask themselves: What is it that arises? Where does the mind dwell, and what is it that dwells? Finally, where does it go, and what is it that goes? The disciples should search for the mind's identity, its shape and color. When it is understood that the mind is like space, the equality of samsara and nirvana is revealed.

It is important for the disciples to become proficient in these preliminaries. {250}

The Main Part

The main part of this text, the introduction to the nature of the mind, has two sections. First, through the introduction to primordial purity (the dharmakāya), the disciples are brought into the experience of it in this present moment. To begin with, a gaṇacakra feast offering complete with tormas is prepared. Prayers are recited, and the key points of bodily posture adopted. The entire lineage prayer should then be chanted and the pointing-out instructions given with the following words:

> Watch the state of self-cognizing awareness in its present immediacy—open, unimpeded, naked. This awareness is luminous. It is free of clinging. It is empty and devoid of self. It is beyond identification. It is the dharmakāya. Remain naturally in this state, without distraction or alteration.

Second, the introduction to spontaneous presence, the state of luminosity, brings freedom in the bardo. Using a crystal held up in the rays of the sun coming in through a skylight, an introduction is given to the nature of the original, primordial ground, to the way of freedom of Samantabhadra, to the way of delusion of ignorant beings, to the nature of the ordinary mind, to the nature of primordial wisdom, to the manner in which the instructions should be practiced, and to the way of freedom in the luminosity of the bardo state.

The skylight is then closed and the introduction to the mind is made in dependence upon a woman through the three stages of penetration, remaining, and withdrawal. The symbols should be placed on the ground. They are lifted up with the crystal and presented by means of example, thesis, and evidence.[2] An introduction to the three kāyas is also given using a crystal, the sun, and a statue. The dharmakāya is introduced by using a crystal, the sambhogakāya is introduced by using a statue, and the nirmāṇakāya is introduced by using the radiating beams of the sun. All these introductions should be performed according to the traditional practice of the lineage. The ray of light from the crystal held up in the sunlight introduces the channel-path that links the heart with the eyes. It indicates the moment when the mind and primordial wisdom are separated, and it introduces the appearances of the ground in the bardo state.[3] And since the kāyas and wisdoms are inseparable in the dimension of the precious spontaneous presence, this clearly indicates the activity for the sake of beings performed by the sambhogakāya and nirmāṇakāya of outwardly radiating luminosity—even while they are still within the inner luminosity of the dharmakāya. {251}

These introductions are an important guide for the path of all three mouth-to-ear transmission lineages.

Conclusion

The concluding section is made up of supplementary instructions. When these have been given—whether in an elaborate or concise way, as befits the situation—they should be sealed as secret.

By the merit of composing these instructions for the path
Of the unwritten mouth-to-ear transmission,
May every being embrace the supreme vehicle
Attaining supreme victory, the level of Samantabhadra.

This completes *A Great Guide for the Supreme Secret Path* of the lineage of the unwritten mouth-to-ear transmission. It was set forth by Natsok Rangdröl, a yogi of the Natural Great Perfection.

Virtue!

The Heart of Practical Instructions[4]

Longchen Rabjam

I bow to glorious Vajrasattva.

To you, spontaneous and enlightened action
Of the triple kāya, radiant with a thousand lights,
To you, O venerable teachers of the transmission lineages
Of the three classes, I bow down.
Here I shall set forth an essential and profound instruction,
A guide to the practice of the sphere of luminosity.

This instruction has three sections: (1) through the definitive key points related to the body, one establishes the foundation [for the practice]; (2) through the definitive key points related to the winds, one endeavors on the path; and (3) through the definitive key points related to awareness, one reaches the vital essence of the matter.

First, Establishing the Foundation through the Definitive Key Points Related to the Body

This refers to the postures and gazes related to the dharmakāya, sambhogakāya, and nirmāṇakāya, as well as to the posture of [vajra-like] inseparability.

For the lion posture of the dharmakāya, keep your body upright and make fists with your hands. Place your fingers on the ground with your arms to right and left of your torso. Push the back of your neck forward and gaze into the sky.

For the elephant posture of the sambhogakāya, crouch down with your knees drawn up against your chest. Touch the ground with your elbows, and cup your chin in the palms of your hands.

For the rishi posture of the nirmāṇakāya, sit on the ground with your arms crossed around your knees pulled up to your chest. {252}

For the posture of vajra-like inseparability, adopt the vajra posture, which is said to be propitious for the state of enlightenment. Sit with your legs crossed, your hands placed in the meditative position. Keep your spine straight like a column of coins, pushing it back slightly in line with your neck.

If you begin in this way, you will find that thanks to these postures, your thoughts will naturally cease, and your winds will be purified and brought under control. Train in whichever of these positions you like, thereby creating an adamantine foundation [for your practice.]

Second, Endeavoring on the Path through the Definitive Key Points of the Breath, or Wind

This has four stages: first the breath is expelled, then it is held outside, then it is drawn in, and finally it is held inside. When expelling the breath, you should exhale as slowly and gently as possible. Then hold your breath outside as much as you can without breathing in. Then inhale gently and hold your breath inside for as long as is naturally possible. The wind or breath is the steed or vehicle of the mind. When the breath is brought under control, the mind is also brought under control. When the breath is held outside, the mind is naturally held within, [becoming still]. This is a wonderful key point. It is imperative that this be done gently, for all forced action will create obstacles. On the other hand, hindrances cannot arise when the breathing exercise is done naturally and without forcing—like the natural, unhindered movement of the breath. Excellent qualities will arise through understanding the key point of slow and gentle breathing.

It is also said that the wind or breath is the most important factor for the maintaining of the state of awareness. Moreover, the intensification and the dissipation of luminous meditative visions also depend on the wind. At first, when the winds are brought under control, the visions of luminosity increase. When finally the impure winds are purified and exhausted, luminosity is deprived of the vehicle or steed that draws it out. {253} It dissolves within and is exhausted. This too is a key point to be understood by all skilled practitioners.

In particular, when strong defilement arises, or when you are angry or irritated, if you breathe out with the sound *ha*, all such feelings will be cleared away quite naturally. By contrast, when you feel devotion, or your concentration is good, and so on, if you hold your breath within, all such qualities will increase. This is also a key pith instruction.

Third, Reaching the Essence of the Matter through the Definitive Key Points Related to Awareness

Here, the instruction refers to three key points: the key point of the sense door, the key point of the visual field, and the key point of awareness.

The key point of the sense door refers to the three ways of gazing. These are the peaceful, lowered gaze of the śrāvakas, the forward-looking gaze of the bodhisattvas, and the upward-looking gaze of the tathāgatas. [In all of these,] it is important to gaze naturally and gently without straining your eyes. If you watch too intensely, your eyes will water and become uncomfortable. And if you have weak eyes, you will be disinclined to practice the gazes. On the other hand, if your way of looking is natural and gentle, the luminous visions will increase and will be without defect.

The key point of the visual field refers to the fact that you must fix your gaze on a cloudless sky. It is important not to shift your gaze from the point in the sky [that you have chosen]. This is vital. If at one moment you gaze here and at another moment you gaze there, there will be nowhere for the visions to arise. It is therefore crucial to keep your gaze focused on one place.

The key point of awareness is as follows. Without straying into the other sense doors, your eyes—the means by which the path of luminosity is revealed—should gaze without blinking and without distraction into the sky. However many thoughts may flash by and memories arise, your gaze should not move from that one place in the sky. It should be kept there steadily like a peg driven into a board.[5] First there will come flashes of light that are dazzlingly white, within which disks of five-colored light will appear. {254} And as you focus your eyes on them, you will experience a state that is at once outwardly luminous, inwardly lucid and fresh, and (between these two) even and without fixation.

Outwardly appearing luminosity appears as skillful means and corresponds to the generation stage on the relative level. The inner state of empty luminosity arises as wisdom and corresponds to the perfection stage on the ultimate level. Thus awareness holds its own place in the fundamental stratum of the dharmakāya. It is then that three events occur: Since awareness remains in the fundamental stratum, the king is seated immovably upon his throne. Since there is neither the unfolding nor the dissolution of thoughts, because the wind is inactive, the minister is detained in prison. Since luminosity manifests in space, while the five sense doors are not distracted elsewhere, the common people are subdued. This wisdom state is inseparable from the dharmatā. Awareness—which is empty, luminous, and unceasing—remains in its natural condition: the three kāyas spontaneously present. It is thus that the goal of the instruction is actualized.

Through continuous practice, day and night, all the qualities indicating that you have achieved proficiency in meditation will be gained. For example, you will have neither an expectation of nirvana nor a dread of samsara; you will not stir from the dharmatā, the fourth time; and you will receive prophecies from the ḍākinīs. The best meditators purify their habitual tendencies and experience the luminous visions of primordial wisdom. As a result, they enter the dimension of precious spontaneous presence in this very life.[6] Meditators of moderate ability recognize the luminosity of the dharmatā [in the bardo] and gain freedom within the dimension of spontaneous presence—that is, luminous primordial wisdom. They take hold of the natural state of awareness. Meditators of least scope will encounter these teachings in their subsequent lives and will attain enlightenment. This explains why the present instruction is called *The Mirror of the Secret Key Points: An Instruction That Places Buddhahood in the Palm of Your Hand.*[7]

This text, distilling all the crucial points of the Great Secret,
Was written on the slopes of Kangri Tökar by the yogi Natsok
  Rangdröl, {255}
For whom all manifold phenomena subsided naturally.
By this virtue, may all beings reach enlightenment.

This completes *The Heart of Practical Instructions*, written by the yogi Longchen Rabjam.

Virtue! Virtue! Virtue!

PART FIVE

Essential Instructions

This section is composed of two items: General Teachings on the Great Perfection by Guru Padmasambhava, followed by the *Meditation Guide for "Finding Rest in the Nature of the Mind,"* the first part of Longchenpa's celebrated Trilogy of Rest.

The texts by Guru Padmasambhava are found in the Nyingma Kama (the orally transmitted texts of the Nyingma school) and in the treasure texts of Nyangral Nyima Özer, Guru Chökyi Wangchuk, and Dorje Lingpa. In both the Nyingma Kama and Kongtrul's *Treasury of Precious Instructions*, the manner in which these texts are laid out is confusing. Although the entire compilation is called *The Heap of Jewels*, this title actually applies only to the first item in the collection. To this the subsequent texts are added, separated from it, and distinguished from each other only by small typographical signs. For ease of identification, the translated texts have been more clearly separated. Several items figure in the compilation. The first, *A Heap of Jewels*, is a lamrim text, an explanation of the common gradual path of sutra and mantra. It contains textual glosses by Padmasambhava himself and is accompanied by a summary exposition in the form of a textual outline. The second text, *The Precious and Illuminating Lamp*, is also a lamrim, a gradual exposition of the inner path of the Secret Mantra. It also contains a few textual glosses and is accompanied by a summary exposition. This second text is prefaced with a historical note that, although not so identified by Kongtrul, is by the great translator Nyak Jñānakumāra. The block print of both the Palpung and Shechen editions is of very poor quality and appears to have been damaged. Its numerous errors created many difficulties for the translation. Fortunately, we discovered an excellent version of all these texts in the new Chinese edition of the extended collection of the orally transmitted texts of the Nyingma school. Here, we discovered another text by Guru Padmasambhava, titled *A Precious Garland*, which proved to be an autocommentary on the second lamrim text and afforded considerable assistance in the translation of its terse and obscure verses.

The compilation also contains three pointing-out instructions composed by Guru Padmasambhava. The first of these is a lengthy explanation in five parts and is followed by the inspiringly beautiful *Staff-Pointing Instruction Given to an Old Man* and *The Finger-Pointing Instruction Given to an Old Woman*. As mentioned in the translators' introduction to the present volume, this collection of texts was included in the extant printed editions of *The Treasury of Precious Instructions* instead of the text from *The Innermost Essence of the Ḍākinīs* mentioned in Kongtrul's catalog.

The second item in this section is Longchenpa's well-known *Meditation Guide*. In one hundred and forty-one instructions, it lays out a gradual path of Great Perfection practice. This text is cherished in the Nyingma school and is traditionally used in retreat in the manner of guiding instructions given according to the meditative experience of the practitioner.

14. General Teachings on the Great Perfection

A Heap of Jewels: An Outer Presentation of the Common Gradual Path of Sutra and Mantra[1]

Guru Padmasambhava

Homage to the Bhagavan, the glorious Vajrasattva! {258}

That beings might investigate phenomena
And set out on the path to freedom,
Thence to gain the fruit that is omniscience,
Here I shall expound *A Heap of Jewels*.

Rely upon a master gifted with six qualities,
And be mindful of four attitudes.
Abandon the three defects of a vessel
And listen to your master,
Whom you should consider in five ways.
Now that you have gained a precious human form
So very hard to find,
Do not make it meaningless, remaining empty-handed.
Reap instead an everlasting harvest.
Now meditate on the five outer aspects of impermanence

And meditate on its three inner aspects in seven ways.
Make effort in this meditation for it has five benefits.

The Same Passage with Inserted Glosses

Rely upon a master gifted with six qualities

Such a master belongs to a lineage of transmission and is thus able to bestow excellent teachings. He has received empowerment and thus is able to grant powerful blessings. He is endowed with wisdom and is therefore strong in his compassion. He is erudite and possesses great spiritual experience. He is in possession of the view and is an accomplished meditator. Learned in the words of the teachings, he lives according to their meaning.

And be mindful of four attitudes.

These attitudes are defined as general, special, perfect, and defective, and each of them is subdivided into four aspects. The general attitude is to consider samsara as a river, the dharma as a boat, your teacher as the captain, and the practice as the crossing of the river. The special attitude is to consider yourself to be sick, your teacher as a physician, the dharma as a medicine, and the practice as the cure for your sickness. The perfect attitude is to think that you have been infected with the contagion of the five poisons, that your teacher is the Buddha, that his teachings are the draft of immortality, and that the practice is the antidote to these same poisons. Finally, the defective attitude is to regard yourself as a king, the Buddha as a merchant, and his dharma as a mere commodity, and to receive his teachings in the manner of a business transaction.

Abandon the three defects of a vessel
And listen to your master,

[The three defects are to behave like] an upturned vessel, a vessel with a hole in its base, and a vessel that contains poison. {259}

Whom you should consider in five ways.

[Think of your teacher] as the embodiment of all the buddhas, as the essence of the vajra holders, and the root of the Three Jewels. Consider him or her as a jewel and superior to all the buddhas.

Now that you have gained a precious human form,
So very hard to find,
Do not make it meaningless, remaining empty-handed.
Reap instead an everlasting harvest.
Now meditate on the five outer aspects of impermanence

These are the change from summer to winter, the four seasons, the change from day to night, "arising, dwelling, ceasing," and finally, the impermanence of pure and impure causes.

And meditate on its three inner aspects in seven ways.

The three inner aspects are the certainty of death, the uncertainty of the time of death, and the fact that you can take nothing with you when you die. The seven ways means that you should bear in mind that anything can be a cause of death, that nowhere is safe from death, that death is unpredictable, that there is no averting it, that you will go quickly, that there is no escape, and finally that it is inevitably rightening.

Make effort in this meditation for it has five benefits.

[Through this meditation,] you will gain faith, you will have devotion to your teacher, you will gain certainty in the teachings, you will be able to engage in the practice, and it will be easy for you to realize emptiness.

Common folk, extremist thinkers, śrāvakas, and pratyekabuddhas
Think of objects and their minds and bodies
In terms of "self," phenomenal and personal.
But such self-clinging has no basis;
There's no self, and all is empty.
All beings undergo four basic sufferings.
Six secondary pains they also undergo,
And countless other lesser sorrows. {260}
These are introduced as being your own mind, by nature empty.
Two causes, good and evil deeds,
Yield two results, your happiness and suffering.
Distinguish well the line dividing sin from virtue,
And cut the stream of negativity by means of the four forces.

Śrāvakas and pratyekabuddhas taken both together,
The bodhisattvas, and the yogis of the Secret Mantra—
These three, in the same order,
Take refuge in the Buddha, dharma, sangha,
For their own sake, for others' sake, and for the sake of both.
Thus there are three ways of taking refuge,
The means to take you far beyond the world.
To wish for buddhahood, to implement this wish,
To taste in your experience the unconditioned dharmatā
Beyond the ordinary mind—
These are the three kinds of bodhicitta,
Dharma of the Mahāyāna.
Reject three kinds of evil deed,
Practice the three kinds of virtue,
Recognize your fundamental nature—
These are three vows that the Buddha has set forth.
The mind that loves is without hatred.
The mind that is compassionate knows no attachment.
The enlightened mind is free of ignorance.
These three minds are Buddha's wisdom.
To purge all evil deeds and inclinations is true discipline;
Bringing benefit is concentration.
Wisdom is the union of skillful means and wisdom.
These three trainings are the Three Collections.

The ground of ultimate and self-arisen nature
Abides within the unborn, empty character.
Appearances arise in endless unimpeded play,
Nondual and free of ontological extremes.
Beings fail to recognize; they understand this wrongly.
Through five poisons and three kinds of action,
They take bodies in the six realms and experience suffering.
From ignorance till age-and-death, they circle constantly.
The ultimate and undetermined state
Gives rise to all kinds of appearance,
Which are but mind's own self-experience.
To realize this—their natural openness and freedom—

Is the view.
Relax. Stay fresh and natural,
And a luminous and naked state devoid of thought will come.
Appearances and mind are one and never parted. {261}
Inseparable luminosity and emptiness—
This is the meditation.
All appearances, arising from conditions,
Gross and subtle, high and low, all thoughts
Are but the mind's display.
Be without depression or conceit in their regard.
Do not cling to them, and they are free and open naturally—
This then is the conduct.
Whatever you may do, remain within the natural state,
Luminous by its very essence.
This is emptiness, and emptiness is ceaseless [luminosity].
Nonexistence, ceaselessness, inconceivability,
Purity, spontaneous presence, truth,
The phenomena belonging
To the view, the meditation, conduct, and result,
And all the other things that should be known—
Of all of these be certain.

The two certainties,[2] exhausted, ripen as the kāyas.
The knowledge of the nature of phenomena,
The knowledge of phenomena in all their multiplicity,
The knowledge [that transcends duality]—
All these will come to flower.
[Altruistic actions] are supported, unsupported, and also one in nature.
[The wisdom mind] is neither one nor many.

Through the merits of this virtuous deed,
May beings, infinite in number as the sky is vast,
Come face-to-face with ultimate reality,
Swiftly to accomplish perfect buddhahood.

This concludes *A Heap of Jewels.*

A Summary Exposition of the Outer Explanation of *A Heap of Jewels*[3]

Homage to all holy teachers.

I. The introduction
  A. Expression of homage (Homage to the Bhagavan . . .)
  B. The promise to explain the teaching
    1. Investigation of phenomena (That beings might investigate . . .)
    2. Setting out on the path to liberation (And set out on the path . . .)
    3. The attainment of the result (Thence to gain . . .)
    4. The name of the instruction (Here I shall expound . . .)
II. The main teaching
  A. An exhortation of expedient meaning
    1. Reliance on a teacher
      a. The qualities of a teacher (Rely upon a master . . .)
      b. The way to rely on the teacher (Being mindful of four . . .)
      c. The way in which one should listen to one's teacher (Abandon the three defects of a vessel . . .)
      d. The way in which one should honor one's teacher (Whom you should consider . . .)
    2. A reflection on the freedoms and advantages of a precious human form
      a. The freedoms and advantages identified (Now that you have gained . . .)
      b. A reflection on the difficulty of obtaining the freedoms and advantages (So very hard to find . . .)
      c. The importance of not wasting them (Do not make it meaningless . . .)
      d. Making one's freedoms and advantages meaningful (Reap instead . . .)
    3. A reflection on impermanence {262}
      a. Five outer aspects of impermanence (Now meditate on the five . . .)
      b. Three inner aspects of impermanence (And meditate on its three . . .)
      c. The way to reflect on impermanence (In seven ways . . .)
      d. Striving in this reflection on account of its benefits (Make effort in this meditation . . .)
    4. Overcoming one's grasping to a self
      a. The agent of self-grasping (Common folk, extremist thinkers . . .)
      b. The objects of self-grasping (Think of objects and their minds . . .)

- c. The ways in which the self is grasped (In terms of "self" . . .)
- d. A refutation of self-grasping by showing that there is no self (But such self-clinging . . .)

5. A reflection on suffering
    - a. The four main sufferings (All beings undergo . . .)
    - b. The six subsidiary sufferings (Six secondary pains . . .)
    - c. The infinite multitude of lesser sufferings (And countless other . . .)
    - d. A presentation of suffering as the mind (These are introduced as . . .)
6. An investigation of karmic cause and effect
    - a. Identifying of the cause (Two causes, good and evil deeds . . .)
    - b. A demonstration of how the result arises (Yield two results . . .)
    - c. Distinguishing virtue from sin (Distinguish well . . .)
    - d. Breaking the continuum of sin (And cut the stream . . .)

B. The general and common instructions

1. Taking refuge (In Buddha, dharma, sangha . . .)
2. Generating bodhicitta (To wish for buddhahood . . .) {263}
3. Taking the vows
    - a. The vows of individual liberation (Reject three kinds of evil deed . . .)
    - b. The vows of bodhicitta (Practice the three kinds of virtue . . .)
    - c. The Secret Mantra vows (Recognize your fundamental nature . . .)
    - d. These three vows are the buddhadharma (These three vows that . . .)
4. Meditating on bodhicitta
    - a. Meditating on loving-kindness (The mind that loves . . .)
    - b. Meditating on compassion (The mind that is compassionate . . .)
    - c. Meditating on bodhicitta (The enlightened mind . . .)
    - d. These three are shown to be the buddha's wisdom mind (These three minds . . .)
5. Educating the mind with the three trainings
    - a. The higher training in discipline (To purge all evil deeds . . .)
    - b. The higher training in concentration (Bringing benefit . . .)
    - c. The higher training in wisdom (Wisdom is the union . . .)
    - d. These trainings correspond to the Tripiṭaka (These three trainings are . . .)

C. The special and uncommon instructions of the Great Perfection

1. The ground
    - a. The fundamental nature
        - i. The self-arisen ultimate nature (The ground of ultimate . . .)
        - ii. Its unborn character (Abides within . . .)

iii. Its unceasing display (Appearances arise . . .)
iv. Their nature is free of ontological extremes (Nondual and free . . .)
b. Delusion
i. The cause of delusion (Beings fail to recognize . . .)
ii. The condition of delusion (Through five poisons . . .)
iii. The result of delusion (They take bodies . . .)
iv. The way beings turn [through the cycle of twelve links] (From ignorance till age-and-death . . .)
2. The path
a. The view that transcends all extremes
i. The fundamental nature (The ultimate and undetermined state . . .)
ii. The mode of arising (Gives rise . . .)
iii. The mode of being (Which are but mind's . . .) {264}
iv. The mode of openness and freedom (To realize this . . .)
b. Meditation on the natural state of awareness
i. The method for settling the mind (Relaxed, stay fresh and natural . . .)
ii. The emergence of experiences (A luminous and naked state . . .)
iii. Presenting appearances as a meditative state (Appearances and mind . . .)
iv. Gaining conviction that thoughts are a state of meditation (Inseparable luminosity and emptiness . . .)
c. Conduct wherein delusion subsides
i. Identifying appearances (Gross and subtle . . .)
ii. Showing that they are the mind (Are but the mind's display . . .)
iii. Preserving the single taste (Be without depression . . .)
iv. Remaining without clinging (Do not cling . . .)
d. Bringing the path to the crucial point
i. Focusing the mind on stillness (Whatever you may do . . .)
ii. Causing the radiance of luminosity to emerge (Luminous by very . . .)
iii. Placing on it the seal of emptiness (This is emptiness.)
iv. Establishing their indivisibility (Emptiness is ceaseless [luminosity].)
e. Instruction for gaining clear confidence
i. Confidence in the fundamental nature thus introduced (Nonexistence, ceaselessness . . .)
ii. Confidence that it is the ground (Purity, spontaneous presence . . .)
iii. Confidence with respect to the path and result (To the view, the meditation . . .)

iv. Confidence with respect to all phenomena (And all the other things . . .)

3. The result

a. The kāyas are the support (The two certainties . . .)

b. The wisdoms are the supported (The knowledge of the nature . . .)

c. How benefit is brought to beings ([Altruistic action] is . . .)

d. How the wisdom mind subsists ([The wisdom mind] is . . .)

III. The conclusion

A. The dedication of merits (Through the merits . . .)

B. The name of the text and the conclusion (This concludes . . .)

The Precious and Illuminating Lamp
A Gradual Path of the Secret Mantra[4]

Guru Padmasambhava

In Sanskrit: *Mantrasayapathakramanāma*
In Tibetan: *gSang sngags lam gyi rim pa rin po che'i gsal ba'i sgron me zhes bya ba*

A Historical Note on the Inner Explanation of the Gradual Path of the Secret Mantra[5]

namo ratna guru

This explanation of the gradual path of the Secret Mantra was composed by the great Master Padmasambhava. Padmasambhava of Oḍḍiyāna was endowed with countless sublime qualities of physical greatness and was perfect in the way he composed pith instructions. {265}

Regarding the greatness of his body, he appeared miraculously on a lotus flower in the western land of Oḍḍiyāna and was thus unstained by the impurity of a womb. And since he brought both birth and death beneath his power, he is undying. As concerns the greatness of his speech, Padmasambhava expounded the dharma in many ways and gained great power of speech, on account of which all the arrogant spirits became subject to his word. As for the greatness of his mind, he knows all phenomena without exception, and endowed with immaculate wisdom, he dwells in the state of nonconceptual concentration. He possesses the two knowledges [of the nature of all phenomena and of the multiplicity of phenomena].

The greatness of his qualities lies in the fact that he possesses the three wheels of the inexhaustible ornaments of the enlightened body, speech, and mind and is able to fulfill all the needs, wishes, and hopes of beings. The greatness of his activities lies in four abilities. He pacifies all defilements and thoughts, causing them to subside right where they stand. He has the power to bring an unbounded increase in life and power. He draws beneath his sway all beings, human or otherwise. Finally, he eradicates all wrong views and evildoers. All this describes a mere fragment of his greatness—for a more detailed account, you must look elsewhere.

Padmasambhava was a perfect author of pith instructions. The best of all authors are those who see the truth of the dharmatā, and Padmasambhava beheld the fundamental nature of phenomena just as it is. Those of moderate strength have looked upon the face of their yidam deity, and Padmasambhava beheld directly the sambhogakāya buddha fields and their yidam deities. Authors of least ability are those who are adept in the various activities. Padmasambhava, for his part, accomplished all of them without impediment—pacifying, increasing, magnetizing, and wrathful subjugating. Such is the author of this text.

ithi

This teaching,
This most *Precious and Illuminating Lamp*,
This path of all enlightened beings,
Past, present, and to come,
Is the key to the entire Tripiṭaka,
The heart of all the tantras and their commentaries,
The vital sap of every pith instruction,
The explanation of the crucial points of certain meaning,
The wisdom of the heart of all the buddhas,
The secret path of Vajrasattva,
The lamp that drives away the dark,
The guiding rail to keep from deviation. {266}
Buddhahood is thereby placed upon your palm;
Samsara's depths are thereby churned.
In this text, *The Precious and Illuminating Lamp*,
The gradual path of Secret Mantra
I shall now set forth.

With devotion, I bow down to the three roots.

Subduing both, possessing both, transcending both:[6]
The twofold supreme glory,[7]

Embodiment of all without exception[8]
And the genuine state devoid of all deceit,[9]
Is the lord Samantabhadra, the sixth of those who go in bliss,
To him I bow respectfully with fervent faith.

I, the yogi Padmasambhava from Oḍḍiyāna,
Will now compose *The Precious Lamp*
For yogis who are fortunate in times to come.
It is a gradual path of practice of the Vajrayāna
That brings accomplishment within a single life.

Recognize the fundamental nature
And the nature of delusion:
The first is nonduality, spontaneous presence,
Primal purity, primordial buddhahood.
The second is ignorance of the essence,
Karma and defilement, wrong view, and sorrow.

The basis for the practice should be marked by five perfections.
Carefully survey the qualities and defects of the place—
Cliffs or forests, charnel grounds or caves.
Have devotion and receive empowerment;
Keep samaya and have the confidence of wisdom.
Begin your practice on a good day of the lunar month,
Beneath propitious stars, on good days of the week,
Before the moon begins to swell.
Gather your provisions, the medicines you need, the substances of offering,
Materials for confession, restoration, and the practice.
Do not be complacent, but with a focused courage
Bring your practice to accomplishment.

Now for the levels of the circle of protection for the practice:
Practice so that all embodied beings

Attain supreme enlightenment.
Set up the protection with the deity's implements,
With wheels or vajras, weapons, fire. {267}
Consider that your body, speech, and mind
Are syllables of the enlightened body, speech, and mind.
Meditate upon Avalokita, Mañjuśrī, and your yidam deity.
Meditate upon the vajra ground, the vajra fence, the vajra tent,
The arrows, and the fire—
And rest within the state of understanding
That there is no object, no agent, and no harm.

Set out upon the path by means of five key points.
Take refuge—common, special, unsurpassed.
Three mantras: white, red, black—
Recite each one a hundred times.
Make offerings and restore samaya.
Meditate upon your freedoms and advantages,
Upon the karmic law, impermanence, the defects of samsara.
Offer both the mandalas—of accomplishing and offering.
With tormas of the various practices,
Gather two accumulations.
Make your daily tormas, three, seven, or eleven.
Make seven pure offerings,
And outer, inner, secret offerings.
These are the preliminaries of the path of Secret Mantra.

Lay the path's foundation with three trainings:
Abandon what is inappropriate,
Place your mind in even meditation,
Recognize your nature.
These three [trainings] are the *śikṣaṇa*:
Śīla, samādhi, and prajñā.
Shrink from harmful action; practice [beneficial deeds]
Conjoined with special means.
Never cease from training in the vision of the truth.
There are, as antidotes, the four and eighty thousand teachings.

By means of the three attitudes of mind, embark upon the path:
Consider beings as your dearest parents;
Wish that they have happiness;
Wish too that they be free from suffering;
Wish and act in such a way that all attain enlightenment.
To these three attitudes there correspond the Three Collections,
The three trainings, and the three experiences:
The enlightened mind.

The essence of the Secret Mantra's special path
Is the granting of the four empowerments—
The vase, the secret, wisdom, and great bliss.

Visualize the outer world and inner beings
As one vast palace thronged with deities.
Freedom from arising and cessation and duality
Is the self-arisen wisdom that transcends conceptual extremes.

When three key points are mastered,
A state of luminosity arises free of ordinary cognition.

Let your outer conduct be the strength behind your path.
Enhance it with your secret and your ultimate behavior.

Keep the five samaya pledges {268}
Linked with meditation, with post-meditation,
With food, with what should be upheld,
And with what should be observed.
For this is the essential nature of the path of Secret Mantra.

Practice these five yogas:
Sleep in the state of dharmakāya beyond the ordinary mind,

And clear away the concept "death."
Rise in the unceasing sambhogakāya,
And clear away the concept "birth."
Bless your food and drink that they become amṛta
According to the four empowerments,
And then enjoy them.
Grasp with skillful means the various [defilements],
Transforming them into the path.
At dawn [when primordial wisdom] arises,
At dusk [when your defilements] manifest,
At death, and in the bardo
Be absorbed in practice.

The way to banish four impediments and faults
Arising on this path will now be shown.
Rectify your dullness, agitation, meditative experience,
And bring them to the path.
Recognize the basis of disease,
Its causes and conditions and results;
Devise a cure and drive it out
By resting in the freedom from all mental movement.
Sever thus the stream [of thoughts],
Allowing wisdom to arise.
Eat food that saps the strength [of all such ailments],
And cast your worries far away without a care.
A streaming forth of letters *hūṃ*—white, red, and black—
Will drive diseases from the body from above and from below.
[All hindering forces are] none other than yourself.
Discard, therefore, all fear and doubt.
Remove the fourfold obscuration
Deriving from degenerate samaya, companions, places, food.

Strike at the key point of this path, and so progress.
Give up your ego-clinging, root of every fault.
Strong practice is the basis of all excellence.

When you stall upon the path,
Enhance your practice with ancillaries,
[With skillful means and wisdom.]
Seize defilements at their vital point,
And carry them upon the path.
Likewise carry thoughts upon the path,
Enhancing thus your practice.
All these are supportive factors of your path.

The manifest results, accomplished on this path,
Are the five enlightened bodies, fivefold enlightened speech,
Five enlightened minds, activities and qualities,
[Altruistic works], supported, unsupported, one in nature.
The [wisdom minds of buddhas] are neither one nor many.
Examine whether what they see is true or false—
Exists or else does not exist. {269}

Definitive teachings show completely and unerringly
This short path for attaining full enlightenment within a single life.
This tradition that combines both skillful means and wisdom
Is the supreme vehicle—unsurpassed, victorious, and overwhelming.

Through the stainless merit of this composition,
May all set out upon the path to ripening and freedom.
May they dispel conceptual obscuration
That conceals their birthright, [buddha nature],
And may they drive away all faults
Quickly to achieve their true and perfect buddhahood.

This concludes *The Precious and Illuminating Lamp*, a gradual path of the Secret Mantra, composed by Padmasambhava from Oḍḍiyāna.

A Textual Outline of the Inner Explanation of *The Precious and Illuminating Lamp: The Gradual Path of the Secret Mantra*[10]

Homage to the glorious Samantabhadra.

I. Introduction
  A. Homage (Subduing both . . .)
  B. Promise to compose (I, the yogi . . .)
II. The teaching itself
  A. The ground
    1. The fundamental nature (The first is nonduality . . .)
    2. Delusion (The second is ignorance . . .)
  B. The path
    1. The preliminaries
      a. The five perfect features of the foundation for practice
        i. The place (The basis for the practice . . .)
        ii. The person (Have devotion and . . .)
        iii. The time (Begin your practice . . .)
        iv. Equipment to be assembled (Gather your provisions . . .)
        v. Methods of practice (Do not be complacent . . .)
      b. Explanation of the levels of the circle of protection {270}
        i. The protection of bodhicitta (Now for the levels of the circle . . .)
        ii. The protection with five weapons (Set up the protection . . .)
        iii. The protection with the three syllables (Consider that your body . . .)
        iv. The protection by the three levels of peaceful and wrathful deities visualized one above the other (Meditate upon Avalokita . . .)
        v. Self-arisen and spontaneous protection (Meditate upon the vajra ground . . .)
        vi. The ultimate protection devoid of characteristics (And rest within the state . . .)
      c. Setting out on the Mahāyāna path by means of five key points
        i. Laying the foundation by taking refuge (Set out upon the path . . .)
        ii. Purifying obscuration with the hundred syllables (Three mantras: white, red, black . . .)
        iii. Training the mind by reflecting on karma and impermanence (Meditate upon your freedoms . . .)

iv. Gathering the accumulations through mandala and torma offerings (Offer both the mandalas . . .)
v. Increasing the accumulation through the making of other offerings (Make seven pure offerings . . .)

2. The path itself
a. The common general path
i. Laying the foundations with the three trainings
A) Identification of the three trainings (Lay the path's foundations . . .)
B) An explanation of the Sanskrit terms (śīla, samādhi . . .)
C) The defining features of the three trainings (Shrink from . . .)
D) The way in which the three trainings arise in the minds of individuals (Never cease from . . .)
E) The number of teachings according to their antidotes (There are, as antidotes, . . .)
ii. A guide for the path through three attitudes
A) Loving-kindness (By means of the three attitudes . . .)
B) Compassion (Consider beings as . . .)
C) Bodhicitta (Wish and act . . .)
D) Their identification with the Tripiṭaka reveals them as the three trainings (To these three attitudes . . .)
b. The path of mantra
i. The empowerment, which brings the mind to ripeness (The essence of the Secret Mantra . . .)
ii. The view that liberates the ripened mind
A) Training in the generation stage (Visualize the outer world . . .) {271}
B) Training in the perfection stage (Freedom from arising . . .)
iii. The meditation whereby one becomes habituated to the view (When three key points . . .)
iv. The conduct that never separates from the training in the view and meditation (Let your outer conduct . . .)
v. The samaya of never transgressing the view, meditation, and conduct (Keep the five samaya pledges . . .)

3. Ancillary factors on the path
a. The key points of the practice of the path of five yogas
i. The yoga of sleep (Sleep in the state of . . .)
ii. The yoga of rising (Rise in the unceasing . . .)
iii. The yoga of eating (Bless your food . . .)

iv. The daily yoga (Grasp with skillful means . . .)
v. The yoga related to important times of the day (At dawn . . . at dusk . . .)
b. Four ways to dispel hindrances on the path
i. Dispelling the obstacle of a weak concentration (Rectify your dullness . . .)
ii. Dispelling the obstacle of physical sickness and pain (Recognize the basis . . .)
iii. Dispelling the obstacles of gods and spirits and thoughts ([All hindering forces] . . .)
iv. Dispelling the hindering obscurations of adventitious circumstances (Remove the four . . .)
c. Making progress on the path
i. Dispelling defects that have hindered progress (Give up your ego-clinging . . .)
ii. Laying the foundations for progress (Strong practice is the basis . . .)
iii. The way to progress
A) Enhancing one's practice on the path (When you stall . . .)
B) Causing to arise what has not yet been acquired
1) Enhancement by means of the defilements (Seize defilements . . .)
2) Enhancement by means of thoughts (Likewise carry thoughts . . .)
C. The result accomplished on the path
1. Identifying the resultant qualities (The manifest results . . .) {272}
2. The way in which beings are benefited ([Altruistic works] . . .)
3. The way of abiding in the fundamental nature (The [wisdom minds of buddhas] . . .)
4. Halting the wrong thoughts of others regarding the compassionate seeing of beings to be trained (Examine whether . . .)
III. Conclusion
A. Showing the greatness of the dharma (Definitive teachings . . .)
B. Dedication of merits to the gaining of omniscience (Through the stainless merit . . .)
C. The title of the text and the conclusion (This concludes . . .)

This concludes the condensed summary of *The Inner Gradual Path of the Secret Mantra.*

The Essence of the Gradual Path of the Secret Mantra

A Pointing-Out Instruction in Five Parts through Which the Nature of the Mind Is Nakedly Shown[11]

Guru Padmasambhava

Homage to all our holy teachers.

This essential pointing-out instruction by Guru Padmasambhava, through which the nature of the mind is nakedly shown, has five parts. The first part is an admonition to watch one's mind. The second reveals the nature of the mind when this has not been seen. The third is an introduction to the nature when it has been seen. The fourth discusses the examples used [to support this introduction]. The fifth concerns the gaining of certainty.[12]

[I. Watching the Mind]

What is your own mind? Look at it. Just bring it to me. Now if you say, "The mind is empty; there is nothing to look at," this only means that you haven't seen it. If you say, "All appearances are the mind," that means that you have seen only the mind's perceptions in general. You are still failing to recognize the mind of this present instant. And, however much you may look for sky, earth, mountains, and so on in your mind, you do not find them there.

[II. The Nature of the Mind That Has Not Yet Been Seen]

Now as for how the nature of the mind is shown, to see the mind's general perceptions does not amount to seeing the mind. You have to recognize *as your mind* whatever is appearing in it right now. Sound, for instance, arises as the mind. When I say, "What is your mind? Look at it!" it is the [sound itself] that is your mind manifesting. And then, what is the "you" [implied in the "your" of "your mind"]? You may reply that the one who is looking is the mind itself. This is a way of pointing out using the example of a mother with her child. {273} Moreover, with "Look at your mind!" is it the sound that is looking at the mind as something over here? Or is your mind grasping the sound as something over there? Or again, are the sound and mind inseparable? Watch! If you answer that either one or the other of the first two options is right, you haven't understood. If you answer that you can't separate them, then you have understood, and that is how the introduction is made.

The objects of the five senses, forms and so on, should be introduced as being the mind in the same way.

[III. The Nature of the Mind That Has Been Seen]

The introduction to the nature of the mind when it has been seen is in three stages: the introduction to the appearing aspect of the mind as a state of natural openness and freedom, the introduction to its fundamental condition as the primordial state of openness and freedom, and the introduction to its nondual ultimate nature.

First of all, when I ask you, "What is it?" Is the mind of the one who watches the watcher itself—or is it something else? If you say it is something else, you haven't understood. If you say it is the watcher, then you have seen it, and the nature of the mind has been introduced. If you are clearly certain that the mind of the watcher is not something else, you have been introduced to the fact that the watcher is the mind's own self-experience. And this will lead you to understand that it is a state of *natural* openness and freedom. If you know that the mind of the watcher is the watcher itself, you will have no thoughts that apprehend it as something other. This is the crucial point of its natural openness and freedom.

Regarding the introduction to the primordial state of openness and freedom, when I say to you, "This mind, which appears to be watching—is this appearance [of the watching mind] a truly existent, autonomous, thing? Or is it by nature empty?" If you say that it is an autonomous thing, you have not understood. If you say that it is empty, then I will ask you further, "Is it empty when you concentrate on it, is it empty after it has vanished, or is it just empty in itself?" If you say that either the first or the second is right, you have not understood. But if you answer that this appearance of the mind watching is empty in itself, its nature has been seen. The nature of the mind has been introduced. If you are clearly certain that the appearance of the watching mind is not an autonomous and truly existing thing, you have been introduced to its emptiness, and this will lead you to the understanding that it is a state of primordial openness and freedom. If you understand that this appearance is empty, you will not take it as something truly existent. This is the crucial point of the primordial openness and freedom of the mind.

For the introduction to the mind's nondual ultimate nature, I ask you, "Is the emptiness of the mind a mere nothingness, or is the mind's emptiness luminous and aware?" If you answer that it is a mere nothingness, you have not understood. If you answer that it is luminous and aware, {274} then I will ask you further, "Is this emptiness separate from luminosity and awareness, or is it identical with them?" If you say that it is separate, you have not understood. If you say that it is identical with them, then the ultimate nature of the mind has been seen. The nature of the mind has been introduced. Seeing that appearance and emptiness cannot be parted, you are introduced to the fact that they are inseparable. And this will lead to the recognition of their nonduality. Abiding in their nonduality, you will not have thoughts of dualistic apprehension, and this is said to be the realization of the mind's nonduality.

[IV. The Examples Used in the Introduction]

The introduction is supported by examples, and these fall into three categories. First, regarding the introduction to the natural state of openness and freedom, it must be said that in their fundamental condition, appearing phenomena do not extend beyond the state of original openness and freedom [in the same way that birds in flight do not go beyond the confines of the sky. Second, regarding the introduction to the primordial state of openness and freedom, it must be said that, in their fundamental condition, phenomena do not extend beyond the state of original openness and freedom],[13] just as on a golden island there is only gold, and in the expanse of water, there is only water. Third, regarding the supporting examples for the introduction to nonduality, all phenomena are nondual in their ultimate nature just as heat is indivisible from fire and humidity is indivisible from water. All this may be understood through observation.

[V. Gaining Certainty]

For this there are three points: gaining certainty in primordial purity, gaining certainty in spontaneous presence, and gaining certainty regarding the nature of all things.

Gaining certainty in primordial purity has in turn three aspects: First, all thoughts—to the effect that the appearances that ceaselessly arise as the mind's display are something other [than the mind]—are themselves pure from the very beginning. This is the primal purity of primordial wisdom. Second, because the character of all arising appearances is empty, phenomena are, from the very beginning, pure or devoid of true existence as autonomous entities. This is the primal purity of the ultimate expanse. Third, because the ultimate nature of all phenomena is the indivisibility of appearance and emptiness, this means that all distinct, dualistic phenomena are pure from the very beginning. This is the primal purity of nonduality.

Gaining certainty in spontaneous presence has again three aspects. First, there is no need to search for the mind's display anywhere other than in variegated manifestation. What arises is the mind itself. This is the spontaneous presence of phenomena. Second, there is no need to search for the character of all manifestations anywhere other than in emptiness. That which arises [phenomenal appearances] is empty in itself. This is the spontaneous presence of the nature of phenomena. Third, there is no need to search for the ultimate nature of everything anywhere other than in the indivisibility of appearance and emptiness. Whatever appears is intrinsically nondual. This is the spontaneous presence of nonduality.

With regard to the gaining of certainty with respect to the nature of all things, all phenomena are your own mind. {275} The cognizing aspect of the mind is utterly unceasing. Its fundamental condition is the complete absence of existence. Its ultimate nature is utterly devoid of ordinary cognition. This reveals the character of all phenomena.

This shows that the ground of all phenomena is the nonduality of appearance and emptiness. The mind's cognizing aspects are utterly unceasing. The fundamental condition of outer appearances is the complete absence of existence. Their ground is empty. Their ultimate nature is utterly devoid of ordinary cognition. Their ground has the character of nonduality.

This refers also to the view—namely, the character of both the generation and perfection stages. The generation stage is unceasing, and the perfection stage is its complete absence of existence. Their nonduality is beyond the reach of ordinary cognition. This refers also to meditation—that is, the character of calm abiding and deep insight. Deep insight is unceasing, calm abiding is the absence of existence, and their nonduality is beyond the reach of ordinary cognition. This refers also to the character of the result—namely, the three kāyas of buddhahood. The sambhogakāya is unceasing. The dharmakāya is the absence of existence. The nirmāṇakāya is beyond the reach of ordinary cognition. This refers also to the primordial wisdom endowed with the two kinds of knowledge. The knowledge of all things is unceasing. The knowledge of their nature refers to the fact that they have no existence. The knowledge of their indivisibility is beyond the reach of ordinary cognition. This refers to the perfection of the factors that are to be eliminated and the qualities of realization. The latter are perfectly unceasing, and that which is to be eliminated is completely without existence.

Knowing all this, you gain certainty that samsara and nirvana, defects and good qualities, gods and demons, and so on are equal. Because they are unceasing, appearances are equal in being the self-experience of awareness. Because they are devoid of existence, they are equal in being empty. Because they are beyond ordinary cognition in their ultimate nature, they are equal in the nonduality [of appearance and emptiness].

Consequently, the ground of all appearances is but the fundamental nature of things. The view is but the nature of the generation and perfection stages. The meditation is but the nature of calm abiding and deep insight. The result is but the mandala of the three kāyas of buddhahood. Once you have recognized that appearances are the self-experience of awareness, there is no cognizing them as being something other. Once you have recognized that they are self-empty, there is no apprehension of a true independent existence of things. Once you have recognized that appearance and emptiness are indivisible, there is no apprehension of their being two separate aspects.

{276} Consequently, emptiness arises as both cause and effect—and to know this is the special feature of omniscience. Thanks to the realization that cause and effect are empty, a clear certainty is gained concerning the great state of equality. All phenomena exist as mere appearances, and this is the power of the relative truth. Phenomena lack true existence, and this is the character of the ultimate truth. Phenomena are neither existent nor nonexistent; they are neither permanent nor annihilated [momentary]. Defects are primordially pure. Good qualities are primordially complete. Ontological extremes are primordially nonexistent. Nonduality refers to the nonexistent two. Union refers to the unfound pair. Freedom from ontological extremes refers to the unfound extremes. The "all-good" refers to the unfound good and bad. Spontaneous presence needs no exertion. Primordial purity is the absence of delusion. All divisions are erased. All foundations are torn out. All separate elements blend together into one. There is not a single phenomenon in samsara and nirvana that is not primordially a state of openness and freedom.

This then is the pointing-out instruction in five parts through which the nature of the mind is nakedly shown, a short teaching belonging to the gradual path of the Secret Mantra called *The Precious and Illuminating Lamp.*

ithi

Instructions for Meditation on the Gradual Path of the Secret Mantra Given in the Manner of an Introduction to the Nature of the Mind[14]

Guru Padmasambhava

The Staff-Pointing Instruction Given to an Old Man: An Introduction to Enlightenment[15]

namo guru

Master Padmasambhava once spent a year in the solitude of Drakpoche. Now during that time, there was living there an old man of sixty years, Ngok Sherab Gyalpo, a person of little study but much devotion and faith. He did not, however, request instruction, and thus the Master did not teach him. But when a year had passed and Guru Rinpoche was minded to depart, Ngok placed gold coins like flowers on a mandala plate and, offering it to him, made the following request: {277}

> Precious Master, think lovingly of me. First of all, I am not a learned man. Second, I am of small intelligence, and finally I am old. Great Master, I beg you to bestow on me, an old man close to death, an instruction that is easy to grasp, cuts through all misunderstandings, and may be realized easily—that brings everything together and is easy to practice.

The Master pointed his staff at the old man's heart and gave him this instruction:

Listen! Watch your own awareness, your enlightened mind. No shape, no color does it have. It is without division or direction. No center does it have and no periphery. First, it has no arising; it is empty. Second, it does not remain; it is empty. Finally, it doesn't go anywhere; it is empty. If you recognize its emptiness, you recognize your own nature and understand the nature of all things. Then the mind is seen by mind; the primal fundamental nature of the mind is understood.

Awareness, the enlightened mind, not existing as a thing, dwells self-arisen in yourself. Do not look for it elsewhere. The truth of dharmatā is easily realized, and yet this same truth of dharmatā cannot be grasped by a mind marked by hopes and fears. Your mind is beyond the extremes of permanence and nothingness. Your mind cannot *become* enlightened, for it is buddhahood itself. Your mind cannot go to hell, for hell itself is your own mind. The mind can have no expectation of buddhahood, for it is [already] buddhahood. There is no fear of hell, for awareness is naturally pure. It cannot be altered. Awareness is dharmatā, which is naturally luminous. The view, the great fundamental nature, is within yourself. It is pointless to look for it elsewhere—be completely sure of this!

Now if you have this understanding, you might wish to bring it into your direct experience. Wherever you may be, your own body is your mountain solitude. {278} Whatever appears outwardly is your mind's self-experience. It is luminous of itself, empty of itself, and arises and subsides of itself. Rest in a state that is free of any movement of thought. It is then that all outer appearances become your friends, for they are pure in nature. Since they are naturally pure, it is easy to bring them onto the path and make them part of your practice.

Inwardly, whatever thought arises in your mind, whatever moves in your mind, has no intrinsic being—it is empty. Moving thoughts are pure in their nature. If you remember this and carry your thoughts onto the path, your practice will be easy.

Secretly, no matter what defilements occur, if you just watch them, they will fade away without leaving any trace. They arise all by themselves and they subside all by themselves. If you bring them onto the path, your practice will be easy.

When you practice in this way, there is no need for you to meditate in sessions. Everything will manifest as your friend and this experience will neither wax nor wane. [Your experience of] dharmatā, primordial wisdom, will be without interruption and your conduct will be free from acceptance and rejection. In any situation, you will never separate from the truth of the dharmatā.

When you gain realization of this, you will understand that though your body has grown old, the enlightened mind cannot age and that there is no such thing as sharp or dull faculties. You will understand that whereas your body, the support of your consciousness, may be destroyed, self-cognizing primordial wisdom, the dharmakāya, continues unchanging without a break. When you gain stability in this understanding, life is neither long nor short. Dharmatā is everywhere. And if you understand the meaning of this, there is no such thing as erudition, vast or small.

Old man, practice this true path! Bind your mind in service to the practice. Never forget my words and what they mean. Never part from diligence; it is your friend! Embrace mindfulness. Take no pleasure in gossip and worthless chatter, and let go of all the ordinary attitudes of mind. Do not cling to your children. Do not crave food or drink. {279} Think of the fundamental nature. Be diligent; in this life there is no time to waste. Practice this instruction—given for an old man close to death.

Pointing his staff at the old man's heart, Master Padmasambhava give him this instruction. And he, Ngok Sherab Gyalpo, gained accomplishment.

The Staff-Pointing Instruction Given to an Old Man—an introduction to enlightenment—was written down for the sake of future generations by Tsogyal, Lady of Kharchen.

Virtue!

The Finger-Pointing Instruction Given to an Old Woman[16]

namo guru

Once, when Master Padmasambhava, invited to Tibet by King Trisong Detsen, was staying at Drakmar, a faithful lady was living there by name of Gedenma. She was advanced in years and of deep piety and was greatly devoted to the Master. Every morning, she would send her servant Rinchen Tso, a woman of Margön, to the Master with a cup of milk and a handful of raisins. Later, when the Master was leaving for Samye, old Gedenma made prostrations on the path and, circumambulating the Master, made this request:

> Great Master! Now that you are leaving, I beg you to give an instruction to me, an old woman who has not long to live. To begin with, I have the body of a woman, and thus I am of lower birth. Then I am of scant intelligence with little knowledge and learning. Finally, I am old—my wits are dull and my eyes are bleary. Therefore, Great Master, I ask you to grant to me, an old woman, a teaching that is without difficulty—that is easy to understand and practice and that will be of great benefit.

The Master said, "Who are you, old woman?" and she replied, "I am the person who sent a servant every morning to bring you, my Master, a cup of milk." The guru said, "Your devoted faith is greater than that of Trisong Detsen himself." {280} And with that, he gave the following instruction to the old lady and her servant.

"Now, old woman," he said. "Sit cross-legged with your back straight and let your mind relax for a while." And pointing his finger at her heart, the Master spoke to her and said,

> Listen now, old woman. What is the difference between the wisdom mind of a truly perfect buddha and the [minds of] beings of the three worlds? It is the realization or lack of realization of the nature of the mind—and nothing else. If you realize the nature of your mind, you are a buddha. If you do not realize it, you wander in samsara. Even though you already possess the primordial wis-

dom of buddhahood, you do not recognize it. It is the cause of buddhahood, and it lies in every sentient being. It is found especially in all humans endowed with freedoms and advantages. It is not that men have a greater cause for buddhahood and women have a lesser cause. So being a woman is not at all a disqualification for the attainment of enlightenment!

In order that beings grasp and realize this primordial wisdom, the Buddha set forth the eighty-four thousand ways of practicing the dharma. And to enable beings to understand their meaning, all is gathered into three statements. These are given as the teacher's instruction, the power of which is unaffected by the weakness of mind and little intelligence of their hearers. These three statements reveal the nature of things, the wisdom mind of all the buddhas. They are as follows. Because the objects of apprehension appearing in the outer world are pure—these appearances are free and open just as they are. Because the inner mind that apprehends them is also pure, awareness, free of fixation, is also free and open just as it is. In between these two, you can recognize your own nature in the pleasant experience of luminosity.

What does it mean to say that the outer objects of apprehension are pure? It means that when you settle in awareness, the enlightened mind—which appears as a state of intrinsic luminosity, undistorted by thought—you do not fixate on the objects that appear. No matter what happens, you do not cling to them as truly existent. {281} It means that you do not fix on anything that appears to you as having real existence—rocks, mountains, fruit trees, forests, houses, castles, riches, grains, enemies or relatives, brothers, sisters or friends, your husband or your children. It means that, although they appear to you, you do not take them as real—you do not cling to them. This is what is called the purity of the outer objects of apprehension. Though it is said that the outer objects of apprehension are pure, this does not mean that they are nonexistent. It is just that there is no fixation, no attachment to them. They are clearly manifest, and yet they are empty. It is like when things are reflected in a mirror, there is nothing [in the mirror] that you can get hold of, nothing that you can cling to. This is the same as saying that sense objects are empty—though they appear, they are empty of themselves.

The inner apprehending mind is also pure. Awareness is open and free in itself. Here is a pith instruction concerning it. Whatever mental states arise—whatever thoughts, shifting memories, or defilements occur—if you do not cling to them, these selfsame movements melt away all by themselves. They are empty and their movement leaves no stain upon awareness. When it is said that inner awareness is not stained, this does not mean that it is a material object like earth or rock. It is rather that awareness is not stained by thought. This is like traveling to an island of gold. When you get there, even the words *stone* and *earth* are not to be found. In the same way, it is said that when you find freedom in self-cognizing primordial wisdom, even the word *thought* will not occur.

Between these two [the outer object and the inner mind], there is the pleasant experience of luminosity, and for this I will give you the following pith instruction. When you are practicing, when you meditate on awareness—stainless, clear, bright, and wide awake—the three experiences of bliss, luminosity, and no-thought will come, unspoiled by attachment and fixation. This is the wisdom mind of all the buddhas. You will recognize your own nature in just the same way that, when something belongs to you, you do not need to meditate in order to persuade yourself that it is yours. A thought that it is not yours will never occur to you. In the same way, when you recognize all on your own that your awareness is the ultimate nature of phenomena, {282} you will have no need to meditate on the fact that all the phenomena of samsara and nirvana are in fact the dharmatā. Even if you don't meditate on this, phenomena are never separate from the ultimate nature. This is the so-called meditation of no meditation. The understanding that all phenomena lack intrinsic being is the child of primordial wisdom. The recognition of awareness, the dharmadhātu, is called the recognition of one's own nature. When you reach that point, there is no such thing as higher or lower birth, greater or lesser activities, sharp or dull intelligence, greater or lesser wisdom, vast or little learning, clear or unclear mind.

So practice this instruction, old woman. It is not difficult. It is easy to understand and practice, and it will bring you immense

> benefit. Do not be afraid of death. In this life, however, there is no time to waste, so be diligent. It is better to meditate for a single instant on awareness than it is to labor for a thousand years as the unpaid servant of your husband and children. Be quick to follow your teacher's instructions. The activities of this life have no end. Bring instead your meditation to its accomplishment. Practice my advice on how to welcome death without any fear.

Because Master Padmasambhava gave this instruction pointing his finger at the woman's heart, it is called *The Finger-Pointing Instruction Given to an Old Woman*. The lady and her servant both attained accomplishment and freedom.

For the sake of future generations, Tsogyal, Lady of Kharchen, set it down in writing.

This concludes *The Finger-Pointing Instruction Given to an Old Woman*.

These stages of the outer and inner paths are the unerring vajra teachings of the great Master Padmasambhava. Their long lineage of oral transmission, beginning with Nyak Jñānakumāra and Nub Sangye Yeshe, is unbroken. Similar to them in word and meaning are the upper and lower treasure teachings [associated respectively with Nyangral Nyima Özer and Guru Chökyi Wangchuk], together with the treasure teachings of Dorje Lingpa. Therefore, they should all be regarded as completely trustworthy. {283} Detailed autocommentaries and ancillary instructions, and so on, also exist.

15. The Excellent Path to Enlightenment

A Three-Part Guide for Meditation on the Three Excellent Instructions of the Text Finding Rest in the Nature of the Mind: A Teaching of the Great Perfection[1]

Longchen Rabjam

Outline

Part one: A guide to the outer expository causal vehicle
- The transmission lineages of the teachers
- The instruction for the practice itself
- The first vajra point: The difficulty of finding freedoms and advantages
  - Instruction 1: The freedoms that are the very nature of precious human existence
  - Instruction 2: The specific advantages of precious human existence
  - Instruction 3: The abyss of evil destiny
  - Instruction 4: The examples that illustrate the difficulty of acquiring a precious human existence
  - Instruction 5: The different kinds and possibilities of beings
  - Instruction 6: The senselessness of allowing this human life to go to waste
  - Instruction 7: The interrelatedness of causes and conditions
  - Instruction 8: The perpetual cycle of birth and death
  - Instruction 9: Praise of the freedoms and advantages of precious human existence
  - Instruction 10: The great joy of possessing freedoms and advantages
- The second vajra point: The transience of life
  - Instruction 11: The impermanence of the physical body
  - Instruction 12: The impermanence of the gods, the lords of beings

Leaving behind hope and fear regarding the result
Instruction 139: The ultimate expanse of dharmatā
Instruction 140: The nature of the kāyas, the display of the ultimate expanse
Instruction 141: The primordial wisdoms displayed within the kāyas

---

oṃ svasti siddhi {286}

The wish-fulfilling tree of freedom,
Growing in the ground of two accumulations,
Gleaming with the fruits and flowers
Of endless perfect qualities,
Casts a cooling shade of happiness and benefit
Over both samsara and nirvana.

To the enlightenment of the victorious ones,
This tree of miracles, I pay homage.

The treasures of holy dharma—outer, inner, secret—
The highway of the ground, path, and result I have traversed.
And now I shall elucidate a threefold excellent instruction
On the very essence of the vehicles of cause, result,
And the supreme and unsurpassed.

This text begins with a presentation of excellent outer instructions on the expository causal vehicle, the common ground of the two vehicles that follow. It goes on to supply excellent and particular inner instructions on the resultant vehicle of the Secret Mantra, the Vajrayāna, and concludes with excellent secret instructions on the unsurpassed vehicle of the Great Perfection, the ultimate and quintessential result.

Part One: A Guide to the Outer Expository Causal Vehicle

Here there are two sections: (1) a description of the transmission lineages of the teachers and (2) the instructions on the practice itself.

The Transmission Lineages of the Teachers

The many levels of teachings that I have studied in relation to the various approaches of the Mahāyāna may be completely subsumed under three topics: {287} first, the tradition of vast activities regarding the gradual training in the teachings; second, the profound and vast tradition of teachings on the grounds and paths, concentration, and experiential signs; and third, the tradition of the profound view, the teaching on the dharmatā, the ultimate and fundamental nature.

The lineage of the first tradition listed here consists of the great and powerful Buddha Śākyamuni, Mañjuśrī, Śāntideva, Eladhari, Mahāśrī, Ratnabhavavajra, Dharmakīrti, Dīpaṃkara, Sumati, Lotsāwa Loden Sherab, Tseponwa Chökyi Lama, Chapa Chökyi Senge, Denpakpa Darma Tashi, Sherab Lodrö, Sherab Wangchuk, Sangye Tsöndru, Wengewa Śākya Senge, Ladrangwa Chöpel Gyaltsen, and Samyepa Tsultrim Lodrö.

The lineage of the second tradition consists of the great and powerful Buddha Śākyamuni, Maitreya, Asaṅga, Vasubandhu, Ārya Vimuktisena, Bhadanta Vimuktisena, Paramasena, Vinītasena, Vairocanabhadra, {288} Haribhadra, Buddhajñāna, Guṇamitra, Ratnasarvaja,[2] Sthirapāla, Loden Sherab, Dre Sherab Bar, Ar Changchub Yeshe, Khu Sherab Tsöndru, Karchung Ringmowa, Zhang Yeba, Nyalzhik, Gyaching Rupa, Chumikpa Senge Pal, Lodrakpa. These were followed by Tsen Gönpa and the two Wengewas, followed by Langdrawa and Chödrakpa—and it was through the last two masters that the lineage came down to me.

The lineage of the third tradition consists of the buddha, Mañjughoṣa, Ārya Nāgārjuna, Candrakīrti, Rikpai Kuchuk, the Older and the Younger Kusali, Lord Atiśa, the Nepali Tangpa Dza, Abhayākara, Changchub Sempa Dawa Gyaltsen, Drolungpa the Great, Chiwo Lhepa Changchub Ö, Ma Śākya Senge, Chim Namkha Drak, Khenpo Möntsul, Lopön Changchub Drub, and Lopön Zhönu Dorje, through whom it came to me, Samyepa Ngaki Wangpo.

There also exists another teaching lineage, not detailed here, that comes down from Atiśa.

To you who are the supreme givers of good fortune,
Of abundant goodness, happiness, and every perfect quality,
Who with clouds of benefit and bliss possess the nature of compassion—
To you, O glorious lords and teachers, I respectfully bow down.

The Instruction for the Practice Itself

This instruction is divided into eight vajra points: (1) the difficulty of finding freedoms and advantages, (2) the transience of life, (3) the sufferings of existence in samsara, (4) the karmic law of cause and result, (5) attendance on a spiritual master, (6) refuge, (7) the four immeasurables, and (8) the cultivation of the attitude of aspiring to supreme enlightenment together with its precepts.

The First Vajra Point: The Difficulty of Finding Freedoms and Advantages

This section is divided into ten reflections on the following topics: (1) the freedoms that are the very nature of precious human existence, {289} (2) the specific advantages of such an existence, (3) the abyss of evil destiny, (4) the examples that illustrate the difficulty of acquiring precious human existence, (5) the different kinds and possibilities of beings, (6) the senselessness of wasting one's human life, (7) the interrelatedness of causes and conditions, (8) the perpetual cycle of birth and death, (9) praise of the freedoms and advantages of a precious human existence, and (10) the great joy of possessing them.

Instruction 1: The Freedoms That Are the Very Nature of Precious Human Existence

It is important that you think of the eight situations in which there is no leisure for the practice of dharma, reflecting that you have not fallen into them and are thus free. This is a matter of great rejoicing, and you should now endeavor in the practice of the dharma. If you had been reborn in hell, you would experience the suffering of extreme heat and cold. You would have no opportunity to practice the dharma. Likewise, if you had been reborn among the hungry ghosts, you would have the burning fire of hunger and thirst. The practice of dharma would be impossible for you. If you had been reborn among the animals, who suffer so much the violence of being devoured by each other and so on, you again would be unable to practice. Reborn as a god of vast longevity, you would spend an entire kalpa in a state devoid of all perception, and then at the moment of death, you would have wrong views. This too is a condition in which the practice of dharma is impossible. If you had been born in some barbarian land, where the light of the teachings does not shine, you would also be unable to practice. If you had been born among those who are outside the dharma, you would have false views and thus be deprived of the practice of the dharma. If you had been born in an age of darkness when the Three Jewels are not proclaimed, you would have no means of practicing the dharma. If you had been born handicapped, your mental faculties would be an unsuitable vessel, and again you would have no chance of practicing the dharma.

Since you have not been born in these eight conditions, you are said to have the freedoms to accomplish the teachings. You should therefore have a clear resolve, thinking that you will now endeavor in the practice of the dharma. You should first take refuge and cultivate the bodhicitta attitude. Reflecting then on the eight situations in which there is no freedom and on the reverse of this, the existential freedom that you have in fact obtained, you should come to the conclusion that the only thing to do is to practice the dharma. Think about this again and again, then dedicate the virtue of doing so, and in the post-meditation period, let your thoughts affect the way you live. {290}

Instruction 2: The Specific Advantages of Precious Human Existence

If a human body is not gained, it is impossible to practice the dharma. But even if you do have the personal advantage of being born a human being, the fact is that if you are born in a place where the dharma is not found, you will be unable to practice. Even if you have the personal advantage of being born in a central land where the dharma is proclaimed, if your sense powers are incomplete, you will be unable to practice the dharma. Even if you have the personal advantage of fully functioning sense powers, if you are born into an evil way of life and indulge in nonvirtue, the practice of dharma will be impossible. But even if you have the personal advantage of a wholesome way of living, and even if you do aspire to goodness, if you have no confidence or faith in the teachings, you will be unable to practice the dharma. By contrast, if you do have faith in the teachings, all these personal advantages will be yours.

If the Buddha had not appeared in the world, not even the name of the dharma would exist. But the Buddha has indeed appeared, and thus you have this sublime circumstantial advantage. On the other hand, if the Buddha had appeared but had not taught, it would have been to no avail. But the Buddha has in fact turned the wheel of dharma three times, and thus you possess this supreme circumstantial advantage. Now granted that the Buddha taught the dharma, this would be of no use if in the meantime the teachings had died out. But in fact, the dharma still exists without decline, and so it is that you have this supreme circumstantial advantage. Again, even if the teachings remain, if no one practices them, no good would come of it. But practitioners of the teachings do exist, and this is a sublime circumstantial advantage. On the other hand, even if there are people who practice the dharma, if there are no propitious circumstances in the form of teachers to set it forth, you would still be ignorant of what to do and what not to do. But the fact is that there are indeed genuine teachers ready to guide you with love and great compassion. So it is that you are in full possession of the five circumstantial advantages.

{291} You should therefore resolve from the core of your being that in this present moment, while you are in possession of these ten perfect advantages, you will put these freedoms and advantages to good use and make them meaningful. First, you should prepare the ground by taking refuge and cultivating the attitude of bodhicitta. Then as the main practice, you should reflect on the advantages of your present situation. Conclude by making the dedication, and in post-meditation bring this reflection to bear on the way you live.

Instruction 3: The Abyss of Evil Destiny

If beings fail to practice the dharma while they possess a body endowed with freedoms and advantages, when they die, they will, through the power of their karma, be born in one of the three evil destinies where even the word *dharma* is not heard. They will meet no spiritual master and, failing to recognize right from wrong, they will accomplish only nonvirtue and never anything wholesome. So it is that they will circle in endless samsara. What a terrible misfortune! Bearing this in mind, give yourself to the dharma in the three stages of preparation, main practice, and conclusion.

Instruction 4: The Examples That Illustrate the Difficulty of Acquiring a Precious Human Existence

Imagine that upon the surface of an ocean troubled by the wind there floats a yoke in constant movement here and there. In the depths of the ocean there lives a blind turtle that comes to the surface once every hundred years. Think to yourself that it is more difficult to escape the evil destinies and to be born in the human state than it is for the turtle to find the yoke and to come to the surface with its head inside it. Take a handful of dried peas, and throw them at a smoothly plastered wall. It is easier for one of the peas to stick to the wall than it is to gain a human birth. Reflect on examples like these in a session with the three stages of preparation, main practice, and conclusion.

Instruction 5: The Different Kinds and Possibilities of Beings

In general, when you reflect on the numbers of beings and on their different possibilities, you are led to the conclusion that to get a human life is almost impossible. And when you think about the number of beings who have no dharma and whose actions are invariably negative, you will understand that an interest in the teachings and the study of them is scarcely within the realms of possibility. {292} And it is even less likely to find beings who are actually willing to commit themselves to the true dharma and to practice it sincerely. Think about the fact that you have met an authentic teacher, that you have heard the profound teachings, and that it is possible for you to train on the path to liberation. Reflect that you have to make an effort to render your precious human life meaningful. Meditate on this in a session with the three stages of preparation, main practice, and conclusion.

Instruction 6: The Senselessness of Allowing This Human Life to Go to Waste

If you come home empty-handed from an island of jewels, what was the point of making the journey? In the same way, if you sail to the island of a precious human life but fail to gather the different jewels of the sublime dharma, if you are distracted by the affairs of this life and fail to set out on the path to freedom, you will be empty-handed even though you gained a precious human life. In a session complete with preparation, main practice, and conclusion, reflect upon your freedoms and advantages.

Instruction 7: The Interrelatedness of Causes and Conditions

The practice of the dharma depends on the mind, a mind that is supported by a body endowed with freedoms and advantages. It is hard to bring together all these favorable conditions. So decide that while you have a body that is free from disease and not in pain, and while you are a free agent and not beneath the power of someone else, you must strive in the dharma by every means. In preparation, take refuge and cultivate the attitude of bodhicitta. Then as your main practice meditate yearningly and repeatedly. In conclusion, make the dedication, and in post-meditation implement this teaching on the path.

Instruction 8: The Perpetual Cycle of Birth and Death

The beings in the three worlds and the six realms are constantly subject to birth and death and to the sufferings that belong to each of these conditions. And at the present time there is for them no freedom, no end in sight. The reason is that when they gain the freedoms and advantages of a precious human life, they fail to practice the dharma and let them go to waste. Therefore, reflect that you must make your freedoms and advantages meaningful. {293} Do so in a session complete with preparation, main practice, and conclusion.

Instruction 9: Praise of the Freedoms and Advantages of Precious Human Existence

It is said that the arhatship of the śrāvakas and pratyekabuddhas and even the enlightenment of the buddhas is achieved on the basis of a body endowed with the freedoms and advantages [of the precious human condition]. The same is true of the accomplishment of the powerful teachings of the Secret Mantra. These freedoms and advantages are described as noble because they are the support for the teachings of both the greater and lesser vehicles. So tell yourself that now that you possess these same freedoms and advantages, you must set out on the path to liberation. Cultivate the attitude of bodhicitta and reflect like this again and again, concluding with the dedication.

Instruction 10: The Great Joy of Possessing Freedoms and Advantages

Once you have taken refuge and cultivated the attitude of bodhicitta, think that in gaining the freedoms and advantages [of the precious human state] you are as happy as someone poor and destitute who has chanced upon a precious jewel. Isn't this just a dream? Can it really be true? You should be really delighted at your situation and tell yourself again and again that you will practice the dharma. Make the dedication, and let this thought affect the way you live.

The Second Vajra Point: The Transience of Life

The impermanence of life can be considered by reflecting on the following twelve things: (1) the physical body; (2) the gods, the lords of beings; (3) the formation and destruction of the universe and its inhabitants; (4) the transience of holy beings; (5) the uncertainty of the time of death; (6) the nature of compounded things; (7) the dreadful circumstances of death; (8) the fact that when beings die, they must go alone; (9) the beings that appear in the course of time; (10) the unreliability of this present life; (11) the uncertainty of the causes of death; (12) the cultivation of a strong awareness of death. {294}

Instruction 11: The Impermanence of the Physical Body

Consider the collection of major and minor members that is your body—and indeed the bodies of other people. For the time being you care for it by supplying it with suitable food and clothing. You keep it clean and smart. But when death comes, this body of yours will be carried away naked and unclothed to some lonely place where the jackals and vultures will eat it.

Its greater and lesser members will fall apart, and even its bones will fall into disconnected fragments. This is what will happen. Therefore, you must tell yourself that you will practice the dharma right now and reflect on this in a session complete with preparation, main practice, and conclusion.

Instruction 12: The Impermanence of the Gods, the Lords of Beings

Even for the gods, Devendra, Śakra, Īśvara, and Viṣṇu, and the great rishi Vyāsa, Vālmīki, and so on, who are beautiful and splendid in form, who can live for an entire kalpa, and who possess great qualities of wisdom, preternatural sight and knowledge, and limitless powers of miraculous display—for all of them there comes the moment of death. How could this not be so for someone like you? Think, therefore, that right now is the time to practice dharma, and reflect on this in a session with preparation, main practice, and conclusion.

Instruction 13: The Formation and Destruction of the World and Its Inhabitants

The world consisting of mountain ranges, countries and regions, and the men and women who inhabit it will all at length be reduced to nothing by the seven fires and the single flood that will bring the present kalpa to an end. And since the age of voidness that will follow will eventually arrive, how could you think that a being like yourself will not perish? Reflect on this in a session with the three stages of preparation, main practice, and conclusion.

Instruction 14: The Impermanence of Holy Beings

Even the seven buddhas,[3] together with their retinues, and in the ages of time that separated them, the pratyekabuddhas and others, together with their own retinues, have {295} at different times appeared and departed from the world. Likewise, their doctrine spread and then declined throughout the endless continuity of time. How could you possibly think that you and your environment will last forever? Therefore, make the strong wish that from now on you will implement the sublime dharma, and reflect on this in a session complete with the three stages of preparation, main practice, and conclusion.

Instruction 15: The Uncertainty of the Time of Death

It is impossible for you to add to your span of life. Every instant it grows less. Day and night bring death nearer and nearer like two marmots, white and black, chewing at the fibers of a rope of grass. There is no certainty where you will die, and many are the circumstances of death. Ask yourself: When will your death come to you? And reflect on this in a session complete with the three stages of preparation, main practice, and conclusion.

Instruction 16: The Impermanence of Compounded Things

Generally speaking, all compounded or conditioned things are impermanent. In particular, the lives of beings—or more specifically, the meeting of body and mind, the support for life—is impermanent. Ponder the fact that whole cities and monasteries, which grew and flourished in the past, are now but desolate and empty ruins, and then ask yourself: When will the time come for your body to be abandoned by your mind—like a city emptied of its people? Reflect on this in a session complete with preparation, main practice, and conclusion.

Instruction 17: The Circumstances of Death

The light of a butter lamp is impermanent. It is quickly exhausted, and it can in an instant be blown out by a sudden gust of wind. In just the same way, beings, once born, draw ever nearer to their deaths, and if there is a cause for their untimely death, such as a disease, an evil force, or some violent harm, they are unable to remain even for another instant. Keep in mind that you have no idea when such a thing will come to you. Prepare by cultivating bodhicitta, reflect like this as your main practice, and conclude with the dedication.

Instruction 18: When Beings Die, They Must Go Alone {296}

When the appearances of this life fade, you set out on the path to your next life. For the last time, you will lie down on your bed, you will eat your last meal, put on your clothes for the last time, and speak your last words. You will have to leave behind your family and friends and everything you have and set out alone. This moment will come and will be very hard for you to bear. Remember that you have no idea when this will happen, and therefore reflect on it now in a session complete with preparation, main practice, and conclusion.

Instruction 19: The Impermanence of Beings That Appear in the Course of Time

Of all the beings, beast or man, who lived more than one hundred years ago, not one is left alive. And in a hundred years' time, most beings now alive upon this earth will be no more. You are no exception to this rule and nor indeed will anyone be in times to come. You should think that just like the changing of the season's crops, all your neighbors and fellow countrymen in the place where you were born, all your relatives and friends, your dogs, your goats and cattle, all your enemies, and all your contemporaries and family will be no more. Reflect in this way in a session consisting of the three stages of preparation, main practice, and conclusion.

Instruction 20: The Unreliability of This Present Life

There is not a single place in the fastness of the mountains, in the heart of the sea, or in the regions of the air that is untouched by death—death that comes, timely or untimely, in every possible way. Especially in regions inhabited by human beings, the circumstances of death are very numerous. Think about the time when you will die, reflecting in a session with preparation, main practice, and conclusion.

Instruction 21: The Uncertainty of the Causes of Death {297}

Even when there are no untimely circumstances, the Lord of Death will come like the shadows of sunset. And yet very many people perish through poison, weapons, fire, water, the attacks of enemies, sickness, evil forces—or just by eating the wrong food, wearing the wrong clothes, or some other mishap. So ask yourself: When will I die? Reflect about it in a session complete with preparation, main practice, and conclusion.

Instruction 22: Cultivating a Strong Awareness of Death

When you go somewhere, ask yourself whether you will die there or whether you will return home. When you are on your way and you halt at a resting place, think that you might die there. You should do this wherever you are and whatever you do. Whether you are eating, walking, lying down, or whatever, tell yourself that this could be your final act. In this way you should earnestly recall the thought that death is always possible. As a preparation for this contemplation, cultivate the attitude of bodhicitta. Then as the main practice, bring up a powerful thought of the presence of death. Finally, make the dedication and in the post-meditation period let this affect the way you live.

The Third Vajra Point: The Sufferings of Samsara

The reflection on the sufferings of samsara has three sections: (1) the cultivation generally of a sense of sorrow or weariness with samsara, then (2) a more specific reflection on suffering itself, and finally (3) an examination of our present situation.

Instruction 23: Cultivating a Sense of Weariness with Samsara

The beings who wander in the three worlds of samsara are truly in a sorry state. Continuously turning in the circle of samsara, there is not a single being who is not connected to every other—whether in the close relation of father, mother, family, and friends, or in the hostile relation of enemies, or in the indifferent relation of anonymity. Moreover, if all the heads and members of the insect bodies that you have assumed [in samsara from time without beginning] were to be gathered together, they would make a mountain higher than Meru itself. {298} The tears that you have wept would fill an ocean and numberless would be the heads and limbs that you have lost in the pursuit of your desires. Though beings may be rich in this present life, endowed with perfect wealth, social connections and influence, it may well be that, after death, they will be reborn in situations of distress and poverty. [Their present life] is like the happiness of a dream, which vanishes when they wake. Since every happiness that beings may experience owing to the appearances of this life, and to which they are so attached, does not go beyond this sorry state of affairs, what is the point of it all? And given that your future lives represent a far greater quantity than this, your present life, you should resolve to adhere to the teachings that lead to freedom, organizing your reflection into a session with preparation, main practice, and conclusion.

The specific reflection on the sufferings of samsara is sixfold.

Instruction 24: The Eight Hot Hells

The beings in the Reviving hell gather together on a ground of glowing coals. Perceiving each other as mortal enemies, they slay one another with the weapons created by their karma. As soon as they die, there comes a voice from the sky crying, "Revive." The slain come back to life and the cycle of dying and resurrection begins again. This is what they must endure until their karma is exhausted.

Beings in the Black Line hell have black lines traced on their bodies by the workers of the Lord of Death who use these lines to cut them into pieces with saws of iron. As soon as their bodies are dismembered, they are joined together again, only to be torn apart once more.

Beings in the hell of Crushing are smashed into powder in valleys that are like iron mortars. They revive only to be pulverized again, crushed between rocky cliffs shaped like horses, camels, and so on.

Beings in the hell of Screaming are boiled in molten metal and their bodies are consumed by fire. They scream and wail in torment. In the Hell of Great Screaming, beings are driven into houses with walls of double-layered incandescent metal, where they are roasted and crushed with hammers ablaze with the fire of the Lord of Death.

Beings in the hell of Heat {299} are boiled in molten iron and copper. Their bodies are filled with fire through and through. Beings in the hell of Great Heat are burned in metal houses blazing with fire. They are impaled, head and shoulders, on tridents and are wrapped in sheets of incandescent metal.

Beings in the hell of Torment Unsurpassed are trapped in buildings of blazing metal. Surrounded by the sixteen additional neighboring hells, they experience the pains of all the other hells together. They are suffused with fire and can do nothing but lament.

As the feeling of pain increases sevenfold at each stage, the suffering increases sevenfold in sequence from one hell to the next. The suffering in these hellish states is beyond all bearing. So you must resolve that you will now do everything necessary to avoid being born there—reflecting in a session complete with preparation, main practice, and conclusion.

Instruction 25: The Neighboring Hells

In addition [to the hells just mentioned] there are sixteen neighboring hells—a set of four in each direction of the hell of Torment Unsurpassed. These are the trench of burning embers, the swamp of rotting corpses, the plain of knives, and the unfordable river of burning ash. When there is a slight lessening of the karma that has caused the experience of the dreadful pain of the burning houses of the hell of Torment Unsurpassed, the beings caught there have the impression that doors open in the four directions, and they escape.

They see what looks like a shady ravine and rush there, only to have their flesh and bones consumed in blazing embers. When they have the impression of escaping from this, they plunge into what looks like a flowing river, which turns out to be a quagmire of rotting corpses in which they are tormented, their bodies gnawed by worms with beaks of iron. They eventually escape and reach what looks like a pleasant plain, only to find that it consists of razor-sharp blades. Their feet are cut to pieces every time they take a step, only to become whole again as they raise them. {300} When they escape, they find themselves rushing into what looks like a pleasant forest. But the leaves of the trees turn into blades that move in the wind. They are sliced to pieces only to be made whole again immediately afterward. As they reach the limits of that place, they find themselves at the foot of a hill on the summit of which they see their former lovers, male or female, calling to them. As they climb up to them, their bodies are cut by the scalpel-like blades of the leaves of the trees. Arriving at the summit of the hill, they encounter carrion crows and vultures that gouge out their brains. Then they see their former lovers calling to them from below. Down they run only to be lacerated once again by the leaves that have now turned upward. Throwing themselves into the embrace of their former lovers, they find that they have now changed into monsters made of red-hot iron that take them into their arms and burn and devour them. Then in the distance, they see a pleasant flowing stream. Falling into it, they sink up to their waists in hot ashes that burn them, flesh and bone. They try to escape, but there on the riverbanks are the guards and minions of the Lord of Death.

Reflect that many times in the past, you have endured all these horrors. Now is the time to rid yourself of them completely. Again, structure your reflection into a session with the three stages of preparation, main practice, and dedication.

Instruction 26: The Eight Cold Hells

In the snowy mountains, caught in middle of ice and snow, in places lashed by freezing blizzards, beings are tormented by the cold. Blisters form on their body, and there their condition is called the hell of Blisters. Then there is the hell of Bursting Blisters, where the swellings burst and become open wounds. Then there are beings whose teeth chatter uncontrollably. This is the hell of Chattering Teeth. Then there is the hell of Lamentation, the "achu hell," corresponding to the noise made by the beings there. Then there is the hell of Groaning, where beings cry with long protracted moans. Then, in the hell of Utpala Wounds, the flesh of the beings there splits open in configurations that look like the four petals of an utpala lotus. This is followed by the hell of Lotus Wounds, where the flesh breaks open in patterns resembling the eight petals of a lotus flower. Finally, in the hell of Great Lotus Wounds, the flesh of the beings there splits apart in wounds of sixteen or thirty-two pieces like lotuses. {301} All these wounds are infested with tiny insects that burrow into the flesh and eat it. And everything is enveloped in the unbearable suffering of cold.

As you reflect on this, feel the relief of not being born in such a situation. And thinking that you must renew your efforts in the dharma, structure your reflection in a session complete with preparation, main practice, and conclusion.

Instruction 27: The Lesser Hells

In the lesser hells, beings take birth crushed in the middle of rocks. They are frozen and paralyzed in glaciers, boiled in hot springs, tormented in cold winter rivers, and tortured in fires. They take the form of logs of wood, and when these are chopped and split, they suffer pain as if their greater and lesser members were being hacked off. They may be born in the form of cooking pots, doors, mats, pillars, fireplaces, ropes, and so on—in the form of things that are in constant use. And because of their karma, they are tormented by the various pains that are associated with such things and that are so difficult to bear. In metallic structures, also, they suffer torments that differ during the day and night. And so it is.

Reflecting on the torment suffered by beings in the mountains, on the shores of the sea, in snow and glacial cold, in places whether deserted or inhabited by human beings, think that you must do everything necessary not to be reborn in such circumstances. And structure your meditation in the three stages of preparation, main practice, and conclusion.

Instruction 28: Pretas, or Hungry Ghosts

The pretas suffering from external obscurations have enormous bodies and tiny limbs. They are constantly tormented by hunger and thirst. They do not even hear the words "food and drink." They are harmed by others. They perceive as repulsive substances even lakes and forests, and so on, but these dry up as soon as they see them.

Pretas suffering from internal obscurations have fires burning in their hearts and lungs and smoke emerges through their mouths and noses. {302} Pretas suffering from specific obscurations suffer because their bodies are infested with other creatures that eat their flesh and drink their blood. Think that you must make sure not to be reborn in such forms, reflecting in a session with preparation, main practice, and conclusion.

Instruction 29: Animals

There are animals that live down in the depths of the great ocean and the seas that lie between the cosmic continents. There are so many of them that they are like the grains of barley packed in a beer barrel. They devour one another and they are dull and without intelligence. Then there are animals like birds and deer that live scattered through the human and divine worlds. Their sufferings are unbounded. They are killed, castrated, beaten, cut, and tormented in every possible way. Think that you must do whatever it takes not to be born in such states, and structure your reflection into a session with preparation, main practice, and conclusion.

Instruction 30: Human Beings

Human beings are tormented by the three and eight kinds of sufferings. In the first case, they experience suffering upon suffering, as when someone already afflicted with leprosy has eczema as well, or when even before an earlier disease or unwanted trouble has finished, another one arrives. The suffering of change is when for example people are at a wedding, rejoicing and dancing, and the house suddenly collapses, causing terrible injury. All-pervading suffering in the making is illustrated by the fact of [ignorantly] consuming poison or doing harm to another—actions that will be productive of suffering in the future. It refers to all the kinds of actions that will produce physical and mental torment at some later time. With the thought that you must now free yourself from all such torments, reflect about them in a session with preparation, main practice, and conclusion.

There now follows a reflection on the four rivers of suffering: birth, old age, sickness, and death. {303}

Instruction 31: Birth

At first, the consciousness in the bardo mixes with the father's semen and the mother's ovum. For seven weeks, a body gradually takes form, beginning with a round and then an oblong embryo. Then as it continues to live inside the body of its mother, developing more and more, it suffers because the womb is evil-smelling, nauseating, and cramped. The fetus also suffers when the mother eats, dresses, or engages in some unsuitable activity. When she is too hot, the fetus feels as though it is in a ditch of fire. When she is cold, it feels as though it has been thrown into snow or cold water. When she eats too much, it feels like it is being crushed by a mountain. When she feels weak and anxious, it feels as though it has been thrown into an abyss and as though it had been turned upside down and shaken. In all these ways, the fetus suffers greatly. When the baby is actually born, it is as if it is passing through the hell of Crushing, and it actually loses consciousness for a while. When the baby is touched, the pain is unbearable, as if its flesh were being sliced by razors. When it is being washed, it feels as if it is being flayed alive—and so on. A baby has countless sufferings to endure. Therefore, no matter where you are born, you are never beyond the reach of pain. Thinking that you must bring the continuum of birth to an end, structure your reflection in three stages: preparation, main practice, and conclusion.

Instruction 32: Old Age

Your strength of body will be lost. It will be hard for you to stand, to sit, and to move around. The clarity of your senses will dim. Your eyes will no longer see well, your hearing will be dull, and your memory will fade. As the power of consciousness is lost, your happiness of mind will evaporate, and you will sink into melancholy. As the channels and winds degenerate, you will become as silly and fretful as a child. Your body and mind will change, and illness and affliction will abound. You will become disagreeable company. You will say that you want to die, but in truth, death will be the very thing that you fear. Countless are the sufferings of age. Therefore, thinking that you must attain enlightenment beyond both birth and death, {304} reflect about this in a session with preparation, main practice, and conclusion.

Instruction 33: Sickness

When the equilibrium of the body's four elements is disturbed, the feeling of pain grows strong. Your physical constitution changes, your body aches and you become miserable. The force of your faculties diminishes, and it is hard to get out of bed. Nothing is pleasant and your mind is constantly disturbed. When obstacles in the form of negative forces appear, grave accidents occur. In terror of imminent death, the mind experiences great dread. Such are the sufferings of illness. Reflecting on how hard it is to bear illness and disease, you should reflect that now is the time to achieve the nectar that frees from torment. And structure your meditation in a session with preparation, main practice, and conclusion.

Instruction 34: Death

Finally, you will come to your last bed. You will eat your last meal. You will dress for the last time. You will speak your final words. No matter how many close friends and attendants you may have, none can give you the slightest shred of help. The feeling of approaching death is one of great dread. The escort of hallucinatory perceptions will arrive, and you must enter the dangerous pathway of the bardo. The elements of your body will dissolve, the appearances of this life will be left behind, and you will set out for the land of your next life. You will lose everything, going forth alone like a hair pulled from a lump of butter. However much food, however much wealth you may possess, you will not be able to take even a handful of ordinary tsampa. However many friends or attendants you may have, not one will be able to keep you company. Those who die go forth alone, and it is a terrible thing. You leave, and there is no returning.

Until now you have spent your time protecting your friends and getting the better of your enemies, planning for the future in terms of house and property, and doting on your children and those close to you with loving attention. What is the point of all this—the affairs of this life? Reflecting thus, you must tread the supreme path of liberation in which there is no death—structuring your meditation in the three stages of preparation, main practice, and conclusion. {305}

Instruction 35: Meeting with Adversity and Separation from What Is Loved

[Meeting with adversity] refers to encounters with unpleasant people and harmful situations. You do not want them, and so you suffer and are unhappy.

[Separation from what is loved is] when your friends and close relations die or move away to some far country, as soon as you think of them—their attractive qualities, their physical appearance and the sound of their voices; your heart will ache, and unhappiness will fall on you. This is what it is like to be deprived of what you like. It is the suffering that comes when pleasant situations change for the worse and your fortune declines.

Moreover, the five aggregates of form, feeling, perception, conditioning factors, and consciousness—all of which perpetuate the samsaric process—are the place where suffering occurs. They are its foundation and its source. Thus, they are sufferings in themselves. For example, when you are pricked by a thorn, the form aggregate is painful. The feeling aggregate knows this to be pain, and perception aggregate detects the pain from one instant to the next; the conditioning factors bring the pain about, while consciousness is aware of the "pain of the thorn." Whatever physical malaise or mental sorrow occurs, it occurs in the aggregates and nowhere else.

Therefore, thinking that you must by all means attain to sublime primordial wisdom—which is free of the five impure aggregates that perpetuate existence and are all part of the truth of suffering—you should structure your reflection into a session with the three stages of preparation, main practice, and conclusion.

Instruction 36: Asuras, or Demigods

The asuras cannot tolerate the glory of the gods and are constantly jealous of them. They wage war against them and are greatly tormented. Their homes are laid waste, and they suffer great harm, afflicted in body and mind. {306} They cry out and struggle even more and thus are in a state of constant tribulation. As you think of this, decide that you will implement the sacred dharma that brings peace, and structure your reflection in a session with the three stages of preparation, main practice, and conclusion.

Instruction 37: Gods

In the celestial regions of the desire realm, the gods live, for a time, in bliss. But death comes to them, and at that moment, thanks to their clairvoyance, they see that their positive karma is now exhausted and that the karmic fruit of previous negative actions will result in their being born in the lower destinies. For seven celestial days, they endure intense suffering greater than that of fishes writhing on hot sand. Likewise in the heavens of the form and formless realms, the gods enjoy for a moment the bliss of meditative concentration. But when their good karma is exhausted, their residual bad karma results in the suffering of falling into the lower states. They will assume once more a bodily aggregate and will thus experience all-pervading suffering in the making. You should think that now is the time to free yourself from the three worlds and the six realms. Structure your meditation in the three stages of preparation, main practice, and conclusion.

Instruction 38: An Examination of the Present Situation

At this present time—when you have gained a human existence endowed with freedoms and advantages and have the liberty to decide for yourself—you cannot stand even the slightest pain, such as a spark of fire falling on your skin. You cannot endure the slightest experience of cold, hunger, thirst, or exhaustion. So after death, how will you possibly bear the terrible, long-lasting tortures of the hot and cold hells, the thirst and hunger of the pretas, the slavery and exploitation of the animals, and so on? Knowing that you cannot bear even the pains and sicknesses of a single day, ask yourself how you can possibly endure the endless sufferings of samsara. And structure your reflection in a session with the three stages of preparation, main practice, and conclusion.

The Fourth Vajra Point: The Karmic Law of Cause and Result

This section consists of three reflections: (1) negative action, (2) positive action, and (3) the fact that everything is the outcome of action. {307}

Instruction 39: The Three Negative Actions of the Body

Of the ten negative actions, three concern the body. The result of taking life will be that in whichever situation you are born, your life will be short and attended by many ills. Your environment will be unpleasant with steep ravines and precipices that are a danger to life. Killing, moreover, results in the suffering of the three lower destinies.

Stealing or taking what is not given results in poverty and in the fact that you must live in environments menaced by frost and hail and famine. And of the three lower destinies it leads to being reborn among the pretas.

Owing to sexual misconduct you will have an unattractive spouse who takes the side of your enemies, and you will find yourself living in environments that are saline, extremely evil-smelling and filthy. Sexual misconduct also results in the sufferings of the lower destinies. With the thought that you must now abandon all such negative actions of the body, you should structure your reflection in a session with the three stages of preparation, main practice, and conclusion.

Instruction 40: The Four Negative Actions of Speech

The result of lying is to be frequently criticized and constantly deceived. Because of divisive speech you will be surrounded by unfriendly people and even those you help will become your enemies. Because of harsh speech, you will be assailed with unpleasant words and whatever you say will result in arguments. Through worthless chatter, your speech will be confused and regarded as unreliable. Through all such actions of speech, you will fall into the lower destinies and suffering will be your lot. Thinking that you must give up all such behavior, structure your reflection in a session with the three stages of preparation, main practice, and conclusion.

Instruction 41: The Three Negative Actions of Mind

Because of covetousness, you will fail to accomplish your goals and instead will get precisely what you do not want. Because of ill will, you will be beset with danger and harm; you will be persecuted and frightened. Because of wrong views, you will belong to mistaken traditions that are either eternalist or nihilist, and you will reject the karmic law of cause and effect. {308} All this will lead to suffering in the lower destinies. Therefore, thinking that you should abandon all such negative attitudes of mind, structure your reflection in a session with preparation, main practice, and conclusion.

Of virtuous actions, there are some that lead to happiness in samsara and others that lead to liberation.

Instruction 42: The Three Virtuous Actions of the Body Leading to Happiness

To refrain from killing leads to a long life free from sickness. To refrain from stealing results in perfect wealth. To refrain from sexual misconduct is the cause of having a beautiful spouse who is not your enemy and with whom you will have a harmonious relationship. You should reflect that you should rely on all such actions because they lead to happiness in the higher destinies, meditating in a session with the three stages of preparation, main practice, and conclusion.

Instruction 43: The Four Virtuous Actions of Speech Leading to Happiness

To refrain from lying leads to happiness and to being the object of general praise. To refrain from divisive speech leads to being surrounded by harmony and respect. To refrain from harsh speech will lead to only hearing pleasant words and praise. To refrain from worthless chatter will lead to being trusted and believed. Thinking that it is by refraining from these four defects that your speech will be virtuous and that you will have every happiness, reflect that you should act accordingly, structuring your meditation in a session with the three stages of preparation, main practice, and conclusion.

Instruction 44: The Three Virtuous Actions of Mind Leading to Happiness

By refraining from covetousness, you will realize all your hopes. Through refraining from malevolence, you will be protected from harm. By abandoning wrong views, you will come to hold the perfect view. Reflect that you must implement all these actions because they lead to a virtuous mind and happiness in the higher destinies, and structure your reflection in a session with preparation, main practice, and conclusion. {309}

Instruction 45: Virtuous Actions Leading to Liberation

You should reflect that these are actions that lead to liberation from samsara and the attainment of the peace of nirvana. All in all, they are distinguished into the actions that lead to the liberation of the śrāvakas and pratyekabuddhas and those that lead to perfect buddhahood.

So if you wish to attain perfect buddhahood, practice the ten virtuous actions, the four samādhis [of form], the four formless samādhis, calm abiding and deep insight, the four boundless attitudes, the six pāramitās, and so on. Without a moment's idleness, prepare by cultivating bodhicitta. Then, as your main practice, reflect on the fact that all your actions are without true existence. In conclusion, make the dedication. This is how you should practice, remembering that if you do not complete the accumulations of merit and wisdom, you will never attain enlightenment.

Instruction 46: Everything Is the Outcome of Action

All happiness and suffering in samsara, all situations high and low, are the product of virtuous or unvirtuous action. In addition, the various kinds of happiness specific to the three kinds of enlightenment are the result of superior actions leading to liberation. This action, or karma, is like a painter, and a single action can have many effects. Your karma will follow you like your shadow. Your karma cannot be transferred to others and the karma of others cannot be transferred to you. It is like the pleasure and pain of different bodies. Because in their great strength, virtue and sin drive you into the higher or lower destinies, they are like great and powerful rulers. Because their range is immense, they are like the vast expanses of the sky. Because they are of a great variety, they are like all the many wares in a market. Because different actions do not blend into one, they are like [the different colors] in a brocade cloak. {310} White and black actions do not change their character. They are like the lotus and the lily of the night. Since all actions performed produce their corresponding result, you must understand that everything is the outcome of your karma. Think that you should be diligent in adopting virtue and abandoning evil, and structure your reflection into a session with the three stages of preparation, main practice, and conclusion.

The Fifth Vajra Point: Following a Spiritual Teacher

This section covers two topics: (1) the teacher's character and (2) the practice of guru yoga. The character of a teacher may be considered under three headings: (1) distinguishing [between true and false teachers], (2) examining the qualifications of a teacher, and (3) celebrating the teacher's qualities.

Instruction 47: Distinguishing between True and False Teachers and Following and Avoiding Them Accordingly

When you follow a genuine spiritual teacher, his or her qualities of virtue and excellence will pass naturally to you—just as when you stand beneath a sandal tree and are enveloped in the sweetness of its perfume. Rely, therefore, on a virtuous teacher and on good companions because by that means your own virtue will develop and flourish. If, however, you keep company with a teacher who is not virtuous, and if you take up with bad friends, you will naturally be stained by their faults. Left in a filthy place, even kuśa grass will end up smelling like rotten fish. This is why you should keep your distance from bad teachers and evil company—for it is important to refrain from negative actions, to rid yourself of them, and to put an end to them. Reflecting in this way, structure your meditation into a session with the three stages of preparation, main practice, and conclusion.

The examination of the qualifications of a spiritual teacher has two parts: (1) the examination of the common qualifications and (2) the examination of the uncommon qualifications.

Instruction 48: The Common Qualifications of a Sublime Teacher

Just as you would rely on a skillful pilot to guide you to an island of jewels, likewise you rely on a teacher, a spiritual friend, to take you to the land of freedom and the attainment of buddhahood. Therefore, make up your mind to follow teachers whose conduct is unblemished in body, speech, and mind; who are adorned with {311} perfect qualities; who have great learning, kindness, boundless wisdom and compassion; who are able to place all those connected with them on the path of liberation; and who are able to endure disappointment, fatigue, and hardship. Make the wish that you will quickly meet such teachers, that you will be guided by their compassion, and that you will never be parted from them. As you reflect in this way, structure your meditation into a session with the three stages of preparation, main practice, and conclusion.

Instruction 49: The Uncommon Qualifications of a Sublime Teacher

Just as in this life, possessions, dominion, power, and every excellence depend upon a gracious sovereign or mighty emperor, likewise the achievement in a single life of the unsurpassed result and of all perfect qualities depends upon a sublime teacher, a holder of the vajra, who is learned and accomplished. Rely, therefore, on such teachers, who are abundant in the empowerments [they have received] and are perfect in the samayas [that they hold], who are learned in the tantras and the pith instructions, who possess the power of the profound stages of approach and accomplishment, who possess the full confidence of the view and the practice of concentration, and who are perfect in their activities for the sake of others. If you have not met such teachers, you should aspire to do so. If you have met them, you should resolve never to leave them. You should resolve to please them at all times and wish to be held in their compassion. Reflecting in this way, structure your meditation into a session with the three stages of preparation, main practice, and conclusion.

Celebrating in Three Stages the Qualities of a Sublime Teacher
Instruction 50: The First Stage

Just as it is rare for the udumbara to flower in this world, so too is it rare for a buddha to appear. It is equally rare for a sublime teacher to come into this world, manifesting through the buddha's compassion. As in the case of {312} your own sublime and glorious teacher at the present time, all true spiritual teachers radiate the light of their unbounded qualities. Liberating beings from the ocean of existence, they are like the captains of great ships. Leading [their disciples] on the path to liberation, they are like skilled guides. Dispelling the defects of both existence and peace, they are like wish-fulfilling jewels. Extinguishing the fire of the defilements, they are like streams of nectar. Sending down a rain of dharma, they are like magnificent clouds. Bringing joy to beings, they are like the resounding of the drums of the gods. Dissipating all the diseases of the three poisons, they are like supreme physicians. Scattering the darkness of ignorance, they are like the lamps of sun and moon. Satisfying every hope and desire, they are like great trees of miracles. Endowed with the splendor of enlightened action, they are like the mandala of the sun. Sublime teachers possess all such qualities and are a great wonder. Now that you have met such a teacher, whom you have taken as your mainstay, you should greatly rejoice and make the wish that in all your lives to come, you will be able to follow, and be held in the compassion of, such a being—so that one day you will have just the same qualities. Reflecting in this way, structure your meditation into a session with the three stages of preparation, main practice, and conclusion.

Instruction 51: The Second Stage

All sublime teachers or virtuous friends have minds as vast as the sky. Their concentration is as brilliant as the sun and moon, and their wisdom is as vast as the ocean. Strong is their compassion like the course of a river, and their minds are as firm as the king of mountains. Like lotus flowers, they are pure and free of every fault. They have an equal love for wandering beings as if they were their very parents. Their excellent qualities are spontaneously present like a hoard of treasure, and like the victorious ones within the world, they have the noble character of guides of beings. The different aspects of each of these qualities are truly innumerable; they are a great wonder. Wishing to please your teacher and to be held in his compassion, structure your reflection {313} into a session with the three stages of preparation, main practice, and conclusion.

Instruction 52: The Third Stage

Just to see, hear, recall, or touch such glorious lords, such sublime teachers, plants within you the seed of liberation. Samsara is destroyed. Thus the activity of sublime teachers is the same as that of all the buddhas. To be guided by them on the path to liberation is a supreme good fortune. Because they perform the activity of all the empowerments, like the heruka in the mandala, they are the fourth jewel. Their kindness toward beings to be trained exceeds even that of the buddhas. You should wish that in all your lives to come, you will be able to follow the teachers who, in this very life, have placed you on the profound path of ripening and liberation. You should wish to please them and to be blessed by their compassion. Contemplating in this way, structure your reflection into a session with the three stages of preparation, main practice, and conclusion.

Guru Yoga

The practice of guru yoga has three sections: (1) the daily practice, (2) the four activities, and (3) the quelling of disease and evil influences and the ransoming of the life force.

Instruction 53: The Daily Practice of Guru Yoga

First take refuge and generate the attitude of bodhicitta. Then, from within the sphere of emptiness, visualize your root teacher above the crown of your head (during the day) or in your heart (during the night). He or she is seated on a lotus and disks of sun and moon and is surrounded by yidam deities and ḍākinīs. Invite the root and lineage teachers, together with the ḍākinīs—who come and dissolve into the visualization. Then pay homage, make offerings, and confess your faults by reciting the following prayer:

> *Namo*. To my guru and my yidam
> And the host of ḍākinīs
> I bow down in reverence.
> I make outer, inner, and secret offerings,
> Confessing all transgressed and spoiled
> Samayas, root and branch.
> Bestow on me empowerment and blessings
> That mature and liberate,
> And be my guide, I pray you,
> Throughout all my lives.

When you have recited this prayer three times, a stream of nectar flows down from the body of your teacher and fills your body. {314} Consider that all diseases, evil forces, sins, and obscurations are cleansed away, and that the realization of the great bliss of the dharmatā arises within you. Rest for a moment in meditation. If you know the Sanskrit form of your teacher's name, recite it enclosed within the syllables *oṃ āḥ hūṃ*—for example, *oṃ guru kumarāja siddhi āḥ hūṃ*.

From the bodies of the guru, the yidam deities, and the ḍākinīs, there falls a stream of light and nectar that clears away the obscurations of your body. You thus receive the vase empowerment, and your body is blessed as the vajra body. From the speech centers of the guru, yidam deities, and ḍākinīs streams of nectar descend and clear away your obscurations of speech. You receive the secret empowerment, and your speech is blessed as vajra speech. Then light rays and nectar emanate from their hearts and purify your mind. You receive the wisdom empowerment, and your mind is blessed as the vajra mind. A stream of light and nectar emanates from the guru, yidam deities, and ḍākinīs and dissipates the stain of taking your body, speech, and mind as distinct and separate entities. Thus you receive the precious word empowerment and your mind is blessed as vajra-like indestructible primordial wisdom. Your body, speech, and mind dissolve into the body, speech, and mind of the guru, who then dissolves into the unborn state of dharmakāya. Rest in a state free of all mental movement and conclude by making the dedication.

Instruction 54: The Four Activities

For the peaceful activity, consider that the visualized field is completely white. Imagining that it projects rays of white light that soothe away all disease, evil forces, negativities, and obscurations, recite the mantra described above, adding the concluding formula *śāntiṃ kuruye svāhā.*

For the activity of increasing, consider that the visualized field is completely yellow. Imagining that it projects rays of yellow light that increase your life span, merit, and wealth, recite the mantra, adding the words *puṣṭiṃ kuruye svāhā.*

For the activity of magnetizing, consider that the visualized field is completely red. Imagining that it projects rays of red light that bring within your power all that is to be accomplished, recite the mantra, adding the words *vāśaṃ kuruye svāhā.*

For the wrathful activity, consider that the visualized field is dark-blue. Visualize rays of fiery, sparkling light {315} that destroy all evil forces and obstacle makers. Recite the mantra, adding the words *dön gek māraya phaṭ.* The other visualizations are as previously described.

Instruction 55: Quelling Disease and Evil Forces and Ransoming the Life Force

First, take refuge and generate the attitude of bodhicitta. Then, from within the sphere of emptiness, visualize in the sky in front of you your own root teacher. He or she is seated above a lotus on a precious lion throne, disks of sun and moon, and a brocade cushion and is inseparable from the lineage teachers and the buddhas. All around are the assemblies of the deities of the yidam mandalas, together with an ocean-like infinity of ḍākinīs and protectors. Below them, visualize all the beings of the six realms and all the harmful forces.

Imagine that your consciousness, in the form of the syllable *hūṃ*, shoots up from your heart and out through the Brahmā aperture. The ḍākas and ḍākinīs of the five families, armed with razor-sharp knives, then cut off the top of your skull just above the eyebrows. They place it on a hearth made of three skulls each as big as Mount Meru itself and pour into it all the flesh and blood of your body. As the fire beneath it burns, the ingredients come to a boil and the nectar of all the buddhas and bodhisattvas of the ten directions rises and fills the skull cup to the brim. This in turn transforms into all the food and drink that one could wish for, as well as the perfect draft of immortality. Countless ḍākas, each holding a skull cup, are then emanated. They offer them simultaneously to all the guests.

The guests who are beyond the world are pleased thereby. The two accumulations are perfected, and the supreme and ordinary siddhis are attained. The guests who are still in samsara are likewise pleased, and all the karmic debts owed to them from beginningless time are discharged. In particular, all kinds of harmful evil forces are appeased and their malevolence and the obstacles they create are dissipated. {316} All the guests are now satisfied, and as you are touched by the beams of light that radiate from them, consider that all your illnesses are brought to an end, that all evil forces are quelled, that your life has been ransomed, and that you have gained accomplishment. Finally, like clouds melting into the sky, everything dissolves into the state beyond reference. And in this state, make the dedication. By this means, the two accumulations are perfected, your life force is ransomed, and death is avoided. Later you will be able to recognize the state of luminosity in the bardo.

The Sixth Vajra Point: Taking Refuge

Here, there are three sections: (1) the different kinds of refuge, (2) the benefits of taking refuge, and (3) the way of taking refuge.

Instruction 56: Different Kinds of Refuge

Those who take refuge in the Three Jewels because they are frightened of the sufferings of the three lower destinies and because they seek the happiness of the upper realms are "beings of lesser scope"—meaning that they exclusively pursue a happiness that is only temporary.

Those who take refuge in the Three Jewels because they fear the sufferings of samsara in its entirety [all six realms both high and low], and who are concerned for the happiness and peace of nirvana only for themselves, are "beings of medium scope." They are so-called because they aim only for their own liberation from samsara.

Those who take refuge in the Three Jewels because they see the suffering of the unnumbered beings in samsara and wish to free them from it are "beings of great scope." They are so-called because their aim is to attain buddhahood for the sake of all beings.

Think that you will turn away from the paths of beings of lesser and medium scope, and that you will emulate the beings of great scope for the sake of all that lives, and structure your meditation in the three stages of preparation, main practice, and conclusion.

Instruction 57: The Benefits of Taking Refuge {317}

If people are prepared to take refuge in the worldly gods, who are themselves in samsara, what possible reason could they have for not taking refuge in the Three Jewels, who dwell in the state of supreme and indestructible liberation? Of course, people do not take refuge in kings and so on, whom they cannot trust and who inflict harm on them. By contrast, by simply taking refuge in the Three Jewels, the seeds of liberation are planted in the mind; actions of great nonvirtue are banished far away and virtue increases. Taking refuge is the basis of all the vows and is the source of all excellent qualities. When you take refuge, you will be protected by the gods and spirits who belong to the side of virtue, and all your hopes and wishes will come to fulfillment. Always mindful of the entire sequence of your lives, you will never part from the light of the Three Jewels. In this and future lives, therefore, you will be happy and will come at last to the attainment of buddhahood. Reflecting on these and the other countless benefits of taking refuge, structure your meditation into a session with the three stages of preparation, main practice, and conclusion.

Instruction 58: The Way of Taking Refuge

First take refuge and generate the attitude of bodhicitta. Then visualize your teacher in the sky in front of you. Inseparable from the Buddha, he or she is seated on a precious lion throne, a lotus, and disks of sun and moon and is surrounded by the bodhisattvas and an infinite assembly of ḍākinīs and dharma protectors, filling the entire sky. Imagining that all the beings on earth do the same, join the palms of your hands and make the following resolution: "From now until I gain the essence of enlightenment, I offer myself to you. I rely on you. I have no other hope, no other refuge." Then, with a pleasant melody, repeat the following words many times:

> I take refuge in my teacher. I take refuge in the Buddha. I take refuge in the dharma. I take refuge in the sangha.

{318} Finally imagine that you and all beings melt into the Three Jewels. The Three Jewels then dissolve into the central figure of the precious Buddha, your teacher, who then dissolves into the dharmakāya, the state of emptiness free of all conceptual construction. Relax in the sphere beyond all reference, and meditate for as long as your mind remains in this state. Then make the dedication. The taking of refuge is the basis of the entire practice of the dharma. It is of crucial importance, and you must practice it earnestly.

The Seventh Vajra Point: Meditating on the Four Boundless Attitudes

This section consists of three instructions: (1) on how to take delight in the four boundless attitudes by reflecting on their benefits, (2) on how to perform the meditation itself, and (3) on how to become skilled in this meditation.

Instruction 59: Taking Delight in the Four Boundless Attitudes by Reflecting on Their Benefits

It is impossible to attain buddhahood without training in the four boundless attitudes. Therefore, meditate on them and enlightenment will be yours. If you train yourself in love, you will be the delight of all beings now, and ultimately you will gain the sambhogakāya. If you train in compassion, no harm will come to you, and you will attain the dharmakāya. If you train in sympathetic joy, you will be free of jealous envy and will attain the nirmāṇakāya. If you train in impartiality, your mind will be fit [for the path], and you will accomplish the svabhāvikakāya. Furthermore, you will gain a divine or human life with happiness and well-being in the desire realm. You will perfectly accomplish the concentrations of form and all the qualities of a pure rebirth. Reflect, therefore, upon the benefits of the four boundless attitudes, and train in them, structuring your meditation into the three sections of preparation, main practice, and conclusion.

How to Meditate on the Four Boundless Attitudes
Instruction 60: Impartiality

Here, there are two things to consider: the object of focus for the meditation and the mental attitude required.

It is important to examine fully and to understand the object of focus of this meditation. At the present time, you are attached to "your own side"—that is, your parents, relatives, and so on. Conversely, you feel aversion for enemies and everything pertaining to them. This makes no sense {319} because those who are your enemies at the present time were your friends in previous lives, and those who are your friends now were once your enemies. There is nothing definitive about the present situation. Moreover, even those who are your enemies now are unable to harm you all the time. Indeed, if you were to comply with them, it is quite possible that they would help you and become your friends. On the other hand, if your friends become verbally abusive, quarreling and fighting with you, if they disagree with you about how property is to be shared, you suffer and your friends in fact behave like enemies. It is moreover quite possible [in the course of the present life] for friends to become enemies and for enemies to become friends. You should therefore abandon the partial attitude of attachment to your own side and of hostility to opponents and consider the essential sameness of friends and enemies. This way of viewing all beings constitutes the focus of this meditation.

Then the correct mental attitude is to meditate on great nonreferential impartiality that is free of biased attachment and aversion. Start by considering one person, then two, then three, working up to a whole town, country, and continent, until you include the entire mass of beings with which the whole of space is filled—structuring your meditation into a session with the three stages of preparation, main practice, and conclusion.

Instruction 61: Love

Here the object of focus is the entire multitude of beings. Among people who are close to you, you wish that those who are without happiness have happiness. Likewise you should wish the same for all who are similarly deprived. With the loving thought that all beings find happiness, you should regard them all as yours and as close to you. Your mental attitude should be the wish that all who are dear to you, beginning with your parents, should be happy. Then gradually extend this wish so that, starting with a single individual, it embraces all beings. Then rest in a state devoid of reference. Structure your meditation in a session with the three stages of preparation, main practice, and conclusion. {320}

Instruction 62: Compassion

The meditation on compassion is likewise twofold. For your object of focus, take someone who is tormented by intense and unbearable suffering. Your mental attitude should be a yearning compassion, a wish that the person in question be freed from pain, gradually extending the range of your concern until, beginning with this one being, it embraces all. Then rest in a state devoid of reference. Structure your meditation in a session with the three stages of preparation, main practice, and conclusion.

Instruction 63: Sympathetic Joy

In the meditation on sympathetic joy, your object of focus ranges from those who are more or less happy right up to beings in the higher realms, who are blissful in every possible way. As for your mental attitude, you should have the wish that they never lose their happiness but rather that their joy and contentment increase—that they be blessed with longevity, have excellent companions and perfect wealth, that they be untouched by harm, have great wisdom, and so forth, until they attain buddhahood. Beginning with a single being, this wish of yours must eventually embrace all. In particular, you should wish this again and again for enemies who harm you and for those who are the object of your jealous envy. Then rest in a state devoid of reference. Structure your meditation in a session with the three stages of preparation, main practice, and conclusion.

Instruction 64: How to Become Skilled in These Meditations

Practice these meditations in different sequences. Beginning with love, go on to compassion, then to joy, and then to impartiality. Or you could reverse the order from impartiality to love. Or again you could proceed stepwise: first love, then joy, then compassion, and finally impartiality. It is thus that you should train yourself in the four boundless attitudes, becoming familiar with them at all times. The meditation should be implemented always in a threefold structure. Begin with a preliminary stage of generating the attitude of bodhicitta and go on to practice the main meditation with great endeavor and in a manner that is free of clinging. Then conclude the session with the dedication. {321}

The Eighth Vajra Point: Cultivating Bodhicitta and Observing Its Precepts

This section consists of three parts: (1) a reflection on the benefits of bodhicitta, (2) the actual cultivation of bodhicitta, and (3) finally the bodhicitta precepts.

Instruction 65: The Benefits of Bodhicitta

Of all the teachings of the Mahāyāna, the cultivation of bodhicitta, the mind of enlightenment, is uniquely and supremely noble. If bodhicitta is not cultivated, buddhahood will never be achieved. If it is cultivated, buddhahood will follow. Moreover, bodhicitta is a protection from the sufferings of samsara. It dissipates the torments of the defilements. It is superior to the attitudes and objectives of the śrāvaka and pratyekabuddha vehicles. Thanks to bodhicitta, the roots of virtue will never be exhausted but will increase. Indeed, thanks to bodhicitta, a great amount of merit is gained. And it is through bodhicitta that the lineage of enlightened beings is perpetuated. Through bodhicitta, the foundations of your happiness are laid and you become an object of reverence for the whole world. Your wishes come to fulfillment. You accomplish great good for others. Thanks to bodhicitta, you will swiftly gain enlightenment—and there are even more benefits besides. For all these reasons, you should think that from this day onward, you will cultivate bodhicitta and endeavor in it, structuring your meditation in a session with the three stages of preparation, main practice, and conclusion.

The actual cultivation of bodhicitta is done in two steps: (1) the preliminary practice in seven branches and (2) the generation of the bodhicitta attitude.

The Preliminary Practice in Seven Branches
Instruction 66: Homage

Prepare offerings, and lay them before a representation of the Three Jewels. Then visualize your teacher in the sky in front of you. Above his head, visualize the Three Jewels surrounded by dense clouds of yidam deities, ḍākinīs, and dharma protectors. Then imagine forms of yourself in countless myriads covering the entire earth, and in company with all the beings of the three worlds and the six realms, make prostration. With melodious song {322} recite *The King of Sovereign Sutras Relating the Great Deeds of [the Buddha's] Past Lives*, *The Confession of Bodhisattva Downfalls*, *The Many Names of the Tathāgatas*, *The Names of the Thousand Buddhas*, the homage from *The Confession and Restoration Prayer Addressed to the Peaceful and Wrathful Deities*,[4] and so on. Stand up straight with your hands joined at your heart, throat, or forehead, then going down with your five limbs touching the ground, make many prostrations, a hundred or a thousand times. This homage should be performed in a session with the three stages of preparation, main practice, and conclusion.

Instruction 67: Making Offerings

In front of a representation of the Three Jewels, place offerings of whatever you can get—especially rows of lamps and fragrant incense. Then imagine that the earth and sky are filled with the offering substances of gods and humankind—incense, flowers, lamps, and so on—as well as vast and sublime palaces and all kinds of landscapes of great beauty. Add to these the seven attributes of royalty, the eight auspicious objects and so on. Imagine also that gods and goddesses perform many kinds of dance and song, emanating massed clouds of offering. Think that you are presenting all this as an offering to the Three Jewels in this and other buddha fields. Make the offerings in the way explained in *The Noble Prayer of Excellent Conduct*, *The Way of the Bodhisattva*, and so on—all in the knowledge that the object of offering, the one who offers, and the offering itself are empty of real existence. And all this should be done according to the threefold structure of preparation, main practice, and conclusion.

Instruction 68: Confession of Unwholesome Acts

Before a representation of the Three Jewels, join your hands and, with feelings of sorrow and remorse, confess all your negative actions of body, speech, and mind—all that you remember and all that you have forgotten, from beginningless time until this present moment—all your lack of respect toward parents, abbot, teacher, spiritual kindred, and every other being, {323} the ten negative actions, the five sins of immediate effect and the five closely related sins, all misuse of religious property, and all avarice and obstruction to the practice of generosity. Imagine all this in the form of a black mass on your tongue.

As you make your confession, imagine that from the body, speech, and mind of the representations of the Three Jewels, there issue rays of light that touch the black coagulated mass [on your tongue] and completely remove it. Promise that by applying the antidotes, you will refrain from repeating all such negativities in the future, and recite the texts of confession of negative deeds drawn from the sutras and the tantras, such as *The Confession of Bodhisattva Downfalls*. Conclude by calling to mind that those before whom the confession is made, the confession of negativity itself, and the one who is making the confession, all are empty of real existence. This should be done in a session complete with preparation, main practice, and conclusion.

Instruction 69: Rejoicing

Prepare by cultivating the bodhicitta attitude. Then sincerely rejoice from the depths of your heart in the virtue of the buddhas who, among other things, have turned the wheel of dharma for the sake of beings. Rejoice in the virtue of the bodhisattvas, who have undertaken great deeds of enlightened courage, and in the virtuous actions of beings that lead to happiness in samsara and to liberation. Rejoice also in your own virtue: all that you have managed to practice in the past, all that you are practicing in the present, and all that you will certainly practice in the future. Begin your reflection in relation to a single being and train yourself to include all. Then rest in the state of emptiness free of reference, and conclude with the dedication.

Instruction 70: Requesting That the Wheel of Dharma Be Turned

Before a representation of the Three Jewels, cultivate the attitude of bodhicitta. Then, out of all those who labor extensively for the benefit of others—the buddhas, the bodhisattvas, teachers, {324} and great masters—focus on those who are not actually teaching the dharma. Emanating a myriad forms of yourself, offer them precious wheels, jewels, and so on, requesting them to turn the wheel of the teachings, just as in the past Brahmā and Indra requested the Buddha to teach. Imagine that they all agree to do so and that a rain of dharma falls. Recite this request in the words of *The Prayer of Excellent Conduct* and other texts. Rest in the state that is free of thought, and conclude with the dedication.

Instruction 71: Requesting the Teachers Not to Pass beyond Sorrow but to Remain for the Sake of Beings

After cultivating the attitude of bodhicitta, imagine that all the teachers and all buddhas and bodhisattvas, who have finished their work for beings in this and other buddha fields, now wish to pass beyond sorrow. In their presence, imagine that you emanate many bodies and pray to them to remain, just as in the past the upāsaka Cunda had done.[5] Then imagine that they accept to remain and work for the sake of beings until the very emptying of samsara. Make this request by reciting verses taken from the sutras and tantras. Finally, after remaining for a moment in the state that is free of thought, make the dedication.

Instruction 72: Dedication

As represented by the specific virtues of the present practice, from the first branch of paying homage and so on, now dedicate all virtue—accumulated by yourself and others throughout the three times—to the achievement of buddhahood for the sake of all beings. Use the words spoken by the noble beings mentioned in the sutras, tantras, and great śāstras. Finally, remain for a moment in the state of emptiness, and once again make the dedication. {325}

Instruction 73: The Actual Cultivation of the Attitude of Bodhicitta

Before a representation of the Three Jewels, join your hands and reflect as follows: "I will generate an attitude of mind turned toward supreme enlightenment for the sake of beings. Never relaxing my efforts, I will train intensely in all the appropriate activities until not even a single being is left in samsara." Express your intention in the following majestic terms:

> I, (*state your name*), from this moment onward until the essence of enlightenment is reached, take refuge in the teachers, the great holders of the vajra. I take refuge in the bhagavan buddhas, supreme of humankind. I take refuge in the sublime teachings of the dharma, the supreme state of peace and freedom from attachment. I take refuge in the sangha, the supreme assemblies of the noble ones who are beyond regress. I pray to you, accept me as your follower, a bodhisattva.
>
> Teachers, great holders of the vajra, bhagavan buddhas, and great bodhisattvas dwelling on the sublime grounds, turn your minds to me. Just as in the past all the buddhas and great heroic bodhisattvas abiding on the grounds cultivated the attitude of mind of wishing to gain supreme enlightenment for the sake of beings, so too, from this moment onward until the essence of enlightenment is reached, I, (*state your name*), will cultivate the attitude of mind that is turned toward the attainment of supreme enlightenment for the sake of beings. I will bear across the stream those who have not crossed. I will free all those who are not yet free. I will bring relief to those not yet relieved. I will lead beyond all suffering all who have not completely passed beyond it.

Recite the above three times. {326} As for ultimate bodhicitta, all learned masters affirm that since this is attained through the strength of authentic meditation, it does not depend on a ritual.

When you have finished the third proclamation [of the vow], you should consider that you have now become a bodhisattva. Your human existence has become meaningful, and you have become an object of reverence for both gods and humankind. The door through which you might fall, by karmic action, into the lower realms is now closed, and you will go from joy to joy in the worlds of the higher destinies, and you will accomplish great work for the benefit of others. You have become the child of all the buddhas, and you will swiftly gain enlightenment. You should rejoice and raise your spirits by reflecting in this way.

The reflection on the precepts of bodhicitta deals first with the precepts of bodhicitta in intention and then with the precepts of bodhicitta in action. The examination of the precepts of bodhicitta in intention is again divided threefold and concerns (1) the cultivation of bodhicitta through the equalizing of self and other, (2) the exchange of self and other, and (3) the cherishing of others.

The Precepts of Bodhicitta in Intention
Instruction 74: The Equalizing of Self and Other

Here, you cultivate bodhicitta by thinking that, for the sake of beings, you will [learn how to] equalize self and other. Then consider as follows. All beings, including yourself, want to be happy and do not want to suffer. They always rejoice and are at ease when things go well. And yet beings are ignorant of the causes of their situation; they are confused about the principle of adopting virtue and rejecting evil. How pitiful it is to see that, as a result, they are always suffering.

And so with a fierce aspiration from the depths of your heart, train yourself to think as follows:

> Alas! May those beings who have no happiness meet with happiness! May those who are worn down by misery be freed from misery! May those who are happy and content continue in their happiness and never lose it! May those who are attached to those who are close and who are hostile to those who are distant abide in an even state of impartiality free from biased attachment and

> aversion! May all beings enter the path to liberation, and may they at all times practice the pure dharma. May all beings, myself included, swiftly come to perfect buddhahood. {327}

Relax for a few moments in the state of emptiness, the lack of intrinsic being in all things. Finally, make a dedication that is uncontaminated by the three spheres [of subject, object, and action].

Instruction 75: The Exchange of Self and Other

First of all, imagine in front of you a single being in distress for whom you feel compassion. Then take all your feelings of happiness and physical well-being, your possessions and roots of virtue and give them to this being as though dressing him or her in your own clothes. Think that, as a result, the being in question feels happy and at ease. Then take in return all the sorrows with which that same being is afflicted and place them upon yourself. Take them eagerly, cultivating a feeling of joy that the suffering is coming to you. It is as if you were exchanging clothes. As you become skilled in this practice, give your own happiness to beings as you breathe out, and as you breathe in, eagerly take their suffering to yourself. This is how you should train, giving and receiving turn by turn. Begin with one being and then extend your scope until you include all beings. Strive in this, day and night, with great endeavor, structuring your meditation in sessions with the three stages of preparation, main practice, and conclusion.

Instruction 76: Cherishing Others More Than Oneself

This means cultivating the kind of love toward others that a mother feels for her only child. First give rise to the attitude of bodhicitta and then imagine that you are in the presence of someone who is dear to you, for whom it is easy to feel love. The idea that such a person is suffering is impossible for you to bear. You would rather take the suffering on yourself and give to that person your own virtue so that they become happy. You think to yourself "It is all right if I have to stay in samsara. It is all right if I fall sick. It doesn't matter if I die. I accept whatever hardships may come. But what I can't stand is that this person should suffer and wander in samsara." With such a thought, give rise in yourself to an extraordinary feeling of love toward that person, and meditate so as to extend it to include all beings. {328} Imagine that you are taking all beings into your charge, all beings as infinite as the sky is vast—all those whom you see or hear about, whether or not they help or harm you. Look on them all with the sublime attitude of bodhicitta. Then, at the end of your meditation session, rest in a state free of reference, and conclude by making the dedication.

The Precepts of Bodhicitta in Action

The precepts of bodhicitta in action consist of the practice of the pāramitās, the six transcendent perfections.

Instruction 77: The Perfection of Generosity

Cultivating the attitude of bodhicitta with the thought that you will practice generosity for the sake of beings, give to those same beings whatever material things you can, as well as the gift of dharma. Then, in your imagination, give to them all your wealth, even your own body, as well as your roots of virtue. You should train yourself, in your imagination and in actual deeds, in ordinary, great, and extreme generosity.[6] Make whatever material offerings you can to the Three Jewels, as well as whatever offerings you can imagine through mental concentration. Give tormas and water offerings to the spirits and hungry ghosts. Then rest in a state that is free of reference, and conclude by making the dedication.

The Perfection of Discipline

The training in the pāramitā of discipline is twofold: (1) training in discipline generally and (2) training in its particular aspects.

Instruction 78: Training in Discipline Generally

Discipline means to abandon negative actions and to commit your mind to virtue. First, cultivate the attitude of bodhicitta. Then, if you have taken monastic as well as bodhisattva vows, you should earnestly implement your earlier precepts belonging to the śrāvakayāna. However, in addition to confession, the vow to refrain from negativity, and reliance on antidotes, you must observe the precepts related to both bodhicitta in intention and bodhicitta in action, taking the vows repeatedly in accordance with their specific rituals. If you are a layperson, you should train in the precepts of bodhicitta. Whether you are ordained or a layperson, you should control your mindstream, bring benefit to others, {329} and take the bodhisattva vows repeatedly according to the prescribed rituals. Then make the dedication in a state that is free of reference.

Training in the Particular Aspects of Discipline

Training in the particular aspects of discipline covers two areas: (1) the pure conduct as described in the *Avataṃsaka Sutra* and (2) the eight thoughts that typify beings of great scope.

Instruction 79: Pure Conduct as Described in the Avataṃsaka Sutra

When bodhisattvas enter a house, they should generate the attitude of bodhicitta with the wish "May all the beings here reach the city of liberation." When they lie down, they should think, "May beings attain the dharmakāya of buddhahood." When they dream, they should think, "May beings understand that all phenomena are dreamlike." When they tie their belts, they should think, "May beings be joined to the roots of virtue." When they sit down, they should think, "May beings attain the vajra throne." When they light a fire, they should think, "May the firewood of their defilements be consumed." As the fire burns, they should think, "May the fire of their wisdom blaze." When they finish cooking, they should think, "May beings obtain the ambrosia of primordial wisdom." When they eat, they should think, "May they consume the food of samādhi." When they go out, they should think, "May beings be freed from the city of samsara." When they go downstairs, they should think, "May I enter samsara for the sake of beings." When they open the door, they should think, "May the door of liberation be opened for them." When they close the door, they should think, "May the door to the lower destinies be closed for them." When they set off on their way, they should think, "May beings set out on the noble path." When they go uphill, they should think, "May all beings be placed in the happiness of the higher destinies." When they go downhill, they should think, "May the continuity of the three lower destinies be severed." When they meet someone, they should think, "May I meet the Buddha." When they walk, they should think, "May I walk for the benefit of all beings." When they lift their feet, {330} they should think, "May beings be released from samsara." When they see people who are well dressed and adorned with jewels, they should think, "May they attain the ornaments of the major and minor marks." When they see people who are unadorned, they should think, "May they gain the spiritual qualities that are the result of training." When they see vessels that are filled, they should think, "May beings be filled with spiritual qualities." When they see vessels that are empty, they should think, "May beings be empty of defects." When they see people who are cheerful, they should think, "May they take joy in the dharma." When they see those who are glum, they should think, "May they be glum regarding compounded phenomena." When they see happy people, they should think, "May they gain the happiness of buddhahood." When they see those who are suffering, they should think, "May the suffering of all beings cease." When they see the sick, they should think, "May beings be cured of their diseases." When they see people expressing their gratitude, they should think, "May they repay the kindness of all the buddhas and bodhisattvas." When they see ungrateful people, they should think, "May their ingratitude be toward those who have wrong views." When they see a dispute taking place, they should think, "May it be possible to remove all disputes." When they see people praising someone, they should think, "May they be praising all the buddhas and bodhisattvas." When they see people discussing the dharma, they should think, "May they gain the self-assurance of the Buddha." When they see sacred images, they should think, "May beings have an unobscured vision of all the enlightened ones." When they see a stupa, they should think, "May beings look upon this stupa as an object of veneration." When they see people engaged in commerce, they should think, "May these beings obtain the seven noble riches." When they see people bowing down, they should think, "May all beings, including the gods, attain the invisible uṣṇīṣa." Cultivating bodhicitta in this way, you should structure your meditation into a session with preparation, main practice, and conclusion.

Instruction 80: The Eight Thoughts That Typify Beings of Great Scope {331}

Once you have cultivated the attitude of bodhicitta, you should think to yourself, "O when will I be able to clear away the sufferings of all beings? O when will I be able to place in a state of great abundance those who are tormented by want? O when will I be able to work for beings in this body of flesh and blood? O when will I be able to help those long imprisoned in the realms of hell? O when will I be able to fulfill the hopes of beings with great wealth both worldly and beyond the world? O when will I be able to become a buddha and remove all the sufferings of beings? O in all my lives to come, may I never be happy with a birth in which I am of no benefit to others, in which I savor only the ultimate truth, in which I utter words that bring no happiness to beings, in which my life, body, intelligence, wealth, and fame are of no help to others, and in which I take pleasure in harming other beings! O may I be happy when the results of the evil actions of others ripen on myself and when my virtuous deeds ripen in the minds of others!" After cultivating all such thoughts, conclude with the dedication.

The Perfection of Patience

The pāramitā of patience can be practiced either with or without an object of reference.

Instruction 81: Patience Practiced with an Object of Reference

Patience with regard to the hardships encountered during the practice of the sacred teachings, patience in the sense of accepting sufferings caused by others, and patience in the sense of fearlessness regarding the great teachings on emptiness are all included in the practice of patience in relation to one's own mental state. However, in the present context, patience should be cultivated mainly in the sense of not allowing anger to develop when harm is done to one by others. {332}

Generate the attitude of bodhicitta thinking that you will practice patience for the sake of all beings. Then, when you are badly treated by the people around you—or when some harm, serious or otherwise, comes to you—don't get irritated. Instead, examine the situation and think as follows:

> This harm has come to me because it is in the nature of beings to do harm—[they cannot help it]. So I must be patient; it is not right to retaliate. After all, this is the returning consequence of the evil I myself have done in the past. Besides, since great merit comes from practicing patience, it makes sense to do so. After all, it is my aggressors who will suffer the consequences of their

> actions, whereas the harm they do to me cannot place me either high or low in samsara. Therefore it makes sense to bear with this offense. If the situation can be improved, then I will do what I can to make it so. But if there is nothing to be done about it, to be impatient and irritated achieves nothing but to make me miserable.

Even if the attacks of others increase, abandon your anger and feelings of outrage, and relax in a peaceful state free of thought. Then make your dedication in a way that is free of the three spheres [of subject, object, and action].

Instruction 82: Patience Practiced without an Object of Reference

Mentally dissect the bodies of your aggressors and yourself down to their infinitesimal particles. They will be found to be empty; they are not part-possessing entities. Then examine the voices [of both yourself and your aggressors], analyzing the sounds by which they are recognized. They vanish of their own accord leaving nothing behind. Examine the nature and identity of [your and their] minds. They are found to be without real being. The enemy (the agent of harm), the harm inflicted (the unpleasant speech, physical injury, unhappiness of mind, and so on), and the object of harm (yourself) are all empty. There is no difference between them. Relax in this state of unborn emptiness, structuring your meditation into a session with the three stages of preparation, main practice, and conclusion.

Instruction 83: The Perfection of Diligence

First cultivate the attitude of bodhicitta. Then reflect that because of your laziness, you cannot accomplish even your own good, let alone the good of others. {333} And since [through bodhicitta] you wish to be of benefit to others, it stands to reason that you must act with diligence. So strive in the ten activities associated with the dharma,[7] the ten pāramitās,[8] the practice of prostration, circumambulation, and so on—as much as you can. Most especially, persevere in the seven-branch practices and the threefold practice [of prostration, confession, and dedication]. Then conclude with dedication in a manner that is free of the three spheres of agent, action, and object.

The Perfection of Meditative Concentration

The perfection of meditative concentration is divided into six reflections.

Instruction 84: The Changing and Impermanent Character of All Things

All that is born dies. Everything that comes together separates. All accumulations are eventually exhausted. Everything that flourishes ends in decline. The appearances of this life are shifting and without a solid core; they are by their very nature impermanent, and those who are attached to them are ruined thereby. Before long, you too will surely die. Whether it will be tomorrow morning or even tonight, there is nothing you can do to escape your death. So what use are the hallucinatory appearances of this life? When death comes, only the profound instructions are certain to be of benefit to you. Therefore, strive in meditative concentration. With the thought that every day, every night, every minute, every second, every instant, you are drawing closer to your death, structure your meditation into a session with the three stages of preparation, main practice, and conclusion.

Instruction 85: The Defects of Desire

Desire for things has many drawbacks. Gathering, protecting, and increasing your possessions take up all your efforts and result in a growth of unvirtuous activity. Desire is the cause of disputes with others, dissatisfaction with what you have, pride, and an increasing possessiveness. It gives rise to the fear of losing what you have, to the dread of being robbed and having all your possessions stolen and shared among the thieves. {334}

All that you have gathered and saved will be left behind at death. You will lose it all. You suffer in direct proportion to the things that you possess and greatly so. Desire is inimical to study, reflection, and meditation, to discipline and all the other factors of liberation. Desire is utterly repudiated and scorned by noble beings. Having reflected in this way, remain in the state of unborn emptiness. Structure your meditation in the three stages of preparation, main practice, and conclusion.

Instruction 86: The Faults of Keeping Company with Childish Beings

First cultivate the attitude of bodhicitta, and then reflect in the following way. It is important to avoid the whole company of ordinary beings—householders or monastics, and so on. This includes family members and people whom you like—friends, enemies, or neither. [You should reflect that childish beings] are by nature unwholesome. They are ungrateful and return harm for the help that is given to them. They have great desire and are dissatisfied with what they have. They are aggressive and speak harshly. They work only to get what they want and thus are naturally harmful to others. Friendship with such beings is short-lived, for when your wealth and prosperity decline, they disparage and abandon you. They care not at all for moral conscience, for the dharma, for samaya, and for the ripening and results of karma. They have many plans and activities. They are very difficult to please and are led astray by unvirtuous things and situations—quarrels, violence, envy, and so on. This is the story of their lives, and in their company, virtue diminishes and nonvirtue grows. {335} For this reason, all noble beings hold such childish beings very much at arm's length. And so, since they create obstacles for the practice leading to supreme liberation, you too should avoid their company. Stay alone instead, and practice peaceful concentration. After reflecting in this way, conclude by making dedication.

Instruction 87: The Defects of Busy Activities

First cultivate the attitude of bodhicitta, and then consider the fact that, in general, all worldly experiences, and specifically the activities of this life, are never-ending and never satisfy. You are constantly busy and distracted and all to no great purpose. However you may strive, it is all futile. However much you may get the better of your enemies, there is no end to them. However much you may do for your friends, the task is endless. Other than as a means of gaining the necessities of life, in terms of food and clothing, no matter what kind of trade, farming, or craft you may be engaged in, it contains not a single atom of meaning, for by practicing it, you do not make the slightest progress on the path of dharma. How futile to consume your time in such constant and distracting activities day and night!

Resolve instead that you will abandon your preoccupation with this life and cultivate meditative concentration instead. And conclude by making dedication.

Instruction 88: The Qualities of Solitude

All the buddhas and bodhisattvas of the past have practiced in peaceful forests, and there they found the nectar of immortality. Think, therefore, that you too will happily go to places of solitude. For in such places, there is none of the distracting bustle of worldly affairs. There is nothing that has to be done. There is neither hurry nor trade, nor farming, nor the company of childish beings. Among the birds and deer, you will be happy. The water you find there and the produce of the trees will provide you with the sustenance that accords with yogic practice, and the cliffs and caves will provide dwelling places that are in harmony with the dharma. In the absence of friends and acquaintances, your virtue will naturally increase. {336} Your awareness will become lucid all by itself, and your wisdom will be limpid and clear. Many are the qualities of solitude! Think that this very day you will set off for a lonely place—and conclude your reflection by making dedication.

Instruction 89: The Actual Practice of Meditative Concentration

Assuming the seven-point posture of Vairocana, take refuge and cultivate the attitude of bodhicitta. Then rest quietly, without distraction, in a state that is free of all thought and fixation, without blocking your perceptions. A concentration will be born in which clinging and thought have ceased. Then conclude with dedication.

The Perfection of Wisdom

The perfection of wisdom has three sections.

Instruction 90: Viewing the Nature of Appearances according to the Eight Examples of Illusion

First cultivate the attitude of bodhicitta, and then reflect as follows. All the things that appear as the five outer objects in fact arise within deluded perception and are without existence. They appear like the visions of a dream. Since they appear abruptly through the interdependence of causes and conditions, they are like magical illusions. Though nonexistent, they seem to exist, just like a trick of sight. In the moment that they appear, they have no true existence and are like mirages. Since there is no locating them, either outside or within, they are like echoes. Devoid of support and supported, they are like cities of the gandharvas in the clouds. Appearing even though they lack intrinsic being, they are like reflections. Arising as anything whatsoever, and being without existence while they appear, they are like the emanated apparition of a city. In the very moment that they appear, phenomena are false, insubstantial, and empty forms. Cultivate this thought in your meditation and in conclusion make the dedication.

Instruction 91: Investigating the Empty Dharmatā

First cultivate the attitude of bodhicitta, and then analyze all gross outer phenomena as they appear, including your own physical body, breaking them down to their infinitesimal particles. {337} By this means, come to the decisive conviction that phenomena are empty and do not exist as real objects. Then analyze the inner apprehending mind into its partless instants, and come to the firm conviction that it is empty and ungraspable. When you have come to the understanding that the object to be apprehended and the mind that apprehends have no existence, rest evenly in the state of emptiness devoid of reference, and make the dedication.

Instruction 92: Resting in the View of the Middle Way Free from Ontological Extremes

First take refuge and cultivate the attitude of bodhicitta. Sit with your body still, your speech silent, and your mind without thought. It is thus that outwardly, while the appearance of objects are unceasing, the conceptual grasping at these objects is stilled. Inwardly, the mental elaborations of clinging and fixation come to stillness in awareness, which is empty and limpid. And in between, the body and mind having no support, the dharmatā, the ultimate truth, manifests. Rest in awareness, empty and luminous like the sky. This is primordial wisdom, ineffable, inconceivable, inexpressible. It is the middle way free from the ordinary mind. It is the state of suchness. Rest evenly therein for as long as it lasts. Then, in the state in which phenomenal appearances are [seen to be] like dreams and magical illusions, make the dedication:

> This then is the causal vehicle of exposition,
> The pathway trod by all the conquerors,

Past, present, and to come.
These are the great teachings that bring benefit
To others and oneself,
The essence of the sutras and the śāstras
That fulfills all present and all ultimate objectives.
Here is how to practice it—
A method wrought into a single path.
May every being, leaving none aside,
Set out upon the path to liberation.
May the kāyas, wisdoms, and enlightened deeds
Be naturally, spontaneously accomplished.

This concludes the first part, excellent in the beginning, of *The Excellent Path to Enlightenment*, the meditation guide for *Finding Rest in the Nature of the Mind: A Teaching of the Great Perfection*. It expounds the topics of the causal expository vehicle. {338}

Part Two: A Guide to the Inner Resultant Vehicle

The second part, excellent in the middle, sets forth a detailed instruction on the inner, particular path of the resultant vehicle of the Secret Mantra. This guiding instruction is twofold and comprises (1) a presentation of the transmission lineages of the teachers and (2) the instructions themselves.

The Transmission Lineages of the Teachers

There are, in general, numerous transmission lineages of teachers who—being learned in the principles of the tantra classes of the Old and New Traditions—brought together the quintessence of all the associated pith instructions. In the present context, however, we will mainly discuss the transmission lineage of *The Great Net of Illusory Manifestations*,[9] the definitive and quintessential teaching of the Secret Mantras of the Old Translation school. This consists of three transmissions: the mind-to-mind transmission of the victorious ones, the knowledge transmission of the vidyādharas, and the hearing transmission of spiritual masters.

The mind-to-mind transmission of the victorious ones passes from the dharmakāya Samantabhadra to the sambhogakāya buddhas of the five families, from them to the lords of the three families of the nirmāṇakāya, and finally to the various nonhuman vidyādharas of the various classes.

The knowledge transmission of the vidyādharas begins with King Jah, who requested teachings from Vajrapāṇi. It then passed to Indrabhūti, to Indrabhūti's son Śākyabhūti, and then to Kukurāja, Nāgārjuna, Padmasambhava, and Vimalamitra.

The hearing transmission of spiritual masters continues with Nyak Jñānakumāra, Ma Rinchen Chok, Kyere Chökyong, Darje Palgyi Drakpa, Nub Sangye Yeshe, the noble minister of Pagor [Vairotsana], Den Yönten Chok, Bek Salwai Changchub, Gya Lodrö Zhönu, Gar Tsultrim Zangpo, Tsur Yeshe Wangpo, Den Chökyi Wangchuk, Zhang Chökyi Lama, Kyi Yönten Jungne, and finally to Lopön Zhönu Döndrub, who bestowed it on me, Ngaki Wangpo of Samye. {339}

Sublime emanations of all the conquerors,
They crossed the ocean of all perfect qualities.
Boundless is the surging power of their activity—
To all these masters I bow down.

A Detailed Exposition of the Meditation Instructions

These instructions are related to the generation and perfection stages of the kriyā, caryā, yoga, and the great anuttarayoga tantras.

Instruction 93: The Instruction Related to Kriyā, or Action, Tantra

The causal expository vehicle and the vehicle of the Secret Mantra both share the same goal: the attainment of the resultant state of buddhahood. Nevertheless, the Mantrayāna is superior in terms of its understanding of the profound and vast aspects of the path of practice. It is superior also in terms of its use of manifold techniques, in terms of the fact that it is not difficult to accomplish, and finally in terms of the acuity of those who practice it. It is indeed the unsurpassed vehicle whereby a person may accomplish buddhahood swiftly. When both vehicles are practiced by a single person, the expository vehicle acts as the support, the point from which to embark on the path of mantra. It is the preliminary, and the mantra path is the main practice.

Now the entrance door of mantra is the vehicle of kriyā tantra, the deities of which are the Great Compassionate One (Avalokiteśvara) and so forth. In preparation, the practitioner engages in purificatory ablutions and ritual cleanliness and then meditates on the deities concerned. In the present case, we may consider the practice of Avalokiteśvara as follows. First take refuge and generate the attitude of bodhicitta. Then visualize in the sky in front of you, seated in vajra posture upon a lotus and a moon disk, the powerful sovereign of the world. He is white in color, with one face and four arms. His hair is bound up on the top of his head, and he wears a precious diadem. He is adorned with short and long necklaces, bracelets, anklets, and a lower garment of silk. His first two hands are joined at the level of his heart, {340} while the second pair of hands holds a mala on his right and a white lotus on his left. In his heart, in the center of a moon disk supported by a lotus, is the syllable *hrīḥ* surrounded by the six syllables of his mantra. Rays of light pour forth from them and, touching all beings, including yourself, cleanse away all negativities and obscurations. Imagine that all beings perform a sweet and melodious recitation of the seven-syllable mantra, *oṃ maṇi padme hūṃ hrīḥ*, at the end of which all beings are once again bathed in the light of the Great Compassionate One. Then, together with yourself, they dissolve into emptiness. The Compassionate One also melts away into the state beyond reference. After resting for a moment in that same state, make the dedication. Of all the methods to purify negative actions and obscurations, this one is supremely profound.

Instruction 94: The Instruction Related to Caryā, or Conduct, Tantra

Here, you visualize yourself as the deity (*samayasattva*) with the wisdom deity (*jñānasattva*) in front of you. In the present instance, let us consider that this is a practice of the lord Acala.[10] First take refuge and generate the attitude of bodhicitta. Then recite the mantra *oṃ svabhāvaśuddhāḥ sarvadharmāḥ svābhāva viśuddho'haṃ*, and consider that all things are empty. From within this state of emptiness, there appears a lotus on which are the disks of sun and moon. On this, you visualize yourself in the form of Acala, white in color, with one face and three eyes, and with bared teeth biting down on his lower lip. His hair and beard are orange in color, in his right hand he brandishes a sword at the level of the top of his head and with his left hand he is making the threatening pointing mudra at the level of his heart. He is kneeling on his right knee, which is resting on a sun disk, while the sole of his left foot presses down onto a moon disk.[11] He is adorned with all the precious ornaments and is clad in a lower garment of silk. In his heart, in the center of a lotus and moon disk, the syllable *hūṃ* is encircled by the root mantra.

Visualize in front of you Acala in the same form. {341} Imagine that the mantra garland turns around the syllable *hūṃ* in your heart, enters the mouth of the deity in front, passes through his body, exits through his navel, and enters through your own. Lights radiate from the turning mantra and gather into you all the perfect qualities of the buddhas and bodhisattvas residing in the ten directions: wisdom, concentration, realization, longevity, merits, and so forth. These dissolve into the syllable *hūṃ* in your heart, and you consider that you now possess them. Recite as much as you can the mantra *oṃ caṇḍa mahāroṣana hūṃ phaṭ*.[12] At the end of the recitation, the mantra garland dissolves into your heart, the wisdom deity departs while the meditational deity melts into the nonreferential state. Conclude the practice with the dedication.

Instruction 95: The Instruction Related to Yoga Tantra

In the practice of yoga tantra, it is said that accomplishment is gained through the invocation and descent of the wisdom deity, the *jñānasattva*, into oneself visualized as the deity, the *samayasattva*. Here the practice is linked with the purification of the lower destinies.[13]

First take refuge and then generate the attitude of bodhicitta. Then, from within the sphere of emptiness, visualize the wrathful Conqueror of the Three Worlds.[14] He is green-blue in color, with one face and two arms. He is holding a vajra and bell. His right leg is bent, his left leg outstretched, and he is standing on a lotus and a sun disk. He is adorned with all the ornaments of the wrathful deities, and the flames that blaze from his body fill the whole of space. The enclosing vajra tent is filled with banners. A multitude of wrathful manifestations radiate from his body.

Touch your thumbs to your middle fingers, turn your hands upward, link your little fingers together and point forward with your index fingers. Recite three times the mantra *oṃ vajra krodha analārka mahākrodha drava drava vidrava vidrava sarva apāya nāśaya nāśaya hara hara praṇaṃ hūṃ phaṭ*.[15] By this means, you will protect yourself and the place. {342} Imagine that from the state of emptiness, in the heart of the deity, upon a lion throne, lotus, and moon disk, you appear in the form of the lord Sarvavid Vairocana. He is white in color and has four faces. He is seated with legs crossed, and his two hands are in the mudra of meditation. His main face is white, the face on the right is yellow, the left face is red, and the face at the back is green. He is adorned with silken garments and precious ornaments. Visualize in his heart a lotus and a moon disk with the syllable *oṃ* surrounded by the root vidyā mantra. Then invite Sarvavid Vairocana from the field of Akaniṣṭha in a form similar to the one visualized, surrounded by many buddhas and bodhisattvas. Recite the syllables *jaḥ hūṃ baṃ hoḥ*, and imagine that he dissolves indivisibly into you visualized as the deity. Then consider that lights radiate from the vidyā mantra in Vairocana's heart. They cleanse away the obscurations of you and all beings of the six samsaric destinies and make offerings to the noble beings and bring benefit to all. As much as you can, recite the mantra *oṃ namo bhagavate sarva durgati pariśodhani rājāya tathāgatāya arhate samyak saṃbuddhaya tadyathā oṃ śodhane śodhane sarva pāpam viśodhanaye svāhā*. Following this recitation, make outer offerings of incense and flowers. Then recite the following praise:

> O Bhagavan Vairocana,
> Making the mudra of concentration,
> You are the primordial wisdom of the dharmadhātu.
> I bow to you, all-knowing lord.

Then, as you pronounce the words *oṃ vajra muḥ*, the invited wisdom deity departs and returns to Akaniṣṭha. You, yourself, in the form of the meditational deity, fade like the mist that forms on a mirror when you blow on it, dissolving into the syllable *oṃ* in the heart [of the deity]. Then the syllable *oṃ* also melts into a state beyond all reference, and you remain for a moment in meditative evenness.

Finally, dedicate your virtue for the welfare of beings. It is taught that because this practice exhausts even the five sins of immediate retribution, it is extremely beneficial. {343}

The Unsurpassed Tantras

The anuttara, or unsurpassed, tantras are divided into three classes.

Instruction 96: The Unsurpassed Father Tantras

All phenomena are, in the three mandalas, the primordial state of buddhahood. By simply calling this to mind, this view is implemented mainly in the generation stage, which corresponds to skillful means. This is the position of tantras such as *The Glorious Assembly of Secrets.* The present account follows *The Display of the Supreme Horse Tantra.*

First take refuge and cultivate the attitude of bodhicitta. Then, within the sphere of emptiness, visualize the syllables *hrīḥ* and *ma* on a lotus and disks of sun and moon. They transform into the father-mother deity, Hayagrīva in union with his consort. The father is standing with one leg extended and the other bent. In his right hand he wields a staff, and with his left hand he makes the threatening mudra at the level of his heart. The mother brandishes a curved knife in her right hand, and with her left she offers to the father a skull cup filled with blood. Both father and mother have one face and three eyes. They are red in color and are adorned with all the ornaments of the wrathful deities. On the crown of the father's head, there is a horse's head, green in color, which fills the ten directions with the scream of its neighing. He wears a cloak of human skin, a kilt of tiger skin, and a garland of skulls. His body is huge with limbs of great thickness, and from his form there blazes a fire like the world-destroying conflagration at the end of the kalpa that consumes the entire thousandfold universe. Visualize in his heart, on a lotus and on disks of sun and moon, the syllable *hūṃ* encircled by the root mantra.

Consider that the wisdom deity dissolves into [the visualized deity]. The deity's head is then adorned with the presence of Amitābha. His heart projects sparks of fire and countless tiny wrathful emanations. Imagine that the entire thousandfold universe is quaking, shaking, and rocking. Then recite as much as possible the mantra *oṃ vajra krodha hayagrīva hulu hulu hūṃ phaṭ*. In conclusion, {344} the entire visualization gradually melts into the syllable *hūṃ* visualized in the heart. This dissolves into the bindu, which disappears into the state devoid of reference. Then rest in the state of dharmatā. In conclusion, make the dedication.

Instruction 97: The Unsurpassed Mother Tantras

All phenomena are the state of buddhahood in that they are the indivisibility of the ultimate expanse and primordial wisdom. This view is implemented through the great bliss of the generation and perfection stages. This is the position of the mother tantras, to which belongs the glorious *Cakrasaṃvara* and so on. The present account follows *The Heruka Galpo Tantra*.

First take refuge, cultivate the attitude of bodhicitta, and meditate on the three concentrations. Then, upon a lotus and disks of sun and moon, visualize yourself in the form of the Great Glorious One. He has three faces, six arms, and four legs, which are spread wide apart in striding posture. The central face is dark-blue, the right face is white, and the left face is red. Each of the faces has three eyes and mouths with fangs bared. The first hand on the right holds a vajra, the second a skull cup, and the third a plow. The first hand on the left holds a bell, the second a trident, and the third a small drum. The consort, Vajra Krodhiśvarī, is blue in color with one face and two arms. With clenched fist, her right arm grips the neck of the heruka, and with her left hand, she offers him a skull cup filled with blood. With both legs she embraces the thighs of the bhagavan. Both deities are adorned with ornaments of jewels and bone and garlands made of human heads. They are resplendent with the eight glorious attributes.[16] They are standing amid a mass of blazing fire. In the heart of the main deity, in the center of a lotus and disks of sun and moon, there is a nine-pronged vajra, the size of a barley grain. In the central prong, or life tree, there is the syllable *hūṃ*, and in the eight surrounding prongs are the eight syllables of the *rulu* mantra facing inward. They are as fine as if they had been written with a single hair. Consider that each of these syllables is blazing with light. Then imagine that the wisdom deity dissolves [into the visualized deity] and seals it with the three syllables. {345} The deity's head is adorned with Akṣobhya, who is the size of a thumb. A mantra garland arises from the syllable *hūṃ* and the eight syllables of the *rulu* mantra and, issuing from the mouth of the father deity, enters the mouth of the mother. Passing through her body and out through her secret space, it dissolves into the lower part of the syllable *hūṃ* in the heart of the father. As the mantra garland turns, the lights that it projects purify the obscurations arising from the karma and defilements of all beings, establishing them in the state of the Great Glorious One. The lights also make offerings to the noble ones and gather a wealth of accomplishments, which dissolve into the syllables of the *rulu* mantra in the [father's] heart. Recite as much as you can *oṃ rulu rulu hūṃ bhyo hūṃ*.

After this, you should implement the perfection stage, which has two aspects. When you practice the perfection stage endowed with form, concentrate for a moment and without distraction on the finely written syllables of the *rulu* mantra in the heart of the deity. Primordial wisdom, empty, luminous, and free of mental elaboration, will manifest—neither in your mental consciousness nor anywhere else. Rest in meditation, relaxing in this state.

When you practice the perfection stage without form, you should consider that all appearances are absorbed and dissolved into the mother deity. The mother then dissolves into the father deity, who then dissolves into the vajra in his heart. The vajra then melts into the eight syllables of the *rulu* mantra, which then dissolve into the *hūṃ*. This dissolves progressively through its constituent parts. The *shabkyu* dissolves into the small *a*, the small *a* into the body of the *ha*, the body into the crescent moon, and the crescent into the bindu, which finally melts into the dharmadhātu. Rest in the state that is beyond seeing and thinking. Finally, make the dedication. Such is this extremely profound path.

The Unsurpassed Nondual Tantras

The unsurpassed nondual tantras are discussed in relation to the practice of *The Great Net of Illusory Manifestations*, which comprises a general meditation on the generation and perfection stages and a particular meditation on the profound path. With regard to the general training, there are four meditations, which purify the habitual tendencies to the four ways of being born. {346}

Instruction 98: Purification of Birth from an Egg

For the highly elaborate generation-stage practice that purifies the habitual tendency to birth from an egg, you should first take refuge and cultivate the attitude of bodhicitta. Then proceed according to the wording of *The Ineffable Absolute Confession*.[17] Invite into the space in front of you the mandala of the peaceful and wrathful deities. Present offerings, sing praises, make prayers, and renew your vows. Afterward, when you pronounce the words *vajra muḥ*, the deities dissolve into emptiness, and you rest in a state of meditative equipoise. Then practice the three concentrations: the concentration on suchness,[18] the all-illuminating concentration,[19] and the concentration on the seed syllable.[20] Imagine that the seed syllables of the deities emerge from a white syllable *A* and descend onto their individual seats in the mandala. As they transform into the deities, the mandala of the illusory manifestations of the peaceful and wrathful deities is generated. The wisdom deities subsequently dissolve into the visualized deities. After making offerings and praise, be diligent in the recitation of the mantra, accompanying this with the radiation and absorption of lights. If you wish to practice in a detailed way, you should enjoy a gaṇacakra feast. It is, however, acceptable not to do so. Subsequently, you should meditate on the two kinds of perfection stage [with form and without form] and conclude with the dedication. For a detailed explanation of this practice, consult *The Precious Net of Peaceful Deities* and *The Ornament of Wrathful Appearances*.[21]

Instruction 99: Purification of Birth from a Womb

The moderately elaborate method for the meditation that purifies the tendency to birth from a womb is the same as the previous meditation except that the visualization and subsequent dissolution of the field of merit are omitted.

Instruction 100: Purification of Birth from Warmth and Moisture

For the condensed meditation practice that purifies the tendency to birth from warmth and moisture, first take refuge and cultivate the attitude of bodhicitta. Then by simply pronouncing the names of the supporting palace and the supported deities of the mandala, visualize the peaceful and wrathful deities within the space of emptiness. Then, as you recite once the passage [in the text] from the line "This completes the empowerment"[22] until "All are male and female deities,"[23] {347} understand that you are already primordially enlightened as the deity itself. In your heart, upon a lotus and disks of sun and moon, visualize Samantabhadra in union with his consort. Consider that from the syllable *hūṃ* in his heart lights radiate. They clean away the obscurations of beings who have no realization (and who, as a result, become deities) and make offerings to the noble ones. The sound of the mantra fills the entire universe. As much as you can, recite the mantra *oṃ āḥ hūṃ oṃ hūṃ trāṃ hrīḥ āḥ*. Then proceed to meditate on whichever of the two kinds of perfection stage is appropriate for you, and conclude with the dedication.

Instruction 101: Purification of Miraculous Birth

For the extremely condensed meditation practice that purifies the tendency toward miraculous birth, first take refuge and cultivate the bodhicitta attitude. Then within the sphere of emptiness, visualize in a single instant the entire mandala. Recite the mantra, and meditate on the perfection stage. In this case, after cultivating bodhicitta, visualize, in the middle of the sky, Samantabhadra seated on disks of sun and moon. He is in vajra posture with his hands in the mudra of meditation. He is in union with his consort and the lights that radiate from them purify the whole of phenomenal existence, transforming it into the buddha field of the five primordial wisdoms. This is a reminder that samsara and nirvana have a single taste. They are pure from the beginning and are the very state of buddhahood. Recite the mantra *oṃ āḥ hūṃ* as much as you can. As you relax in this way, an inconceivable state of luminosity will arise. Afterward, make the dedication. Here, as the saying goes, "To meditate on one buddha is to meditate on all." This is because one is meditating on the sovereign of all enlightened families, the ruler of all mandalas, the self-arisen primordial lord, the exalted sire of all the buddhas. As it is said in *The Secret Essence Tantra*,

> Within the sky's immaculate expanse, upon a sun and moon,
> Meditate upon the king of primal wisdom united with his consort.
> In this way you meditate on every mandala
> Of the victorious ones without exception. {348}

The Special Meditation on the Profound Path

The profound path has three instructions: (1) an instruction on the blessings that bring accomplishment, (2) an instruction on the preliminaries that clear the way, and (3) an instruction on the particular main practice.

Instruction 102: The Blessings That Bring Accomplishment

Take refuge and generate the attitude of bodhicitta. Then, visualizing yourself in the form of a deity, consider that above your head is the deity of your guru yoga practice in union with his consort, surrounded by ḍākas and ḍākinīs also in union. Make offerings and praise to them. Imagine that from the point of their union, a stream of nectar falls and dissolves into [the centers of] your body, speech, and mind. It is thus that you receive the first three empowerments. The deities then melt into a state of bliss and descend into your heart. The precious word empowerment is received, coming naturally to birth, endowed with the nature of the vajra of nondual primordial wisdom. Relax in meditation for a while and then conclude with the dedication. Thanks to this practice, blessings are authentically received, and realization arises all by itself. All obstacles to the path are dispelled, hindrances and deviations are eliminated, and the two kinds of accomplishment are gained. This is an extremely secret instruction.

The Preliminary Practice That Clears the Way

The preliminary practice that clears the way comprises three trainings: (1) the training on the channels, the key point of the fence of emptiness; (2) the training on the winds, the key point of the life force; and (3) the training on the essence drops, the key point of effort.

Instruction 103: Training on the Channels, the Key Point of the Fence of Emptiness

Meditate on the preliminaries as has just been explained [in the previous instruction]. Then visualize and concentrate on the subtle channels—that is, rasanā, lalanā, and the ever-trembling central channel, all of which run through the four chakras. The channels are like three perfectly hollow pillars. The main or central channel resembles an inflated membrane. Meditate on it first as being as thin as a bamboo arrow, then as wide as an incense holder, then as wide as a milk-churn, {349} and finally as being wide enough to contain your entire body. This is a crucial instruction for causing the wind-mind to enter the central channel quite naturally.

Instruction 104: Training on the Winds, the Key Point of the Life Force

In the center of the four chakras, visualize the two channels, rasanā and lalanā, to the right and left of the central channel. These two channels curve down at your forehead so that their upper extremities enter your two nostrils. At a distance of four finger widths below your navel, their lower ends curve into the central channel. When you exhale your stale breath, all diseases, negativities, and obscurations are cleared away. When you breathe in, the entire world, animate and inanimate, the universe and the beings it contains, together with all the qualities of the buddhas and bodhisattvas, enter you in the form of wind, passing through your nostrils and into the rasanā and lalanā channels and, through them, into the central channel. As you concentrate on this, hold the gentle vase breath in a relaxed and leisurely manner. This way of holding the breath quite naturally is an excellent key point. If you practice thus, the wind will be freed of defects, and you will be able to hold and refine it quite easily.

Instruction 105: Training on the Essence Drops, the Key Point of Effort

This is a reference to the practice of tummo. First, meditate on the wind as previously described. Then, within the central channel, in the center of the chakra of manifestation at the level of the navel, meditate on the quintessence of the fire element. It is the size of a needle point or a mustard grain and is in the form of the end stroke of the Tibetan letter *A*. It is very hot to touch. As the winds from the rasanā and lalanā channels pass through their lower ends and into the central channel, they ignite the quintessence of fire, and this blazes up like a horsehair and touches the letter *haṃ*, which is the size of a pea and is upside down in the central channel running through the middle of the chakra of great bliss. Tiny drops of the white and red essences drip down and feed the fire at the level of your navel. {350} As the fire increasingly blazes up, more essence drops drip from the syllable *haṃ* and fill the central channel. Meditate undistractedly until all the empty radial channels of the four chakras fill up with the essence drops. Great bliss will arise naturally throughout your body and mind.

The Particular Main Practice

The particular main practice comprises three key instructions. These concern (1) the primordial wisdom supported from above, (2) the primordial wisdom supported from below, and (3) the inconceivable primordial wisdom of Samantabhadrī.

The Primordial Wisdom Supported from Above

The key point of the primordial wisdom supported from above has four parts [corresponding to the four chakras].

Instruction 106: A Pith Instruction on the Chakra of Great Bliss

In the middle of each of the four chakras, primordial wisdom is displayed in the form of a drop, the size of a mustard seed. It is a blend of the refined white and red essences. Upon this support, visualize a sphere of five-colored lights the size of a pea. As the refined essence (the size of a mustard seed) in the crown of the head melts through the effect of the heat of the essence and the lights in the throat, drops of bodhicitta enter the radial channels of the chakra in the crown of the head and drip continuously down as if they formed a single hair, and enter the essence-support in the throat. Considering that you are filled with an immeasurable bliss, hold the gentle vase breath.

Instruction 107: A Pith Instruction on the Chakra of Enjoyment

Then, through the effect of the heat of the essence and the lights located in the heart, the essence-support in the throat melts, and [drops of bodhicitta] enter the radial channels of the chakra of enjoyment [in the throat], as well as the essence-support in the heart. Consider that an immaculate bliss arises.

Instruction 108: A Pith Instruction on the Chakra of Ultimate Reality

Then, through the effect of the heat of the essence and lights located in the navel, the essence-support in the heart melts, the essence drops enter the radial channels of the chakra of ultimate reality [in the heart], as well as the essence-support in the navel. Consider that supremely blissful primordial wisdom is born. {351}

Instruction 109: A Pith Instruction on the Chakra of Manifestation

Finally, the heat of the essence-support and lights in the heart descends and the essence-support in the navel melts. This essence has the form of a vapor. It is not gross but subtle and fine, and it enters the radial channels of the chakra of manifestation [in the navel], the rasanā and lalanā channels, and the central channel. Consider that you are pervaded by an utterly peaceful bliss and that the wisdom of the four joys is born.

The Primordial Wisdom Supported from Below

The key instruction on the primordial wisdom supported from below also has four stages.

Instruction 110: The First Stage

The rays projected from the light in your heart center reach down to your navel. There the essence-support becomes smaller and finer, is gathered upward, and dissolves into the essence drop and lights in the heart. Rest in the state that then arises.

Instruction 111: The Second Stage

The rays of light then reach up to your throat, the essence drop of which, becoming smaller and finer, is gathered into the heart. Rest in the state that then arises.

Instruction 112: The Third Stage

The rays of light then strike upon the support for the essence drop in the crown of your head. This becomes smaller and finer and is gathered into the heart. Rest in the state that then arises.

Instruction 113: The Fourth Stage

Then the essence drop draws in the essences present in the radial channels of the heart chakra, and these gather in the supported sphere of light that is the size of a pea. The lights of five colors dissolve into the central light, which is blue like the sky. Its radiance becomes more and more subtle, and finally, without thinking of anything at all, you should rest in meditative evenness in the pure ultimate expanse of great emptiness—Samantabhadrī, the dharmatā.

Instruction 114: The Key Instruction on the Inconceivable Primordial Wisdom of Samantabhadrī

Keep your body as motionless as the king of mountains, your speech as silent as that of a dumb person, and your mind in a space-like state without thought. {352} This state of emptiness, devoid of mental activity, is the actual primordial wisdom of Samantabhadrī, the dharmatā. The pristine, vivid appearance of luminous, limpid awareness is the primordial wisdom of the ground, the dharmakāya Samantabhadra. The indivisibility of these two states—namely, the awareness that seamlessly pervades the outer and inner spheres—is the inseparability of the ultimate expanse and primordial wisdom, the union of Samantabhadra and Samantabhadrī, the uncontrived, innate primordial wisdom—which we refer to as the Great Perfection.

These then are the quintessential and definitive crucial instructions for the ultimate and unsurpassed perfection stage of *The Net of Illusory Manifestations.*

This is the path of the Secret Mantra Vajrayāna,
The teachings of the supreme secret, vast and deep,
Which swiftly bring the accomplishment of perfect buddhahood.
O you who are so fortunate, practice it with zeal.
Through this merit may all beings, leaving none aside,
Embrace the Vajra Vehicle of Secret Mantra.
And riding on the wheels of the two stages, night and day,
May they attain the wish-fulfilling land of their accomplishment.
When through these powerful means,
Samsara, with its various worlds of beings,
Blends, in one taste, with the state beyond all sorrow,
May the benefit of others be spontaneously achieved,
And may a rain of dharma fall.

This concludes the second part, excellent in the middle, of *The Excellent Path to Enlightenment*, the meditation guide for *Finding Rest in the Nature of the Mind: A Teaching of the Great Perfection*. It expounds the Secret Mantra Vajrayāna.

Part Three: A Guide to the Secret and Unsurpassed Vehicle

The third part of this guide, excellent in its ending, is a detailed exposition of the gradual instructions belonging to the secret, definitive, and quintessential resultant vehicle of the unsurpassed Great Perfection. {353}

This vehicle is greatly superior to both the causal and resultant vehicles, marked as these are by the attitudes of adopting, rejecting, and effortful activity. It openly reveals primordial wisdom, self-arisen and primordially present of itself, the dharmatā beyond the intentional striving of body, speech, and mind, the actual, definitive, quintessential meaning of the vajra peak of ati. The instructions for the practice are set forth in two sections: (1) a description of the transmission lineages of its teachers and (2) the instructions themselves.

The Transmission Lineages of the Teachers of the Great Perfection

Generally speaking, the Great Perfection is a quintessential teaching gathered into three classes of instruction: the mind class, the space class, and the pith-instruction class, each of which has its own distinct lineage of transmission. Of these, the third is the most important since it expounds crucial teachings that act like the cauterization of the body's vital points. It includes the unsurpassed pith-instruction class, which sets forth introductory teachings for those who perceive appearances as sense objects,[24] as well as the trekchö teachings for students of the highest caliber.[25] As a means to setting forth these teachings in accordance with their respective practices, we will first consider the mind-to-mind transmission of the victorious ones, the transmission through symbols of the vidyādharas, and the hearing transmission of spiritual masters.

The [lineage of the] mind-to-mind transmission of the victorious ones passes from the dharmakāya Samantabhadra to an infinite array of sambhogakāya deities, both peaceful and wrathful, and thence to the great nirmāṇakāya Vajradhara, the teacher Vajrasattva, and to the Lord of Secrets, Vajrapāṇi.

The lineage of the transmission through symbols of the vidyādharas passes from the nirmāṇakāya Garab Dorje to the guru Mañjuśrīmitra, then to the learned Śrīsiṃha, the victorious Jñānasūtra, and the paṇḍita Vimalamitra.

The hearing transmission of spiritual masters passes through Nyang Tingdzin Zangpo, Neten Dangma Lhungyi Gyaltsen, Chetsun Senge Wangchuk,

Tulku Gyalwa Zhangtön, Guru Khepa Nyibum, the Lord of Dharma Guru Jober, Trulzhik Senge Gyapa, the great siddha Dawa Munsel, the precious Lord of Dharma Kumaradza, who reached the level of vidyādhara, and from him, as we have said, to the omniscient Ngaki Wangpo [Longchenpa]. {354}

Dharmakāya Samantabhadra—nature, utterly immaculate;
Sambhogakāya of great bliss—luminous and present of itself;
Nirmāṇakāya—various emanations striving for the benefit of beings:
To the teachers of the three transmission lineages, I reverently bow.

A Detailed Exposition of the Instructions

This explanation is threefold: (1) instructions on how to reach certainty [concerning the ground] by means of the view, (2) instructions on how to preserve this state by means of meditation, and (3) instructions on how to leave behind hope and fear regarding the result.

First, How to Reach Certainty by Means of the View

Decisive certainty [with regard to the ground nature] is achieved in two stages: (1) through a demonstration that the outwardly appearing object of apprehension is empty and beyond all reference and (2) through a demonstration that the inner apprehender is groundless and rootless. The first of these two stages is again divided twofold: (1) with the help of the eight examples of illusion, it is demonstrated that appearing phenomena are like the unreal images seen in a mirror, and (2) it is demonstrated that when appearances are investigated, they are not found: they are referenceless and empty.

Instruction 115: Appearing Phenomena Are Like Unreal Images Seen in a Mirror

All things appearing as the objects of the five senses—the visible forms and so on that populate phenomenal existence, both samsara and nirvana, the universe and its inhabitants—occur as the mere self-experience [either of the ordinary mind or of primordial wisdom]. They are without existence. These appearances—those that occur to the pure perception of the sugatas and those that appear to the deluded perception of sentient beings—are referred to respectively as the appearances of primordial wisdom and the appearances of the ordinary mind. Now both these kinds of phenomena—in the very moment of their being perceived—simply appear but lack intrinsic being, just like reflections seen in a mirror or rainbows in the sky.

The pure appearances of primordial wisdom are not stained by either an object or a subject of apprehension. They are beyond the extremes of existence and nonexistence. They are without birth and cessation. They are without movement and change and are therefore free of the characteristics of conditioned compounded entities. They are the appearances of uncompounded, empty forms, beyond all mental elaboration.

The deluded experiences of the ordinary mind, on the other hand, are the objects [of an apprehender that] clings to self [personal and phenomenal]. They are individually established as either existent or nonexistent and lack the characteristics of uncompounded things. Compounded or conditioned appearances are the adventitious self-experience of the mind. They simply appear as the fully developed manifestation of habitual tendencies. Consequently, there arises the understanding that the deluded appearances of the ordinary mind, the appearing objects of apprehension, are without true existence. {355}

Outer phenomena in all their variety are, like the visions of a dream, the fully developed manifestation of habitual tendencies. They simply appear, as it were, to those who are intoxicated by the sleep of ignorance. In truth, they have not the slightest existence. When they appear, however, they are not actually the mind. For their color, size, and materiality, and so on, are all at variance with the way in which the mind itself is defined. Neither are they other than the mind, for, apart from being hallucinatory appearances, they are not truly existent objects. Appearing to the mind, they are just the manifestation of the full development of habitual tendencies that have formed in the mindstream from beginningless time. They are like the images that appeared in your dream last night, when you dreamed about a magical spectacle that you witnessed the day before. However you perceive phenomena, they clearly appear and yet are nonexistent. They are like dreams, magical illusions, mirages, echoes, tricks of sight, water moons, emanated apparitions, and cities of the gandharvas. They have no support, no abode, and no intrinsic being. They are undefinable.

With the thought that they are nothing more than clear appearances, empty by their nature, get used to a clear and vivid understanding that everything that appears to you and everything you do—in terms of self and other, enemies and friends, towns and regions, houses and neighborhoods, food, drink, possessions, and all actions of eating, sleeping, going and sitting—is destitute of real existence. And you should engage in this meditation according to the threefold structure of preparation, main practice, and conclusion.

Instruction 116: When Investigated, Phenomenal Appearances Are Found to Be Empty and beyond Reference

When phenomena, great or small, are examined down to their atomic constituents, no partless particles can be found. Form is therefore empty. {356} When investigated in terms of its quality and identity, sound is also empty. When examined as to its aspects and nature, smell is empty. Analyzed in terms of different savors, taste is empty. Examined with regard to its sources, touch is also empty. And though they are different in the way that they appear as objects of the senses, they are all equal in terms of their empty nature. However, the emptiness of the different objects of sense cannot in itself be distinguished [in relation to these same objects]. It is like pure space; it is not differentiated [into several emptinesses]. At the same time, it is not one. The appearing objects of the senses are by nature empty. Apply this in your meditation in the three stages of preparation, main practice, and conclusion.

Reflection on the Fact That the Inner Apprehender Is Groundless and Rootless

The reflection on the fact that the inner apprehender is groundless and rootless is divided into two parts: (1) it is demonstrated that the [eight] consciousnesses are self-illuminating and without support, and (2) when investigated, these consciousnesses are shown to be groundless and rootless.

Instruction 117: The [Eight] Consciousnesses Are Self-Illuminating and without Support

The five sense consciousnesses arise as their five objects, form and so on. The mental consciousness[26] takes as its object the mind-created "object universal." The defiled mental consciousness[27] perceives this as something to be accepted or rejected, liked or disliked. The mental consciousness, which takes as its object things in a neutral sense [as neither attractive nor repulsive], arises subsequent to the six sense consciousnesses.[28] The ālayavijñāna, or the consciousness of the universal ground, is nonconceptual; it is self-illuminating and does not engage with objects [of cognition]. Whatever the eight or six consciousnesses cognize, they are clear, vivid, unsupported and self-illuminating. Although clearly manifest, they are insubstantial. Though nonexistent, they appear. They are like clean air, like a fresh breeze free of dust. Naturally clear, they are like the unclouded sky—like the wind, they move freely and yet are quite ungraspable. In the very moment that they seem to apprehend something, they are a wide-open clarity beyond identification. {357} When you watch them as they arise, when you watch them as they persist—when, in a state of relaxed calm, you watch the manner in which the apprehending consciousnesses appear—you realize that though they are nonexistent, they clearly appear. Without distinction, they are all empty, and being unsupported, they are self-illuminating. This reflection should be implemented according to the three stages of preparation, main practice, and conclusion.

Instruction 118: When Examined, the [Eight] Consciousnesses Are Shown to Be Rootless and Empty

The unsupported, self-illuminating mind is by nature free of outer appearances, inner aggregates, and any movement between them.[29] If you examine and analyze this same indwelling mind as to its shape and color, the three aspects of its arising, remaining, and ceasing, its nature and identity, and so on, you will understand its fundamental nature and see that it does not exist as anything whatsoever. You will see that it is rootless, unsupported, and lies beyond the extremes of existence and nonexistence. And when you make this investigation, the only important thing is your devotion to your teacher.

Second, How to Preserve the State of Certainty by Means of Meditation

This has two sections. There is, first, (1) a general exposition of the meditation of practitioners of the three capacities and, second, (2) a special explanation of a particular meditation endowed with skillful means. For the general explanation suited to the three capacities of beings, since the meditation practice is more easily understood in relation to the realization of the view, the text *Finding Rest in the Nature of the Mind* deals first with the meditation of beings of highest capacity. Here, however, we will adopt the gradual approach beginning with the meditation suitable for those of least capacity. We will then proceed with the meditation for those of moderate capacity and conclude with the practice suited to those of highest capacity.

Calm Abiding

Practitioners of least capacity begin by training in calm abiding. They then move on to the cultivation of deep insight, and finally they cultivate the two together. The practice of calm abiding comprises three trainings: (1) the subduing of thoughts, (2) focusing the mind [on a visible form] and (3) a meditation in relation to mental objects.

Instruction 119: The Subduing of Thoughts

First of all, practice guru yoga. Of the details pertaining to the seven-point posture of Vairocana, make sure that you place your hands on your knees and have your neck slightly bent. {358} Visualize your three channels. From the ends of rasanā and lalanā a luminous wind is exhaled.[30] It is like a long, twisted rope of five colors—brilliantly white like smoke, intense blue, glowing red, radiant yellow, dark-green, and pale-blue. The wind is then inhaled and kept within. Count from one to five cycles on the beads of your mala moving them one by one. This will cause gross thoughts to subside.

Instruction 120: Focusing the Mind [on a Visible Form]

Begin with the preliminary practice just described. As the main practice, place an object in front of you—an image, a book, a stone, or piece of wood—and look at it without distraction with a steady, unmoving gaze. Remaining in this way, you should completely abandon and eliminate whatever presents itself (sounds, smells, or unfolding thoughts) and stare intently at the object of focus. When your mind becomes concentrated and one-pointed, close your eyes and meditate by focusing one-pointedly on the vivid mental image of the object. If thoughts appear, open your eyes and look again at the object of focus. As you practice in this way, a state of calm abiding will arise in which the mind is one-pointedly held on any of the appearing objects of the five senses together with their mental images.

Instruction 121: Focusing the Mind on Other Sense Objects

You should, in addition, train yourself using sound as an object. Practice the preliminaries as before, and then, as the main practice, meditate focusing your hearing unwaveringly on the sound of a person's voice, on the sound of the wind, the barking of a dog, and so on. Once again, look inwardly and focus on the mental image of the sound [rather than the sound itself]. {359} As you alternately practice these two methods, your mind will be held on [the experience of] sound. As you practice in this way—and also in relation to smell, taste, and touch—the result will be that in your subsequent meditation you will not be disturbed by the five sense objects, which will instead become your helpers. This is a key point of great importance.

Instruction 122: Meditation in Relation to Mental Objects

Practice the preliminaries as previously. Then for the main practice, visualize yourself undistractedly in the form of a deity. When your concentration becomes one-pointed, modify your visualization and benefit beings through the radiation and absorption of lights. Otherwise, with a clear one-pointed mind, free of distraction, and focusing on beings, meditate on loving-kindness and the rest of the four boundless attitudes. By interchanging these two practices, you will acquire a calm abiding in which your mind is held in a state where movement and stillness are the same. Thanks to this and the previous key point, calm abiding is accomplished without hindrance.

Deep Insight

Deep insight is cultivated in two stages: first, (1) the mind is settled evenly in a state in which the outer appearing objects of apprehension are referenceless and space-like, and second, (2) the inner apprehender is also shown to be rootless and empty.

Instruction 123: Outer Appearing Objects Are Referenceless and Space-Like

Practice the preliminaries as previously. For the main part of the meditation, consider that appearing objects in all their variety are like the things you see in your dreams or when you observe a magical illusion. If you investigate them, you can see that they are empty, for they do not exist even on the level of infinitesimal particles. Rest in the state of perfect meditative evenness in which these objects—together with the cognitions that evaluate them—appear despite the fact that they are empty. This is a crucial point whereby you realize that both the objects and the perceptions of those objects are devoid of self.

Instruction 124: The Inner Apprehender Is Rootless and Empty

{360} Regarding the nature of the mind that evaluates both the object and the subject [of cognition], when you examine the mind's past and future, when you search for its existence or nonexistence, when you look for its arising, remaining, and ceasing, its shape, color, and so on, you find nothing at all. It is then that you should rest, completely relaxed, in a state of mind that is devoid of all support and fixation. This will bring you to the understanding that self and self-clinging are both empty.

Instruction 125: The Meditation on the Union of Calm Abiding and Deep Insight

In this meditation, mental calm and deep insight—which previously were cultivated separately—are blended together. As before, practice the preliminaries. Then, for the main practice, whatever may appear to you, do not examine it but settle in a state that is even in its natural flow, comfortable in its easy relaxation, clear in being traceless, open in its vastness, and spacious in being free of all limitations. At that time, a state of mind will arise that is like space, in which there is neither outside nor inside nor anything in between. Its stillness is calm abiding. Its luminosity is deep insight. The union of the two is spontaneous and indivisible.

For practitioners of moderate capacity, the meditation has three parts: (1) a meditation on the space-like empty state, (2) a meditation that is like a limpid mirror, and (3) a meditation in which arising thoughts are like waves [that sink back into the water].

Instruction 126: The Meditation on the Space-Like Empty State

Sit in the seven-point posture of Vairocana with your body as unmoving as the king of mountains. Do not block your sense faculties but leave them open and clear, limpid like the moon reflected in a pool. Do not rest on the appearance of what you perceive, but rest focused on its emptiness, free and relaxed, in a state of wide-open clarity in which there is neither outside nor inside nor anything in between. In this way, you will come to realize that everything is empty like a seamless space. {361}

Instruction 127: The Meditation That Is Like a Limpid Mirror

The key points concerning the body and sense faculties are as previously described. In the present case, however, do not focus on emptiness but meditate limpidly, lucidly, and vividly and in a state in which phenomena themselves clearly appear without your fixating on them. By doing this you will come to the realization that phenomena are insubstantial, ungraspable.

Instruction 128: The Meditation in Which Thoughts Arise Like Waves

The key points for the body and sense faculties are as before. The difference is that you should now focus on the arising of thoughts—they emerge and sink back—within the limpid state of awareness. Since they are without support, if you do not fixate on them, they subside—and you realize that they are like waves sinking back into the water.

Instruction 129: The Meditation for Practitioners of Highest Capacity

The meditation of such practitioners has the nature of an uninterrupted stream like a vast, pure river. Thanks to the understanding that thoughts are the dharmakāya, the discursive activity [of such meditators] arises and subsides as the play of the dharmatā. Thus without accepting, without rejecting, without obscuration, and without deviation, everything bears witness to the proficiency of their realization. Indeed, when one reaches the precious isle of gold, one will not find ordinary stones even if one looks for them. In the same way, whatever arises in the minds [of such practitioners] arises as self-arisen primordial wisdom. The cognitions of the apprehender[31] are, from the very first, a state of openness and freedom. They are nothing other than the wisdom of Samantabhadra. Whatever appears as an object of the senses arises as a form of emptiness. These cognitions of the apprehended[32] are, from the very beginning, open and free. They do not fall outside the vast expanse of Samantabhadrī. All phenomena, apprehended separately as "the mind and its objects," are nirvana within the nondual expanse of the great perfection. They arise within the vast expanse of primordial wisdom where there is neither out nor in. They are even in the vast expanse where there is neither up nor down. {362} They arise as self-arisen primordial wisdom where there is neither direction nor frontier. They arise as the display of dharmatā beyond all partiality. Thus, these yogis, free of the duality of self and other, attain the fundamental nature. They reach the primordial expanse devoid of place and time. And even if these yogis, whose minds have reached the level of exhaustion, experience thoughts—within the state wherein phenomena are exhausted—this is itself a moment of bliss.

This then is a presentation of uninterrupted realization. When awareness is stripped to its very nakedness, the mind soars. It is open, unimpeded, and bare. And once there is a clear certainty regarding this natural state of nonmeditation, it must be maintained.

The Special Meditation Endowed with Skillful Means

Now the special meditation endowed with skillful means has three methods. Of these, the first two correspond to auxiliary and proficiency stages and act simply as stepping stones to the final method. The meditation has four stages: calm abiding, deep insight, their union, and the gaining of a deep confidence [with regard to the primordial expanse of nonaction]. With regard to the first, there is the practice of calm abiding and then the enhancement of calm abiding. In the first case, calm abiding may be practiced either with an appearing object of without an appearing object.

Instruction 130: The Practice of Calm Abiding with an Appearing Object

Here, as described earlier, you may concentrate on an outer object of focus, such as the image of a deity. In the case of calm abiding in which an inner appearing object is used, when your mind is not still and you are experiencing too many thoughts, you should visualize in your heart a white lotus or crossed vajra, and so on, the base of which descends lower and lower until it makes contact with the golden foundation of great strength. As a result, your mind will become still. If you meditate one-pointedly in this way—stabilizing your mind and dissolving the visualization in your heart—a state of no-thought will arise.

Instruction 131: Calm Abiding without an Appearing Object

In this case, you rest in a state that is without any mental activity. This is like resting in the state of emptiness that arises as a result of investigating the status of outer and inner entities. {363} Similarly, it is like when you have meditated on the form of a deity in which all other thoughts have subsided—there comes a point when the deity itself also disappears, and you rest in that state. Train yourself in this way and an experience of calm abiding will arise that is free of any reference. It is like directly seeing something but without identifying it. This is a particularly profound key point.

Instruction 132: The Enhancement of Calm Abiding

As you move around a little or sit, observe the condition of your calm abiding. Combine it a little with speaking and reflecting on something and again observe it. As you get used to this, your calm abiding will increase. If it becomes stagnant, allow your mind to be distracted and agitated. Then, as you return to meditation, your calm abiding will be very clear.

The Cultivation and Enhancement of Deep Insight

There now follows the cultivation and then the enhancement of deep insight. Deep insight is cultivated in two ways: first (1) by using phenomenal appearances and second (2) by using emptiness.

Instruction 133: Deep Insight Cultivated with Regard to Phenomenal Appearances

Thinking that all phenomenal appearances are magical illusions or the visions of a dream, meditate from time to time on the unreality of whatever appears. There is an important difference in thinking that phenomena are *like* magical illusions and thinking that they *are* magical illusions. Previously it was shown how phenomena are like magical illusions. Here, however, you should meditate on them as actually being magical illusions.

Instruction 134: Deep Insight Cultivated with Regard to the Emptiness [of Phenomena]

The closer you observe phenomena from the moment that they appear, the more you see that they are clear, empty, and traceless. Rest in a space-like state without thinking of anything. Previously, the emptiness of phenomena was set forth through analysis and investigation. Now, however, the pure emptiness of phenomena is directly encountered. There is, therefore, a great difference between these two instances.

Instruction 135: The Enhancement of Deep Insight {364}

In whatever you do, train in mingling both appearance and emptiness—an emptiness that is the subsiding of all reference points.[33] If your meditation stagnates, then without being distracted for a single instant, train [by turning your attention] relaxedly to a physical form or some other sense object [and regard it] as ungraspable, as appearing but empty. In this way, you will accomplish deep insight.

Regarding the union of calm abiding and deep insight, there is first (1) the union itself and then (2) the enhancement of this union.

Instruction 136: The Union of Calm Abiding and Deep Insight

In order to cultivate the union of calm abiding and deep insight, adopt the key points of bodily posture. Then, without picking or choosing with regard to whatever appears or arises, closely watch your awareness, the ground from which the appearance has arisen. To refrain from investigating the appearing object but to leave it as it is constitutes a most profound and important crucial point. As you remain steadily in the state wherein movement and stillness are equal, stillness is not disturbed by movement. It is thus that awareness—the blending of the three factors of emptiness, luminosity, and movement—the fundamental stratum of the three kāyas is reached.

Instruction 137: Enhancing the Union of Calm Abiding and Deep Insight

When the sky is cloudless and clear, turn your back to the sun and focus your gaze on the open expanse of space. When, as illustrated by the outer pure sky, the inner sky of the mind also becomes pure, there instantaneously arises the secret pure sky of the essence of luminosity—the dharmatā beyond center and periphery. This is the extremely profound instruction of the Nepali master Kāmaśrī. If your meditation stagnates, train in calm abiding and deep insight separately. If you are drowsy, refresh yourself; if you are agitated, just relax. The key point is to train in the union of calm abiding and deep insight bringing it to bear on whatever you do.

Instruction 138: Gaining a Deep Confidence in the Primordial Expanse of Nonaction

As you meditate in this way, {365} your experiences, your mental stillness, your thoughts both good and bad, all appearances, whether pure or hallucinatory—all are of one taste in the great emptiness devoid of all support. This is the great exhaustion of phenomena beyond the ordinary mind, a great and seamless equality, a vast and groundless immensity. Therefore, do not grasp at anything. Do not think of anything. Do not ask anyone about anything. Do not rely on anything. Cut through all the fetters of pride, of hope and fear. Take as your destination the exhaustion of phenomena that lies beyond the ordinary mind. Have confidence in the primordial expanse of nonaction. Do not turn back. Gain conviction in the actual way of being of things—a conviction that transcends the intellect.

Third, Leaving Behind Hope and Fear regarding the Result

Here, there are three things to be considered: (1) the ultimate expanse of dharmatā in itself; (2) the nature of the kāyas, which are the appearances of the ultimate expanse; and (3) the primordial wisdoms displayed within the kāyas.

Instruction 139: The Ultimate Expanse of Dharmatā

The ultimate expanse of dharmatā is neither samsara nor nirvana. It is beyond all delimitation; it falls into neither of these two extremes but provides the ground for the manifestation of both of them. It is referred to as the ultimate expanse, the ultimate truth, the final point of all realization, the last of all exhaustions, the final destination, the primordial dharmadhātu. And this is none other than self-arisen, self-cognizing primordial wisdom. It is self-knowing awareness itself, free of all mental activity. It is free of all delimitations and falls into no extreme. It is what the teacher introduces you to—it is not to be looked for anywhere else. As it is said in *The Secret Essence Tantra*,

> The nature of the mind is perfect buddhahood.
> Nowhere else should buddhahood be sought.
> Even though they looked for it,
> Not even the victorious ones would find it somewhere else.

Since the ultimate expanse of buddhahood is veiled by adventitious impurities, its nature is said to be pure. But it is not just that. You should know that, in itself, it is neither good nor bad. Be completely certain that, in its present immediacy, empty awareness is the spontaneous presence of the dharmadhātu. {366}

Instruction 140: The Nature of the Kāyas, the Display of the Ultimate Expanse

The kāyas—of which by nature there are five—are the display of the ultimate expanse. This ultimate expanse is the state of the inseparability of the kāyas and wisdoms. The aspect of the absence of arising and cessation, movement and change of this ultimate expanse is the dharmakāya. It is the great ineffable state, inconceivable, and inexpressible. The sambhogakāya is gathered within the ultimate expanse of luminosity. It transcends the extremes of permanence and nothingness, and it manifests spontaneously as the major and minor marks of buddhahood. The nirmāṇakāya arises unceasingly. It is the aspect of cognizant power, which radiates everywhere impartially. The abhisambodhikāya, the body of manifest enlightenment, is the aspect of the primordially pure ultimate expanse, which is spontaneously endowed with the ten strengths, the four fearlessnesses, and so on—in other words, all the qualities of buddhahood, which are as many as the grains of sand in the Ganges river. The unchanging vajrakāya is by nature the ultimate expanse, which throughout the passage of time is changeless and unmoving.

Despite the difference implied by the presence or removal of adventitious stains, awareness—at this very moment—subsists in the state of sentient beings as the five kāyas. In other words, its nature is empty, its character is luminous, and its manifestation is unceasing. Anything whatever can arise, and yet the nature of awareness does not change. You should be completely certain that the five kāyas are not to be sought elsewhere. They are your great, spontaneously present, birthright. Be completely convinced that awareness—empty, open, and unimpeded—is the spontaneous presence of the five kāyas.

Instruction 141: The Primordial Wisdoms Displayed within the Kāyas

The primordial wisdom of the dharmakāya is completely beyond word, thought, and expression. The primordial wisdom of the sambhogakāya possesses five characteristics. The primordial wisdom of the nirmāṇakāya consists of what is referred to as [the two knowledges:] the knowledge of the nature of phenomena as it is and the knowledge of the phenomena in their multiplicity. {367} Whether or not these wisdoms are unstained or stained by adventitious impurities, they are naturally and completely present in the ultimate expanse and are thus complete within awareness—even in this present moment [when one is on the path]. Empty awareness, self-cognizing awareness, the traceless self-subsiding of the five poisons, and nature and specificity (the nature of phenomena and phenomena themselves)—all is simply awareness.[34]

More particularly, even though a casually arising thought of desire is an ordinary defilement, nevertheless, when you recognize its nature and when you are able to rest in this recognition, this same thought arises as a state of bliss that is completely free of clinging—it is all-perceiving primordial wisdom. When dislike arises in relation to a given thing, this is ordinary aversion. But when you recognize its nature, it arises as a limpid, luminous state free of mental elaboration—it is mirrorlike primordial wisdom. When you are caught in a state of not knowing, this is ignorance. But if you recognize the nature of this unknowing, it arises as a nonconceptual, luminous state—it is the primordial wisdom of the dharmadhātu. To claim that you are better than others is ordinary pride. But when you recognize its nature, you realize the nondual equality of yourself and others—this is the primordial wisdom of equality. When you feel competitive rivalry with others, this is ordinary jealousy. But when you recognize its nature, it arises as limpid impartiality, and this is the all-accomplishing primordial wisdom.

Even though, within awareness, the five poisons manifest as the display of your failure to recognize this same awareness, nevertheless, when you do recognize it, these same poisons arise as the creative power or display of the five primordial wisdoms. Being completely certain, therefore, that in this very moment, the kāyas inseparably united with the wisdoms constitute your natural birthright, have no more hope or fear. Rest instead in a state of powerful and decisive certainty. With these words, you have been properly introduced to your own nature.

These then are the topics
Of the supreme and secret Great Perfection,
Preeminent and placed above
The causal and resultant vehicles.

Not within the range of all,
This is the vajra peak reserved
For those of supreme mind and fortune. {368}

Through the merit of expounding them,
May every wandering being achieve
Samantabhadra's state of great perfection.

This concludes the third part, excellent in its ending, of *The Excellent Path to Enlightenment*, the meditation guide for *Finding Rest in the Nature of the Mind: A Teaching of the Great Perfection.* It expounds the topics of the unsurpassed Great Perfection.

The essential meanings of the perfect path of cause and fruit,
The key points utterly profound of all the sutras, tantras,
Treatises, and pith instructions in their vast array,
Are gathered here within this guide.
It is my offering to those of perfect fortune.

My faithful followers of future generations,
Children of my lineage,
Supreme guides in your turn
Of fortunate disciples on the path to freedom,
With these instructions train your students perfectly
Throughout the year, in brief, or mid-length,
Detailed, or extremely detailed courses.

In a brief course, every subject
Is considered for one day—
And thus in four months, one and twenty days,
The treasury of outer, inner, and secret dharma
Will stand open.

In a mid-length course, each topic
Should be contemplated
For the space of three days.
Thus your students, in the space
Of one year, two months, and three days,
Will find the signs of warmth of understanding
Of the vehicles of cause, result, and unsurpassed instruction.
They will find conviction
In this path to liberation
And the essence of enlightenment.

In the detailed exposition, every subject
Is reflected on for five days.
Thus if, within one year, eleven months, and fifteen days,
All is covered, your disciples
Will attain the essence of the Triple Gem,
The truth sublime and ultimate.

In the extremely detailed exposition,
Every topic is considered over seven days,
And thus within two years, six months, and twenty-seven days,
The instructions for the meditation on the supreme vehicle
Will be perfectly concluded.

Your followers will enter irreversibly
The essence of enlightenment.

May all such fortunate and diligent disciples,
Heirs of the victorious ones,
Upholders of the supreme lineage,
Devote themselves to that state where
The aims of self and other are perfected.
May they swiftly journey into peace,
The essence of enlightenment. {369}

Therefore, for the beings
Of generations that are now to come
I give this good advice,
The essence of definitive instruction.
I join my hands and cry to them:
"Do not be idle, but practice day and night
With confidence and diligence
Upon the path to liberation!"

These instructions were set forth
Upon the slopes of Kangri Tökar
By Stainless Rays of Light,
The sun of concentration
And accomplishment of luminosity,
Arising from the vast expanse of wisdom.

By this virtue, may we—I and every being—
Traverse the tangled mirkwood of samsara,
Entering the path of peace and liberation
Leading to supreme enlightenment.
May we come to utter freedom, perfect buddhahood.
For as long as there remains the buddhadharma,
May these spiritual instructions
Appear for beings throughout all the world.
Upheld with deep respect and confidence a hundredfold,
May it be spread and flourish everywhere and always!

The Excellent Path to Enlightenment, a guide for meditation on the three excellent parts expounded in *Finding Rest in the Nature of the Mind: A Teaching of the Great Perfection*, was composed by Drime Özer, a yogi of the supreme vehicle—one who was rich with great learning in the Buddhist scriptures. It was written on the slopes of Kangri Tökar, on an excellent high throne, in the palace of Samantabhadra, in the garden that brings forth the flowers of the clouds. May its auspicious glory shine in all directions, causing everything to turn to virtue and propitiousness.

Virtue! Virtue! Virtue!

PART SIX

Texts Taken from The Trilogy of Natural Openness and Freedom

Longchenpa's *Trilogy of Natural Openness and Freedom* consists of three root texts referring in sequence to the nature of the mind, the dharmatā, and the state of equality. These root texts are in verse, and each is accompanied by a meditation guide. In Longchenpa's catalog of his own works,[1] titles are given for what appear to be autocommentaries on the three sections of the trilogy. Alas, they seem to have been lost. In the present volume of *The Treasury of Precious Instructions*, Jamgön Kongtrul decided to include only the meditation guide and an accompanying prayer—but not the root text itself—of the first part of the trilogy, *The Natural Openness and Freedom of the Nature of the Mind*. For the second and third parts of the trilogy, only root texts, but no meditation guides, are included. There is no obvious explanation for this inconsistency.

The second and third parts of the trilogy, *The Natural Openness and Freedom of the Dharmatā* and *The Natural Openness and Freedom of the State of Equality*, are each divided into three subsections—the former according to ground, path, and result and the latter according to view, meditation, and action. Other than this, these two root texts are composed in uninterrupted verse. As an aid to the reader and in order to create a system of reference useful for the student, we have divided both these poems into short stanzas of unequal length according to the perceived manner in which the content of the two texts is developed. It should be remembered that there are no such stanzas in the root texts themselves and that this arrangement is no more than the artificial but well-intentioned suggestion of the translators.

Of general interest is the fact that, according to Nyoshul Khen Rinpoche, this trilogy is, to all intents and purposes, a meaning commentary on the mind-class teachings of the Great Perfection, specifically the *All-Creating King Tantra*, which is one of its most important scriptures.

In the absence of auto- and other commentaries, the translation of the root texts, which are in part extremely terse, was not easy and, despite our best efforts and the help of Tibetan scholars, remains in part conjectural.

16. A Prayer Belonging to *The Natural Openness and Freedom of the Nature of the Mind*[1]

Longchen Rabjam

Take refuge by reciting, {371}

With all the beings of the six realms, I devotedly take refuge
In the teacher, yidam deity, and the host of ḍākinīs,
Buddha, dharma, and the noble sangha,
Who fill the vast expanses of the sky.

Cultivate the attitude of bodhicitta by reciting,

Lord Buddha and your bodhisattva heirs, please think of me.
Just as the victorious ones, past, present, and to come,
Have brought to birth the attitude of bodhicitta,
Likewise for the benefit of beings,
I too will cultivate this attitude.
By training well and step-by-step
In all the precepts as they have been taught,
May I, in all my deeds, bring benefit to others
And drive away the suffering of wandering beings.

oṃ āḥ hūṃ vajra guru padma siddhi huṃ
I pray to you, O dharmakāya Samantabhadra in union with your consort.

oṃ āḥ hūṃ vajra guru padma siddhi hūṃ
I pray to you, sambhogakāya Amitābha in union with your consort.

oṃ āḥ hūṃ vajra guru padma siddhi hūṃ
I pray to you, nirmāṇakāya lord of Oḍḍiyāna in union with your consort.

oṃ āḥ hūṃ vajra guru padma siddhi hūṃ
I pray to you, O Drime Özer, scion of the Conqueror.

oṃ āḥ hūṃ vajra guru padma siddhi hūṃ
I pray to you, O Khedrub Delek Gyatso.

oṃ āḥ hūṃ vajra guru padma siddhi hūṃ
I pray to you, renunciant Mati Maṅgala.

oṃ āḥ hūṃ vajra guru padma siddhi hūṃ
I pray to you, O bodhisattva Guṇa Śrī.

oṃ āḥ hūṃ vajra guru padma siddhi hūṃ
I pray to you, O Tulku Samdrub Gyalpo.

oṃ āḥ hūṃ vajra guru padma siddhi hūṃ
I pray to you, O Trulzhik Namkha Zhönu.

oṃ āḥ hūṃ vajra guru padma siddhi hūṃ
I pray to you, O bodhisattva Chöying Dorje.

oṃ āḥ hūṃ vajra guru padma siddhi hūṃ
I pray to you, O Khedrub Lodrö Gyaltsen.

oṃ āḥ hūṃ vajra guru padma siddhi hūṃ
I pray to you, my root teacher, who have been most kind.

oṃ āḥ hūṃ vajra guru padma siddhi hūṃ
I pray to you, the assemblies of the deities of the yidam mandala.

oṃ āḥ hūṃ vajra guru padma siddhi hūṃ
I pray to you, O ḍākinīs and dharmapālas, protectors of the Buddha's word.

oṃ āḥ hūṃ vajra guru padma siddhi hūṃ {372}
I pray to you, my precious teacher. Purify the obscurations of my body, speech, and mind that I may thus accomplish your body, speech, and mind, attaining buddhahood within this very life.

oṃ āḥ hūṃ vajra guru padma siddhi hūṃ

Son of all the buddhas, spontaneously present as the primordial wisdom of Mahāsāgara, mind of all the sugatas of the three times and the ten directions, Padmasambhava—throughout the three times I bow before your stainless lotus feet and come to you for refuge. In your great love, I pray you, be my guide.

Lord, primordial and perfect Buddha,
Treasure, source of all the qualities of supreme bliss,
Supreme master of all buddhas,
Samantabhadra, father-mother, I bow down to you.

Embodiment of the five wisdoms and five families,
Vajradhara's very nature,
Who display appearances of peace and wrath past numbering,
O Amitābha, father-mother, I bow down to you.

Emanation of the ocean of the buddhas gone in bliss,
Self-arisen on a lotus-stem,
Ablaze with all the great and lesser marks of buddhahood,
Pema Jungne, Lotus-Born, to you I bow.

In ultimate nature, you are Samantabhadra.
In luminous character, you are the sugata Amitābha,
In cognizant potency you are the nirmāṇakāya Padma—
Śākya Senge, Lion of the Śākyas, I bow down to you.

Through the enlightened deeds of your three kāyas,
You fulfill the hopes of beings to be trained.
You emanate a sparkling cloud of ḍākinīs,
Pema Gyalpo, Lotus King, to you I bow.

Knowing all things in their nature and their multiplicity,
Sounding thus the dharma drum in manifold variety,
You drive away all māras and all tīrthikas,
Loden Chokse, Intelligence and Love Supreme, to you I bow.

Upon the snowy mountain of all-knowing wisdom
You attained the state of supreme freedom
In a throng of countless retinues. {373}
Senge Dradok, Lion's Roar, to you I bow.

From the clouds of your compassion all arrayed,
Lightning garlands flash, and falling rains of joy and benefit
Enlarge with excellence the minds of beings.
Padmasambhava, to you I bow.

The sun's disk of your love and wisdom
Brings to flower the lotus of the sacred teachings
And shines upon the path of living beings—
Nyima Özer, Light Rays of the Sun, to you I bow.

With fierce emanations you subdue,
And with your ninefold dance of terrible demeanor,
You cut down all the evil gods and spirits.
Pema Tötreng, Lotus Garlanded with Skulls, to you I bow.

From brilliant clouds of ḍākinīs,
There falls a rain of nectar-like accomplishment.
You who pleased the greatly blissful Conqueror,
O Kharchen Tsogyal, I bow down to you.

You who perfectly beheld all things that can be known,
Who held the precious treasuries of sacred dharma,

Who caused an increase of deep treasures of the mind,
O Drime Özer, I bow down to you.

Through the union of your view and action,
You achieved the level of supreme vidyādhara,
And upheld all the teachings of the essence unsurpassed.
To you, O Delek Gyatso, I bow down.

Father of all beings, holder of the lineage of teachings,
Who, endowed with bodhicitta, perfect in your realization,
Placed beings on the path of ripening and freedom,
To you, O Mati Maṅgala, I bow.

Through the great strength of your prayers and training in past lives,
You manifestly realized voidness and compassion
And gloriously and with love have guided beings on the path.
To you, O Guṇa Śrī, I bow.

You who have absorbed the meaning of the sutras and the tantras,
Whose realization shone with the adornment of the threefold training,
Who upheld the essence of the Buddha's teaching,
To you, O Tulku Samgyal, I bow down.

Utter freedom, dharmadhātu, equality itself,
And supreme luminosity of stainless primal wisdom—
From these, like day from night, you have been never parted,
Namkhai Zhönu, I bow down to you. {374}

Dharmakāya, spontaneously present from the first,
Displayed as rūpakāya, whose illusory forms
With plenteous skill set beings free,
To you, O Khalong Yangpa, I bow down.

You severed with the blade of your awareness-wisdom
All the fetters that deprive our nescient minds

Of deep emptiness's light,
To you, O Mati Dhvaja, I bow down.

Through the great strength of your training in past lives,
You understood spontaneously and without effort
The meaning of the vajra essence unsurpassed,
To you, my own root teacher, I bow down.

With emanations of a whole array of means
Within the display of the dharmadhātu,
You perform the four activities,
O ḍākinīs and faithful guardians of the teachings, I bow down to you.

And to all vidyādharas residing in the ten directions,
To the dharma of the blissful buddhas, and the host of noble ones,
And to the ocean the greatly blissful ḍākinīs,
And all those worthy of respect, I bow.

Virtue!

17. An Essential Meditation Guide for the Stages of the Path according to *The Natural Openness and Freedom of the Nature of the Mind: A Teaching of the Great Perfection*[1]

Longchen Rabjam

Homage to glorious Vajrasattva. {376}

You whose nature is primordially unborn—
Nondual dharmakāya, indescribable, beyond the reach of thought—
Samantabhadra, self-arisen, sovereign nature of the mind—
To you, perfection of the ground beyond all change and movement,
I bow down.

Teachings, thanks to which a yogi surely gains
The fruit within a single life—instructions where
The blessing power of holy beings is made manifest,
That show how what arises all subsides
When there is no accepting or rejecting—
Here I will explain in written form.

The utterly perfect Buddha, skilled in means and filled with great compassion, expounded countless vehicles and teachings in accordance with the various dispositions and capacities of beings. The meaning of them all is subsumed in awareness, the enlightened mind. There are many instructions on how to meditate on awareness, but their effectiveness is weakened by the strong clinging to extremes by which beings are hampered. Only a few paths lead directly to freedom in a single life.

{377} The following instructions, which accord with *The Natural Openness and Freedom of the Nature of the Mind*, constitute a supremely secret method that brings about the instantaneous subsiding of all accepting and rejecting in the openness and freedom of the ground. These instructions, which transcend those of every other vehicle, are presented in three stages: (1) the transmission lineages of the teachers, (2) the teaching transmitted by them, and (3) the sealing of the teaching with secrecy on account of their great value.

The Transmission Lineages of the Teachers

Within the dharmadhātu, the palace of Akaniṣṭha, the dharmakāya Samantabhadra gave instructions to the sambhogakāya Amitābha, who then transmitted them to the nirmāṇakāya Padmasambhava. The latter instructed Yeshe Tsogyal, who in turn instructed Guru Śīlamati. From him the transmission passed to Khedrub Delek Gyatso, then to Mönlam Özer, Lord of Dharma, who bestowed it on me.

The Teaching Transmitted

The teaching transmitted by this lineage comprises three topics: (1) instructions for practice whereby freedom is found in this very life, (2) instructions on luminosity, the ground for the appearance of the bardo state, and (3) instructions regarding the final result. {378}

The Instructions for the Practice whereby Freedom Is Found in This Very Life

Here, there are three sections: (1) the preliminary practices, (2) the main practice, and (3) the conclusion.

The Preliminary Practices

There are seven preliminary practices.

First, the Reception of Blessing Power by Means of Guru Yoga

Sit on a comfortable seat. Take refuge in the Three Jewels and generate the bodhicitta attitude. Then, in a single instant, visualize above the crown of your head a lotus and disks of sun and moon, on which is seated Master Padmasambhava inseparable from your own root teacher. Attired as a heruka, he blazes with the major and minor marks of buddhahood. Blue in color, he is holding a vajra and a bell and is in union with his consort. He is adorned with jeweled ornaments and ornaments of bone. In his lap, embracing him, is the Lady of Kharchen, red in color. She is holding a curved blade and a skull cup. Imagine that they are surrounded by a throng of lineage teachers and countless buddhas, bodhisattvas, ḍākas, and ḍākinīs. Mentally pay homage, presenting offerings and confessing your negative actions. Rejoice in all good deeds, and request the teachers to turn the wheel of the dharma, imploring them not to pass into nirvana. Then pronounce the following prayer:

> I pray you, precious teacher, bestow on me your blessing power that all the obscurations of my body, speech, and mind be purified. Accomplishing your body, speech, and mind, may I attain buddhahood in this very life.

Light pours from the body of your teacher and his retinue, cleansing away the obscurations of body, speech, and mind of yourself and all beings. The whole of phenomenal existence is transmuted and becomes the expression of the teacher. In the form of light, the [blessings of the] body, speech, and mind of the teacher and his retinue enter through the crown of your head and give rise to the primordial wisdoms of bliss, luminosity, and no-thought. Imagine that an extraordinary realization of a state of openness and freedom instantaneously arises in your being. Remain focused on this in meditation, holding your breath for a short while. {379} Then, in conclusion, make the dedication in the understanding that all things are illusory. If you practice in this way for seven days, you will quite suddenly receive extraordinary blessings and the signs that the level of the teacher has been attained.

Second, the Mandala Offering whereby the Two Great Accumulations Are Perfected

Visualize your teacher and the host of deities of the yidam mandala in the sky in front of you. Place as many heaps of offering substances as possible on the mandala plate. Then consider that, symbolized by the four continents of this universe, all the buddha fields of the ten directions—all of which have the nature of different jewels—are filled with an array of objects of enjoyment both human and divine. They are overflowing with infinite clouds of outer and inner offerings, ocean-vast. Make an offering of all this—together with your own body, possessions, and merit—to the invited guests, imagining that they are very pleased to receive them. Make effort in this mandala offering, day and night, for seven days. The purpose of this practice, the accumulation of merit and wisdom, will thus be perfectly fulfilled, and an extraordinary realization will arise in your mind.

Third, the Recitation of the Hundred-Syllable Mantra through Which the Two Obscuring Veils Are Dispelled

Within the state of emptiness, instantaneously visualize yourself in the form of Vajrasattva—white in color, with one face and two arms, and holding a vajra and a bell. Adorned with precious ornaments, he is seated cross-legged in vajra posture. In his heart, in the middle of a lotus and upon disks of sun and moon, is the syllable *hūṃ* encircled by the hundred-syllable mantra. Imagine that rays of light pour from the mantra and purify the obscurations of yourself and all beings. Recite the hundred syllables as much as you can for a period of seven days. The purpose of this practice is to cleanse away the obscurations produced by evil deeds and to realize swiftly the fundamental nature of phenomena.

Fourth, a Meditation on the Impermanence of Life as a Means to Generate a Sense of Weariness with Samsara and a Determination to Leave It {380}

To be sure, even this life, adorned as it is with precious freedoms and advantages, is fleeting and transient. Consider the impermanence of outer phenomena, which change with the passage of time—days, months, and years. Consider too that no beings can escape death. Think of your own dead relatives, and understand that your life too will pass. Your body will disintegrate, its components scattered, just like a bursting bubble. And there is no certainty that you will not die this very day.

Think now, therefore, that you will die for sure and imagine that today is in fact your last day in this world—that the elements of your body will dissolve, and your mind and body will separate. Sincerely meditate like this for seven days. The aim of this practice is to call to mind the impermanence of all things, to reduce your preoccupation with the future, and to inspire you with diligence in the dharma.

Fifth, the Practice of Taking Refuge, a Preliminary to the Path

Visualize the Three Jewels in the sky in front of yourself: the buddhas and bodhisattvas, past, present, and to come, residing in the ten directions; the hosts of deities of the yidam mandala; the śrāvaka and pratyekabuddha arhats; and so on. With the intention to take them as your protectors until you gain enlightenment, recite as much as you are able,

> I take refuge in the teacher,
> I take refuge in the Buddha,
> I take refuge in the dharma,
> I take refuge in the sangha.

Imagine that, like parents with their darling children, the objects of refuge think of you with great love and compassion. Recite the prayer of refuge from the depths of your heart, imagining that all beings are loudly reciting the prayer along with you. Strive in this practice for seven days. Its purpose is to banish all obstacles to the practice of the dharma and to bring about an increase in spiritual realization.

Sixth, the Practice of Bodhicitta, Which Gives Authenticity to the Implementation of the Dharma

{381} Picture in front of you all the sufferings of the hot and cold hells; the hunger and thirst of the famished pretas; the slavery and exploitation of the animal kingdom; the sufferings of birth, old age, sickness, and death of the human state; the conflicts of the asuras; and the horror of the death and fall of the gods. Reflect too upon the causal process of the karmic law, which leads to suffering, and consider that suffering is indeed the general condition of samsara. Wish that all beings, constantly tormented by the sorrows of samsara, come to abide in the four measureless attitudes. Through the dedication of your body, wealth, and virtuous action, may they have happiness here and now. May they be free from suffering. May they possess an open impartiality free of attachment to what is close and aversion to what is distant and alien. Wishing also that, on the ultimate level, they come to buddhahood, take the vow of bodhicitta, reciting the short ritual formula as follows:

> O enlightened lords and all your offspring, think of me.
> Just as all the buddhas, past, present, and to come,
> Have brought to birth the attitude of bodhicitta,
> Likewise, for the benefit of beings,
> I too will cultivate this attitude.
> And in the precepts, just as they have taught,
> I will step-by-step correctly train myself
> And drive away the sorrows of all beings.
> May all I do bring benefit to others.

Train yourself in the alternate practice of taking all the sufferings of beings upon yourself and giving them your happiness. For seven days, meditate on heartfelt compassion. The purpose of this practice is to convert all your exertions of body and speech into actions done for the benefit of others, transforming them into the true path of the Mahāyāna. {382}

Seventh, the Implementation of the Quintessential, Definitive Teaching, Which Gives Rise to the Realization of the Fundamental Nature

This requires three things: (1) training in calm abiding, (2) the cultivation of deep insight, and (3) the recognition of their union.

Calm Abiding

Sit cross-legged in a state of meditative evenness in which past thoughts have ceased and subsequent thoughts have not yet arisen. Rest in the present moment where you are not thinking of anything at all. Make effort in this practice for seven days. The purpose of this exercise is, first, to suppress ordinary negative thoughts, thus preventing [the mind] from being overshadowed thereby, and second, to make it easier to distinguish the mental states of clarity and dullness and thus to recognize whatever thoughts adventitiously arise.

Deep Insight

Examine the whole variety of thoughts that now seem to arise even more grossly than before. When they proliferate with great intensity, look for the place from where they arise. Search your whole body, its upper and lower parts, and in between. Look for the shape and color of your thoughts, their identity. Seeing that they arise from nowhere, you will come to understand that the mind itself is rootless and unborn.

When thoughts remain with overwhelming force, examine where they dwell.[2] Are they outside or inside the body or somewhere in between? What is their color, how can they be identified? You will see that the mind itself—unceasing, clear, and empty—is a state of utter purity. The thoughts themselves arise quite suddenly and disappear you know not where. But when they have ceased, by looking for where they have gone, you will recognize that they subside without trace just where they are, and you will understand the ungraspable quality of awareness.

The Union of Calm Abiding and Deep Insight

Relax your mind and body in a state that—even, serene, clear, and lucid—is beyond all thoughts and memories. The stilling of the movement of past thoughts is calm abiding. The vivid, clear display of awareness is deep insight.[3] {383} These two states occur together, simultaneously united. The purpose of this meditation is to identify the methods of meditative concentration. Meditate for a day on each of these three stages.

The Main Practice, the Introduction to the Nature of the Mind

Leave your body and mind in a state of deep relaxation, for it is on the basis of the mind of the present instant that recognition occurs. The outer vessel of the universe and the beings that dwell within it—all phenomena of samsara and nirvana—are simply the ways in which the mind manifests.

They are like the dreams you had last night. And the mind—empty in nature and luminous in character—arises in the various manifestations that occur,[4] which are like forms reflected in a spotless mirror. They appear and yet are ungraspable, for they are beyond the conceptual extremes of existence and nonexistence. This means that the dharmatā is none other than the mind in the immediacy of the present moment, unfolding as it does in various ways. As the great Master Padmasambhava has said,

> If you understand that this, the thought, is dharmatā,
> You will not meditate upon the dharmadhātu as some other thing.
> It is enough to know the way of thoughts and their subsiding.
> This thought itself is dharmakāya.
> This is the supreme path, alone preeminent.
> Phenomenal existence bears Samantabhadra's seal.[5]
> Those who abandon thought and meditate on no-thought
> See phenomenal existence as their enemy.
> Their "freedom" is delusion.[6]

Therefore, do not meddle with the mind of the present instant, but deeply relax and leave it as it is in its natural flow. No matter what thoughts arise, do not reject them, do not indulge in them—but just rest on them quite naturally, quite directly. The mind is open and free when its ultimate nature is seen. It is open and free when its character is understood, and likewise its manifestations are completely open and free. This is how the mind is. Therefore, whatever thoughts arise, pay no attention to them. {384} The mind will remain in the flow of awareness and its natural perfection will manifest all by itself. When that moment comes, you will rest in awareness. Thoughts no longer bother you—you will not reject some and indulge in others. You will rest in awareness devoid of movement and change—a state in which the primordial wisdoms of bliss, luminosity, and no-thought instantaneously subside.

When you refrain from conceptually apprehending the mind of the present instant as this or that, thoughts simultaneously arise and vanish all on their own. And as they disappear, rest without any contrivance until the next thought appears. Again, when thoughts occur, do not get caught up in those whose nature you fail to recognize. Just rest in them freely, rest in them openly, and let them go without holding onto them. It's as though you are putting things into a vessel that is open at the bottom. Get used to awareness that is open, immediate, naturally free, and unhindered, without conceptualizing it by thinking, "This is it."[7]

In brief, since the view and meditation regarding the immediate subsiding of thoughts as soon as they arise (as well as all the other ways of subsiding) occur all on their own—bursting forth from the depths [of the mind]—both the factors to be eliminated and the antidotes to them vanish all by themselves in the state of openness and freedom. Since phenomenal existence arises as the dharmatā, meditation is uninterrupted. Since in the absence of fixation, empty thoughts are open and free, defilements are themselves the corresponding pure primordial wisdoms. Since all perfect qualities are spontaneously present and complete, they are beyond the sphere of effortful practice and striving. Since everything arises as the fundamental nature, deviations and obscurations are in their nature pure, and dharmatā is found within. Ordinary thoughts and recollections, in their present freshness, are therefore the natural state of dharmakāya. As the great Master Padmasambhava has said,

> Refrain from meditating
> On the nature of the mind—it cannot be conceived—
> But rest in evenness.
> Even if you meditate, it is of no importance[8]—
> Just rest quite naturally.
>
> Do not wander in distraction.
> Just be focused and attentive.
> Even if you wander, it's of no importance—
> Just rest quite naturally.
>
> Do not watch.
> Instead rest freely.
> Even if you watch, it is of no importance—
> Just stay as you are.
>
> Do not think.
> Just stay alert.
> Even if you think, it is of no importance—
> Just stay as you please.[9] {385}

Do not dissolve your thoughts.
Instead stay clear and vivid.
Even if you do dissolve them, it's of no importance—
Just stay quiet.

Don't be tightly focused.
Just stay naturally relaxed.
Even if you focus tightly, it's of no importance—
Just be restrained.

Do not alter anything.
Instead stay clear and vivid.
Even if you alter something, it's of no importance—
Just stay clearly present.

Don't affirm.
Instead rest free of effort.
Even if you do affirm, it is of no importance—
Just be your natural self.

Don't negate.
Just be spontaneous.
Even if you do negate, it is of no importance—
Just rest in unborn nature.

Do not be discouraged.
Instead remain alert.
Even if you are discouraged, it's of no importance—
Just stay quietly serene.

Don't make an effort.
Rest at ease.
Even if you do make effort, it's of no importance—
Just be spontaneous.

Do not settle.
Just remain ungrounded.

Even if you settle, it's of no importance—
Just rest in relaxation.[10]

No matter how the mind of the present moment arises, it is spontaneously perfect. When you leave it uncontrived in its natural flow, there is no grasping at phenomena outside or within. Since there is no acceptance or rejection with regard to mental states, the nonduality of the mind is uninterrupted. Full-blown thoughts do not run wild and uncontrolled,[11] and therefore there is freedom from the kind of mind that belongs to the desire realm. As it unfolds, consciousness arises in its natural flow with the result that the deviations of the form and formless realms are transcended. Since there is no grasping at specific things, calm abiding occurs spontaneously. Since the fresh and uncontrived state arises on its own, deep insight is also present spontaneously. And since the unfolding of the mind is not separate from its intrinsic stillness, calm abiding and deep insight are spontaneously united. Since the mind's movement instantaneously subsides in its own nature, wisdom is spontaneously present. Since stillness is blissful,[12] meditative absorption is spontaneously achieved.

Since there is no fixation on the simultaneous arising and subsiding of thoughts, primordial wisdom is present all by itself. Since there is no fixation on defects,[13] these subside in an open state devoid of clinging. Since all enlightened qualities arise within primordial wisdom, which is awareness, they develop and increase. And since the grounds and paths[14] are perfectly included in the natural state, the supreme accomplishment of Mahāmudrā is achieved within this very life. {386}

In awareness, uncontrived, open, naturally occurring,
No matter what arises, leave it in the great arising.
Blissful mind devoid of clinging—
Sovereign absence of all reference—
Holds the everlasting realm of unborn dharmakāya.

This is how the nature of the mind is introduced.

Conclusion

There are three parts to the conclusion: (1) the training in the post-meditation period, (2) the dispelling of hindrances and (3) the enhancement of the practice.

Training in the Post-Meditation Period

Following the actual meditation—in the course of which you have become proficient in leaving in its natural flow all that arises in the mind of the present moment—train yourself in seeing clearly that outer appearances, inner mental states, and meditative experiences are, in the very moment of their being perceived, devoid of intrinsic being, that they are just like magical illusions, dreams, the moon reflected in the water, or emanated apparitions. This training will cause your assumptions of the true existence of phenomena to subside. And even in your dreams, you will be without clinging, and you will remain in the dharmakāya.

Dispelling Hindrances in the Form of Diseases and Negative Forces

If you examine illness and negative forces—the illusory display of your thoughts—you will surely find that they are neither outside nor inside you, nor somewhere in between. So convert them into a practice on the unborn nature, and be happy. In your meditation, imagine that you are piercing the place of your disease and relieving its pain. And cultivate bodhicitta regarding the negative forces, training yourself in viewing their lack of intrinsic being. This will certainly cause them to subside.

Enhancement of the Practice

If your training in virtuous practice becomes lackluster and you are failing to make progress, pray fervently to your teacher. Cultivate a strong sense of weariness with samsara and a determination to free yourself from it. Accumulate merit by offering gaṇacakra feasts and so on—and meditate on loving-kindness, compassion, and bodhicitta. Go to a very solitary place, such as a charnel ground, a lonely valley, or a mountain top. Visualize your teacher above the crown of your head, and then run and jump, crying out whatever words come into your mind. And mentally imagine yourself in situations of happiness or suffering, indulgence or rejection. Then, all of a sudden, cause these experiences to subside and merge with the nature of your mind. {387} After practicing like this for several days, you will gain an extraordinary understanding. These are the concluding crucial points of the training.

Yogis who proceed in this way acquire a fearless confidence regarding birth and death. For them the objects and subjects of apprehension subside in and of themselves. And in this very life, such yogis will see directly all the qualities of the supreme and common accomplishments.

If one were to explain these topics in detail, there would be no end to it. So here I have set them forth very briefly. This completes the teaching for the attainment of freedom in this life.

The Instructions on Luminosity, the Ground for the Appearance of the Bardo State

Earlier, while in the bardo of the present life (between birth and death), yogis have meditated on the crucial points of natural openness and freedom so that even in their dream bardo, the fundamental nature, primordially free and open, manifests without their clinging to it. When the moment of death arrives and the earth element dissolves into the water element, the yogis lose their physical strength. When the water element dissolves into the fire element, all the liquids in their bodies dry. When the fire element dissolves into the wind element, warmth gradually withdraws, beginning with the extremities. And when the wind element dissolves into consciousness, respiration ceases.

When [the consciousness of] form dissolves into [the consciousness of] sound, the eyes no longer see. When [the consciousness of] sound dissolves into [the consciousness of smell], the ears cease to hear. When [the consciousness of] smell dissolves into [the consciousness of] taste, the nose no longer smells. When [the consciousness of] taste dissolves into [the consciousness of] touch, the tongue no longer tastes. When [the consciousness of] touch dissolves into [the consciousness of] mental phenomena, the body can no longer feel. When [the consciousness of] mental phenomena dissolves into the mind,[15] all gross thoughts of apprehended objects and apprehending mind cease. It is like losing consciousness or fainting. The eight consciousnesses thus dissolve into the universal ground.

In the very moment that yogis settle in meditative absorption, they gain freedom as one of the buddhas of the five families, and the primordial ground is reached. They come to the five endowments and the great endowment of perfection. In the very instant that they settle, relaxed and devoid of conceptual target, upon the blue light—recognizing it as the primordial wisdom of the dharmadhātu—they find freedom as Sarvavid Vairocana. {388} Similarly, when they settle in the white light, recognizing it as mirrorlike primordial wisdom, they are enlightened as Akṣobhya. When they settle in the yellow light, recognizing it as the primordial wisdom of equality, they are enlightened as Ratnasambhava. When they settle in the red light, recognizing it as all-discerning primordial wisdom, they are enlightened as Amitābha. When they settle in the green light, recognizing it as all-accomplishing primordial wisdom, they are enlightened as Amoghasiddhi. Subsequently, they strive for the benefit of beings by means of nirmāṇakāya manifestations. They gain manifest enlightenment in the primordial ground.

Moreover, in their previous existence these yogis have grown used to the crucial point of thoughts naturally and instantaneously subsiding. And, within the recognition of the self-arising of thoughts, they have acknowledged the primordial wisdoms of bliss, luminosity, and no-thought as being spontaneously and effortlessly present. Now, therefore, in the instant that they blend these wisdoms with the luminosity of the bardo state, they gain freedom.

Because the ultimate nature of awareness is empty, it does not dwell anywhere. Because its character is luminous, the ground of manifestation is unceasing. Because its manifestations are manifold, the yogis remain in a state in which whatever arises subsides without exception. These are the three endowments of the yogis. [The distinct experiences of the process of dissolution of the four elements is their fourth endowment. And the fact that these yogis find freedom as one of the five buddhas through the integration of luminous primordial wisdom is their fifth endowment.][16]

When they strive for the benefit of beings by means of nirmāṇakāya manifestations, this constitutes their endowment of perfection. Subsequently, when the sambhogakāya dissolves into the dharmakāya and the yogis seize the stronghold of the dharmatā beyond movement and change, they rest in the great, perfect equality of the dharmakāya. And this constitutes their endowment of great perfection.

These, then, are the instructions for the gaining of freedom in the bardo state for yogis of moderate capacity.

Additional Instructions for Yogis of Basic Capacity, Whose Remaining Karma Continues to Unfold in the Bardo of Becoming

When beings fail to recognize luminosity in the bardo state, they assume a mental body. During the first half of the bardo period, this appears in the form of the body of their previous existence. During the second half of the bardo, it appears in the form to be assumed in the next life. [In such a mental body,] beings are in possession of the full complement of sense powers, and owing to the miraculous power of karma, they are able to go wherever they want. Unimpeded, they can go anywhere except a mother's womb[17] and vajrāsana, the vajra seat. Many experiences of happiness and sorrow arise, just as in the dream state. The duration of the bardo is not fixed. Some beings take birth quickly, whereas others remain in the bardo for forty-nine days or more. {389}

It is a suffering to realize that one is dead. But if at that time, one remembers the instructions that one has previously received, if one is adept in not holding onto appearances and mental states, and if one prays to one's teacher, one has a chance of gaining freedom. At that time too, it is also very important to remember the pure buddha fields, to know that the appearances of the bardo are unreal, and to have fervent faith and devotion. It is said that in such a situation, there are some who take birth in the pure buddha fields and gain enlightenment there.

The best way of navigating the experiences of the bardo is to realize that they are unreal. The intermediate approach is to train oneself in perceiving them as being like the magical, illusion-like appearances of the generation and perfection stages, and of the pure fields.[18] The most basic way is to train in choosing the door of a good rebirth. For birth among the gods, this will appear as a garden or an immeasurable palace. For birth among the asuras, it will appear as a wheel of light. For human birth, it will appear as a pleasant house, a beautiful grove of trees, or as a group of many people. The door to animal birth will look like a cave or shelter of grass, whereas in the case of birth among the pretas, it will look like a deep ravine, a cave, or a pile of filth. The door to birth in hell will look like a deep darkness or a deluge of rain.

It is important not to be attached to any of these places of birth. Instead, one should imagine the excellent place of birth of the celestial or human realms as a divine mansion. One should visualize within it a seed syllable, such as *hūṃ*, and allow one's consciousness to enter it. With the thought that in one's next life, one must meet the dharma and gain supreme accomplishment, one should visualize oneself in the form of one's yidam deity. It is thus that one will take birth as a god or a human being endowed with all the freedoms and advantages. One will meet with teachers and virtuous friends, and in that very lifetime one will reach supreme accomplishment.

This completes the instructions for the bardo state.

Instructions regarding the Accomplished Result

Whether one gains freedom in this very life, in one's next life, or in the bardo state, the result is certainly the same: unsurpassed buddhahood. {390} Through directly realizing that the nature of the mind, in its openness and freedom, is utterly pure and luminous, one captures the citadel of the immaculate dharmakāya. And at that time, like the sun and moon rising in the sky, the sambhogakāya appears within the state of dharmakāya and, endowed with the five certainties, brings benefit to the beings dwelling on the grounds of realization. Likewise, the various forms of the nirmāṇakāya also appear and spontaneously accomplish the welfare of beings.

In particular, if what one perceives in the bardo state is recognized as the luminosity of the ground, the citadel of the dharmakāya is captured, and within that state, the benefit of beings is secured by means of both the sambhogakāya and the nirmāṇakāya.

If what one perceives is recognized as the display of the five primordial wisdoms, the citadel of the sambhogakāya is captured and the benefit of beings is secured by means of the nirmāṇakāya. Subsequently, the nirmāṇakāya dissolves into the sambhogakāya, the sambhogakāya dissolves into the dharmakāya, and one rests in the primordial ground. Then, from within that primordial ground the two rūpakāyas appear, thanks to which the benefit of beings occurs.

If what one perceives is recognized as the pure bodies and fields of the nirmāṇakāya, [the citadel of the nirmāṇakāya is attained]. The appearances of the nirmāṇakāya dissolve into the sambhogakāya, which then dissolves into the dharmakāya, and subsequently the benefit of beings is once more secured through the emergence of the two rūpakāyas.

Both samsara and nirvana are perfectly contained within awareness in its present immediacy. If this awareness, which is one's very nature, is not recognized, the various visions of samsaric experiences of happiness and suffering unfold like dreams within the sleep of ignorance, and beings wander through the three worlds and the six realms. By contrast, if awareness is recognized and one becomes fully acquainted with it, the nirvanic visions of the various sambhogakāya buddha fields appear, also in the manner of dreams, and one accomplishes the benefit of beings in a dreamlike way.

Whatever appearances of samsara or nirvana are perceived, if in the very moment of their appearing,[19] [they are seen to be] without true existence, they disappear—just as dreams do when one wakes from sleep. They become of one taste with the dharmakāya, free of all mental elaboration, which (in terms of the present metaphor) resembles the experience of daytime appearances.

If one fails to recognize the empty nature of awareness in its present immediacy, {391} it is through ignorance that one mistakes it for the mind and the formless realm, which is qualified by an absence of cognitive activity. If the luminous character of awareness is not recognized, it is through aversion that it is mistaken for speech and the form realm, [which is associated with luminosity]. If the various manifestations of awareness are not recognized, then it is through attachment that they are mistaken for the body and the desire realm, which is qualified by bliss.

It is there that unvirtuous deeds cause one to wander in the lower destinies. Contaminated virtue, unrelated to meditative concentration, causes one to wander among the gods and humans of the desire realm. The luminous clarity of concentration leads to wandering in the form realm. The stillness aspect of concentration leads to wandering in the formless realm. So it is that one is constantly engulfed in suffering.

When, however, one recognizes and beholds awareness in its present immediacy, its empty nature appears as the dharmakāya free from all elaboration,[20] its luminous character appears as the sambhogakāya endowed with the five certainties, and its various manifestations are the nirmāṇakāya appearing according to the needs of beings and spontaneously accomplishing their welfare.

Within the space-like dharmakāya, free from all the extremes of conceptual elaboration, there appears the highest sambhogakāya buddha field of Dense Array. Here, until samsara is completely emptied, the peaceful and wrathful sambhogakāya buddhas, adorned with all the major and minor marks, take delight in instructing their retinues who are their own self-experience, together with the bodhisattvas residing on the grounds of realization.

From within that state, there emanate countless manifestations corresponding to the varying perceptions of beings in all the ten directions of the six worlds. With their inexhaustible deeds of body, speech, and mind endowed with the wisdom that knows the nature of things and the wisdom that knows all things in their multiplicity, they bring benefit to beings. Such is the enlightened activity of their unbounded compassion.

In its ultimate nature or inner luminosity,[21] the primordial wisdom of the buddhas who thus appear encompasses the fivefold greatness of the sambhogakāya. In its form—that is, the outwardly radiating luminosity—it encompasses the twofold greatness of the nirmāṇakāya. {392} The five inner primordial wisdoms are the wisdom of the dharmadhātu, mirrorlike wisdom, the wisdom of equality, all-discerning wisdom, and all-accomplishing wisdom. As for the two primordial wisdoms of outwardly radiating luminosity, these are the knowledge of phenomena in their multiplicity (that is, of all things distinctly and without confusion), and the knowledge of the nature of things, the single taste of their ultimate nature.

This brings to an end the teaching on the stages of the arising of the result, which occurs at the conclusion of the path.

Great is the chariot of the perfect path
Pursued by beings of good fortune.
It is primordial wisdom,
Nondual, open, free, and uncontrived.
It is the free and open "mind of now,"
Where arising and subsiding coincide.
Without before and after,
It is a free and open state.
It is not altered by the apprehended.
Neither does the apprehender stain it.
Defiled afflictions that arise
Are all indeed primordial wisdom.
These teachings that my teacher
In his kindness gave to me,
I have written down for sake of future generations.
All who yearn for freedom
From existence in samsara
Should depend on them.
But those with minds that keenly wish

To seize on things as this or that,
Accepting and rejecting,
Do not have the karmic fortune for these nondual teachings.
For on this path, all things
Are savored as primordial wisdom.
And thus the everlasting kingdom
Of the dharmakāya is attained.

My friends!
Within the quintessential mansion
Free of all extremes,
Taste the richness of the nature of the mind,
Securing thus with certainty
The fruit of great bliss in this very life.
And then you will secure quite naturally
The benefit of beings.

This life of ours is like the scudding clouds,
Our body coreless like a bubble.
Rare it is to hear the teachings,
Rare to practice what one heard.
So stir up, quickly now, the strength of effort.
With good deeds swiftly ripening in flower and fruit,
May wandering beings all attain
The state of buddhahood.

While staying in the Orgyen fortress
On the white brow of the snowy peaks,
I, Drime Özer, wrote this down.
May every being in the three states of existence
All together and spontaneously
Achieve by virtue of this merit
The level of Samantabhadra.

This concludes *An Essential Meditation Guide for the Stages of the Path*, instructions for *The Natural Openness and Freedom of the Nature of the Mind: A Teaching of the Great Perfection*, composed by Longchen Rabjam.

The Sealing of the Teaching with Secrecy

A seal of secrecy is placed upon this teaching, for it is the epitome of the most hidden pith instructions. To teach it to more than three fortunate disciples at a time will incur the punishment of the ḍākinīs. Therefore, keep it strictly hidden. May Black Lekden, glorious protector; Ekajaṭī, guardian of the tantras; and Rāhula, upāsaka planetary spirit, protect this teaching very closely.

Virtue! Virtue! Virtue!

18. The Natural Openness and Freedom of the Dharmatā

A Teaching of the Great Perfection[1]

Longchen Rabjam

In Sanskrit: *Mahāsandhidharmadhātvātmakonāma* {396}
In Tibetan: *rDzogs pa chen po chos nyid rang grol zhes bya ba*

The Ground

Homage to glorious Samantabhadra!

The state of luminosity, primordially unborn,
Equality, the vast immensity ungraspable,
The mind's unmoving nature,
Is Akaniṣṭha of great bliss,
The triple kāya spontaneously present,
Wherein I bow down to the perfect ground
Beyond all change and movement. (1)

Enlightened is the nature of the minds
Of me and every other being,
And yet because of ignorance,
We wander in the wasteland of existence.
Wishing that we all be freed therefrom,
I will describe the pathway of the perfect chariot:
A definitive and quintessential teaching. (2)

My friends, samsara's fathomless abyss,
Storm-tossed with waves of every pain,
Has come about through ignorance,
Through our deluded clinging to a self.
How important then its antidote:
The view, the recognition
of the nature of phenomena! (3)

All things in phenomenal existence,
Samsara and nirvana,
Are, from the very first, unborn, primordial equality.
Beyond the reach of proof and refutation,
They are not permanent or ceasing.
They do not come; they do not go. (4) {397}

The space-like state of nondual dharmatā,
Untouched by ontological extremes,
Appears as anything at all,
As manifold, distinct phenomena.
Yet in the very instant that such things appear,
They are beyond the mind's elaborations.
They are not extramental things;
They are the way the mind appears.
They are not mind or things arising from the mind. (5)

All things appearing as five objects of the senses
Are like the black hairs seen by those whose vision is impaired.
They appear and yet do not exist.
To apprehend them dualistically is a delusion.
When dreaming, you may see yourself surrounded
By a herd of elephants or soldiers, all illusory,
And thinking they are different from yourself,
You are alarmed.
But are they different from you,
Or are they in your mind?
At that moment, they have no existence
Either in the outer or the inner world.

For those who know their nature,
All such terrors vanish there and then. (6)

So it is that taking dualistically what is not dual,
The ignorant believe them true,
And thus they are deluded in samsara.
The wise perceive as nondual what appears dualistically,
And thus they find their freedom
In the state beyond samsara, painful by its nature. (7)

Kyeho! Appearances are unborn from the first. {398}
However various, they are not different—
All are like reflections in a glass.
Their appearance and their empty nature are not separate
But are a nondual unity, like water and its wetness.
Like a phantom city, like a magical illusion,
They are free from ontological extremes.
In their moment of arising, they're primordially unborn.
Although appearing to remain,
They do not dwell; they are the dharmakāya.
In the very moment that they cease, they do not cease,
For they transcend both growth and diminution.
However they appear, it is not thus that they exist.
No matter how they are examined,
They lack intrinsic being.
All are free and open from the very first,
Samantabhadra's very state. (8)

Phenomena are groundless, rootless,
And devoid of any substance.
In them there is nothing to identify—
Nothing you can cling to, saying "this."
They are like space, without creator and bereft of function.
All there is, whatever there may be—
Nothing can be pointed out as "this." (9)

It is hard to see the quintessential nature of the mind,
The state that is innate and uncontrived,

By means of the one-sided statements in the tenet systems
With their various categories of view, of meditation, and of action.
The śrāvakas and the pratyekabuddhas,
The cittamātrins—even the svātantrika madhyamikas—
Distinguish the two no-selves of phenomena and person
And stray in the four aspects of the practice:[2]
Space-like view and meditation and the rest.
And thus for many countless kalpas they must practice. (10)

Through all the many transformations and contrivance
Of the generation and perfection stages of the tantras,
Be they kriyā, caryā, yoga, or anuttara—
You do not even come close to the natural state,
Innate and uncontrived, spontaneously present,
For you are tangled in the web of concepts. (11)

Those engaged in view and meditation, action and result
Identify the awakened mind, declaring "It is this."
Some there are who block their feelings and perceptions.
Others cut the continuity of the three times
And say the present state of mind is open, unimpeded.
Others count their thoughts as they arise and cease
And say their moving waves are but the nature, uncontrived.
Likewise, there are others, fettered by their lust, {399}
Who bind the winds and practice sexual union,
Claiming that the vibrant pleasure is the mind's true nature.
Those who are entangled in the net
Of their accepting and rejecting, turn by turn,
Will never see the ultimate quintessence.
All such beings are deceived
By doctrines that the mind conceives
And thus are caught in this existence
With no chance of freedom. (12)

Kyema! Not knowing how to estimate a jewel,
These people throw away a wishing-gem and search for trinkets.
They spurn the nature of the mind, supreme and uncontrived,
And get entangled in the snake pit

Of contrivance and manipulation, hope and fear.
Through all such mental efforts, they are never freed.
Because a thing sought for implies a seeker, they are led astray. (13)

Ema! If you wish to find the nature of your mind,
What use to you is much investigation and analysis?
Whatever may appear, there is no way to grasp it, saying
"It is this" or "It appears as that."
There is no need to take or leave what is beyond such grasping,
Free from ontological extremes.
All is unreal. Do not change or contrive anything. (14)

All these appearances—the objects of the senses and the mind—are empty.
What view is needed, therefore, that declares them to be so?
And if they are not empty, then no view will make them so.
What point is there in all this meaningless fatigue? (15)

In just the same way, there's no need to meditate
Upon the generation and perfection stages.
It does not matter how you see phenomena,
Things that you accept or else reject.
If they exist in truth, there is no need for all your efforts,
And if they don't exist, such efforts have no purpose—
Coal will not turn into gold.
Imputed by the mind, phenomena have no existence.
Don't distort this fact by alteration, change, or antidotes. (16)

Herein lies the meaning of the vajra essence, unsurpassed.
There is no mantra and no tantra, no claims of tenet systems,
No view, no meditation, no action, no result—
Nothing to identify as "this."
All is but a single mandala; all, perfect equality.
There the tenet systems are no more.
There is no view, no meditation, no action, no result.
Samsara and nirvana are completely equal—
The great and all-pervading dharmatā. {400}
Not bound, not freed, enlightened from the first,

They are the state of dharmakāya,
Sovereign of nonaction, perfect of itself. (17)

The illusory and various display of rūpakāya,
Phenomenal existence, is not separate
From primordial wisdom, the three kāyas.
Beyond acceptance and rejection,
All things are completely pure,
An awe-inspiring vast immensity.
Phenomena are perfect of themselves.
They are all equal;
They are the unborn sovereign state
Without periphery, or center, or direction.
When there is no subject-object clinging to them,
This is what is meant by "nature uncontrived."
There is no need to spurn or to accept,
No need for affirmation or negation.
All is one sole state of evenness.
This then is the great perfection,
The highest peak of all the views.
Recognize this sovereign state
Beyond all target and fixation.
All focusing entangles you.
But when all arises for you
In the freedom from conceptual fixation,
It is actually primordial wisdom [that arises],
The primal flow, self-empty, the nature, fresh and uncontrived.
Reach decisive certainty about the view,
Devoid of clinging, free from all positions. (18)

Kyeho! At all these various appearances, one has to laugh!
Leave them unexamined, and they have existence well enough.
Investigate them, and you will find nothing to identify.
Look more closely—they transcend all ontological extremes.
And when you turn and watch the mind discerning this,
You will not discover it—past, present, or to come.
It does not arise, remain, or cease.
No color does it have, no shape; it cannot be identified.

When it seems that it arises,
There is nothing that arises and no place for such arising.
You do not see it inside, and you do not see it outside.
It is beyond the two extremes of seer and of seen.
It seems to move outside toward external objects,
Yet there is no movement.
For it is in the mind itself that all such things arise.
If the mind did stray externally, it would become inanimate.
And there would be two kinds of momentary mind: [the conscious and material]. (19)

The ground of such arising is utterly without existence.[3]
Like space, it is primordially free and open.
The arisings are not different from it;
They are like the things reflected in a mirror.
Indeed, the ground and the arisings are not separate
But are like water and the waves that form in it.
There is no need to take or to reject—
All are but the state of great perfection. {401}
By nature, they are buddhahood primordially pure. (20)

Appearances and the mind
Are from the very first without intrinsic being.
Today I realized what my glorious teacher taught me.
I am decisively convinced
That each and every thing is dharmakāya.
Concerning this, I have no doubts or misconceptions.
No one do I need to ask, for I have seen the mind's true nature,
The innate, uncontrived condition of no-action. (21)

Now I see that movement, stillness—
Both are the display of dharmakāya.
No need is there to take one and reject the other.
No matter what arises, it is but a great adornment,
While stillness is the one state of unmoving dharmatā.
Everything is perfect of itself
Beyond both change and movement.
Now I have attained the wisdom mind

Of the victorious ones, past, present, and to come.
Present of itself, it is the great bliss
Perfectly included in the ground—Samantabhadra.
At all times it is free of change and movement.
Everything is even, free, and open in the primal ground. (22)

Kyema! As long as you possess a mind that clings
To one side or another,
There is no chance of liberation, for you are thereby bound.
But when there are no sides,
When clinging to extremes subsides,
This is nonduality itself,
There is no other nonduality.
It is not seen by watching; it is not found by searching.
You cannot point to it as "this" or "that."
Do not with the grasping mind
Imprison or set free the natural, "ordinary" state. (23)

If you posit nonduality[4] and freedom from extremes,
You bind the quintessential nature of the mind
In the extreme of "freedom from extremes."
You may assert the two truths,
And yet, in doing so, you fall to that extreme.
You may assert their union, but this is not
The fundamental, uncontrived condition.
However you reflect,
You fall into the ambush of conceptual fixation.
You do not have enough of subject-object apprehension,
The beginningless delusion.
Still you are caught up
In the persistent patterns of your mind's examination. (24)

Kyema! How pitiful is this deluded mind!
When you identify things, saying "this,"
You do not have the view.
You have fallen in the trap
Of the mind's multifarious elaboration.
There is no need for this. {402}

No matter what occurs, be unconcerned.
Awareness has no high or low, no narrow and no wide.
Let go, therefore, of clinging and fixation. (25)

Appearances and minds
Are not to be fixated on with words like "It is this."
So do not think in terms of antidotes and something to reject.
Do not contrive; do not change anything.
Just leave alone whatever happens.
This is the quintessence of definitive instruction. (26)

All phenomena in their variety are equal in their nature.
Whatever may arise is simply this: nondual primordial wisdom.
Do not use your mind to search
For what cannot be realized by discursive intellect.
Do not be entangled by an apprehended object;
Do not be polluted by an apprehending mind. (27)

Those who understand that all things are like space,
Who look on them as magical illusions,
Who do not fix on anything as real,
Possess the supreme sovereign view of nonduality.
It is a marvelous wonder,
The highest realization free from all extremes. (28)

Samsara and nirvana are not two;
They are awareness pure and simple.
When this is recognized, you see
That they are groundless, rootless, and devoid of substance.
Bondage, freedom likewise are not two—
This is the meaning of the great perfection,
Which is forever dwelling in the minds of every being. (29)

And that it might be seen,
The Rays of Stainless Light arose to demonstrate
This unexampled teaching, so profound.
Recognize, I beg you, through this view,
The playful, magical, ungraspable illusion

Of appearances and mind.
Recognize it as awareness, free from all extremes. (30)

This completes the first chapter, "Freedom Gained by Realization of the Ground," of *The Natural Openness and Freedom of the Dharmatā: A Teaching of the Great Perfection.*

The Path

Here is the nondual path
That takes you to the supreme vajra peak.
No matter what arises is awareness.
Do not cling to it as real.
When you watch it nakedly,
Remaining in the state of evenness,
This limpid state and your own mind,
Like water into water poured,
Are indivisible, not two,
In natural openness and freedom.
Bliss, luminosity, and no-thought all arise. (1)

And even when your mind stirs once again,
Stay firm, unwavering—
And you will be within its unborn nature,
The state of dharmakāya.
Thoughts arising and subsiding are
The rūpakāya, the state beyond all sorrow.
No need is there to take or to reject. {403}
Movement and stillness—leave them to themselves.
Do not mentally contrive or tamper with
The union of stillness and arising,
Of calm abiding and deep insight,
Of skillful means and wisdom. (2)

By affirming or negating, adopting or rejecting
Even just a little, you are caught in hope and fear,

The trap of dualistic clinging.
You will not reach the goal that you desire.
Instead you deviate into erroneous paths.
It's important therefore not to take or spurn whatever may arise. (3)

The mind, my friends, is like a camel:
It does the contrary of what one wants.
When you try to hold it still, it moves.
When you want to think, it stubbornly stays still.
But when it is relaxed and in its natural flow,
It is a state that's free and open, uncontrived.
The subject and the object of your apprehension
Subside right where they stand.
And in that very state you find your mind at ease. (4)

So let go of the mind that fixes on phenomena.
No matter what arises, simply stay without concern,
Not meddling, not involved.
The appearing object and the apprehending mind
Will be a single nondual state of openness and freedom.
Awareness unobstructed, primordial wisdom
Luminous and empty, will arise. (5)

When thoughts in their variety unfold,
They are themselves the appearing skillful means.
When they subside, the wisdom of deep insight
Is present of itself spontaneously.
When you rest within that state,
There is a limpid calm abiding
Where bliss and luminosity and no-thought—
All such concentrations—
Are, of themselves, spontaneously present.
Unmade and indestructible, this is the supreme natural state.
Movement ceases, overwhelmed by stillness. (6)

Unbounded is the excellence
Of unfolding and of stillness in the natural flow.
Thanks to the unfolding, there's no drowsiness,

And clinging to the stillness of the mind is halted.
The wisdom of deep insight uproots[5] all defilement
And is completely free of states of mind
Belonging to the form and formless realms.
Through stillness, there's no agitation,
And the threads of all discursiveness are snapped.[6]
The primordial wisdom of the state of calm abiding
Quells defilement, and it is completely free
From the desire realm's mental states. (7)

In meditation of this kind—
Unfabricated, present of itself—
There is no acceptance, no rejection.
Appearances and mind are both your friends.
The apprehending mind and what is to be apprehended
Are free and open. Perfect qualities are present. {404}
Thus the mind is purified—
And this is the great meditation, unsurpassed. (8)

When you rise from this
Into the free state of post-meditation,
Appearances resemble dreams and magical illusions.
They are like mirages, like tricks of sight,
Like echoes,[7] cities of gandharvas,
Like the moon's reflected images in water,
And like emanated apparitions.
All are empty by their nature,
Appearing yet nonexistent, unreal, intangible,
Uncertain, evanescent, insubstantial, undefinable.
You experience appearances without regarding them as real. (9)

Sincerely cultivate from time to time
A weary sorrow with samsara and the will to leave it.
Be at all times mindful of your death,
And do not fret about the future.
Be impartial in your pure perception.
Let there be no break in your devotion.
Exert yourself in refuge, bodhicitta,

And the path of two accumulations.
Contemplate the karmic law of virtue and nonvirtue,
Remembering the defects of samsara. (10)

In brief, keep mindful watch upon your mind.
Constantly rely on carefulness and introspective vigilance.
School yourself from time to time
In the illusory condition of phenomenal existence,
And mingling meditation with post-meditation,
Bring adverse circumstances to the path. (11)

By various means, enhance
Your view and meditation.
Leave the six sense consciousnesses free and open;
Watch the spectacle created by the five sense doors.
Sometimes rest one-pointedly in your mind's limpid state.
It's thus that calm abiding's single-pointed concentration is achieved.
Moreover, do not keep your mind in stillness.
Outer things and inner thoughts,
As well as the five poisons—let them all unfold.
Train then in deep insight where they instantly subside.
Thus all adversity, affirming and negating,
Arises as the play of your own mind. (12)

Sometimes go to mountain tops,
To charnel grounds, or lonely valleys[8]—
Places that inspire you with joy, or fear, or grief.
Physically express yourself by jumping, running,
Dancing, and gesticulating.
Verbally express yourself by shouting, singing, weeping.
Mentally imagine all the joys and sorrows
Of the beings in the six migrations. (13)

Do not be idle for an instant.
Diligently train in letting every situation
Sink into its natural openness and freedom.
Ask yourself, your view, your meditation, and your action—
Have they hit their mark? {405}

Then train yourself in seeing all phenomenal existence
As a dream or magical illusion.
Swiftly you will gain supreme and common siddhis;
All untoward events, adversities, and obstacles will be dispelled. (14)

At other times, when great misfortunes—
Plague or evil forces—strike,
Go to haunted places where
The dead and evil spirits walk:
Lake islands, forests, rocks, ravines, and lonely trees.
Take refuge, cultivate the attitude of bodhicitta,
And turn with great devotion to your teacher.
Imagine that your body grows as vast as Sumeru itself,
And break and scatter it in pieces in the ten directions
According to the wish of all such evil forces.
Thus they will be satisfied and all the karmic debts
Of beings in the six migrations paid. (15)

Decide that all things that appear and are considered
To be plagues or demons, ghostly phantoms
Are your mind and that your mind is empty.
Put aside the agitation of your thoughts
And be at peace in scorn of all such apparitions,
Leaving all such self-arisen various displays
To dissipate quite naturally.
Diseases, evil forces, obstacles will thus be pacified,
And you will neither grasp at happiness nor shrink from pain.
You will see that everything resembles space—
That there is neither apprehending subject
Nor something to be apprehended.[9]
Within the natural state without contrivance,
You will thus receive the empowerment of the power of awareness. (16)

Moreover in six periods, by day and night,
Train yourself as follows.
At dawn, allow your nonconceptual sense cognitions
To rest within the limpid state,
Just like the stars and planets in the sky.

In the morning, rest nakedly in deep insight
In which the states of movement and of stillness
Both subside in that state where they are not different.
At midday, train impartially in pure perception and devotion,
And see the whole array of things as dreams and magical illusions.
In the afternoon and evening, cultivate a sense of sadness at samsara
And the determination to escape from it.
Sincerely reflect upon impermanence and death.
At nightfall make an offering of your body as a sacred feast.
Cultivating loving-kindness and compassion,
Train in bliss and luminosity and no-thought.
At midnight, let your thoughts arising and dissolving
To enter and to dissipate
Within the unborn nature of your mind.
Then sleep, and thus your slumber and your dreams
Will both arise as one vast luminosity. (17) {406}

By training in such conduct in these six times of the day,
You will quell the mental states and habits of samsara,
And make your way to peace, the state beyond all sorrow—
The natural openness and freedom of the mind.
Various perfect qualities you will acquire:
Supernatural vision, clairvoyance, and the rest.
First, your bad dreams will be changed to good,
Then you will recognize that they are dreams.
Finally, they'll vanish in the ultimate expanse.
Then samsara, in its openness and freedom,
Will subside into nirvana.
The grounds and paths will be completed.
The generation and perfection stages
Will attain their final goal—and in this very life
Your mind will come to perfect buddhahood.
This then is the quintessential vehicle,
The definitive instruction. (18)

Signs that the essential teaching
Has been well applied will manifest
As follows in your training stage by stage.

From the bottom of your heart
You will be conscious of impermanence,
And thus you will not fret about the future.
You will feel sorrow at samsara and decide to leave it.
Unlimited compassion will be born in you.
You will be impartial and endowed with pure perception.
You will be devoted and have understanding.
Craving and fixation will decline,
And deluded clinging to things' real existence will collapse. (19)

These signs that you have set out on the unmistaken path
Will increase more and more, and you will gain
The sublime ground of realization.
Well trained in view, in meditation, and in action
To see all things as unborn magical illusions,
You will seize the everlasting realm, the luminosity of dharmatā,
Within the quintessential nature of your mind,
The sublime mansion of your freedom. (20)

When yogis lay aside their bodies
Contrived of the four elements—
When earth and water, fire and wind merge one into the other
And consciousness dissolves in space
And space into the luminosity of dharmakāya—
The six consciousnesses, the senses and their objects,
And the consciousness of universal ground
All dissolve into the universal ground itself,
Which then dissolves into the dharmakāya.
At that moment, with the gradual arising
Of light, its increase, culmination, and its utter culmination—
Luminosity's four stages utterly devoid of ordinary mind[10]—
The eighty mental states[11] all disappear.
Yogis who succeed in recognizing these four stages
Find their freedom in the space of dharmakāya. (21)

Then the bardo of the five sambhogakāya families
Will gradually arise in the five days of pure samādhi.[12] {407}
Yogis who succeed in recognizing them

Are freed in the sambhogakāya.
When this occurs, they emanate in various forms of nirmāṇakāya
bardo[13]
And bring about the benefit of beings.
This done, they merge with the sambhogakāya,
Which then dissolves into the dharmakāya,
Which rests unmoving in the vast expanse of bliss. (22)

From inner luminosity, the kāyas and the wisdoms
Never separate. Undivided and all-knowing,
They dwell within the subtle primal wisdom
Of the ground of all arising.
Like space, they are unborn and are unceasing
And are spontaneously present of themselves.
When there are beings to be guided,
This inner luminosity radiates outwardly
In form of five sambhogakāya families, which are in turn
The ground for the arising of the nirmāṇakāya.
Then afterward, as previously said,
They spontaneously[14] [dissolve into] the ground.
This is how practitioners of moderate ability
Gain freedom in the bardo. (23)

When the bardo of becoming manifests by stages,
And when various appearances occur as in a dream,
Practitioners of least ability will know them as untrue,
As limpid magical illusions.
Then, by means of practice of the generation and perfection stages,
By refuge, bodhicitta, and by guru yoga,
They overturn samsara's cause.
They block the womb door and by meditation,[15]
They transfer their consciousness to some pure field
Or, for the next life, gain a form endowed with seven riches.
And practicing the dharma, they gain freedom.
This is a most profound and crucial teaching. (24)

Night and day, my friends, do not be idle!
Strive with diligence!

Train in the view and practice meditation.
Insistently enhance your practice with your conduct.
Do not wander for a single second into ordinariness.
Instead make effort in the practice as has been explained.
If you don't succeed in mastering your mind within this present
moment,
No freedom will be gained in any future moment of the mind.
Your life is swiftly gone; samsara has no end.
So strive now, I beseech you, to be free from it! (25)

If briefly told, this wandering in beginningless samsara
Comes from grasping at a self and ingrained dualistic clinging. {408}
Proceed at all times in the view that everything is empty,
Devoid of true existence.
And effortlessly train in your mind's sovereign nature. (26)

For as long as you possess a mind deluded by self-clinging,
It is vital that you train in view and meditation,
Adopting what is good, rejecting evil.
But when dualistic clinging vanishes right where it stands,
There'll be no need for antidotes to things that should be spurned.
View and meditation will be both transcended.
Phenomenal existence will arise as dharmakāya. (27)

Kyeho! My friends, samsara and nirvana are not different.
All is the display of the mind's nature,
The single ultimate expanse.
The ground is free and open, and free and open is the path.
Free and open from the very first is the result.
Everything is free and open.
All is but the play of an illusion
Where, without substance and ungraspable, all things appear.
All things are illusory, so give up clinging and fixation.
For in the final truth, there's no delusion, none who is deluded.
There is no meditation and no absence of the same.
Once you have decisive certainty that this is so,
What point is there in much activity—in all those things to do?
No matter what appears, be free of all fixated clinging.

Be free of wanting, free of clinging, free of all concern,
Free of all one-sided partiality.
Phenomena are empty; they're devoid of self.
None is different, all spontaneously present.
There is no samsara; there is no nirvana.
This is the view of all the sutras, all the tantras, all the pith instructions. (28)

Drime Özer, Stainless Rays of Light,
The son of the victorious ones,
Revealed in their entirety these quintessential teachings.
All you of future times who wish for freedom in this very life,
Take up this deep instruction, practice it with diligence. (29)

This completes the second chapter, "Freedom Gained by Meditating on the Path," of *The Natural Openness and Freedom of the Dharmatā: A Teaching of the Great Perfection.*

The Result

And so, when perfect realization of the ground and path is gained,
The activities of mind in their variety sink back
Into the stainless nature of pure mind.
The everlasting kingdom of the sovereign dharmakāya—
The single taste of primal wisdom and the ultimate expanse—is reached. (1) {409}

It's then that in the space-like nature, free of mental movement,
Transcending all delimitation, beyond extreme positions,
The changeless and unmoving dharmatā
Endowed with twofold purity
Is found the Dense Array, Akaniṣṭha, utterly immaculate,
The exclusive self-experience of sambhogakāya.[16] (2)

In this pure field of luminosity's five primordial wisdoms,
Appear the mandalas of the five families
Of peaceful and of wrathful deities.

They fill the whole of space: the zenith and the nadir,
The main and intermediate directions.
Countless are the deities together with their retinues,
All equal in their realization.
They are aglow with shining rays of light,
All beautiful with the major and the minor marks of buddhahood.
All in turn possess five kāyas and five wisdoms.
Motionless and wordless, they utterly transcend expression.
All have the ten strengths and other perfect qualities
In ocean-like profusion. Deploying their activities
In the display of the three kāyas,
They are the primordial sambhogakāya teachers. (3)

From within that state,
The teacher-guides in their five families
Appear in worlds of beings to be guided.[17]
They are like moons appearing in the water,
Which are but the reflections
Of the [single] moon aloft, up in the sky.
For those upon the grounds of realization,
They appear as different teachers of five families:
Vairocana, Akṣobhya, Ratnasambhava,
Amitābha and Amoghasiddhi,
Who dwell in Akaniṣṭha, Abhirati, Śrīmat, Sukhāvatī,
Sukarmasiddhi.
They purify all ignorance and anger,
Pride, attachment, jealousy.
They show their perfect form as though it were a mirror
And thus contrive the benefit of their disciples,
Who see that their own bodies are not equal
To the radiant light forms of the victorious ones.
And, therefore, they refine their realization of the dharmatā
By removing one by one the stains of the ten grounds
Until they reach the Ground of Universal Light.
Such is the enlightened action of the teacher-guides,
Who appear as long as there are beings to be guided.
Present everywhere, like space itself, {410}
They are nirmāṇakāya, luminous in character. (4)

From within that state,
Six munis in their countless manifestations
Set forth their inconceivable instructions
For the benefit of beings in the world of the six destinies.
Their bodies, speech, and minds,
Appearing in accordance
With the varying perceptions of these six migrations,
Are wheels of endless ornaments of various kinds.
As they appear, so too do they bring benefit.
They are renowned as the nirmāṇakāya guides of beings. (5)

From within this state again
Emerges the diversified nirmāṇakāya,
Supports of the enlightened body, speech, and mind,
Both naturally occurring and contrived—
Statues, paintings, sacred texts,
Pools and bridges, residences, pleasant groves,
Earth and water, fire and wind, lotuses and wishing trees,
Jewels and lamps and healing drafts,
Delicious sustenance and garments,
Ornaments and every other thing—
All performing their enlightened action.
Bringing temporary happiness,
They at last place every being on the perfect path.
Material and inanimate, they nonetheless
Produce the benefit of beings.
The compassion, marvelous and unending, of the conquerors
Is called diversified nirmāṇakāya
That manifest in various forms. (6)

Countless are the teachers of the triple kāya.
When there are no more beings to be taught,
Such guides dissolve sink back into the ultimate expanse.
Their nature, as has been described, is indivisible.
And yet if we describe in further detail,
Each one dissolves into the other,
Starting from below, [the nirmāṇakāya,] and
Remaining at the last within the one expanse of bliss,

The dharmakāya, present of itself.
They dwell forever in the inner luminosity—
The subtle primal wisdom of the ground of all arising—
The peace that is omniscience.
When there are beings to be trained,
As previously declared, these same guides gradually appear,
Beginning from above, [the dharmakāya].
They work for beings' good and know their every need.
Such is the result, definitive and ultimate. (7)

Drime Özer, Stainless Rays of Light,
Arose and set this forth.
Let all the fortunate who wish to tread this final, perfect path
Capture the everlasting kingdom of spontaneous presence.

{411} This completes the third chapter, "Freedom as the Supreme Result," of *The Natural Openness and Freedom of the Dharmatā: A Teaching of the Great Perfection.*

Stainless Rays of Light arose and has set forth
This teaching, both profound and vast.
By its virtue may all beings
Dispel the darkness of existence.
And like the lotus of enlightenment,
May their minds burst into flower.

May this essential teaching, well composed,
A tracery of clouds to grace the throat of Kangri Tökar,
Send down ambrosial rain to satisfy the fortunate.
May the radiance of the perfect path shine out in all the ten directions.

The Natural Openness and Freedom of the Dharmatā: A Teaching of the Great Perfection was written upon the slopes of Kangri Tökar by the yogi Drime Özer, Stainless Rays of Light, who was himself blessed and guided by Senge Dradok, the glorious master of Oḍḍiyāna.

sarva mangalaṃ

19. The Natural Openness and Freedom of the State of Equality

A Teaching of the Great Perfection[1]

Longchen Rabjam

In Sanskrit: *Mahāsandhisamatānāma* {414}
In Tibetan: *rDzogs pa chen po mnyam nyid rang grol zhes bya ba*

Homage to glorious Samantabhadra!

The dharmakāya is equality,
The primordial enlightened state,
And therefore the abyss of all-embracing space,
Unspeakable, beyond the reach of thought.
Nonabiding and nonreferential,
It is the state of great perfection.
To this enlightened mind, this utter purity, I bow.

The View

The vajra peak of all the vehicles
Transcends the law of cause and fruit
And is beyond adopting and rejecting, hope and fear.
All things, whatever they may be,
Are without identity. Unconfined, they fall to no extreme.
Listen now to what this means. (1)

The state of primal openness and freedom
Of phenomenal existence, samsara and nirvana,

Is the place of Akaniṣṭha.
Its unceasing, various display
Is the palace of primordial wisdom.
Here the teacher, the unchanging dharmatā,
The state of perfect evenness,
Reveals the teaching that transcends
Adoption and rejection and all effortful exertion.
He reveals this to his retinue: the triple kāya—
The universe and its inhabitants, six kinds of beings.
He does this in the pure and timeless time,
Beyond past, present, and to come—
For in the ground, these three times are no more. (2)

The outer and the inner dharma, boundless though it is,
Is set forth in nine vehicles of teaching, {415}
Which in their nature correspond to levels of capacity.
Yet ultimately all resemble space.
There are no vehicles;
There is no wish for freedom from samsara.
There is no coming and no going.
There is nothing to be spurned, no antidotes for doing so.
Nothing is discarded, nothing gained.
All is dharmatā, the state bereft of movement and of change. (3)

However things appear, they lack intrinsic being.
Outer and inner entities, described as causes and results,[2]
Are but the enlightened mind,
Primordial luminosity, spontaneously present.
There is nothing to assert and nothing to negate;
There is just primordial wisdom, self-arisen.
What is there to strive for
Through one's inner or external efforts?
The uncontrived and natural state, the dharmatā,
Is without change or movement through the lapse of the three times.
Simply leave things as they are.
If there's a point of reference, "this" or "that,"
There is a dualistic apprehension.
Do not negate, do not affirm,

Do not accept, do not reject,
But simply rest in this, your natural condition. (4)

Do not spurn defilements;
They are the five primordial wisdoms.
In the instant they arise,
When there is neither taking nor rejecting,
They naturally subside.
There is no need for cleansing or transforming.
The mind itself is pure, the state of great perfection.
In this very instant, present of itself,
It is a self-arisen and primordial state. (5)

Common things in their variety
Are but a great, spontaneous, perfect mandala. {416}
Within the uncreated, self-arisen palace beyond measure,
Form, feeling, and perception,
Conditioning factors, consciousness
Are the buddhas of the five enlightened families.
The elements of earth and water, fire and wind and space
Are the five female buddhas.
Phenomenal existence, therefore, is completely pure.
No need is there to take some things, rejecting others.
Remedies, transforming antidotes—
None of these serve any purpose.
All has the same taste, the state of great perfection.
Understand that all is pure primordially,
Perfectly included in the ground. (6)

Rootless and primordially empty, the nature of the mind
Is uncreated buddhahood, spontaneously present.
If you rest within it, leaving it just as it is,
You dwell within the equal state.
Without beginning, without an end, it does not change
From earlier to later: it is outside time.
It does not fall to one side or another: it defies evaluation.
It is beyond all deviation and all obscuration.
Therein there are no grounds to be traversed, no paths to tread.

The training and progression you desire,
Regarding that which is without existence,
Are nothing more than changing and contriving space itself. (7)

Self-arisen wisdom, free of every change and alteration,
Is like an ocean clear primordially of all turbidity,
In which the moon appears.
All pure and impure things
Are but the great display of the one ultimate expanse:
This is the most profound and quintessential teaching. (8)

Dharmatā, immense and all-creating,
Is the essence of all things.
Its nature, present of itself, is infinitely vast.
Its character is luminous,[3]
And its cognizant potency unceasing.
Just as it is, it is primordially, spontaneously present. (9)

Not the slightest atom of phenomena
Is found outside this single, ultimate expanse,
The dharmatā, which is like space.
Phenomena are simply void appearances,
The spectacle of dharmatā itself,
Its natural play, spontaneously present. (10)

The universe and its inhabitants, phenomenal existence,
And even all the buddhas, past, present, and to come,
Are nowhere to be found but in the state of suchness.
They are uncreated from the very first
And are by nature utterly immaculate.
Therefore, they are not produced in time.
Cognition with regard to their identity subsides.[4]
Effortful exertion thus is needless,
For all these things transcend causality. (11)

Self, other, all there is—there's no identifying them.
However you impute them, that is how they are— {417}

No more than adventitious labels.
When you investigate, they're nowhere to be found,
For they are merely imputations, empty by their nature.
To say or to deny that they exist is ordinary mind.
Freedom from this mind is dharmakāya.
There is no other freedom.
No matter what arises, there is nothing to be grasped at. (12)

Concerning the sole, space-like, nature,
Many tenets have appeared, contrived by intellect.
All are gathered in the great perfection, the enlightened mind,
Which is like space, is all-pervading, and contains all things,
And thus is the great source of everything. (13)

All things in their variety
Are its equal, perfect play.
Joy and sorrow, high and low,
Are like the moon reflected in the water.
They are but a magical illusion.
Nonexistent yet appearing,
They do not stain the enlightened mind;
They are the nondual state, spontaneous and perfect. (14)

In whatever way phenomena appear,
It is not thus that they exist.
Causes and effects are not two different things;
They are free of the ascription—or negation—of existence.
Adherents of the vehicles that depend on right and wrong
Will never reach the true and ultimate reality.
For ultimately, good and bad are unborn and primordially pure.
In the very moment they appear,
Phenomena are themselves beyond all reference—
Untouched by concepts of an apprehended object
And an apprehending subject.
Apart from ultimate reality, there is nothing to be found.
Since it transcends the law of cause and fruit,
The adherents of such vehicles will never see the natural state.[5] (15)

If you still affirm the conditioned workings of causality,
Consider now the nature of appearances.
What is the first cause, productive
Of the five external objects of the senses?
What is the mind, and what gives rise to it?
If you thus investigate,
You find that they are not substantial things
But are like space.
They lie outside the process of causality
And thus are the primordial state of dharmatā.
They have not been created; they have not come into being—
Indeed, they are spontaneously present.
What in their regard is to be gained
By clinging and exertion? (16)

All things from the first are empty and devoid of self.
And yet, by ignorantly clinging to them,
Beings wander in this circle of existence.
They undergo their various joys and pains, {418}
And yet in truth these are, like dreams, without existence.
Understand that, by their nature, they are uncreated.
They are the pure, enlightened state—
Empty, groundless, rootless—from the very first. (17)

Whatever is imputed by the mind is empty by its nature.
Neither different nor the same, phenomena
Are taken to be true by the unwise, who thus are bound.
But freedom is not gained
By those entrapped by different tenet systems.
If causal and resultant teachings, expedient and definitive—
Doctrines all imputed by the intellect—are followed,
There will be no ending to samsara's stream. (18)

And so it is that the three causal vehicles,
Which cleanse the mind with antidotes
And thwart what is to be rejected,
Do not, within three countless kalpas and the rest,

Bring freedom in primordial wisdom,
Self-arisen, fresh, and uncontrived. (19)

Of the twofold vehicle asserting the result,
There are three outer tantras of which, in kriyā[6]—
By virtue of its style of lord and servant—
There is an attitude of dualistic grasping,
Of adoption and rejection,
With respect to the pure dharmatā,
The single ultimate expanse of all.
Thus it gives no liberation from the snare of hope and fear,
For it is marred through taking one as two. (20)

Through its mistaken dualistic clinging
Arising from its style of friend and kin,
The ubhaya[7] also mars the dharmatā, which is by nature pure.
Because it differentiates a taking and rejecting
With regard to that which is but one,
The ultimate quintessence is not seen. (21)

Through the five factors of awakening,
Through the four powers of manifesting
That belong to yoga tantra,[8]
The state of suchness is quite simply obscured.
That which is unborn primordially
Is not to be accomplished at some later stage.
Thus the nature of the mind,
The ultimate quintessence, is not seen.
And so, for these three outer tantras—
Respectively for sixteen, seven, and three lifetimes—
Freedom in the unspoiled nature is prevented. (22)

Of the three inner tantras,
Mahāyoga[9] fabricates a pure mind through four phases
Of approach and of accomplishment
And through the sending out and gathering in of light.
If the mind is pure primordially, it needs no fabrication;

It does not need to be transformed.
And if it is not pure, such things will not affect it—
One may just as well attempt to tie the sky in knots. {419}
The final nature, which transcends acceptance and rejection,
Is not seen. (23)

Anuyoga,[10] through its causal process,
Distorts and fabricates the one quintessence,
The indivisibility of primal wisdom and the ultimate expanse.
Indeed, to nondual, space-like nature,
Of what relevance is bliss and emptiness? (24)

And atiyoga[11] binds the quintessential and enlightened mind,
Where generation and perfection are not two,
To that state which is free of all extremes.
But this does no more than entrammel the mind's nature
With the noose of space. (25)

Those who place their trust in a one-sided emptiness
Do not know the suchness that appears in all phenomena.
They do not understand the perfect evenness of things.
All such "knowers of the mind" are based
Upon a yoga that accords with nihilism. (26)

These people, through their effortful exertion,
And their taking and rejecting,
Confine their stainless minds
Within a state that's free of reference.
Powerless to realize quintessential suchness
And with fortune, teaching, tenet all deficient,
They do not see the suchness
That transcends both getting and rejecting. (27)

Following the paths and training on the grounds,
These people are tormented by the ills of effort.
They bind themselves within existence
With their vows and their samayas.
They fail to reach the state of self-arisen primordial wisdom. (28)

Enlightenment itself is of a space-like nature.
And the enlightened mind[12] likewise is of a space-like nature.
So who is there to tread the path to their enlightenment?
Give up your wish to journey to the vast expanse of space.
Behold what lies beyond adoption and rejection,
Beyond all action and exertion. (29)

All teachings are unborn and free of obscuration.
But because of the mind's clinging to them,
Deviation, obscuration both arise.
To journey toward that which lacks intrinsic being is to deviate.
To watch what is not watchable gives rise to obscuration. {420}
However much you strive and strain according to the scriptures
Of the vehicles of cause and fruit, you deviate into samsara.
And thus obscured, you do not see the natural true state. (30)

When you who are [already] good pursue the good,
As much as you pursue, so much are you obscured and deviate.
Therefore, if you wish to see it, do not seek it
But rely upon the clear conviction that you *are* this good.
To seek the mind with pure mind is an error also,
For what is sought for is the very seeker.
This very thing is pure from the beginning.
So rest at ease, not searching for it
With contriving and transforming antidotes. (31)

Through viewing the nine vehicles
As awareness, one and self-arisen,
There will be no obscuration and no deviation.
For these very vehicles are like ripples on the water.
Awareness is not seen through looking,
Neither is it found by searching.
Rest, therefore, within the nature
That is from the first beyond removal and addition. (32)

"Primordial wisdom," "ignorance,"
"The profound," "the peaceful," and "the subtle"—
None of them exists.

That which is nondual and not dependent
Lies beyond the false ascriptions and denials of tenet systems.
Because this nature, from the first just as it is,
Is present of itself, whatever there may be is of that very nature.
Rest within the nature that is everything. (33)

For what is present of itself, there is no need for effort.
When you watch a nonexistence, is there something to be seen?
Therefore, clearly watch the nature of unborn phenomena,
The suchness that transcends the causal law. (34)

Here then is the essence of the teacher's pith instructions:
The ultimate expanse of dharmatā is free of edge and center.
Without dependence on the causal path
And on the generation and perfection stages,
Qualities of excellence are complete, spontaneously present,
In the sovereign nature of the mind. (35)

Through concentration where there is an expectation
Of the state of nonattachment,
The quintessential nature of the mind cannot be seen.
It lies beyond the range of contemplation.
Through intellectual investigation
That increases manifold conceptual elaboration,
The primordial fundamental nature is not seen.
It lies beyond the intellect.
Through the ocean-like infinity of precious methods,
Suchness as it is from the beginning is not seen. (36)

If you are free of hope and hesitation,
Leaving everything just as it is, {421}
You will see this very suchness
Without watching and no matter where you are.
If on the contrary you claim
That excellence derives from some contrivance,
And if you are consumed by doubt and hesitation,
This very suchness will be veiled. (37)

All the various classes of instruction have but one objective:
The quintessential nature of the mind,
The uncontrived and genuine natural state.
It is the pure field of the triple kāya—
Endowed with the perfections
Of the place wherein the teacher sets forth
Teachings for his retinue.
With this understanding, stay relaxed and free of fabrication. (38)

The earlier and later, the past, the present, and the future,
Samsara and nirvana—all are but the mind in its display.
All without exception have the one, sole, final nature.
It is the vast, spontaneous quintessence—
Suchness, the enlightened mind,
Primordial enlightenment, the very present dharmatā. (39)

Now has dawned the wisdom, unmade, pure from the beginning.
It cannot be revealed or taught through various symbols.
Words and scriptures just give mental understanding.
The mind that has attained the summit
Of the different vehicles
Encompasses the enlightened mind,
For it has realized suchness.
This culminating vehicle explains
That all is linked with the one ultimate expanse.
It is the ultimate and secret essence
Of all the vehicles without exception.
Therein the nature of the mind is seen. (40)

Those of lower fortune never understand.
For them, it is like setting up an image
In front of people blind from birth.
How can they understand by means of signs and symbols?
But those who have good fortune
Are like lotuses that open in the radiance of the sun.
Through the kindness of their teachers,
Realization manifests, arising from within. (41)

Not thinking of phenomena or of their nature,
Rest at ease and fresh in that equality
That is your nature throughout the three times.
Primordial enlightenment is completely pure by nature.
Do not fetter it with adventitious clingings,
But enjoy it freely at your pleasure.
Phenomena and the nature of phenomena
Are the equal state of dharmatā.
When awareness self-arisen manifests
In all the things that may appear,
Do not tamper with them.
Rest in the primordial nature,
Which in itself is free and open. (42)

Within the display of the dharmakāya,
The mind's nature uncontrived,
Realization and the lack of realization are the same.
They are not drawn together with the peg
Of an unwavering samādhi. {422}
There is not a single grain of good or bad, decline and loss.
Do not let yourself be fettered by view, meditation, action. (43)

Concerning the primordial condition,
There is no distraction nor the absence of distraction.
A deluded mind of hope and fear, of single-pointed focus,
Which clings to the "nonreferential," fetters you.
And yet the mind and the mind's nature are not two.
Emptiness and nonemptiness are indeed an equal state,
Where arising and remaining are primordial.
Do not react with wanting or aversion.
Do not repress; do not encourage.
But let it be as it appears.[13] (44)

In the dharmakāya, pure like space
And free of ordinary cognition,
All the various appearing things and states of mind
Are simply the great showing of awareness' display—
The appearance of birth in that which is unborn.

It lies beyond the mind's elaboration.
Do not, with agitated thinking, tamper
With whatever is perceived and noticed.
No matter what it is, no matter what arises in this state,
Just let its display manifest. (45)

Everything is but the all-pervading dharmatā.
Don't reject it; don't accept it.
Just stay within the very state of suchness.
As long as you refrain from mental movement,
You will be within equality itself.
If you find there is no high or low—
Just as it is primordially—
You are in the primal nature.
Rest in suchness without center or periphery,
Free of ordinary cognition. (46)

Beyond all striving,
Dharmakāya has no form—
It is not something to be shown.
It is freedom from attachment.
It is a state of peace, of insubstantial suchness.
Like space beyond the reach of action,
The nature of the mind cannot be meditated on.
Realization and the lack of it are equal.
Therefore, freely rest just as you please. (47)

Those who enter on the path that is no path
Have one great illness that torments their minds—
The poison of exertion.
However much they strive, they're caught up
In the causal process of samsara.
Never can they reach the path of liberation. (48)

The coarse mind that has grown accustomed
To actions, good and evil, white and black,
Belongs to the desire realm,
For it gives rise to higher and lower destinies.

The mind that's clear and luminous, and moist with virtue,
Represents the realm of form, for it brings forth
The four kinds of samādhi. {423}
The mind that is completely motionless, devoid of thought,
Exemplifies the formless realm,
For it is caught in the four spheres
(Boundless space and the remaining three).
Those who in whatever way contrive
The genuine and natural mind
Will give rise to a state of blank no-thought
Without a chance of freedom from samsara. (49)

The three times are but one—
A great primordial enlightenment,
Equality that is by nature
One immense expanse of space devoid of thought.
Even its mere name cannot be found.
There is nothing to compare it with,
No features does it have.
Its wondrous, marvelous, great display,
Perfectly contained within the ground,
Is inexpressible, ineffable,
Spontaneously present of itself.
Beyond becoming, it is a field of purity
Unmoving by its nature.
This never-waning victory banner
Is the great expanse, the universal essence,
The luminosity of mind's own nature. (50)

When, free of stress or laxity, you rest in it,
Even the accumulations, its adornments,
Are a nondual suchness present of itself
Beyond the mind's elaboration.
Do not define as this or that
The objects of the sense powers and the mind,
Appearing without effort and yet empty.
Just rest at ease in natural relaxation. (51)

However they appear,
They are the uncontrived state of the dharmakāya,
Spontaneously present as a sovereign equality
Beyond all dualistic knowing.
This sovereign equality is suchness without stain,
Transcending all acceptance and rejection.
It is buddhahood completely uncontrived,
A state beyond the law of cause and fruit.
It is the present mind, right now and in this very moment,
Unborn and perfect in itself.
No matter what arises, do not tamper with it—
This is the very meaning of the view,
The state of natural great perfection. (52)

Unmoving dharmatā is one and only one,
Yet, various and unceasing,
Each and every thing appears within it.
Completely peaceful, pure like unborn space,
Primordial wisdom, without origin and free of obscuration,
Is the all-pervading, supreme, secret state
Of great perfection, free of all extremes.
This groundless, rootless, insubstantial nature
Does not need to be accomplished
Through exertion or the practice of the teachings.
Be sure you understand this state just as it is. (53) {424}

The teaching that proclaims
The secret, ocean-vast, is this:
Awareness,[14] present of itself, is perfect.
Beyond acceptance and rejection,
Its display as it arises is immensely vast,
Free and open from the very first.
And in its openness and freedom,
Mind is but the natural flow of the primordial state.
When your realization of it,
Like the king of mountains, is unshakable,
You will enjoy the vast expanse

Of the great sphere [of dharmakāya],
All-pervading, present of itself. (54)

This completes the first chapter of *The Natural Openness and Freedom of the State of Equality: A Teaching of the Great Perfection*, which treats of freedom through the realization of the ground by practitioners of supreme capacity.

Meditation

When in the view you rest at ease
In that great effort [that is free of effort],
In the mind's own natural flow,
All that arises naturally subsides,
And a state occurs that's limpid, ocean-vast.
You do not meditate and yet are not distracted,
Free of thoughts and words, of apprehender-apprehended.
Awareness, self-arisen, unaltered and unspoiled—
This is natural meditation, pure from the beginning.
By focusing your mind in meditation,
Do not distort the dharmatā,
Where realization and nonrealization are the same.
Remain in the primordial state,
Where movement is not different from remaining still. (1)

Without projection, without dissolution, without meditation—
Such is "ordinary" mind: awareness in its natural condition,
Equal, perfect, uncompounded.
When you are clearly certain that this lies
Beyond both meditation and nonmeditation,
Rest at ease, relaxed in suchness, just as it has ever been. (2)

As long as mind contrives the generation and perfection stages,
As long as it contrives the concentrations
Marked by bliss, by luminosity, and no-thought—
And even primal wisdom free of dualistic knowing—
Habitual tendencies will be produced, the causes of samsara.

Practices endowed with characteristics
And even those without—which are themselves
Like space, completely peaceful—
Result in rebirth in the higher realms and thus produce samsara. (3)

When neither karma nor habitual propensities are formed,
When concentration is not cultivated, and when mind,
With its detecting and discerning, is transcended,
No existence comes therefrom, no suffering of existence. (4)

Unborn and immaculate, free of attributes, expectancy,[15]
Sovereign meditation, effortless and uncontrived,
Does not in the slightest waver from the state of suchness.
The realization of the ground by virtue of the view, {425}
However it may be explained,[16]
Means simply that the mind is left alone
And free of taking and rejecting.
It is awareness in its primal, unconditioned state,
Which holds the everlasting kingdom
Of the dharmakāya sovereign and impregnable. (5)

The one sole ultimate expanse, the primal ground,
Is reached now in this present moment.
The triple kāya, the result,
Is not to be accomplished at some future point.
That nature that we call enlightenment or buddhahood
Is manifest, and fear and doubt both fall away.
The level of Samantabhadra, self-arisen and spontaneous,
Is present of itself in natural rest, supreme and uncontrived. (6)

The quintessential nature of the mind
Is found within a stream-like continuity of nonmeditation,
A path in which sporadic practice has no place.
Free of deviation, free of obscuration,
It is contained within the single vast expanse of bliss.
Not existent and not nonexistent,
The mind finds ease.
Neither both nor neither,

It is a single state of evenness.
All is perfectly included in the ground;
All things are Samantabhadra. (7)

Reach a clear conviction that awareness,
Which cannot be identified by attributes like color,
Does not exist and is not nonexistent.
Do not alter it, but just rest naturally relaxed.
The unfolding and subsiding of your various thoughts
Are but the radiance of primordial wisdom self-arisen,
Like water and its waves.
They are neither good nor bad,
For all are self-arisen and devoid of effortful exertion. (8)

Consider that they are pure from the beginning
In their natural openness and freedom.
Let them be without rejecting them—
For all are but a single, perfect state.
Neither tense nor too relaxed,
Within the state of supreme
Self-arisen primal wisdom,
You will effortlessly pass beyond all thought and recollection.
Such is the pure meditation
On the luminous condition of the mind. (9)

Everything within phenomenal existence
Is unborn and empty.
Rest in suchness with your three doors all relaxed.
The essence of conventional truth
Is posited as the awareness state,
Where inner apprehender
And the outer apprehended objects are not different.
No matter what appears, do not cling to it,
But keep the view where what arises naturally
Naturally subsides within awareness. (10)

This is the unmoving state, {426}
Where meditation session and post-session are the same,

Where the three times are the "no-time,"
Their equality, spontaneously present.
No matter how sense objects and the mind appear,
They are the state of dharmatā.
To settle in this very ground is supreme meditation.
All discursive thoughts are thus transcended,
Perfectly and of their nature gathered
In this one sole, space-like meditative evenness.
They all arise as the unborn display of supreme bliss. (11)

This self-arisen quintessential nature,
On which you cannot meditate,
Is "ordinary mind," unaltered, uncontrived.
When it unfolds, it naturally subsides.
When it is still, it is equality.
Defilements are the five primordial wisdoms
Of luminous and empty suchness.
Thus there is no need to spurn them,
Purify, or change them with the use of antidotes.
They are the display of the primordial state,
The unborn, space-like dharmakāya. (12)

This quintessence, self-arisen primal wisdom,
Is free of attributes; you cannot meditate on it.
Therefore, abandon meditation.
In a mind that's free of thought, of hope and fear,
There is no bondage and no freedom from the very first.
There is neither ground nor root. (13)

That which fetters it is also free and open.
For defilement is not different from its antidote,
Both are suchness.
And within the field of suchness,
Good qualities and defects are not different.
Remain relaxed and free within awareness, all-creating. (14)

Its uncontrived and natural state,
Which does not fall to one side or another,

Is described as empty and devoid of features.
It cannot be observed.
Place your mind in suchness,[17]
In this one sole ultimate expanse. (15)

Listen to this one sole and definitive instruction.
Worldly deeds and situations never cease
As long as you continue with activity.
If you leave it, they will cease.
There is no call, therefore, for effort in the dharma.
However much you analyze, by so much are you bound.
Hope for an accomplishment
And fear of failure are a trap.
So just rest in the uncontrived and natural flow.
Rest in the state of suchness. (16)

Past phenomena have ceased,
And thus they are not things on which to meditate.
Future things are not yet born
And so are not among the objects of your meditation.
In the mind subsisting in the present moment,
There is no subject and no object of the meditation.[18]
The three times are but the equality
That transcends all meditative objects. {427}
Therefore, do not meditate by focusing your mind.
Leave self-occurring thoughts just as they come. (17)

The final teaching upon inconceivable great bliss
Refers to the supreme state of equality—
The ultimate quintessence,
Where skillful means and wisdom are not two.
It is unborn and falls to neither side,
Beyond all increase and decrease.
Do not arrest perception.
Its objects[19] are the state of suchness, ungraspable, unfindable.
Both defects to be spurned and antidotes to them
Are open—free right where they are. (18)

Nonmeditation, relaxed and free,
Is the perfect equal state that, free of limits,
Does not fall into extremes
Of wide and narrow, high and low.
Within this state where, without being rejected,
There is neither hope nor fear,
Rest in the enlightened mind,
Where expectation and discursiveness disintegrate—
The pure state of the all-illuminating nature. (19)

All the various sights and sounds are states of mind.
The nature of the mind is motionless, the primal state.
Be certain that phenomena and the nature of phenomena,
The dharmas and the dharmatā,
Are both without existence.
Rest in evenness devoid of agitated thoughts and memories,
In the perfect equal state
Wherein samsara and nirvana are not found. (20)

Do not merge them; do not think of them as different.
They are the expanse of spontaneous presence
Beyond all hope and fear.
Allow your mind to rest therein,
Undistracted, free of all elaboration,
In a manner free of limitation,
Not falling into one side or another. (21)

Heighten and expand awareness,
Allowing it to spread through center and periphery.
Don't grasp at it, but do not let it go.
See it solely as the state of luminosity,
The primal state, the single, even,
All-pervading, ultimate expanse.
And luminous primordial wisdom, free of thought,
Will rise up from within. (22)

There are some who wish to implement
The teachings on the nondual state,

But do not go beyond instructions that the mind contrives.
The lower and the higher vehicles are equal—
Both are destitute of the quintessence.
The actual ultimate in itself
Is inexpressible, unborn, completely pure.
And yet such people labor to transform and fabricate {428}
The mind itself, unmoving buddha nature,
And claim that it is later purified.
Abandoning samsara, they search for their nirvana.
These fools will never see the ultimate quintessence. (23)

Those who think that meditation
Leads later to the space-like, stainless qualities
Of excellent nonmeditation,
Will never look upon this very essence of the view,
For how could pure nonmeditation
Arise as a result of meditation? (24)

For us, by contrast, all such qualities arise
Through growing used to direct realization—
A realization that must be devoid
Of change and fluctuation in its quality.
Wise are those who know that this is so. (25)

Foolish people do not understand—
They cling to the validity of causes and results.
Inferring that phenomena arise dependent
On substantial causes and conditions,
They practice with exertion to achieve
The insubstantial nature of the mind.
Having seen that shoots are generated from their seeds,
They want results from cleaning something
That is nothing more than space—
An utter, contradictory, irrelevance!
What point is there in meddling
With a mind that has no substance?
Do not try to manufacture insubstantial suchness,
Like growing saplings in the garden of the sky. (26)

The various array of things is inconceivable.
Those, like earth,[20] that seem to be substantial
Are by causes brought into existence
And then transformed through circumstances,
Which thus produce a multiplicity.
But space and spotless suchness are not made[21]
Through effort and through striving.
They are beyond all movement and all change.
It is by such exertions that deluded habit fills the mind.
However much one effortfully strives,
The current of samsara is not cut. (27)

The nature of the mind is motionless;
It does not move or change throughout the lapse of time.
So do not try to make or change the nature of the mind,
The state of pure enlightenment,
But simply rest in suchness.
Ah, do not tire yourself in fabricating space! (28)

Accomplishment and nonaccomplishment
Are both without intrinsic being.
Do not believe, therefore,
That realization and the lack of it are different. {429}
Whatever may arise within the self-arisen dharmatā,
Leave it as it is.
If you stay without contrivance,
There will be no break in the primordial condition,
Quintessential luminosity.
And so, whatever may befall,
Just leave it in its natural, great state. (29)

A limpid state of mind as luminous as sun and moon
Will come to birth, accompanied by happiness and joy
And other beneficial qualities.
For this mind, there's neither high nor low—
The mind and body are suffused
With effortless and all-encompassing contentment. (30)

The openness and freedom of all things
Is primordial suchness that exceeds all reference.
This sovereign, pure, and uncreated nature
Unfolds in luminous appearances
Of primal wisdom free of all extremes.
Remain in meditation that does not distort this suchness,
The ultimate, unchanging essence,
All-encompassing and uncontrived. (31)

If all you do arises as this meditation,
Then even though you do not meditate,
You're free from all distraction.
For this is the consummate meditation
Of supreme spontaneous presence. (32)

The phase of action, conduct,
Which brings progress to your view and meditation
Is also like a magical illusion, like an apparition,
Like the moon's reflection,
Not separate from the water that reflects it.
In the six periods of your daily conduct,
Act in the manner of Samantabhadra.
But if you find there's good or bad,
Your conduct is not right.
You should know that conduct must be free
Of taking and rejecting, free of hope and fear. (33)

If you crave or are attached,
If you adopt or else reject,
Then no matter what the object of desire may be,
Your conduct is not right.
Conjurers experience the illusions they create,
And yet they do not cling to them.
Likewise in their conduct, yogis do not cling,
Experiencing objects as the play of their awareness. (34)

Things have no identity at all.
Though they do not exist, they yet appear.

Therefore, do not cling to them.
Behave and act in harmony with suchness—
The state of great perfection, nondual, free and open. (35)

If your mind acts dualistically,
Discerning "this" and "that,"
It is deluded, and it does not see the nature uncontrived.
You may think that your conduct is beyond extremes, {430}
And yet you still fall into them.
You're still caught in the trap of
Taking magical illusions for reality. (36)

In the supreme ultimate reality,
The openness and freedom of your mind,
To have or not to have right conduct makes no difference;
It makes no difference whether you adopt or else reject.
Do not be tormented by the illness of exertion.
And as much as this is nondual, likewise rest therein. (37)

All things have the nature of equality,
Of the single ultimate expanse—
Primordial wisdom, great perfection of the nature of the mind.
Enjoy at ease this self-arisen, ultimate quintessence. (38)

It is perfect of itself spontaneously,
So do not strive for it by making effort.
It is the fundamental nature;
So do not contrive or alter it.
It is primordial—and so there is no need to gain it now.
Therein there's nothing to be added, nothing to remove,
So do not try to purify or to transform it.
Therein there are no sides and no divisions.
Therefore, do not cling to it as this or that.
It is beyond samsara and nirvana.
Therefore, have no hope or fear.
It is beyond both good and bad,
So be without acceptance and rejection. (39)

However you may meditate, however you behave,
You do not move outside the mind itself.
What purpose is there in adopting or rejecting,
In confessing faults and making offerings?
A concentration that confines you
Is an ailment for the mind.
Do not distort with clinging the mind's purity.
Instead be like a king—enjoy whatever may occur. (40)

If for you there is no good or bad,
No accepting or rejecting, your conduct is correct.
The slightest clinging or fixation
That occurs through saying "this"
Is said to be great deviation
And an obscuration of the state of suchness.
Not clinging to the limitless expanse of space,
Enjoy instead the mind's pure nature,
Which space itself exemplifies. (41)

Appearing objects are but skillful means;
The mind itself is wisdom.
Enjoy them in a carefree way,
Without regarding them
As subjects and as objects of your apprehension.
Merit, wisdom, and the generation and perfection stages
Are completely pure,
An illusory display that, without ceasing,
Is spontaneously present. (42)

The unborn nature of phenomena and mind is dharmakāya.
Their unceasing character is empty, luminous sambhogakāya.
Their variety, arising and immediately subsiding, is nirmāṇakāya.
Savor all phenomena as great primordial wisdom,
The simultaneous three kāyas. (43) {431}

When phenomena appear to you
As a display untouched by ordinary cognition,
You will have in your possession

All the excellence of both the causal and resultant vehicles.
The nature of the mind, moreover,
Is a precious treasury of meditative absorption.
Therein, samsara and nirvana are the same,
The state of great perfection. (44)

Seeing their primordially pure nature
Is called the ground of Perfect Joy.
Freedom from the stain of dualistic clinging
Is the ground called the Immaculate,
And this is followed by the grounds called
Luminous and Radiant.
Then come those that are not everyone's domain:
The Hard to Keep, the Clearly Manifest,
Then that which from existence is the Far Progressed,
Which then is followed by the ground of dharmatā, Immovable.
Then follows supreme Perfect Intellect
And finally the Cloud of Dharma,
Stainless sunlight of primordial wisdom.
These then are the ten grounds
Classified according to their share of realization. (45)

The understanding of the meaning of the nondual state
Occurs on the path of accumulation.
Its practice is the path of joining.
The supreme realization is the path of seeing,
And subsequent habituation to what is seen
Is then the path of meditation.
And when the everlasting realm is captured,
This is said to be the resultant path of no more learning. (46)

Because within the ground,
The three doors, being pure,
Are great primordial wisdom,
There are four empowerments:
Vase, secret, wisdom, and the word.
All the many qualities of pairings like
The mind and object,

Appearances and emptiness,
Generation and perfection
Are effortlessly present of themselves
Within the state of great perfection. (47)

You will see this state when you transcend
Conditioned things and thoughts.
By watching it you will not see it.
By meditating you will not accomplish it.
You will not find it through analysis,
For it transcends all action and exertion. (48)

The immutable quintessence of the mind is buddhahood.
In terms of presence, it subsists from the beginning
In samsara and nirvana.
In terms of its pervasiveness,
It spreads throughout the three times all at once.
In terms of what it is, it is the dharmadhātu,
Which transcends the causal law.
It is like space. It's not a substance that has aspects to be seen. (49)

Primordial wisdom, self-arisen,
Does not wander from the ground.
It is like the ocean and is by nature limpid luminosity.
It does not cognize objects dualistically
But is present as their suchness.
Not depending on conditions,
It lies within you like your very countenance. {432}
Were it to depend on objects,
It would not be self-arisen from the first.
It would arise from something other than itself
And therefore would be variously changing. (50)

Therefore, it is self-arisen
And does not change throughout the lapse of time.
It is the unobstructed ground of all arising,
The indivisibility of the three kāyas.
Empty is its nature, luminous its character,

Unceasing its cognizant power—
These three facets are the essence of awareness,
Inner luminosity, unmoving, present of itself. (51)

And what arises as primordial knowing[22]
That cognizes objects in a dualistic way
Is called primordial knowing of creative power—
The radiance of awareness.
It is like a wave [upon the sea]
And like a form appearing in a mirror.
Such knowing manifests when there's an object present.
Without an object, no cognition manifests—
The two are thus connected.
Since it arises in *oneself*,
This knowing has been labeled "*self*-arisen."
But being discontinuous, it comes from something other—
It is something that arises through conditions.
It is an unobstructed play, unfolding and resorbing. (52)

Thus primordial wisdom, self-arisen,
Abiding as the ground, is indeed the ultimate expanse,
Whereas primordial knowing
Is the knowing that arises in relation to an object.
When you rest within the very nature of primordial knowing,
It is not separate from primordial wisdom. (53)

Those who do not understand this
Are but foolish meditators.
Some strive just to stay within the ultimate expanse.
They stop their feelings and perceptions
Through the concentration of their minds.
They gain the habits of the form and formless realms,
And thus samsara is contrived. (54)

Some say that the outwardly directed
Primal knowing that cognizes objects
Subsides all by itself,
And therefore they encourage thoughts

To rise and dissipate.
But this discursive movement
Fetters them in the desire realm.
They fail to realize the inseparable union
Of primordial wisdom and the ultimate expanse. (55)

Others hinder the true essence,
Which is the nature of the mind,
By practicing the different causal processes of
Generation and perfection.
For them there is no chance for freedom
From the city of samsara.[23] (56)

In our case, when one neither takes nor spurns arisings,
Being convinced that in the limpid, ultimate expanse
They *are* awareness,
And when awareness and arisings
Are thus gathered into one expanse of bliss,
Wherein they are inseparable, {433}
The mind's proliferation and its stillness are not different.
They are free and open in the great and perfect state of evenness.[24]
This is the natural state, the primal state,
The state of great perfection.
No need for acceptance, no need for rejection—
Everything is pure primordially. (57)

Within the nature of the mind,
Which from the first is free of all discursive thought,
If there's no indulgence in what may now arise,
Appearances and mind subside within the field
Of dharmakāya, free of ordinary knowing.
And at no later stage but now
Is suchness, the perfection of equality, achieved. (58)

When there occur the six sense objects
In the one primordial wisdom, self-arising,
There's no need to examine them.

Just leave them as they are.
And like the nondual clarity
Of mirror and reflected images,
So too is the spontaneous nonduality
Of the ultimate expanse and primal wisdom. (59)

Although this primal wisdom manifests in objects,
When thoughts do not unfold in their regard,
These objects are but a display, reflection-like,
Of the mind's limpid nature.
Since it knows primordially
All things as but a single ultimate expanse,
This uncontrived, unaltered, self-arisen primal wisdom
Reveals that they transcend causality. (60)

Because phenomena, displayed by mind,
Are products of habitual tendencies,
Beings wander in samsara
Through karmic causes and effects.
Various experiences of joy and sorrow, good and bad,
Occur like fruits of different seeds. (61)

Because the nature of the mind,
Both luminous and uncontrived, transcends causality,
It is beyond all striving from the very first.
It is like space—it is not born,
It does not cease, and it does not subsist.
Throughout the three times, therefore,
It is free of change and movement.
It is inexpressible and inconceivable.
Since it is without exertion, present of itself spontaneously,
It is free of defects and good qualities.
Since its display is ceaseless,
It is the vast expanse of ultimate reality.
Do not tamper with this one sole nature. (62)

This nature is not reached by following the path.
It is not rendered pure through being purified.
It is not found by searching.
Therefore, just stay naturally relaxed.
The perfect qualities of kāyas and of wisdoms
Are present of themselves. {434}
It is by staying in suchness free of all contrivance
That you will accomplish them.
Therefore, do not strive. The great space
Of the nature of the mind is pure primordially.
There is no need to strive for it
In terms of causes and results. (63)

The dharmakāya of your mind
Is present of itself spontaneously.
If you wish to come to it,
Then, no matter what appears—
Things or mental states—do not fixate on them.
If there is no clinging to them as specific things,
The dharmakāya is made manifest.
Refrain from fixed ideas like "it is one" or "it is everything."
Just stay relaxed and free within equality,
Awareness free of all extremes. (64)

Regarding this, the final nature of all things,
There's nothing to be done—
It is not reached through action.
Therefore, do not tamper with this natural state,
Which is beyond all grasping.
There's no ascertaining it by saying
"All there is, whatever it may be,
Is simply this."
Rest, therefore, within the vast expanse without extremes,
The state of great perfection.
If you find a resting place,
It's not the great perfection.
Therefore, don't identify this state as "this" or "that." (65)

This completes the second chapter of *The Natural Openness and Freedom of the State of Equality: A Teaching of the Great Perfection*, which treats of freedom through the practice of the path.

The Result

When thus the ground and path,
Awareness and the ultimate expanse,
Attain their culmination, this is the result,
Primordially present of itself
And perfectly included in the ground:
It is, for your own sake, the dharmakāya.
For others' sake, the twofold rūpakāya. (1)

The ultimate expanse and primal wisdom
Are indivisible, are not two things.
Samsara and nirvana are not two.
When they rest peacefully
Within the single ultimate expanse, awareness,
Free of mind's elaboration,
This is called Samantabhadra's Ground of Indivisibility.
It is the state of nonabiding dharmakāya,
The exhaustion of all thought—
The dharmatā, which by its nature is primordially pure. (2)

Within this state, there is a subtle primal wisdom,
The inner luminosity, omniscience,
The unobstructed ground of all arising,
Which from the kāyas and primordial wisdoms is inseparable.
It is the Ground of Motionless Absorption
Of perfect, great equality. (3)

Thence outwardly emerge
The luminous appearances—
The play, unfolding and resorbing,
Of Samantabhadra father-mother.
It is the Ground of the Great Wheel of the Collection.[25] (4)

Thence there manifest the buddha fields {435}
Of the five peaceful buddha families,
The spontaneous and perfect,
Pure, exclusive self-experience of luminosity.
For each of these five, there are five perfections:
The pure field, teacher, teaching, retinue, and time.
Each family has the nature of the five primordial wisdoms:
Dharmadhātu, mirrorlike, equality, all-perceiving, all-accomplishing.
All this is called the Ground of Dense Array. (5)

Thence the wrathful buddha fields appear,
Spontaneous, perfect mandalas of the five families—
The space-like union of the kāyas and primordial wisdoms.
This is called the Ground of Vajra Holders. (6)

Thence for bodhisattvas who reside on the ten grounds
Appear the buddhas Vairocana and Akṣobhya,
Ratnasambhava and Amitābha and Amoghasiddhi,
Who, to cleanse the minds of these, their retinue,
Act like mirrors and contrive their benefit.[26]
This is called the Ground of the Lotus Free of All Desire. (7)

Thence, for impure beings to be guided,
There appear six munis, guides of beings,
With diverse emanations, animate, inanimate,
And a manifold array of everything required.
In brief, enlightened teachers manifest
To work the benefit of beings,
Appearing in accordance with their shared perceptions.
This is called the Ground of Universal Light.
And like the radiance of the sun illuminating the four continents,
Like lotuses in flower that bring joy to all,
The radiant beams of the nirmāṇakāya are all-enveloping. (8)

Samantabhadra's Ground of Indivisibility,
Together with the Ground of Meditative Absorption
Are grounds belonging to the nondual dharmakāya—
The stilling of all mental movement.

Great Collection, Dense Array, and Vajra Holders
Are grounds of luminosity: the sambhogakāya's self-experience.
The Lotus Ground and that of Universal Light
Are grounds of the nirmāṇakāya—
Of luminous character, guide of beings, and diversified.
These spontaneously accomplish
Countless exploits of enlightened action. (9)

All the kāyas, primal wisdoms, and pure fields
Are space-like: everlasting, all-pervading, unconditioned— {436}
Appearing without interruption till all beings are freed.
Such is the ultimate, primordial state,
The result according to the Natural Great Perfection.
Not causally produced, it is primordial wisdom, present of itself. (10)

When you see that mind's pure, uncreated nature
Is beyond all action, all exertion,
When you gain mastery in leaving it just as it is
Within its natural state—free and open from the outset—
You will realize the primordial and spontaneous presence. (11)

This completes the third chapter of *The Natural Openness and Freedom of the State of Equality: A Teaching of the Great Perfection*, which treats of the result that is spontaneously present.

Upon the slopes of Kangri Tökar, the essential jewel,
Stainless Rays of Light has rendered visible
This supreme, marvelous teaching.
May its virtue dissipate the dark of beings' minds.

May this glorious blossom, honey-filled and grown
From my mind's clear intelligence, bring joy.
May the music of this teaching, well explained, resound,
Rejoicing those who have the fortune to receive it.

This completes *The Natural Openness and Freedom of the State of Equality*, composed upon the slopes of Kangri Tökar by Drime Özer, a yogi who was adopted by the mighty Padmasambhava, the glorious master of Oḍḍiyāna.

Virtue! Virtue! Virtue!

PART SEVEN

CONCLUDING RITUAL TEXTS

This section comprises two texts both composed by Jamgön Kongtrul. The first is a very long sādhana of homage to the forty lineage holders of *The Heart Essence of Vimalamitra*, from Samantabhadra until Kongtrul's own teacher, Jamyang Khyentse Wangpo. It concludes with a gaṇacakra offering.

The second text is a sādhana of Ekajaṭī and the six protectors belonging to her retinue. As specified in the colophon, Ekajaṭī is the main guardian of the Heart Essence teaching—her single tress, her one eye, one tooth, one breast, and (sometimes) one leg are emblematic of the one sole sphere of the dharmakāya. She is regarded as a transmundane protector, Samantabhadrī herself manifesting in the form of a wisdom mamo. The sādhana concludes with an empowerment of the dharma protectors, thereby rounding off in the traditional way the collection of extraordinary texts contained in this volume.

20. An Ornament for Samantabhadra's Display

A Ritual of Homage Addressed to the Lineage Teachers of the Pith-Instruction Class of the Heart Essence of the Great Perfection[1]

Jamgön Kongtrul Lodrö Taye

Homage to the teachers and to the primordial expanse of self-cognizing awareness!

In bodies of pure light, all impurities exhausted, {438}
They came in one life to the ground of openness and freedom.
Inseparable they are from the primordial lord.
In their bodies of great transference,
They labor for the benefit of beings for as long as space endures.

To Vimalamitra, crown jewel of the learned masters,
To the lake-born Vajradhara beyond both birth and death,
And to the all-perfect Drime Özer, Stainless Rays of Light, and all the rest—
To the venerable root and lineage masters, I reverently bow.

A rite of prayer and homage I shall now compose.
It is not just my own devising or devoid of a true source,
But it is glorious with the blessing power of secret vajra speech
That I and those of equal fortune may increase
The great accumulations of wisdom and of merit.

It is said in *The Great Array of Ati Tantra*,

To meditate without distraction on your teacher's form
Is one hundred thousand times superior
To meditating on one hundred thousand deities.

To make just three prayers to your teacher
Is more than one hundred thousand times more powerful
Than billions of recitations in the phases of approach and of accomplishment.

The appearance of your teacher's form within your mind
Is twenty thousand times superior
To a kalpa's practice on the perfection stage.

And in the scriptures, it is also said,

Abandon every other offering.
Strive instead in offerings to your teacher!
By pleasing him you will achieve {439}
Omniscience in this very life!

As these texts say, to please the teachers and make offerings to them is the essence of the practice of those who have entered the path of the Vajrayāna. For such teachers, who followed the path of the vajra essence of luminosity (the pinnacle of all vehicles and doctrines), who accomplished the state of the primordial lord Samantabhadra, and who appeared among us in an uninterrupted line, [are so extraordinary that] it is hardly possible to hear their names even in a hundred eons of time. This being so, there is no need to speak of finding people who actually have faith and devotion and who wish to emulate them. Consequently, those who have the good fortune to have entered this path and who follow in this tradition should consider the practice (of praying to the masters of the lineage) as their special pledge and duty.

Therefore, when an elaborate ritual of homage is to be offered to the masters of the Great Perfection—such as on the eighteenth day of the twelfth Tibetan month, the feast day of the omniscient Longchen Rabjam—clean the place of worship thoroughly and adorn it with various decorations. Then, in front of the images of your teacher and the Three Jewels, place on a clean table a tripod with an accomplishment mandala composed of five heaps. Place all around the seven traditional offerings (two of water and the five objects of enjoyment), multiplied a hundredfold, or as many as you can. Alternatively, you may place in the center of the table four sets of offerings arranged clockwise in the four directions. In addition, prepare an offering mandala, a conch shell, flowers, and, if you wish, the articles for the offering of gaṇacakra. In the case of a daily practice or for a ritual of less complexity, use whatever you can find—for example, a mandala and a single set of offerings. {440} For yogis whose practice is without elaboration, it is sufficient to rely on meditative concentration.

First take refuge, reciting as follows:

> All things are from the very beginning the state of buddhahood. Yet beings fail to recognize this and therefore wander in samsara. Alas for them! I will place them all in the state of perfect enlightenment.

Recite the following verse three times:

> In the hosts of teachers, yidam deities, and ḍākinīs,
> Together with the Buddha, dharma, and the noble sangha,
> Who fill the whole of space, the vast expanses of the sky,
> I and every being respectfully take refuge.

Then repeat three times,

> Together with my mothers, all beings infinite as space is vast,
> I take refuge in the teacher.
> I take refuge in the Buddha.
> I take refuge in the dharma.
> I take refuge in the sangha.

Then recite the following:

> I take refuge in my teacher, the buddha dharmakāya.
> I take refuge in my teacher, the sambhogakāya.
> I take refuge in my teacher, the nirmāṇakāya, which appears in various forms.
> I take refuge in my teacher, the abhisambodhikāya, the body of manifest enlightenment.
> I take refuge in my teacher, the unchanging vajrakāya, indestructible.
> I take refuge in my kind root teacher.
> I take refuge in all the yidam deities of the mandalas.
> I take refuge in the hosts of ḍākinīs and protectors.

Bless me so that evil actions, sins, and obscurations all be purified.
Bless me so that all adversity and obstacles subside.
Bless me so that I may see the dharmatā directly.
Bless me to intensify my experience of awareness.
Bless me to attain the climax of awareness.
Bless me to attain the exhaustion of phenomena in the dharmatā.

Now meditate on the four unbounded attitudes:

May all beings have happiness and the cause of happiness . . .

The Self-Visualization

It is said in *The Secret Essence Tantra*,

> If you meditate on the king of primal wisdom in union with his consort,
> Upon the disks of sun and moon in the middle of the limpid sky,
> You meditate on the mandalas of all the conquerors without exception.

Contemplating the unborn nature of your mind, recite as follows:

This mind, which has no root,
Is itself the root of all phenomena. {441}
The nature of the mind itself is syllables—
A precious wish-fulfilling cloud of syllables.[2]
A is not found even in the midpoint
Between nonemptiness and emptiness.
All things are simply names—and buddhas
Dwell in strings of syllables.
a a a

Then reflect as follows:

In that state wherein phenomena are neither one nor many, I meditate upon Samantabhadra and Samantabhadrī in union, who appear in the center of a pure, unclouded sky amid the radiating beams of sun and moon. Samantabhadra's hands are in the mudra of meditation. Since he is the nature of the dharmakāya, he is naked and unadorned. Within a fence and in the center of a tent contrived of beams of five-colored light, he is in a mansion made equally of layers of light that pervade the whole of space. As its radiance fills the entire sky, I imagine that the whole of phenomenal existence is ablaze with light.

As much as possible, recite the syllables *oṃ āḥ hūṃ a a a*, and rest in a space-like state. It is thus that you meditate on the mandalas of all the buddhas without exception, for you meditate on their source. Then, in this same state of mind, in a single instant, visualize yourself as a deity.

All phenomena, outer and inner, are the state of great equality, and in this vajra expanse, they are primordially unborn. They are the state of natural great perfection. Therein, upon a white lotus and a moon disk, I appear in the form of Vajrasattva, white in color, with one face and two arms. In his right hand, he holds a vajra at his heart; in his left, he holds a bell at the level of his hip. Arrayed in silken garments and adorned with precious ornaments, he sits in vajra posture. In his forehead, inside a globe of five-colored light, there is a white syllable *oṃ*. In his throat, inside a globe of five-colored light, there is a red syllable *āḥ*. In his heart, inside a globe of five-colored light, there is a blue syllable *hūṃ*. {442}

The whole world is the pure field of Akaniṣṭha.
All beings are pure deities, male and female.
I and every being, all without exception, dwell by nature
In unborn great luminosity, spontaneously perfect.

As you recite these words, consider that the universe and the beings it contains, palaces, deities, and substances of offering are but the display of self-arisen, primordial wisdom, spontaneously perfect.

The Front Visualization

In the space-like vast expanse of primal buddhahood, pure from
 the beginning,
In the center of a mass of rainbow light and disks of light,
 spontaneously present,

Awareness ripens as the form of the primordial lord,
Manifesting as the lord and teacher who reveals the path—
Vimalamitra appearing in a body of light.
His color is light-green; he is arrayed in robes of a renunciant and wears the hat of a paṇḍita.
His hands placed in the mudra of absorption
Hold a long-life vase marked with a vajra.
In vajra posture, he is seated on a lotus and a lunar disk.
Above his head is Garab Dorje in nirmāṇakāya aspect.
Radiant like the moon, he makes the dharma-teaching mudra.
Above his head is glorious Vajrasattva,
And above him is Samantabhadra, Changeless Light.
In front of him sits Padmasambhava,
And to his right, behind, and to his left
Sit Mañjuśrīmitra, Śrīsiṃha, and Jñānasūtra.
In front of Padmasambhava is the omniscient Dorje Zijitsal,
Attired in the three dharma robes and wearing a paṇḍita's hat.
Making the earth-touching mudra,
He holds utpala lotuses with sword and book.
Around him sit Vairotsana, Tsogyal, Tingdzin Zangpo,
The dharma king together with his son,
Then Dangma Lhungyal, the mighty Chetsun,
Pema Ledrel, Rangjung Dorje, and the rest—
All the teachers of the Heart Essence
Of the oral and the treasure lineages.
In various attire, ablaze with glowing splendor,
They watch the unborn sky with vajra gaze.
In inconceivable absorption in the state of luminosity,
They turn their loving minds to their devoted children.
Likewise, the Three Jewels—residing in the ten directions and the fourfold time, {443}
Together with the three roots, and the guardians and protectors of the doctrine, all without exception—
Appear, spontaneous and perfect,
In the vast and all-pervading primal sphere.

You may now engage in the various practices through which accumulations are gathered, such as prostrations and the making of offerings. In order to dispel your dualistic perception, pray that the wisdom beings enter into you.

oṃ āḥ hūṃ
From the palace of the dharmadhātu,
Come, I pray you, unborn teachers!
From the palace of the sambhogakāya,
Come, I pray you, teachers of pure speech!
From the palace of the nirmāṇakāya,
Compassionate ones, I pray you,
Come in rainbow lights a-swirling!
Come in spheres of light a-whirling!
Upon a seat of sun and moon above my head,
Stay firmly, never leaving me!
With body, speech, and mind, I bow devotedly
And lay before you outer, inner, secret offerings.
All spoiled and broken pledges I confess regarding the enlightened body, speech, and mind.
I implore you to bestow empowerments that ripen and instructions that set free.

oṃ
To you the dharmakāya, unborn, limpid clarity,
To you the vajra body indestructible, I pray:
Grant bliss-bestowing blessing to my body.

āḥ
To you, the sound of dharmatā, unceasing speech,
To you, resounding vowels and consonants, I pray:
Grant power-bestowing blessings to my speech.

hūṃ
To you, the enlightened mind, primordially pure, Samantabhadra's vast expanse,
To you, the freedom from all thought, I pray:
Bless me to attain the state of the exhaustion of phenomena.

Homage and Prostration

oṃ āḥ hūṃ
Resplendent teachers endowed with boundless wisdom and compassion, who by your very nature are glorious Samantabhadra, source of all the buddhas—I devotedly bow down to you and take refuge. I pray you, guide me with great bliss.

Primordial Lord, Unchanging Light,
Chief source of every mandala,
Who have found the ocean of knowledge and primordial wisdom— {444}
To you Samantabhadra, father-mother, I bow down.

Within the dharmakāya, nonabiding, unobservable,
The sambhogakāya's luminous primordial wisdom
Possesses a wish-granting, precious treasure—
To unnumbered deities, the peaceful and the wrathful, I bow down.

To you who have unchanging, omnipresent wisdom,
Who are great bliss supreme, unmoving,
Wish-fulfilling precious treasure unsurpassed—
To you the mighty Vajradhara, I bow down.

To you, illusory deity of luminous, primordial wisdom,
Blazing with the glory of the major and the minor marks,
Perfect buddha, spontaneous presence of the triple kāya—
To you, O Vajrasattva, I bow down.

To you the holder of the vajra body, speech, and mind,
The conquerors' great secret,
Sire of beings and lord of strength and power—
To you, O Vajrapāṇi, I bow down.

To you who journeyed to the other shore of means and wisdom
And gained the endless primal wisdom, ocean-vast, of utter freedom,

The supreme friend of every wandering being—
Garab Dorje, I bow down to you.

To you who gained supreme and unsurpassed accomplishment,
Who are a wish-fulfilling treasure, source of perfect teachings,
Who bring the teachings raining down on beings—
To you, Mañjuśrīmitra, I bow down.

In the vast expanse of striving in both love and knowledge,
You are the spreading sunlight of primordial wisdom,
To you who dissipate the darkness in the ten directions—
To you, Śrīsiṃha, I bow down.

Within the mandala of pure compassion,
Radiating light of beneficial wisdom,
Illuminator of the perfect path for wandering beings—
To you, O Jñānasūtra, I bow down.

You who, with a thousand lights of love and knowledge
unsurpassed,
Brought the lotus of the teaching bursting into flower,
Scattering the darkness of the ignorance of beings—
To you, Vimalamitra, I bow down.

O you, the sun who rose upon a self-arisen lotus,
Enlightened Lotus-Born,
Who send forth glowing clouds of ḍākinīs—
Padmasambhava, to you I bow.

Lord of the mandala of this exalted land,
Boundless in your works of knowledge and of love,
Who with many emanations have protected beings—
Trisong Detsen, dharma king, to you I bow.

Treasury of concentration and of unforgetting memory, {445}
Illusory embodiment of luminosity,
Sovereign of clairvoyance and of miraculous power—
Tingdzin Zangpo, I bow down to you.

Holder of a treasury of deep and sacred teachings,
Who gained the core of luminosity while in the bardo,
Compassionate lord, skilled in the methods of great love—
Dangma Lhungyal, I bow down to you.

Through the great strength of your striving to be free,
You found the nectar of primordial wisdom free of stain.
Within your body of light, all qualities are spontaneously perfect.
Senge Wangchuk, I bow down to you.

Through the union of skillful means and wisdom,
You constantly remained within the state of spotless luminosity,
Changeless and spontaneously present.
Gyalwa Zhangtön, I bow down to you.

Liberation's supreme wisdom you have found,
Endowed with clouds of essence of dhāraṇīs on the final ground of realization,
And dispelled the darkness of the ignorance of beings.
To learned Khepa Nyibum, I bow down.

Unsurpassed in utterly completing great accumulations,
Who are the form of emptiness endowed with sublime qualities,
Who realized the essential core of the definitive instructions—
Guru Jober, I bow down to you.

You who realized the illusions that are pure and perfect[3]
And of compassion and of emptiness had perfect mastery,
Who journeyed to nirmāṇakāya buddha fields of luminous character—
To you, O Senge Gyapa, I bow down.

You who perfectly beheld the truth of dharmatā
And who with yogic deeds, the display of primal wisdom,
Strove for the welfare of unnumbered beings—
To you, accomplished master Melong, I bow down.

You for whom the fields of pure, essential luminosity
Were always present of themselves, who were yourself
A wish-fulfilling treasure of clairvoyant knowledge and the clouds
of dhāraṇīs—
To you, O Kumaradza, I bow down.

You who had a perfect understanding of all that may be known,
Holder of the precious treasuries of sacred dharma,
Who widely spread the deep mind treasures—
Omniscient Lord of Dharma, I bow down to you.

From within the mandala of loving-kindness and compassion,
You radiated beams of happiness and welfare,
Directly showing forth the dharmatā as something visible—
O Khyabdal Lhundrub, I bow down to you. {446}

Your illusory form of spotless, primal wisdom
Is beyond extremes of going, coming, permanence, and
nothingness.
You truly saw the mandala of all that may be known.
To you, O Drakpa Özer, I bow down.

With compassion and great love,
You constantly held beings in your care
As if they were your very children.
Great Trulzhik, I bow down to you.

All-knowing in the sciences and topics to be known,
Who with compassion acted for the benefit of beings,
Emanation of Avalokita and father of all beings—
Dawa Drakpa, I bow down to you.

Completely free of all obscuring veils,
Endowed with concentration and supreme samādhi,
You reached the dharmakāya, end of the four visions—
Kunzang Dorje, I bow down to you.

You held aloft the victory banner of the precious sacred dharma.
According to the wants of beings, you rained down teachings that both liberate and ripen.
Joyous friend of all the fortunate—
Gyaltsen Palzang, I bow down to you.

A shining light upon compassion's perfect path,
Protector of the dharma realm of the Great Vehicle,
Spontaneously accomplishing the twofold aim of self and other—
Natsok Rangdröl, I bow down to you.

To you who gained primordial wisdom of immutable great bliss,
Whereby all dualistic clinging fell apart,
And hope and fear, acceptance and rejection subsided in the space of emptiness—
To you, O Tendzin Drakpa, I bow down.

You traversed the ocean of the sutras and the tantras,
And were the wish-fulfilling gem of the completely secret teachings,
Vidyādhara and granter of all wishes—
Dongak Tendzin, I bow down to you.

Vajradhara, who without mistake revealed
The essential path of all victorious ones,
Lord of Dharma unmatched by any rival—
Trinle Lhundrub, I bow down to you.

Embodiment of changeless primal wisdom,
Great teacher of the supreme vajra vehicle,
Fearless, universally victorious Lord—
Gyurme Dorje, I bow down to you.

Through the union of both view and action,
You gained the accomplishment of the supreme absorption.
Holder of the doctrine, unsurpassed and quintessential— {447}
Rinchen Namgyal, I bow down to you.

Meditating on primordial wisdom, self-arisen,
You gained supreme, unbroken, seamless realization.
Establisher of every being in the state of buddhahood—
Mingyur Paldrön, I bow down to you.

You who realized that awareness, cognizant self-arisen power,
Is the openness and freedom of the dharmakāya,
And through unbounded actions wrought the benefit of beings—
Oḍḍiyāna, I bow down to you.

To you who realized the expanse, primordially pure and
self-arisen,
Where samsara and nirvana are both equal in the openness and
freedom of the ground,
To you who were the guide of beings—
Trinle Namgyal, I bow down.

In your sky-like realization, free of all extremes,
The mandalas of sun and moon of luminosity shone forth,
Dispelling all the gloom of beings' ignorance.
Dharmatārā, I bow down to you.

Your knowledge of the nature and the multiplicity of things came
fully into flower,
And lovingly you set free beings infinite as space is vast
And brought them to the primal state.
Dorje Ziji, I bow down to you.

Beyond the ordinary mind, within the state of primal openness
and freedom,
Relaxed, you are immersed within this natural flow
And with compassion cherish beings like their very mother.
To you, my own root teacher, I bow down.

Beginning with the mention of Rinchen Namgyal and until this point, the lineage of the teachers of the secret cycle of the Great Perfection has been slightly altered.

The nature is a vast expanse, beyond expression.
The character is luminous, the sambhogakāya.
The cognizant power utterly pervades all beings.
To you who are this supreme refuge, I bow down.

Within compassion's vast expanse, you found primordial openness
and freedom.
Its luminous appearance blossomed into one vast buddha field,
A spacious state that unites all things in equality.
To you whom no example can encompass, I bow down.

Though dwelling at all times in meditative evenness,
In enjoyment of primordial Samantabhadra,
You bring about the benefit of others like a wish-fulfilling gem.[4]
To you, who grant all wishes, I bow down.

By means of concentration and clairvoyant sight,
You lead to the primordial expanse
All beings to be trained within the world. {448}
To you who are our guide, I bow.

You are a great ship that delivers
From the vast sea of their suffering
All who wander unprotected in samsara.
To you, great loving one, I bow.

To those who in this world are long fatigued,
Caught in the deceptive round of karma and defilement,
You show the direct path where things to be abandoned and their
antidotes both naturally subside.
To you who are our teacher, I bow down.

Whoever sees you gains great faith.
Whoever hears you cuts the web of doubt.
Whoever touches you gains blessings and accomplishment.
To you who are beyond compare, I bow.

Indeed, to everyone
Who sees and gazes on your body,
Who hears and keeps your words in mind—
To all these beings, at all times, I bow.

And to the buddhas of the ten directions,
To the bodhisattvas in their mandalas spontaneously present,
And to the dharma and the supreme gathering of noble ones,
With intense devotion, I bow down.

To images and stupas and the rest,
Supreme fields wherein beings garner merit,
To all, as many as they are, without exception,
I bow down with brilliant faith.

To the enlightened mind, the source of all samsara and nirvana,
To the sublime essence unsurpassed of luminosity,
And to the buddha element, the tathāgatagarbha,
In great wonder, I bow down.

To those who tread the path of liberation,
Who hear the tuneful sound of the Three Jewels—
To all of every race and kind,
That I might gain my freedom, I bow down.

The world and all who dwell therein—phenomenal existence—
Are from the very first Samantabhadra's own display.
Their nature is primordially pure.
In the state of nonduality, I bow to them.

You, O teacher, supreme virtuous friend,
You are our lord and our protector,
Giver of intelligence to those confused and ignorant,
Revealer of the path for those who lost their way,
Lamp for those who wander in the dark,
Precious jewel, dispeller of our pain, {449}
I bow before the sunlight of your feet.

I bow before the moonlight of your body.
Prostrating to your lotus feet I bow.
And thus with joy and with respect,
With praises I bow down to you.

ho
Perfect Buddha, precious nature of the mind,
Sacred dharma utterly unstained by the impurity of thought,
Assembly of perfect yogis—to you I go for refuge.
To all those who are free of craving, I respectfully bow down.
From this day forward, that I might become the sustenance of beings,
I offer myself in service to you, lords of refuge,
And pray that you accept me in your goodness.
Look down upon me with the beauteous countenance of loving-kindness,
Restoring my transgressions, all my errors,
And the weakening and breaking of samaya.

Now, as your principal offering, present the mandala of the three kāyas. Wipe the mandala plate thoroughly, and sprinkle it with saffron water. In the best case, place on it fifteen heaps of flowers or grains, and so on. In the next best case, arrange nine heaps or at least five heaps.

oṃ āḥ hūṃ
The golden ground is of vast strength. Upon it is Sumeru, king of mountains. In the east is Purvavideha, in the south is Jambudvīpa, in the west is Aparagodānīya, and in the north is Uttarakuru. Then there are [the subcontinents of] Deha and Videha, Cāmara and Aparacāmara, Satha and Uttaramantrina, and Kurava and Kaurava. Then there are the seven golden mountain ranges, the seven seas of enjoyment, the seven precious attributes of royalty, the eight auspicious substances, the treasure vase, the wish-fulfilling tree, the bountiful cow, the untilled harvest; the pleasures that delight the senses; the most beautiful goddesses; the sun, the moon. In the center, there is everything that is pleasing to the senses of both gods and humankind. All this I offer, well arranged, together with an infinite array of universal systems. {450} In addition, I offer the endless buddha fields based

upon the inexhaustible wheels of the body, speech, and mind of Mahāsāgara in the aspects of the five families (the lord Bhagavan Vairocana and so on) in all the ten directions, all of them adorned with the Mahābrahmā's Eon.[5] All this—visualized as the inconceivable cloud of offering of Samantabhadra—I offer to the teachers, to the hosts of deities of the yidam mandalas, and to the infinite assemblies of protectors.

Universes, each with its Mount Meru and four continents,
As many as the atoms in unnumbered buddha fields
In all the ten directions,
And clouds of offerings to the sugatas
Of things delightful to the senses of the gods and humankind,
Pleasantly adorned with Mahābrahmā's Eon—
For the infinite prosperity of every being—
I offer to the fields of merit:
Teachers, hosts of deities of the yidam mandalas,
And the infinite assemblies of the protectors.

This precious mandala, this pleasing cloud of offerings,
Endowed with boundless riches of the conquerors,
This ornament of boundless space, I offer.
May I enjoy the nirmāṇakāya buddha fields of luminous character.

oṃ āḥ hūṃ
In the blissful buddha field of Akaniṣṭha, Dense Array, where all appears but is devoid of intrinsic being—in an utterly delightful, measureless, square palace, with four gates and four pediments, are jeweled parasols, dharma wheels, beautiful gazelles, silken victory banners, delightful tassels, tiny moonlike trinkets moving in the wind, jewel-handled tail fans, strings of little golden bells, a vajra and a precious crest jewel. It consists of five concentric walls, each surmounted with a precious cornice and adorned with friezes made of different jewels and balconies and trellises of gems. {451} These are further surmounted with parapets and a high dome. There is a ledge for the offering goddesses—of charm, of garlands, of song, of dance, of flowers, of incense, of light, of scent, of food, and of music. On all sides, inconceivable clouds of

offerings are laid out, both outside and within. This place—the buddha field called Drumbeat of Brahmā, beautifully adorned with a cloudlike fabric of primordial wisdom—I offer to the teachers, to the hosts of deities of the yidam mandalas, together with infinite assemblies of protectors, all within the wheel of everlasting continuity, until the very emptying of samsara.

A place of perfect bliss
With endless banks of clouds shot through with rays of light,
Foursquare with four doors and four pediments,
Adorned with walls of the five wisdoms,
With goddesses of charm, of garlands,
Precious song and dance,
Who send forth shining clouds of offerings—
All this I offer to the teachers,
To the hosts of deities of the yidam mandalas,
And to the infinite assemblies of protectors.

I offer the jeweled palace of great bliss of Akaniṣṭha,
Canopied with clouds of various offerings,
Considering that it fills the whole of space.
May I enjoy the sambhogakāya buddha fields of spontaneous
presence.

oṃ āḥ hūṃ
The buddha field of luminous dharmatā is by nature primordially pure. It is empty like space, without center or periphery. It is bright like the sun and moon and is spontaneously present. Within it, samsara and nirvana are not separate either in the past, the present, or the future. It is the great wellspring of countless buddha fields and of the manifestation of the six classes of beings. This precious dimension of spontaneous presence is the expanse of the inseparable three kāyas. {452} It is the fourth time, the primordial wisdom of equality. It is the buddha field of the everlasting youthful vase body, which, beyond outside and in, is at all times placed within. It radiates beams of blue, yellow, red, white, and green light in all the ten directions. Its unbounded space is beautifully adorned with the kāyas and the great light of

the primordial wisdoms. This perfect realm of boundless array is the buddha field of the Luminous Vajra Essence, which is by nature completely pure and spontaneously present. All this—the supreme offering of primordial wisdom in the state of the utterly pure expanse of realization—I offer to the teachers, to the hosts of deities of the yidam mandalas, and to the infinite assemblies of protectors.

The field of luminosity, primordially pure,
Unborn, spontaneously perfect, unconditioned,
The palace of five wisdoms,
Where all samsaric things are nowhere to be found
And where conceptual elaboration all subsides—
This place, spontaneously present and endowed
With rays of light of the activities of the three kāyas,
I offer to the teachers,
To the hosts of deities of the yidam mandalas,
And to the infinite assemblies of protectors.

The field of the five primal wisdoms of luminosity, spontaneously
  present,
Is primordially adorned with kāyas and with disks of light.
I offer well this spotless self-display of awareness.
May I enjoy the dharmakāya field of Samantabhadra.

Now offer the mandala in the usual way. The threefold wiping of the mandala plate removes the impurities of your body, speech, and mind. Imagine that from the syllable *bhrūṃ*, there appears a pure buddha field complete with golden mountains and four continents. Its beautiful ground is filled with an unlimited array of things delightful to the senses of both gods and humankind belonging to the desire and form realms. It is endowed with the joys of the formless concentrations and with immeasurable palaces of pure lands, with wish-fulfilling trees and so forth, as well as with the boundless, joyful bliss of the śrāvakas, pratyekabuddhas, bodhisattvas, and buddhas. {453} Make three, eight, or twelve heaps of offering and present them.

oṃ āḥ hūṃ
The essence of an ocean of boundless forms and arrays consisting of all beings without exception that pervade the whole of space to its farthest limits in the different realms of the universes in

the ten directions—an essence adorned with Mahāsāgara—all the clouds of celestial and human arrays of offering as vast as the expanses of the sky, I devotedly offer to the ocean-like assemblies of the victorious ones and to all those worthy of offering.

The golden ground adorned with mighty Sumeru,
Arrayed with the four continents, subcontinents, the sun and moon, the stars and planets—
I offer this endowed with perfect substances delightful to the gods and humankind
And all the ornaments of the universes of four continents.

Lakes of precious water strewn with flowers, immeasurable palaces of immaculate pure lotuses upheld by stems of wishing gems, and ravishing pagodas above, below, and on the earth, celestial parks aglow with glorious splendor—all this I offer to the teacher of all beings and to all his heirs.

I make offerings of gold and silver, precious sapphire,
Emerald, coral, lapis lazuli,
A beauteous array of glowing, wish-fulfilling jewels,
Excellent vases, sublime wishing trees.

I make offerings of fragrant lotuses, lilies of the night, utpala flowers radiantly bright, and ravishing, resplendent blossoms. I offer celestial and human maidens adorned with fine and tinkling bracelets, with anklets made of gems, all of them singing melodies of praise. I offer parasols, sweet music, and all the glorious riches found both on the earth and in the other higher realms.

The seven jewels I offer, and the eight auspicious substances,
Palaces immeasurable, fair and fine and ravishing,
Glorious garlands and the perfect attributes of royalty.
May I naturally accomplish the riches of the conquerors.

I offer the delightful abodes of the gods absorbed in samādhi with their immeasurable palaces of clear light, adorned with the many gods and goddesses of fine appearance, the peaceful groves of the unmoving absorptions with and without form, {454} where the concentration that enjoys primordial wisdom is encountered. I offer all the ocean-like infinity of the enjoyments of the three realms, material and immaterial.

Clouds of outer, inner, secret offerings, endless as the ocean,
Arising from the clouds of the essence of the dhāraṇīs
Of śrāvakas, pratyekabuddhas, bodhisattvas, and victorious ones,
I offer to the teachers and the hosts of deities of the yidam
mandalas.

To the pure buddha fields replete with the riches of the buddhas and their bodhisattva children, filled with divine and human pleasures and dense clouds of infinite victorious ones, to the magnificent space-pervading fields of the sambhogakāya with their measureless palaces of primordial wisdom, and to the essence of the dharmakāya fields—to all these arrays without exception, may all beings in a single multitude progress.

Through the presentation to the fields of perfect merit
Of precious mandalas and clouds of Samantabhadra offerings,
The boundless riches of samsara and nirvana,
May all beings attain the city of their freedom.

The reason for making these offerings is that the two common accumulations are thereby perfected and the pure buddha fields enjoyed. Then as a means to the enjoyment of the buddha fields of the five primordial wisdoms, two special accumulations must be gathered. To that end, arrange the five mandalas, each of five heaps of substances, and imagine that all the buddha fields are filled with various kinds of fragrant incense, grains, medicines, gems, and flowers.

oṃ āḥ hūṃ
Buddha fields adorned on every side by netlike clouds of wishing gems, each consisting of a golden ground and of jewel mountains, forests of medicinal trees, massing clouds of incense, storehouses of grains, gardens of flowers, trees of miracles, wish-fulfilling jewels, and so on, innumerable cloud banks of celestial and human offerings that fill the endless reaches of space—all these I offer to the teachers, to the hosts of deities of the yidam mandalas,

and the infinite assemblies of protectors in a wheel of everlasting continuity until the very emptying of samsara. {455}

All buddha fields, with foundations of fine gold,
Enameled with a range of precious stones, aglow with wondrous jewels,
Pervading the expanse of space, which has no center, no periphery—these clouds of boundless offerings
I offer to the teachers,
To the host of deities of the yidam mandalas,
And to the infinite assemblies of protectors.

Imagining that space unbounded is replete
With various wondrous gems, I offer them.
May every being spontaneously accomplish their immediate needs and wishes,
And ultimately may they taste the five primordial wisdoms.

Buddha fields with grounds all carpeted with grains of different kinds,
Richly planted with medicinal trees, with flowers, untilled harvests, cultivated fruits,
Granaries bursting with the wealth of many cereals, and fair palaces, immeasurable,
A sublime glorious source of all that could be wished for, resembling samādhi's hundred savors—
All this I offer to the teachers,
To the hosts of deities of the yidam mandalas,
And to the infinite assemblies of protectors.

Imagining that space unbounded is replete
With boundless wealth of many grains, I offer them.
May all beings in this moment have unbounded wealth
And ultimately may they all enjoy the fields of the five kāyas.

All buddha fields suffused with purest perfume—the ground of the pure mind,
Arrayed with different sandal trees and fragrant incense powders piled up like Mount Meru,

Adorned with meres of fragrant wish-fulfilling waters—all these limpid offering clouds of sweetest scent
I offer to the teachers,
To the hosts of deities of the yidam mandalas,
And to the infinite assemblies of protectors.

Imagining that space unbounded is replete
With nectar clouds of incense and of medicines, I offer them.
May every being now possess untroubled senses {456}
And ultimately have enjoyment of Samantabhadra's field.

Buddha fields adorned with gleaming grounds of healing substances,
Beautifully filled with mountain-heaps of medicines,
Ablaze with glory of auspiciousness and splendor to subdue all illnesses—all this
I offer to the teachers,
To the hosts of deities of the yidam mandalas,
And to the infinite assemblies of protectors.

Imagining that space unbounded is replete
With supreme nectars, offering clouds of panaceas, I offer them.
May beings all be blessed with long life free of every ailment,
And ultimately may they all enjoy the field of perfect bliss.

Buddha fields all stocked with jewels,
And lotus lakes, and stacked arrays of flowers, and perfect woven garlands of utpala lotuses,
With earth and sky made beautiful with rains of heavenly blossoms—all this
I offer to the teachers,
To the hosts of deities of the yidam mandalas,
And to the infinite assemblies of protectors.

Imagining that endless space is filled
With ravishing gems all beauteously aglow, I offer them.
May every being now possess vast wisdom,
And ultimately may they all enjoy the field of the five lights.

It is said that this offering produces countless benefits: a long life free of illness and endowed with wealth and all enjoyments, an increase in realization of primordial wisdom of the four visions, and so on. If you are unable to make these three kinds of mandala offering, you should offer only the common mandala or the mandala of the three kāyas. In any case, the offering is accompanied with the oblation of various substances.

oṃ āḥ hūṃ
Vast space is the great element:
It is the treasure house of five great elements.
From space comes all that one might wish.
May the offering of all desirable things arise!

Bless the offerings by reciting the following mantra three times.

namo ratna trayāya oṃ namo bhagavate {457} *vajra sārapramardhane tathāgatāya arhate samyaksaṃbuddhāya tadyathā oṃ vajre vajre mahāvajre mahātejo vajre mahā vidyā vajre mahā bodhi maṇḍāpasaṃkrama vajra sarva karma āvaraṇa viśodhana vajre svāhā*

I make offering with vast and unsurpassed oblations
In actual substance or else emanated by my mind.
Flowers, incense, lamps, and food and water,
Canopies and floating tassels, music,
Victory banners, tail fans, ceramic drums, and so forth,
Together with my body, wealth, and day-to-day possessions—
All these I offer to the Buddha, teacher of all beings,
Together with his heirs.

Ravishing and measureless, many-storied palaces, adorned with nets of jewels
In heavens of the gods or other worlds,
Together with a falling rain of tuneful praise, with song and dance and music,
And all sublime adornments hundredfold, all these I offer.

I offer jeweled mountains, forests, lotus lakes,
The haunt and habitat of water birds,

Healing plants, sweet fragrances, and wishing trees
That bend beneath the weight of fruit and flowers.

I offer thousand-petaled lotuses alive with bees,
And bracelets made of lilies of the night,
Utpalas that open in the light of the unclouded sun and moon,
And every other ravishing, delightful thing.

The cooling scent of sandal wafting through the vault of heaven,
Fragrant breezes, bliss-bestowing perfumes,
Pleasant caves and cliffs and valleys filled with healing plants
And lakes of cooling water—this I offer.

The uneclipsed full moon in autumn nights,
Encircled by a garland of the moving stars,
And beauteous skies ablaze with networks of a thousand solar lights,
And everything that ornaments the universes of four continents—all this I offer.

A myriad meadows with their circling hills, {458}
All without exception filled with an array of all that might be wished,
And buddha fields in all the ten directions, many as the drops of water in the sea—
I take them all within my mind and to the Powerful Sage and to his heirs I offer them.

Excellent vases, wish-fulfilling trees, and cows of plenty,
The seven emblems of a king, the eight auspicious substances,
The seven precious articles, and all the rest, all in teeming quantity,
I offer to the great compassionate ones, the sublime objects of all offering.

With concentrated mind I offer
Endless clouds of outer, inner, secret offerings,
Pervading all the reaches of the sky.
Delightful floating clouds of flowers, with wondrous bright pavilions,

Nectar clouds of frankincense and healing drafts,
Splendid lamps, food fit for gods, and symphonies of music,
With endless praises, tuneful song, I offer.

I send out clouds of various offering goddesses,
Of charm, of garlands, and of precious song and dance,
All carrying endless clouds of gifts.
May the buddhas and their heirs without exception all be pleased.

There now follows the confession of past misdemeanors. Stir up, to the point of tears, a sense of sorrow for your wrong actions, and recite as follows:

Kye! Kye! Teacher, precious one,
I have no other hope but you.
Protect me now, who am protectorless.
I pray you, turn your loving eyes to me!
Ignorant I am and foolish;
The demon of dark ignorance oppresses me.
With great remorse I now confess
The spoiling of samaya, root and branch:
My lack of faith in you, O Lord,
And in your bodhisattva children,
As well as all ill-feeling for my vajra kin,
And all transgressions of the three vows.
Purify me now at once, I pray.

Kyema! In samsara that has no beginning,
I have perpetrated evil deeds unknowingly.
In the past, I wandered in samsara,
And even now, I wander still.
I pray you, guard me, be my refuge!

As you see, my faults are those
Of but an ignorant and foolish child. {459}
It is right that you should think of me
With even more compassion.
For just as in the case of common worldly folk,

A mother is forgiving of her children's faults
And gives them her protection.

Compassionate lord and father of all beings,
When you look on me and all the beings of the six migrations,
If you do not care and grant us your compassion,
What truth is in the famous saying,
"Your enlightened deeds
Bring benefit to beings to be guided"?

The buddhas of the past in countless number
Left us all behind, departing for their freedom.
The śrāvakas and the pratyekabuddhas also
Only strove for their own peace.
Will you now do the same and leave without us?

All the victors of the ten directions
Implored you to appear
For our sake as our teacher.
Are you now willing to abandon us?

Like some false escort in a fearful land,
Will you now betray us?
You may dismiss us, thinking, "It's their karma ripening,"
But then what use are your compassionate thoughts
For those who do not have such evil karma?
Even flesh-devouring spirits overlook
Their former wrath when they receive the offerings
And hear the words of truth.
So how could you, the loving father
Of all wandering beings,
Not acknowledge this confession of our faults?

If I pray before a wish-fulfilling jewel,
All my wishes will be granted.
Therefore, loving master, skilled in means,
How could you not fulfill my hopes?

Alas, compassionate lord,
If now I fail to cleanse away my sins,
I will be born again and burn for ages
In the fires of hell, so difficult to bear.
If you do not guard me, even though I am at risk,
What sort of "lord of great compassion" could you be?

Alas, Alas! I pray you, cleanse away
My evil actions, leaving none aside.
In this very instant, think of me! {460}
Grant me blessing and empowerment.
Bestow the common and supreme accomplishments.
Dispel all obstacles, all hindering, misleading forces.
In this very life, fulfill my wishes,
Allowing me to spend my days and nights in practice of the teachings.
Turn aside untimely death, and let my death
Be without sudden pain and violence
So that in the bardo I might master luminosity.
Lead me to a pure celestial field.

Pray in this way with great yearning, and joyfully consider that your spoiled and broken samayas have been restored. The remaining sections of the seven-branch practice now follow:

From time without beginning and through force of habit,
The evils I have done and the defilements I have gathered,
All causes of samsara, I confess and break with them.
At all times I rejoice in beings' boundless merit.
For the freeing of all beings, leaving none aside,
I request the turning of the wheel of dharma, unsurpassed.
Until the very emptying of samsara's sea,
I pray you to remain here constantly, not leaving for nirvana.
By the merit of this practice, may I and every being
Reach buddhahood together, all without exception.

Prayers and praises now follow. In the spirit of the prayers addressed by Terchen Rinpoche (Terdak Lingpa) to the great paṇḍita Vimalamitra, to the Great Master of Orgyen, and to the omniscient Longchenpa, recite prayers and expressions of praise as much as you can to different teachers. In general, recite the lineage prayers of the Heart Essence and *The Innermost Essence of the Master,* as well as the prayers belonging to the mind and space classes of the Great Perfection. If you are unable to recite them all, recite at least the prayer called *The Mass of Wish-Fulfilling Clouds,* which is in *The Innermost Essence of the Master: The Wish-Fulfilling Gem.* And add to it the following list of lineage masters:

oṃ āḥ hūṃ
Primordial protector, Samantabhadra father-mother,
I pray you, look with your compassionate eyes.
Bless me now that in this very instant I might realize
The luminous essence of the self-arisen nature of the mind.

Victorious buddhas, peaceful, wrathful, present of yourselves,
I pray you, look with your compassionate eyes.
Bless me now that in this very instant I might see {461}
The great radiant light of luminous primordial wisdom.

Mighty Vajradhara, sovereign of great bliss,
I pray you, look with your compassionate eyes.
Bless me now that in this very instant I might realize
The free and open ground of both samsara and nirvana—the dharmakāya, nature of the mind.

Vajrasattva, illusion of primordial wisdom,
I pray you, look with your compassionate eyes.
Bless me now that in this very instant I might reach
Great blissful Akaniṣṭha, changeless and spontaneously present.

Vajrapāṇi, lord of every mandala,
I pray you, look with your compassionate eyes.
Bless me now that in this very instant I might journey
On the royal road of the Secret Mantra to buddhahood in but a single life.

Garab Dorje, emanation of victorious ones,
I pray you, look with your compassionate eyes.
Bless me now that in this very instant my form of flesh
Dissolve into the body of the light of primal wisdom.

Mañjuśrīmitra, perfect wisdom's emanation,
I pray you, look with your compassionate eyes.
Bless me now that in this very instant I be liberated
From the sea of pain arisen through the power of karma and
defilement.

Śrīsiṃha, sovereign of the supreme mind,
I pray you, look with your compassionate eyes.
Bless me now that in this very instant I might reach
The isle of jewels, the scriptures of the ocean of the teachings.

Jñānasūtra, you who gained supreme accomplishment,
I pray you, look with your compassionate eyes.
Bless me now that in this very instant I might gain
The wish-fulfilling cloud of all accomplishments, supreme and
ordinary.

Vimalamitra, great in learning and accomplishment,
I pray you, look with your compassionate eyes.
Bless me now that in this very instant I might master
And perceive directly the four visions of luminosity.

Padmasambhava, great one, self-arisen,
I pray you, look with your compassionate eyes.
Bless me now that in this very instant every obstacle,
All hindering, deceptive forces, all subside without exception.

Tingdzin Zangpo, you who mastered your own mind,
I pray you, look with your compassionate eyes.
Bless me now that in this very instant I perfect
The sublime luminosity, transcending night and day.

Great dharma king who gathered both immense accumulations,
I pray you, look with your compassionate eyes. {462}
Bless me now that in this very instant, I might gain
The supreme realm, the sevenfold quality of noble wealth.

Dangma Lhungyal, shining light upon the isle of liberation,
I pray you, look with your compassionate eyes.
Bless me now that in this very instant I set free
All beings all together in the essence of enlightenment.

Senge Wangchuk, who achieved the body of light,
I pray you, look with your compassionate eyes.
Bless me now that in this very instant I might enter the expanse
Of the primordial ground, exhaustion of hallucinatory experience.

Gyalwa Zhangtön, king of the spontaneous presence,
I pray you, look with your compassionate eyes.
Bless me now that in this very instant I might realize
The inseparable union of the kāyas and primordial wisdoms.

Learned Nyima Bum, who absorbed the treasury of scriptures,
I pray you, look with your compassionate eyes.
Bless me now that in this very instant
With the sun of wisdom I dispel the gloom of ignorance.

Guru Jober, propagator of the sacred dharma,
I pray you, look with your compassionate eyes.
Bless me now that in this very instant I accomplish
Great waves of action for the welfare of all beings.

Senge Gyapa, for whom delusions of duality collapsed,
I pray you, look with your compassionate eyes.
Bless me now that in this very instant I might end
Attachment to this life, samsara's false appearances.

Great siddha Melong, you who gained supreme accomplishment,
I pray you, look with your compassionate eyes.
Bless me now that in this very instant I spontaneously accomplish
The twofold goal and reach the radiant dharmatā.

Kumaradza, great vidyādhara,
I pray you, look with your compassionate eyes.

Bless me now that in this very instant realization's light may blaze
And compassion come in massing clouds.

Natsok Rangdröl, illusory display of luminosity,
I pray you, look with your compassionate eyes.
Bless me now that in this very instant I might see phenomenal existence,
The universe and beings, as dreams and magical illusions.

Khyabdal Lhundrub, great scholar and accomplished master,
I pray you, look with your compassionate eyes.
Bless me now that in this very instant I gain mastery
Of love, compassion, and the supreme attitude of bodhicitta.

Drakpa Özer, manifesting as the son of the Victorious One,
I pray you, look with your compassionate eyes.
Bless me now that in this very instant I might cause to flourish
The teachings of the luminous vajra essence.

Sangye Önpo, great destroyer of delusion, {463}
I pray you, look with your compassionate eyes.
Bless me now that in this very instant I might see
The pointless nature of this present life's activities.

Dawa Drakpa, emanation of the supreme Hayagrīva,
I pray you, look with your compassionate eyes.
Bless me now that in this very instant I might realize
All samsara and nirvana as a sole and single sphere.

Kunzang Dorje, unrivaled great accomplished master,
I pray you, look with your compassionate eyes.
Bless me now that in this very instant I might realize
Dharmakāya, the union inseparable of space-awareness.

Kunga Gyaltsen, propagator of the path profound,
I pray you, look with your compassionate eyes.
Bless me now that in this very instant I might see
Phenomena as free and open in the vast expanse of luminosity, the state of equality.

Natsok Rangdröl, lamp of sacred doctrine,
I pray you, look with your compassionate eyes.
Bless me now that in this very instant I might cleanse in the primordial expanse
All false thoughts of apprehender-apprehended.

Tendzin Drakpa, destroyer of delusion,
I pray you, look with your compassionate eyes.
Bless me now that in this very instant I gain mastery
Of the four visions, accomplishing the body of light of primal wisdom.

Dongak Tendzin, knower of all things,
I pray you, look with your compassionate eyes.
Bless me now that in this very instant I achieve
My goal and mightily perform enlightened deeds.

Trinle Lhundrub, rebirth of Nubchen Sangye Yeshe,
I pray you, look with your compassionate eyes.
Bless me now that in this very instant I attain
Primordial purity, luminous and empty, the exhaustion of phenomena in the dharmatā.

Terdak Lingpa, king of dharma in the triple world,
I pray you, look with your compassionate eyes.
Bless me now that in this very instant I perfect
The twofold goal, accomplishing the four activities.

Rinchen Namgyal, Vimalamitra's emanation,
I pray you, look with your compassionate eyes.
Bless me now that in this very instant I bring forth
Great waves of deeds and aspirations for the doctrine and all beings.

Mingyur Paldrön, you who were the appearing form of Tsogyal in reality,
I pray you, look with your compassionate eyes.
Bless me now that in this very instant I dispel deluded thought,
Production of the wind-mind, into the exhaustion of the dharmatā.

Oḍḍiyāna, illusory emanation of Yudra Nyingpo,
I pray you, look with your compassionate eyes.
Bless me now that in this very instant all cognitions of the apprehended
And appearing things subside within the groundless state devoid of true existence.

Trinle Namgyal, the display of Mañjuśrī,
I pray you, look with your compassionate eyes.
Bless me now that in this very instant, the cognitions of an apprehender
Sink into awareness, empty, luminous, and unimpeded. {464}

Trinle Chödrön, of mighty realization and experience,
I pray you, look with your compassionate eyes.
Bless me now that in this very instant all self-clinging
Sink in the expanse of dharmatā beyond all action.

Mañjughoṣa, you who are omniscient,
I pray you, look with your compassionate eyes.
Bless me now that in this very instant and through various emanations
I achieve the good of beings who fill the whole of space.

My own root teacher, you of peerless kindness,
I pray you, look with your compassionate eyes.
Bless me now that in this very instant I might look upon
The face of the primordial nature, openness and freedom, transcending ordinary mind.

While it is not necessary in the main text, if you wish and when performing the ritual of homage, you may add here a brief mention of the names of other lineage masters. Recite as follows:

I pray you, lineage teachers of the secret cycle of the Great Perfection,
Tingdzin Zangpo, Lodrö Wangchuk,
Rinchen Barwa, Lhungyi Gyaltsen, and the others of the lineage,
Bless me to attain the state of dharmatā, exhaustion of phenomena.

I pray you, lineage teachers of the space class of the Great
Perfection,
Vairotsana, Pangtön Mipham Gönpo,
Changchub Gyaltsen, Rinchen Yik and others of the lineage,
Bless me that my form of flesh dissolve in light.

I pray you, lineage teachers of the mind class of the Great
Perfection,
Vairotsana, Yudra Nyingpo, Trisong Detsen, dharma king,
The three ancestral masters—Nyak, great Nub, and Zur—and all
the rest,
Bless me that hallucinatory appearances sink back into the
ground.

I pray you, teachers of the lineage of the Heart Essence,
Pema Ledrel, Gyalse Lekpa,
Ngaki Wangpo, Rangjung Dorje, and the rest,
Bless me to perfect the experience of the four visions.

Between the stanza mentioning the name of the master Khyabdal Lhundrub and until Rangjung Dorje, the listed names have been added [to Longchenpa's list].

Furthermore, with great respect I pray to you, victorious ones,
Together with your heirs, residing in the ten directions,
To the śrāvakas, pratyekabuddhas, the assembly of all noble ones
and all practitioners.
I pray you bless me, look upon me with compassion.

Kyema, kyehu!
With your great love and your compassionate hands,
Protect me now, a poor and wretched being, long-tormented
By my karma and defilement, difficult to bear.
I pray you in this instant, be my guide.

Though buddha from the very first, {465}
Through ignorant delusion, I am wandering in existence.
How wearisome it is, samsara that is like a dream.
I pray you, be my refuge and protector.

Hard it is for me and beings without end
To cross samsara's shoreless sea.
I pray you save us from this vast abyss of suffering
With the unsurpassed great ship of primal wisdom.

My long-accustomed habit of subject-object grasping at
hallucinatory appearance
Is, in form, like Sumeru, the towering king of mountains.
With the vajra of supreme primordial wisdom, utter freedom,
I pray you, in this instant bring it all to nothing.

The total dark of ignorance is deep indeed.
Hard it is to fathom its duration—no sign is there that it will ever
end.
I pray you, with the rays of your primordial wisdom,
Scatter these great waves of darkness that enshroud the heart of
luminosity.

However much I strive, I just create the cause of sorrow and
defilement.
From worldly deeds so utterly bereft of meaning
Completely turn away my mind, I pray, and grant
That I might pass my days and nights in spiritual practice.

The heaving swell of misled mental states,
The various thoughts pursuing the five objects of the senses,
With all the tendencies of the eight consciousnesses and the
ground of all,
I pray you, make them all subside into the dharmadhātu.

The conceptual habits and defilements of the mind in the desire
realm,
The clarity of the realm of form,
Together with the mental stasis of the formless realm—
I pray you, purify all these samsaric states and their propensities.

I pray you turn me from the sordid mind of striving only for myself,
Of seeking to accomplish peace for me alone.

Embarking on the supreme path of outer, inner, and secret
teachings,
May I mightily secure the benefit of others.

Purify the karma, the defilements, and habitual tendencies
Of all who go astray on vile, mistaken paths.
Drive the horses of their minds, and herd them
To the wish-fulfilling city of their freedom.

For us who dwell for endless and unstarted time
In dark and turbid seas of obscuration, {466}
There is no point when we might free ourselves by our own
strength.
I pray you, you who have great love, come set us free.

From strong defilement hard to bear,
From torments of samsara rank with many sorrows,
From carelessness and indolence and evil influence of others—
I pray you in this moment grant us your protection.

Give me the conviction that phenomena are essenceless,
Impermanent, unstable, deceptive magical illusions.
And grant that I may spend my nights and days
In weary sadness with samsara and the wish to leave it.

Grant that in some pleasant solitude upon a noble mountainside,
I might master concentration, clairvoyance, and awareness
And with the twofold aim spontaneously achieved,
Depart for the pure celestial land of perfect bliss.

Grant that I might strive alone, enduring in the practice,
Undistracted for an instant by the interests of this life,
That, walking in the footsteps of the masters of the past,
At all times pleasing to my teacher, I might gain accomplishment.

Grant that with samaya and the vows unbroken and unspoiled,
I realize without mistake the view, the meditation, action, and
result.

I pray that, day and night not stirring from the state of luminosity,
I might secure the twofold aim of self and others.

Grant that through the generation and perfection stages, I attain
the utter purity of phenomenal existence.
With the ḍākinīs and the protectors gathered in vast clouds,
And with the two attainments pouring down like rain,
Grant that I might be proficient in the four enlightened deeds.

Cause my pure perception and devotion to arise impartially,
And grant that nothing interrupt my love and my compassion.
May the excellent experience and realization of the view and
meditation blaze,
And may the benefit of beings be everywhere achieved.

Grant that, through this aspiration pure and perfect,
All beings, leaving none aside, be all together and at once set free.
I pray that they might reach within this very life
Samantabhadra's blissful buddha field, spontaneously present.

If you are unable to recite the foregoing prayer, through lack of time or some other constraint, it is sufficient to recite the lineage prayers composed by Terchen Rinpoche[6] for *The Innermost Essence of the Master* and the Heart Essence. {467}

There now follows the ritual for keeping the samaya pledges fresh. With your hands joined, recite as follows.

O you my teacher, holder of the vajra,
And you the blissful buddhas of five families,
Think of me, I pray.

From now until I gain the essence of enlightenment,
I take refuge in the Three Jewels, unsurpassed,
Of Buddha, dharma, sangha.
And in my teacher also I take refuge.
I confess my evil conduct
And rejoice in every virtue.
I cultivate the enlightened attitude.

The samayas of the five enlightened families
I will properly preserve—
Keeping vajra, bell, and every other substance of samaya.
At no time will I ever spurn
The unsurpassable Three Jewels,
And will never leave the vajra master.
The vajra kindred I will never denigrate.
Refraining from all injury to living beings,
I will not disdain the noble ones.
I will not vilify the lower vehicles
And will not abandon the mantrikas.
The recitations of approach and of accomplishment
I will complete and meditate upon the mandala.
I will live by the samaya pledges and the vows
And will refrain from all deluded deeds.
I will utterly subdue my mind
And secure the highest benefit of beings
Who live in all directions till the very end of space.
I will set free all those who are not free.
I will carry over those who have not crossed.
I will bring relief to those not yet relieved
And place all beings in the state beyond all sorrow.

The following sections of the seven-branch practice may now be added. If you wish to make a gaṇacakra feast offering, bless the assembled substances by reciting *oṃ āḥ hūṃ* and sprinkling them with amṛta. Recite the following:

The fire, wind, and water that arise from primordial wisdom,
  self-cognizing,
Cleanse away the impurity of clinging to phenomena as real.
Within the space-like vessel, luminous and empty, primordial
  wisdom manifests
As gaṇacakra—every object pleasing to the senses, all
  spontaneously perfect.
oṃ āḥ hūṃ oṃ āḥ hūṃ oṃ āḥ hūṃ

The raining down of blessings on the gaṇacakra offering is as follows:

oṃ āḥ hūṃ {468}
Equal are samsara and nirvana, the great and all-pervading sphere!
In ultimate Akaniṣṭha, awareness present of itself,
You are the glorious embodiments of the kāyas and the wisdoms never parted,
Although the space of luminosity is beyond both staying and departing,
O vidyādharas and teachers, together with the mandalas of the victorious ones,
Think of your devoted children with compassion.
Rain down great blessings; grant the great and infinite empowerments.
Bless the universe and its inhabitants as the buddha field of the sambhogakāya's self-experience.
Bless all these samaya substances as the mandala of primal wisdom.
vajra samāveśaya a āḥ jaḥ hūṃ baṃ ho

Now offer the first part of the feast. Recite the following prayers three times:

oṃ āḥ hūṃ
In the vast external universe, the buddha field of Mahābrahmā,
Phenomena, both pure and impure, are heaped up as the offerings of gaṇacakra.
I offer them to you, my teacher, the expanse of self-arisen nirmāṇakāya.
I pray you, cause hallucinatory appearance to subside into the ground.

Within the central channel, where the essence of the five winds gathers,
The samaya substances of the sixteen joys of great bliss all collect.
I offer them to you, my teacher, luminous expanse of the sambhogakāya.
I pray you, cause immaculate primordial wisdom to increase.

In the vast expanse, the rootlessness of all phenomena,
Are limitless clouds of offerings, massing clouds of undivided dharmatā, free and open from the very outset.

I offer them to you, my teacher, the expanse of openness and
freedom of the dharmakāya.
I pray you, empty out the ground and root of birth and death.

In the blazing light of the direct perception of awareness,
Experiences intensify, and from primordial wisdom everything
delightful to the senses is projected.
I offer it to you, assembly of my teachers—awareness ripened into
forms—
I pray you, grant me the accomplishment of phenomenal
exhaustion that transcends the ordinary mind.

oṃ āḥ hūṃ
Holy root and lineage masters of the four times and the ten
directions,
Lineage of the mind-to-mind transmission,
Lineage of the symbolic transmission of vidyādharas,
Lineage of the hearing transmission of the yogis,
Hosts of deities of the yidam mandalas,
Five classes of the ḍākinīs,
Infinite assemblies of protectors,
Guests of both samsara and nirvana—
I offer you this feast; be pleased to take it!
gaṇacakra khāhi {469}

For the confession of mistakes, recite as follows:

Overwhelmed by ignorant delusion,
I have transgressed and spoiled the root and branch samayas
And those of the enlightened body, speech, and mind.
With deep remorse, I openly confess my faults.

Overpowered by deluded habits accrued from time without
beginning,
Every violation, every breach, conscious or unconscious,
I confess them all to you, O great compassionate ones.
I pray you to bestow accomplishment of utter purity.

Uncompleted recitations of approach and of accomplishment,
spoiled offerings of the first part, ritual uncleanness,
Failure to make offerings at the proper times, laziness, parsimony,
Lack of realization of the view, unclear and muddled meditation,
Careless deeds—all this I openly confess.

Contempt toward the teacher, his family and consort, and the
vajra kindred,
All accidental negativity, defilement,
And all obscurations, passing and enduring,
I openly confess with great remorse.
I pray you to bestow accomplishment of utter purity.

ho
In the ultimate natural state, there are no faults and no mistakes,
And therefore no confession—nothing in the slightest to confess.
Yet by confessing faults just on the level of relative illusion,
May they be purified within the nondual state of mind.

The apprehension of duality is the natural cause of impaired
precepts.
In the space of nonduality, all is from the outset present of itself.
All is but the space-like state of great perfection,
Ultimate reality, unborn, completely pure.

The offerings are made and received with symbolic gestures, and the yogis enjoy the feast in the manner of an inner fire offering.

ho
The aggregates, the elements, the sense fields of my body
Are by nature the three perfect seats,
The deities of the mandala of the hundred families.
All movements are great bliss.
In keeping with the vajra pledges unsurpassed,
I enjoy this feast
As a great cloud of bodhicitta
In the state of evenness without duality.
Completing the accumulations of the yogic path,

And unobscured by food, {470}
May I and all who have participated generously in this offering
Experience the result of the Great Vehicle.

Reciting this, enjoy the feast in the state of all-embracing dharmatā. Sing appropriate vajra songs, songs of realization of the lineage masters and so on. In brief, recite these vajra words taken from *The Union of the Sun and Moon Tantra*:

ema kiri kīrī maṣṭa bāli bāli samitra suru suru kutāli masu masu ekarā sulibhataye cakira bhulisalaye samunta carya subhaye bhetasanabhya kuliye sakaridhūkana matari baitana baralihisana makhatatakilanī saṃbhara tam eka citatamra suryabhaṭara evaśanasa dranbhiti saghurālasa masmin sagulitayasa agurā agurā paga kharnalī nara nāra ethara saṭala sirna sirṇā bhesarasapalaṃ bhundha bhundha cikṣapakelaṃ sasā rirī lilī i ī mimī rararā

Then recite,

Because it is unborn, it is unceasing.
It does not come, it does not go, and it is everywhere pervading.
No movement is there in the supreme, ultimate reality of great bliss.
Like space itself, it has no need to be set free.
Rootless and without support,
It is great dharmatā, without abode, impossible to grasp,
Primordial state of openness and freedom, vast spontaneous equality.
Unfettered, it is not to be set free.
It is the all-embracing perfect dwelling, present from the first,
All-pervading, even, utterly without a dwelling place,
It is the great immensity, the great expanse of space.
Great ultimate reality, it is the blazing mandala of sun and moon,
Spontaneously present, object of direct experience,
The vajra mountain, the great lotus,
The sun, the lion, body of primordial wisdom,
Peerless music of the roar of dharmatā,
At play within the vast expanse of space.
It is buddha, equal of all buddhas,

Immense Samantabhadra, peak of all phenomena,
Samantabhadrī's space-like womb—
The luminous expanse, spontaneous presence, primordial great perfection. *Ho!*

As you recite this, meditate on its profound meaning. In conclusion, offer the remainder of the feast, purifying it with *raṃ yaṃ khaṃ* and blessing it with *oṃ āḥ hūṃ*.

In this vast palace of the gaṇacakra, luminous primordial wisdom,
O you, the guests of the remainder—thoughts arising, tending to the objects of the senses— {471}
Powerful mamos, *gings* and hosts of *laṅka* spirits,
Accept this illusory display of the remainder of the gaṇacakra feast.
Drive back, I pray, the army of samsara. Churn the depths of conditioned existence,
Bringing all to freedom in the vast expanse of primal purity.
ma ma hriṃ hriṃ balinda khāhi

To the sound of cymbals, carry the remainder outside. In conclusion, first recite the following short seven-branch practice:

To all those worthy of respect
I bow in veneration,
Prostrating with as many bodies
As there are specks of dust within this buddha field.

To all the worthy objects of my offerings
I offer clouds of outer, inner, and secret gifts,
Both in reality and imagined by my mind,
Extending to the farthest limits of the sky.

I honor all victorious ones
With the great offering of natural equality,
Immaculate and vast as space. I worship them
With joyful evenness, the most sublime enlightenment.

My body and enjoyments, all my merits and belongings—
I offer them to every being.

To all beings I present the offering
Of primordial wisdom, perfect freedom.

Reaching to the buddha fields in all the ten directions,
As long as there are buddhas and beings residing there,
May my wish-fulfilling clouds of offering
Be placed before them without interruption.

In the presence of all those reverend objects, I confess
All obscurations of my body, speech, and mind.
With great remorse I now declare that henceforth,
At the cost of life and limb, I will refrain from them.

All transgressions of the three vows,
Of śrāvakas, of bodhisattvas,
And of vidyādharas of Secret Mantra—
Each and every one I now confess.

All transgression of my body, speech, and mind
Regarding the three secrets
Of the vajra body, speech, and mind—
Each and every one I now confess.

I confess with sorrow and regret all breaches and all spoilings
Of the root and fivefold branch samayas:[7]
Things that should be known, things not to be spurned, things
  that should be eagerly accepted,
Things that should be trained in, things that are to be performed.

I, unwise and ignorant, have perpetrated
Deeds that are the causes of samsara,
Impeding liberation.
I confess them all that they be cleansed away. {472}

The natural purity of all phenomena
Is a vast immensity commensurate with space.
May the enlightened mind, beyond acceptance and rejection,
Be perfected as the vast expanse of dharmatā.

I take delight in all the virtues
Of victorious ones and sentient beings.
I pray that the wheel of dharma now be turned
According to the needs and wishes of all beings.

Buddhas and their bodhisattva heirs,
And you, the supreme teachers of all beings,
For as long as there are beings left,
I pray you free them all without exception.

O teachers, may your lives be stable like the mountains,
May you remain like kingly Sumeru itself,
And from samsara to nirvana, I pray that you may lead
All beings numerous as space is vast.

Beings helplessly engulfed and sinking
In the ocean of their karma and defilement,
I pray you, with the ship of your compassion,
Bring them all to safety each and every one.

With the rays of your primordial wisdom,
Dispel the gloom of ignorance,
And soothe those tortured by the fires
Of sorrow and defilement.

I pray you, halt the twelve dependent links
That, turning like a chariot wheel,
Are the foundation of illusory samsara,
Where beings turn protectorless.

Destroy the mill of mental movement
Arising though the mind's dysfunction.
I pray you that my mind be turned away
From worldly deeds bereft of meaning.

At all times, night and day, I pray you
Let no evil attitudes arise within my mind.

Grant that, striving in the good that leads to liberation,
I may gain enlightenment.

For ages equal to the ocean's drops,
May I pay honor to the buddhas, the victorious ones.
May I at all times please my glorious teachers
And uphold the sacred dharma, so profound.

Spontaneously to gain the twofold aim of self and others,
May I strive with effort in the study, contemplation, meditation
on the teachings.
Blessed with all the perfect attributes of sevenfold wealth,
May I at all times labor for the benefit of beings. {473}

At all times and from this day forward,
May I be the ground of beings' sustenance.
May all who see or hear, remember me or touch me
Come to unsurpassed enlightenment.

There may be some who hate and scorn me,
Who revile or criticize—
All this is perfect! May it be the cause of their enlightenment.
May they become the first of my disciples.

Those who look to me with faith,
Who with devotion praise and think of me—
May they gain a treasure of accomplishment.
May they be blessed by ḍākinīs.

May I become the basis for the ending of the faults
Of those who now rely on me.
May they embark upon the path to freedom.
May their virtues constantly increase.

May just the utterance of my name
Become a source of beings' safety.
May just my clothing, hair, or nails
Become for them a great defense.

May just the thought of me
Protect them from the fear of thieves and robbers.
May it bring about for them
Their every wished-for goal.

From now until the end of time to come,
May I become for all beings their protector.
May I become their refuge, friend, and guardian.
May I fulfill their every hope.

May I become for every being
The wish-fulfilling jewel itself.
May I dispel their poverty
And satisfy their hopes and wishes.

May my body, my possessions,
Together with my every virtue,
Become the ground of happiness for beings,
A spring of boundless benefit for others.

May all my wishes be directed
Solely to the benefit of beings.
With patience in the face of boundless difficulties,
May I accept all harm and bring to others benefit.

As long as living beings remain,
I will labor for their good.
May I only gain enlightenment
When all have found their freedom from samsara. {474}

Perfecting the four visions,
The pathway of the vajra heart of luminosity,
May I attain the body of great transference
And bring unbounded benefit to beings.

May every being who relies on me
Attain the fields of the nirmāṇakāya—

In this life, in the bardo state, or their next existence.
May they all accomplish freedom in the primal ground.

May all my undertakings
Be for the benefit of beings.
May they cross the ocean of existence
And attain in one life their enlightenment.

May the supreme teachings, unsurpassed,
The secret treasure of victorious ones,
Like the sun that rises in the sky,
Flourish and spread in every land.

Now invoke the promise of the teachers and receive empowerment:

Teachers, holders of the vajra,
Sole friends in the three worlds of samsara,
Refuge of those who wander unprotected,
Great stair that leads to liberation,
Lost in darkness, I now come to you for refuge,
Ignorance-dispelling light!
Protect me, who, protectorless,
Am sinking in the murky ocean of samsara.
Cool me with the draft of self-arisen wisdom,
For I am tortured in the fires of the three poisons.
My body of flesh, my speech, and mind,
Entrapped in ignorant delusion—
Cause them to dissolve in light
That I attain remainderless nirvana.
O my teachers, precious buddhas,
I have no other hope but you.
I pray you, look upon me with compassionate eyes
And free me from the ocean of samsara.
Grant that I achieve within this very life all excellence,
And free me from all obstacles and hindrances.
Grant that at the moment of my death,
I recognize deep luminosity.
And be delivered from the bardo's dangerous paths.

I pray that all my deeds of body, speech, and mind
Be always for the benefit of others,
And that from this day forward,
Every circumstance be changed into the supreme path
That leads me to enlightenment.

However much I labor, freedom is so hard to gain.
Lords, protectors, in the boat of your compassion, {475}
Bring me and all who are protectorless
To the very land of liberation.

May any who have faith in me,
Or those who scorn and criticize,
Be free of evil actions and defilements,
May they be delivered from the river of existence.

And when at last my simple name
Will bring to beings all that they desire,
May clouds pour down a rain of offerings
In all the buddha fields that fill the ten directions.

By this virtue may all beings
Be liberated from samsara.
May they gain the two supreme primordial wisdoms,
Spontaneously accomplishing the twofold goal.

In conclusion, consider as follows:

The whole of phenomenal existence and the mandala of the teachers melt into light. This dissolves into the retinue, which then dissolves into the main teacher. The main teacher comes with great joy and rests above the crown of my head. From the big toe of his foot there issues a stream of nectar that, entering through the crown of my head and the heads of all beings, spreads through our bodies, inside and out. This purifies the obscurations of the body, and we gain the accomplishment of the enlightened body. The stream of nectar then flows to our throats. The obscurations of speech are purified, and we gain the accomplishment of enlightened speech. The stream of nectar then flows to our hearts. The obscurations of mind are purified, and we gain the accomplishment of the enlightened mind. The stream of nectar then descends to our navels. All impurities are cleansed away, and we gain the accomplishment of enlightened qualities. The stream of nectar then descends to the secret center, and we gain the accomplishment of enlightened activities. With great joy, the teacher melts into light and dissolves into us. The teacher's body, speech, and mind mingle inseparably with our bodies, speech, and minds.

Rest in meditative evenness in the state of primordial purity, the expanse of luminous wisdom. When you arise from this meditation, consider as follows:

All appearances are the teacher's body.
All sounds are the teacher's speech.
All thoughts are the teacher's mind.
Phenomenal existence is the display of primordial wisdom.

Seal your practice with appropriate prayers of dedication, such as,

By this merit may I swiftly gain
The accomplishment of my glorious teacher.
[May all beings, leaving none aside,
Attain likewise his level.] {476}

Consider that the earth and sky are filled with dense clouds of teachers, hosts of the deities of the yidam mandalas together with an infinite multitude of dharma protectors, who rain down a shower of flowers and sing auspicious prayers. In one voice with them, chant as follows:

While never stirring from the ultimate expanse, your auspicious prayers are all accomplished.

The perfect buddha, nondual union of the kāyas and the wisdoms,
Primordial lord, the glory of samsara and nirvana,
Samantabhadra, you and a vast multitude of buddhas of the five families—
May your auspicious presence bestow prosperity and happiness!

The supreme path, the essence of luminosity, causes all mental movement to subside.
It is altogether pure, uncluttered, free of all defilement.
It is the vast domain of self-cognizing primal wisdom.
May the auspicious sunlight of the sacred dharma grant prosperity and happiness!

Owners of the wish-fulfilling treasury of freedom, field of beings' merit,
Assembly of the noble ones, with all vidyādharas and multitudes of the protectors,
Send out radiant clouds of worldly ḍākinīs, performers of activities.
May your auspicious granting of supreme accomplishment bestow prosperity and happiness!

As a conclusion to this and other prayers of good wishes, play music and scatter a rain of flowers.

All happiness and well-being in this and future lives
Derive from making offerings in honor of the teacher.
The samayas and the vows take root therein.
It brings an increase to experience and realization like the waxing moon.
It is the chief of virtuous deeds, and you should strive therein.
This common ritual veneration of the teachers,
Well known in all the tenet systems,
I composed according to the words of Ngaki Wangpo the omniscient.
It is easy for the fortunate to implement.
Through this merit, may all beings and myself
Be guided by our teachers, perfect and sublime.
Thus may I, in one life and one body,
Gain freedom in the primordial ground.
And through countless emanations may I liberate
All beings infinite as space itself.

Since this ritual was required for the completion of the accumulations [of merit and wisdom] of myself and others, and since the "second omniscient master," Dorje Ziji, granted me the permission to compose it, I, Karma Ngaki Wangpo Yönten Gyatso Lodrö Tayepai De, the very last of the disciples of Karma Tai Situ, lord of the teachings of ultimate meaning—and linked as I am by constant aspiration with the superlative Kagyu lineage—composed this text on the excellent day of the manifest enlightenment in the primordial place of freedom of the omniscient Drime Özer, in the meditation retreat of Tsadra Rinchen Drak, in the heart of Dewakoti, the mandala of the luminous mind of the Great and Glorious One.

May virtue and good fortune increase!

21. An Authorization Ritual for the Practice of Ekajaṭī, Protectress of the Doctrine, together with the Six Guardians of Her Retinue[1]

Jamgön Kongtrul Lodrö Taye

oṃ svasti {480}

Samantabhadrī, mother of all victorious ones,
Adopts the manner of a wisdom mamo
To guard the teachings of the Secret Mantra.
Bowing to her, I shall now explain her sādhana.

The empowerment of the wisdom mamo Ekajaṭī and her retinue of six or four attendant guardians—together with the associated sādhana—comprises three sections: (1) the preparation of the materials required, (2) the main part of the sādhana, and (3) the ritual of empowerment.

The Preparation of the Required Materials

Upon a square support and in the middle of a star made of two superimposed triangles, which serves as the triangular ritual receptacle, arrange seven heaps of black grain corresponding to the positions of the respective protectors. In the center, on a tripod, place the glorious torma of the protectress of Secret Mantra surrounded by the four smaller, similar tormas of her retinue and four lotus petals. In the east is the three-cornered torma for Sokdrubma, surrounded by three similar [smaller] tormas. In the south is the three-cornered torma for Rishi Rāhula, twisted clockwise, surrounded by eight [smaller] tormas of similar form. In the west is the three-cornered torma for Yakṣa (the dark-red *shenpa* spirit) marked with circular ornaments and surrounded by eight [smaller] tormas. {481} In the north is the torma for Damchen Dorje Lekpa. Placed on a square castle-shaped structure, it is three-cornered, marked with a goat's head, and surrounded by the six [smaller] tormas. In the northeast is the torma for Lekden: a dark-red, three-cornered torma surrounded by the six similar tormas of his retinue. Finally, there is a three-cornered torma for Rematī surrounded by four [smaller] tormas.

All should be decorated with various foodstuffs of good quality but mainly with meat and blood. Stick arrows in each of the main tormas, which are colored and equipped with images according to the protector in question. In the east [of the tormas], place the general offering torma of the principal deity and her retinue, with amṛta and rakta to the right and left. On the south side, place a torma made in the shape of Mount Meru with its four terraces. Place five butter lamps on its summit, one in the center and the others in the four directions. On the west side, place a ritual arrow decked with silken ribbons and articles that are the supports of the guardians. On the north side, place a skull cup filled with the substances of samaya. In addition, according to traditional practice, place together a representation of Mount Meru, silken ensigns, victory banners, a garland of hearts, and all the substances needed for the exorcism, rakta, white mustard, phurbas, and swords—all surrounded by various offerings. {482}

The Sādhana of Ekajaṭī

First of all, perform the self-visualization according to the sādhana of any appropriate peaceful or wrathful yidam deity, and bless the general offering torma. Cleanse and purify the representation [of Ekajaṭī and the other protectors] in front of yourself. Then imagine that, within the sphere of emptiness in the space in front of you, in the center of a great charnel ground, there issues from the syllable *yaṃ* a deep-red fire, blazing like the fires at the end of time, stirred up by a tempestuous wind. Within this expanse, there is a syllable *raṃ*, which transforms into an ocean of rakta with heaving waves. Therein, a syllable *keṃ* transforms into a Mount Meru made of bones all mixed and piled together. On its summit, a syllable *bhrūṃ* transforms into a blazing palace made of skulls. It is of immeasurable size and decked with dreadful and terrifying ornaments. In its center is a throne composed of a lotus, a sun disk, and the bodies of enemies and obstacle-producing spirits. Upon this, a dark, maroon-colored syllable *trak* appears and transforms into the glorious wisdom mamo, the protectress of Secret Mantra. She is dark in color like a dense cloud of maroon-colored smoke. She has one face and two arms and is an unbearable form of ferocious wrath. She has a single, glaring, round, red eye set in her forehead and in her gaping mouth she has a single fang curving downward like a crescent moon. Her tongue is curled back, and she is roaring with the ferocious sounds of *hūṃ* and *bhyo*. Amid her flying red hair, she has a single, iron-hard, upward-pointing tress. At the level of her heart, she has a single breast from which there flows a stream of amṛta. In her right hand, she is brandishing at the level of her head a staff emblazoned with a flayed human skin. From her left hand, in which she holds the heart of an enemy, there emanates a piśācī in the form of an iron wolf. She wears a crown and a necklace made of dry skulls. Her upper body is draped with a human skin and a cloud of rainbows, and as her lower garment, she wears a kilt of tiger skin. She is adorned with the five kinds of bone ornaments. With her left leg outstretched, she stands in dancing posture on a corpse. {483} She is encircled by an inconceivable assembly of the mamos of phenomenal existence: the three emanated mamos; the three gings of union, liberation, and killing; the five wisdom mamos; the fourteen mistresses; the fifty-eight menmo spirits; and so forth.

On the mamo's left side, in the northeasterly direction, is black Dugön Lekden, who is as black as the clouds at the end of time. He has one face, four arms, and three eyes. In his two right hands he holds a curved knife and a poisonous plant. In his two left hands, he holds a skull cup filled with blood and a demon's lasso. He is arrayed in three capes of black silk, and he wears a diadem of dry skulls and a garland of freshly severed heads. He rides upon a diabolical black horse. He is the personification of fierce wrath and majesty. His retinue is the millionfold warband of the gods.

On his left is the glorious goddess Rematī. Dark-blue in color, she is emaciated and gaunt. She has one face and two arms. In her right hand, she holds a sword; and in her left, a bag of pestilential sickness. She is arrayed in the attire of the mamos. In the midst of a tempestuous black wind, she rides a three-legged mule and is surrounded by a myriad host of mamos.

In front of mamo Ekajaṭī, the syllable *bhyo* transforms into black Sokdrubma, the female black shenpa spirit. Fierce and wrathful, she holds in her right hand a razor-sharp knife, and with her left hand she is devouring the lungs and heart of an enemy. She is arrayed in human skins and is adorned with skulls, bones, and serpents. She rides upon a black gale that engulfs the whole of existence. She is surrounded by myriads of flesh-devouring spirits and mamos. On her right flank, they have the heads of jackals; on her left, the heads of pigs; and in front, the heads of owls.

To the right of Ekajaṭī, the syllable *tri* transforms into the planetary spirit Rāhula. He is dark-maroon in color and has nine heads and four arms. In his two upper hands, he holds a sea-monster banner of victory and a lasso made of snakes. In his two lower hands, he holds a bow with an arrow thrust into the heart of an enemy. His entire body is filled with eyes, and his lower part is like a coiling serpent. He is arrayed in the terrifying attire of the charnel ground. {484} All around him is a host of terrifying spirits: the planetary spirits, the four sisters of varying countenance, the spirits of the constellations, and so on.

To the rear of Ekajaṭī, the syllable *kṣa* transforms into Yakṣa, the dark-red shenpa spirit. He has one face and four arms. In his two right hands, he holds a curved blade and a sword; in his two left hands, he holds a skull and a lasso made of a snake. He is arrayed in a cape of red silk and the clothing of the charnel ground. He is riding on a garuḍa and is surrounded by a host of flesh-devouring shenpa spirits, such as the eight classes of emissaries.

Again, on the left of Ekajaṭī, the syllable *tri* transforms into supreme Dorje Lekpa. He is red in color. In his right hand, he brandishes a vajra aiming at the head of an enemy, and in his left hand, he has a human heart. He is arrayed in splendid clothing and a mantel of white silk. He is riding on an orange-colored goat and is surrounded by a host of arrogant spirits: the four classes of mighty *ging*; three hundred and sixty *tsen* gods and demonic upāsakas; twelve joyful female spirits; and snarling, bare-fanged, devouring spirits.

All around on the outer rim, there is an inconceivable host of wisdom protectors and fierce worldly guardians of male and female lineages together with their delegated emissaries. All are terrifying and dreadful in their form. Their actions change according to desire and need, and thus they are like wishing jewels that satisfy the hopes and expectations of practitioners. They all have the syllable *oṃ* in their foreheads, *āḥ* in their throats, and *hūṃ* in their hearts.

The Summoning

Beams of light radiate from the syllable *hūṃ* in your heart and invite the wisdom mamo together with her retinue to arise from the dharmadhātu, the expanse of the mother, and to come from the continent in the southern ocean, from the summit of Mount Meru, from the eight great charnel grounds, and from all other sacred lands and places, which are their fields of joyful enjoyment. *vajra samā jaḥ*

Consider that you summon them with the following words:

bhyo
From the expanse of mother Samantabhadrī of great bliss,
Self-arisen wisdom, the expanse beyond all mental movement,
The mandala of dharmakāya beyond all reference,
Arise through your compassion in a manifested form,
Great queen of all the ḍākinīs,
Mistress of the three worlds, Lady of the Single Tress, {485}
Protectress of the Secret Mantra, mother who brings freedom,
Wrathful lady, dark-maroon in color. I pray you, come to me!
In answer to my faithful pledges of samaya,
Come, O come to me, my dear and only mother!
Now I, your vajra sibling, cry to you.
Guardian, sister, come to me!

hūṃ
From the charnel ground of Ucala,
Come, black Lekden, come, I pray.
From the mandala of black cyclonic wind,
Queen of the desire realm, come, I pray.

bhyo
Sky-going lady, ferocious shenpa spirit,
From the charnel ground, I pray you, come!
Lord of frightful spirits, Great Rāhula,
From the sky, I pray you, come!
From the charnel ground of spreading joy,
I pray you, liberating ging, great Yakṣa, come!

From the place of your samaya,
Dorje Lekpa Tikletsal, I pray you, come!
All you guardians who protect the teachings,
With your servants, with your envoys,
To this place of samaya I summon you.
I pray you, come and your activities perform!

oṃ roru ekajaṭī nying khama rulu rulu hūṃ bhyo hūṃ bhyo jaḥ jaḥ trak rakṣa saparivāra ehyehi vajra sāmaja jaḥ hūṃ baṃ hoḥ

The Request to Remain

hūṃ
Dark-maroon and wrathful Lady of the Copper Face,
Arisen from the dharmadhātu,
Protectress of the Secret Mantra, along with all your retinue,
Remain upon this seat of blazing fire all prepared.
trak rakṣa saparivāra samaya tiṣṭha lhan

Homage

Glorious mistress of the wisdom ḍākinīs,
Lady of the Single Tress, protectress of the Secret Mantra,
Together with your retinue of powerful protectors,
I bow down to you.
atipū hoḥ pratīccha hoḥ

Offerings

hūṃ
Clouds of secret offerings from all the infinite pure fields,
Lovely flower garlands, floating incense clouds,
Bright and sparkling light, bubbling scented waters,
Foodstuffs of a hundred tastes, music of hundred tuneful melodies, {486}
Flesh, bones, hearts, the body's inner organs,
A sea of marvelous drinks of rakta and amṛta,
Tormas, inconceivable, of food and drink, delightful to the senses,

Fair forms and pleasant sounds, sweet smells and pleasing tastes,
Objects pleasing to the touch—all these clouds of offerings brought by offering goddesses,
I lay before you. Savor them with pleasure and engage in your activities!

oṃ trak rakṣa saparivāra puṣpe . . . śabda amṛta rakta balinda pañca kāma guṇa pratīccha svāhā

Praise

bhyo
From the charnel ground ablaze with fire as at the end of time,
Wrathful mistress, dark-maroon, of overwhelming presence, come!
Your body is like space, your raiment like a southern cloud.
Devouring a heart, you suck out all the heart blood of samaya breakers.
With your staff made of a corpse, you split apart the hearts of all your enemies.
Great terrifying lady with your single tress erect,
With the one eye on your forehead, you behold the three worlds of existence.
With the single fang within your mouth, you slay your enemies.
With the single dug upon your breast, you feed the supreme yogis like your babes.
This red torma now accept; enjoy this flesh and blood!

By force of your samaya pledges, slay all those of spoiled samaya—
O mamo, take the life force that you relish
And accomplish the deeds that we entrust to you.
The time to act according to your pledge is now at hand. *Samaya.*

hūṃ
Mother Ekajaṭī, glorious queen,
With one face and two arms and shouts of *rulu*,
Supreme mamo of Samantabhadrī's space,
Mistress of the wisdom and the worldly guardians, to you I offer praise.

hūṃ
Glorious protector and unvanquished master of the triple world,
Black Lekden who lay in ruins the three cities,
Your great excellence is equal to the confines of the sky,
Mahākāla with your retinue, to you I offer praise.

bhyo
Rematī, O demoness of great ferocity,
Clothed in darkness, riding your three-legged mule, {487}
Ranging through the universe three thousandfold,
You snatch away the lives of beings,
Protectress of the teachings, to you I bow in praise.

bhyo
Black she-shenpa spirit wearing human skin,
Holding in your hands a heart together with a satchel of disease.
Encircled by a busy host of ḍākinīs, a millionfold,
Black Revatī together with your fearful company, to you I offer praise.

hūṃ
Great Rishi Rāhula, planetary spirit,
Of smoky color, with nine heads and a thousand burning eyes,
Holding in four hands an arrow, bow, a sword, and flag of victory,
I praise you with your company of the four sisters and eight kinds of spirits.

hūṃ
Dark-red Yakṣa riding a garuḍa, copper-red in color,
With one face and four arms, you hold a curved blade and a blood-filled skull cup,
A sword that pierces an enemy's heart, and a lasso made of a black snake—
Great ferocious one, to you and all your retinue I offer praise.

hūṃ
Great guardian Damchen, dark-red Tikletsal,
With one face and two hands that hold a vajra and an enemy's heart,

Garlanded with skulls and clothed in human skin and kilt of tiger fur.
To you with all your kin, three hundred and sixty strong, I offer praise.

hūṃ
To you, the hosts of guardians,
Who took the oath in Vajradhara's presence,
To you, the treasure keepers and twelve tenma goddesses,
To you the place gods, and the owners of the ground of the Tibetan lands, I offer praise.

If you wish, you can also recite the praises of the varying attributes of mamo Ekajaṭī mentioned in *The Secret Tantra of the Wrathful Goddess*, together with particular praises addressed to the four guardians—whatever you are familiar with.

Mantra Recitation

In the hearts of mamo Ekajaṭī and those of her retinue, upon a solar disk, visualize the appropriate seed syllables surrounded by their respective mantras. Invoke them by sending rays of light from the heart of yourself (visualized as a deity) and consider that they perform without impediment all the activities entrusted to them.

The mantra for mamo Ekajaṭī:

oṃ mama ekajaṭī tri trak rakṣa nying rakma rulu rulu hūṃ bhyo hūṃ {488}

For Gönpo Lekden:

oṃ mahākāla trakṣad mahākāla siddhi tri yaṃ du jaḥ jaḥ

For Rematī:

oṃ trak rakṣa rematī rulu rulu hūṃ bhyo hūṃ

For Sokdrubma:

oṃ khikhale nakmo sö sokmati sö nying khakha bam yama sö ca baṃ bitimu sö ghaya sö niya sö rakma nira büd

For the planetary spirit Rāhula:

hrīḥ śaga ruram nage citta traṃ mamo yong ṭha gram hahe yoga śala jaḥ jaḥ

For Yakṣa:

oṃ ehe marutse guṇa hri hri ghraṃ bhyo śaraṃ bhyo surāja dhri kahala ghanda caya jaḥ jaḥ

For Damchen Dorje Lekpa:

oṃ vajra sādhu samaya he cha hü cha lege ebhaga śaya jaḥ

Recite the mantras of Ekajaṭī and her retinue as much as you can, and then make offerings and praise. If you wish to offer a gaṇacakra feast and recite the prayer of confession and restoration, do so now. At the end of your session, present the torma, make offerings and praise, request forgiveness for faults, dissolve the [wisdom] protectors [into the supports], and request [the worldly protectors] to depart. Finally, make prayers of aspiration and good wishes.

The Empowerment Ritual of Ekajaṭī

The master should perform the self-visualization practice as well as the front visualization as previously explained. The disciples should purify themselves and make prostration. First, a torma is given to the obstacle makers and the empowerment is introduced with the following words:

Ekajaṭī is the chief protector of the Secret Mantra teachings of the Vajrayāna in general and of the atiyoga teachings of the great secret in particular. She is the buddha Samantabhadrī manifesting in the form of a wisdom mamo in order to subdue evil forces and to protect the teachings. She is known as Lady of the Single Tress, the great protectress of Secret Mantra, and as Vajra Lady of the Copper Face. The teachings concerning her are found mainly in *The Secret Tantra of the Wrathful Goddess*. But many tantras of both atiyoga and mahāyoga contain teaching on her. She may be practiced either as a yidam deity or as a protector of the doctrine. Here she is propitiated in her role as dharma protector. Moreover, Ekajaṭī may be practiced as a single mamo on her own or in a group of many protectors. In the present case, she is in the company of a host of other protectors, according to a ritual composed by the great omniscient Lord of Dharma (Longchenpa). This is taken from the tradition of the lineage teachers of the Great Heart Essence belonging to the pith-instruction class of the Great Perfection. {489}

When the master has finished his preparations, the disciples should offer a mandala and recite the following formula three times:

> *Ema!* Master, hold me in your mind.
> That I might now protect the doctrine,
> I pray you grant the empowerment of the proud and powerful protectors
> Who have been commanded by the sugata.

The master gives his consent by saying,

> Approach, O fortunate and noble child.
> It is good that you should wish to guard the doctrine.
> The granting of empowerment of the fierce and powerful protectors
> Will enable you to be a guardian of the Buddha's teaching.

The disciples now accumulate merit by using whichever seven-branch prayer they know. The water of the oath is now administered to the disciples.

> This is the water of your hell!
> If you break samaya, it will burn you.
> If you keep samaya, you will gain accomplishment.
> The vajra samaya should be kept without transgression.
> *samaya amṛta hūṃ*

The disciples are now bound under oath.

With the tormas in front of them, the master and the disciples now visualize themselves as deities according to whichever practice they are engaged in. They should imagine that before them is a great charnel ground in the middle of which there is a seat contrived of a lotus, a solar disk, and the bodies of enemies and obstacle makers. On this stands the glorious wisdom mamo Ekajaṭī, protectress of Secret Mantra. To the northeast is black Dugön Lekden in union with his consort. To the east is the female shenpa spirit. To the south is the planetary demon Rāhula. To the west is the dark-red shenpa Yakṣa. To the north is Damchen Dorje Lekpa. All are with their retinues, surrounded by inconceivable armies of wisdom protectors and worldly guardians of both male and female lineages, together with their delegated emissaries. Their forms are of incomparable majesty, and they have expressions of joy. Their speech is the thunderous proclamation of the mantras *hūṃ* and *bhyo*, and their blissful, luminous minds rejoice in their activities for the protection of the doctrine. {490}

The master and disciples consider that the dharma protectors are actually present in that place. Then, as the disciples feel a fervent devotion toward the master, rays of light are projected from the latter's heart, and these invoke the mind of mamo Ekajaṭī visualized in front.

The master then says to the disciples,

> Imagine that from Ekajaṭī's three centers there emanate countless rays of light—red, white, and blue in color—which dissolve into your three centers.

Placing the torma on the heads of the disciples, the master says,

> *hūṃ*
> Through the empowerment of Ekajaṭī, the glorious queen—
> With her one face, two arms, and shouts of *rulu!*—
> Supreme mamo of the space of Samantabhadrī,
> That I grant to you, my fortunate and noble children,
> May you gain the power to accomplish this guardian of the Secret
>   Mantra
> And spontaneously perform the four activities.
>
> *oṃ mama ekajaṭī trak rakṣa nyingkha rakma rulu rulu hūṃ bhyo hūṃ*
> *kāya abhiṣiñca oṃ vāka abhiṣiñca āḥ citta abhiṣiñca hūṃ*

As the mantra is recited, the torma is placed against the three places of the disciples, who now consider that the body, speech, and mind of mamo Ekajaṭī mingle inseparably with their body, speech, and mind. They have assumed the great power of the mamo, who then fulfills the activities entrusted to her and follows them like their shadow. This completes the empowerment of the body.

The Empowerment of the Mamo's Speech

The master and disciples visualize themselves as Ekajaṭī. In their hearts and in the heart of the deity visualized in front, there is a lotus and a sun disk, on which the seed syllable [of Ekajaṭī] stands surrounded by her mantra. As the disciples generate a strong feeling of devotion toward their master, a garland of the mantra of Ekajaṭī issues from his mouth and enters the mouths of the disciples. Passing through their bodies, it enters Ekajaṭī's [secret] space and issues from her mouth. It enters the secret space of the master, and thus the mantra garland turns like a firebrand. Its rays of light dissolve into the seed syllable and mantra in the heart of the disciples. It is thus that they receive the accomplishment of the mamo's mantra. {491} With this visualization, they recite the mantra:

> *om mama ekajaṭī trak rakṣa nyingkha rakma rulu rulu hūṃ bhyo hūṃ*

The disciples recite the mantra three times. They then cast a flower in the direction of the master and repeat after him,

> You have granted me [the empowerment of] the protectress of the
> Secret Mantra.
> Cause her to become my guardian.

The disciples say this three times, whereupon the master places a flower on their heads and says three times,

> I have granted you [the empowerment of] the protectress of the
> Secret Mantra.
> I pray that she be with you at all times.

This completes the empowerment of speech.

The Empowerment of the Mamo's Mind

The master says,

> Mamo Ekajaṭī, visualized in front of you, now melts into light and, disappearing like the haze on the surface of a mirror, dissolves into you. You yourselves now melt into light and dissolve into the state of emptiness devoid of mental elaboration, like a rainbow vanishing in the sky. Rest meditatively within this state. This is a very important point. The reason for becoming inseparable from the protectress is to protect you from being harmed by her.

This completes the empowerment of the mamo's mind.

Following the same procedure, the torma empowerment of Lekden is now bestowed:

> *hūṃ*
> Fortunate and noble children, now I give to you
> The empowerment of the glorious protector
> Black Lekden, unvanquished master of the triple world,
> Bringer of destruction to the three cities,
> Whose qualities of greatness are as vast as space itself—
> Mahākāla with his retinue.
> By this means, may you be able to accomplish
> This guardian of the Secret Mantra,
> Spontaneously engaging in the four activities.
>
> *oṃ mahākāla trakṣad mahākāla siddhi tri yamadu jaḥ jaḥ kāya vāka citta abhiṣiñca hūṃ*

The deity's mantra is then transmitted in the same way as for Ekajaṭī, except that for the four guardians of the male lineage, the turning garland of the mantra passes through the mouth and navel. The deity then dissolves into light.

The torma empowerment of Rematī is now bestowed:

> *bhyo*
> Fortunate and noble children, now I give to you
> The empowerment of Rematī, the demoness of great ferocity.

Clothed in darkness, she rides upon a three-legged mule {492}
And ranges through the universe to snatch away the breath of
beings' lives.
Together with her retinue, she is the guardian of the teachings.
By this means, may you be able to accomplish
This guardian of the Secret Mantra,
Spontaneously engaging in the four activities.

oṃ trak rakṣa rematī rulu rulu hūṃ bhyō jaḥ hūṃ kāya abhiṣiñca hūṃ vāka abhiṣiñca hūṃ citta abhiṣiñca hūṃ

The deity's mantra is then transmitted and the deity dissolves into luminosity.

The torma empowerment of Sokdrubma is now bestowed:

bhyo
Fortunate and noble children, now I give to you
The empowerment of the black she-shenpa wearing human skin,
Holding in her hands a heart and satchel of disease,
Encircled by a busy host of ḍākinīs a millionfold—
Black Revatī, together with her fearful company.
By this means, may you be able to accomplish
This guardian of the Secret Mantra,
Spontaneously engaging in the four activities.

oṃ khi khale nakmo sö sokmati sö nying khakha bam yama sö ca bam bitimu sö bhaya sö niya sö rakma nira bü kāya abhiṣiñca hūṃ vāka abhiṣiñca hūṃ citta abhiṣiñca hūṃ

The deity's mantra is then transmitted with the same visualization as before. The deity dissolves, melting into luminosity.

The torma empowerment of Rāhula is now bestowed:

hūṃ
Fortunate and noble children, now I give to you
The empowerment of the great rishi Rāhula, planetary spirit.
Of smoky color, with nine heads and a thousand burning eyes,
He holds in his four hands an arrow, bow, a sword, and flag of
victory.

He is accompanied by the four sisters and the eight classes of spirits.
By this means, may you be able to accomplish
This guardian of the Secret Mantra,
Spontaneously engaging in the four activities.

hrīḥ śaga ruram nāge citta traṃ mama yo ṭhagram hahe yogi śala jaḥ jaḥ kāya abhiṣiñca hūṃ vāka abhiṣiñca hūṃ citta abhiṣiñca hūṃ

The deity's mantra is then transmitted and the deity dissolves into luminosity.

The torma empowerment of Yakṣa is now bestowed:

hūṃ
Fortunate and noble children, now I give to you
The empowerment of dark-red Yakṣa riding a garuḍa copper-red in color.
With one face and four arms he holds a curved blade and a skull cup filled with blood,
Together with a sword that pierces an enemy's heart and a lasso of black snakes— {493}
The great ferocious one with all his retinue.
By this means may you be able to accomplish
This guardian of the Secret Mantra,
Spontaneously engaging in the four activities.

oṃ ehe marutse guṇa hrīḥ hrīḥ ghram bhyo śaram bhyo surāja dhri kahala ghana caya jaḥ jaḥ kāya abhiṣiñca hūṃ vāka abhiṣiñca hūṃ citta abhiṣiñca hūṃ

Once the empowerment has been given and the mantra of the deity transmitted, the deity dissolves into luminosity.

The torma empowerment of Damchen Dorje Lekpa is now bestowed:

hūṃ
Fortunate and noble children, now I give to you
The empowerment of the great guardian Damchen, dark-red Tikletsal,
Together with three hundred and sixty of his kin.

With one face and two hands he holds a vajra and an enemy's heart.
He is garlanded with skulls and clothed in human skin and kilt of tiger fur.
By this means may you be able to accomplish
This guardian of the Secret Mantra,
Spontaneously engaging in the four activities.

oṃ vajra sādhu samaya hecha hūcha lege ebhaga śaya jaḥ jaḥ kāya abhiṣiñca hūṃ vāka abhiṣiñca hūṃ citta abhiṣiñca hūṃ

The deity's mantra is then transmitted and the deity dissolves into luminosity.

The empowerment of the samaya substances is now bestowed. Place the skull cup in the disciples' hands and say,

hūṃ
Through the granting of empowerment
Of this true and secret kapāla,
The basis for the palace of the eight clans of the spirits,
May those eight clans be now sent forth to do their work.
kapāla abhiṣiñca maṃ

Present the torma with these words:

Through the granting of empowerment
With this torma with four terraces and five lamps—
Of Mount Meru and the three planes of existence—
May all the oath-bound guardians be pleased.
oṃ balinda abhiṣiñca maṃ

Present the representation of Mount Meru with these words:

Through the granting of empowerment
Of the support of the enlightened body,
Mount Meru and four continents,
May all the oath-bound guardians
Become your servants, brought beneath your power.
oṃ ratna mandala abhiṣiñca maṃ

Present the silken ensign with these words:

Through the granting of empowerment of this fine ornament,
This silken ensign of various colors, {494}
This ornament of the enlightened body,
With many ribbons fluttering in the air,
May you possess the perfect ornament.
pataṃka abhiṣiñca maṃ

Present the victory banner with these words:

To you, the children of my lineage, I grant
Empowerment of this beautiful victory banner
Of power and prosperity.
May your wishes thereby be spontaneously fulfilled.
oṃ dvāja abhiṣiñca maṃ

Present the garland of hearts with these words:

hūṃ
To you, the children of my lineage, I grant
Empowerment of the hearts of various living beings—
The samaya substances that correspond to them.
May they be always with you, never parting.
cittamāla abhiṣiñca maṃ

Present the offering torma of the ferocious ones with these words:

hūṃ
To you, the children of my lineage, I grant
Empowerment of this substance of samaya,
An offering of torma to the ferocious ones.
May you have the power to summon them—the guardians of the doctrine, all without exception.
mahā balinda abhiṣiñca maṃ

Present the substances of exorcism with these words:

To you, the children of my lineage, I grant
Empowerment of the glorious weapons of the delegated emissaries,
The substances that exorcise the harmful spirits.
May you accomplish all fierce activities.
māraya abhiṣiñca maṃ

Present the rakta with these words:

To you, the children of my lineage, I grant
Empowerment of this rakta, the destruction of all craving,
The lethal weapon, the mamos' plague.
May you accomplish the ferocious mantra spells.
oṃ mahā rakta abhiṣiñca maṃ

Present the white mustard with these words:

White mustard is connected with the king of rishis,
The lethal arrow of the emissaries.
By the empowerment of this devastating weapon,
May all activities without exception be accomplished.
śāriraṃ abhiṣiñca maṃ

Present the phurba with these words:

To you, the children of my lineage, I grant
Empowerment of this phurba,
The glorious weapon of the emissaries.
May all enemies and hindrance makers be destroyed.
om kīlaya abhiṣiñca maṃ

Present the sword with these words:

To the children of my lineage I grant
Empowerment of this blazing perilous weapon, {495}
Which eradicates both birth and death.
May the life vein of all enemies and hindrances be cut.
oṃ khāṭvaṅga abhiṣiñca maṃ

It is thus that the empowerments are gradually bestowed. The empowerments of the samaya substances—from the kapāla until the offering torma—are empowerments of qualities, whereas the empowerments of the substances of exorcism and those that follow are empowerments of activities. Before bestowing the empowerment of the substances of exorcism, the master should dissolve the object of exorcism into the symbolic effigy. He entrusts the substances of exorcism to his disciples, and they throw them one by one on the effigy, with the result that the enemy to be exorcised is eradicated and the goal of the empowerment achieved. The text for the empowerment of the samaya substances composed by the Omniscient One appears to be based on the empowerment of the Mighty Guardians contained in the Eight Great Mandalas text called *Union of the Sugatas*.[2] It is presented here in the same way.

There now follows a torma ritual of conjuration. All the tormas, the supports of the dharmapālas, are placed together on one tray. Visualizing them in the form of the dharmapālas that they represent, the master places them in the hands of the disciples and says,

> Above these tormas—visualized in the form of the glorious wisdom mamo, protectress of Secret Mantra, and the other six guardians, together with their consorts and retinues—consider that your root and lineage teachers and all the buddhas and bodhisattvas are gathered like great banks of clouds.

All the mantras of the dharmapālas are now recited, and then the master continues,

> Glorious wisdom mamo, protectress of the Secret Mantra, dark-maroon in color, queen of wrathful goddesses; black Dugön Lekden with your consort; black Shenpa Sokdrubma; Rishi, great planetary spirit; dark-red Yakṣa Shenpa; Damchen Dorje Lekpa—with all your retinues, servants, emissaries, and minions, do not transgress the orders and the samaya pledges of Samantabhadra, Vajrasattva, and the others—all the teachers of the lineage: (*the master enumerates them by name*).
>
> Through your enlightened body, speech, mind, qualities, and activities, grant power and accomplishment to these vajra disciples. {496} Raise up their strength, I pray, as protectors of the Buddha's teaching. And as great guardians of these disciples, stay as close to them as if you were their shadows. Drive away all evil, and foster and bring forth propitious circumstances.

In this way, the master gives appropriate orders to the protectors. Thereupon, both the master and the disciples think in the following way:

> Finally, the teachers and the yidam deities dissolve into the mamo and her retinue, who now melt into light and dissolve into the disciples.

The usual conclusion is now performed: the proclamation of samaya, the taking of the promise to observe it, the making of offerings, and so on. The ritual is brought to a close by offering the torma as before, by making an offering of thanksgiving, by asking forgiveness, by dissolving some of the deities and requesting the others to depart, and finally by making prayers of aspiration and good wishes.

This then is a description of the practice related to the seven protectors. If a sādhana of the five protectors is used, the tormas for Lekden and Rematī are not made and the associated recitation and meditation are omitted. The remaining protectors are as described. Separate sādhanas [for the protectors] exist, also composed by omniscient [Longchenpa] himself, but their [scriptural] sources and view are mostly in harmony with the ritual described here.

The mantra protectress propitiated in this ritual is not only the guardian of the Secret Mantra in general. She is also the special protectress of the Great Heart Essence, or Nyingtik, teachings, with which her tantra, sādhana, and pith instructions are specifically linked. Lekden in union with his consort—also known as the protector with the curved blade and skull cup from the temple of Zha—is associated with the form of Lekden figuring in the present sādhana. His sādhana, composed by Master Padmasambhava, was discovered in the Zha temple by Chilha Garab, who gave it to Nyö Lotsāwa. The latter had received [a similar teaching] from Balim Atsama. Deciding that both teachings came to the same crucial point, Nyö Lotsāwa devised a practice on Lekden that combined the teachings of both the oral transmission (*kama*) and the discovered treasures (*terma*). In the present sādhana, therefore, Lekden is visualized holding in his right hand a curved blade (instead of a lasso) and in his left hand a lasso (instead of a khaṭvāṅga). With the exception of Faceless Shona, the other deities are the same.

In the Nyö tradition, Rematī is generally considered as having four arms. Sometimes, however, she has two. Occasionally, the visualization is stipulated as being optional. For the most part, however, her appearance corresponds to the description given in the present sādhana. Sokdrubma is a special protector of *The Heart Essence of the Ḍākinīs*. The planetary spirit Rāhula and the shenpa spirit Yakṣa are also associated with these treasure teachings. {497}They are the peerless protectors of the Vajrayāna teachings. Damchen Dorje Lekpa is the special guardian of the treasure teachings of the Heart Essence.

The sādhanas composed by Master Padmasambhava and the great Nyangben are linked with the present ritual. The combined practice of the main protectress and her retinue, as set forth in the present ritual, is the usual traditional method and is imbued with the blessings of the teachers of the lineage. Specifically, the omniscient Lord of Dharma, who himself beheld the face of Ekajaṭī and the others, composed two sādhanas based on his experience: *A Treasure Mine of Accomplishment*[3] and *A Wish-Fulfilling Tree.*[4]

Moreover, these seven protectors all have their own tantras and sādhanas, together with pith instructions replete with profound and secret crucial points. They are distinguished from the other protectors owing to their great power and blessings.

Though indivisible in the unchanging dharmatā,
The protectors of the vajra essence
Appear distinctly, in a group of seven.
This is their profound, essential sādhana.

This concludes the section devoted to the sādhana conjoined with the empowerment ritual of the glorious protectress of Secret Mantra with the six or four guardians of her retinue.

May good fortune increase!

Abbreviations

BDRC	Buddhist Digital Resource Center (formerly Tibetan Buddhist Resource Center), http://www.bdrc.org.
DNZ	Jamgön Kongtrul Lodrö Taye. *The Treasury of Precious Instructions. gDams ngag rin po che'i mdzod.* 18 vols. Delhi: Shechen Publications, 1999.
KSG	*Expanded Collection of the Nyingma Kama. sNga' gyur bka' ma shin tu rgyas pa.* Chengdu: Si khron mi rigs dpe skrun khang, 2009.
LYT	*The Innermost Essence of the Master. bLa ma yang tig (yid bzhin nor bu).* In *sNying thig ya bzhi.* Delhi: Shechen, 2021.
NG	Collected Tantras of the Ancients. *rNying ma rgyud 'bum.* 26 vols. Dege: Dege Parkhang, 1991.
P.T.	Peking Tengyur
THL	Tibetan and Himalayan Library. https://www.thlib.org.
Toh.	*A Complete Catalog of the Tibetan Buddhist Canons,* edited by Hakuju Ui et al. Sendai, Japan: Tohoku University, 1934.
TPQ, Book 1	Jigme Lingpa and Kangyur Rinpoche. *Sutra Teachings.* Treasury of Precious Qualities, vol. 1. Boston: Shambhala, 2011.
TPQ, Book 2	Jigme Lingpa and Kangyur Rinpoche. *Vajrayāna and the Great Perfection.* Treasury of Precious Qualities, vol. 2. Translated by Padmakara Translation Group. Boston: Shambhala, 2013.
VNT	*The Heart Essence of Vimala. Bi ma'i snying thig.* In *sNying thig ya bzhi.* Delhi: Shechen, 2021.
ZYT	*The Profound Innermost Essence. Zab mo yang tig.* In *sNying thig ya bzhi.* Delhi: Shechen, 2021.

Notes

Series Introduction

1. 'Jam dbyangs mkhyen brtse dbang po (1820–1892), mChog 'gyur bDe chen gling pa (1829–1870), Mi pham rgya mtsho (1846–1912), and many more masters were involved in this movement, including Kongtrul's guru Si tu Pad ma nyin byed (1774–1853). See Smith, *Among Tibetan Texts*, 247–50; Jamgön Kongtrul, *The Treasury of Knowledge, Book 8, Part 4: Esoteric Instructions*, 25–48; Ringu Tulku, *The Ri-me Philosophy of Jamgön Kongtrul the Great*; etc.
2. The specific text by Shes rab 'od zer that expounds the eight chariots is *Meditation's Ambrosia of Immortality* (*sGom pa 'chi med kyi bdud rtsi*). A study of this has been made by Marc-Henri Deroche: "'Phreng po gter ston Shes rab 'od zer (1518–1584) on the Eight Lineages of Attainment." According to Deroche, "This text may be considered as an (if not the) original source of the '*ris med* paradigm' of the eight lineages of attainment" (17). It is interesting to note that the eight lineages are arranged in a different sequence in that text—Nyingma, Kadampa, Shangpa Kagyu, Lamdre, Marpa Kagyu, Zhije, Jordruk, Dorje Sumgyi Nyendrub—which may have been more chronological than Kongtrul's preferred order.
3. This idea is developed in the volume on esoteric instructions in *The Treasury of Knowledge*, where Kongtrul describes in incredibly condensed detail the basic principles and sources of these eight lineages. It is expounded in the catalog of *The Treasury of Precious Instructions* (*DNZ*, vol. 18), published in English as *The Catalog of "The Treasury of Precious Instructions,"* trans. Richard Barron (Chökyi Nyima). Also see Stearns, *Luminous Lives*, 3–8.
4. Jamgön Kongtrul Lodrö Taye, *Catalog*, 21.
5. *The Treasury of Precious Instructions. gDams ngag rin po che'i mdzod* (*DNZ*), 12 vols. (Delhi: N. Lungtok and N. Gyaltsan, 1971–1972). Known as the Kundeling printing.
6. *The Treasury of Precious Instructions. gDams ngag rin po che'i mdzod* (hereafter *DNZ*), 18 vols. (Delhi: Shechen Publications, 1998). Known as the Shechen printing.

Translators' Introduction

1. Jamgön Kongtrul Lodrö Taye, *Catalog*, vii.
2. See Richard Barron, *The Autobiography of Jamgön Kongtrul: A Gem of Many Colors*, translated by Richard Barron (Ithaca, NY: Snow Lion, 2003), 269–70, cited in Jamgön Kongtrul Lodrö Taye, *Catalog*, xv.
3. See *Chos dbyings rin po che'i mdzod kyi 'bru 'grel 'od gsal thig le nyag gcig* (Beijing: Mi rigs dpe skrun khang, 2005), 133–34.
4. The following account, which is no more than the bare bones of a much more complex and in some places bewildering story, is based on the detailed histories by Nyoshul Khen Rinpoche, Tulku Thondup, and Philippe Cornu.
5. See *TPQ, Book 2*, 323–24.
6. *sems sde*, *klong sde*, and *man ngag gi sde.*
7. See *Chos dbyings rin po che'i mdzod kyi 'bru 'grel 'od gsal thig le nyag gcig*, 37–38.
8. *sNying thig ya bzhi.*
9. *Zab mo yang tig.*
10. The title of the omitted text is *Pad lugs mkha' 'gro yang tig khrid yig rin chen gser phreng.*

Part One: Primary Texts for the Heart Essence Teachings

1. See *dNgos gzhi 'od gsal snying po'i don khrid*, in *LYT*, vol. 1. (*e*), 344.

1. The Three Testaments of the Buddha: The Quintessence of the Key Points of the Pith-Instruction Class of the Luminous Great Perfection

1. *'Od gsal rdzogs pa chen po man ngag sde'i gnad kyi bcud phur sangs rgyas kyi 'das rjes gsum*, *DNZ*, vol. 2 (*kha*), 1–7. Second source: *VNT*, vol. *e*, 287–95.
2. Respectively, *Theg mchog rin po che'i mdzod* and *bLa ma yang tig yid bzhin nor bu.*

2. The Parting Testaments of the Four Vidyādharas

1. *Rig 'dzin bzhi'i zhal chems 'das rjes kyi yi ge*, *DNZ*, vol. 2 (*kha*), 7–15. Second source: *VNT*, vol. *e*, 304–31.
2. *dGa' rab rdo rje'i zhal chems tshig gsum gnad du brdeg pa.*
3. This refers to the miraculous circumstances of Garab Dorje's birth. His mother, an ordained nun and a virgin, frightened and ashamed by her pregnancy, tried to rid herself of her child and left the baby for dead in an ashpit. Days later, he was discovered very much alive and radiant with health.
4. *'Jam dpal bshes gnyen gyi zhal chems sgom nyams drug pa.*

5. We have adopted the wording of *VNT*, which has *yul la snang ba'i ye she*, rather than the Shechen edition, which has *'di ni snang ba'i ye shes*.
6. We have followed the wording of *VNT*, which has *gnas brten pa lus gyi yul dang*, rather than the Shechen edition, which has *gnas brten pa yul gyi yul dang*.
7. The Tibetan text reads *rgya mdud kyi dril lugs kyis lu gu rgyud kyi khungs bcad pa'o*.
8. *Śrīsiṃha'i zhal chems gzer bu bdun pa*.
9. We have followed the wording of *VNT*, which has *mi 'gyur sa la gzer chen btab pa'i phyir*, rather than the Shechen version, which has *mi 'gyur la la gzer chen btab pa'i phyir*.
10. Here *VNT* reads *rig pa chos min gyi gzer*.
11. *Ye she mdo'i zhal chems bzhag thabs bzhi pa*.

3. The Net of Purity: A Ritual for the Elaborate Empowerment

1. *sPros bcas kyi dbang chog tshangs pa'i drwa ba*, *DNZ*, vol. 2 (*kha*), 17–34.
2. *dBang gi gnad yig*. Source not located.
3. *dBang bzhi'i dus dang mtshan ma bstan pa'i phra tig*, *VNT*, vol. 4 (*ya*), 220–21.

4. A Clear Exposition of the Names for the Elaborate Mandala

1. *dKyil 'khor spros bcas kyi ming gi rim pa gsal bar byed pa*, *DNZ*, vol. 2 (*kha*), 35–38.

5. The Net of Precious Gems: A Ritual for the Unelaborate Empowerment

1. *sPros med kyi dbang chog rin po che'i drwa ba*, *DNZ*, vol. 2 (*kha*), 39–61.
2. *Phra tig rin chen dag*. The source has not been located.
3. *sPros pa med pa'i dbang gi phra tig*, *VNT*, vol. 4 (*ya*), 283.
4. For a discussion of the different kinds of nirmāṇakāya, see *TPQ, Book 2*, 293ff.
5. For a discussion of the ever-youthful vase body, see *TPQ, Book 2*, 236.
6. *dBang gi phra tig*. Source not located.
7. *bLa ma yang tig* (*yid bzhin nor bu*).
8. *gNad yig*. Source not located.
9. For a discussion of the qualities of realization and elimination, see *TPQ, Book 1*, 215ff and 387ff.
10. *Byin rlabs sprin phung ye shes 'bebs pa*.
11. *gNad yig bum pa'i brda' don*.
12. The translation of the eight following lines is conjectural. It is a highly technical description of the mandala. We have been unable to find precise information

regarding its details. The Tibetan text reads as follows: *gru bzhi pa ni cha bzhir bgo // nang gi cha gnyis bum pa'i lto // gsum pa phyed bgos phyi thig gi // g.yas g.yon lto ba'i bzhi cha re//mtshan ma byas la gyen mthur gdab // de yang phyed du bgos pa yi // shar dang lho ni bum pa'i gsham // nub dang byang ni kha yin te // logs zur gang rung rtse nas bskor // logs na bskor na bzhi pa yis // shar lho'i phyogs la bum gdan bya // nub byang sgangs po kha rgyan bri // zur nas bskor na shar dang lho'i // bzhi pa ril po bum pa'i gdan.*

6. The Net of Lotuses: A Ritual for the Extremely Unelaborate Empowerment

1. *Shin tu spros med kyi dbang chog pad ma'i drwa ba*, *DNZ*, vol. 2 (*kha*), 63–79.
2. See chapter 2, note 3.
3. The eye of flesh refers to the ability to see all forms, gross or subtle, of the trichiliocosm.
4. *Phra tig rin chen rgyan spras*. Source not located.

7. The Adornment of the Four Continents: An Offering Ritual of the Five Mandalas

1. *gLing bzhi rgyan gyi man dal*, *DNZ*, vol. 2 (*kha*), 81–86.

8. The Net of Light: A Ritual for the Supremely Unelaborate Empowerment

1. *Rab tu spros med kyi dbang chog 'od kyi drwa ba*, *DNZ*, vol. 2 (*kha*), 87–99.
2. "King Free of Doubt," an alternative name for the buddha Amoghasiddhi.
3. The Tibetan for this obscure expression reads *lcags sdong gi 'dril stabs kyi kha sbubs la mtha' dril cig.*
4. This is probably a reference to the empowerment ritual given in *VNT*.
5. *dBang rnam par phye ba* . Source not located.
6. *Phra tig*. The full title of this text is *shin tu spros pa med pa'i dbang gi phra tig.* See *VNT*, vol. *ma*, 333.

9. The Wish-Fulfilling Net: An Offering Ritual of the Five Mandalas of the Five Offering Substances

1. *lNga tshan lnga'i man dal 'bul ba'i cho ga yid bzhin drwa ba*, *DNZ*, vol. 2 (*kha*), 101–2.

10. The Wish-Fulfilling Sea: A Ritual for the Offering of Gaṇacakra

1. *Tshogs mchod kyi rim pa yid bzhin rgya mtsho*, *DNZ*, vol. 2 (*kha*), 103–13. Second source: *LYT*, vol. 1 (*e*), 297.

11. The Heart Essence Mother and Child: The Stainless Words, a Guide That Brings Together the Two Traditions, Mother and Child, of the Secret Heart Essence of the Great Perfection

1. *rDzogs pa chen po gsang ba snying thig ma bu'i bka' srol chu bo gnyis 'dus kyi khrid yig dri med zhal lung*, *DNZ*, vol. 2 (*kha*), 115–231.
2. In the light of what Kongtrul says in his colophon, we have interpreted this line as referring to the great treasure revealer Terdak Lingpa and his daughter and lineage holder, Mingyur Paldrön.
3. *A ti bkod pa chen po'i rgyud*.
4. *Rig pa rang shar gyi rgyud*.
5. *bDud rtsi 'byung ba'i rgyud*.
6. *Dam tshig mchog gi rgyud*.
7. *kLong gsal gyi rgyud*.
8. Ibid.
9. Ibid.
10. This refers to the four volumes of the pith instructions of the Heart Essence (Nyingtik) that had been written in different inks and concealed by Vimalamitra in the cliff of Trakmar Gekong near Samye Chimpu.
11. Most histories of Buddhism in Tibet list Nyima Bum as the son of Zhangtön.
12. More commonly known as Melong Dorje.
13. In other words, conceptual obscurations and the obscurations created by defilement.
14. *sGra thal 'gyur rtsa ba'i rgyud*.
15. The text is not located.
16. *Kar ma snying thig* (*Karma Nyingtik*).
17. *Bi ma'i snying thig* (*Vima Nyingtik*, or *VNT*).
18. *Pad ma snying thig* (*Pema Nyingtik*).
19. *Bi ma'i snying thig ma bu*.
20. Probably Tai Situ Pema Nyinche Wangpo (1774–1853), the root teacher of Jamgön Kongtrul.
21. Orgyen Terdak Lingpa Gyurme Dorje (O rgyan gter bdag gling pa 'gyur med rdo rje, 1646–1711), also called Minling Trichen and Minling Terchen, the founder of the great monastery of Mindröling, a major treasure revealer (*gter ston*) renowned for his vast learning and high accomplishment. He played a

crucial role in the preservation of the teaching and practice of the Nyingma tradition.

22. Mingyur Paldrön (Mi 'gyur dpal sgron), daughter of Terdak Lingpa, was responsible for the restoration of Mindröling monastery following the Dzungar invasion of 1717. A brilliant teacher, she wrote several important meditation manuals and played a decisive role in the preservation of the teachings of the Great Perfection. See https://treasuryoflives.org/biographies/view/Mingyur-Peldron.
23. *sGra thal 'gyur gyi rgyud.*
24. *bDe chen lam bzang.* See Kongtrul's colophon to the present guide, p. 266.
25. *mKha' 'gro snying thig* (*Khandro Nyingtik*).
26. *mKha' 'gro yang tig* (*Khandro Yangtik*).
27. Katok Rikdzin Tsewang Norbu (Ka thog rig 'dzin tshe dbang nor bu, 1698–1755). Master of wide, eclectic, and nonsectarian interests—as it were, rime *avant la lettre*. He was instrumental in the preservation of the then-suppressed Jonang tradition.
28. *rDor sems snying tig.*
29. *Bai ro snying tig.*
30. *gSang ba snying thig gi bab lugs chen mo 'am yang tig lo rgyus rin po che'i phreng ba* (*LYT*).
31. *Nges shes 'dren pa'i lcags kyu.*
32. Līlavajra, *Dam tshig phra rgyas, Samayānuśayanirdeśa* (P.T. 4745).
33. See *TPQ, Book 2*, 210ff.
34. *Dri med rgyal po bshags pa'i rgyud.*
35. *Dam tshig mchog gi rgyud.*
36. For a definition of the buddha fields of luminous character, see *TPQ, Book 2*, 294–5.
37. *dMigs gtad gsal bar byed pa'i sgron me nyams su len pa'i sgom khrigs chen mo.* This is a text belonging to *The Agate-Lettered Instructions* (*Phra yig can*), *VNT*, vol. 2 (*wam*), 48.
38. *'Od gsal snying po'i don khrid*, *LYT*, vol. 1 (*e*), 333–88.
39. *gNad gsum chos nyid 'khor lo* (*LYT*).
40. The syllable *hūṃ* emits rays of light, and as they are gathered back, one receives empowering blessings. One then transforms into a three-pronged vajra, and one stands in the vajra posture. Then the teacher, in the form of the letter *hūṃ*, shoots into the center of oneself visualized as a vajra, and one's mind and the teacher's mind become one.
41. *Zangs yig can*, *VNT*, vol. *e*, 362.
42. The tummo fire is blissful, bright, hot, and swift.
43. *Yi ge dmar ru'i rgyab yig.* This text belongs to *The Agate-Lettered Instructions* (*VNT*).
44. The text continues with the words *lnga tshom lta bu'i ka dpe ma mi dgos*, the meaning of which is obscure.

45. *sNyan brgyud chung ngu ye shes rang snang* (*LYT*).
46. *bLa ma yang tig yid bzhin nor bu* (*LYT*).
47. *ba byung.*
48. For an explanation of the cosmic buddha Mahāsāgara (Gangs chen mtsho), see *TPQ, Book 2*, 440n465.
49. *Tshangs chen gyi bskal pa chen po*, a name of the nirmāṇakāya field.
50. *Tshangs pa rnga sgra'i zhing khams*, a name of the sambhogakāya field.
51. *dNngos grub rgya mtsho* (*LYT*).
52. *Chos spyod chen mo*. Source not located.
53. The four features of the vase breath are inhaling, filling up, turning, and expelling the breath like an arrow.
54. *bDe stong bdud rtsi'i sprin phung* (*LYT*).
55. *ro ma.*
56. *rkyang ma.*
57. The *A*-stroke is a fiery flame visualized in the shape of the inverted downward stroke of the Tibetan letter *A*. It is located at the junction of the three channels, four fingers below the navel center.
58. *Sems nyid ngal gso'i don khrid*. See p. 329.
59. *'Byung bzhi zad pa'i rgyud.*
60. *'dus shes dang rlung thams cad dran pa rang yal du btang nas.*
61. *'dzin yul tshor sogs sdud byed kyi dwangs ma mig gi shes pa rang dag.*
62. *lTa sgom 'byed pa'i lde'u mig sbas pa mig 'byed, VNT*, vol. *e*, 375.
63. The Tibetan text has *de dag la'ang chos can spyi ste rdzogs pa chen po spyi dang / chos nyid rang gi bye brag ces yang gsang thig le'i man ngag.*
64. Mingyur Paldrön in *The Excellent Path of Great Bliss* specifies these as "who is watching," "what is watched (the nature of phenomena)," "how this nature is watched (that is, without biased partiality)," and "what is attained by watching (the dharmakāya in which there is neither out nor in)." Collected Works of Minling Jetsun Mingyur Paldrön, vol. 2. (*wam*), 443–44. Dehra Dun: Mindröling Monastery, 2017.
65. *sGron ma skor bzhi*. This cycle belongs to *The Copper-Lettered Instructions* (*VNT*).
66. *sPyod pa bsdus pa'i sgron ma* (*VNT*).
67. *'khor 'das ru shan.*
68. *Khregs chod ye babs sor bzhag* (*LYT*).
69. Respectively, *rGyab yig nam mkha' dri med* and *rTog med nam mkha'i sprin phung*. Both texts belong to *LYT*.
70. *Tshig gsum gnad du rdeg pa*, the first of *The Parting Testaments of the Four Vidyādharas*, found in *The Gold-Lettered Instructions* (*VNT*).
71. *bzhi cha gsum bral.*
72. *tha mal gyi rig pa.*
73. *Yang gsang sgra rgyud.*
74. *Nor bu phra bkod pa'i rgyud.*

75. *rMad byung gi rgyud.*
76. Source not located.
77. Such as the thought that it is something important, something that one should do.
78. *khregs chod ye babs sor bzhag* (LYT).
79. This is perhaps a reference to the teaching tradition of Terdak Lingpa recorded in *The Excellent Path of Great Bliss* by Mingyur Paldrön.
80. *Nam mkha' 'dri med* and *rTog med nam mkha'i sprin phung* (LYT).
81. *Tshogs mchod yid bzhin rgya mtsho.* See p. 127.
82. *Hevajra tantra. dPal kye rdo rje'i rgyud.* (BDRC UT3JT13352_011_0000, p 32.)
83. *'das rjes.* This is *The Second Testament of the Buddha, DNZ*, vol. 2 (*kha*), 4. It is also found in *The Gold-Lettered Instructions* (*VNT*).
84. *kLong gsal gyi rgyud.*
85. *bDud rtsi ljon shing 'od gsal gyi gnad yig* (*LYT*).
86. *mngon sum rang thog tu dbab pa.*
87. *nyams len lag len du 'dril ba'i khyad par.* In the present text, the second and seventh features have exactly the same names (*nyam myong gong 'phel gyi khyad par*). This is undoubtedly a scribal error. For the sake of clarity, we have adopted the wording of Mingyur Paldrön's *Excellent Path of Great Bliss.*
88. Like an arrow maker examining an arrow.
89. Usually, the nirmāṇakāya gaze is directed slightly downward, as it is mentioned below in the key point for the sense door.
90. And pass into the wrong channel.
91. Source not located. The explanation of these seven complementary postures is given in *Thod rgal gyi gdams pa*, in The Collected Works of Terdak Lingpa Gyurme Dorje, vol. 14, p. 53. Dehra Dun: Khochhen Tulku, 1998.
92. *Yang zab chos nyid kyi 'khor lo* (*not located*).
93. *Nyams len gnad kyi sgron me, LYT*, vol. 2 (*wam*), 187.
94. *gNad gsum chos nyid kyi 'khor lo* (*LYT*).
95. *Nyams len gnad kyi sgron me, LYT*, vol. 2 (*wam*), 187–89.
96. *khra khang*, a structure with apertures in the four directions.
97. *mngon sum rang gnad du phab pa'i don*—an introduction that strikes at the actual key point—that is, direct perception of awareness.
98. For a discussion of the cause tantra, see *TPQ, Book 2*, 98.
99. *sGron ma 'bar ba'i rgyud.*
100. The Tibetan text here is obscure. We have followed the oral explanation of Dilgo Khyentse Rinpoche.
101. This quotation is from *The Third Testament* of the second cycle of *The Three Testaments* (*VNT*, vol. *e*, 301).
102. *gSang ba spyod rgyud.*
103. *sGom khrigs chen mo.* See this chapter, note 36.
104. *Dung yig can* (*VNT*).

105. *dPe don gsal byed sgron me* (*LYT*).
106. *chos nyid mngon sum.*
107. *nyams snang gong 'phel.*
108. *rig pa tshad phebs.*
109. *chos nyid zad sa.*
110. *rtsa ka ti shel gyi sbu gu can.*
111. Although not named here, this is "the lamp of flesh—namely, the heart" (*tsitta sha'i sgron ma*).
112. *shes rab rang byung gi sgron ma.*
113. *dbyings rnam par dag pa'i sgron ma.*
114. *thig le stong pa'i sgron ma.*
115. Spirits that have animal heads and human bodies, renowned for the beauty of their voices.
116. *gNad gsum chos nyid 'khor lo* (*LYT*).
117. *Yang zab ye shes 'khor lo* (*LYT*).
118. *'byams pa bzhi.*
119. *Yang zab ye shes 'khor lo*, *LYT*, vol. 2 (*wam*), 265.
120. *Zangs yig can*, *VNT*, vol. 1 (*e*).
121. *Gegs sel bdud rtsi'i ljon shing* (*LYT*).
122. *Gegs sel sgron ma snang byed* (*LYT*).
123. *Gegs sel ye shes dri med* (*LYT*).
124. *mda' srong gi mig.*
125. *'Od gsal ye shes 'khor lo.* (Source not located.)
126. *Natural Rest in the Primordial Flow*, *Khregs chod ye babs sor gzhag*, *LYT*, vol. 1 (*e*), 386–88.
127. *Khregs chod kyi rgyab yig nam mkha' dri med* (*LYT*).
128. *Nyi zla kha sbyor gyi rgyud.*
129. *dus ma 'gyur bar snang ba 'gyur.*
130. A day of samādhi (*bsam gtan gyi zhag*) corresponds to the period during which a practitioner was able to remain in concentration without any interruption by thoughts.
131. *Nyams len gnad kyi sgron me* (*LYT*).
132. *chos nyid bar do'i snang ba la 'jug pa shes pa'i gnad.*
133. *grol ba lus kyi gnad.*
134. *mthar phyin pa ngo shes pa'i gnad.*
135. *'Pho ba 'od gsal snying po. LYT*, vol. 2 (*wam*), 313–16.
136. *gzhan snang longs spyod rdzogs pa.* This is another name for the nirmāṇakāya of luminous character. See *TPQ, Book 2*, 293ff and 465n557.
137. *'Das rjes don khrid.* Although the title of this text seems to refer to a commentary on the *Three Testaments*, it in fact refers to nothing more than the *Testaments* themselves. See the Shechen Collection of Rare Books. The quotation given here has not been located. *Zhe chen mkhar dmar gsang sngags bstan rgyas gling du bzhugs pa'i dpe dkon phyogs bsdus*, vol. 53, 3–10. (BDRC MW2PD17514)

138. *Yid bzhin nor bu skor gsum, LYT*, vol. 2 (*wam*).
139. *bDud rtsi'i rgyal po* (*LYT*).

12. The Luminous Lamp: An Empowerment Ritual for the Secret Cycle of the Great Perfection

1. *gSang skor gyi dbang gi lag len gsal ba'i sgron me, DNZ*, vol. 2 (*kha*), 233–46. Second source: *ZYT*, vol. 2 (*wam*), 33–51.
2. *gSang ba gnad kyi me long.* See "The Heart of Practical Instructions," in chapter 13, p. 289.
3. *de bzhin du thog ma'i sangs rgyas dang sems can 'od mthong ba las rang ngo ma shes 'khrul pa shar.* The text here is a paraphrase of the original tantra, and its meaning is obscure. The translation is conjectural.
4. *dBang rin po che'i 'khor lo* (BDRC MW1KG14783_E1B05B, p. 36b).

13. Guiding Instructions

1. *mChog gsang lam khrid chen mo, DNZ*, vol. 2 (*kha*), 247–55. Second source: *ZYT*, vol. 2 (*wam*), 51–55.
2. *brda skor sa la bkod pa / de shel gyis bteg la dpe don rtag gsum gyis ngo sprad.* After careful inquiry, we have been unable to elucidate the meaning of this obscure passage.
3. At this point in *The Profound Innermost Essence*, from which this text is taken, there is the following statement: *sgra 'od zer gsum gyi 'char tshul ngo sprad pa*, "the way of arising of sounds, lights, and rays is also introduced."
4. *Lag khrid snying po. DNZ*, vol. 2 (*kha*), 251–55. Second source: *ZYT*, vol. 2 (*wam*), 147–53.
5. Here, the Shechen edition has *mig kho na nas dvangs phyin par lam ston nas / nam mkha'i dkyil der tse re ma yengs bar gtad pas / dran rtog yal yul ji shar ba gcig las ma 'phags pa byang bu la brtod pa 'phar ba bzhin dvangs zin nas.* We have followed the version in *The Profound Innermost Essence*, vol. 2 (*wam*), 151, which has *mig kho nas dangs phyin par lam ston nas / nam mkha'i dkyil der tse re ma yengs par gtad pas / dran rtog yal yul ji ltar shar yang sa gcig las ma 'phags pa byang bu la rtod pa 'phar ba bzhin rang sa zin nas.*
6. For the discussion of precious spontaneous presence, see *TPQ, Book 2*, 239–40.
7. See ch. 12, note 2.

14. General Teachings on the Great Perfection

1. *sLob dpon rin po che pad ma 'byung gnas kyis mdzad pa'i phyi chos mdo sngags thun mong gi lam rim rin chen spungs pa, DNZ*, vol. 2 (*kha*), 257–64. Second source: *KSG*, vol. 83, 153–57. Chengdu: Si khron mi rigs dpe skrun khang, 2009.

2. *Textual gloss:* With the exhaustion of [conceptual] certainty regarding the ground, the fundamental nature is actualized. With the exhaustion of [conceptual] certainty regarding the path, the path itself is perfected.
3. *Phyi bshad rin chen spungs pa'i bsdus don.*
4. *gSang sngags lam gyi rim pa rin po che gsal ba'i srong me. DNZ*, vol. 2 (*kha*), 265–72. Second source: *KSG*, vol. 83, 157–63.
5. *Nang bshad gsang sngags lam rim gyi lo rgyus.* This note was composed by Nyak Jñānakumāra.
6. *Textual gloss:* The subduing of both the object and subject of apprehension, the possession of both the wisdom that knows the nature of phenomena and the wisdom that knows phenomena in their multiplicity, and the transcending of both permanence and annihilation. ["Subduing," "possessing," and "transcending" translate the three elements of the expression *bcom ldan 'das*, the Tibetan equivalent of the Sanskrit *bhagavan.*]
7. *Textual gloss:* The twofold supreme glory refers to the ground and the result.
8. *Textual gloss:* The embodiment of all the wisdom of the buddhas.
9. *Textual gloss:* The genuine state free of all deceit corresponds to the domain of action free of delusion.
10. *Nang chos gsang sngags lam rim sa bcad.*
11. *gSang sngags lam rim gyi snying po sems nyid gcer ston lag khrid lnga pa. DNZ*, vol. 2 (*kha*), 272–76. Second source: *KSG*, vol. 83, 163–67.
12. This explanatory passage is by Nyak Jñānakumāra.
13. The example for the first point and the beginning of the second point are missing in the Shechen edition. We have therefore added the text (in brackets) taken from *KSG*, vol. 83, 166.
14. *gSang sngags lam gyi rim pa'i don khrid ngo sprod du gdab pa. DNZ*, vol. 2 (*kha*), 276–83. Second source: *KSG*, vol. 83, 167–73.
15. *rGan po mkhar btsug gi gdams pa sangs rgyas ngo sprod.*
16. *rGan mo mdzub btsug gi gdams pa.*

15. The Excellent Path to Enlightenment: A Three-Part Guide for Meditation on the Three Excellent Instructions of the Text *Finding Rest in the Nature of the Mind: A Teaching of the Great Perfection*

1. *rDzogs pa chen po sems nyid ngal gso'i gnas gsum dge ba gsum gyi don khrid byang chub lam bzang, DNZ*, vol. 2 (*kha*), 285–369. Second source: Collected Works of Longchenpa (Varanasi: Dodrubchen, 1965), 1–105.
2. In the Dodrubchen edition, this is spelled *Ratnaparvartha.*
3. The "seven buddhas of antiquity," *saptatatathāgata*, are the last three of the thousand buddhas of the *vyūhakalpa* (the glorious eon), followed by the first four of the thousand buddhas of the present *bhadrakalpa* (the good eon), of whom Śākyamuni is the fourth and last.

4. Respectively, *rtogs pa brjod pa'i mdo sde dbang po'i rgyal po*, *byang chub ltung bshags*, *de bzhin gshegs pa'i mtshan mang*, *sangs rgyas stong rtsa*, and *zhi khro skong gi phyag*.
5. It is uncertain whether Cunda the upāsaka is the same person as Cunda the blacksmith, who is said to have served the Buddha his last meal.
6. For the different kinds of generosity, see *TPQ, Book 1*, 281–82.
7. The ten dharma activities are as follows: copying scriptures, making offerings, giving alms, listening to the teachings, reading the scriptures, memorizing them, instructing others, reciting prayers, reflecting, and meditating.
8. Pāramitās number seven to ten are not so much separate perfections as they are qualities accompanying the previous six pāramitās. They are skillful means, strength, aspiration, and primordial wisdom. See *TPQ, Book 2*, 280.
9. *sgyu 'phrul drwa ba chen po.*
10. Mi g.yo ba.
11. In this visualization, the sun and moon disks are side by side, not one on top of the other.
12. The Dodrubchen edition has *oṃ vajra caṇḍa mahāroṣana hūṃ phaṭ.*
13. Although not specifically identified as such, this could be an abbreviated reference to *The Sarvadurgatipariśodhana Tantra: The Tantra of the Purification of All the Lower Destinies.*
14. *khro bo 'jig rten gsum las rnam par rgyal ba.*
15. Dodrubchen has *oṃ vajrasatva krodha ānalārga mahākrodha drava drava vidrava vidrava sarva apāya nāśaya nāśaya hara hara prana hūṃ phaṭ.*
16. For the eight glorious attributes, see *TPQ, Book 2*, 465n553.
17. *brjod med don gyi gshags pa.*
18. *de bzhin nyid kyi ting nge 'dzin.*
19. *kun tu snang ba'i ting nge 'dzin.*
20. *rgyu'i ting nge 'dzin.*
21. Respectively *zhi ba rin po che'i drwa ba* and *khro bo snang ba rgyan.*
22. *'di ni dbang rdzogs.*
23. *thams cad lha dang lha mo'i ngang.*
24. *dmigs pa yul gyi blo can.* See *TPQ, Book 2*, 269.
25. *rig pa rang snang gi blo can.* See *TPQ, Book 2*, 265, 455n507.
26. *yid kyi shes pa.*
27. *nyon yid kyi shes pa.*
28. This is what the text says in both the Shechen and Dodrubchen editions. Normally, the sixth consciousness is the mental consciousness itself.
29. *de ltar rang gsal rten med kyi shes pa'ang phyi snang ba / nang phung po / bar 'gyu ba.* This is an attempted translation of an obscure sentence, which is nevertheless present in both the Shechen and Dodrubchen editions.
30. The text appears to stipulate that the wind emerges from the lower ends (*mar sna*) of rasanā and lalanā. This is difficult to envisage and is at variance with the autocommentary on the part of the root text in question. For the sake of easy

comprehension, and after consultation with competent authorities, we have omitted this detail.

31. *'dzin rtog.*
32. *gzung rtog.* See Longchen Rabjam, *Finding Rest in the Nature of the Mind, Sems nyid ngal gso*, in Collected Works of Longchenpa, 199.
33. The translation is not certain. The text reads *spyod lam gang byed dang snang stong gtad yal stong pa gnyis bsres nas bsgom zhing.*
34. The meaning of this literal translation is not certain. The text reads *rig stong so sor rang rig / dug lnga rang grol rjes med / ngo bo dang khyad par ram / chos can dang chos nyid rig pa'i cha tsam la tshang zhing.*

Part Six: Texts Taken from The Trilogy of Natural Openness and Freedom

1. *bsTan bcos kyi dkar chag rin po che'i mdzod khang.* See Nyoshul Khenpo Jamyang Dorje, *A Marvelous Garland of Rare Gems: Biographies of Masters of Awareness in the Dzogchen Lineage*, translated by Richard Barron (Junction City, CA: Padma, 2005), 142.

16. A Prayer Belonging to *The Natural Openness and Freedom of the Nature of the Mind*

1. *Sems nyid rang grol gyi gsol 'debs, DNZ*, vol. 2 (*kha*), 371–74.

17. An Essential Meditation Guide for the Stages of the Path according to *The Natural Openness and Freedom of the Nature of the Mind: A Teaching of the Great Perfection*

1. *rDzogs pa chen po sems nyid rang grol gyi lam rim snying po'i don khrid, DNZ*, vol. 2 (*kha*), 375–94. Second source: Collected Works of Longchenpa, 34–56.
2. The Shechen edition has *rtog pa de nyid 'phro brdo ba'i tshe*, "when thoughts unfold with great force." Since the notion of unfolding has already been dealt with in the preceding paragraph, we have followed the more easily intelligible reading of the Dodrubchen edition: *gnas brdo ba'i tshe.*
3. This is the expression in the Shechen edition: *rig rtsal sa le gsal ba lhag mthong.* The Dodrubchen edition has *rig ge gsal ba lhag mthong*, "the state of clarity and knowing is deep insight."
4. *mtshan nyid sna tshogs su 'char ba.*
5. This renders the text in the Shechen edition: *snang srid rgyas theb kun bzang ba.* The Dodrubchen edition reads *snang srid rgya theg kun bzang ba*: "it is the universal vehicle, Samantabhadra."
6. Source not located.
7. Here the Shechen edition has *rig pa zang thal skad cid ma'i rang 'gros rtsar shor*

nang shor la 'di yin gza' gtad med pa. The meaning is scarcely intelligible. By contrast, the Dodrubchen edition (which we have followed) has *rig pa zang thal skad cig ma rang grol thal grol 'di yin gza' gtad med pa'i ngang la goms par mdzod.*

8. The Shechen edition has *gal med,* "it is not important." The Dodrubchen edition has *'gal med,* "there is no conflict."
9. The Dodrubchen edition has *'di gar shog,* "stay in the here and now."
10. Source not located.
11. The Shechen edition has *dregs pa'i rtog pa,* "conceited, prideful thoughts." The Dodrubchen edition reads *rags pa'i rtogs pa,* "gross, unsubtle thoughts."
12. The Shechen edition reads *gnas pa bde bas,* "since stillness is blissful." The Dodrubchen edition reads *gnas pa med pas,* "since there is no stillness."
13. The Shechen edition has *skyon thams cad 'dzin pa'i cha las grol bas.* The Dodrubchen edition has *skyon thams cad 'dzin pa'i cha las grub pas,* "since all defects are produced from clinging."
14. The Shechen edition has *sa lam rang lugs su rdzogs te.* The Dodrubchen edition has *sems rang lugs su rdzogs,* "the mind is perfect in its natural state."
15. Here, "the mind" (*sems*) no doubt refers to the consciousness of the universal ground.
16. The fourth and fifth endowments are omitted in the Shechen edition. They are added here taken from the Dodrubchen edition: *de nas 'byung bzhi thim tshul gyi snang ba tha dad pa ni bzhi ldan no / de nas 'od gsal ye shes la 'jug pas sku lngar grol ba ni lnga ldan no.*
17. The Shechen edition has *sangs gnas*: "the place of purity [of buddhahood]." The Dodrubchen edition has *mngal gnas,* "the place of the womb," which corresponds to what is usually said.
18. The Shechen edition has *bskyed rdzogs dvangs shing dag pa*: "the pure and clear stages of generation and perfection." We have followed the more plausible text in the Dodrubchen edition, which has *bskyed rdzogs dang zhing dag pa.*
19. *'khor 'das gang ltar snang dus nyid nas.* The Dodrubchen edition here is less plausible, *kha dog gang ltar,* "whatever colors appear."
20. The Shechen edition has *chos sku dang bral ba,* "without the dharmakāya." The Dodrubchen edition, which we have followed, has the easier reading: *chos sku spros pa bral ba.*
21. Here the Shechen edition has *stong gsal,* "empty luminosity." We have followed the reading of the Dodrubchen edition, which has *nang gsal,* "inner luminosity."

18. The Natural Openness and Freedom of the Dharmatā: A Teaching of the Great Perfection

1. *rDzogs pa chen po chos nyid rang grol, DNZ,* vol. 2 (*kha*), 395–411. Second source: Collected Works of Longchenpa, 60–79.
2. The Shechen edition has *dngos gzhi'i lta bsgom mkha' sogs gzhir gol bas.* We have followed the slightly more plausible Dodrubchen reading, which has *bzhi*

(four) instead of *gzhi* (ground). In any case, the meaning of the word *mkha'* (space) is obscure. Unable to clarify it with certainty, we have associated it with *lta ba* (the view).

3. The Shechen edition has *brtan med*, "unstable." The Dodrubchen edition, which has been followed here, has *gtan med*, "utterly without existence."
4. The Shechen edition has *snying med*, "without courage, essence." The Dodrubchen edition, which is followed, has *gnyis med*, "nonduality."
5. The Shechen edition has *rtsal 'byin*, "give skill." The Dodrubchen edition, which is followed, has *rtsad 'byin*, "eradicate."
6. The Shechen edition has *bgod*, "divide." The Dodrubchen edition, which is followed, has *'gog*, "stop."
7. Words appear to be missing from this line in the Shechen edition. Following the Dodrubchen edition, we have added "echoes" (*brag cha*). Moreover, Dodrubchen also gives here the usually cited example of "the cities of the gandharvas" (*dri za'i grong khyer*) instead of the somewhat redundant "reflection" found here in the Shechen edition.
8. The Shechen edition has *long*, "time, leisure." The Dodrubchen edition reads *lung*, "valley."
9. The Shechen edition has *gzung 'dzin mi rtogs shing*, "they do not realize the object to be apprehended and the apprehending subject." The Dodrubchen edition, which we have followed, has *gzung 'dzin med rtogs shing*, "they will realize that there is neither apprehending subject nor something to be apprehended."
10. For the four stages of luminosity, see *TPQ, Book 2*, 172.
11. For the eighty mental states, see *TPQ, Book 2*, 173ff.
12. A day of samādhi (*bsam gtan gyi zhag*) corresponds to the period during which a practitioner was able to remain in concentration without any interruption by thoughts.
13. For example, as the six munis that appear in the six realms.
14. *lhun gyis grub.*
15. The Shechen edition has *bsgom*, "to meditate." The Dodrupchen edition has 'dam, "to choose." Neither of these alternatives seems plausible.
16. For the specific meaning of the exclusive self-experience of the sambhogakāya, see *TPQ, Book 2*, 292.
17. The Dodrubchen edition, which is adopted, has *rigs lnga*, "five families." The Shechen edition has *rigs gsum*, "three families."

19. The Natural Openness and Freedom of the State of Equality: A Teaching of the Great Perfection

1. *rDzogs pa chen po mnyam nyid rang grol. DNZ*, vol. 2 (*kha*), 413–36. Second source: Collected Works of Longchenpa, 99–126.
2. The Shechen edition reads *rgyu 'bras mi 'dog*, which is almost certainly a scribal

error. We have followed the wording of the Dodrubchen edition, which reads *rgyu 'bras ming 'dogs.*

3. Here the order of the Tibetan terms is *rang bzhin* (*stong pa*), *ngo bo* (*gsal ba*). This wording, found in the *All-Creating King Tantra,* is adopted by Longchenpa here. The *All-Creating King* was translated in the early period, and it was only later that the traditional order (*ngo bo stong pa, rang bzhin gsal ba*) came to be generally accepted. To avoid confusion for the reader, we have adopted this later usage. It should be noted that both terms, *ngo bo* and *rang bzhin*, are practically synonymous.
4. *glo bur mi sbyor ngo bo'i shes pa grol.* This is a conjectural rendering of a particularly obscure expression.
5. We have followed the Dodrubchen edition, which reads *rgyu 'bras 'das pas*, as distinct from the Shechen edition, which reads *rgyu 'bras 'das pa'i*. (The adherents of such vehicles never see the natural state, which transcends the law of cause and fruit).
6. For a presentation of kriyā tantra, see *TPQ, Book 2*, 100–103.
7. For ubhaya tantra, see ibid., 103–4.
8. For yoga tantra, see ibid., 104–6.
9. For mahāyoga, (that is, the generation stage), see ibid., 135–53.
10. For anuyoga (that is, the perfection stage), see ibid., 155–79.
11. For atiyoga (that is, the Great Perfection), see ibid., 231 and following.
12. The Shechen edition gives on both occasions (lines 1 and 2) *byang chub nyid*, "enlightenment itself." We have followed the Dodrubchen edition, which reads on the second line *byang chub sems.*
13. The Shechen edition reads *yan du chug*, "make it free." We have followed the Dodrubchen edition, which reads *yin du chug.*
14. The Shechen edition reads *lhun rdzogs rol pa*, "perfect and spontaneous display." We have followed the Dodrubchen edition, which reads *lhun rdzogs rig pa.*
15. This is a reference to the three doors of perfect liberation, which constitute the nature of awareness. See *TPQ, Book 1*, 437, and *Book 2*, 265.
16. The Shechen edition reads *gang shar bshad kyang*, "however what arises is explained." We have followed the Dodrubchen edition, which reads *gang ltar bshad kyang.*
17. The Shechen edition reads *de bzhin nyid du sems dpa' zhog*, "place the bodhisattva in suchness." We have followed the Dodrubchen edition, which reads *de bzhin nyid du sems la zhog.*
18. The Shechen edition reads *sgom du sgom byed med*, "there is no meditator in meditation." We have followed the Dodrubchen edition, which reads *sgom dang sgom byed med.*
19. The Shechen edition reads *sprul rnam*, "all apparitions." We have followed the Dodrubchen edition, which reads *yul rnam.*
20. The Shechen edition reads *so so'i dngos por snang ba'i chos*, "phenomena that

appear as individual things." We have followed the Dodrubchen edition, which reads *sa sogs dngos por snang ba'i chos.*

21. The Shechen edition reads *mkha' dang nyid chos de bzhin dag pa la.* (The text here is clearly garbled.). We have followed the Dodrubchen edition, which reads *mkha' dang de bzhin nyid chos dag pa la.*
22. In the present context, the Tibetan word *ye shes* has two meanings: "primordial wisdom," which does not cognize dualistically, and "primordial knowing," which, owing to coemergent ignorance, cognizes objects dualistically from the very beginning.
23. The Shechen edition reads *'khor ba'i grangs las*, "from the number of samsara." We have followed the Dodrubchen edition, which reads *'khor ba'i grong las.*
24. The Shechen edition reads *rdzogs pa chen por grol* "free in great perfection." We have followed the Dodrubchen edition, which reads *mnyam rdzogs chen por grol.*
25. That is, the Wheel of the Collection of Syllables (*yi ge'i 'khor lo tshogs chen*). This refers to the luminous, nondual primordial wisdom. See *TPQ, Book 2*, 388n183.
26. For a detailed description, see *TPQ, Book 2*, 296–97.

20. An Ornament for Samantabhadra's Display: A Ritual of Homage Addressed to the Lineage Teachers of the Pith-Instruction Class of the Heart Essence of the Great Perfection

1. *rDzogs pa chen po man ngag snying thig gi bla ma brgyud pa'i rim pa mchod pa'i cho ga kun bzang rnam par rol ba'i rgyan, DNZ*, vol. 2 (*kha*), 437–77.
2. See *TPQ, Book 2*, 388n183.
3. *yang dag sgyu ma.* The perfectly pure illusions are the phenomena of nirvana—namely, the display of the kāyas and wisdoms.
4. The text here contains an unintelligible expression: *nor ba dri bzhin*, which is probably a scribal error for *yid bzhin nor bu*, "wish-fulfilling gem."
5. Mahābrahmā's Eon is the name of the nirmāṇakāya buddha field.
6. Terdak Lingpa.
7. For the root and branch samayas of the Great Perfection, see *TPQ, Book 2*, 211ff.

21. An Authorization Ritual for the Practice of Ekajaṭī, Protectress of the Doctrine, together with the Six Guardians of Her Retinue

1. *bKa' srung e ka dza ti de bdun gyi rjes gnang, DNZ*, vol. 2 (*kha*), 479–97.
2. *bKa' brgyad bde gshegs 'dus pa*, a terma text discovered by Nyang Nyima Özer (1124–1192).
3. *dNgos grub 'byung gter.*
4. *dPag bsam ljon shing.*

Bibliography

1. The Present Texts

The Source Volume

Jamgön Kongtrul Lodrö Taye, comp. *The Treasury of Precious Instructions. gDams ngag rin po che'i mdzod.* Vol. 2 (*kha*). Delhi: Shechen Publications, 1999.

The Translated Texts

Jamgön Kongtrul Lodrö Taye ('Jam mgon kong sprul blo gros mtha' yas). *An Authorization Ritual for the Practice of Ekajaṭī, Protectress of the Doctrine, together with the Six Guardians of Her Retinue. sNgags srung e ka ja ṭī sde bdun gyi rjes gnang.* In *DNZ*, vol. 2 (*kha*), 479–97.

———. *The Heart Essence Mother and Child: The Stainless Words, a Guide That Brings Together the Two Traditions, Mother and Child, of the Secret Heart Essence of the Great Perfection. rDzogs pa chen po gsang ba snying thig ma bu'i bka' srol chu bo gnyis 'dus kyi khrid yig dri med zhal lung.* In *DNZ*, vol. 2 (*kha*), 115–231.

———. *An Ornament for Samantabhadra's Display: A Ritual of Homage Addressed to the Lineage Teachers of the Pith-Instruction Class of the Heart Essence of the Great Perfection. rDzogs pa chen po man ngag snying thig gi bla ma brgyud pa'i rim pa mchod pa'i cho ga kun bzang rnam par rol pa'i rgyan.* In *DNZ*, vol. 2 (*kha*), 437–77.

Longchen Rabjam (kLong chen rab 'byams). *The Adornment of the Four Continents: An Offering Ritual of the Five Mandalas. Man dal 'bul ba'i cho ga gling bzhi rgyan gyur.* In *DNZ*, vol. 2 (*kha*), 81–86.

———. *A Clear Exposition of the Names for the Elaborate Mandala. dKyil 'khor spros bcas ming gi rim pa gsal bar byed pa.* In *DNZ*, vol. 2 (*kha*), 35–38.

———. *A Great Guide for the Supreme and Secret Path. mChog gsang lam khrid chen mo.* In *DNZ*, vol. 2 (*kha*), 247–51. Second source: *ZYT*, vol. 2 (*wam*), 51–55.

———. *An Essential Meditation Guide for the Stages of the Path according to the Natural Openness and Freedom of the Nature of the Mind: A Teaching of the Great Perfection. rDzogs pa chen po sems nyid rang grol gyi lam rim snying po'i don khrid.* In *DNZ*, vol. 2 (*kha*), 375–93. Second source: Collected Works of Longchenpa, 34–56. Varanasi: Dodrubchen, 1965.

———. *The Excellent Path to Enlightenment: A Three-Part Guide for Meditation on the Three Excellent Instructions of the Text "Finding Rest in the Nature of the Mind: A Teaching of the Great Perfection." rDzogs pa chen po sems nyid ngal gso'i gnas gsum dge ba gsum gyi don khrid byang chub lam bzang.* In *DNZ*, vol. 2 (*kha*), 285–369. Second source: Collected Works of Longchenpa, 1–105. Varanasi: Dodrubchen, 1965.

———. *The Heart of Practical Instructions. Lag khrid snying po.* In *DNZ*, vol. 2 (*kha*) 251–55. Second source: *ZYT*, vol. 2 (*wam*), 147–53.

———. *The Luminous Lamp: An Empowerment for the Secret Cycle of the Great Perfection. gSang skor gyi dbang gi lag len gsal ba'i sgron me.* In *DNZ*, vol. 2 (*kha*), 233–46. Second source: *ZYT*, vol. 2 (*wam*), 33–51.

———. *The Natural Openness and Freedom of the Dharmatā: A Teaching of the Great Perfection. rDzogs pa chen po chos nyid rang grol.* In *DNZ*, vol. 2 (*kha*), 395–411. Second source: Collected Works of Longchenpa, 60–79. Varanasi: Dodrubchen, 1965.

———. *The Natural Openness and Freedom of the State of Equality: A Teaching of the Great Perfection. rDzogs pa chen po mnyam nyid rang grol.* In *DNZ*, vol. 2 (*kha*), 413–36. Second source: Collected Works of Longchenpa, 99–126. Varanasi: Dodrubchen, 1965.

———. *The Net of Light: A Ritual for the Supremely Unelaborate Empowerment. Rab tu spros med kyi dbang chog 'od kyi drwa ba.* In *DNZ*, vol. 2 (*kha*), 87–99. Second source: *LYT*, vol. 1 (*e*), 263–79.

———. *The Net of Lotuses: A Ritual for the Extremely Unelaborate Empowerment. Shin tu spros med kyi dbang chog pad ma'i drwa ba.* In *DNZ*, vol. 2 (*kha*), 63–79. Second source: *LYT*, vol. 1 (*e*), 237–57.

———. *The Net of Precious Gems: A Ritual for the Unelaborate Mandala. sPros med kyi dbang chog rin po che'i drwa ba.* In *DNZ*, vol. 2 (*kha*), 39–61. Second source: *LYT*, vol. 1 (*e*), 204–30.

———. *The Net of Purity: A Ritual for the Elaborate Empowerment. sPros bcas kyi dbang chog tshangs pa'i drwa ba.* In *DNZ*, vol. 2 (*kha*), 17–34. Second source: *LYT*, vol. 1 (*e*), 174–200.

———. *A Prayer Belonging to the Natural Openness and Freedom of the Nature of the Mind. Sems nyid rang grol gyi gsol 'debs.* In *DNZ*, vol. 2 (*kha*), 371–74.

———. *The Wish-Fulfilling Net: An Offering Ritual of the Five Mandalas of the Five Substances. lNga tshan lnga'i man dal 'bul ba'i cho ga yid bzhin drwa ba.* In *DNZ*, vol. 2 (*kha*), 101–2.

———. *The Wish-Fulfilling Sea: A Ritual for the Offering of Gaṇacakra. Tshogs mchod kyi rim pa yid bzhin rgya mtsho.* In *DNZ*, vol. 2 (*kha*), 103–13.

Padmasambhava (Pad ma 'byung gnas). *The Essence of the Gradual Path of Secret Mantra: A Pointing-Out Instruction in Five Parts through Which the Nature of the Mind Is Nakedly Shown. gSang sngags lam rim gyi snying po sems nyid gcer ston lag khrid lnga pa.* In *DNZ*, vol. 2 (*kha*), 272–76. Second source: *KSG*, vol. 83, 163–67.

———. *A Heap of Jewels: An Outer Presentation of the Common Gradual Path of Sutra and Mantra Composed by the Precious Master Padmasambhava. sLob dpon rin po che pad ma 'byung gnas kyis mdzad pa'i phyi chos mdo sngags thun mong gi lam rim rin chen spungs pa.* In *DNZ*, vol. 2 (*kha*), 257–64. Second source: *KSG*, vol 83. 153–57.

———. *Instructions for Meditation on the Gradual Path of the Secret Mantra Given in the Manner of an Introduction to the Nature of the Mind. gSang sngags lam gyi rim pa'i don khrid ngo sprod du gdab pa.* In *DNZ*, vol. 2 (*kha*), 276–83. Second source: *KSG*, vol. 83, 167–73.

———. *The Precious and Illuminating Lamp: A Gradual Path of the Secret Mantra. gSang sngags lam rim rin po che gsal ba'i sgron me.* In *DNZ*, vol. 2 (*kha*), 265–72. Second source: *KSG*, vol. 83, 157–63.

The Testaments of the Four Vidyādharas. Rig 'dzin bzhi'i zhal chems 'das rjes kyi yi ge. In *DNZ*, vol. 2 (*kha*), 7–15. Second source: *VNT*, vol. 1 (*e*), 304–31.

The Three Testaments of the Buddha: The Quintessence of the Key Points of the Pith Instruction Class of the Luminous Great Perfection. 'Od gsal rdzogs pa chen po man ngag sde'i gnad kyi bcud phur sangs rgyas 'das rjes gsum la sogs. In *DNZ*, vol. 2 (*kha*), 1–7. Second source: *VNT*, vol. 1 (*e*), 287–95.

2. Works Cited in the Texts

Scriptures (Kangyur)

The All-Creating King Tantra. Kun byed rgyal po. (NG 10)

The Assembly of Secrets Tantra. Guhyasamājatantra. gSang ba 'dus pa. (Toh. 442)

The Blazing Lamp Tantra. sGron ma 'bar ba'i rgyud. (*NG* 104)

Cakrasaṃvara Tantra. Cakrasaṃvaratantra. bDe mchog 'khor lo'i rgyud. (Toh. 385)

The Display of the Supreme Horse Tantra. rTa mchog rol pa'i rgyud. (*NG* 848)

The Essence of the Sun Tantra. Nyi ma'i snying po'i rgyud. (*not located*)

The Exhaustion of the Four Elements Tantra. 'Byung bzhi zad pa'i rgyud. (*not located*)

The Great Array of Ati Tantra. A ti bkod pa chen po'i rgyud. (*NG* 277)

The Great Net of Illusory Manifestations Tantra. Māyājālatantra. sGyu 'phrul drwa ba chen po'i rgyud. (Toh. 466)

The Heruka Galpo Tantra. He ru ka gal po'i rgyud. (*NG* 646)

The Luminous Expanse Tantra. kLong gsal gyi rgyud. (*NG* 139)

The Most Secret Words Tantra. Yang gsang sgra sgyud. (*NL*)

The Secret Essence Tantra. Guhyagarbhatantra. gSang ba snying po'i rgyud. (Toh. 832, *NG* 524)

The Source of Amṛta Tantra. bDud rtsi 'byung ba'i rgyud. (BDRC MWONGMCP37782)

The Stainless King of Confession Tantra. Dri med rgyal po bshags pa'i rgyud. (*NG* 557)

The Supreme Samaya Tantra. Dam tshig mchog gi rgyud. (*not located*)

The Tantra of the Array of Studded Jewels. Nor bu phra bkod pa'i rgyud. (*NG* 109)

The Tantra of Awareness Self-Arisen. Rig pa rang shar gyi rgyud. (*NG* 96)

The Tantra of Marvels. rMad byung gi rgyud. (BDRC WAOMGMCP48754)
The Tantra of Secret Action. gSang ba spyod rgyud. (*not located*)
The Tantra of Self-Arisen Perfection. rDzogs pa rang byung gi rgyud. (*NG* 94)
The Union of the Sun and Moon Tantra. Nyi zla kha sbyor gyi rgyud. (*NG* 214)
The Wheel of Precious Empowerments Tantra. dBang rin po che'i 'khor lo rgyud. (BDRC MW1KG14783_E1B05B, p. 36b)
The Word-Transcending Tantra. sGra thal 'gyur rtsa ba'i rgyud. (*NG* 95)

Treatises (Tengyur)

Līlavajra. *Subtle and Extensive Samayas. Samayānuśayanirdeśa. Dam tshig phra rgyas.* (P.T. 4745)

Tibetan Works

Karmapa Rangjung Dorje. *The Heart Essence of Karmapa. Kar ma snying thig.* (not located)
Longchen Rabjam. *The Innermost Essence of the Ḍākinīs. mKha' 'gro yang tig.* In *sNying thig ya bzhi*. Delhi: Shechen, 2021.
———. *The Innermost Essence of the Master: The Wish-Fulfilling Gem. bLa ma yang tig* (*yid bzhin nor bu*). In *sNying thig ya bzhi*. Delhi: Shechen, 2021.
———. *The Precious Treasury of the Supreme Vehicle. Theg mchog rin po che'i mdzod.* Collected Works of Longchenpa. Varanasi: Dodrubchen, 1965.
———. *The Profound Innermost Essence. Zab mo yang tig.* In *sNying thig ya bzhi*. Delhi: Shechen, 2021.
Padmasambhava. *The Heart Essence of the Ḍākinīs. mKha' 'gro snying thig.* In *sNying thig ya bzhi*. Delhi: Shechen, 2021.
———. *The Heart Essence of Padma. Pad ma'i snying thig.* In *sNying thig ya bzhi*. Delhi: Shechen, 2021.
Vairotsana. *The Heart Essence of Vairotsana. Bai ro snying tig.* (*not located*)
———. *The Heart Essence of Vajrasattva. rDor sems snying tig.* Delhi: Shechen, 2008.
Vimalamitra. *The Heart Essence of Vimala. Bi ma'i snying thig.* In *sNying thig ya bzhi*. Delhi: Shechen, 2021.
———. *The Secret Heart Essence [of Vimala]. gSang ba snying thig.* In *sNying thig ya bzhi*. Delhi: Shechen, 2021.

3. Reference Bibliography

Tibetan Texts

Collected Tantras of the Ancients. rNying ma rgyud 'bum. Dege: Dege Parkhang, 1991.
Collection of Rare Books Belonging to Zhechen Kharmar Sangngak Tengye Ling. Zhe chen mkhar dmar gsang sngags bstan rgyas gling du bzhugs pa'i dpe dkon phyogs bsdus. Vol. 53, 3–10. BDRC MW2PD17524.
Expanded Collection of the Nyingma Kama. sNga 'gyur bka' ma shin tu rgyas pa. Vol. 83, 153–73. Chengdu: Si khron mi rigs dpe skrun khang, 2009.

Guru Padmasambhava. *The Precious Garland (Rin chen phreng ba).* In *KSG*, vol. 83.

Khangsar Tenpai Wangchuk (Khang sar bsTan pa'i dbang phyug). *An Offering to Please the Omniscient Lord: A Word Commentary on "The Precious Treasury of the Fundamental Nature." rDzogs pa chen po gnas lugs rin po che'i mdzod kyi 'bru 'grel dpal ldan bla ma'i zhal lung kun mkhyen dgyes pa'i mchod sprin.* Beijing: Mi rigs dpe skrun khang, 2005.

———. *The One Sole Sphere of Luminosity: A Word Commentary on "The Precious Treasury of the Dharmadhātu." Chos dbyings rin po che'i mdzod kyi 'bru 'grel 'od gsal thig le nyag gcig.* Beijing: Mi rigs dpe skrun khang, 2005.

Longchen Rabjam. *Finding Rest in the Nature of the Mind. Sems nyid ngal gso.* Collected Works of Longchenpa. Varanasi: Dodrubchen, 1965.

———. *The Great Chariot: An Autocommentary on "Finding Rest in the Nature of the Mind." rDzogs pa chen po sems nyid ngal gso'i 'grel pa shing rta chen po.* Collected Works of Longchenpa. Varanasi: Dodrubchen, 1965.

Mingyur Paldrön (Mi 'gyur dpal gron). *The Excellent Path of Great Bliss: Instructions on the Heart Essence Mother and Child. sNying thig ma bu'i khrid yig bde chen lam bzang.* In Collected Work of Minling Jetsun Mingyur Paldrön, vol. 2 (*wam*), 329–467. Dehra Dun: Mindröling Monastery, 2017.

Terdak Lingpa Gyurme Dorje (gTer bdag gling pa 'gyur med rdo rje.) *Instructions on Tögal. Thog rgal gyi gdams pa.* In Collected Works of Terdak Lingpa Gyurme Dorje, vol. 14, 53. Dehra Dun: Khochhen Tulku, 1998.

Texts in English Translation

Dudjom Rinpoche, Jigdral Yeshe Dorje. *The Nyingma School of Tibetan Buddhism: Its Fundamentals and History.* Translated by Gyurme Dorje. Boston: Wisdom, 1991.

Jamgön Kongtrul Lodrö Taye. *The Autobiography of Jamgön Kongtrul: A Gem of Many Colors.* Translated by Richard Barron. Ithaca, NY: Snow Lion, 2003.

———. *The Catalog of "The Treasury of Precious Instructions."* Translated by Richard Barron (Chökyi Nyima). New York: Tsadra, 2013.

Jigme Lingpa and Kangyur Rinpoche. *Sutra Teachings.* Treasury of Precious Qualities, vol. 1. Boston: Shambhala, 2011.

———. *Vajrayāna and the Great Perfection.* Treasury of Precious Qualities, vol. 2. Translated by Padmakara Translation Group. Boston: Shambhala, 2013.

Longchen Rabjam. *La Liberté Naturelle de l'Esprit.* Translated by Philippe Cornu. Paris: Edition du Seuil, 1994.

Nyoshul Khenpo Jamyang Dorje. *A Marvelous Garland of Rare Gems: Biographies of Masters of Awareness in the Dzogchen Lineage.* Translated by Richard Barron. Junction City, CA: Padma, 2005.

Tulku Thondup. *Masters of Meditation and Miracles.* Boston: Shambhala, 1996.

———. *The Tantric Tradition of the Nyingmapa: The Origin of Buddhism in Tibet.* Marion, MA: Buddhayana, 1984.

Online Reference Sources
84000: Translating the Words of the Buddha. https://www.84000.com.
Buddhist Digital Resource Center. https://www.bdrc.org.
Tibetan and Himalayan Library. https://www.thlib.org.
Treasury of Lives. https://www.treasuryoflives.org.

Index